The Phenomenology
of Mind

G. W. F. HEGEL

TRANSLATED,
WITH AN INTRODUCTION AND NOTES,
BY

J. B. BAILLIE

DOVER PUBLICATIONS, INC.
Mineola, New York

DOVER PHILOSOPHICAL CLASSICS

Bibliographical Note

This Dover edition, first published in 2003, is an unabridged republication of the second revised edition of the J. B. Baillie translation, originally published by the Macmillan Company, London and New York, in 1931 [first publication: 1910].

Library of Congress Cataloging-in-Publication Data

Hegel, Georg Wilhelm Friedrich, 1770–1831.
  [Phänomenologie des Geistes. English]
  The phenomenology of mind / G.W.F. Hegel ; translated, with an introduction and notes, by J.B. Baillie. — [2nd, rev. ed.].
      p. cm. — (Dover philosophical classics)
  Originally published: London ; New York : Macmillan Co., 1910.
  Includes bibliographical references and index.
  ISBN 0-486-43251-3 (pbk.)
    1. Spirit. 2. Consciousness. 3. Truth. I. Title. II. Series.

B2928.E5B3 2003
193—dc21

                                                                2003051274

Manufactured in the United States of America
Dover Publications, Inc., 31 East 2nd Street, Mineola, N.Y. 11501

Contents

[In the following table of contents the matter within square brackets is inserted by the translator.]

INTRODUCTION

A. CONSCIOUSNESS

B. SELF-CONSCIOUSNESS

Prefatory Note to the Second Edition

THE translation has been carefully revised and the previous edition has been extensively altered. A translation of a work of such originality and profound insight into the operations of the human spirit—a profundity which is often dark as well as deep—must necessarily be in large measure an interpretation of the thought as well as a rendering of the language of the text. The changes which have been introduced have brought the translation closer to the text; it is hoped that they have also made the meaning clearer to the reader.

In the revision of the translation, invaluable assistance has been received from the suggestions and criticisms of Professor Joachim of Oxford.

The resetting of the translation, which the numerous alterations have involved, has made it possible to produce the work in the more convenient form of a single volume, in place of the two volumes in which the translation originally appeared.

The "Translator's Introduction" has been as a whole recast for the new edition and considerable additions have been made. The present Introduction may prove more helpful towards an understanding of the work, and may also serve as a short introduction to Hegel's system generally.[1]

Dr. Georg Lasson of Berlin, the learned and indefatigable editor of Hegel's works, has given generous help in connection with the present as with the previous edition of the translation.

I am greatly indebted to Dr. Turner of the Department of Philosophy in Liverpool University for having so kindly undertaken the arduous labour of correcting the proofs. I am also much obliged to the proprietors and publishers of Hastings's *Encyclopœdia of Religion and Ethics* for their cordial assistance.

---

[1]For a fuller introduction to the system the reader may be referred to my article on Hegel in Hastings's *Encyclopœdia of Religion and Ethics.*

The text from which the translation has been made is primarily that of the second edition, published in 1841, and edited by Schulze. The text of the first edition (1807) has been referred to; and the scholarly edition of Dr. G. Lasson (Leipzig, 1907), with its excellent Introduction, has been of great service. A second edition of Lasson's recension appeared in 1921, and in 1928 the same editor brought out as a third edition of the work a reproduction of the text of Hegel's original edition (1807).

An index has been made for the present edition of the translation. This may usefully supplement the detailed table of contents. It has been found impracticable, however, to give the references to such terms as "universality," "negation," which, while important, recur throughout the whole work.

J. B. BAILLIE

THE UNIVERSITY, LEEDS
April 1931

Translator's Introduction

I

THE *Phenomenology of Mind* was the first fruit of Hegel's intellectual maturity. It appeared in 1807 when he was thirty-seven years of age. It was also the last work to engage his attention. He had begun to revise the book with a view to a second edition in the autumn of 1831, a revision which was to be confined to minor alterations of the text without any change in the form or substance of the argument. He had reached about half-way through the Preface a few weeks before his death in November of that year.

It had been preceded by several miscellaneous publications on theological and philosophical subjects. The most important of these were his essays contributed to the *Critical Journal of Philosophy*[1] (first published in 1802), and the essay on the "Difference between the philosophical systems of Fichte and Schelling."[2] The latter was issued separately in 1801, and was at once a critical exposition of the work of his chief contemporaries and marked a turning point in his own philosophical development. These earlier writings proclaimed the advent of a master mind of uncommon speculative ability. But there was little in them to indicate constructive originality or to suggest the direction in which his mind was to evolve.[3] The years between 1803 and 1806 seem to have been decisive for his development. His lectures to his students disclose the beginnings of a systematic scheme of thought. The study of history and of the history of philosophy in particular, on which he first lectured in 1805, transformed the whole conception of the problem of philosophy, as hitherto understood by himself and his contem-

---

[1]Contained in vol. i. Hegel's Werke, ed. Michelet: and also in Hegel's *Vermischte Schriften*, vol. i., ed. Förster and Boumann (1834).
[2]Hegel's Werke, vol. i.
[3]Some attempt has been made by the translator to trace the course of Hegel's development at this early stage in *The Origin and Significance of Hegel's Logic* (1902). See also W. Dilthey, *Die Jugendgeschichte Hegels* (1905).

poraries. He saw, as no philosopher since Aristotle had seen, the necessity for establishing his own philosophical position, not by the refutation of the philosophical theories of the past, but by incorporating them within his own system. He sought to do so by giving logical continuity to what in appearance was mere historical sequence, and by shewing that his own distinctive principle of synthesis was at once the presupposition, the outcome, and the completion of the theories of his predecessors. He further conceived, as no one before him had done, that, in order to vindicate his principle completely, it must necessarily contain within its sway every fundamental type of experience in which mind had been historically realized. The principle would thus connect together, interpret and explain, and itself be the final result of all experience as historically known. The systematic elaboration of this conception found expression in his first complete treatise — the *Phenomenology of Mind*.

In its plan, its purpose, its method and its manner of execution, the work is unique in the history of philosophy. The subject in front of the author's mind throughout the argument may be said to be the whole range of human experience as historically realized in different forms and at different stages, more particularly in Western Europe. Movements of human history which have marked epochs in the development of the human race are treated as typical or permanent embodiments of attitudes of mind or principles in operation in the spirit of man, and are discussed in shadowy form through which the historical reality implied is only dimly visible. Tracts of experience which have each formed from time to time the subject of separate analysis by different thinkers are here regarded as fragments of a single system. Types and processes of science lose their self-containedness and are reduced to phases of the necessary movement of human intelligence. The importance of religion in human experience is not allowed to obscure the fact that religion is but one necessary act in the drama of human existence. To philosophy there is also assigned its appointed relative place; but all philosophies are taken to be aspects of a single mood of the mind, and the array of philosophical theories constituting the history of philosophy are abbreviated into central principles which together involve a single comprehensive truth controlling the minds of individual philosophers even though unknown to themselves.

So exhaustive an analysis of the life-history of the human spirit, so sustained an effort to reduce its varied and involved forms of expression to their simple leading principles, and to express these controlling ideas in an orderly, connected system, had certainly never before been compressed within the compass of a single treatise. The courage which made such an effort possible was, no doubt, in large measure due to the state of the intellectual atmosphere at the time when the book was written, an atmosphere surcharged with beliefs and ideas, which were capable of stimulating and sustaining philosophical enthusiasm, or of exciting and intoxicating speculative ambition. Influenced as Hegel undoubtedly was by the confident aspirations of his contemporaries, he yet saw the necessity for chaining speculative imagination to the solid ground of tried and verifiable experience. The wealth of familiar and accessible truth in science, history, and ordinary experience, must be at our disposal before philosophy can take with assurance the high road of comprehensive, systematic knowledge. The constant, if cryptic, reference throughout the whole of the treatise to facts of nature, human nature, and human history, amply testifies at any rate to the seriousness with which Hegel endeavoured to meet this demand of all true philosophy. In this sense, the work is in large measure a reaction against the ingenious manipulation of principles *in abstracto*, which characterized the theories of his immediate predecessors before the appearance of the *Phenomenology* in 1807. It is, therefore, small surprise that, though the appearance of the book was hailed with great expectation, the work was received with coldness and dissatisfaction by those who had, up to this point, been Hegel's teachers and friends.

But while an enormous wealth of representative material lies behind the treatise, partly illuminating the argument, partly determining the course of its development, it need not be supposed that the author intended to lay claim to omniscience. From first to last it is apparent that the author was limited by the information available at his time, by the scientific views prevalent during his day, and by his own selective interest in the material presented before him. Only in one department was his knowledge sufficiently adequate to reduce this limitation to smaller dimensions. This was the department of History, and more especially the History of Philosophy. But here, it may well be said, the material was regarded as primarily representative, and typical of movements of the human spirit, so that errors of fact or of detail are, for the purpose of the argument, insignificant. Even so, his selection of such material is governed by his interest in the problem of the *Phenomenology*, by his personal predilections, and also by the philosophical principle which he adopted. A selection under such conditions imposes restrictions on the character of the argument of the treatise. Such limitations are doubtless inevitable, and they help us to explain many of the peculiarities, the omissions, and the defects, of the work. Subjects are treated in the book with a fullness, and even diffuseness of analysis, which must now seem utterly out of proportion to the value of what is discussed. For example, Hegel devotes much labour to demonstrating the hollow pretentiousness of the pseudo-sciences of

"Phrenology" and "Physiognomy," and endeavours to bring to light the truth which they had misconstrued.[4] The explanation is that in his day these twin scientific impostures had great success, and won much favour from learned and unlearned alike. The scientific function of "Observation," again, is dealt with at an inordinate length, doubtless because of the success which attended the scientific investigation of nature towards the end of the 18th century.[5] So, too, the constantly recurring reference to states of spiritual life which were familiar features of the Romantic movement, is only to be explained by the outstanding historical importance of this movement at the time the book was written.

The omissions from the treatise are as remarkable as the exaggerated attention devoted to some aspects of experience relatively to others. In a work ostensibly dealing with the whole range of human experience, it seems surprising to find no specific discussion of our knowledge of space or of number, or of the sphere of fact dealt with by chemistry; or again, to take another domain of experience remote from these, there is no mention at all of important fine arts, like music or painting. Such omissions are all the more striking when we bear in mind Hegel's keen appreciation of the value of both pure science and fine art, and when we remember that, in his later works, a full and elaborate treatment is given to the subjects just mentioned. It is not enough to plead in excuse that he is dealing in this work with the main types of experience, and that what is not explicitly discussed is implied in the analyses of the types selected; for it seems obvious that the kinds of knowledge and of art above referred to, play an unique part in experience, and are not simply specific forms of more general types of experience.

Looking at the plan of the treatise as a whole and the method of treatment assigned to the forms of experience brought under review, an impartial critic is bound to admit that the scheme of the work is unbalanced. The discussion of some parts is foreshortened; in other cases, subjects are treated with an elaborateness of detail in which the main idea is overborne by the sheer mass of the material used to elucidate it. At times, indeed, the writer seems to have become so absorbed with the particular subject in hand, that for the time being he seems to have lost perspective. In such cases, the author's description of his work as his "voyage of discovery" is rather an explanation than a defence of his procedure. For the business of a writer is to determine the chart of his argument before he sets out on his literary expedition,

---

[4]This truth finds ample recognition not merely in ordinary experience but in the recent work of scientific investigators such as Lombroso.
[5]*Vide* p. 271.

and not to draw it afterwards in order to discover what coasts of truth he has visited. Hegel himself felt that in many parts the argument had been overweighted,[6] and expressed the hope, in a letter to his friend Niethammer, that he might be able, in a second edition, to "unload some of the ballast, and get the ship to float more easily."[7] The last part of the work in particular seems hurried and condensed. To the discussion of "Religion" and "Absolute Knowledge," in both of which he was supremely interested, one would naturally have expected the author to have devoted the greatest elaboration. For it was one of the main objects of his task to explain and justify the place of Philosophical Knowledge in the plan of human experience. Yet the analysis of "Religion" seems fragmentary, and inadequate to the theme; while the statement of "Absolute Knowledge" is brief and elliptical to the verge of obscurity. This is in striking contrast to the long and carefully-wrought argument dealing with the sphere of moral and social experience which immediately precedes the section on Religion. The defect certainly demands some explanation, and this seems to be found in the circumstances under which this last part of the treatise was written.

In a letter to Schelling, in which Hegel promises to send him a copy of the book,[8] Hegel asks indulgence for the unsatisfactory character of the last parts of the work, and says, as if by way of explanation, that the "composition of the book was concluded at midnight before the battle of Jena." This sounds rather fanciful. "On the night before the battle" there could have been no serious cannonade to disturb Hegel's meditations. In point of fact, the Prussian General himself did not expect Napoleon to attack on October 14th (the day of the battle); and it is extremely unlikely that Hegel could have been so certain of Napoleon's plans as to feel constrained to hurry on the completion of his book in case of eventualities. No doubt, after the battle, affairs in Jena were uncomfortable, and sufficiently uncertain to induce Hegel to carry about in his pocket the MS. finished on the night of the 13th, and to defer till the 20th, when things had quieted down, the despatch of his MS. to Bamberg.

The real explanation was much more commonplace. Hegel had made an unfortunate arrangement with his publisher. Instead of waiting till the MS. of the work was actually finished before sending it to the publisher, Hegel arranged to let the publisher have it in instalments. The publisher, who was both printer and bookseller, was to pay

---

[6]*Briefe*, i. p. 80. See also the letter to Schelling, *Briefe*, i. p. 102.
[7]It was a quarter of a century before the wish had the prospect of being fulfilled, and then, unfortunately, the author, as above stated, died before he had revised many pages.
[8]*Briefe*, i. p. 102.

so much a sheet, the first payment to be made when half the entire MS. was in his hands. Printing began in February, 1806. When Hegel had sent what he took to be half the MS. of the book, and demanded payment accordingly, the publisher declared himself unable to feel satisfied that this really was half the MS. Payment was therefore refused, and further, the edition of one thousand copies, originally agreed upon, was altered now to one of seven hundred and fifty, with a corresponding diminution of payment to the author. Hegel, being much in need of the money, appealed in despair to his friend Niethammer, then living in Bamberg (the place of publication), and asked his good offices to urge the publisher to forward the money. The publisher was obdurate. Finally, Niethammer made a new contract with the publisher, whereby Niethammer agreed to pay the publisher so much should Hegel fail to send the last of the MS. by October 18, 1806. This new contract was made on September 29th. By great effort, Hegel managed to send off large instalments on the 8th and on 10th of October, promising faithfully to send the last remaining instalment by the 13th. Meanwhile, Napoleon appeared on the scene, and hostilities with Prussia were definitely declared from Bamberg on October 7. The proximity of this Zeitgeist on horseback added to Hegel's anxieties and difficulties; for there could be no certainty that postal arrangements would be efficiently carried out and the MS. safely reach its destination, either in due time or at all. Hegel was doubtless perturbed, for the loss of time would be serious to his friend, and the loss of the MS. irreparable to himself. It was in these circumstances that the last part of the *Phenomenology* was composed. With his mental energies strained to keep pace with the flight of time, his personal honour at stake, with the roll of war in his ears, and an illiberal publisher master of his financial resources—Hegel could hardly be expected to be in the appropriate frame of mind necessary to compose the dialectic hymn of Absolute Knowledge. There is thus some excuse, and at any rate sufficient explanation, for the curtailed analysis, and the condensed utterance, which characterize these last stages of the work.

But these defects, avoidable and unavoidable, to which reference has been made, do not seriously impair the monumental greatness of the work. No man can escape from the limitations of his own individuality, any more than he can avoid the restrictions imposed upon him by the circumstances of his time. The very attempt to rise above them requires their assistance to support the effort. We cannot, therefore, expect that the work before us, which, as we shall see, is so closely concerned with history, should be unaffected by the conditions under which historical phenomena exist.

II

(a)

The argument of the *Phenomenology* presents unusual difficulties even to the trained student of philosophy. It has been said that a great man lays the world under the obligation to understand him. The obligation is not easily fulfilled when a man of genius of the highest order produces a philosophical interpretation of experience so novel in its design, so subtle in the texture of its thought, so comprehensive in its range and penetrating in its vision. It is impossible to trace the stages in the construction of the system. He made his "voyage of discovery" alone, and we are only made aware of his arrival at his destination. It has been customary to seek and to find the origins of his thought in his immediate predecessors, Kant, Fichte, and Schelling.[9] At best, however, these provide merely clues to Hegel's main principles. The partial and formal similarity of principle does not account for the manner in which the principle was completely transformed by Hegel. If we attach sole importance in his development to these predecessors we overlook the profound influence on Hegel's mind exercised by Greek thought on the one hand and by history on the other; both of these being almost wholly ignored by the three thinkers named. On the whole, perhaps, the significance of these philosophers for Hegel appears to have been much exaggerated. His mind was much too original to remain under their influence; and the easy mastery of their doctrine in his early critical writings shows that he quickly passed beyond them.

It may be of some assistance in appreciating the point of view of the *Phenomenology* if we put the argument in the setting of Hegel's philosophy as a whole. This will throw light not only on the principle which operates throughout the argument, but also on his method of procedure, and on the place which the *Phenomenology* occupies in his scheme of thought.

And first it is essential to understand what he meant by philosophy and what he expected philosophy, as a form of human activity, to accomplish.

Hegel differs from other philosophers in nothing more than the care which he bestowed on the consideration of the place of philosophy in the plan of human experience. In this he reminds us of Plato and Aristotle rather than of any modern thinker. In a sense one might say that his conception of philosophy contains a kind of epitome of

[9] See, for example, Hutchison Stirling's *Secret of Hegel* (1st edition, 1865; 2nd edition, 1898). This is still the most stimulating introduction to the study of Hegel in English. Stirling, however, has little to say of the *Phenomenology* and does not seem to have recognized its importance.

his whole system. He constantly recurs to the topic whenever a relevant opportunity arises, and had no doubt as to what he meant by philosophy.

The essential elements in Hegel's conception are determined by reference to the object with which philosophy deals; the medium in which it works; and the method by which it carries on its process to a final result. These factors are closely connected, but each is distinct from the others.

In Hegel's view the object of philosophy is described in general terms as the Whole, the Absolute, or God. This is reality without qualification, and hence, abstractly considered, can only be described as what *is* simply, or what is not finite, not a part. The specific meaning assigned to this object varies with each philosophy, but it is one and the same object with which all philosophies deal. Even when a philosophy denies that any definite meaning can be attached to such an object, it is just the reference to this object which makes such a denial a contribution to philosophy. Whatever philosophy may or may not achieve, it has always been concerned with what is ultimate. This does not require demonstration; it is so much historical fact.

Again, the medium in which philosophy moves is that of the supreme achievement of thought—a notion. This has certain characteristics, negative and positive. Negatively, it is not derived from nor dependent on sensation or perception, and hence is not a mere general concept. It is not a purely formal "abstract" universal, and hence a notion has no rigid fixity of outline, empty of all specific content and applicable to any, and does not exclude all relationship with other notions. Positively characterized, a notion operates freely and independently within itself and under its own conditions. It is the ultimate principle controlling and penetrating all thought wherever it appears, whether in sensation, perception, or abstract reflexion. It is universal, but is a concrete universal, that is, holds within itself the particular and is the organic unity of universality and particularity. It is a single identity in and through difference. And each notion directly refers to and connects itself intimately with other notions, so as to form an organically articulated system, a self-contained structure of notions.

The method by which philosophy proceeds is that of development of the notion. Development here does not mean development in time, but development in expression and coherence of the elements involved in the notion; it is a development in terms of and for the purposes of complete thought. The notion is an operative individual unity, and thus is a process which can be realized with more or less completeness. The unity of the elements in the notion may be implicitly asserted or explicitly affirmed; it may be immanent or fully unfolded. The elements in the notion may be taken by themselves, and each may in turn be said to be the whole notion; but each inevitably calls for the others as soon as the one-sided affirmation is clearly made and seen, because nothing short of the whole notion can express its meaning, and its unity is indissoluble. One partial affirmation, therefore, gives rise to another, till the notion is fully unfolded and installed as an explicit unity of all its elements. The partial affirmation of the notion is, relatively to the whole, an abstract affirmation; the complete explicit co-ordination of all the elements within the unity of the whole notion makes impossible any abstract isolation of elements, and so cancels all one-sided affirmations. Relatively to these abstract affirmations, the whole notion, as explicitly containing and co-ordinating all its elements, is concrete. From this point of view the development of the notion is described by Hegel as a process of the notion from abstract to concrete.[10] The notion itself determines these stages; it *is* these stages, and it is the process of removing the one-sidedness of each till the unity of the whole is completely realized. Looking at the process as a growth from a lower to a higher degree of articulation of the nature of the whole, it is spoken of as a process from "potentiality" to "actuality." Looking at the notion as an individual concentration of the highest activity of mind, which is essentially self-consciousness, the process is described as the notion gradually "coming to consciousness of itself." Taking the stages of the notion as stages in a self-distinguishing and self-relating principle, the identity as such of the notion is spoken of as the notion "in itself," the notion "implicit"; the diversity as such, which the notion contains, is described as the notion "for itself," the notion "explicit"; while the union of these two aspects in a single articulate totality is the notion "in and for itself," the notion completely "realized." These different ways of regarding the process in the life of the notion are closely connected, and are, in fact, alternative expressions which are employed according to the context and to suit the convenience of the exposition.

The conception of philosophy above delineated marks off philosophy as a form of knowledge from all other forms in which knowledge exists, and is from first to last the region within which philosophy in Hegel's sense lives and moves. It no doubt requires justification, and Hegel gives a justification of this conception; but it is a justification in terms of and satisfactory to philosophy itself, not one that any other form of knowledge would accept or give. And indeed no other form of knowledge, except philosophy, requires or is able to guarantee the point of view of philosophy. Each form of knowledge takes its own way and keeps within its own conditions and limits, without giving any

---

[10]See *Gesch. der Philos.*, xiii. 54.

pragmatic justif ?

other justification of itself except the success with which it accomplishes its aim. Philosophy alone must try to justify its own conception, because it is and claims to be the most comprehensive type of knowledge; and without such a justification from itself it would require a still higher form of knowledge to justify it, and so on *ad infinitum*. The only way it can prove that it is the final or "absolute" form of knowledge is by showing that it can account for its own conception; and if it can do so there is no further form of knowledge possible or required. In that sense philosophy is without presuppositions because it leaves nothing, not even itself, unexplained and external to the control of its own principle. What this justification is, we shall presently see.

The conception of philosophy is of importance not merely to make clear from the outset what Hegel means by philosophy, but also to understand his manner of treating the different parts that fall within his scheme of philosophy. The treatment is throughout uniform in character. The Absolute is the fundamental object from first to last. The Absolute is one and is apprehended in the form of the notion: it is the notion *par excellence*. But the Absolute expresses itself in different ways, each of which is an embodiment of the notion. And conversely, wherever we have a notion, there in some way we have an expression of the Absolute, the ultimately real. The process of revealing what the notion contains is, as just indicated, that of development. Hence in every part of philosophy the same mode of exposition is adopted. This principle of development has to deal sometimes with material which has no temporal nature at all, sometimes with material which has a temporal character, or only exists in a temporal sequence. In all cases the development is a logical sequence, for only so is the content of the notion coherently and systematically connected in the way demanded by philosophy. In the case where the content is bound up with temporal conditions, the development of that content in logical form consists either in adopting the content which time offers and arranging it to meet the requirements of the logical development of the notion considered, or in regarding the temporal sequence of the content as in essence following the same course as the logical sequence of the notion. An illustration of the former appears in the treatment of the various historical forms assumed by the idea of freedom in human history; the course of the history of philosophy in Europe is an illustration of the latter.

Following this clue of the inseparable connexion of the notion with the principle of logical development, we can see how it comes about that in every part of Hegel's scheme of philosophy there are only two questions to be considered: what is the notion dealt with in the part in question, and how is the development of the content of that notion to be expressed in terms of the peculiar character of the notion in question?

Thus we have the notion of philosophy itself as a factor in the life-history of the human experience of the individual mind. The development of this notion in and through the various forms of concrete human experience gives us the philosophical interpretation and vindication of the place of philosophy in experience. This part of the system of philosophy is worked out in the *Phenomenology of Mind.*

Philosophy, as a human effort to express the ultimate notion of the Absolute, is subject to the conditions of race, culture, and civilization in the midst of which it appears. The one notion is, as already said, dealt with all along, but it expresses itself differently owing to the variety of conditions just mentioned. It is thus one philosophy which works itself out under these conditions; the different expressions of this one philosophy constitute a variety of philosophical systems. These systems appear at different times, and necessarily make philosophy take on a historical character. Taken together, they constitute the history of philosophy; and these systems are but forms of one philosophy, being the work of the one notion which animates them all. The logical development of the expressions of this one system through all its historical conditions constitutes what Hegel understands by the *History of Philosophy.* The logical development here is inseparable from the direct historical sequence in which the different systems have appeared. The historical direction is the logical direction, because there is one notion or one absolute system working through all and animating the various minds concerned; and the way in which its content actually appears is a historical sequence. Thus Hegel's *History of Philosophy* is not a mere narrative of theories succeeding one another in time, but an integral part of his own philosophy; it is a philosophical interpretation of the history of philosophical theories.

The notion of the Absolute, which is the ultimate object of philosophy, has, like every other notion, its own moments or aspects, each of which is the Absolute, but is capable of distinction from the others, and capable of separate logical development. Its very concreteness makes it necessary for philosophy to take it in detachments, so to say, in order exhaustively to express its content. But its single concrete reality cannot be broken up into separate components. It remains in its concreteness as the all-comprehensive and supreme principle operating in each of its aspects, and containing all the results of the development of each in turn. It is the presupposition and final result of that development. The aspects are themselves, therefore, but stages in the evolution of its concrete single reality, and must be so treated; and the development of the different stages forms a continuous development of the entire content of the notion of the Absolute. This comprehensive development of the notion of the Absolute is the entire system of the philosophy of the Absolute. It forms a single body of philosophical science, with distinct members. This constitutes what Hegel calls the *Encyclopædia of the Philosophical Sciences*. It is thus not a mere collection of sciences, or a dictionary of philosophical knowledge; it is a philosophically connected whole of Science.

It has just been said that each of the aspects of the notion of the Absolute can be treated by itself, but that each must be looked on as a specific embodiment of that notion. The first aspect logically is that of the notion in its bare concentrated universality, the notion "in itself," the notion as self-identical. This aspect must cover the whole domain of the Absolute, but must do so always with this character of universality, and self-identity. Whatever the Absolute contains must be expressible from this point of view; and, since the Absolute is the totality of all reality, there will be a multiplicity of universals within it. The notion as self-identical, in short, is capable of logical development in terms of its universality alone; such development will unite all its universals into an organized whole, or Science, of all the ultimate universal elements of the Absolute as it is or was "in its essence before the creation (i.e. differentiation) of nature and finite spirit."[11] This is carried out in the science of *Logic*—the science of the pure universal principles by which the Absolute lives and moves in a uniformly coherent intelligible system. Such a system is the ground-plan of the whole of reality, the network of notions which holds together and constitutes the essence of all that is.

The second aspect of the notion of the Absolute is the sheer opposite of the first, is the aspect of pure dispersion, the notion "for itself" (i.e. *out of* itself), the notion as self-externalized. This again covers the whole domain of the Absolute, is the Absolute in this peculiar form. The fundamental oneness of the Absolute must not therefore be lost sight of when viewing this phase of its externalization; it is a differentiation *within* the one, or the one resolved into pure self-externality. Without this implication of the oneness of the Absolute, it would be impossible to have a science or intelligible system of the Absolute in this form of pure difference. The Absolute in its aspect of self-dispersion is the world of Nature, inorganic and organic, as realized in space and time—the universal media of thoroughgoing externalization—whose very essence consists in keeping its contents apart from one another down to the minutest particular detail. Space is the universal objective unchanging form of permanence which takes and holds within itself the infinitely detailed

---

[11]*Logik*: Einleitung (W.W. III: p. 33: ed. 1841).

content of nature. Time is the universal objective unchanging form of succession into which all the content of nature falls. These forms are inseparable. Hence every part and element of nature is in reality a unitary focus of space and time — an event. Nature, however, makes a whole by itself, and that wholeness of Nature is once more the unity of the Absolute as such expressed in and through the form of Nature. This makes possible an intelligible system of Nature, and such a system is the *Philosophy of Nature* — the philosophical development of the notion in the form of self-externalization.

The third aspect of the notion of the Absolute is the explicit union of the first (pure universality) and the second (pure difference) in a synthesis which avoids these abstract extremes and expresses the concreteness of the Absolute in its highest possible form. It contains the principle that gives rise to each of the preceding extremes. It is, therefore, a principle of universality and also a principle of self-differentiation. The term combining these two functions in one reality is that of mind or spirit, which, being essentially self-conscious, is at once a conscious unity in all its processes and the conscious source of endless differences and distinctions within itself. It is supremely an identity which maintains itself through its differences and refers them to itself. It is thus the realized embodiment of the concrete forms of the notion, and the type of all such concreteness. The notion of the Absolute fully realized, "in and for itself," is thus "Mind," and the logical evolution of the notion as mind is the *Philosophy of Mind*. This completes and exhausts the notion of the Absolute; it contains all that fell within the content of the other stages of that notion, for mind is the source of universals, and mind as the soul of an organized body sums up in its organic embodiment the processes of nature. In the logical evolution of mind, therefore, the philosophy of the Absolute comes full circle: and the crowning stage in the development of mind is the philosophy of the Absolute itself. The final outcome and expression of Absolute Mind is the truth of the Absolute revealed in and through philosophy.

Since the notion of the Absolute is embodied with varying degrees of completeness throughout all the system, any part may be taken by itself and worked out into systematic form in exactly the same way that reality as a whole is developed. Each part forms a realm by itself, and its detailed contents can be logically evolved from it. Hegel dealt with four parts or stages in the philosophy of mind in this way. One of these has already been mentioned — the *Phenomenology of Mind* — mind as creating "experience." The other three are (*a*) mind as "objective," as the source of social and moral activity, (*b*) mind as expressing itself in the realm of art, (*c*) mind as realized in the life of religion. These are respectively worked out as subforms of his comprehensive system, under the titles *Philosophy of Law, Aesthetic,* and *Philosophy of Religion.* In each case exactly the same plan is pursued: we have the notion of "social mind" delineated and then logically developed through all its forms and stages; and similarly of Art and Religion.

(b)

It was pointed out above that the medium in which philosophy works is that of the "notion." For the proper understanding of Hegel's system it is essential to make clear what the notion in his sense means, and how he arrives at it. Hegel no doubt expounds the principle repeatedly, but always in terms of his own theory, and thus takes for granted precisely what the interpreter of the system wishes to have explained. Nowhere does he trace how he personally arrived at this principle, and nowhere does he show how it is derivable from thought as commonly accepted. On the contrary, he proceeds in the opposite way; he recasts the meaning of ordinary thought by reference to the notion previously accepted as true and as having a specific significance from the outset. Yet there can be no question that this principle was not arrived at without a struggle, and did not spring from his mind, like Minerva from the head of Jupiter. The principle is not self-evident, and needs both explanation and justification.

In default of any historical evidence of how Hegel reached this principle, we must fall back on the epistemological grounds for adopting it. These are mainly two, and are not strictly separable. In the first place, Hegel regarded the world as a single unified whole, which maintained its unity through endless multiplicity of real individuals, and in a certain sense could itself be looked upon as the supreme form of individuality. The world was not a mere process, nor a static reality; for the former makes unity or singleness impossible, and the latter is in contradiction with the plain facts of life in nature and man. The world is a process that is self-contained, and so as a whole is at rest with itself: it is a process *sub specie temporis,* but a unified whole *sub specie æternitatis.* Its unity is all-pervading, and is maintained in and through the process of its finite parts. The question for philosophy is how best to conceive the principle which thus constitutes the nature of the Absolute a self-complete and self-contained single whole. This resolves itself into the further question what form of finite reality furnishes the most adequate homologue, is nearest in structure, composition, and process to this supreme individual. For man, the solution must be found in the highest individuality known to him. But for man the central individuality in all finitude, that which supplies him with the very standard for determining the nature and degree of individuality among finite beings, is the human individual as a realized self-conscious mind.

This must be the clue and the basis for the comprehension of the Absolute, as it is the final source of the interpretation of all that is finite.

But self-conscious mind (or spirit) reveals its activity in many ways, through sensation and perception as well as through ideas. To make use of mind as a working principle of explanation we must therefore find the highest and at the same time the most universal function of its activity, that which is the controlling essence of its individuality, dominating all its modes of expression, making them what they are, and holding them together as phases of its own individuality. This is nothing other than its supreme function of consciously uniting its own differences in a single focus of self-hood: not "referring its content to the unity of the self," but realizing singleness of being or self-hood through the function of combining differences in a unity. The conscious operation of that function *is* the reality of the self; the self of the individual mind is at once the unity and the differences, is a concrete function, and is single from first to last. As Hegel puts it (*Gesch. der Philos.* xiii. 45), "the being of mind is its *act*, and its act is to be aware of itself." This supreme function is not an abstract operation; it is the essential principle operating throughout all the process and expressions of the life of mind, and such an essence is in no way and in no sense separate from its expressions. The statement of this essence is no doubt formal; but the essence itself is only a form in the sense that form is inseparable from content. We never have the form "by itself" in experience, and hence can never treat it as abstract when making use of it for purposes of explanation. It is not admissible, therefore, to start from it as an abstract form and try to deduce out of it analytically further principles or forms of unity. For, if we take it as abstract at all, we can extract nothing out of it; at best we can only repeat it; and, if we seem to derive further principles from it, we have not, to begin with, taken it as abstract.

It is by the use of this supreme function of mind, then, that we have to proceed when we employ self-conscious mind as the clue to interpret reality, finite and absolute. This highest function Hegel, following the traditional usage of philosophers, calls "reason." Since in it the self always operates in a conscious way (it is the conscious unifying of differences), reason is essentially cognitive in character, but "cognitive" only in the general sense of full awareness. Reason does not here mean simply reflective activity, nor merely intuitive activity; it is both at once in an indivisible act. It can be called reflective when we consider the aspect of distinguishing and relating the elements involved; and intuitive when we consider the aspect of uniting these differences into a single whole. But these are, after all, aspects; the function is one and individual. Reason is therefore "mediate" and "immediate" in its operation; and wherever it operates this holds true. This means, however, that as a function it is self-complete, directing itself and determining it-self according to its own law or method of procedure: it is its own world and the law of its world. It is the realized limit of knowing. In other forms of knowledge, something is "given" as an "immediate," and "re-ceived" by reflexion as material to be worked upon or "thought about"; and these factors in the process are assigned to distinct sources. Both factors must exist if knowledge in any sense is to take place; and the aim of knowledge is to transform and permeate the "given" by the process of reflexion. The limiting case of such a process is when the immedi-ate and the mediating activity are merely aspects of a single operation. Such a limit is reason. But it is an actual limit, not an imaginary or "ideal" limit; for reason is but the highest function of mind, and mind is through and through actual. Reason is thus not a point of view, but an active function, not external to its contents, but holding its contents (its immediate) within itself. It is in this sense that reason is described as "concrete" and not abstract. It is concrete, as the essential function of mind must be; and mind is, as already indicated, the very type and standard of what is concrete and individual.

But a further stage is required before we can make effective use of this principle. So far we have treated reason as a function. Now that function operates within a certain range and for an end. It is a function which operates in an individual way, grasps a whole in its singleness, as a unity in and through differences. The end is its product, the outcome and summary of its operation. In a sense this product may be described as the function itself, the function in its single completeness. The dis-tinction between them, such as it is, consists in the product being regarded as the function brought to rest, while the function is the prod-uct in course of being brought about. This product Hegel calls a "no-tion" (*Begriff*). A notion may be called the object of reason, but only if the connexion between reason and its object be considered as close as that between function and product just mentioned. A specific notion is reason in one of its manifestations of its function; and, if we look at rea-son simply as the most general function of self-conscious mind, we can speak of reason itself as "the notion" (*der Begriff*) *par excellence*. Hence we often find Hegel using precisely the same expressions in describing the operation of "the notion" as when describing the function of rea-son. The notion is spoken of as "conscious of itself," and "determining itself," and as "uniting its differences," etc.—expressions which seem to create difficulty until we see that for Hegel "the notion" *is* reason, in the sense just described. He does not mean that the notion works in-dependently of the vital energy of mind. The notion is reason in the full plenitude of its power, and is indistinguishable from it except as function and end are distinguishable in the operation of reason. The notion is thus not "endowed" with activity by reason; nor again is the notion the "expression" of reason, if this implies that the expression is separable from the source or force from which it proceeds. And what is true of "the notion" *par excellence* holds good of any notion in which reason is embodied.

This step is highly important for Hegel's view. For now it becomes possible to link his theory with the language in which philosophy from its inception has clothed its thoughts in detail. For philosophy has itself created and creates that language, because it is the function of grasping a unity with its differences. That language is animated throughout by the activity of reason; and the results of its activity appear in the manifold "categories" with which philosophy deals. Wherever we have a function of thought-unity in and through differences, there we have a category, and there we have the operation of reason. Hence we can treat a category as a specific realization of the operation of reason, and can trace its source to the one supreme function of self-conscious mind. Hegel does not require to create the world of reason out of his own mind, nor to dictate to experience the kind or number of categories which constitute reality. The work has been already done in the course of the history of philosophy, and he has but to put the results together; while experience alone can let us see what the categories are which constitute reality. The complicated culture of European life is, so to say, strewn with categories, some having names derived from one language, some with names derived from another. Again, he does not require to be constantly appealing to the nature of reason to verify or justify his categories; he is sure that reason is present wherever this function of unity in and through difference is exercised and concentrated into the summary form of a category. And, finally, reason, while the supreme essential function of mind, must articulate itself into a plurality of categories, because mind is the absolutely concrete with an endless variety of content due to the fact that it gathers up into itself the entire realm of finitude. It is, as already said, the standard of all individuality, and is the standard because it contains all that the other types of individuality contain, and more than is contained by any other single type.

The plurality of categories referred to, being all in the long run expressions of the one supreme activity of reason, are necessarily connected with one another through their common derivation from a single source. Together they form a system so organically connected that any one category involves all the others, and can be clearly interpreted only in the light of the entire system. Each mirrors the whole system in itself; and the whole system can be said to be the unfolding of "the notion" *par excellence*. This supreme notion gathers up into itself all the plurality of the various categories, and in this respect assumes a distinct name—"the Idea." Such a system is, again, self-complete and self-contained, because, as we saw, reason is a self-complete and self-determined function carrying its own "immediate" within itself. Such a system can thus constitute an organic whole of "knowledge," the knowledge which reason has of itself in its character of the essence of mind. This does not mean that the system defies or is independent of experience and reality; for the notions are the controlling principles of experience and reality. It means simply that, since the notions are concrete in the sense explained, they can and do form a distinctive subject-matter for systematic treatment.

Recurring to our starting-point, we can now see how Hegel proceeds to work in interpreting the Absolute. Self-conscious mind is the clue, and the activity of reason is its principle and supreme function. The Absolute is interpretable only in terms of mind, for mind is the highest type of individuality with which we have any acquaintance. It is needless to ask what the absolute may be over and above mind; for over and above mind there is nothing higher to which to appeal in an intelligible way. To be intelligible is to be mentally constituted, and intelligibility is the presupposition and result of philosophy in the sense of complete knowledge. Moreover, mind *qua* mind is homogeneous with itself, whether mind be finite or absolute. This is especially so if we take the essence of mind, for that essence is identical in all the shapes and forms of mind. The essence of mind is, as said, reason. The operation of reason is thus the same in finite and absolute mind; it is the function that grasps individuality in its concrete singleness. If the Absolute is the supreme individual, reason *qua* reason is adequate to its comprehension. But not only is reason adequate to the comprehension of the Absolute, in the sense of being able to undertake this task. It might make this claim and still be a mere unrealized point of view, or at best enunciate merely abstract propositions identical in significance. But we are not left in darkness regarding the detailed content of the Absolute. For we are able to evolve coherently and in terms of reason the varied content of finite mind. And, if we accomplish this, we *ipso facto* have expressed the content of the Absolute, for the result so realized is the articulation of the one supreme function of reason, which constitutes finite and absolute mind alike. The evolution of such a result is made possible because mind, and therefore reason, is the spokesman and interpreter of the totality of finite individual things. Mind supplies the standard of their individuality in each case, and brings to the consciousness of its own individuality the constitutive principle of each. All individuals, so to say, come to light in finite self-conscious mind. But the Absolute itself is expressed in terms of the whole of finitude; and, when the Absolute is viewed as mind, its expression is not merely inseparable from but is identical with itself, for mind is conscious self-expression. Hence, if reason is adequate to the comprehension of the totality of finitude, and accomplishes this result in coherent systematic form, the result so achieved can be taken as the evolved and connected content of Absolute Reality. And this is just what Hegel means by comprehending the Absolute. Thus it is through the notion and in terms of the notion—which is the form with which reason works, the language of its activity—that the Absolute is expressed. The notion, as above indicated, is the beginning and end of Hegel's system. Wherever reason grasps individuality in its singleness, there we have a notion; and, since its function is to grasp in this and in no other way, the totality of finitude is for it a realm or system of notions; while again the system of notions is the comprehension and indeed the self-comprehension of the Absolute.

The second line of thought by which Hegel reaches his notion, and secures its validity as a principle of interpretation, is equally important. The distinction of subject and object, within which human conscious experience exists, is held to be a distinction within a single unity, and the form in which this unity in difference reaches its highest expression is self-consciousness. In this form the distinction in question becomes a self-distinction, and the unity is the single self functioning in and through both factors alike and at once; while, as already indicated, the essential nature of self-consciousness is the activity of reason. By this line of thought Hegel seeks, on the one hand, to avoid the dangers of subjective idealism to which his principle is liable, and into which certain of his immediate predecessors, notably Fichte, fell when developing the implications of Kant's theory; and, on the other, to steer clear of the abstractness of the bare unity of subject and object propounded by Schelling, which possessed objectivity at the price of being inarticulate.

The argument by which he established this position is contained in the first half of the *Phenomenology of Mind*. Briefly stated,[12] it consists in showing that, wherever subject and object stand in the relation which constitutes experience, the unifying principle is that of thought. This is at once a function of the subject and the controlling centre of the reality of the object; and these are inseparable in the life of experience. This unity is not apparent, but is only implicit at the lower levels of experience, where subject and object seem more opposed than united, as, for example, in such levels as those of sensation and perception. But analysis of these types of experience brings to light the

[12] cp. Philos. d. Rechts: Einleitung §26: W.W. VIII (1854).

underlying principle of unity. The very process of experience from the lower to the higher forms is necessitated by the demand for the explicit in place of the implicit unity; and is at once the gradual evolution of the essential unity of subject and object and the growing awareness of the universality of thought which permeates the component factors constituting experience. We cannot say that the subject dominates the object any more than that the object directs the activity of the subject: they are inseparable elements and develop *pari passu*. It follows that the process reaches its goal, and experience its truest type, when subject and object are transparent to each other, when the subject is aware of itself in its object, and the object responds and corresponds to the functions of the subject. The distinction between the two is as real as ever, and their unity contains them as factors of a specific process. This stage is that of consciousness of self. From this point of view, so attained in the course of experience, the levels below this stage are now seen to be not merely preparatory steps to the attainment of self-consciousness, but are themselves implicitly constituted by self-consciousness, which was operative in them from the first, and from which, in fact, by abstraction they obtained their place as forms of experience and as stages in the evolution of experience. Experience is thus constituted and permeated by self-consciousness; indeed its significance consists in its being the process of manifesting or evolving consciousness of self, in the subject's becoming gradually aware of or finding itself in its object, and so coming to be "at home" in its world.

In this way the principle of reason, which, as we saw, was taken to be the essential activity of self-consciousness, is liberated from all one-sidedness, especially the one-sidedness of finite subjectivity, and is adequate to meet the mind's demands for unity with its object, whatever the object may be. There is no need for distrust or hesitation on the part of reason in dealing with the world; it has but to "let itself go," and the whole domain of concrete individuality in all its manifold forms will straightway give up its essential meaning without reserve, and without retaining the least part of the only secret worth knowing, the secret of the "thing itself." Reason is the open secret of the world, because it opens all secrets. It makes the world after its own image, because it finds its own likeness in the face of the world.

> The fast-bound substance of the universe has no power within it capable of withstanding the courage of man's knowledge: it must give way before him, and lay bare before his eyes, and for his enjoyment, its riches and its depths (Hegel's address to his students in Berlin, October 22, 1818).

In the light of the foregoing we can see at once the central position which Hegel's logic holds in his theory. For logic, as he understands it,

is the science of the notions which constitute the sole and only outcome of the activity of reason. The totality of all the notions is the
totality of the constitutive principles of reality in all its forms of individuation; and the science of this totality thus must cover the whole of
reality, finite and absolute. And since these notions so systematized
exhaustively reveal all that reason can obtain in the way of complete
knowledge, the science of logic is straightway identical with metaphysic.[13]

III

The translator has prefixed to most of the sections short statements of
an explanatory nature. These may help the reader to follow Hegel's
train of thought in those sections and to trace the connexion between
the successive stages of the argument.[14]

Some indication of the character and plan of the work as a whole
may also be useful by way of introduction.

In general terms, the *Phenomenology of Mind* is a comprehensive
and connected survey of the ways in which experience appears. The
survey seeks to accomplish a threefold result: (1) to shew that the various forms of experience constitute a continuous and connected series
of stages of mind, that the life of mind is a whole and a single continuous movement: (2) to vindicate for each typical form of experience a
necessary place in the plan of the whole: (3) to prove that the self-
comprehension of Spirit as supreme reality, complete spiritual self-
consciousness, is the necessary demand, the inevitable outcome, and
the final consummation of the entire process of experience. These
three aspects of the argument essentially involve one another. Without
some single principle present throughout the series of forms, they
could not be connected together: Spirit is this principle. Without some
single end dominating the movement from first to last the movement
could not be continuous nor have a meaning: "Absolute Knowledge" is
this end. Unless each stage had a definite positive value of its own, no
connexion could be established between them; the moments of

---

[13]A translation of the so-called larger *Logic* has recently been made by W. H. Johnston
and L. G. Struthers and forms part of the *Library of Philosophy*, published by Messrs.
George Allen & Unwin, 1929.

[14]They are no substitute for a commentary. A full commentary on the work is very much
required, and some day, it is hoped, may be provided.

Commentaries on the early part of the work have been supplied by W. Purpus, *Die
Dialektik der Sinnlichen Gewissheit bei Hegel* (1905) and *Zur Dialektik des
Bewusstseins nach Hegel* (1908). See also Gabler's *Kritik des Bewusstseins* (1901), and
Rosenkranz: Hegel als Deutscher National Philosoph.

experience would be illusory, and experience as a whole meaningless. They can only possess positive significance if they are affirmed as moments in the process of spiritual self-realization; and the whole process of experience is necessary if spirit is to come completely into its own and be the one Absolute Reality.

There seems no reason to doubt that all three aspects were present in the author's mind before he proceeded to work out the argument of the treatise. A perusal of his "Preface" and "Introduction" makes this clear. The ways in which he varies the description of the character of the treatise arise from laying emphasis on one or other of the features of the argument. The term "Phenomenology of Mind" has in view the fact that we are here dealing with the procession of the modes of mind, and the forms in which its experience "appears." The term "Science of the Experience of Consciousness," by which he described it on the title page of the first edition, lays stress on the second aspect above noted— the constructive interpretation of the positive value of each phase of experience. "The development of Science," or again, the "development of the natural consciousness up to the level of science," by which he designates the work, refers to the relation of the movement of experience to its final outcome and end—a relation in virtue of which he also speaks of the work as a "first part" of a "System of Science," and as an "introduction" to Speculative Science in general. It is a "part" of a system, because it involves the same principle and method as the whole and deals with a specific problem. It is a "first" part and an "introductory" part because it is necessary to show that and how Philosophical Science is related to other forms of experience before Science can define its province and secure its freedom. The "second" part of the system consists of the whole range of philosophical knowledge (Logic, Philosophy of Nature, and Philosophy of Mind—together the "Encyclopædia of the Philosophical Sciences").[15]

To interpret experience in the manner above indicated, the factors and the process constituting experience must apply both to experience as a whole and to every form in which experience appears. The term "experience" is indefinite, and has been used by different thinkers for

---

[15]In the *Philosophy of Mind*, Phenomenology appears as a stage in the evolution of Mind. This has given rise to some confusion. The explanation seems simple. Experience, with which the *Phenomenology* deals, is rooted in the distinction between subject and object. This distinction, however, arises in the "evolution" of mind out of an earlier stage of life and more particularly "soul-life," viz. at that stage where consciousness dawns. Before the stage of consciousness there is life and there is soul, but neither of these as such involves the distinction between subject and object. The *Philosophy of Mind* traces the various stages in the "evolution" of mind. Amongst these stages consciousness falls, and with it the distinction between subject and object on which Experience, and so Phenomenology, rests.

different purposes. Hegel takes experience to mean the inseparable and continuous interrelation of subject and object. The interrelation takes the form of conscious awareness of an object. The moments are distinct, and the unity of these factors is simply the mental process of holding them together in a single mental situation and distinguishing them from each other within that situation. The moments are inseparable, and have neither existence nor significance except in conscious relation to each other. Till the distinction arises there is no experience; after it disappears there is equally no experience. Kant held that the relation disappeared if a particular kind of element (a sense-"datum") disappeared or could not be produced. From this followed his view of things *per se*, "apart from experience," and of "ideas of reason" beyond the bounds of experience. Both notions are connected together. Hegel rejected this whole scheme. The subject-object relation was maintained as the essential nature of experience, but Hegel extended the term "experience" to each and every conscious relation of subject and object. In this way Hegel was in closer touch with fact and common usage.

In this way the problem of interpreting experience assumes a new form. The component factors, subject and object, are distinguishable but inseparable and irreducible. Experience is therefore not to be explained, as had previously been supposed, by resolving the object into terms of the subject or the subject into terms of the object. To be conscious is to experience, and to be is to be experienced. From this point of view everything falls within experience, and experience contains all reality and even the appearance of reality. And experience as a whole consists of experiences, of forms and types of experience: one we call perceptual experience, another scientific experience, another moral experience, another religious experience, etc. As forms of experience they have certain features in common. They are discovered and not produced or invented by the mind; they are "given." In each case the subject is on the one hand directly aware of its object, the object is "immediately" present to the subject, and their unity is implicit; on the other hand the process of consciously relating these factors (of "mediating" them) is that of bringing out the unity or universal which holds them together so as to constitute a single experience. These two aspects are found in all types of experience, and they are inseparable aspects in all experience. But the manner in which they appear varies from one kind of experience to another. The way in which objects are "given" in perception is very different from the way in which objects are "given" in moral experience, or in science: and similarly the process of conscious interrelation (or "mediation") differs in each kind of experience.

This anticipates another point. The forms of experience have, as in-

dicated, features in common. They also differ specifically from one another, and each type has its own claims, its own process, and its own
value. And in general this is clearly recognized in ordinary life: for no
one would identify perceptual experience with scientific experience, or
confuse either of these with moral experience. At the same time they
all fall within the whole experience of one mind, and some connexion
between them is both possible and necessary if experience is to be interpreted. Hegel's interpretation consists in regarding the various forms
of experience as differing not only in kind but in degree of completeness from one another. This implies a standard or end to which to refer
each type of experience. The standard consists in the conscious interpenetration of the two factors constituting experience—subject and object. This is realized in varying degrees in different types of experience:
at the lowest—in sense-experience—the subject least of all finds itself
in its object: at the highest—Absolute Knowledge—the object is the
very substance of the mind, and this is the culmination of experience.
Between these two the various kinds of experience realize the end or
principle of all experience in varying degrees. Hegel connects the various types of experience with one another by treating them as a series
of stages in the development of experience at its highest: thereby he at
once gives value to each kind of experience, links all forms of experience together as stages in a continuous process and shows experience
to be a systematic whole, permeated by a single principle—self-
conscious Reason or Spirit—whose highest realization is itself the final
outcome of the whole process. Such an interpretation of experience is
what he means by a scientific (philosophical) explanation of it.

We next ask, how are the forms of experience to be found? Whose
experience is under consideration? What determines the selection of
the types to be considered? The answer lies in the nature of system
which the treatise seeks to furnish. The system of experience has a logical and an historical aspect. On the one hand it seeks to be a coherently ordered whole: as such, it must work with universals, for the coherence which every scientific system requires can only be obtained by
connecting universals. On the other hand, its facts are the manifestations in time of the content and processes of conscious individual experience: as such, they are historical phenomena, for history is precisely the co-existence and succession in time of the appearances of a
living individuality. But the "system of experience" does not appear *qua*
system, for experience, regarded historically, is a disjointed series of
events and occurrences. It is equally clear that every individual does
not as a fact go through, either successively or otherwise, each and all
of the forms which the human spirit historically assumes. For the purposes of a system of experience we must therefore combine these two

aspects. The science requires generality, the experience requires individuality; the generality of science must be individualized, the individuality of experience must be generalized. The generality of science is satisfied if we abstract a form of experience from a given historical or individual situation, and treat this form as a typical moment of experience; the individuality of experience is satisfied if at any time, or in any individual situation, the typical form has been, or is, actually realized; both are satisfied at once if the experience considered by this system is treated as the experience of a generalized individual. The series of forms of experience, analyzed and connected in the *Phenomenology*, constitutes the experience of such a typified individual. This working conception enables us to treat experience as a whole, and at the same time to embrace the various modes of experience as these appear discretely in history. Without it, we should either have history alone, which is inexhaustible and so cannot be a whole; or a mere connexion of abstract ideas, which cannot as such be experience.

In this way Hegel determines the principle on which the forms of experience are selected, and the manner in which historical phenomena are treated in the argument. Those selected are, in the main, the constant or recurrent forms of experience. We do not find every possible form of experience discussed, but only such forms as serve the main idea of the discussion. Idiosyncrasy and eccentricity are no doubt of interest in human experience, but they have a significance for purposes of biography or autobiography; they are off the main track of common experience, and do not play a necessary part in the development of the essential substance of the human spirit. Nor do we find all the forms of experience that might have been expected to have a place in the general plan of experience. As already indicated the selection of the forms of experience is subject to certain limitations under which the author worked. Again, historical phenomena are throughout the argument invariably treated as individual instances of a type of experience, not as mere historical fact. This accounts for one of the most perplexing difficulties in following the discussion at certain points. Concrete historical facts are before the mind of the author, inspiring and suggesting the course of his analysis; but in many cases hardly a single hint is given of the particular facts in question. It would seem as if history were treated as a mere illustrative footnote to a typical movement of experience, instead of being, as it is, the substance of the movement analyzed. The particular time at which the historical facts appeared is a matter of indifference to the type of experience; still more so the thousand and one details which fitted them into one historical epoch as distinct from another. Hence, at certain stages of the argument, currents of history similar or identical in general character, but far removed in point of time, may operate simultaneously in determining the nature of the discussion, and elements may be drawn, now from one, and now from another. The reason, and the justification, for such procedure is that while history may not repeat itself, types of experience do, as we see, e.g., from the simple facts of language, custom, and tradition. And, indeed, it may be said that only when a form of experience has been repeatedly manifested in human history are we in a position to regard it as a type, and thus essential to the unfolding of the complete meaning of human experience. That type and historical fact should thus be indissolubly blended in the argument of the *Phenomenology* is a necessary characteristic and condition of such a system of experience. Whether the author has successfully interwoven the two in his analysis may doubtless be questioned. It may be said that sometimes he mistakes a side-track for the high road, sometimes takes an incident for a type, sometimes takes aspects of a type for the whole type, sometimes repeats types at different stages of the development of the whole. But at any rate there need be no doubt regarding his intention and aim.

The method of connecting the successive "moments" of experience is, as already indicated, that of logical development. It is one and the same in its procedure in each type of experience and in experience as a whole. Hegel fully explains in his "Preface" and "Introduction" the significance of the method and how it controls the argument in the case of the present treatise. Nothing further therefore need be said here on this point. But it should not be supposed that his actual application of the method was carried through by its own, or by his own, spontaneous inspiration, without suggestion and assistance from other sources. So far from dispensing with assistance in the construction of this system of experience, he maintains that the method really operates, unconsciously, in all minds and in all experience. And there can be no doubt that in the working out of the system the author was guided to a very large extent by results achieved by others, and by facts and suggestions drawn from familiar sources. It is not difficult to trace the profound influence of Greek thought not only in his conception of the method, but also in determining the analysis. For example both the beginning and the conclusion of his system of experience are directly derived from Greek thought. The discussion of "sense-certainty" in the first stage of the *Phenomenology* is little more than a fresh restatement of the analysis and criticism of the nature of αἴσθησις, found in Greek philosophy, especially in Plato and Aristotle.[16] The conception of "Absolute Knowledge" with which the *Phenomenology* concludes is a reproduction of

---

[16]This has been well brought out by Purpus in his pamphlet, *Die Dialektik der Sinnlichen Gewissheit bei Hegel*, Nürnberg, 1905.

Aristotle's interpretation of the divine thought. "Pure thought thinks that which is the most divine and most precious, and it does not change. . . . Since it is the most excellent thing, it thinks itself, and its thinking is the thinking on thinking. . . . In productive activity, apart from the matter, the substance or formal essence is the object, and in theoretical activity the object is the concept or function of thinking. Therefore thought and the object of thought, not being different in the cases where there is no matter, will be the same, and thinking will be one with the object of thought. . . . The position in which human thought finds itself at a particular time . . . is that in which the divine thought, the thought which thinks *itself*, is throughout all eternity."[17]

Again, the order in which the various forms of experience are placed between the upper and lower limits of experience was probably suggested by the mental development of the individual and the historical development of mankind. This was inevitable, for the very nature of experience, as we have seen, involves process in time, and this occurs in a definite order. If that order coincides with the necessary order required by a logically constructed system, the coincidence may be a chance, but it facilitates and gives vividness to the analysis. Moreover, it is of the essence of the argument to look upon historical process, whether in the individual unit, or in the larger area of spiritual life found in society, as the condition by which the individual and universal elements of experience become concretely identified and harmonized. Thus, e.g., the "psychological" process of mental development provides the suggestion for the "dialectical" process of mind from sense-knowledge to perception, or again, from consciousness to self-consciousness; the historical evolution of Greek and Roman society suggests the "dialectical" transition from the custom-constituted to the law-constituted order of society; the historical connexion between the individualism of the eighteenth century and the ethical philosophy of his own day suggests the "dialectical" connexion between the atomistic freedom of a revolutionary epoch and the inner freedom of conscience.

IV

It is manifest that such a system is no more than an orderly arrangement of the ways in which experience appears. It does not expound all the truth that the various modes of experience themselves contain. Each mode forms a nucleus of a sphere of truth all its own, the elaboration of which is a separate undertaking by itself. The substance of the truth which each contains is only relevant to the argument, and is only

---

[17]*Metaphysics*, 1074*b*, 25–1075*a*, 10.

introduced so far as is necessary to bring out the peculiar nature of the
kind of experience each mode embodies.

Again, the *Phenomenology* is distinct from empirical psychology on
the one hand, and the concrete life of individual experience on the
other. The growth in mental life of the distinction between subject and
object is presupposed before experience can be said to exist, and the
growth of that distinction in time it is part of the work of psychology to
trace. On the other hand, relatively to the living agent in concrete experience, the phenomenological observer is like the historian or the
dramatist who perceives and understands the play of the forces controlling the living agent, and traces the connexion of the moving principles that operate unseen, and certainly unforeseen, in the production
of the result.

It is equally clear from what has been said that the *Phenomenology* is
not a complete system of philosophy. It is at most a part, and, as the author insisted, the introductory part to a comprehensive philosophical
system. The exhaustive elaboration of "Absolute Knowledge" would
alone be a complete system of philosophy. All that is done in the
Phenomenology to provide such a system is to show that "Absolute
Knowledge" as a mode of spiritual life has its roots in experience, and
is the consummation and final cause of the whole process of experience. The author endeavoured in his other works to construct the entire system of "Absolute Knowledge"; but the success or incompleteness of this achievement does not affect the value of the argument of
the *Phenomenology*, which justifies the standpoint of "Absolute
Knowledge."

It is improbable that the argument of this treatise as a whole will meet
with general acceptance even from those who are capable of appreciating it. In the nature of the case this is not to be expected. Philosophy
as an attitude of mind towards the world, and a philosophical system as
the expression of such an attitude, occupy a region midway between
poetry on the one hand and science on the other. It is an activity of that
imagination which is "reason in her most exalted mood," and an attempt to articulate this in the form of a connected scheme of thought.
It always implies an individual point of view and a perspective of the
world, which are central and final for the individual, but are different
in each case. There is thus no final philosophical theory for all men,
any more than there is one poetic vision for all. If philosophy were to
claim the universality of science the history of philosophical systems
would refute the claim, since no two philosophers agree in the theories
they advance. The value of a philosophical system is therefore not to be
measured by its general acceptance but by the success and consistency

with which it expresses a specific view of the world; by the extent to which it stimulates the mind to enjoy the liberty of pursuing thought for its own sake; and by the light it affords in solving the problems which the world presents in a different form to every one who possesses the philosophical frame of mind.

Viewed in this way the *Phenomenology* has more than a disciplinary interest to students of philosophy. It is a supreme expression of the idealistic outlook on the universe, "on man, on nature and on human life," and will doubtless have much to give for generations to come to those who understand.

At the present time the *Phenomenology* may prove of assistance in approaching the profoundly important philosophical problems which have been raised by the novelty, the complexity, and the range of modern science, by the freshened interest in morality and religion, and by the immense expansion of historical knowledge. These must necessarily compel the mind to consider fundamental principles and to attempt to reach a central point of view. How necessary this is those are best able to judge who find fanciful spiritism masquerading as philosophy and capable scientists propounding primitive metaphysics.[18] The accumulated wealth of knowledge of all kinds cannot entitle us to assume the airs of intellectual arrogance, or to indulge in the luxuries of intellectual self-complacency. The most comprehensive scientific theory of recent times—that of Relativity—no more solves the fundamental problem of the nature of human experience as a whole than did the equally comprehensive theory of evolution put forward in the middle of last century. That problem remains the same now as it has always been. Whatever may be said for Hegel's argument, his claim that the speculative outlook on the universe is a necessary demand of human experience and has an unique contribution to make to its fulfilment, can hardly be disputed. The composer and the conductor of the orchestra are as necessary to the performance as the various instrumentalists.

It is also important to recognize the value of his contention that human experience is essentially a reasonable process, and that every type of experience has its own substantial part to play in the complete drama of human life. In actual experience we neither confound one type of experience with another—morality, science, art and religion— nor would we attempt to resolve one into another. Each has its limits:

---

[18]E.g., one writer of distinction states that scientific thought, in spite of its immense achievement, supplies only a "symbolic" scheme of an "unknown background," and that it is doubtful if anyone knows what is meant by the reality or existence of anything "but our own Egos."

none can rightly trespass on the domain of another: and no single experience can alone satisfy the whole mind. Each constitutes a level of experience; each has a reality and a truth of its own to supply to the human spirit.[19] Some individuals may lay emphasis on one more than on another; but this is a matter of individual selection and not a method of determining that one is primary and another secondary, that one gives reality and another appearance, or that one is true and another false.

Again, a new significance, not without interest in our day, is given to the familiar but much misunderstood statement that the individual is a representative of humanity. In Hegel's view this is not an incidental feature, but a principle underlying human experience. The individual is potentially capable of accomplishing all that humanity has explicitly realized: the wealth of human resources is his rightful inheritance and endowment: the achievement of humanity is his own fulfilment, its range and its height the measure of his stature and his worth. The accomplishment of the drama of human life in time and space is the *Divina Commedia* of his own spirit as he passes from the level of nature through the refining processes of the moral order until he attains his reconcilement in religion and the beatific vision of the spirit of the universe, seen by

l'eterna luce
Che vista sola sempre amore accende.

This self-manifestation of the Absolute Spirit to man is at once the consummation of his experience and the discovery that the Divine Spirit has been the immanent agency operative throughout experience, giving reality to each stage and continuity to the whole process. For it is of the essence of Hegel's argument that the Absolute Spirit takes upon itself and makes its own the stupendous labour of the world's history; that in so doing it infuses the component parts with spiritual significance, embodies itself in human form, and, in the process, at once eternal and in time, reconciles the world to itself and itself to the world.[20] For the individual these altitudes of vision where the world is transfigured are not a permanent residence, and the formulation of the experience well-nigh defeats human effort.

---

[19] On this view a "conflict between science and religion" becomes impossible: as it would be meaningless to speak of a conflict between science and art or between science and morality.

[20] Students of religion will doubtless recognize that such a view is in agreement with essential doctrines in the catholic faith of Christendom. This was no accident of Hegel's scheme of thought: it seems to have been one of the purposes which provided a controlling motive for his work.

> 'tis a thing impossible to frame
> Conceptions equal to the soul's desires;
> And the most difficult of tasks to keep
> Heights which the soul is competent to gain.[21]

But for the Absolute Spirit, the universe being eternal, as Hegel after Aristotle maintained, the process is eternally being fulfilled and eternally complete.

---

[21]*Excursion:* Bk IV.

The Phenomenology
of Mind

PREFACE: ON SCIENTIFIC KNOWLEDGE

IN THE case of a philosophical work it seems not only superfluous, but, in view of the nature of philosophy, even inappropriate and misleading to begin, as writers usually do in a preface, by explaining the end the author had in mind, the circumstances which gave rise to the work, and the relation in which the writer takes it to stand to other treatises on the same subject, written by his predecessors or his contemporaries. For whatever it might be suitable to state about philosophy in a preface—say, an historical sketch of the main drift and point of view, the general content and results, a string of desultory assertions and assurances about the truth—this cannot be accepted as the form and manner in which to expound philosophical truth.

Moreover, because philosophy has its being essentially in the element of that universality which encloses the particular within it, the end or final result seems, in the case of philosophy more than in that of other sciences, to have absolutely expressed the complete fact itself in its very nature; contrasted with that the mere process of bringing it to light would seem, properly speaking, to have no essential significance. On the other hand, in the general idea of e.g. anatomy—the knowledge of the parts of the body regarded as lifeless—we are quite sure we do not possess the objective concrete fact, the actual content of the science, but must, over and above, be concerned with particulars. Further, in the case of such a collection of items of knowledge, which has no real right to the name of science, any talk about purpose and such-like generalities is not commonly very different from the descriptive and superficial way in which the contents of the science—these nerves and muscles, etc.—are themselves spoken of. In philosophy, on the other hand, it would at once be felt incongruous were such a method made use of and yet shown by philosophy itself to be incapable of grasping the truth.

In the same way too, by determining the relation which a philosophical work professes to have to other treatises on the same subject,

an extraneous interest is introduced, and obscurity is thrown over the
point at issue in the knowledge of the truth. The more the ordinary
mind takes the opposition between true and false to be fixed, the more
is it accustomed to expect either agreement or contradiction with a
given philosophical system, and only to see reason for the one or the
other in any explanatory statement concerning such a system. It does
not conceive the diversity of philosophical systems as the progressive
evolution of truth; rather, it sees only contradiction in that variety. The
bud disappears when the blossom breaks through, and we might say
that the former is refuted by the latter; in the same way when the fruit
comes, the blossom may be explained to be a false form of the plant's
existence, for the fruit appears as its true nature in place of the blossom.
These stages are not merely differentiated; they supplant one another
as being incompatible with one another. But the ceaseless activity of
their own inherent nature makes them at the same time moments of an
organic unity, where they not merely do not contradict one another,
but where one is as necessary as the other; and this equal necessity of
all moments constitutes alone and thereby the life of the whole. But
contradiction as between philosophical systems is not wont to be conceived in this way; on the other hand, the mind perceiving the contradiction does not commonly know how to relieve it or keep it free from
its onesidedness, and to recognize in what seems conflicting and inherently antagonistic the presence of mutually necessary moments.

The demand for such explanations, as also the attempts to satisfy this
demand, very easily pass for the essential business philosophy has to undertake. Where could the inmost truth of a philosophical work be
found better expressed than in its purposes and results? and in what way
could these be more definitely known than through their distinction
from what is produced during the same period by others working in the
same field? If, however, such procedure is to pass for more than the beginning of knowledge, if it is to pass for actually knowing, then we
must, in point of fact, look on it as a device for avoiding the real business at issue, an attempt to combine the appearance of being in earnest
and taking trouble about the subject with an actual neglect of the subject altogether. For the real subject-matter is not exhausted in its purpose, but in working the matter out; nor is the mere result attained the
concrete whole itself, but the result along with the process of arriving
at it. The purpose by itself is a lifeless universal, just as the general drift
is a mere activity in a certain direction, which is still without its concrete realization; and the naked result is the corpse of the system which
has left its guiding tendency behind it. Similarly, the distinctive difference of anything is rather the boundary, the limit, of the subject; it is
found at that point where the subject-matter stops, or it is what this

subject-matter is *not*. To trouble oneself in this fashion with the purpose and results, and again with the differences, the positions taken up and judgments passed by one thinker and another, is therefore an easier task than perhaps it seems. For instead of laying hold of the matter in hand, a procedure of that kind is all the while away from the subject altogether. Instead of dwelling within it and becoming absorbed by it, knowledge of that sort is always grasping at something else; such knowledge, instead keeping to the subject-matter and giving itself up to it, never gets away from itself. The easiest thing of all is to pass judgments on what has a solid substantial content; it is more difficult to grasp it, and most of all difficult to do both together and produce the systematic exposition of it.

The beginning of culture and of the struggle to pass out of the unbroken immediacy of naïve psychical life has always to be made by acquiring knowledge of universal principles and points of view, by striving, in the first instance, to work up simply to the *thought* of the subject-matter in general, not forgetting at the same time to give reasons for supporting it or refuting it, to apprehend the concrete riches and fullness contained in its various determinate qualities, and to know how to furnish a coherent, orderly account of it and a responsible judgment upon it. This beginning of mental cultivation will, however, very soon make way for the earnestness of actual life in all its fullness, which leads to a living experience of the subject-matter itself; and when, in addition, conceptual thought strenuously penetrates to the very depths of its meaning, such knowledge and style of judgment will keep their due place in everyday thought and conversation.

The systematic development of truth in scientific form can alone be the true shape in which truth exists. To help to bring philosophy nearer to the form of science—that goal where it can lay aside the name of *love* of knowledge and be actual *knowledge*—that is what I have set before me. The inner necessity that knowledge should be science lies in its very nature; and the adequate and sufficient explanation for this lies simply and solely in the systematic exposition of philosophy itself. The external necessity, however, so far as this is apprehended in a universal way, and apart from the accident of the personal element and the particular occasioning influences affecting the individual, is the same as the internal: it lies in the form and shape in which the process of time presents the existence of its moments. To show that the time process does raise philosophy to the level of scientific system would, therefore, be the only true justification of the attempts which aim at proving that philosophy must assume this character; because the temporal process would thus bring out and lay bare the necessity of it, nay, more, would at the same time be carrying out that very aim itself.

When we state the true form of truth to be its scientific character—
or, what is the same thing, when it is maintained that truth finds the
medium of its existence in notions or conceptions alone—I know that
this seems to contradict an idea with all its consequences which makes
great pretensions and has gained widespread acceptance and conviction at the present time. A word of explanation concerning this contradiction seems, therefore, not out of place, even though at this stage it
can amount to no more than a dogmatic assurance exactly like the view
we are opposing. If, that is to say, truth exists merely in what, or rather
exists merely *as* what, is called at one time intuition, at another immediate knowledge of the Absolute, Religion, Being—not being in the
centre of divine love, but the very Being of this centre, of the Absolute
itself—from that point of view it is rather the opposite of the notional
or conceptual form which would be required for systematic philosophical exposition. The Absolute on this view is not to be grasped in conceptual form, but felt, intuited; it is not its conception, but the feeling
of it and intuition of it that are to have the say and find expression.[1]

If we consider the appearance of a claim like this in its more general
setting, and look at the level which the self-conscious mind at present
occupies, we shall find that self-consciousness has got beyond the substantial fullness of life, which it used to carry on in the element of
thought—beyond the state of immediacy of belief, beyond the satisfaction and security arising from the assurance which consciousness
possessed of being reconciled with ultimate reality and with its all-
pervading presence, within as well as without. Self-conscious mind has
not merely passed beyond that to the opposite extreme of insubstantial
reflection of self into self, but beyond this too. It has not merely lost its
essential and concrete life, it is also conscious of this loss and of the
transitory finitude characteristic of its content. Turning away from the
husks it has to feed on, and confessing that it lies in wickedness and sin,
it reviles itself for so doing, and now desires from philosophy not so
much to bring it to a knowledge of what it is, as to obtain once again
through philosophy the restoration of that sense of solidity and substantiality of existence it has lost. Philosophy is thus expected not so
much to meet this want by opening up the compact solidity of substantial existence, and bringing this to the light and level of self-
consciousness—is not so much to bring chaotic conscious life back to
the orderly ways of thought, and the simplicity of the notion, as to run
together what thought has divided asunder, suppress the notion with its
distinctions, and restore the *feeling* of existence. What it wants from

---

[1]Hegel has in mind the views of Jacobi and the Romantics, Schlegel and
Schleiermacher.

philosophy is not so much insight as edification. The beautiful, the holy, the eternal, religion, love—these are the bait required to awaken the desire to bite: not the notion, but ecstasy, not the march of cold necessity in the subject-matter, but ferment and enthusiasm—these are to be the ways by which the wealth of the concrete substance is to be stored and increasingly extended.[2]

With this demand there goes the strenuous effort, almost perfervidly zealous in its activity, to rescue mankind from being sunken in what is sensuous, vulgar, and of fleeting importance, and to raise men's eyes to the stars; as if men had quite forgotten the divine, and were on the verge of finding satisfaction, like worms, in mud and water. Time was when man had a heaven, decked and fitted out with endless wealth of thoughts and pictures. The significance of all that is, lay in the thread of light by which it was attached to heaven; instead of dwelling in the present as it is here and now, the eye glanced away over the present to the Divine, away, so to say, to a present that lies beyond. The mind's gaze had to be directed under compulsion to what is earthly, and kept fixed there; and it has needed a long time to introduce that clearness, which only celestial realities had, into the crassness and confusion shrouding the sense of things earthly, and to make attention to the immediate present as such, which was called Experience, of interest and of value. Now we have apparently the need for the opposite of all this; man's mind and interest are so deeply rooted in the earthly that we require a like power to have them raised above that level. His spirit shows such poverty of nature that it seems to long for the mere pitiful feeling of the divine in the abstract, and to get refreshment from that, like a wanderer in the desert craving for the merest mouthful of water. By the little which can thus satisfy the needs of the human spirit we can measure the extent of its loss.

This easy contentment in receiving, or stinginess in giving, does not suit the character of science. The man who only seeks edification, who wants to envelop in mist the manifold diversity of his earthly existence and thought, and craves after the vague enjoyment of this vague and indeterminate Divinity—he may look where he likes to find this: he will easily find for himself the means to procure something he can rave over and puff himself up withal. But philosophy must beware of wishing to be edifying.

Still less must this kind of contentment, which holds science in contempt, take upon itself to claim that raving obscurantism of this sort is something higher than science. These apocalyptic utterances pretend to occupy the very centre and the deepest depths; they look askance at

---

[2]Cp. pp. 119 ff.

all definiteness and preciseness (ὅρος) of meaning; and they deliberately hold back from conceptual thinking and the constraining necessities of thought, as being the sort of reflection which, they say, can only
feel at home in the sphere of finitude. But just as there is a breadth
which is emptiness, there is a depth which is empty too: as we may have
an extension of substance which overflows into finite multiplicity without the power of keeping the manifold together, in the same way we
may have an insubstantial intensity which, keeping itself in as mere
force without actual expression, is no better than superficiality. The
force of mind is only as great as its expression; its depth only as deep as
its power to expand and lose itself when spending and giving out its
substance. Moreover, when this unreflective emotional knowledge
makes a pretence of having immersed its own very self in the depths of
the absolute Being, and of philosophizing in all holiness and truth, it
hides from itself the fact that instead of devotion to God, it rather, by
this contempt for all measurable precision and definiteness, simply at-
tests in its own case the fortuitous character of its content, and in the
other endows God with its own caprice. When such minds commit
themselves to the unrestrained ferment of sheer emotion, they think
that, by putting a veil over self-consciousness, and surrendering all understanding, they are thus God's beloved ones to whom He gives His
wisdom in sleep. This is the reason, too, that in point of fact what they
do conceive and bring forth in sleep is dreams.

   For the rest it is not difficult to see that our epoch is a birth-time, and
a period of transition. The spirit of man has broken with the old order
of things hitherto prevailing, and with the old ways of thinking, and is
in the mind to let them all sink into the depths of the past and to set
about its own transformation. It is indeed never at rest, but carried
along the stream of progress ever onward. But it is here as in the case
of the birth of a child; after a long period of nutrition in silence, the
continuity of the gradual growth in size, of quantitative change, is sud-
denly cut short by the first breath drawn—there is a break in the
process, a qualitative change—and the child is born. In like manner
the spirit of the time, growing slowly and quietly ripe for the new form
it is to assume, disintegrates one fragment after another of the structure
of its previous world. That it is tottering to its fall is indicated only by
symptoms here and there. Frivolity and again ennui, which are spreading in the established order of things, the undefined foreboding of
something unknown—all these betoken that there is something else
approaching. This gradual crumbling to pieces, which did not alter the
general look and aspect of the whole, is interrupted by the sunrise,
which, in a flash and at a single stroke, brings to view the form and
structure of the new world.

But this new world is perfectly realized just as little as the new-born child; and it is essential to bear this in mind. It comes on the stage to begin with in its immediacy, in its bare generality. A building is not finished when its foundation is laid; and just as little is the attainment of a general notion of a whole the whole itself. When we want to see an oak with all its vigour of trunk, its spreading branches, and mass of foliage, we are not satisfied to be shown an acorn instead. In the same way science, the crowning glory of a spiritual world, is not found complete in its initial stages. The beginning of the new spirit is the outcome of a widespread revolution in manifold forms of spiritual culture; it is the reward which comes after a chequered and devious course of development, and after much struggle and effort. It is a whole which, after running its course and laying bare all its content, returns again to itself; it is the resultant abstract notion of the whole. But the actual realization of this abstract whole is only found when those previous shapes and forms, which are now reduced to ideal moments of the whole, are developed anew again, but developed and shaped within this new medium, and with the meaning they have thereby acquired.

While the new world makes its first appearance merely in general outline, merely as a whole lying concealed and hidden within a bare abstraction, the wealth of the bygone life, on the other hand, is still consciously present in recollection. Consciousness misses in the new form the detailed expanse of content; but still more the developed expression of form by which distinctions are definitely determined and arranged in their precise relations. Without this last feature science has no general intelligibility, and has the appearance of being an esoteric possession of a few individuals—an esoteric possession, because in the first instance it is only the essential principle or notion of science, only its inner nature that is to be found; and a possession of few individuals, because, at its first appearance, its content is not elaborated and expanded in detail, and thus its existence is turned into something particular. Only what is perfectly determinate in form is at the same time exoteric, comprehensible, and capable of being learned and possessed by everybody. Intelligibility is the form in which science is offered to everyone, and is the open road to it made plain for all. To reach rational knowledge by our intelligence is the just demand of the mind which comes to science. For intelligence, understanding (*Verstand*), is thinking, pure activity of the self in general; and what is intelligible (*Verständige*) is something from the first familiar and common to the scientific and unscientific mind alike, enabling the unscientific mind to enter the domain of science.

Science, at its commencement, when as yet it has reached neither detailed completeness nor perfection of form, is exposed to blame on that account. But it would be as unjust to suppose this blame to attach to its essential nature, as it is inadmissible not to be ready to recognize the demand for that further development in fuller detail. In the contrast and opposition between these two aspects (the initial and the developed stages of science) seems to lie the critical knot which scientific culture at present struggles to loosen, and about which so far it is not very clear. One side parades the wealth of its material and the intelligibility of its ideas; the other pours contempt at any rate on the latter, and makes a parade of the immediate intuitive rationality and divine quality of its content. Although the first is reduced to silence, perhaps by the inner force of truth alone, perhaps, too, by the noisy bluster of the other side, and even though having regard to the reason and nature of the case it did feel overborne, yet it does not therefore feel satisfied as regards those demands for greater development; for those demands are just, but still unfulfilled. Its silence is due only in part to the victory of the other side; it is half due to that weariness and indifference which are usually the consequence when expectations are being constantly awakened by promises which are not followed up by performance.

The other side[3] no doubt at times makes an easy enough matter of having a vast expanse of content. They haul on to their territory a lot of material, that, namely, which is already familiar and arranged in order; and since they are concerned more especially about what is exceptional, strange, and curious, they seem all the more to be in possession of the rest, which knowledge in its own way was finished and done with, as well as to have control over what was unregulated and disorderly. Hence everything appears brought within the compass of the Absolute Idea, which seems thus to be recognized in everything, and to have succeeded in becoming a system *in extenso* of scientific knowledge. But if we look more closely at this expanded system we find that it has not been reached by one and the same principle taking shape in diverse ways; it is the shapeless repetition of one and the same idea, which is applied in an external fashion to different material, the wearisome reiteration of it keeping up the semblance of diversity. The Idea, which by itself is no doubt the truth, really never gets any farther than just where it began, as long as the development of it consists in nothing else than such a repetition of the same formula. If the knowing subject carries round everywhere the one inert abstract form, taking up in external fashion whatever material comes his way, and dipping it into this element, then this comes about as near to fulfilling what is wanted—viz. a self-origination of the wealth of detail, and a self-determining distinction of shapes and forms—as any chance fancies

---

[3]Schelling and his school.

about the content in question. It is rather a monochrome formalism, which only arrives at distinction in the matter it has to deal with, because this is already prepared and well known.

This monotonousness and abstract universality are maintained to be the Absolute. This formalism insists that to be dissatisfied therewith argues an incapacity to grasp the standpoint of the Absolute, and keep a firm hold on it. If it was once the case that the bare possibility of thinking of something in some other fashion was sufficient to refute a given idea, and the naked possibility, the bare general thought, possessed and passed for the entire substantive value of actual knowledge; similarly we find here all the value ascribed to the general idea in this bare form without concrete realization; and we see here, too, the style and method of speculative contemplation identified with dissipating and resolving what is determinate and distinct, or rather with hurling it down, without more ado and without any justification, into the abyss of vacuity. To consider any specific fact as it is in the Absolute, consists here in nothing else than saying about it that, while it is now doubtless spoken of as something specific, yet in the Absolute, in the abstract identity A = A, there is no such thing at all, for everything is there all one. To pit this single assertion, that "in the Absolute all is one," against the organized whole of determinate and complete knowledge, or of knowledge which at least aims at and demands complete development—to give out its Absolute as the night in which, as we say, all cows are black—that is the very *naïveté* of emptiness of knowledge.

The formalism which has been deprecated and despised by recent philosophy, and which has arisen once more in philosophy itself, will not disappear from science, even though its inadequacy is known and felt, till the knowledge of absolute reality has become quite clear as to what its own true nature consists in. Having in mind that the general idea of what is to be done, if it precedes the attempt to carry it out, facilitates the comprehension of this process, it is worth while to indicate here some rough idea of it, with the hope at the same time that this will give us the opportunity to set aside certain forms whose habitual presence is a hindrance in the way of speculative knowledge.

In my view—a view which the developed exposition of the system itself can alone justify—everything depends on grasping and expressing the ultimate truth not as Substance but as Subject as well. At the same time we must note that concrete substantiality implicates and involves the universal or the immediacy of knowledge itself, as well as that immediacy which is being, or immediacy *qua* object *for* knowledge. If the generation which heard God spoken of as the One Substance[4] was

---

[4]Spinoza.

shocked and revolted by such a characterization of his nature, the reason lay partly in the instinctive feeling that in such a conception self-consciousness was simply submerged, and not preserved. But partly, again, the opposite position, which maintains thinking to be merely subjective thinking, abstract universality as such, is exactly the same bare uniformity, is undifferentiated, unmoved substantiality.[5] And even if, in the third place, thought combines with itself the being of substance, and conceives immediacy or intuition (*Anschauung*) as thinking, it is still a question whether this intellectual intuition does not fall back into that inert, abstract simplicity, and exhibit and expound reality itself in an unreal manner.[6]

The living substance, further, is that being which is truly subject, or, what is the same thing, is truly realized and actual (*wirklich*) solely in the process of positing itself, or in mediating with its own self its transitions from one state or position to the opposite. As subject it is pure and simple negativity, and just on that account a process of splitting up what is simple and undifferentiated, a process of duplicating and setting factors in opposition, which [process] in turn is the negation of this indifferent diversity and of the opposition of factors it entails. True reality is merely this process of reinstating self-identity, of reflecting into its own self in and from its other, and is not an original and primal unity as such, not an immediate unity as such. It is the process of its own becoming, the circle which presupposes its end as its purpose, and has its end for its beginning; it becomes concrete and actual only by being carried out, and by the end it involves.

The life of God and divine intelligence, then, can, if we like, be spoken of as love disporting with itself; but this idea falls into edification, and even sinks into insipidity, if it lacks the seriousness, the suffering, the patience, and the labour of the negative. *Per se* the divine life is no doubt undisturbed identity and oneness with itself, which finds no serious obstacle in otherness and estrangement, and none in the surmounting of this estrangement. But this "per se" is abstract generality, where we abstract from its real nature, which consists in its being objective to itself, conscious of itself on its own account (*für sich zu sein*); and where consequently we neglect altogether the self-movement which is the formal character of its activity. If the form is declared to correspond to the essence, it is just for that reason a misunderstanding to suppose that knowledge can be content with the "per se," the essence, but can do without the form, that the absolute principle, or absolute intuition, makes the carrying out of the former, or the develop-

---

[5]Kant and Fichte.
[6]Schelling.

ment of the latter, needless. Precisely because the form is as necessary to the essence as the essence to itself, absolute reality must not be conceived of and expressed as essence alone, i.e. as immediate substance, or as pure self-intuition of the Divine, but as form also, and with the entire wealth of the developed form. Only then is it grasped and expressed as really actual.

The truth is the whole. The whole, however, is merely the essential nature reaching its completeness through the process of its own development. Of the Absolute it must be said that it is essentially a result, that only at the end is it what it is in very truth; and just in that consists its nature, which is to be actual, subject, or self-becoming, self-development. Should it appear contradictory to say that the Absolute has to be conceived essentially as a result, a little consideration will set this appearance of contradiction in its true light. The beginning, the principle, or the Absolute, as at first or immediately expressed, is merely the universal. If we say "all animals," that does not pass for zoology; for the same reason we see at once that the words absolute, divine, eternal, and so on do not express what is implied in them; and only mere words like these, in point of fact, express intuition as the immediate. Whatever is more than a word like that, even the mere transition to a proposition, is a form of mediation, contains a process towards another state from which we must return once more. It is this process of mediation, however, that is rejected with horror, as if absolute knowledge were being surrendered when more is made of mediation than merely the assertion that it is nothing absolute, and does not exist in the Absolute.

This horrified rejection of mediation, however, arises as a fact from want of acquaintance with its nature, and with the nature of absolute knowledge itself. For mediating is nothing but self-identity working itself out through an active self-directed process; or, in other words, it is reflection into self, the aspect in which the ego is for itself, objective to itself. It is pure negativity, or, reduced to its utmost abstraction, the process of bare and simple becoming. The ego, or becoming in general, this process of mediating, is, because of its being simple, just immediacy coming to be, and is immediacy itself. We misconceive therefore the nature of reason if we exclude reflection or mediation from ultimate truth, and do not take it to be a positive moment of the Absolute. It is reflection which constitutes truth the final result, and yet at the same time does away with the contrast between result and the process of arriving at it. For this process is likewise simple, and therefore not distinct from the form of truth, which consists in appearing as simple in the result; it is indeed just this restoration and return to simplicity. While the embryo is certainly, in itself, implicitly a human being, it is not so explicitly, it is not by itself a human being (*für sich*);

man is explicitly man only in the form of developed and cultivated reason, which has made itself to be what it is implicitly. Its actual reality is
first found here. But this result arrived at is itself simple immediacy; for
it is self-conscious freedom, which is at one with itself, and has not set
aside the opposition it involves and left it there, but has made its account with it and become reconciled to it.

What has been said may also be expressed by saying that reason is
purposive activity. The exaltation of so-called nature at the expense of
thought misconceived, and more especially the rejection of external
purposiveness, have brought the idea of purpose in general into disre-
pute. All the same, in the sense in which Aristotle, too, characterizes
nature as purposive activity, purpose is the immediate, the undisturbed,
the unmoved which is self-moving; as such it is subject. Its power of
moving, taken abstractly, is its existence for itself, or pure negativity.
The result is the same as the beginning solely because the beginning is
purpose. Stated otherwise, what is actual and concrete is the same as its
inner principle or notion simply because the immediate *qua* purpose
contains within it the self or pure actuality. The realized purpose, or
concrete actuality, is movement and development unfolded. But this
very unrest is the self; and it is one and the same with that immediacy
and simplicity characteristic of the beginning just for the reason that it
is the result, and has returned upon itself—while this latter again is just
the self, and the self is self-referring and self-relating identity and
simplicity.

The need to think of the Absolute as subject, has led men to make
use of statements like "God is the eternal," the "moral order of the
world," or "love," etc. In such propositions the truth is just barely stated
to be Subject, but not set forth as the process of reflectively mediating
itself with itself. In a proposition of that kind we begin with the word
God. By itself this is a meaningless sound, a mere name; the predicate
says afterwards *what* it is, gives it content and meaning: the empty beginning becomes real knowledge only when we thus get to the end of
the statement. So far as that goes, why not speak alone of the eternal,
of the moral order of the world, etc., or, like the ancients, of pure conceptions such as being, the one, etc., i.e. of what gives the meaning
without adding the meaningless sound at all? But this word just indicates that it is not a being or essence or universal in general that is put
forward, but something reflected into self, a subject. Yet at the same
time this acceptance of the Absolute as Subject is merely anticipated,
not really affirmed. The subject is taken to be a fixed point, and to it as
their support the predicates are attached, by a process falling within the
individual knowing about it, but not looked upon as belonging to
the point of attachment itself; only by such a process, however, could

the content be presented as subject. Constituted as it is, this process cannot belong to the subject; but when that point of support is fixed to start with, this process cannot be otherwise constituted, it can only be external. The anticipation that the Absolute is subject is therefore not merely not the realization of this conception; it even makes realization impossible. For it makes out the notion to be a static point, while its actual reality is self-movement, self-activity.

Among the many consequences that follow from what has been said, it is of importance to emphasize this, that knowledge is only real and can only be set forth fully in the form of science, in the form of system; and further, that a so-called fundamental proposition or first principle of philosophy, even if it is true, is yet none the less false just because and in so far as it is merely a fundamental proposition, merely a first principle. It is for that reason easily refuted. The refutation consists in bringing out its defective character; and it *is* defective because it is merely the universal, merely a principle, the beginning. If the refutation is complete and thorough, it is derived and developed from the nature of the principle itself, and not accomplished by bringing in from elsewhere other counter assurances and chance fancies. It would be strictly the development of the principle, and thus the completion of its deficiency, were it not that it misunderstands its own purport by taking account solely of the negative aspect of what it seeks to do, and is not conscious of the positive character of its process and result. The really positive working out of the beginning is at the same time just as much the very reverse, it is a negative attitude towards the principle we start from, negative, that is to say, of its one-sided form, which consists in being primarily immediate, a mere purpose. It may therefore be regarded as a refutation of what constitutes the basis of the system; but more correctly it should be looked at as a demonstration that the *basis* or principle of the system is in point of fact merely its *beginning*.

That the truth is only realized in the form of system, that substance is essentially subject, is expressed in the idea which represents the Absolute as Spirit (*Geist*)—the grandest conception of all, and one which is due to modern times and its religion. Spirit is alone Reality. It is the inner being of the world, that which essentially is, and is *per se*; it assumes objective, determinate form, and enters into relations with itself—it is externality (otherness), and exists for self; yet, in this determination, and in its otherness, it is still one with itself—it is self-contained and self-complete, in itself and for itself at once. This self-containedness, however, is first something known by us, it is implicit in its nature (*an sich*); it is Substance spiritual. It has to become self-contained *for itself*, on its own account; it must be knowledge of spirit, and must be consciousness of itself as spirit. This means, it must be presented to itself as an object, but at the same time straightway annul and transcend this objective form; it must be its own object in which it finds itself reflected. So far as its spiritual content is produced by its own activity, it is only *we* [the thinkers] who know spirit to be for itself, to be objective to itself; but in so far as spirit knows itself to be for itself, then this self-production, the pure notion, is the sphere and element in which its objectification takes effect, and where it gets its existential form. In this way it is in its existence aware of itself as an object in which its own self is reflected. Mind, which, when thus developed, knows itself to be mind, is science. Science is its realization, and the kingdom it sets up for itself in its own native element.

A self having knowledge purely of itself in the absolute antithesis of itself, this pure ether as such, is the very soil where science flourishes, is knowledge in universal form. The beginning of philosophy presupposes or demands from consciousness that it should feel at home in this element. But this element only attains its perfect meaning and acquires transparency through the process of gradually developing it. It is pure spirituality as the universal which assumes the shape of simple immediacy; and this simple element, existing as such, is the field of science, is thinking, which can be only in mind. Because this medium, this immediacy of mind, is the mind's substantial nature in general, it is the transfigured essence, reflection which itself is simple, which is aware of itself as immediacy; it is being, which is reflection into itself. Science on its side requires the individual self-consciousness to have risen into this high ether, in order to be able to live with science, and in science, and really to feel alive there. Conversely the individual has the right to demand that science shall hold the ladder to help him to get at least as far as this position, shall show him that he has in himself this ground to stand on. His right rests on his absolute independence, which he knows he possesses in every type and phase of knowledge; for in every phase, whether recognized by science or not, and whatever be the content, his right as an individual is the absolute and final form, i.e. he is the immediate certainty of self, and thereby is unconditioned being, were this expression preferred. If the position taken up by consciousness, that of knowing about objective things as opposed to itself, and about itself as opposed to them, is held by science to be the very opposite of what science is: if, when in knowing it keeps within itself and never goes beyond itself, science holds this state to be rather the loss of mind altogether—on the other hand the element in which *science* consists is looked at by consciousness as a remote and distant region, in which consciousness is no longer in possession of itself. Each of these two sides takes the other to be the perversion of the truth. For the naïve consciousness, to give itself up completely and straight away to science is

in itself/for itself
universal/particular
sense-consciousness /
self-consciousness } vs. science
understanding
The Phenomenology of Mind   15

to make an attempt, induced by some unknown influence, all at once to walk on its head. The compulsion to take up this attitude and move about in this position, is a constraining force it is urged to fall in with, without ever being prepared for it and with no apparent necessity for doing so. Let science be *per se* what it likes, in its relation to naïve immediate self-conscious life it presents the appearance of being a reversal of the latter; or, again, because naïve self-consciousness finds the principle of its reality in the certainty of itself, science bears the character of unreality, since consciousness "for itself" is a state quite outside of science. Science has for that reason to combine that other element of self-certainty with its own, or rather to show that the other element belongs to itself, and how it does so. When devoid of that sort of reality, science is merely the content of mind *qua* something implicit or potential (*an sich*); purpose, which at the start is no more than something internal; not spirit, but at first merely spiritual substance. This implicit moment (*Ansich*) has to find external expression, and become objective on its own account. This means nothing else than that this moment has to establish self-consciousness as one with itself.

It is this process by which science in general comes about, this gradual development of knowing, that is set forth here in the *Phenomenology of Mind*.[7] Knowing, as it is found at the start, mind in its immediate and primitive stage, is without the essential nature of mind, is sense-consciousness. To reach the stage of genuine knowledge, or produce the element where science is found—the pure conception of science itself—a long and laborious journey must be undertaken. This process towards science, as regards the content it will bring to light and the forms it will assume in the course of its progress, will not be what is primarily imagined by leading the unscientific consciousness up to the level of science: it will be something different, too, from establishing and laying the foundations of science; and anyway something else than the sort of ecstatic enthusiasm which starts straight off with absolute knowledge, as if shot out of a pistol, and makes short work of other points of view simply by explaining that it is to take no notice of them.

The task of conducting the individual mind from its unscientific standpoint to that of science had to be taken in its general sense; we had to contemplate the formative development (*Bildung*) of the universal [or general] individual, of self-conscious spirit. As to the relation between these two [the particular and general individual], every moment, as it gains concrete form and its own proper shape and appearance, finds a place in the life of the universal individual. The par-

---

[7] "Being the first part of the *System of Science*" (first edition; omitted in later edition).

ticular individual is incomplete mind, a concrete shape in whose existence, taken as a whole, one determinate characteristic predominates, while the others are found only in blurred outline. In that mind which stands higher than another the lower concrete form of existence has sunk into an obscure moment; what was formerly an objective fact (*die Sache selbst*) is now only a single trace: its definite shape has been veiled, and become simply a piece of shading. The individual, whose substance is mind at the higher level, passes through these past forms, much in the way that one who takes up a higher science goes through those preparatory forms of knowledge, which he has long made his own, in order to call up their content before him; he brings back the recollection of them without stopping to fix his interest upon them. The particular individual, so far as content is concerned, has also to go through the stages through which the general mind has passed, but as shapes once assumed by mind and now laid aside, as stages of a road which has been worked over and levelled out. Hence it is that, in the case of various kinds of knowledge, we find that what in former days occupied the energies of men of mature mental ability sinks to the level of information, exercises, and even pastimes, for children; and in this educational progress we can see the history of the world's culture delineated in faint outline. This bygone mode of existence has already become an acquired possession of the general mind, which constitutes the substance of the individual, and, by thus appearing externally to him, furnishes his inorganic nature. In this respect culture or development of mind (*Bildung*), regarded from the side of the individual, consists in his acquiring what lies at his hand ready for him, in making its inorganic nature organic to himself, and taking possession of it for himself. Looked at, however, from the side of universal mind *qua* general spiritual substance, culture means nothing else than that this substance gives itself its own self-consciousness, brings about its own inherent process and its own reflection into self.

Science lays before us the morphogenetic process of this cultural development in all its detailed fullness and necessity, and at the same time shows it to be something that has already sunk into the mind as a moment of its being and become a possession of mind. The goal to be reached is the mind's insight into what knowing is. Impatience asks for the impossible, wants to reach the goal without the means of getting there. The length of the journey has to be borne with, for every moment is necessary; and again we must halt at every stage, for each is itself a complete individual form, and is fully and finally considered only so far as its determinate character is taken and dealt with as a rounded and concrete whole, or only so far as the whole is looked at in the light of the special and peculiar character which this determination gives it.

Because the substance of individual mind, nay, more, because the universal mind at work in the world (*Weltgeist*), has had the patience to go through these forms in the long stretch of time's extent, and to take upon itself the prodigious labour of the world's history, where it bodied forth in each form the entire content of itself, as each is capable of presenting it; and because by nothing less could that all-pervading mind ever manage to become conscious of what itself is—for that reason, the individual mind, in the nature of the case, cannot expect by less toil to grasp what its own substance contains. All the same, its task has meanwhile been made much lighter, because this has historically been implicitly (*an sich*) accomplished, the content is one where reality is already cancelled for spiritual possibilities, where immediacy has been overcome and brought under the control of reflection, the various forms and shapes have been already reduced to their intellectual abbreviations, to determinations of thought (*Gedankenbestimmung*) pure and simple. Being now a thought, the content is the property of the substance of mind; existence has no more to be changed into the form of what is inherent and implicit (*Ansichseins*), but only the implicit— no longer merely something primitive, nor lying hidden within existence, but already present as a recollection—into the form of what is explicit, of what is objective to self (*Fürsichseins*).

We have to state more exactly the way this is done. At the point at which we here take up this movement, we are spared, in connexion with the whole, the process of cancelling and transcending the stage of mere existence. This process has already taken place. What is still to be done and needs a higher kind of transformation, is to transcend the forms as ideally presented and made familiar to our minds. By that previous negative process, existence, having been withdrawn into the mind's substance, is, in the first instance, transferred to the life of self only in an immediate way. The property the self has thereby acquired, has still the same character of uncomprehended immediacy, of passive indifference, which existence itself had; existence has in this way merely passed into the form of an ideal presentation. At the same time, by so doing, it is something familiar to us, something "well-known," something which the existent mind has finished and done with, and hence takes no more to do with and no further interest in. While the activity that is done with the existent is itself merely the process of the particular mind, of mind which is not comprehending itself, on the other hand, *knowledge* is directed against this ideal presentation which has hereby arisen, against this "being-familiar" and "well-known"; it is an action of *universal* mind, the concern of *thought*.

What is "familiarly known" is not properly known, just for the reason that it is "familiar." When engaged in the process of knowing, it is the commonest form of self-deception, and a deception of other people as well, to assume something to be familiar, and give assent to it on that very account. Knowledge of that sort, with all its talk, never gets from the spot, but has no idea that this is the case. Subject and object, and so on, God, nature, understanding, sensibility, etc., are uncritically presupposed as familiar and something valid, and become fixed points from which to start and to which to return. The process of knowing flits between these secure points, and in consequence goes on merely along the surface. Apprehending and proving consist similarly in seeing whether every one finds what is said corresponding to his idea too, whether it is familiar and seems to him so and so or not.

Analysis of an idea, as it used to be carried out, did in fact consist in nothing else than doing away with its character of familiarity. To break up an idea into its ultimate elements means returning upon its moments, which at least do not have the form of the given idea when found, but are the immediate property of the self. Doubtless this analysis only arrives at thoughts which are themselves familiar elements, fixed inert determinations. But what is thus separated, and in a sense is unreal, is itself an essential moment; for just because the concrete fact is self-divided, and turns into unreality, it is something self-moving, self-active. The action of separating the elements is the exercise of the force of Understanding, the most astonishing and greatest of all powers, or rather the absolute power. The circle, which is self-enclosed and at rest, and, *qua* substance, holds its own moments, is an immediate relation, the immediate, continuous relation of elements with their unity, and hence arouses no sense of wonderment. But that an accident as such, when out loose from its containing circumference,—that what is bound and held by something else and actual only by being connected with it,—should obtain an existence all its own, gain freedom and independence on its own account—this is the portentous power of the negative; it is the energy of thought, of pure ego. Death, as we may call that unreality, is the most terrible thing, and to keep and hold fast what is dead demands the greatest force of all. Beauty, powerless and helpless, hates understanding, because the latter exacts from it what it cannot perform.[8] But the life of mind is not one that shuns death, and keeps clear of destruction; it endures death and in death maintains its being. It only wins to its truth when it finds itself utterly torn asunder. It is this mighty power, not by being a positive which turns away from the negative, as when we say of anything it is nothing or it is false, and, being then done with it, pass off to something else: on the contrary, mind is this power only by looking the negative in the face, and

---

[8]This is directed against Novalis and the cult of beauty.

cf. Milton, Areopag.

dwelling with it. This dwelling beside it is the magic power that converts the negative into being. That power is just what we spoke of above as subject, which by giving determinateness a place in its substance, cancels abstract immediacy, i.e. immediacy which merely *is*, and, by so doing, becomes the true substance, becomes being or immediacy that does not have mediation outside it, but is this mediation itself. *appropri-ation*

This process of making what is objectively presented a possession of pure self-consciousness, of raising it to the level of universality in general, is merely one aspect of mental development; spiritual evolution is not yet completed. The manner of study in ancient times is distinct from that of the modern world, in that the former consisted in the cultivation and perfecting of the natural mind. Testing life carefully at all points, philosophizing about everything it came across, the former created an experience permeated through and through by universals. In modern times, however, an individual finds the abstract form ready made. In straining to grasp it and make it his own, he rather strives to bring forward the inner meaning alone, without any process of mediation; the production of the universal is abridged, instead of the universal arising out of the manifold detail of concrete existence. Hence nowadays the task before us consists not so much in getting the individual clear of the stage of sensuous immediacy, and making him a substance that thinks and is grasped in terms of thought, but rather the very opposite: it consists in actualizing the universal, and giving it spiritual vitality, by the process of breaking down and superseding fixed and determinate thoughts. But it is much more difficult to make fixed and definite thoughts fuse with one another and form a continuous whole than to bring sensuous existence into this state. The reason lies in what was said before. Thought determinations get their substance and the element of their existence from the ego, the power of the negative, or pure reality; while determinations of sense find this in impotent abstract immediacy, in mere being as such. Thoughts become fluent and interfuse, when thinking pure and simple, this inner immediacy, knows itself as a moment, when pure certainty of self abstracts from itself. It does not "abstract" in the sense of getting away from itself and setting itself on one side, but of surrendering the fixed quality of its self-affirmation, and giving up both the fixity of the purely concrete—which is the ego as contrasted with the variety of its content—and the fixity of all those distinctions [the various thought-functions, principles, etc.] which are present in the element of pure thought and share that absoluteness of the ego. In virtue of this process pure thoughts become notions, concepts, and are then what they are in truth, self-moving functions, circles, are what their substance consists in, are spiritual entities.

This movement of the spiritual entities constitutes the nature of scientific procedure in general. Looked at as the concatenation of their content, this movement is the necessitated development and expansion of that content into an organic systematic whole. By this movement, too, the road, which leads to the notion of knowledge, becomes itself likewise a necessary and complete evolving process (*Werden*). This preparatory stage thus ceases to consist of casual philosophical reflections, referring to objects here and there, to processes and thoughts of the undeveloped mind as chance may direct; and it does not try to establish the truth by miscellaneous ratiocinations, inferences, and consequences drawn from circumscribed thoughts. The road to science, by the very movement of the notion itself, will compass the entire objective world of conscious life in its rational necessity.

Further, a systematic exposition like this constitutes the first part of science,[9] because the positive existence of mind, *qua* primary and ultimate, is nothing but the immediate aspect of mind, the beginning; the beginning, but not yet its return to itself. The characteristic feature distinguishing this part of science [Phenomenology] from the others is the element of positive immediate existence. The mention of this distinction leads us to discuss certain established ideas that usually come to notice in this connexion.

The mind's immediate existence, conscious life, has two aspects—cognition and objectivity which is opposed to or negative of the subjective function of knowing. Since it is in the medium of consciousness that mind is developed and brings out its various moments, this opposition between the factors of conscious life is found at each stage in the evolution of mind, and all the various moments appear as modes or forms (*Gestalten*) of consciousness. The scientific statement of the course of this development is a science of the experience through which consciousness passes; the substance and its process are considered as the object of consciousness. Consciousness knows and comprehends nothing but what falls within its experience; for what is found in experience is merely spiritual substance, and, moreover, object of its self. Mind, however, becomes object, for it consists in the process of becoming an other to itself, i.e. an object for its own self, and in transcending this otherness. And experience is called this very process by which the element that is immediate, unexperienced, i.e. abstract—whether it be in the form of sense or of a bare thought—externalizes itself, and then comes back to itself from this state of estrangement, and by so doing is at length set forth in its concrete nature and real truth, and becomes too a possession of consciousness.

---

[9]*v.* note p. 15.

The dissimilarity which obtains in consciousness between the ego and the substance constituting its object, is their inner distinction, the factor of negativity in general. We may regard it as the defect of both opposites, but it is their very soul, their moving spirit. It was on this account that certain thinkers[10] long ago took the void to be the principle of movement, when they conceived the moving principle to be the negative element, though they had not as yet thought of it as self. While this negative factor appears in the first instance as a dissimilarity, as an inequality, between ego and object, it is just as much the inequality of the substance with itself. What seems to take place outside it, to be an activity directed against it, is its own doing, its own activity; and substance shows that it is in reality subject. When it has brought out this completely, mind has made its existence adequate to and one with its essential nature. Mind is object to itself just as it *is*, and the abstract element of immediacy, of the separation between knowing and the truth, is overcome. Being is entirely mediated; it is a substantial content, that is likewise directly in the possession of the ego, has the character of self, is notion. With the attainment of this the Phenomenology of Mind concludes. What mind prepares for itself in the course of its phenomenology is the element of true knowledge. In this element the moments of mind are now set out in the form of thought pure and simple, which knows its object to be itself. They no longer involve the opposition between being and knowing; they remain within the undivided simplicity of the knowing function; they are the truth in the form of truth, and their diversity is merely diversity of the content of truth. The process by which they are developed into an organically connected whole is Logic or Speculative Philosophy.

Now, because the systematic statement of the mind's experience embraces merely its ways of appearing, it may well seem that the advance from that to the science of ultimate truth in the form of truth is merely negative; and we might readily be content to dispense with the negative process as something altogether false, and might ask to be taken straight to the truth at once: why meddle with what is false at all? The point formerly raised, that we should have begun with science at once, may be answered here by considering the character of negativity in general regarded as something false. The usual ideas on this subject particularly obstruct the approach to the truth. The consideration of this point will give us an opportunity to speak about mathematical knowledge, which non-philosophical knowledge looks upon as the ideal which philosophy ought to try to attain, but has so far striven in vain to reach.

Truth and falsehood as commonly understood belong to those

---

[10]Leucippus and Democritus.

sharply defined ideas which claim a completely fixed nature of their own, one standing in solid isolation on this side, the other on that, without any community between them. Against that view it must be pointed out, that truth is not like stamped coin[11] that is issued ready from the mint and so can be taken up and used. Nor, again, is there something false, any more than there is something evil. Evil and falsehood are indeed not so bad as the devil, for in the form of the devil they get the length of being particular subjects; *qua* false and evil they are merely universals, though they have a nature of their own with reference to one another. Falsity (that is what we are dealing with here) would be *otherness*, the negative aspect of the substance, which [substance], *qua* content of knowledge, is truth. But the substance is itself essentially the negative element, partly as involving distinction and determination of content, partly as being a process of distinguishing pure and simple, i.e. as being self and knowledge in general. Doubtless we can know in a way that is false. To know something falsely means that knowledge is not adequate to, is not on equal terms with, its substance. Yet this very dissimilarity is the process of distinction in general, the essential moment in knowing. It is, in fact, out of this active distinction that its harmonious unity arises, and this identity, when arrived at, is truth. But it is not truth in a sense which would involve the rejection of the discordance, the diversity, like dross from pure metal; nor, again, does truth remain detached from diversity, like a finished article from the instrument that shapes it. Difference itself continues to be an immediate element within truth as such, in the form of the principle of negation, in the form of the activity of Self. All the same, we cannot for that reason say that falsehood is a moment or forms even a constituent part of truth. That "in every case of falsity there is something true" is an expression in which they are taken to be like oil and water, which do not mix and are merely united externally. Just in the interest of their real meaning, precisely because we want to designate the aspect or moment of complete otherness, the terms true and false must no longer be used where their otherness has been cancelled and superseded. Just as the expressions "unity of subject and object," of "finite and infinite," of "being and thought," etc., are clumsy when subject and object, etc., are taken to mean what they are *outside* their unity, and are thus in that unity not meant to be what its very expression conveys; in the same way falsehood is not, *qua* false, any longer a moment of truth.

Dogmatism as a way of thinking, whether in ordinary knowledge or in the study of philosophy, is nothing else but the view that truth consists in a proposition, which is a fixed and final result, or again which

---

[11]Cp. Lessing, *Nathan der Weise*, IV. 6. (L.)

is directly known. To questions like, "When was Cæsar born?", "How many feet make a furlongs?", etc., a straight answer ought to be given; just as it is absolutely true that the square of the hypotenuse is equal to the sum of the squares of the other two sides of a right-angled triangle. But the nature of a so-called truth of that sort is different from the nature of philosophical truth.

As regards truth in matters of historical fact—to deal briefly with this subject—so far as we consider the purely historical element, it will be readily granted that they have to do with the sphere of particular existence, with a content in its contingent and arbitrary aspects, features that have no necessity. But even bare truths of the kind, say, like those mentioned, are impossible without the activity of self-consciousness. In order to know any one of them, there has to be a good deal of comparison, books must be consulted, or in some way or other inquiry has to be made. Even in a case of direct perception, only when we know it along with the reasons behind it, is it held to be something of real value; although it is merely the naked fact itself that we are, properly speaking, supposed to be concerned about.

As to mathematical truths, we should be still less inclined to consider anyone a geometer who had got Euclid's theorems by heart (*auswendig*) without knowing the proofs, without, if we may say so by way of contrast, getting them into his head (*inwendig*). Similarly, if anyone came to know by measuring many right-angled triangles that their sides are related in the way everybody knows, we should regard knowledge so obtained as unsatisfactory. All the same, while proof is essential in the case of mathematical knowledge, it still does not have the significance and nature of being a moment in the result itself; the proof is over when we get the result, and has disappeared. *Qua* result the theorem is, no doubt, one that is seen to be true. But this eventuality has nothing to do with its content, but only with its relation to the knowing subject. The process of mathematical proof does not belong to the object; it is a function that takes place outside the matter in hand. Thus, the nature of a right-angled triangle does not break itself up into factors in the manner set forth in the mathematical construction which is required to prove the proposition expressing the relation of its parts. The entire process of producing the result is an affair of knowledge which takes its own way of going about it. In philosophical knowledge, too, the way existence, *qua* existence, comes about (*Werden*) is different from that whereby the essence or inner nature of the fact comes into being. But philosophical knowledge, for one thing, contains both, while mathematical knowledge sets forth merely the way an existence comes about, i.e. the way the nature of the fact gets to *be* in the sphere of knowledge as such. For another thing, too, philosophical knowledge unites both these particular movements. The inward rising into being, the process of substance, is an unbroken transition into outwardness, into existence or being for another; and conversely, the coming of existence into being is withdrawal into the inner essence. The movement is the twofold process in which the whole comes to be, and is such that each at the same time posits the other, and each on that account has in it both as its two aspects. Together they make the whole, through their resolving each other, and making themselves into moments of the whole.

In mathematical knowledge the insight required is an external function so far as the subject-matter dealt with is concerned. It follows that the actual fact is thereby altered. The means taken, construction and proof, contain, no doubt, true propositions; but all the same we are bound to say that the content is false. The triangle in the above example is taken to pieces, and its parts made into other figures to which the construction in the triangle gives rise. It is only at the end that we find again reinstated the triangle we are really concerned with; it was lost sight of in the course of the construction, and was present merely in fragments, that belonged to other wholes. Thus we find negativity of content coming in here too, a negativity which would have to be called falsity, just as much as in the case of the movement of the notion where thoughts that are taken to be fixed pass away and disappear.

The real defect of this kind of knowledge, however, affects its process of knowing as much as its material. As to that process, in the first place we do not see any necessity in the construction. The necessity does not arise from the nature of the theorem: it is imposed; and the injunction to draw just these lines, an infinite number of others being equally possible, is blindly acquiesced in, without our knowing anything further, except that, as we fondly believe, this will serve our purpose in producing the proof. Later on this design then comes out too, and is therefore merely external in character, just because it is only after the proof is found that it comes to be known. In the same way, again, the proof takes a direction that begins anywhere we like, without our knowing as yet what relation this beginning has to the result to be brought out. In its course, it takes up certain specific elements and relations and lets others alone, without its being directly obvious what necessity there is in the matter. An external purpose controls this process.

The evidence peculiar to this defective way of knowing—an evidence on the strength of which mathematics plumes itself and proudly struts before philosophy—rests solely on the poverty of its purpose and the defectiveness of its material, and is on that account of a kind that philosophy must scorn to have anything to do with. Its purpose or principle is quantity. This is precisely the relationship that is non-essential,

quantity

alien to the character of the notion. The process of knowledge goes on, therefore, on the surface, does not affect the concrete fact itself, does not touch its inner nature or notion, and is hence not a conceptual way of comprehending. The material which provides mathematics with these welcome treasures of truth consists of space and numerical units (*das Eins*). Space is that kind of existence wherein the concrete notion inscribes the diversity it contains, as in an empty, lifeless element in which its differences likewise subsist in passive, lifeless form. What is concretely actual is not something spatial, such as is treated of in mathematics. With unrealities like the things mathematics takes account of, neither concrete sensuous perception nor philosophy has anything to do. In an unreal element of that sort we find, then, only unreal truth, fixed lifeless propositions. We can call a halt at any of them; the next begins of itself *de novo*, without the first having led up to the one that follows, and without any necessary connexion having in this way arisen from the nature of the subject-matter itself. So, too—and herein consists the formal character of mathematical evidence—because of that principle and the element where it applies, knowledge advances along the lines of bare equality, of abstract identity. For what is lifeless, not being self-moved, does not bring about distinction within its essential nature; does not attain to essential opposition or unlikeness; and hence involves no transition of one opposite element into its other, no qualitative, immanent movement, no *self*-movement. It is quantity, a form of difference that does not touch the essential nature, which alone mathematics deals with. It abstracts from the fact that it is the notion which separates space into its dimensions, and determines the connexions between them and in them. It does not consider, for example, the relation of line to surface, and when it compares the diameter of a circle with its circumference, it runs up against their incommensurability, i.e. a relation in terms of the notion, an infinite element, that escapes mathematical determination.

Immanent or so-called pure mathematics, again, does not oppose time *qua* time to space, as a second subject-matter for consideration. Applied mathematics, no doubt, treats of time, as also of motion, and other concrete things as well; but it picks up from experience synthetic propositions—i.e. statements of their relations, which are determined by their conceptual nature—and merely applies its formulae to those propositions assumed to start with. That the so-called proofs of propositions like that concerning the equilibrium of the lever, the relation of space and time in gravitation, etc., which applied mathematics frequently gives, should be taken and given as proofs, is itself merely a proof of how great the need is for knowledge to have a process of proof, seeing that, even where proof is not to be had, knowledge yet puts a value on the mere semblance of it, and gets thereby a certain sense of satisfaction. A criticism of those proofs would be as instructive as it would be significant, if the criticism could strip mathematics of this artificial finery, and bring out its limitations, and thence show the necessity for another type of knowledge.

As to time, which, it is to be presumed, would, by way of the counterpart to space, constitute the object-matter of the other division of pure mathematics, this is the notion itself in the form of existence. The principle of quantity, of difference which is not determined by the notion, and the principle of equality, of abstract, lifeless unity, are incapable of dealing with that sheer restlessness of life and its absolute and inherent process of differentiation. It is therefore only in an arrested, paralysed form, only in the form of the quantitative unit, that this essentially negative activity becomes the second object-matter of this way of knowing, which, itself an external operation, degrades what is self-moving to the level of mere matter, in order thus to get an indifferent, external, lifeless content.

Philosophy, on the contrary, does not deal with a determination that is non-essential, but with a determination so far as it is an essential factor. The abstract or unreal is not its element and content, but the real, what is self-establishing, has life within itself, existence in its very notion. It is the process that creates its own moments in its course, and goes through them all; and the whole of this movement constitutes its positive content and its truth. This movement includes, therefore, within it the negative factor as well, the element which would be named falsity if it could be considered one from which we had to abstract. The element that disappears has rather to be looked at as itself essential, not in the sense of being something fixed, that has to be cut off from truth and allowed to lie outside it, heaven knows where; just as similarly the truth is not to be held to stand on the other side as an immovable lifeless positive element. Appearance is the process of arising into being and passing away again, a process that itself does not arise and does not pass away, but is *per se*, and constitutes reality and the life-movement of truth. The truth is thus the bacchanalian revel, where not a member is sober; and because every member no sooner becomes detached than it *eo ipso* collapses straightway, the revel is just as much a state of transparent unbroken calm. Judged by that movement, the particular shapes which mind assumes do not indeed subsist any more than do determinate thoughts or ideas; but they are, all the same, as much positive and necessary moments, as negative and transitory. In the entirety of the movement, taken as an unbroken quiescent whole, that which obtains distinctness in the course of its process and secures specific existence, is preserved in the form of a self-recollection, in which existence is self-knowledge, and self-knowledge, again, is immediate existence.

It might well seem necessary to state at the outset the chief points in connexion with the *method* of this process, the way in which science operates. Its nature, however, is to be found in what has already been said, while the proper systematic exposition of it is the special business of Logic, or rather is Logic itself. For the method is nothing else than the structure of the whole in its pure and essential form. In regard, however, to what has been hitherto currently held on this point, we must be sensible that the system of ideas bearing on the question of philosophical method, belongs also to a stage of mental culture that has now passed away. This may perhaps seem somewhat boastful or revolutionary; and I am far from adopting an attitude of that sort; but it is significant that the scientific régime bequeathed by mathematics—a régime of explanations, divisions, axioms, an array of theorems, with proofs, principles, and the consequences and conclusions drawn from them—all this has already come to be generally considered as at any rate out of date. Even though there is no clear idea why it is unsuitable, yet little or no use is made of it any longer; and even though it is not condemned outright, it is all the same not in favour. And we must be so far prejudiced in favour of what is excellent to believe that it can turn itself to practical account, and make itself acceptable. But it is not difficult to see that the method of propounding a proposition, producing reasons for it and then refuting its opposite by reasons too, is not the form in which truth can appear. Truth moves itself by its very nature; but the method just mentioned is a form of knowledge external to its material. Hence it is peculiar to mathematics and must be left to mathematics, which, as already indicated, takes for its principle the relation of quantity, a relation alien to the notion, and gets its material from lifeless space, and the equally lifeless numerical unit. Or, again, such a method, adopting a freer style, one involving more of arbitrariness and chance, may have a place in ordinary life, in a conversation, or in supplying matter-of-fact instruction for the satisfaction of curiosity rather than knowledge, very much as a preface does. In every-day life the mind finds its content in different kinds of knowledge, experiences of various sorts, concrete facts of sense, thoughts, too, and principles, and, in general, in whatever lies ready to hand, or passes for a solid stable entity, or real being. The mind follows wherever this leads, sometimes interrupting the connexion by an unrestrained caprice in dealing with the content, and takes up the attitude of determining and handling it in quite an external fashion. It runs the content back to some touchstone of certainty or other, even though it be but the feeling of the moment; and conviction is satisfied if it reaches some familiar resting-place.

But when the necessity of the notion banishes from its realm the loose procedure of the "raisonnements" of conversation, as well as the pedantic style of scientific pomposity, its place, as we have already mentioned, must not be taken by the disconnected utterance of presageful surmise and inspiration, and the arbitrary caprice of prophetic utterance; for this does not merely despise that particular form of scientific procedure, but contemns scientific procedure altogether.

Now that the triplicity, adopted in the system of Kant—a method rediscovered, to begin with, by instinctive insight, but left lifeless and uncomprehended—has been raised to its significance as an absolute method, true form is thereby set up in its true content, and the conception of science has come to light. But the use this form has been put to in certain quarters has no right to the name of science. For we see it there reduced to a lifeless schema, to nothing better than a mere shadow, and scientific organization to a synoptic table. This formalism—about which we spoke before in general terms, and whose procedure we wish here to state more fully—thinks it has comprehended and expressed the nature and life of a given form when it proclaims a determination of the schema to be its predicate. The predicate may be subjectivity or objectivity, or again magnetism, electricity, and so on, contraction or expansion, East or West, and such like—a form of predication that can be multiplied indefinitely, because according to this way of working each determination, each mode, can be applied as a form or schematic element in the case of every other, and each will thankfully perform the same service for any other. With a circle of reciprocities of this sort it is impossible to make out what the real fact in question is, or what the one or the other is. We find there sometimes constituents of sense picked up from ordinary intuition, determinate elements which to be sure should mean something else than they say; at other times what is inherently significant, viz. pure determinations of thought—like subject, object, substance, cause, universality, etc.— these are applied just as uncritically and unreflectingly as in every-day life, are used much as people employ the terms strong and weak, expansion and contraction. As a result that type of metaphysics is as unscientific as those ideas of sense.

Instead of the inner activity and self-movement of its own actual life, such a simple determination of direct intuition (*Anschauung*)—which means here sense-knowledge—is predicated in accordance with a superficial analogy, and this external and empty application of the formula is called "construction." The same thing happens here, however, as in the case of every kind of formalism. A man's head must be indeed dull if he could not in a quarter of an hour get up the theory[12] that there are enervating, innervating, and indirectly enervating diseases and as many cures, and who could not—since not so long ago instruction of that sort sufficed for the purpose—in as short a time be turned from being a man who works by rule of thumb into a theoretical physician. Formalism in the case of speculative Philosophy of Nature (*Naturphilosophie*) takes the shape of teaching that understanding is electricity, animals are nitrogen, or equivalent to South or North and so on. When it does this, whether as badly as it is here expressed or even concocted with more terminology, such forceful procedure brings and holds together elements to all appearance far removed from one another; the violence done to stable inert sense-elements by connecting them in this way, confers on them merely the semblance of a conceptual unity, and spares itself the trouble of doing what is after all the important thing—expressing the notion itself, the meaning that underlies sense-ideas. All this sort of thing may strike anyone who has no experience with admiration and wonder. He may be awed by the profound genius he thinks it displays, and be delighted at the happy ingenuity of such characterizations, since they fill the place of the abstract notion with something tangible and sensuous, and so make it more pleasing; and he may congratulate himself on feeling an instinctive mental affinity for that glorious way of proceeding. The trick of wisdom of that sort is as quickly acquired as it is easy to practise. Its repetition, when once it is familiar, becomes as boring as the repetition of any bit of sleight-of-hand once we see through it. The instrument for producing this monotonous formalism is no more difficult to handle than the palette of a painter, on which lie only two colours, say red and green, the former for colouring the surface when we want a historical piece, the latter when we want a bit of landscape. It would be difficult to settle which is greater in all this, the agreeable ease with which everything in heaven and earth and under the earth is plastered with that botch of colour, or the conceit that prides itself on the excellence of its means for every conceivable purpose; the one lends support to the other. What results from the use of this method of sticking on to everything in heaven and earth, to every kind of shape and form, natural and spiritual, the pair of determinations from the general schema, and filing everything in this manner, is no less than an "account as clear as noonday"[13] of the organized whole of the universe. It is, that is to say, a synoptic index, like a skeleton with tickets stuck all over it, or like the rows

---

[12]Cp. John Brown, *Elementa medicinae*, 1780 (L.)

[13]Expression adopted from Fichte's "Sonnenklarer Bericht an das Publikum uber das eigentliche Wesden der neuesten Philosophie."

of boxes kept shut and labelled in a grocer's stall; and is as intelligible as either the one or the other. It has lost hold of the living nature of concrete fact; just as in the former case we have merely dry bones with flesh and blood all gone, and in the latter, there is shut away in those boxes something equally lifeless too. We have already remarked that the final outcome of this style of thinking is, at the same time, to paint entirely in one kind of colour; for it turns with contempt from the distinctions in the schematic table, looks on them as belonging to the activity of mere reflection, and lets them drop out of sight in the void of the Absolute, and there reinstates pure identity, pure formless whiteness. Such uniformity of colouring in the schema with its lifeless determinations, this absolute identity, and the transition from one to the other—these are the one as well as the other, the expression of inert lifeless understanding, and equally an external process of knowledge.

Not only can what is excellent not escape the fate of being thus devitalized and despiritualized and excoriated of seeing its skin paraded about by lifeless knowledge and the conceit such knowledge engenders; but rather, such a fate lets us realize the power the "excellent" exercises over the heart (*Gemüth*), if not over the mind (*Geist*). Moreover, we recognize thereby, too, the constructive unfolding into universality and determinateness of form which marks the complete attainment of excellence, and which alone makes it possible that this universality can be turned to superficial uses.

Science can become an organic system only by the inherent life of the notion. In science the determinateness, which was taken from the schema and stuck on to existing facts in external fashion, is the self-directing inner soul of the concrete content. The movement of what is partly consists in becoming another to itself, and thus developing explicitly into its own immanent content; partly, again, it takes this evolved content, this existence it assumes, back into itself, i.e. makes *itself* into a moment, and reduces itself to simple determinateness. In the first stage of the process negativity lies in the function of distinguishing and establishing existence; in this latter return into self, negativity consists in the bringing about of determinate simplicity. It is in this way that the content shows its specific characteristic not to be received from something else, and stuck on externally; the content gives itself this determinate characteristic, appoints itself of its own initiative to the rank of a moment and to a place in the whole. The pigeon-holing process of understanding retains for itself the necessity and the notion controlling the content, that which constitutes the concrete element, the actuality and living process of the subject-matter which it labels: or rather, understanding does not retain this for itself, on the contrary, understanding fails to know it. For if it had as much insight as that, it would surely show that it had. It is not even aware of the need for such insight; if it were, it would drop its schematizing process, or at least would no longer be satisfied to know by way of a mere table of contents. A table of contents is all that understanding gives, the content itself it does not furnish at all.

If the specific determination (say even one like magnetism) is one that in itself is concrete or actual, it all the same gets degraded into something lifeless and inert, since it is merely predicated of another existing entity, and not known as an immanent living principle of this existence; nor is there any comprehension of how in this entity its intrinsic and peculiar way of expressing and producing itself takes effect. This, the very kernel of the matter, formal understanding leaves to others to add later on. Instead of making its way into the inherent content of the matter in hand, understanding always takes a survey of the whole, assumes a position above the particular existence about which it is speaking, i.e. it does not see it at all. True scientific knowledge, on the contrary, demands abandonment to the very life of the object, or, which means the same thing, claims to have before it the inner necessity controlling the object, and to express this only. Steeping itself in its object, it forgets to take that general survey, which is merely a turning of knowledge away from the content back into itself. But being sunk into the material in hand, and following the course that such material takes, true knowledge returns back into itself, yet not before the content in its fullness is taken into itself, is reduced to the simplicity of being a determinate characteristic, drops to the level of being one aspect of an existing entity, and passes over into its higher truth. By this process the whole as such, surveying its entire content, itself emerges out of the wealth wherein its process of reflection seemed to be lost.

In general, in virtue of the principle that, as we expressed it before, substance is implicitly and in itself subject, all content makes its reflection into itself in its own special way. The subsistence or substance of anything that exists is its self-identity; for its want of identity, or oneness with itself, would be its dissolution. But self-identity is pure abstraction; and this is just thinking. When I say Quality, I state simple determinateness; by means of its quality one existence is distinguished from another or is an "existence"; it is for itself, something on its own account, or subsists with itself because of this simple characteristic. But by doing so it is essentially Thought.

Here we find contained the principle that Being is Thought: here is exercised that insight which usually tends to deviate from the ordinary non-conceptual way of speaking of the identity of thought and being. In virtue, further, of the fact that subsistence on the part of what exists is self-identity or pure abstraction, it is the abstraction of itself from

itself, in other words, is itself its own want of identity with itself and dissolution—its own proper inwardness and retraction into self—its
process of becoming.

Owing to the nature which being thus has, and so far as what is has
this nature from the point of view of knowledge, this thinking is not an
activity which treats the content as something alien and external; it is
not reflection into self away from the content. Science is not that kind
of Idealism which stepped into the place of the Dogmatism of mere assertion and took the shape of a Dogmatism of mere assurance, the
Dogmatism of mere self-certainty. Rather, since knowledge sees the
content go back into its own proper inner nature, the activity of knowledge is absorbed in that content—for it (the activity) is the immanent
self of the content—and is also at the same time returned into itself, for
this activity is pure self-identity in otherness. In this way the knowing
activity is the artful device which, while seeming to refrain from activity, looks on and watches how specific determinateness with its
concrete life, just where it believes it is working out its own self-
preservation and its own private interest, is, in point of fact, doing the
very opposite, is doing what brings about its own dissolution and makes
itself a moment in the whole.

While, in the foregoing, the significance of Understanding was
stated from the point of view of the self-consciousness of substance; by
what has been here stated we can see clearly its significance from the
point of view of substance *qua* being. Existence is Quality, self-
identical determinateness, or determinate simplicity, determinate
thought: this is existence from the point of view of Understanding. On
this account it is νοῦς, as Anaxagoras first thought reality to be. Those
who succeeded him grasped the nature of existence in a more determinate way as εἶδος or ιδέα, i.e. as determinate or specific universality,
kind or species. The term species or kind seems indeed too ordinary
and inadequate for Ideas, for beauty, holiness, eternal, which are the
vogue in these days. As a matter of fact, however, idea (ιδέα) means
neither more nor less than kind, species. But we often find nowadays
that a term which exactly designates a conception is despised and rejected, and another preferred to it which hides and obscures the conception, and thus sounds more edifying, even though this is merely due
to its being expressed in a foreign language.

Precisely for the reason that existence is designated a species or kind,
it is a naked simple thought: νοῦς, simplicity, is substance. It is on account of its simplicity, its self-identity, that it appears steady, fixed, and
permanent. But this self-identity is likewise negativity; hence that fixed
and stable existence carries the process of its own dissolution within itself. The determinateness appears at first to be so solely through its re-

lation to something else; and its process seems imposed and forced upon it externally. But its having its own otherness within itself, and the fact of its being a self-initiated process—these are implied in the very simplicity of thought itself. For this is self-moving thought, thought that distinguishes, is inherent inwardness, the pure notion. Thus, then, it is the very nature of understanding to be a process; and being a process it is Rationality.

In the nature of existence as thus described—to be its own notion and being in one—consists logical necessity in general. This alone is what is rational, the rhythm of the organic whole: it is as much knowledge of content as that content is notion and essential nature. In other words, this alone is the sphere and element of speculative thought. The concrete shape of the content is resolved by its own inherent process into a simple determinate quality. Thereby it is raised to logical form, and its being and essence coincide; its concrete existence is merely this process that takes place, and is *eo ipso* logical existence. It is therefore needless to apply a formal scheme to the concrete content in an external fashion; the content is in its very nature a transition into a formal shape, which, however, ceases to be formalism of an external kind, because the form is the indwelling process of the concrete content itself.

This nature of scientific method, which consists partly in being inseparable from the content, and partly in determining the rhythm of its movement by its own agency, finds, as we mentioned before, its peculiar systematic expression in speculative philosophy. What is here stated describes in effect the essential principle; but cannot stand for more at this stage than an assertion or assurance by way of anticipation. The truth it contains is not to be found in this exposition, which is in part historical in character. And just for that reason, too, it is not in the least refuted if anyone assures us on the contrary that this is not so, that the process instead is here so and so; if ideas we are all used to, being truths accepted or settled and familiar to everyone, are brought to mind and recounted; or, again, if something new is served up and guaranteed as coming from the inner sanctuaries of inspired intuition.

Such a view is bound to meet with opposition. The first instinctive reaction on the part of knowing, when offered something that was unfamiliar, is usually to resist it. It seeks by that means to save freedom and native insight, to secure its own inherent authority—against alien authority—for that is the way anything apprehended for the first time appears. This attitude is adopted, too, in order to do away with the semblance of a kind of disgrace which would lie in the fact that something has had to be learnt. In like manner, again, when the unfamiliar or unknown is received with applause, the reaction is in the same way an exaltation of freedom and native authority. It consists in something analogous to ultra-revolutionary declamation and action.

Hence the important thing for the student of science is to make himself undergo the strenuous toil of conceptual reflection, of thinking in the form of the notion. This demands concentrated attention on the notion as such, on simple and ultimate determinations like being-in-itself, being-for-itself, self-identity, and so on; for these are elemental, pure, self-determined functions of a kind we might call souls, were it not that their conceptual nature denotes something higher than that term contains. The interruption by conceptual thought of the habit of always thinking in figurative ideas (*Vorstellungen*) is as annoying and troublesome to this way of thinking as to that process of formal intelligence which in its reasoning rambles about with no real thoughts to reason with. The former, the habit, may be called materialized thinking, a fortuitous mental state, one that is absorbed in what is material, and hence finds it very distasteful at once to lift its self clear of this matter and be with itself alone. The latter, the process of *raisonnement*, is, on the other hand, detachment from all content, and conceited superiority to it. What is wanted here is the effort and struggle to give up this kind of freedom, and instead of being a merely arbitrary principle directing the content anyhow, this freedom should sink into and pervade the content, should let it be directed and controlled by its own proper nature, i.e. by the self as its own self, and should observe this process taking place. We must abstain from interrupting the immanent rhythm of the movement of conceptual thought; we must refrain from arbitrarily interfering with it, and introducing ideas and reflections that have been obtained elsewhere. Restraint of this sort is itself an essential condition of attending to and getting at the real nature of the notion.

There are two aspects in the case of that ratiocinative procedure which mark its contrast from conceptual thinking and call for further notice. *Raisonnement*, in the first place, adopts a negative attitude towards the content apprehended; knows how to refute it and reduce it to nothingness. To see what the content is *not* is merely a negative process; it is a dead halt, which does not of itself go beyond itself, and proceed to a new content; it has to get hold of something else from somewhere or other in order to have once more a content. It is reflection upon and into the empty ego, the vanity of its own knowledge. Conceit of this kind brings out not only that this content is vain and empty, but also that to see this is itself fatuity too: for it is negation with no perception of the positive element within it. In that this reflection does not even have its own negativity as its content, it is not inside actual fact at all, but for ever away outside it. On that account it imagines that by asserting mere emptiness it is going much farther than insight that embraces and reveals a wealth of content. On the other hand, in the case of conceptual thinking, as was above indicated, the negative aspect falls within the content itself, and is the positive substance of that content, as well as being its inherent character and moving principle as by being the entirety of what these are. Looked at as a result, it is determinate specific negation, the negative which is the outcome of this process, and consequently is a positive content as well.

In view of the fact that ratiocinative thinking has a content, whether of images or thoughts or a mixture of both, there is another side to its process which makes conceptual comprehension difficult for it. The peculiar nature of this aspect is closely connected with the essential meaning of the idea above described, in fact, expresses the idea in the way this appears as the process of thinking apprehension. For just as ratiocinative thinking in its negative reference, which we have been describing, is nothing but the self into which the content returns; in the same way, on the other hand, in its positive cognitive process the self is an ideally presented subject to which the content is related as an accident and predicate. This subject constitutes the basis to which the content is attached and on which the process moves to and fro. Conceptual thinking goes on in quite a different way. Since the concept or notion is the very self of the object, manifesting itself as the development of the object, it is not a quiescent subject, passively supporting accidents: it is a self-determining active concept which takes up its determinations and makes them its own. In the course of this process that inert passive subject really disappears; it enters into the different constituents and pervades the content; instead of remaining in inert antithesis to determinateness of content, it constitutes, in fact, that very specificity, i.e. the content as differentiated along with the process of bringing this about. Thus the solid basis, which ratiocination found in an inert subject, is shaken to its foundations, and the only object is this very movement of the subject. The subject supplying the concrete filling to its own content ceases to be something transcending this content, and cannot have further predicates or accidents. Conversely, again, the scattered diversity of the content is brought under the control of the self, and so bound together; the content is not a universal that can be detached from the subject, and adapted to several indifferently. Consequently the content is in truth no longer predicate of the subject; it is the very substance, is the inmost reality, and the very principle of what is being considered. Ideational thinking (*vorstellen*), since its nature consists in dealing with accidents or predicates, and in exercising the right to transcend them because they are nothing more than predicates and accidents—this way of thinking is checked in its course, since that which has in the proposition the form of a predicate is itself the substance of the statement. It is met by a counter-thrust, as we may say. Starting from the subject, as if this were a permanent base on which to proceed, it discovers, by the predicate being in reality the substance, that the subject has passed into the predicate, and has thereby ceased to be subject: and since in this way what seems to be predicate has become the entire mass of the content, whole and complete, thinking cannot wander and ramble about at will, but is restrained and controlled by this weight of content.

Usually the subject is first set down as the fixed and objective self; from this fixed position the necessary process passes on to the multiplicity of determinations or predicates. Here the knowing ego takes the place of that subject and is the function of knitting or combining the predicates one with another, and is the subject holding them fast. But since the former subject enters into the determinate constituents themselves, and is their very life, the subject in the second case—viz. the knowing subject—finds that the former,—which it is supposed to be done with and which it wants to transcend, in order to return into itself,—is still there in the predicate: and instead of being able to be the determining agency in the process of resolving the predicate—reflectively deciding whether this or that predicate should be attached to the former subject—it has really to deal with the self of the content, is not allowed to be something on its own account (*für sich*), but has to exist along with this content.

What has been said can be expressed in a formal manner by saying that the nature of judgment or the proposition in general, which involves the distinction of subject and predicate, is subverted and destroyed by the speculative judgment; and the identical proposition, which the former becomes [by uniting subject and predicate], implies the rejection and repudiation of the above relation between subject and predicate. This conflict between the form of a proposition in general and the unity of the notion which destroys that form, is similar to what we find between metre and accent in the case of rhythm. Rhythm is the result of what hovers between and unites both. So in the case of the speculative or philosophical judgment; the identity of subject and predicate is not intended to destroy their distinction, as expressed in propositional form; their unity is to arise as a harmony of the elements. The form of the judgment is the way the specific sense appears, or is made manifest, the accent which differentiates the meaning it contains: that the predicate expresses the substance, and the subject itself falls within the universal, is however the unity wherein that accent dies away.

To explain what has been said by examples let us take the proposition God is Being. The predicate is "being": it has substantive significance, and thus absorbs the meaning of the subject within it. Being is meant to be here not predicate but the essential nature. Thereby, God seems to cease to be what he was when the proposition was put forward, viz. a fixed subject. Thinking [i.e. ordinary reflection], instead of getting any farther with the transition from subject to predicate, in reality finds its activity checked through the loss of the subject, and it is thrown back on the thought of the subject because it misses this subject. Or again, since the predicate has itself been pronounced to be a subject, to be *the* being, to be the essential reality, which exhausts the nature of the subject, thinking finds the subject directly present in the predicate too: and now, instead of having, in the predicate, gone into *itself*, and preserved the freedom characteristic of ratiocination, it is absorbed in the content all the while, or, at any rate is required to be so.

Similarly, when it is said: "the real is the universal," the real, *qua* subject, passes away in its predicate. The universal is not only meant to have the significance of a predicate, as if the proposition stated that the real is universal: the universal is meant to express the essential nature of the real. Thinking therefore loses that fixed objective basis which it had in the subject, just as much as in the predicate it is thrown back on the subject, and therein returns not into itself but into the subject underlying the content.

This unaccustomed restraint imposed upon thought is for the most part the cause of the complaints concerning the unintelligibility of philosophical writings, when otherwise the individual has in him the requisite mental cultivation for understanding them. In what has been said we see the reason for the specific charge often made against them, that a good deal has to be read repeatedly before it can be understood—an accusation which is meant to convey something improper in the extreme, and one which if granted to be sound admits of no further reply. It is obvious from the above what is the state of the case here. The philosophical proposition, being a proposition, calls up the accepted view of the usual relation of subject and predicate, and suggests the idea of the customary procedure which takes place in knowledge. Its philosophical content destroys this way of proceeding and the ordinary view taken of this process. The common view discovers that the statement is intended in another sense than it is thinking of, and this correction of its opinion compels knowledge to recur to the proposition and take it now in some other sense.

There is a difficulty which might well be avoided. It consists in mixing up the methods of procedure followed by speculation and ratiocination, when what is said of the subject has at one time the significance of its conceptual principle, and at another time the meaning of its predicate or accidental quality. The one mode of thinking invalidates the other; and only that philosophical exposition can manage to become plastic in character which resolutely sets aside and has nothing to do with the ordinary way of relating the parts of a proposition.

As a matter of fact, non-speculative thinking has its rights too, which are justifiable, but are disregarded in the speculative way of stating a proposition. Abolishing the form of the proposition must not take place only in an immediate manner, through the mere content of the proposition. On the contrary, we must give explicit expression to this cancelling process; it must be not only that internal restraining and confining of thought within its own substance; this turning of the conception back into itself has to be expressly brought out and stated. This process, which constitutes what formerly had to be accomplished by proof, is the internal dialectical movement of the proposition itself. This alone is the concrete speculative element, and only the explicit expression of this is a speculative systematic exposition. *Qua* proposition, the speculative aspect is merely the internal restriction of thought within its own substance where the return of the essential principle into itself is not yet brought out. Hence we often find philosophical expositions referring us to the inner intuition, and thus dispensing with the systematic statement of the dialectical movement of the proposition, which is what we wanted all the while. The proposition ought to express *what* the truth is: in its essential nature the truth is subject: being so, it is merely the dialectical movement, this self-producing course of activity, maintaining its advance by returning back into itself. In the case of knowledge in other spheres this aspect of expressly stating the internal nature of the content is constituted by proof. When dialectic, however, has been separated from proof, the idea of philosophical demonstration as a matter of fact has vanished altogether.

On this point it may be mentioned that the dialectical process likewise consists of parts or elements which are propositions. The difficulty indicated seems therefore to recur continually, and seems to be a difficulty inherent in the nature of the case. This is like what happens in the ordinary process of proving anything; the grounds it makes use of need themselves to be based on other grounds again, and so on *ad infinitum*. This manner of furnishing grounds and conditions, however, concerns that type of proof from which the dialectical movement is distinct and hence belongs to the process of external knowledge. As to what this movement is, its element is the bare concept; this furnishes a content which is through and through subject *impliciter* and *per se*. There is to be found, therefore, no sort of content standing in a relation, as it were, to an underlying subject, and getting its significance by being attached to this as a predicate. The proposition as it appears is a mere empty form.

Apart from the sensuously apprehended or ideally presented (*vorgestellten*) self, it is in the main the mere name *qua* name which denotes the subject pure and simple, the empty unit without any conceptual character. For this reason it would e.g. be expedient to avoid the name "God," because this word is not in its primary use a conception as well, but the special name of an underlying subject, its fixed resting-place; while, on the other hand, being or the one, singleness, subject, etc., themselves directly indicate conceptions. Furthermore, if speculative truths are stated about that subject [God], even then their content is devoid of the immanent notion, because that content is merely present in the form of a passive subject, and owing to this the speculative truths easily take on the character of mere edification. From this side, too, the obstacle, arising from the habit of putting the speculative predicate in the form of a proposition, instead of taking it as an inherent essential conception, is capable of being made greater or less by the mere way philosophical truths are put forward. Philosophical exposition, faithfully following its insight into the nature of speculative truth, must retain the dialectical form, and exclude everything which is not grasped conceptually and is conception.

Just as much as in the procedure of ratiocination, the study of philosophy finds obstruction, too, in the unreasoning conceit that builds itself on well-established truths, which the possessor considers he has no need to return upon and reconsider, but rather takes to be fundamental, and thinks he can by means thereof propound as well as decide and pass sentence. In this regard, it is especially needful to make once again a serious business of philosophy. In all spheres of science, art, skill, and handicraft it is never doubted that, in order to master them, a considerable amount of trouble must be spent in learning and in being trained. As regards philosophy, on the contrary, there seems still an assumption prevalent that, though every one with eyes and fingers is not on that account in a position to make shoes if he only has leather and a last, yet everybody understands how to philosophize straight away, and pass judgment on philosophy, simply because he possesses the criterion for doing so in his natural reason—as if he did not in the same way possess the standard for shoemaking too in his own foot. It seems as if the possession of philosophy lay just in the want of knowledge and study, as if philosophy left off where the latter began. It is commonly held to be a formal kind of knowledge devoid of all substantial content. There is a general failure to perceive that, in the case of any knowledge and any science, what is taken for truth, even as regards content, can only deserve the name of "truth" when philosophy has had a hand in its production. Let the other sciences try as much as they like to get along by ratiocination or *raisonnement* without philosophy, they are unable to keep alive without it, or to have any spiritual significance and truth in them.

As regards philosophy in its proper and genuine sense, we find put forward without any hesitation, as an entirely sufficient equivalent for the long course of mental discipline—for that profound and fruitful process through which the human spirit attains to knowledge—the direct revelation of the divine and the healthy common sense of mankind, unconcerned with and undisciplined by any other knowledge or by proper philosophical reflection. These are held to be a good substitute for real philosophy, much in the way that chicory is lauded as a substitute for coffee. It is not a very pleasing spectacle to observe uncultivated ignorance and crudity of mind, with neither form nor taste, without the capacity to concentrate its thoughts on an abstract proposition, still less on a connected statement of such propositions, confidently proclaiming itself to be intellectual freedom and toleration, and even the inspiration of genius. This last used once upon a time, as everyone knows, to be all the vogue in the case of poetry, as it is now in philosophy. Instead of poetry, however, the efforts of this form of inspiration, when it had any sense at all, resulted in the production of trivial prose, or, if it went beyond that, it produced raving harangues. In the same way here in the case of philosophy; philosophizing by the light of nature, which thinks itself too good for conceptual thinking, and, because of the want of it, takes itself to have direct intuitive ideas and poetical thoughts,—such philosophizing trades in arbitrary combinations of an imagination merely disorganized through thinking—fictitious creations that are neither fish nor flesh, neither poetry nor philosophy.

On the other hand again, when instinctive philosophy follows the more secure course prescribed by healthy common sense, it treats us to a rhetorical *mélange* of commonplace truths. When it is charged with the triviality of what it offers, it assures us, in reply, that the fullness and richness of its meaning lie deep down in its own heart, and that others must feel this too, since with such phrases as the "heart's natural innocence," "purity of conscience," and so on, it supposes it has expressed things that are ultimate and final, to which no one can take exception, and about which nothing further can be required. But the very problem in hand was just that the best must not be left behind hidden away in secret, but be brought out of the depths and set forth in the light of day. It could quite well from the start have spared itself the trouble of bringing forward ultimate and final truths of that sort; they were long since to be found, say, in the Catechism, in popular proverbs, etc. It is an easy matter to grasp such truths in their indefinite and crooked inaccurate form, and in many cases to point out that the mind convinced

distinctive kind of universality
for philosophy.

of them is conscious of the very opposite truths. When it struggles to get itself out of the mental embarrassment thereby produced, it will tumble into further confusion, and possibly burst out with the assertion that in short and in fine the matter is settled, the truth is so and so, and anything else is mere "sophistry"—a password used by plain common sense against cultivated critical reason, like the phrase "visionary dreaming," by which those ignorant of philosophy sum up its character once for all. Since the man of common sense appeals to his feeling, to an oracle within his breast, he is done with any one who does not agree. He has just to explain that he has no more to say to any one who does not find and feel the same as himself. In other words, he tramples the roots of humanity underfoot. For the nature of humanity is to impel men to agree with one another, and its very existence lies simply in the explicit realization of a community of conscious life. What is anti-human, the condition of mere animals, consists in keeping within the sphere of feeling pure and simple, and in being able to communicate only by way of feeling-states.

When a man asks for a royal road to science, no more convenient and comfortable way can be mentioned to him than to put his trust in "healthy common sense." And for the rest, to keep abreast of the times and advance with philosophy, let him read reviews of philosophical works, and even go the length of reading the prefaces and first paragraphs of the works themselves; for the latter give the general principles on which everything turns, while the reviews along with the historical notice provide over and above the critical judgment and appreciation, which, being a judgment passed on the work, goes farther than the work that is judged. This common way a man can take in his dressing-gown. But spiritual elation in the eternal, the sacred, the infinite, moves along the highway of truth in the robes of the high priests—a road that, from the first, is itself immediate being in its innermost, the inspiration of profound and original ideas and flashes of elevated thought. All the same, those depths do not yet reveal the well-spring of inner reality; nor, again, are these sky-rockets the empyrean. True thoughts and scientific insight can only be won by the labour of the notion. Conceptions alone can produce universality in the knowing process. This universality is critically developed and completely finished knowledge. It is not the common indefiniteness and inadequacy of ordinary intelligence. Nor, again, is it that extraordinary kind of universality where the powers and potencies of reason are spoiled and ruined by genius through indolence and self-conceit. It is truth which has successfully reached its own inherent native form. It is this universality which is capable of being the property of every self-conscious reason.

Since I have taken the self-development of the notion to be the medium wherein science really exists, and since in those respects to which I have drawn attention, as well as in others, current ideas about the nature of truth and the shape it assumes deviate from my view, and indeed are quite opposed to my position, the consideration of this divergence of view does not seem to promise well for a favourable reception of an attempt to expound the system of science in this sense. In the meantime, I may call to mind that while e.g. the supreme merit of Plato's philosophy has sometimes been held to consist in his myths which are scientifically valueless, there have also been times, spoken of even as times of mere sentimental enthusiasm, when the Aristotelian philosophy has been respected on account of its speculative depth of insight, and when the *Parmenides* of Plato—perhaps the greatest literary product of ancient dialectic—has been taken to be the positive expression of the divine life, the unveiling and disclosing of its inmost truth. I may reflect, too, that notwithstanding much cloudy obscurity which was the product of ecstasy, this misunderstood ecstasy was in point of fact meant to be nothing else than the activity of the pure notion; furthermore, that what is best in the philosophy of our time takes its value to lie in its scientific character; and that, even though others take a different view, it is only in virtue of its scientific character that recent philosophy really gains validity and acceptance. Thus, then, I may hope too that this attempt to justify the claim of science to be a conceptual process, and systematically to develop and present science in this its own peculiar medium, will manage to make a way for itself by the inherent truth of the result accomplished. We may rest assured that it is the nature of truth to force its way to recognition when the time comes, and that it only appears when its time has come, and hence never appears too soon, and never finds a public that is not ripe to receive it. And, further, we may be sure that the individual thinker requires this result to take place, in order to give him confidence in regard to what is no more as yet than a matter for himself singly and alone, and in order to find his assurance, which in the first instance merely belongs to a particular individual, realized as something universal. In this connection, however, it is very often necessary to distinguish the public from those who take upon themselves to be its representatives and spokesmen. The public takes up an attitude in many respects quite different from the latter, indeed, even opposed to them. Whereas the public good-naturedly and generously will rather take the blame upon itself when a philosophical work is not quite acceptable or intelligible to it, these "representatives," on the contrary, convinced of their own competence, put all the blame on the authors. The influence of the work on the public is more silent than the action of those "representatives," who are like the dead burying their dead.

While the general level of insight at the present time is in the main more highly cultivated, its curiosity more quickened and alert, and its judgment more swiftly made up and pronounced, so that the feet of those who will carry you out are already at the door: at the same time we have often to distinguish from all this the slower and more gradual effect which rectifies the direction of attention caught and compelled by imposing assurances, corrects, too, contemptuous censure, and after a little provides a contemporary audience for one part, while another after a temporary vogue finds no audience with posterity any longer.

For the rest, at a time when the universal nature of spiritual life has become so very much emphasized and strengthened, and the mere individual aspect has become, as it should be, correspondingly a matter of indifference, when, too, that universal aspect holds, by the entire range of its substance, the full measure of the wealth it has built up, and lays claim to it all, the share in the total work of mind that falls to the activity of any particular individual can only be very small. Because this is so, the individual must all the more forget himself, as in fact the very nature of science implies and requires that he should; and he must, moreover, become and do what he can. But all the less must be demanded of him, just as he can expect the less from himself, and may ask the less for himself.

INTRODUCTION

IT IS natural to suppose that, before philosophy enters upon its subject proper—namely, the actual knowledge of what truly is—it is necessary to come first to an understanding concerning knowledge, which is looked upon as the instrument by which to take possession of the Absolute, or as the means through which to get a sight of it. The apprehension seems legitimate, on the one hand that there may be various kinds of knowledge, among which one might be better adapted than another for the attainment of our purpose—and thus a wrong choice is possible: on the other hand again that, since knowing is a faculty of a definite kind and with a determinate range, without the more precise determination of its nature and limits we might take hold on clouds of error instead of the heaven of truth.

This apprehensiveness is sure to pass even into the conviction that the whole enterprise which sets out to secure for consciousness by means of knowledge what exists *per se*, is in its very nature absurd; and that between knowledge and the Absolute there lies a boundary which completely cuts off the one from the other. For if knowledge is the instrument by which to get possession of absolute Reality, the suggestion immediately occurs that the application of an instrument to anything does *not* leave it as it is for itself, but rather entails in the process, and has in view, a moulding and alteration of it. Or, again, if knowledge is not an instrument which we actively employ, but a kind of passive medium through which the light of the truth reaches us, then here, too, we do not receive it as it is in itself, but as it is through and in this medium. In either case we employ a means which immediately brings about the very opposite of its own end; or, rather, the absurdity lies in making use of any means at all. It seems indeed open to us to find in the knowledge of the way in which the *instrument* operates, a remedy for this parlous state; for thereby it becomes possible to remove from the result the part which, in our idea of the Absolute received through that instrument, belongs to the instrument, and thus to get the truth in

44

its purity. But this improvement would, as a matter of fact, only bring us back to the point where we were before. If we take away again from a definitely formed thing that which the instrument has done in the shaping of it, then the thing (in this case the Absolute) stands before us once more just as it was previous to all this trouble, which, as we now see, was superfluous. If the Absolute were only to be brought on the whole nearer to us by this agency, without any change being wrought in it, like a bird caught by a limestick, it would certainly scorn a trick of that sort, if it were not in its very nature, and did it not wish to be, beside us from the start. For a trick is what knowledge in such a case would be, since by all its busy toil and trouble it gives itself the air of doing something quite different from bringing about a relation that is merely immediate, and so a waste of time to establish. Or, again, if the examination of knowledge, which we represent as a medium, makes us acquainted with the law of its refraction, it is likewise useless to eliminate this refraction from the result. For knowledge is not the divergence of the ray, but the ray itself by which the truth comes in contact with us; and if this be removed, the bare direction or the empty place would alone be indicated.

Meanwhile, if the fear of falling into error introduces an element of distrust into science, which without any scruples of that sort goes to work and actually does know, it is not easy to understand why, conversely, a distrust should not be placed in this very distrust, and why we should not take care lest the fear of error is not just the initial error. As a matter of fact, this fear presupposes something, indeed a great deal, as truth, and supports its scruples and consequences on what should itself be examined beforehand to see whether it is truth. It starts with ideas of knowledge as an instrument, and as a medium; and presupposes a distinction of ourselves from this knowledge. More especially it takes for granted that the Absolute stands on one side, and that knowledge on the other side, by itself and cut off from the Absolute, is still something real; in other words, that knowledge, which, by being outside the Absolute, is certainly also outside truth, is nevertheless true — a position which, while calling itself fear of error, makes itself known rather as fear of the truth.

This conclusion comes from the fact that the Absolute alone is true or that the True is alone absolute. It may be set aside by making the distinction that a knowledge which does not indeed know the Absolute as science wants to do, is none the less true too; and that knowledge in general, though it may possibly be incapable of grasping the Absolute, can still be capable of truth of another kind. But we shall see as we proceed that random talk like this leads in the long run to a confused distinction between the absolute truth and a truth of some other sort, and that "absolute," "knowledge," and so on, are words which presuppose a meaning that has first to be got at.

With suchlike useless ideas and expressions about knowledge, as an instrument to take hold of the Absolute, or as a medium through which we have a glimpse of truth, and so on (relations to which all these ideas of a knowledge which is divided from the Absolute and an Absolute divided from knowledge in the last resort lead), we need not concern ourselves. Nor need we trouble about the evasive pretexts which create the incapacity of science out of the presupposition of such relations, in order at once to be rid of the toil of science, and to assume the air of serious and zealous effort about it. Instead of being troubled with giving answers to all these, they may be straightway rejected as adventitious and arbitrary ideas; and the use which is here made of words like "absolute," "knowledge," as also "objective" and "subjective," and innumerable others, whose meaning is assumed to be familiar to everyone, might well be regarded as so much deception. For to give out that their significance is universally familiar and that everyone indeed possesses their notion, rather looks like an attempt to dispense with the only important matter, which is just to give this notion. With better right, on the contrary, we might spare ourselves the trouble of taking any notice at all of such ideas and ways of talking which would have the effect of warding off science altogether; for they make a mere empty show of knowledge which at once vanishes when science comes on the scene.

But science, in the very fact that it comes on the scene, is itself a phenomenon; its "coming on the scene" is not yet *itself* carried out in all the length and breadth of its truth. In this regard, it is a matter of indifference whether we consider that it (science) is the phenomenon because it makes its appearance alongside another kind of knowledge, or call that other untrue knowledge its process of appearing. Science, however, must liberate itself from this phenomenality, and it can only do so by turning against it. For science cannot simply reject a form of knowledge which is not true, and treat this as a common view of things, and then assure us that itself is an entirely different kind of knowledge, and holds the other to be of no account at all; nor can it appeal to the fact that in this other there are presages of a better. By giving that assurance it would declare its force and value to lie in its bare existence; but the untrue knowledge appeals likewise to the fact that it *is*, and assures us that to it *science* is nothing. One barren assurance, however, is of just as much value as another. Still less can science appeal to the presages of a better, which are to be found present in untrue knowledge and are there pointing the way towards science; for it would, on the one hand, be appealing again in the same way to a merely existent fact; and, on the other, it would be appealing to itself, to the way in which it exists in untrue knowledge, i.e. to a bad form of its own existence, to its appearance, rather than to its real and true nature (*an und für sich*). For this reason we shall here undertake the exposition of knowledge as a phenomenon.

Now because this exposition has for its object only phenomenal knowledge, the exposition itself seems not to be science, free, self-moving in the shape proper to itself, but may, from this point of view, be taken as the pathway of the natural consciousness which is pressing forward to true knowledge. Or it can be regarded as the path of the soul, which is traversing the series of its own forms of embodiment, like stages appointed for it by its own nature, that it may possess the clearness of spiritual life when, through the complete experience of its own self, it arrives at the knowledge of what it is in itself.

Natural consciousness will prove itself to be only knowledge in principle or not real knowledge. Since, however, it immediately takes itself to be the real and genuine knowledge, this pathway has a negative significance for it; what is a realization of the notion of knowledge means for it rather the ruin and overthrow of itself; for on this road it loses its own truth. Because of that, the road can be looked on as the path of doubt, or more properly a highway of despair. For what happens there is not what is usually understood by doubting, a jostling against this or that supposed truth, the outcome of which is again a disappearance in due course of the doubt and a return to the former truth, so that at the end the matter is taken as it was before. On the contrary, that pathway is the conscious insight into the untruth of the phenomenal knowledge, for which that is the most real which is after all only the unrealized notion. On that account, too, this thoroughgoing scepticism is not what doubtless earnest zeal for truth and science fancies it has equipped itself with in order to be ready to deal with them — viz. the *resolve*, in science, not to deliver itself over to the thoughts of others on their mere authority, but to examine everything for itself, and only follow its own conviction, or, still better, to produce everything itself and hold only its own act for true.

The series of shapes, which consciousness traverses on this road, is rather the detailed history of the process of training and educating consciousness itself up to the level of science. That resolve presents this mental development (*Bildung*) in the simple form of an intended purpose, as immediately finished and complete, as having taken place; this pathway, on the other hand, is, as opposed to this abstract intention, or untruth, the actual carrying out of that process of development. To follow one's own conviction is certainly more than to hand oneself over to authority; but by the conversion of opinion held on authority into opinion held out of personal conviction, the content of what is held is not necessarily altered, and truth has not thereby taken the place of error. If we stick to a system of opinion and prejudice resting on the authority of others, or upon personal conviction, the one differs from the other merely in the conceit which animates the latter. Scepticism, directed to the whole compass of phenomenal consciousness, on the contrary, makes mind for the first time qualified to test what truth is; since it brings about a despair regarding what are called natural views, thoughts, and opinions, which it is matter of indifference to call personal or belonging to others, and with which the consciousness, that proceeds straight away to criticize and test, is still filled and hampered, thus being, as a matter of fact, incapable of what it wants to undertake.

The completeness of the forms of unreal consciousness will be brought about precisely through the necessity of the advance and the necessity of their connection with one another. To make this comprehensible we may remark, by way of preliminary, that the exposition of untrue consciousness in its untruth is not a merely negative process. Such a one-sided view of it is what the natural consciousness generally adopts; and a knowledge, which makes this one-sidedness its essence, is one of those shapes assumed by incomplete consciousness which falls into the course of the inquiry itself and will come before us there. For this view is scepticism, which always sees in the result only pure nothingness, and abstracts from the fact that this nothing is determinate, is the nothing of _that out of which_ it comes as a result. Nothing, however, is only, in fact, the true result, when taken as the nothing of what it comes from; it is thus itself a determinate nothing, and has a _content_. The scepticism which ends with the abstraction "nothing" or "emptiness" can advance from this not a step farther, but must wait and see whether there is possibly anything new offered, and what that is— in order to cast it into the same abysmal void. When once, on the other hand, the result is apprehended, as it truly is, as _determinate_ negation, a new form has thereby immediately arisen; and in the negation the transition is made by which the progress through the complete succession of forms comes about of itself.

The goal, however, is fixed for knowledge just as necessarily as the succession in the process. The terminus is at that point where knowledge is no longer compelled to go beyond itself, where it finds its own self, and the notion corresponds to the object and the object to the notion. The progress towards this goal consequently is without a halt, and at no earlier stage is satisfaction to be found. That which is confined to a life of nature is unable of itself to go beyond its immediate existence; but by something other than itself it is forced beyond that; and to be thus wrenched out of its setting is its death. Consciousness, however, is to itself its own notion; thereby it immediately transcends what is limited, and, since this latter belongs to it, consciousness transcends its own self. Along with the particular there is at the same time set up the "beyond," were this only, as in spatial intuition, *beside* what is limited. Consciousness, therefore, suffers this violence at its own hands; it destroys its own limited satisfaction. When feeling of violence, anxiety for the truth may well withdraw, and struggle to preserve for itself that which is in danger of being lost. But it can find no rest. Should that anxious fearfulness wish to remain always in unthinking indolence, thought will agitate the thoughtlessness, its restlessness will disturb that indolence. Or let it take its stand as a form of sentimentality which assures us it finds everything good in its kind, and this assurance likewise will suffer violence at the hands of reason, which finds something *not* good just because and in so far as it is a *kind.* Or, again, fear of the truth may conceal itself from itself and others behind the pretext that precisely burning zeal for the very truth makes it so difficult, nay impossible, to find any other truth except that of which alone vanity is capable — that of being ever so much cleverer than any ideas, which one gets from oneself or others, could make possible. This sort of conceit which understands how to belittle every truth and turn away from it back into itself, and gloats over this its own private understanding, which always knows how to dissipate every possible thought, and to find, instead of all the content, merely the barren Ego — this is a satisfaction which must be left to itself; for it flees the universal and seeks only an isolated existence on its own account (*Fürsichseyn*).

As the foregoing has been stated, provisionally and in general, concerning the manner and the necessity of the process of the inquiry, it may also be of further service to make some observations regarding the method of carrying this out. This exposition, viewed as a process of relating science to phenomenal knowledge, and as an inquiry and critical examination into the reality of knowing, does not seem able to be effected without some presupposition which is laid down as an ultimate criterion. For an examination consists in applying an accepted standard, and, on the final agreement or disagreement therewith of what is tested, deciding whether the latter is right or wrong; and the standard in general, and so science, were this the criterion, is thereby accepted as the essence or inherently real (*Ansich*). But, here, where science first appears on the scene, neither science nor any sort of standard has justified itself as the essence or ultimate reality; and without this no examination seems able to be instituted.

This contradiction and the removal of it will become more definite if, to begin with, we call to mind the abstract determinations of knowledge and of truth as they are found in consciousness. Consciousness, we find, *distinguishes* from itself something, to which at the same time it *relates* itself; or, to use the current expression, there is something *for* consciousness; and the determinate form of this process of relating, or of there being something for a consciousness, is knowledge. But from this being for another we distinguish being in itself or *per se*; what is related to knowledge is likewise distinguished from it, and posited as also existing outside this relation; the aspect of being *per se* or in itself is called Truth. What really lies in these determinations does not further concern us here; for since the object of our inquiry is phenomenal knowledge, its determinations are also taken up, in the first instance, as they are immediately offered to us. And they are offered to us very much in the way we have just stated.

If now our inquiry deals with the truth of knowledge, it appears that we are inquiring what knowledge is in itself. But in this inquiry knowledge is *our* object, it is *for us*; and the essential nature (*Ansich*) of knowledge, were this to come to light, would be rather its being *for us*: what we should assert to be its essence would rather be, not the truth of knowledge, but only our knowledge of it. The essence or the criterion would lie in us; and that which was to be compared with this standard, and on which a decision was to be passed as a result of this comparison, would not necessarily have to recognize that criterion.

But the nature of the object which we are examining surmounts this separation, or semblance of separation, and presupposition. Consciousness furnishes its own criterion in itself, and the inquiry will thereby be a comparison of itself with its own self; for the distinction, just made, falls inside itself. In consciousness there is one element *for* an other, or, in general, consciousness implicates the specific character of the moment of knowledge. At the same time this "other" is to consciousness not merely *for it*, but also outside this relation, or has a being in itself, i.e. there is the moment of truth. Thus in what consciousness inside itself declares to be the essence or truth we have the standard which itself sets up, and by which we are to measure its knowledge. Suppose we call knowledge the notion, and the essence or truth "being" or the object, then the examination consists in seeing whether the notion corresponds with the object. But if we call the inner nature of the object, or what it is in itself, the notion, and, on the other side, understand by object the notion *qua* object, i.e. the way the notion is *for* an other, then the examination consists in our seeing whether the object corresponds to its own notion. It is clear, of course, that both of these processes are the same. The essential fact, however, to be borne in mind throughout the whole inquiry is that both these moments, notion and object, "being for another" and "being in itself," themselves fall within that knowledge which we are examining. Consequently we do not require to bring standards with us, nor to apply *our* fancies and thoughts in the inquiry; and just by our leaving these aside we are enabled to treat and discuss the subject as it actually is in itself and for itself, as it is in its complete reality.

But not only in this respect, that notion and object, the criterion and what is to be tested, are ready to hand in consciousness itself, is any addition of ours superfluous, but we are also spared the trouble of comparing these two and of making an examination in the strict sense of the term; so that in this respect, too, since consciousness tests and examines itself, all we are left to do is simply and solely to look on. For consciousness is, on the one hand, consciousness of the object, on the other, consciousness of itself; consciousness of what to it is true, and consciousness of its knowledge of that truth. Since both are for the same consciousness, it is itself their comparison; it is the same consciousness that decides and knows whether its knowledge of the object corresponds with this object or not. The object, it is true, appears only to be in such wise for consciousness as consciousness knows it. Consciousness does not seem able to get, so to say, behind it as it is, not for consciousness, but in itself, and consequently seems also unable to test knowledge by it. But just because consciousness has, in general, knowledge of an object, there is already present the distinction that the inherent nature, what the object is in itself, is one thing to consciousness, while knowledge, or the being of the object *for* consciousness, is another moment. Upon this distinction, which is present as a fact, the examination turns. Should both, when thus compared, not correspond, consciousness seems bound to alter its knowledge, in order to make it fit the object. But in the alteration of the knowledge, the object itself also, in point of fact, is altered; for the knowledge which existed was essentially a knowledge of the object; with change in the knowledge, the object also becomes different, since it belonged essentially to this knowledge. Hence consciousness comes to find that what formerly to it was the essence is not what is *per se*, or what was *per se* was only *per se for consciousness*. Since, then, in the case of its object consciousness finds its knowledge not corresponding with this object, the object likewise fails to hold out; or the standard for examining is altered when that, whose criterion this standard was to be, does not hold its ground in the course of the examination; and the examination is not only an examination of knowledge, but also of the criterion used in the process.

This dialectic process which consciousness executes on itself—on its knowledge as well as on its object—in the sense that out of it the new and true object arises, is precisely what is termed Experience. In this connection, there is a moment in the process just mentioned which should be brought into more decided prominence, and by which a new light is cast on the scientific aspect of the following exposition. Consciousness knows something; this something is the essence of what is *per se*. This object, however, is also the *per se*, the inherent reality, *for consciousness*. Hence comes ambiguity of this truth. Consciousness, as we see, has now two objects: one is the first *per se*, the second is the existence *for consciousness* of this *per se*. The last object appears at first sight to be merely the reflection of consciousness into itself, i.e. an idea not of an object, but solely of its knowledge of that first object. But, as was already indicated, by that very process the first object is altered; it ceases to be what is *per se*, and becomes consciously something which is *per se* only *for consciousness*. Consequently, then, what this real *per se* is for consciousness is truth: which, however, means that this is the essential reality, or the object which consciousness has. This new object contains the nothingness of the first; the new object is the *experience* concerning that first object.

In this treatment of the course of experience, there is an element in virtue of which it does not seem to be in agreement with what is ordinarily understood by experience. The transition from the first object and the knowledge of it to the other object, in regard to which we say we have had experience, was so stated that the knowledge of the first object, the existence *for consciousness* of the first *ens per se*, is itself to be the second object. But it usually seems that we learn by experience the untruth of our first notion by appealing to some other object which we may happen to find casually and externally; so that, in general, what we have is merely the bare and simple apprehension of what is in and for itself. On the view above given, however, the new object is seen to have come about by a transformation or conversion of consciousness itself. This way of looking at the matter is *our* doing, what *we* contribute; by its means the series of experiences through which consciousness passes is lifted into a scientifically constituted sequence, but this does not exist for the consciousness we contemplate and consider. We have here, however, the same sort of circumstance, again, of which we spoke a short time ago when dealing with the relation of this exposition to scepticism, viz. that the result which at any time comes about in the case of an untrue mode of knowledge cannot possibly collapse into an empty nothing, but must necessarily be taken as the negation of that of which it is a result—a result which contains what truth the preceding mode of knowledge has in it. In the present instance the position takes this form: since what at first appeared as object is reduced, when it passes into consciousness, to what knowledge takes it to be, and the implicit nature, the real in itself, becomes what this entity *per se*, is *for consciousness*; this latter is the new object, whereupon there appears also a new mode or embodiment of consciousness, of which the essence is something other than that of the preceding mode. It is this circumstance which carries forward the whole succession of the modes or attitudes of consciousness in their own necessity. It is only this necessity, this origination of the new object—which offers itself to consciousness without consciousness knowing how it comes by it—that to us, who watch the process, is to be seen going on, so to say, behind its back. Thereby there enters into its process a moment of being *per se* or of being for us, which is not expressly presented to that consciousness which is in the grip of experience itself. The *content*, however, of what we see arising, exists for it, and we lay hold of and comprehend merely its formal character, i.e. its *bare* origination; *for it*, what has thus arisen has merely the character of object, while, *for us*, it appears at the same time as a process and coming into being.

In virtue of that necessity this pathway to science is itself *eo ipso* science, and is, moreover, as regards its content, Science of the Experience of Consciousness.

The experience which consciousness has concerning itself can, by its essential principle, embrace nothing less than the entire system of consciousness, the whole realm of the truth of mind, and in such wise that the moments of truth are set forth in the specific and peculiar character they here possess—i.e. not as abstract pure moments, but as they are for consciousness, or as consciousness itself appears in its relation to them, and in virtue of which they are moments of the whole, are embodiments or modes of consciousness. In pressing forward to its true form of existence, consciousness will come to a point at which it lays aside its semblance of being hampered with what is foreign to it, with what is only for it and exists as an other; it will reach a position where appearance becomes identified with essence, where, in consequence, its exposition coincides with just this very point, this very stage of the science proper of mind. And, finally, when it grasps this its own essence, it will connote the nature of absolute knowledge itself.

A. CONSCIOUSNESS[1]

I

CERTAINTY AT THE LEVEL OF SENSE-EXPERIENCE —
THE "THIS," AND "MEANING"

THE knowledge, which is at the start or immediately our object, can be nothing else than just that which is immediate knowledge, knowledge of the immediate, of what *is*. We have, in dealing with it, to proceed, too, in an immediate way, to accept what is given, not altering anything in it as it is presented before us, and keeping mere apprehension (*Auffassen*) free from conceptual comprehension (*Begreifen*).

The concrete content, which sensuous certainty furnishes, makes this *prima facie* appear to be the richest kind of knowledge, to be even a knowledge of endless wealth — a wealth to which we can as little find any limit when we traverse its *extent* in space and time, where that content is presented before us, as when we take a fragment out of the abundance it offers us and by dividing and dividing seek to penetrate its *intent*. Besides that, it seems to be the truest, the most authentic knowledge: for it has not as yet dropped anything from the object; it has the object before itself in its entirety and completeness. This bare fact of *certainty*, however, is really and admittedly the abstractest and the poorest kind of *truth*. It merely says regarding what it knows: it *is*; and its truth contains solely the *being* of the fact it knows. Consciousness, on its part, in the case of this form of certainty, takes the shape merely of pure Ego. In other words, I in such a case am merely *qua* pure This, and the object likewise is merely *qua* pure This. I, *this* particular conscious I, am certain of *this* fact before me, not because I *qua* consciousness have developed myself in connection with it and in manifold ways set thought to work about it: and not, again, because the fact, the thing, of which I am certain, in virtue of its having a multitude of distinct qualities, was replete with possible modes of relation and a

---

[1]The reader may be referred to the analysis of Sensation and Perception in Plato's *Theaetetus*, and to Bradley's *Appearance and Reality*, Chaps. II, V, VIII and XIX.

variety of connections with other things. Neither has anything to do with the truth sensuous certainty contains: neither the I nor the thing has here the meaning of a manifold relation with a variety of other things, of mediation in a variety of ways. The I does not contain or imply a manifold of ideas, the I here does not *think*: nor does the thing mean what has a multiplicity of qualities. Rather, the thing, the fact, *is*; and it *is* merely because it is. It *is*—that is the essential point for sense-knowledge, and that bare fact of *being*, that simple immediacy, constitutes its truth. In the same way the certainty *qua relation*, the certainty "of" something, is an immediate pure relation; consciousness is I—nothing more, a pure *this*; the *individual* consciousness knows a pure *this*, or knows what is *individual*.

But, when we look closely, there is a good deal more implied in that bare pure being, which constitutes the kernel of this form of certainty, and is given out by it as its truth. A concrete actual certainty of sense is not merely this pure immediacy, but an example, an instance, of that immediacy. Amongst the innumerable distinctions that here come to light, we find in all cases the fundamental difference—viz. that in sense-experience pure being at once breaks up into the two "thises," as we have called them, one this as I, and one as object. When *we* reflect[2] on this distinction, it is seen that neither the one nor the other is merely immediate, merely *is* in sense-certainty, but is at the same time *mediated*: I have the certainty through the other, viz. through the actual fact; and this, again, exists in that certainty through an other, viz. through the I.

It is not only we who make this distinction of essential truth and particular example, of essence and instance, immediacy and mediation; we *find* it in sense-certainty itself, and it has to be taken up in the form in which it exists there, not as we have just determined it. One of them is put forward in it as existing in simple immediacy, as the essential reality, the *object*. The other, however, is put forward as the non-essential, as *mediated*, something which is not *per se* in the certainty, but there through something else, ego, a state of knowledge which only knows the object because the *object* is, and which can as well be as *not* be. The object, however, is the real truth, is the essential reality; it *is*, quite indifferent to whether it is known or not; it remains and stands even though it is not known, while the knowledge does not exist if the object is not there.

We have thus to consider as to the object, whether in point of fact it does exist in sense-certainty itself as such an essential reality as that certainty gives it out to be; whether its meaning and notion, which is to be

---

[2]I.e. for the purposes of philosophical analysis.

essential reality, corresponds to the way it is present in that certainty. We have for that purpose not to reflect about it and ponder what it might be in truth, but to deal with it merely as sense-certainty contains it.

Sense-certainty itself has thus to be asked: What is the This? If we take it in the two-fold form of its existence, as the *Now* and as the *Here*, the dialectic it has in it will take a form as intelligible as the This itself. To the question, What is the Now? we reply, for example, the Now is night-time. To test the truth of this certainty of sense, a simple experiment is all we need: write that truth down. A truth cannot lose anything by being written down, and just as little by our preserving and keeping it. If we look again at the truth we have written down, look at it *now, at this noon-time*, we shall have to say it has turned stale and become out of date.

The Now that is night is kept fixed, i.e. it is treated as what it is given out to be, as something which *is*; but it proves to be rather a something which is *not*. The Now itself no doubt maintains itself, but as what is *not* night; similarly in its relation to the day which the Now is at present, it maintains itself as something that is also not day, or as altogether something negative. This self-maintaining Now is therefore not something immediate but something mediated; for, *qua* something that remains and preserves itself, it is determined through and *by means* of the fact that something else, namely day and night, is *not*. Thereby it is just as much as ever it was before, Now, and in being this simple fact, it is indifferent to what is still associated with it; just as little as night or day is its being, it is just as truly *also* day and night; it is not in the least affected by this otherness through which it is what it is. A simple entity of this sort, which is by and through negation, which is neither this nor that, which is a *not-this*, and with equal indifference this as well as that—a thing of this kind we call a Universal. The Universal is therefore in point of fact the truth of sense-certainty, the true content of sense-experience.

It is as a universal, too, that we[3] give utterance to sensuous fact. What we say is: "This," i.e. the universal this; or we say: "it is," i.e. being in general. Of course we do not present before our mind in saying so the universal this, or being in general, but we *utter* what is universal; in other words, we do not actually and absolutely say what in this sense-certainty we really *mean*. Language, however, as we see, is the more truthful; in it we ourselves refute directly and at once our own "meaning"; and since universality is the real truth of sense-certainty, and lan-

---

[3] I.e. the naïve consciousness here analysed.

guage merely expresses *this* truth, it is not possible at all for us even to express in words any sensuous existence which we "mean."

The same will be the case when we take the *Here*, the other form of the This. The Here is e.g. the tree. I turn about and this truth has disappeared and has changed round into its opposite: the Here is not a tree, but a house. The Here itself does not disappear; it *is* and remains in the disappearance of the house, tree, and so on, and is indifferently house, tree. The This is shown thus again to be *mediated simplicity*, in other words, to be *universality*.

Pure being, then, remains as the essential element for this sense-certainty, since sense-certainty in its very nature proves the universal to be the truth of its object. But that pure being is not in the form of something immediate, but of something in which the process of negation and mediation is essential. Consequently it is not what we *intend* or "mean" by being, but being with the characteristic that it is an abstraction, the purely universal; and our intended "meaning," which takes the truth of sense-certainty to be *not* something universal, is alone left standing in contrast to this empty, indifferent Now and Here.

If we compare the relation in which knowledge and the object first stood with the relation they have come to assume in this result, it is found to be just the reverse of what first appeared. The object, which professed to be the essential reality, is now the non-essential element of sense-certainty; for the universal, which the object has come to be, is no longer such as the object essentially was to be for sense-certainty. The certainty is now found to lie in the opposite element, namely in knowledge, which formerly was the non-essential factor. Its truth lies in the object as my (*meinem*) object, or lies in the "meaning" (*Meinen*), in what I "mean"; it *is*, because I know it. Sense-certainty is thus indeed banished from the object, but it is not yet thereby done away with; it is merely forced back into the I. We have still to see what experience reveals regarding its reality in this sense.

The force of its truth thus lies now in the I, in the immediate fact of my seeing, hearing, and so on; the disappearance of the particular Now and Here that we "mean" is prevented by the fact that *I* keep hold on them. The Now is daytime, because *I* see it; the Here is a tree for a similar reason. Sense-certainty, however, goes through, in this connection, the same dialectic process as in the former case. I, *this* I, see the tree, and assert the tree to be the Here; *another* I, however, sees the house and maintains the Here is not a tree but a house. Both truths have the same authenticity—the immediacy of seeing and the certainty and assurance both have as to their specific way of knowing; but the one certainty disappears in the other.

In all this, what does not disappear is the I *qua* universal, whose seeing is neither the seeing of this tree nor of this house, but just seeing *simpliciter*, which is mediated through the negation of this house, etc., and, in being so, is all the same simple and indifferent to what is associated with it, the house, the tree, and so on. I is merely universal, like Now, Here, or This in general. No doubt I "mean" an individual I, but just as little as I am able to say what I "mean" by Now, Here, so it is impossible in the case of the I too. By saying "this Here," "this Now," "an individual thing," I say all Thises, Heres, Nows, or Individuals. In the same way when I say "I," "this individual I," I say quite generally "all I's," every one is what I say, every one is "I," this individual I. When philosophy is requested, by way of putting it to a crucial test—a test which it could not possibly sustain—to "deduce," to "construe," "to find a priori," or however it is put, a so-called *this thing*, or *this particular man*,[4] it is reasonable that the person making this demand should say *what* "this thing," or *what* "this I," he means: but to say this is quite impossible.

Sense-certainty discovers by experience, therefore, that its essential nature lies neither in the object nor in the I; and that the immediacy peculiar to it is neither an immediacy of the one nor of the other. For, in the case of both, what I "mean" is rather something non-essential; and the object and the I are universals, in which that Now and Here and I, which I "mean," do not hold out, do not exist. We arrive in this way at the result, that we have to put the *whole* of sense-certainty as its essential reality, and no longer merely one of its moments, as happened in both cases, where first the object as against the I, and then the I, was to be its true reality. Thus it is only the whole sense-certainty itself which persists therein as immediacy, and in consequence excludes from itself all the opposition which in the foregoing had a place there.

This pure immediacy, then, has nothing more to do with the fact of otherness, with Here in the form of a tree passing into a Here that is not a tree, with Now in the sense of day-time changing into a Now that is night-time, or with there being an other I to which something else is object. Its truth stands fast as a self-identical relation making no distinction of essential and non-essential, between I and object, and into which, therefore, in general, no distinction can find its way. I, *this* I, assert, then, the Here as tree, and do not turn round so that for me Here might become *not* a tree, and I take no notice of the fact that another I finds the Here as not-tree, or that I myself at some other time take the Here as not-tree, the Now as not-day. I am directly conscious, I intuit and nothing more, I am pure intuition; I *am—seeing, looking*. For my-

---

[4]Cf. Encyclo. §250.

self I stand by the fact, the Now is day-time, or, again, by the fact the Here is tree, and, again, do not compare Here and Now themselves with one another; I take my stand on *one* immediate relation: the Now is day.

Since, then, this certainty wholly refuses to come out if we direct its attention to a Now that is night or an I to whom it is night, we will go to it and let ourselves point out the Now that is asserted. We must let ourselves *point it out* for the truth of this immediate relation is the truth of *this ego* which restricts itself to *a* Now or *a* Here. Were we to examine this truth *afterwards*, or stand at a distance from it, it would have no meaning at all; for that would do away with the immediacy, which is of its essence. We have therefore to enter the same point of time or of space, indicate them, point them out to ourselves, i.e. we must let ourselves take the place of the very same I, the very same This, which is the subject knowing with certainty. Let us, then, see how that immediate is constituted, which is *shown* to us.

The Now is pointed out; this Now. "Now"; it has already ceased to be when it is pointed out. The Now that is, is other than the one indicated, and we see that the Now is just this—to be no longer the very time when it is. The Now as it is shown to us is one that *has been*, and that is its truth; it does not have the truth of being, of something that *is*. No doubt this is true, that it *has* been; but what *has* been is in point of fact not genuinely real, it is *not*, and the point in question concerned what is, concerned being.

In thus pointing out the Now we see then merely a process which takes the following course: *First* I point out the Now, and it is asserted to be the truth. I point it out, however, as something that *has been*, or as something cancelled and done away with. I thus annul and pass beyond that first truth and in the *second* place I now assert as the second truth that it *has* been, that it is superseded. But, *thirdly*, what *has* been *is not*; I then supersede, cancel, its *having* been, the fact of its being *annulled*, the second truth, negate thereby the negation of the Now and return in so doing to the first position: that Now *is*. The Now and pointing out the Now are thus so constituted that neither the one nor the other is an immediate simple fact, but a process with diverse moments in it. A *This* is set up; it is, however, rather an *other* that is set up; the *This* is superseded: and this otherness, this cancelling of the former, is itself again annulled, and so turned back to the first. But this first, reflected thus into itself, is not exactly the same as it was to begin with, namely something immediate: rather it is a something reflected-into-self, a simple entity which remains in its otherness, what it is: a Now which is any number of Nows. And that is the genuinely true Now; the Now is simple day-time which has many Nows within it—hours. A

Now of that sort, again—an hour—is similarly many minutes; and this Now—a minute—in the same way many Nows and so on. Showing, indicating, pointing out [the Now] is thus itself the very process which expresses what the Now in truth really *is*: namely a result, or a plurality of Nows all taken together. And the pointing out is the way of getting to know, of *experiencing, that Now is a universal*.

The Here pointed out, which I keep hold of, is likewise a *this* Here which, in fact, is not *this Here*, but a Before and Behind, an Above and Below, a Right and Left. The Above is itself likewise this manifold otherness—above, below, etc. The Here, which was to be pointed out, disappears in other Heres, and these disappear similarly. What is pointed out, held fast, and is permanent, is a negative This, which only is so when the Heres are taken as they should be, but therein cancel one another; it is a simple complex of many Heres. The Here that is "meant" would be the point. But it *is* not: rather, when it is pointed out as *being*, as having existence, that very act of pointing out proves to be not immediate knowledge, but a process, a movement from the Here "meant" through a plurality of Heres to the universal Here, which is a simple plurality of Heres, just as day is a simple plurality of Nows.

It is clear from all this that the dialectic process involved in sense-certainty is nothing else than the mere history of its process—of its experience; and sense-certainty itself is nothing else than simply this history. The naïve consciousness, too, for that reason, is of itself always coming to this result, which is the real truth in this case, and is always having experience of it: but is always forgetting it again and beginning the process all over. It is therefore astonishing when, in defiance of this experience, it is announced as "universal experience"—nay, even as a philosophical doctrine, the outcome, in fact, of scepticism—that the reality or being of external things in the sense of "Thises," particular sense objects, has absolute validity and truth for consciousness. One who makes such an assertion really does not know what he is saying, does not know that he is stating the opposite of what he wants to say. The truth for consciousness of a "This" of sense is said to be universal experience; but the very opposite is universal experience. Every consciousness of itself cancels again, as soon as made, such a truth as e.g. the Here is a tree, or the Now is noon, and expresses the very opposite: the Here is not a tree but a house. And similarly it straightway cancels again the assertion which here annuls the first, and which is also just such an assertion of a sensuous This. And in all sense-certainty what we find by experience is in truth merely, as we have seen, that "This" is a universal, the very opposite of what that assertion maintained to be universal experience.

We may be permitted here, in this appeal to universal experience, to anticipate[5] with a reference to the practical sphere. In this connection we may answer those who thus insist on the truth and certainty of the reality of objects of sense, by saying that they had better be sent back to the most elementary school of wisdom, the ancient Eleusinian mysteries of Ceres and Bacchus; they have not yet learnt the inner secret of the eating of bread and the drinking of wine. For one who is initiated into these mysteries not only comes to doubt the being of things of sense, but gets into a state of despair about it altogether; and in dealing with them he partly himself brings about the nothingness of those things, partly he sees these bring about their own nothingness. Even animals are not shut off from this wisdom, but show they are deeply initiated into it. For they do not stand stock still before things of sense as if these were things *per se*, with being in themselves: they despair of this reality altogether, and in complete assurance of the nothingness of things they fall-to without more ado and eat them up. And all nature proclaims, as animals do, these open secrets, these mysteries revealed to all, which teach what the truth of things of sense is.

Those who put forward such assertions really themselves say, if we bear in mind what we remarked before, the direct opposite of what they mean: a fact which is perhaps best able to bring them to reflect on the nature of the certainty of sense-experience. They speak of the "existence" of external objects, which can be more precisely characterized as actual, absolutely particular, wholly personal, individual things, each of them not like anything or anyone else; this is the existence which they say has absolute certainty and truth. They "mean" this bit of paper I am writing on, or rather *have* written on: but they do not say what they "mean." If they really wanted to *say* this bit of paper which they "mean," and they wanted to *say* so, that is impossible, because the This of sense, which is "meant," cannot be reached by language, which belongs to consciousness, i.e. to what is inherently universal. In the very attempt to say it, it would, therefore, crumble in their hands; those who have begun to describe it would not be able to finish doing so: they would have to hand it over to others, who would themselves in the last resort have to confess to speaking about a thing that has no being. They "mean," then, doubtless this bit of paper here, which is quite different from that bit over there; but they speak of actual things, external or sensible objects, absolutely individual, real, and so on; that is, they say about them what is simply universal. Consequently what is called unspeakable is nothing else than what is untrue, irrational, something barely and simply "meant."

If nothing is said of a thing except that it is an actual thing, an ex-

---

[5]Cf. Analysis of *Desire*, p. 220 ff.

ternal object, this only makes it the most universal of all possible things, and thereby we express its likeness, its identity, with everything, rather than its difference from everything else. When I say "an individual thing," I at once state it to be really quite a universal, for everything is an individual thing: and in the same way "this thing" is everything and anything we like. More precisely, as this bit of paper, each and every paper is a "this bit of paper," and I have thus said all the while what is universal. If I want, however, to help out speech—which has the divine nature of directly turning the mere "meaning" right round about, making it into something else, and so not letting it ever come the length of words at all—by pointing out this bit of paper, then I get the experience of what is, in point of fact, the real truth of sense-certainty. I point it out as a Here, which is a Here of other Heres, or is in itself simply many Heres together, i.e. is a universal. I take it up then, as in truth it is; and instead of knowing something immediate, I "take" something "truly," I *per-ceive* (*wahrnehme*, per-cipio).

II

PERCEPTION: OR THINGS AND THEIR DECEPTIVENESS[1]

In this as in the preceding section apprehension is effected under conditions of sense. But whereas in the preceding type of consciousness the universality which knowledge implies and requires no sooner appeared than it melted away, here in Perception we start from a certain stability in the manner of apprehension, and a certain constancy in the content apprehended. The universality in this case satisfies more completely the demands of knowledge. The problem for further analysis is to find the form which the universal here assumes and to determine the way in which the unity of the object (the "thing") holds together its essential differences. The result shows that the unity of the thing *qua* unity is only admissible as an unqualified or non-sensuous unity. It is a universal, but as such, not conditioned by sense; it is a pure or "unconditioned" universal—a thought proper. Being undetermined by sense, it transcends sense-apprehension, and so transcends perception proper, and compels the mind to adopt another cognitive attitude in order to apprehend it. This new attitude is Understanding.

The following section is thus indirectly an analysis and a criticism of the doctrine which reduces or confines knowledge to perception. It shows that the position "esse est percipi" must give way to the principle "esse est intelligi."

Immediate certainty does not make the truth its own, for its truth is something universal, whereas certainty wants to deal with the This.

---

[1]Cp. *Wissenschaft der Logik*, Buch 2, Absch. 2, Kap. 1. Das Ding und seine Eigenschaften, etc.

Perception, on the other hand, takes what exists for it to be a universal. Universality being its principle in general, its moments immediately distinguished within it are also universal; *I* is a universal, and the *object* is a universal. That principle has *arisen* and come into being for *us* who are tracing the course of experience; and our process of apprehending what perception is, therefore, is no longer a contingent series of acts of apprehension, as is the case with the apprehension of sense-certainty; it is a logically necessitated process. With the origination of the principle, both the moments, which as they appear merely fall apart as happenings, have at once together come into being: the one, the process of pointing out and indicating, the other the same process, but as a simple fact—the former the process of perceiving, the latter the object perceived. The object is in its essential nature the same as the process; the latter is the unfolding and distinguishing of the elements involved; the object is these same elements taken and held together as a single totality. *For us* (tracing the process) or in itself,[2] the universal, *qua* principle, is the essence of perception; and as against this abstraction, both the moments distinguished—that which perceives and that which is perceived—are what is non-essential. But in point of fact, because both are themselves the universal, or the essence, they are both essential: but since they are related as opposites, only one can in the relation (constituting perception) be the essential moment; and the distinction of essential and non-essential has to be shared between them. The one characterized as the simple fact, the object, is the essence, quite indifferent as to whether it is perceived or not: perceiving, on the other hand, being the process, is the insubstantial, the inconstant factor, which can be as well as not be, is the non-essential moment.

This object we have now to determine more precisely, and to develop this determinate character from the result arrived at: the more detailed development does not fall in place here. Since its principle, the universal, is in its simplicity a mediated principle, the object must express this explicitly as its own inherent nature. The object shows itself

---

[2]This expression refers to the distinction already made in the Introduction, between the point of view of the *Phenomenology* and that of the actual consciousness whose procedure is being analysed in the *Phenomenology*. That is "for us" which we (i.e. the philosophical "we") are aware of by way of anticipation, but which has not yet been evolved objectively and explicitly; it is intelligible, but not yet intellectually realized. That is "in itself" (*an sich*), which is implicit, inherent, or potential, and hence not yet explicitly developed. The terms "for us" and "in itself" are thus strictly alternative: the former looks at the matter from the point of view of the philosophical subject, the latter from the point of view of the object discussed by the philosopher. The implicit nature of the object can only be "for us" who are thinking about the object: and what *we* have in mind can only be *implicitly* true of the object. The alternative disappears when the explicit nature of the object is what "we" explicitly take the object to be.

by so doing to be the *thing with many properties*. The wealth of sense-knowledge belongs to perception, not to immediate certainty, where all that wealth was merely something alongside and by the way; for it is only perception that has negation, distinction, multiplicity in its very nature.

The This, then, is established as *not* This, or as superseded, and yet not *nothing* (*simpliciter*), but a determinate nothing, a nothing with a certain content, viz. *the This*. The sense-element is in this way itself still present, but not in the form of some particular that is "meant"—as had to be the case in immediate certainty—but as a universal, as that which will have the character of the *property*. Cancelling, superseding, brings out and lays bare its true twofold meaning which we found contained in the negative: to supersede (*aufheben*) is at once to negate and to preserve. The nothing being a negation of the This, preserves immediacy and is itself sensuous, but a universal immediacy. Being, however, is a universal by its having in it mediation or negation. When it brings this explicitly out as a factor in its immediacy, it is a specifically *distinct determinate property*. As a result, there are many such properties set up at once, one the negation of the other. Since they are expressed in the simple form of the universal, these determinate characters—which, strictly speaking, become properties only by a further additional characteristic—are self-related, are indifferent to each other, each is by itself, free from the rest. The simple self-identical universality, however, is itself again distinct and detached from these determinate characteristics it has. It is pure self-relation, the "medium" wherein all these characteristics exist: in it, as in a bare, simple unity, they interpenetrate without affecting one another; for just by participating in this universality they are indifferent to each other, each by itself.

This abstract universal medium, which we can call "Thinghood" in general or pure essential reality, is nothing else than the Here and Now as this on analysis turned out to be, viz. a simple togetherness of many Heres and Nows. But the many (in the present case) are in their determinateness themselves simply universals. This salt is a simple Here and at the same time manifold: it is white, and *also* pungent, *also* cubical in shape, *also* of a specific weight, and so on. All these many properties exist in a simple Here, where they interpenetrate each other. None of these has a different Here from the others; each is everywhere in the same Here where the others are. And at the same time, without being divided by different Heres, they do not affect each other in their interpenetration; its being white does not affect or alter the cubical shape it has, and neither affects its tart taste, and so on: on the contrary, since each is simple relation to self, it leaves the others alone and is related to these merely by being *also* along with them, a relation of mere indifference. This "Also" is thus the pure universal itself, the "medium," the "Thinghood" keeping them together.

In this relation, which has emerged, it is merely the character of positive universality that is first noticed and developed. But there is still a side presented to view which must also be taken into account. It is this. If the many determinate properties were utterly indifferent to each other, and were entirely related to themselves alone, they would not be determinate; for they are so, merely in so far as they are *distinguished* and related to others as their opposites. In view of this opposition, however, they cannot exist together in the bare and simple unity of their "medium," which unity is just as essential to them as negation. The process of distinguishing them, so far as it does not leave them indifferent, but effectually excludes, negates one from another, thus falls outside this simple "medium." And this, consequently, is not merely an "also," an unity indifferent to what is in it, but a "one" as well, an *excluding* repelling unity.

The "One" is the moment of negation, as, in a direct and simple manner, relating itself to itself, and excluding an other: and is that by which "Thinghood" is determined *qua* Thing. In the property of a thing the negation takes the form of a specific determinateness, which is directly one with the immediacy of its being, an immediacy which, by this unity with negation, is universality. *Qua* "one," however, negation, the specific quality, takes a form in which it is freed from this unity with the object, and exists *per se* on its own account.

These moments taken together exhaust the nature of the Thing, the truth of perception, so far as it is necessary to develop it here. It is (1) a universality, passive and indifferent, the "also" which forms the sole bond of connection between the qualities, or rather constituent elements, "matters," existing together; (2) negation, likewise in a simple form, or the "one," which consists in *excluding* properties of an opposite character; and (3) the many properties themselves, the relation of the two first moments—the negation, as it is related to that indifferent element, and in being so expands into a manifold of differences, the focal point of particularity radiating forth into plurality within the "medium" of subsistence. Taking the aspect that these differences belong to a "medium" indifferent to what is within it, they are themselves universal, they are related merely to themselves and do not affect each other. Taking, however, the other aspect, that they belong to the negative unity, they at the same time mutually exclude one another; but do so necessarily in the shape of properties that have a separate existence apart from the "also" connecting them. The sensuous universality, the immediate unity of positive being and negative exclusion, is only then a property, when oneness and pure universality are evolved from it and distinguished from one another, and when that sensuous universality combines these with one another. Only after this relation of the unity to those pure essential moments is effected, is the "Thing" complete.

This, then, is the way the "Thing" in perception is constituted, and consciousness is perceptual in character so far as this "Thing" is its object: it has merely to "take" the object (*capio* — per-*ception*) and assume the attitude of pure apprehension, and what comes its way in so doing is truth (*das Wahre*). If it did something when taking the given, it would by such supplementation or elimination alter the truth. Since the object is the true and universal, the selfsame, while consciousness is the variable and non-essential, it may happen that consciousness apprehends the object wrongly and deceives itself. The percipient is aware of the possibility of deception; for, in the universality forming the principle here, the percipient is directly aware of otherness, but aware of it as null and naught, as what is superseded. His criterion of truth is therefore *selfsameness*, and his procedure is that of apprehending what comes before him as selfsame. Since, at the same time, diversity is a fact for him, his procedure is a way of relating the diverse moments of his apprehension to one another. If, however, in this comparison a want of sameness comes out, this is not an untruth on the part of the object (for the object is the selfsame), but on the part of perception.

Let us now see what sort of experience consciousness forms in the course of its actual perception. We, who are analysing the process, find this experience already contained in the development (just given) of the object and of the attitude of consciousness towards it. The experience will be merely the development of the contradictions that appear there.

The object which I apprehend presents itself as purely "one" and single: also, I am aware of the "property" (*Eigenschaft*) in it, a property which is universal, thereby transcending the particularity of the object. The first form of being, in which the objective reality has the sense of a "one," was thus not its true being; and since the *object* is the true fact here, the untruth falls on my side, and the apprehension was not correct. On account of the *universality* of the *property* (*Eigenschaft*) I must rather take the objective entity as a *community* (*Gemeinschaft*) in general. I further perceive now the property to be determinate, opposed to another and excluding this other. Thus, in point of fact, I did not apprehend the object rightly when I defined it as a "commonness" or community with others, or as continuity; and must rather, taking account of the *determinateness* of the property, isolate parts within the continuity and set down the object as a "one" that excludes. In the disintegrated "one" I find many such properties, which do not affect one another, but are indifferent to one another. Thus I did not apprehend the object correctly when I took it for something that excludes. The object, instead, just as formerly it was merely continuity in general, is now a universal common medium where many properties in the form of sense universals subsist, each for itself and on its own account, and, *qua* determinate, excluding the others. The simple and true fact, which I perceive, is, however, in virtue of this result, not a universal medium either, but the particular property by itself, which, again, in this form, is neither a property nor a determinate being, for it is now neither attached to a distinct "one" nor in relation to others. But the particular quality is a property only when attached to a "one," and determinate only in relation to others. By being this bare relation of self to self, it remains merely sensuous existence in general, since it no longer contains the character of negativity; and the mode of consciousness, which is now aware of a being of sense, is merely a way of "meaning" (*Meinen*) or "intending," i.e. it has left the attitude of perception entirely and gone back into itself. But sense existence and "meaning" themselves pass over into perception: I am thrown back on the beginning, and once more dragged into the same circuit, that supersedes itself in every moment and as a whole.

Consciousness, then, has to go over this cycle again, but not in the same way as on the first occasion. For it has found out, regarding perception, that the truth and outcome of perception is its dissolution, is reflection out of and away from the truth into itself. In this way consciousness becomes definitely aware of how its perceptual process is essentially constituted, viz. that this is not a simple bare apprehension, but in its apprehension is at the same time reflected out of the true content back into itself. This return of consciousness into itself, which is immediately involved and implicated in that pure apprehension—for this return to self has proved to be essential to perception—alters the true content. Consciousness is aware that this aspect is at the same time its own, and takes it upon itself and by so doing consciousness will thus get the true object bare and naked.

In this way we have, now, in the case of perception, as happened in the case of sensuous certainty, the aspect of consciousness being forced back upon itself; but, in the first instance, not in the sense in which this took place in the former case—i.e. not as if the truth of perception fell within it. Rather consciousness is aware that the untruth, that comes out there, falls within it. By knowing this, however, consciousness is able to cancel and supersede this untruth. It distinguishes its apprehension of the truth from the untruth of its perception, corrects this untruth, and, so far as itself takes in hand to make this correction, the truth, *qua* truth of perception, certainly falls within its own consciousness. The procedure of consciousness, which we have now to consider, is thus so constituted that it no longer merely perceives, but is also conscious of its reflection into self, and keeps this apart from the simple apprehension proper.

To begin with, then, I am aware of the "thing" as a "one," and have to keep it fixed in this true character as "one." If in the course of perceiving something crops up contradicting that, then I must take it to be due to my reflection. Now, in perception various different properties also turn up, which seem to be properties of the thing. But the thing is a "one"; and we are aware in ourselves that this diversity, by which the thing ceases to be a unity, falls in us. This thing, then, is, in point of fact, merely white to *our* eyes, *also* tart to *our* tongue, and *also* cubical to *our* feeling, and so on. The entire diversity of these aspects comes not from the thing, but from us; and we find them falling apart thus from one another, because the organs they affect are quite distinct *inter se*, the eye is entirely distinct from the tongue, and so on. We are, consequently, the universal medium where such elements get dissociated, and exist each by itself. By the fact, then, that we regard the characteristic of being a universal medium as *our* reflection, *we* preserve and maintain the selfsameness and truth of the thing, its being a "one."

These diverse aspects, which consciousness puts to its side of the account, are, however, each by itself just as it appears in the universal medium, specifically determined. White is only in opposition to black, and so on, and the thing is a "one" just by the fact that it is opposed to other things. It does not, however, exclude others from itself, so far as it is "one"; for to be "one" is to be in a universal relation of self to self, and hence by the fact of its being "one" it is rather like all. It is through the determinate characteristic that the thing excludes other things. Things themselves are thus determinate in and for themselves; they have properties by which they distinguish themselves from one another. Since the property is the *special* and *peculiar* property [the *proper* property] of the thing, or a specific characteristic in the thing itself, the thing has *several* properties. For, in the first place, the thing is true being, is a being inherently in itself; and what is in it is so as its own essential nature, and not on account of other things. Hence, in the second place, the determinate properties are not on account of other things and *for* other things, but inherent in that thing itself. They are, however, determinate properties *in it* only by the fact that they are several, and maintain their distinction from one another. And, in the third place, since they are thus within "thinghood," they are self-contained, each in and for itself, and are indifferent to one another. It is, then, in truth the thing itself which is white, and *also* cubical, and *also* tart, and so on; in other words, the *thing* is the "also," the general medium, wherein the many properties subsist externally to one another, without touching or affecting one another, and without canceling one another; and, so taken, the thing is taken as what it truly is.

Now, on this mode of perception arising, consciousness is at the same time aware that it reflects itself also into itself, and that, in perceiving, the opposite moment to the "also" crops up. This moment, however, is the unity of the thing with itself, a unity which excludes distinction from itself. It is consequently this unity which consciousness has to take upon itself; for the thing as such is the subsistence of many different and independent properties. Thus we say of the thing, "it is white, and *also* cubical, and *also* tart," and so on. But so far as it is white it is *not* cubical, and so far as it is cubical and also white it is not tart, and so on. Putting these properties into a "one" belongs solely to consciousness, which, therefore, has to avoid letting them coincide and be *one* (i.e. one and the same property) in the thing. For that purpose it introduces the idea of "in-so-far" to meet the difficulty; and by this means it keeps the qualities apart, and preserves the thing in the sense of the "also." Quite rightly consciousness at first makes itself responsible for the "oneness" in such a way that what was called a property is represented as being "free matter" (*materia libera*).[3] In this way the thing is raised to the level of a true "also" since it thus becomes a collection of component elements (materials or matters), and instead of being a "one" becomes a mere enclosure, a circumscribing surface.

If we look back on what consciousness formerly took upon itself, and now takes upon itself, what it previously ascribed to the thing, and now ascribes to it, we see that consciousness alternately makes itself, as well as the thing, into both a pure atomic many-less "one," and an "also" resolved into independent constituent elements (materials or matters). Consciousness thus finds through this comparison that not only *its* way of taking the truth contains the diverse moments of apprehension and return upon itself, but that the truth itself, the thing, manifests itself in this twofold manner. Here we find, as a result of experience, that the thing exhibits itself, in a determinate and specific manner, to the consciousness apprehending it, but *at the same time* is reflected back into itself out of that manner of presenting itself to consciousness; in other words, the thing contains within it opposite aspects of truth, a truth whose elements are in antithesis to one another.

Consciousness, then, gets away also from this second form of perceptual procedure, that, namely, which takes the thing as the true self-same, and itself as the reverse, as the factor that leaves sameness behind and goes back into self. Its object is now the entire process which was previously shared between the object and consciousness. The thing is

---

[3]An expression drawn from the physics of Hegel's day.

a "one," reflected into self; it is *for* itself; but it is also for an other; and, further, it is an other for itself *as* it is for another. The thing is, hence, for itself and *also* for another, a being that has difference of a twofold kind. But it is also "one." Its being "one," however, contradicts the diversity it has. Consciousness would, consequently, have again to make itself answerable for putting the diversity into the "one," and would have to keep this apart from the thing. It would thus be compelled to say that the thing "in-so-far as" it is for itself is not for another. But the oneness belongs to the thing itself, too, as consciousness has found out; the thing is essentially reflected into self. The "also," the distinction of elements indifferent to one another, falls doubtless within the thing as well as the "oneness," but since both are different, they do not fall within the same thing, but in different things. The contradiction which is found in the case of the objective content as a whole is assigned to and shared by two objects. The thing is, thus, doubtless as it stands (*an und für sich*) selfsame, but this unity with itself is disturbed by other things. In this way the unity of the thing is preserved, and, at the same time, the otherness is preserved outside the thing, as well as outside consciousness.

Now, although the contradiction in the object is in this way allotted to different things, yet the isolated individual thing will still be affected with distinction. The different things have a subsistence on their own account (*für sich*); and the conflict between them takes place on both sides in such a way that each is not different from itself, but only from the other. Each, however, is thereby characterized as a something distinctive, and contains *in it* essential distinction from the others; but at the same time not in such a way that this is an opposition within *its* being; on the contrary, it is by itself a simple determinate characteristic which constitutes its essential character, distinguishing it from others. As a matter of fact, since the diversity lies in it, this diversity does indeed necessarily assume the form of a *real* distinction of manifold qualities within it. But because the determinate characteristic gives the essence of the thing, by which it is distinguished from others, and has a being all its own, this further manifold constitution is something indifferent. The thing thus no doubt contains in its unity the qualifying "in-so-far" in two ways, which have, however, unequal significance; and by that qualification this oppositeness becomes not a real opposition on the part of the thing itself, but—so far as the thing comes into a condition of opposition through its absolute distinction—this opposition belongs to the thing with reference to an other thing lying outside it. The further manifoldness is doubtless necessarily in the thing too, and cannot be left out; but it is unessential to the thing.

This determinate characteristic, which constitutes the essential char-

acter of the thing and distinguishes it from all others, is now so defined
that thereby the thing stands in opposition to others, but must therein
preserve itself for itself (*für sich*). It is, however, a thing, a self-existent
"one," only so far as it does not stand in relation to others. For in this
relation, the connection with another is rather the point emphasized,
and connection with another means giving up self-existence, means
ceasing to have a being on its own account. It is precisely through the
absolute character and its opposition that the thing relates itself to
others, and is essentially this process of relation, and only this. The relation, however, is the negation of its independence, and the thing collapses through its own essential property.

The necessity of the experience which consciousness has to go
through in finding that the thing is destroyed just by the very characteristic which constitutes its essential nature and its distinctive existence on its own account, may, as regards the bare principle it implies,
be shortly stated thus. The thing is set up as having a being of its own,
as existing for itself, or as an absolute negation of all otherness; hence
it is absolute negation merely relating itself to itself. But this kind of
negation is the cancelling and superseding of *itself*, or means that it has
its essential reality in an other.

In point of fact the determination of the object, as it (the object) has
turned out, contains nothing else. It aims at having an essential property, constituting its bare existence for itself, but with this bare self-
existence it means also to embrace and contain diversity, which is to be
necessary, but is at the same time not to constitute its essential characteristic. But this is a distinction that only exists in words; the *non-*
essential, which has all the same to be *necessary*, cancels its own
meaning, or is what we have just called the negation of itself.

With this the last qualifying "in-so-far," which separated self-
existence and existence for another, drops away altogether. The object
is really in one and the same respect the opposite of itself—for itself "so
far as" it is for another, and for another "so far as" it is for itself. It is for
itself, reflected into self, one; but all this is asserted along with its opposite, with its being for another, and for that reason is asserted merely
to be superseded. In other words, this existence for itself is as much
unessential as that which alone was meant to be unessential, viz. the relation to another.

By this process the object in its pure characteristics, in those features
which were to constitute its essential nature, is superseded, just as the
object in its sensible mode of existence became transcended. From
being sensible it passed into being a universal; but this universal, because derived from sense, is essentially conditioned by it, and hence is,
in general, not a genuine self-identical universality, but one affected

with an opposition. For that reason this universality breaks up into the extremes of singleness and universality, of the "one" of the properties and the "also" of the free constituents or "matters." These pure determinations appear to express the essential nature itself; but they are merely a self-existence which is fettered at the same time with existence for an other. Since, however, both essentially exist in a single unity, we have before us now *unconditioned absolute universality*; and it is here that consciousness first truly passes into the sphere of *Understanding*, of Intelligence.

Sensible singleness thus disappears in the dialectic process of immediate certainty, and becomes universality, but merely sensuous universality. The stage of "meaning" has vanished, and perceiving takes the object as it inherently is in itself, or, put generally, as a universal. Singleness, therefore, makes its appearance there as true singleness, as the inherent nature of the "one," or as reflectedness into self. This is still, however, a conditioned self-existence alongside which appears another self-existence, the universality opposed to singleness and conditioned by it. But these two contradictory extremes are not merely alongside one another, but within one unity; or, what is the same thing, the common element of both, self-existence, is entirely fettered to its opposite, i.e. is, at the same time, *not* an existence-for-self. The sophistry of perception seeks to save these moments from their contradiction, tries to keep them fixed by distinguishing between "aspects," by using terms like "also" and "so far as," and seeks in like manner to lay hold on the truth by distinguishing the unessential element from an essential nature opposed thereto. But these expedients, instead of keeping away deception from the process of apprehension, prove rather to be of no avail at all; and the real truth, which should be got at through the logic of the perceptual process, proves to be in one and the same "aspect" the opposite (of what those expedients imply), and consequently to have as its essential content undifferentiated and indeterminate universality.

These empty abstractions of "singleness" and its antithetic "universality," as also of "essence," that is attended with a "non-essential" element, an element which is all the same "necessary," are powers the interplay of which constitutes perceptual understanding, often called "sound common sense" (*Menschenverstand*). This "healthy common sense," which takes itself to be the solid substantial type of conscious life, is, in its process of perception, merely the sport of these abstractions; it is always poorest where it means to be richest. In that it is tossed about by these unreal entities, bandied from one to the other, and by its sophistry endeavours to affirm and hold fast alternately now one, then the exact opposite, it sets itself against the truth, and imagines philosophy has merely to do with "things of the intellect" (*Gedankendinge*), merely manipulates "ideas." As a matter of fact, philosophy does have to do with them, too, and knows them to be the pure essential entities, the absolute powers and ultimate elements. But in doing so, philosophy knows them at the same time in their determinate and specific constitution, and is, therefore, master over them; while that perceptual understanding takes them for the real truth, and is led by them from one mistake to another. It does not get the length of being aware that there are such simple essentialities operating within it and dominating its activity; it thinks it has always to do with quite solid material and content; just as sense-certainty is unaware that its essence is the empty abstraction of pure being. But in point of fact it is these essential elements in virtue of which perceptual understanding makes its way hither and thither through every kind of material and content; they are its principle of coherence and control over its varied material; they alone are what constitutes for consciousness the essence of sensuous things, what determines their relations to consciousness; and they are that in the medium of which the process of perceiving, with the truth it contains, runs its course. The course of this process, a perpetual alternate determining of the truth and superseding of this determination, constitutes, properly speaking, the constant everyday life and activity of perceptual intelligence, of the consciousness that thinks it lives and moves in the truth. In that process it advances, without halt or stay, till the final result is reached, when these essential ultimate elements or determinations are all alike superseded; but in each particular moment it is merely conscious of one given characteristic as the truth, and then, again, of the opposite. It no doubt suspects their unessentiality; and, to save them from the impending danger, it takes to the sophistry of now asserting to be true what it had itself just affirmed to be not true. What the nature of these untrue entities really wants to force this understanding to do—viz. to bring together and thereby cancel and transcend the ideas about that "universality" and "singleness," about "also" and "one," about that "essentiality" which is necessarily connected with an "unessentiality," and about an "unessential" that is yet "necessary"—understanding strives to resist by leaning for support on the qualifying terms "in-so-far," "a difference of aspect," or by making *itself* answerable for one idea in order to keep the other separate and preserve it as the true one. But the very nature of these abstractions brings them together as they are and of their own accord. "Sound common sense" is the prey of these abstractions; they carry understanding round in their whirling circle. When understanding tries to give them truth by at one time taking their untruth upon itself, while at another it calls their deceptiveness a mere appearance due to the uncertainty and unreliability of things, and separates the essential from an element which is necessary to them, and yet is to be unessential, holding the former to be their truth as against the latter:—when understanding takes this line, it does not secure them *their* truth, but convicts *itself* of untruth.

III

FORCE AND UNDERSTANDING—THE WORLD OF APPEARANCE AND THE SUPERSENSIBLE WORLD[1]

The term "force" holds primarily with reference to the realm of Nature, whether physical or vital: but it is also used, more or less analogically, in reference to other spheres, e.g. morality. It is the objective counterpart of the activity of "understanding"; it is objectively the same kind of relation of unity to differences which is subjectively realized when the mind understands. Force is a self-conditioned principle of unity; the differences are the "expressions of force," the unity evolves the differences out of itself. Understanding similarly is a self-conditioned process; it consists in reducing differences to some ultimate unity, which is capable of deriving or "explaining" those differences from itself. The "unconditioned universal" to which we are led by the analysis of perception takes shape, therefore, as "force." The question is, How are the elements of this unconditioned universal related, and how do they hold together? The answer is found in the highest achievement of the operation of understanding—the establishment of a "kingdom of laws," which in its entirety is the meaning of the world so far as understanding goes. But laws *per se* are looked on as an inner realm, which merely "appears" in the detailed particulars which those laws control, and in which those laws are made manifest. The differences, in fact, are "phenomena," the laws *per se* are behind the scenes:—the world as a whole thus becomes distinguished into a realm of phenomena and a realm of noumena. These two realms set a new problem to the mind, and must again be brought together in a completer way than understanding can do. This new state of consciousness is "self-consciousness."

In this section we have at once an analysis of empiricism and a criticism of the Kantian solution of the problem of empiricism. It is shown that if phenomena are appearances of noumena, then the noumena do appear, and are, in fact, nothing except so far as they appear: otherwise the noumena, so far being "hidden," are worse than appearances, they are illusion. The phenomena are not merely appearances "to the mind," but appearances of something that does make itself manifest. If phenomena are thus not external to and still less independent of noumena, noumena are just as truly immanent in phenomena. Treated in any other way, noumena can at best be only another kind of phenomena; and this raises anew precisely the problem which the opposition of phenomena or noumena was intended to solve. Phenomena are related to noumena as the trees to the wood, not as a compound to its atoms. The

---

[1]Cp. *Wissenschaft der Logik*, Buch 2, Absch. 2, Kap. 3.

solution of the difficulty is thus only to be found in the type of consciousness which contains both—and this, Hegel says, is self-consciousness.

CONSCIOUSNESS has found "seeing" and "hearing," etc., pass away in the dialectic process of sense-experience, and has, at the stage of perception, arrived at thoughts which, however, it brings together in the first instance in the unconditioned universal. This unconditioned element, again, if it were taken as inert essence bare and simple, would itself be nothing else than the one-sided extreme of self-existence (*Fürsichseyn*); for the non-essential would then stand over against it. But if thus related to the latter, it would be itself unessential, and consciousness would not have got disentangled from the deceptions of perception; whereas this universal has proved to be one which has passed out of such conditioned separate existence and returned into itself.

This unconditioned universal, which henceforward is the true object of consciousness, is still *object* of consciousness; consciousness has not yet grasped its principle, or notion, *qua* notion. There is an essential distinction between the two which must be drawn. On the one hand, consciousness is aware that the object has passed from its relation to an other back into itself, and thereby become inherently and implicitly (*an sich*) notion; but, on the other hand, consciousness is not yet the notion explicitly or *for* itself, and consequently it does not know itself in that reflected object. We (who are analysing experience) found this object arise through the process of consciousness in such a way that consciousness is implicated and involved in the development of the object, and the reflection is the same on both sides, i.e. there is only one reflection. But because in this movement consciousness had as its content merely the objective entity, and not consciousness as such, the result has to be given an objective significance *for consciousness*; consciousness, however, still withdrawing from what has arisen, so that the latter in objective form is the essential reality to consciousness.

Understanding has, indeed, *eo ipso*, done away with its own untruth and the untruth in its object. What has thereby come to view is the notion of the truth as implicit inherent truth, which is not yet notion, or lacks a consciously explicit existence for itself (*Fürsichseyn*), and is something which understanding allows to have its way without knowing itself in it. It pursues its own nature by itself, so that consciousness has no share in its process of free realization, but merely looks on and apprehends that realization as a naked fact. It is, consequently, *our* business in the first instance to step into its place and *be* the notion, which works up into shape what is contained in the result. With this complete formation of the object, which is presented to consciousness as a bare existent fact (*ein Seyendes*), mere implicit awareness then first becomes to itself conceptual consciousness, conscious comprehension.

The result arrived at was the unconditioned universal, in the first instance in the negative and abstract sense that consciousness negated its one-sided notions and abstracted them: it surrendered them. This result, however, has inherently a positive significance; it has established the unity of existence-for-self, and existence-for-another; in other words, absolute opposites are immediately posited as one and the same reality. At first this seems to affect merely the formal relation of the moments to one another. But to be for-self and to be for-another constitutes the content itself as well, because the opposition, looked at truly, can have no other nature than what has come about in the result—viz. that the content, taken in perception for truth, belongs, in point of fact, solely to the form, and is dissipated into its unity. This content is at the same time universal; there can be no other content which by its peculiar constitution would refuse to return into this unconditioned universality. Such a content would be some specific way or other of being for-itself and taking up a relation to something else. But to be in general for-self and to stand in relation to something else constitutes the very nature and meaning of that whose truth lies in being unconditionally universal; and the result is through and through universal.

Since, however, this unconditioned universal is an object for consciousness, the distinction of form and content makes its appearance within it: and, in the shape of content, the moments have the aspect in which they were first presented—that of being on one side a universal medium of many substantial elements, and, on the other, a unit reflected into self, where their substantial independence is overthrown and done away with. The former dissolves the independence of the thing, is the condition of passivity which consists in being something for something else; the latter is its individual subsistence, its being something on its own account (*für sich*). We have to see what shape these moments take in the unconditioned universal which is their essential nature. It is obvious at the outset that by existing only in this universal they do not at all lie any longer apart from one another, but rather are in themselves essentially self-cancelling aspects, and what is established is only their transition into one another.

One moment, then, appears as universal medium, or as the subsistence of independent constituents, as the reality that has stepped aside. The independence of these constituent elements, however, is nothing else than this medium; i.e. this universal is simply and entirely the plurality of such diverse universals. That the universal is *per se* in undivided unity with this plurality means, however, that these elements are each where the other is; they mutually permeate one another—without touching one another, because, conversely, the manifold diversity is equally independent. Along with that, too, goes the fact that they are absolutely pervious and porous, or are cancelled and superseded. To be thus superseded, again, or the reduction of this diversity to bare and simple self-existence, is nothing else than the medium itself, and this is the independence of the different elements. In other words, the elements set up as independent pass directly over into their unity, and their unity directly into its explicit diversity, and the latter back once again into the reduction to unity. This process is what is called *Force*. One of its moments, where force takes the form of a dispersion of the independent elements each with a being of its own, is the *Expression* of Force; when, however, force takes the form of that wherein they disappear and vanish, it is *Force proper*, force withdrawn from expressing itself and driven back into itself. But in the first place force driven back into itself *must* express itself; and, secondly, in that expression it is still force existing within itself, as much as in thus being within itself it is expression.

When we thus keep both moments in this immediate unity, it is Understanding, to which the conception of force belongs, that is, properly speaking, the principle which carries the different moments *qua* different. For *per se* they are not to be different; the distinction consequently exists only in thought. Stated otherwise, only the mere conception of force has been put forward in the above, not its realization. In point of fact, however, force is the unconditioned universal, which is in itself just what it is for something else, or which holds difference within itself—for difference is nothing else than existence-for-an-other. Hence for force to be what it truly is, it has to be completely set free from thought, and put forward as the substantial reality of these differences, that is, first the substance *qua* the entire force remaining essentially self-contained (*an und für sich*), and then its differences as substantial entities, or as moments subsisting each on its own account. Force as such, force as driven back within itself, is in this way by itself an excluding unit, for which the unfolding of the elements or differences is another thing subsisting separately; and thus there are set up two sides, distinct and independent. But force is also the whole, or it remains what, in its very conception, it is; that is to say, these differences remain mere forms, superficial vanishing "moments." The differences between force proper, withdrawn into itself, and force unfolded and expressed in independent constituent elements, would at the same time have no being at all if they had no subsistence; i.e., force would have no being if it did not really exist in these opposite ways. But to exist in this way as opposite aspects means nothing else than that both moments are themselves at the same time independent. It is this process we have now to deal with—the process by which both moments get

themselves fixed as independent and then cancel their independence
again.

   Looked at broadly, it is manifest that this process is nothing else than
the process of perceiving, where the aspects, both percipient and content perceived, are at once inseparably united as regards the process of
grasping the truth, and yet, by that very fact, each aspect is at the same
time reflected into itself, is something on its own account. In the present case these two aspects are elements or moments of force; they subsist within one unity, just as much as this unity, which appears as the
middle term for the distinct and independent extremes, always gets broken up into these very extremes, which only are through this taking
place. Thus the process, which formerly took the shape of the self-
negation of contradictory *conceptions*, here assumes *objective* form, and
is a movement of force, the result of which is to bring out the "unconditioned universal" as something which is not objective—which is the
inner (unperceived) being of things.

   Force, as thus determined, since it is taken *as* force, or as reflected
into itself, is the one side of its notion and meaning: but a substantiated
extreme, and, moreover, the extreme established with the specific character of oneness. In virtue of this, the subsistence of the differentiated
elements falls outside it, and is something other than it. Since of necessity *it* has to *be* this subsistence, i.e., to *express*, externalize itself, its
expression takes the form that the other approaches it and incites it.
But, in point of fact, since it must necessarily express itself, it has within
itself this other, which to begin with took up a position as something
outside it. We must withdraw from the position which sets up force as
a one, and its essence—self-expression—as an other approaching it
from outside. Force is rather itself this universal medium for the subsistence of the moments as differentiated elements; or, in other words,
it *has* expressed or externalized itself, and what was to be something
outside it attracting or inciting it is really force itself. It thus exists now
as the medium of the differentiated elements which are evolved. But all
the same it is in its very nature one and single, and has essentially the
form of being that in which these subsisting elements are superseded.
This oneness is in consequence now something *other* than, external to,
force, since force takes its place as the medium for the elements to exist
in; and force therefore has this its essential being outside itself. Since,
however, it must of necessity be this essential nature, which as yet it is
not affirmed to be, this other comes forward soliciting or inciting it to
reflect into self, to turn this pseudo-external factor into an aspect of itself; in other words, this other cancels its external expression. In point
of fact, however, it is force itself that is thus reflected into self, that is
the sublation of the external expression. The oneness vanishes as it ap-

peared, viz. as something external; force is that very other, is force thrust back into itself.

What took the character of an external other, and incited force at once to expression and to return into self, turns out directly to be itself force: for the other shows itself to be universal medium as well as one and single, and shows this in such a way that each of the forms assumed appears at the same time to be merely a vanishing moment. Consequently force, in that there is an other for it, and it is for an other, has as a whole not yet developed its complete meaning. There are two forces present at the same time; the notion of both is no doubt the same notion, but it has passed out of its unity into duality. Instead of the opposition continuing to be entirely and essentially a mere moment, it appears to have escaped from the control of the unity and to have become, owing to this diremption, two quite independent forces. We have now to see more precisely what sort of situation this independence introduces.

To begin with, the second force stands towards the force incited in the character of inciting force, and, moreover, with respect to its content, plays the part of universal medium. But since that second force consists essentially in an alternation of these two moments and is itself force, it is likewise, in point of fact, universal medium only then when it is incited or solicited to being so; and in the same way, too, it is negative unity, or incites and leads to the retraction of force, only by being incited thereto. As a result, this distinction, which took place between one force regarded as inciting and the other as incited, turns also into one and the same reciprocal interchange of characteristics.

The interplay of the two forces in this way arises from and consists in the two being thus determined with opposite characteristics, in their being for one another in virtue of this determination and in the complete and direct exchange of their characteristics—a transition from one to the other, whereby alone these determinations, in which the forces seem to appear independently, have being. For example, the inciting force is set up as universal medium, and, on the other hand, the force incited as a force repressed. But the former is universal medium just by the very fact of the latter being repressed: that is to say, this latter is really what incites the former, and makes it the medium it claims to be. The former gets the character it has only through the other, and is an inciting force only so far as it is incited by the latter to be so. And it loses just as readily this character given to it, for this character passes, or rather has already passed, into the character of the other. The former, acting in an external way, takes the part of universal medium, but only by its having been incited by the other force to do so. This means, however, that the latter *gives* it that position, and is really *itself* essentially universal medium: it gives the inciting agency this character just because this other character is essentially its own, i.e. because it is really its own self.

To complete our insight into the principle of this process, we may notice, further, that the distinctions themselves reveal distinction in a twofold manner. They are, on the one hand, distinctions of content, since one extreme is force reflected into itself, while the other is a medium for the constituent elements involved: on the other hand, they appear as distinctions of form, since one incites and the other is incited, the former being active, the latter passive. As regards the distinction of content, they are in fact distinct, or distinct for *us* [who are analysing the process]; as regards distinction of form, however, they are independent, in their relation parting asunder of themselves, and standing opposed. In the perception of the movement of force, consciousness becomes aware that the extremes, in both these aspects, are nothing *per se*, that rather these sides, in which their distinction of nature was meant to consist, are merely vanishing moments, an immediate transition of each into its opposite. For us, however [who are analysing the process], it was also true, as stated above, that *per se* the distinctions, *qua* distinctions of content and form, vanished: and on the side of form, the active, inciting, or independent factor was in its very nature the same as what, from the side of content, was presented as repressed force, force driven back into itself; the passive, incited, or related factor was, from the side of form, the same as what, from the side of content, took shape as universal medium for the many constituent elements.

From this we see that the notion of force becomes actual when resolved into two forces, and we see too how it comes to be so. These two forces exist as independent entities: but their existence lies in a movement each towards each, of such a kind that in order to be, each has in reality to get its position purely through the other; that is to say, their being has purely the significance of disappearance. They are not like extremes that keep to themselves something positively fixed, and merely transmit an external property to one another through their common medium and by external contact: they are what they are solely in this medium and in their contact with each other. We have there immediately both force as it is independently, force repressed within itself, and also its expression, force inciting and force being incited. These moments are thus not allotted to two independent extremes, offering each other only an opposite pole: rather their true nature consists simply in each being solely through the other, and in each ceasing *eo ipso* to be what it thus is through the other; since it is the other. They have thus, in point of fact, no substances of their own which could support and maintain them. The notion of force rather maintains itself as the essence in its very actuality: force when actual exists wholly and only in its expression; and this, at the same time, is nothing else than a process of cancelling itself. This actual force, when represented as detached from its expression and existing by itself, is force driven back into itself; but this feature is itself, in point of fact, as appears from the foregoing, merely a moment in the *expression* of force. The true nature of force thus remains merely the thought or idea of force; the moments in its realization, its substantial independence and its process, rush, without let or hindrance, together into one single undivided unity, a unity which is not force withdrawn into itself (for this is merely one of those moments), but is its notion *qua* notion. The realization of force is, then, at the same time dissipation or loss of reality; it has thereby become something quite different, viz. this universality, which understanding knows from the start or immediately to be its essential nature, and which shows itself, too, to be the essence of it in what is supposed to be its reality, in the actual substances.

So far as we look on the first universal as the notion of understanding, where force does not yet exist for itself, the second is now its essential reality, as it is revealed in and for itself. Or, conversely, if we look on the first universal as the immediate, which should be an actual object for consciousness, then this second has the characteristic of being the negative of sensuously objective force: it is force, in the form in which, in its true being, force exists merely as object for understanding. The first would be force withdrawn into itself, i.e., force as substance; the second, however, is the inner being of things *qua* inner, which is one and the same with the notion *qua* notion.

This true being of things has here the characteristic that it does not exist immediately for consciousness; rather, consciousness takes up a mediated relation to the inner; in the form of understanding it looks through the intervening play of forces into the real and true background of things. The middle term combining the two extremes, understanding and the inner of things, is the explicitly evolved being of force, which is now and henceforth a vanishing process for understanding itself. Hence it is called Appearance (*Erscheinung*); for being which is *per se* straightway non-being we call a show, a semblance (*Schein*). It is, however, not merely a show, but appearance, a totality of seeming (*Schein*). This totality as totality or universal is what makes up the inner world, the play of forces in the sense of its reflection into itself. There consciousness has before itself in objective form the things of perception as they truly are, i.e. as moments turning, without halt or separate subsistence, directly into their opposite, the "one" changing immediately into the universal, the essential becoming at once something unessential, and vice versa. This play of forces is consequently the development of the negative; but its true nature is the positive element, viz. the universal, the implicit object, the object existing *per se*.

The being of this object for consciousness is mediated through the movement of appearance, by which the content of perception and the sensuous objective world as a whole, get merely negative significance. There consciousness is turned back upon itself as the truth; but, being consciousness, it again makes this truth into an inner being of the object, and distinguishes this reflection of things from its own reflection into self: just as the mediating process likewise is for it still an objective process. This inner nature is therefore for it an extreme placed over against it. But it is on that account the truth for it, because therein, as in something essentially real, it possesses at the same time the certainty of its own self, the moment of its own self-existence. But it is not yet conscious of this basis [its self-existence], for the independence, its being on its own account, which should have the inner world within it, would be nothing else than the negative process. This negative process, however, is for consciousness still objective vanishing appearance, and not yet its own proper self-existence (*Fürsichseyn*). Hence the inner is no doubt taken to be notion, but consciousness does not yet know the nature of the notion.

Within this inner truth, this absolute universal which has got rid of the opposition between universal and particular, and become the object of understanding, is a supersensible world which henceforth opens up as the true world, lying beyond the sensuous world which is the world of appearance. Away remote from the changing vanishing present (*Diesseits*) lies the permanent beyond (*Jenseits*): an immanent inherent reality (*ein Ansich*), which is the first and therefore imperfect manifestation of *Reason*, i.e. it is merely the pure element where the truth finds its abode and its essential being.

Our object henceforward has thus the form of a syllogistic inference (*Schluss*), whose extremes are the inner being of things and understanding, and its middle term the sphere of appearance. The course of this inferential process, however, furnishes the further characterization of what understanding detects in the inner world by the aid of the middle term; and gives rise to the experience understanding goes through regarding this relation of the terms when joined and united together.

The inner world is so far for consciousness a bare and simple beyond, because consciousness does not as yet find itself in it. It is empty, for it is the nothingness of appearance, and positively the naked universal. This type of inwardness suits those who say that the inner being of things cannot be known;[2] but the reason for the position would have

---

[2]Cp. Goethe, "*Im innern der Natur*," etc.

to be taken in some other sense. Certainly there is no knowledge to be had of this inner world, as we have it here; not, however, owing to reason being too short-sighted, or limited, or whatever you care to call it (on this point there is as yet nothing known at this stage; we have not gone deep enough for that yet), but on account simply of the nature of the case, because in the void there is nothing known, or, putting it from the point of view of the other side, because its very characteristic lies in being *beyond* consciousness.

The result is, of course, the same if you place a blind man amid the wealth of the supersensible world (if it has a wealth, whether this be a content peculiarly its own, or whether consciousness itself be this content), and if you place one with sight in absolute darkness, or, if you like, in pure light, supposing the supersensible world to be this. The seeing man sees in that pure light as little as in absolute darkness, and just as much as the blind man in the ample wealth which lay before him. If there were nothing more to be done with the inner sphere and with our being bound up along with it by means of the world of appearance, then there would be nothing left but to stop at the phenomenal world, i.e. take something for truth about which we know that it is not true. Or in order that there may be something in this empty void—which, while it originally came about as a state devoid of *objective* things, has, however, since it is emptiness pure and simple, to be taken to be also devoid of all *mental* relations and distinctions of consciousness *qua* consciousness—in order that in this complete vacuity, which is even called the holy of holies, the inner sanctuary, there may yet be *something*, we should be driven to fill it up with dreamings, *appearances*, produced by consciousness itself. It would have to be content with being treated so badly, for it would not deserve anything better, since even dreams are something better than its own barren emptiness.

The inner world, or the supersensible beyond, has, however, *arisen*: it comes to us out of the sphere of appearance, and the latter is its mediating agency: in other words, appearance is its essential nature and, in point of fact, its filling. The supersensible is the established truth of the sensible and perceptual. The truth of the sensible and the perceptual lies, however, in being appearance. The supersensible is then *appearance qua appearance*. We distort the proper meaning of this, if we take it to mean that the supersensible is therefore the sensible world, or the world as it is for immediate sense-certainty and perception. For, on the contrary, appearance is just not the world of sense-knowledge and perception as positively *being*, but this world as superseded or established in truth as an inner world. It is often said that the supersensible is *not* appearance; but by appearance is thereby meant not *appearance*, but rather the sensible world taken as itself real actuality.

Understanding, which is our object here, finds itself in this position, that, for it, the inner world has come about to begin with, only as the implicit inherent being, universal and still without a filling. The play of forces has simply and solely this negative significance of not being something *per se*; and its only positive significance is that of being the mediating agency, but outside understanding. The relation of understanding to the inner world through mediation is, however, its own process, by which the inner world will be found to receive fullness of content.

The play of forces is what understanding has directly to do with; but the real truth for it is the inner world bare and simple. The movement of force is consequently the truth only by being in like manner something simple. Regarding this play of forces, however, we saw that its peculiarity lay in this, that the force which is awakened into activity by another force is just on that account the inciting agency for this other force, which thereby itself only then becomes an inciting force. We have here in this way merely direct and immediate interchange or complete exchange of the characteristic which constitutes the sole content of what comes before us, viz. the fact of being either universal medium or negative unity. It ceases immediately on its entrance in determinate form to be what it was on entering: it awakens or incites, by its appearance in determinate shape, the other side, which thereby gives itself expression, i.e. the latter is now directly what the first was to be. Each of these two sides, the relation of inciting and the relation of the opposed determinate content, is on its own account an absolute process of permutation and transposition. But these two relations are again themselves one and the same, and the formal distinction of being incited and of inciting to activity is the same as the distinction of content, i.e. the distinction between the incited factor as such, viz. the passive medium, on the one side, and the inciting factor, viz. the active medium, the negative unity, or the "one" on the other side. In this way there disappears all distinction of contrasted and opposed particular forces, which were meant to be present in this process; for they rested solely on the above distinctions. And, along with both those distinctions, the distinction between the forces collapses likewise into merely one. There is thus neither force nor inciting and being incited to action, nor the characteristic of being a stable medium and a unity reflected into self, there is neither a particular which is something on its own account, nor are there diverse opposites. What is found in this flux of thoroughgoing change is merely difference as universal difference, or difference into which the various opposites have been resolved. This difference as universal, consequently, is what constitutes the ultimate simple element in that play of forces, and is the resultant truth of that process. It is the *Law* of Force.[3]

The absolute flux of the world of appearance passes into bare and simple difference through its relation to the simplicity of the inner being, the simplicity apprehended by understanding. The inner being is in the first instance merely the implicit universal. This implicit simple universal, however, is essentially absolute universal difference as well; for it is the outcome of the change itself, or change is its very nature. But change, when planted in the inner reality as it [change] truly is, forthwith is taken up into that reality as equally absolute universal difference at peace with itself, and remaining at one with itself. In other words, negation is an essential moment of the universal; and negation or mediation in what is universal is universal difference. This difference is expressed in the law, which is the stable presentment or picture of unstable appearance. The supersensible world is in this way a quiescent "kingdom of laws," no doubt beyond the world of perception—for this exhibits the law only through incessant change—but likewise present in it, and its direct immovable copy or image.

This kingdom of laws is indeed the truth for understanding; and that truth finds its content in the distinction which lies in the law. At the same time, however, this kingdom of laws is only the preliminary truth and does not give all the fullness of the world of appearance. The law is present therein, but is not all the appearance present; under ever-varying circumstances the law has an ever-varying actual existence. Thereby appearance continues to keep one aspect which is not in the inner world; i.e. appearance is not yet in very truth established as *appearance*, as that whose independent being has been done away with. This defect in the law has to be brought out in the law itself. What seems defective in it is that while it no doubt has difference within it, it contains this in a merely universal indeterminate way. So far, however, as it is not *law* in general, but *a* law, it has determinateness within it; and as a result there are found an indeterminate plurality of laws. But this plurality is rather itself a defect; it contradicts the principle of understanding, for which, since it is consciousness of the simple inner being, truth is the inherently universal *unity*. It must, therefore, let the many laws coalesce into a single law, just as, e.g., the law by which a stone falls, and that by which the heavenly bodies move have been conceived as one law. When the laws thus coincide, however, they lose

[3]Cp. Helmholtz, "It is precisely in the purest form of the expression of force—viz. in mechanical force which acts on a mass-point—that we find most clearly brought out that force is merely the objectified law of action."—*Lectures and Addresses*, v., Eng., trans., Vol. I., p. 326.

their specific character. The law becomes more and more abstract and superficial, and in consequence we find as a fact, not the unity of these various determinate laws, but a law which leaves out their specific character; just as the one law, which combines in itself the laws of falling terrestrial bodies, and of the movements of celestial bodies, does not, in point of fact, express both kinds of laws. The unification of all laws in universal attraction expresses no further content than just the bare concept of the law itself, a concept which is therein set down as existing. Universal attraction says merely that everything has a constant distinction for anything else. Understanding pretends by that to have found a universal law which gives expression to universal reality as such; but, in point of fact, it has merely found the conception of law itself, although in such a way that it at the same time thereby declares all reality to be in its very nature conformed to law. The idea of universal attraction has, therefore, to this extent great importance, that it is directed against that unthinking way of representing reality, to which everything appears in the shape of accident and chance, and for which determinateness, specificity, takes the form of sensuous independence.

In contrast, then, with determinate laws stands universal attraction, or the bare conception of law. In so far as this pure conception is looked on as the essentially real, or as the true inner being, the determinateness characterizing the specific law itself belongs still to the sphere of appearance, or rather to sensible existence. But the pure conception of law transcends not merely the law, which, being itself a determinate law, stands contrasted with other determinate laws, but also transcends law as such. The determinateness, of which we spoke, is itself strictly a mere vanishing moment which can no longer come forward here as an essential entity (*Wesenheit*), for it is only the law which is the truth here: but the conception of law is turned against the law itself. That is to say, in the law distinction itself is immediately apprehended and taken up into the universal, thereby, however, making the moments, whose relation it expresses, subsist as mutually indifferent and inherently real entities. These parts of the distinction found in the law are, however, at the same time themselves determinate aspects. The pure concept of law, as universal attraction, must, to get its true significance, be so apprehended that in it, as the absolutely single and simple, the distinctions which are present in law as such, return again themselves into the inner being, *qua* bare and simple unity. This unity is the inner "necessity" of the law.

The law is thereby present in a twofold form. In one case it is there as law in which the differences are expressed as independent moments; in the other it is in the form of a simple withdrawal into itself, which again can be called Force, but in the sense not of repressed force [spoken of above], but force in general, or the concept of force, an abstraction which absorbs the distinctions involved in what attracts and is attracted. In this sense, e.g., simple electricity is force; the expression of difference falls, however, within the law; this difference is positive and negative electricity. In the case of the motion of falling bodies force is the simple element, gravity, which has the law that the magnitudes of the different factors in the motion, the time spent, and the space traversed, are to one another in the relation of root and square. Electricity itself is not difference *per se*, is not in its essential nature a twofold entity consisting of positive and negative electricity; hence it is often said it *has* the law of being so and so in the way indicated, or again, that it *has* the *property* of expressing itself in this fashion. This property is doubtless the essential and peculiar property of this force, i.e. it belongs to it necessarily. But necessity is here an empty phrase; force *must*, just because it must, duplicate itself in this manner. Of course, if positive electricity is given, negative electricity is inherently necessary; for the positive element only is by being related to a negative; in other words, the positive element in its very self involves difference from itself, just in the same way as the negative does. But that electricity as such should break itself up into parts in this way—this is not in itself a necessity. Electricity *qua* simple force is indifferent to its law—to be in the form of positive and negative; and if we call the former its notion and the latter its being, then its notion is indifferent to its being; it merely has this as a property, which just means that this is not *per se* necessary to it. This indifference takes another form when it is said that to be positive and negative is involved in the definition of electricity, or that this is neither more nor less than its notion and its essence. Its being in that case would mean its existence in general. But in that definition the necessity of its existence is not contained; it exists either because we find it, i.e. its existence is not necessary at all, or else it exists through other forces, i.e. the necessity of its existence is an external necessity. But in that the determinateness of being through another is what the necessity consists in, we are back again to the plurality of determinate laws, which we have just left in order to consider law as law. It is only with the latter that we can compare its notion as notion, or its necessity. This necessity, however, has in all these forms shown itself to be just an empty phrase.

There is still another way than that just indicated in which the indifference of law and force, or of notion and being, is found. In the law of motion, e.g., it is necessary for motion to be broken up into the elements time and space, or again, into distance and velocity. Since motion is merely the relation of these factors, motion, the universal, has in this way certainly distinct parts in its own self. But now these parts, time and space, or distance and velocity, do not express in themselves this origination from a single unity. They are indifferent the one to the other. Space is thought of as able to be without time, time without space, and distance at least without velocity—just as their magnitudes are indifferent the one to the other, since they are not related like positive and negative, and consequently do not refer to one another by their very nature. The necessity of partition into distinct factors, then, we certainly do have here; but not the necessity of the parts as such for one another. On that account, however, that first necessity too is itself a merely delusory false necessity. For motion is not itself thought of as something simple or as bare essence, but as, from the first, divided into elements; time and space are in themselves its independent parts or its real elements: in other words, distance and velocity are modes of being, or ways of thinking, each of which can very well be without the other; and motion is consequently no more than their superficial relation, not their true nature. If it is represented as simple essence or as force, motion is no doubt gravity; but this does not contain these distinctions at all.

The distinction is, then, in both cases no distinction of an inherent or essential kind. Either the universal, force, is indifferent to the division into parts, which is found in the law, or else the distinctions, the parts of the law, are indifferent to one another. Understanding, however, does have the notion of this distinction *per se*, just by the fact that law is in part the inner being, the inherent nature, but is at the same time something distinguished within the notion. That this distinction is thereby *inner* distinction is shown by the fact that law is bare and simple force, or is the notion of that distinction, and thus is a distinction of the notion. But still this inner distinction falls to begin with only within understanding, and is not yet established in the fact itself. It is thus only its own necessity to which understanding gives expression—the distinction, that is to say, is one which it makes only so as at the same time to express that the distinction is not to be a distinction in the nature of the fact itself. This necessity, which is merely verbal, is thus a rehearsal of the moments which make up the cycle of necessity. They are no doubt distinct, but their distinction is at the same time explicitly stated to be not a distinction of the fact itself, and consequently is itself again straightway cancelled and transcended. This process is called *Explanation*. A law is expressed; from this its inherently universal element or ground is distinguished as force; but regarding this distinction, it is asserted that it is no distinction, rather that the ground has entirely the same constitution as the law. For example, the particular occurrence of lightning is apprehended as universal, and this universal is expressed as the law of electricity; the explanation thereupon merges the law in force as the essence of the law. This force is, then, so constituted that, when it finds expression, opposite electrical discharges appear, and these again disappear into one another. In other words, force has exactly the same constitution as law; both are thus declared to be in no way distinct. The distinctions are pure universal expression or law and pure force; but both have the same content, the same constitutive character; thus the distinction between them *qua* distinction of content, i.e. of fact, is also again withdrawn.   *of opposition*

In this tautological process understanding, as the above shows, holds fast to the changeless unity of its object, and the process takes effect solely within understanding itself, not in the object. It is an explanation that not only explains nothing, but is so plain that, while it makes as if it would say something different from what is already said, it really says nothing at all, but merely repeats the same thing over again. So far as the fact itself goes, this process gives rise to nothing new; the process is only of account as a process of understanding. In it, however, we now get acquainted with just what we missed in the case of the law—absolute change itself; for this process, when looked at more narrowly, is directly the opposite of itself. It sets up, that is, a distinction which is not only for us no distinction, but which it itself cancels as distinction. This is the same process of change which was formerly manifested as the play of forces. In the latter we found the distinction of inciting and incited force, or force expressing itself, and force withdrawn into itself; but these were distinctions which in reality were no distinctions, and therefore were also immediately cancelled again. We have here not merely the naked unity, so that no distinction could be set up at all; the process we have is rather this, that a distinction is certainly made, but because it is no distinction, it is again superseded.

Thus, then, with the process of explaining, we see the ebb and flow of change, which was formerly characteristic of the sphere of appearance, and lay outside the inner world, finding its way into the region of the supersensible itself. Our consciousness, however, has passed from the inner being as an object over to understanding on the other side, and finds the changing process there.

The change is in this way not yet a process of the fact itself, but rather presents itself before us as pure change, just by the content of the moments of change remaining the same. Since, however, the notion *qua* notion of understanding is the same as the inner nature of things, this change becomes for understanding the law of the inner world. Understanding thus learns that it is a law in the sphere of appearance for distinctions to come about which are no distinctions. In other words, it learns that what is selfsame is self-repulsive, and, similarly, that the distinctions are only such as in reality are none and cancel one another, or that what is not selfsame is self-attractive. Here we have a second law, whose content is the opposite of what formerly was called law, viz. the invariable and unchanging self-identical distinction; for this new law expresses rather the process of like becoming unlike, and unlike becoming like. The notion demands of the unreflective mind to bring both laws together, and become conscious of their opposition. Of course the second is also a law, an inner self-identical being; but it is rather a selfsameness of the unlike, a constancy of inconstancy. In the play of forces this law proved to be just this absolute transition and pure change; the selfsame, force, split into an opposition, that in the first instance appeared as a substantial independent distinction, which, however, in point of fact proved to be none. For it is the selfsame which repels itself from itself, and this element repelled is in consequence essentially self-attracted, for it is the same; the distinction made, since it is none, thus cancels itself again. The distinction is hence set forth as a distinction on the part of the fact itself, or as an absolute (objective) distinction; and this distinction on the part of the fact is thus nothing but the selfsame, that which has repelled itself from itself, and consequently only set up an opposition which is none.

By means of this principle, the first supersensible world, the changeless kingdom of laws, the immediate ectype and copy of the world of perception, has turned round into its opposite. The law was in general, like its differences, self-identical; now, however, it is established that each side is, on the contrary, the opposite of itself. The self-identical repels itself from itself, and the self-discordant sets up to be selfsame. In truth only with a determination of this kind is distinction inner distinction, or immanent distinction, when the like is unlike itself, and the unlike like itself.

This second supersensible world is in this way the inverted world (*verkehrte Welt*), and, moreover, since one aspect is already present in the first supersensible world, the inverted form of this first. The inner being is, thereby, in its character of appearance, completed. For the first supersensible world was only the immediate raising of the world of perception into the element of universality. It has its necessary counterpart in this world of perception, which still retains as its own the principle of change and alteration. The first kingdom of laws dispenses with this principle, but receives it in the form of an inverted world.

By the law of this inverted world, then, the selfsame in the first world is the unlike of itself, and the unlike in the first is equally unlike to itself, or it becomes like itself. Expressed in determinate moments, this will assume the form that what by the law of the first is sweet, is, in this inner, inverted reality, sour; what is there black is here white. What, by the law of the first, was north pole in the case of the magnet, is, in its other supersensible inner world (viz. in the earth), south pole; while what was there south pole is here north pole. Similarly, what by the first law is in the case of electricity the oxygen pole becomes in its other supersensible reality hydrogen pole; and conversely, what is there the pole of hydrogen becomes here the pole of oxygen. To take another sphere of experience: revenge on an enemy is, according to the primitive immediate law, the supreme satisfaction of injured individuality. This law, however—that of standing up against one who does not treat me as a substantial self, showing him that I am a substantial being, and even doing away with *him* as a reality—this law is transmuted by the principle of the other world into the very opposite, the reinstatement of myself as the true reality through the removal of the alien hostile being is turned into self-destruction.[+] If now this inversion, which is brought out in the punishment of crime, is made into a law, it also is again only the law of a world which has an inverted supersensuous world standing in antithesis to itself, where that which is despised in the former comes to honour, and that which in the former is honoured meets with contempt. The punishment which, by the law of the former, disgraces a man and annihilates him, turns round in *its* inverted world into the pardoning grace which preserves his being and brings him to honour.

Looked at on the surface, this inverted world is the antithesis of the first in the sense that it has the latter outside itself, and repels that world from itself as an inverted reality; that the one is the sphere of appearance, while the other is the inherent being; that the one is the world as it is for an other, the other again the world as it is for itself. In this way, to use the previous examples, what tastes sweet is properly, or inwardly in the thing, sour; or what is north pole in the case of the actual magnet belonging to the sphere of appearance, would be, in the inner or essential being, south pole. What is shown to be oxygen pole in electricity as a phenomenon, would be hydrogen pole in the case of electricity not falling within the sphere of appearance. Or again, an act which in appearance is a crime would in its inner nature be capable of being really good—a bad act may have a good intention; punishment is only in appearance punishment; in itself or in another world it might well be, for the criminal, a benefit. But such oppositions of inner and outer, appearance and supersensible, in the sense of two sorts of reality, are no longer to be found here. The differences repelled are not divided anew and assigned to two substances such as would support them and lend

---

[+]The primitive procedure of individual vengeance finds its inner meaning revealed in the ethically justifiable procedure of punishment. But ethical punishment is really self-punishment (cp. Plato's *Gorgias*). Punishment, however, Hegel goes on to say, has an inner meaning of its own too.

them a separate subsistence, the result of which would be that understanding would leave the inner region, and fall back again on its previous position. The one aspect or substance would be once more the
world of perception, where the one of those two laws would carry on its
existence, and in opposition to it an inner world, just such a sensible
world as the first, but in the sphere of ideas; one that could not be indicated, seen, heard, and tasted as a sensible world, and yet would be
thought of as such a sensible world. But in point of fact, if the one element set up is a perceived reality, and its inherent being, as its inverted
form, is at the same time a sensuously represented element, then sour,
which would be the inherent nature of the sweet thing, is a real thing
just as much as the latter, viz., a sour thing; black, which would be the
inherent nature of white, is the actual black; the north pole, which is the
true reality of the south pole, is the north pole present in the same magnet; the oxygen pole, the inherent nature of the pole of hydrogen, is the
given oxygen pole of the same voltaic pile. The actual crime, however,
finds its inversion and its inherent nature _qua_ possibility, in the intention as such, but not in a good intention; for the truth of intention is simply the deed itself. The crime, so far as its content goes, recoils upon itself, finds its inversion in actual punishment; this is the reconciliation of
the law with the reality set up against it in crime. Finally, the actual punishment carries its inverted reality with it in such a way that it is a kind
of realization of the law, whereby the activity, which the law exercises in
the form of punishment, is cancelled in the process, a manner of realization through which the law, from being actively operative, becomes
again quiescent and authoritative, and the conflict of individuality with
it, and of it with individuality, is extinguished.

From the idea, then, of inversion which constitutes the essential nature of one aspect of the supersensible world, we must dissociate the
sensuous idea of keeping distinctions substantively fixed in a different
element that sustains them; and this absolute notion of distinction must
be set forth and apprehended purely as _inner_ distinction, self-repulsion
of the selfsame as selfsame, and likeness of the unlike as unlike. We
have to think pure flux, opposition within opposition itself, or
Contradiction. For in the distinction, which is an internal distinction,
the opposite is not only one of two factors—if so, it would not be an opposite, but a bare existent—it is the opposite of an opposite, or the other
is itself directly and immediately present within it. No doubt I put the
opposite here and the other, of which it is the opposite, there; that is, I
place the opposite on one side, taking it by itself without the other. Just
on that account, however, since I have here the opposite all by itself, it
is the opposite of its _own_ self, that is, it has in point of fact the other immediately within itself. Thus the supersensible world, which is the in-

verted world, has at the same time reached out beyond the other world and has in itself that other; it is to itself conscious of being inverted (*für sich verkehrte*), i.e. it is the inverted form of itself; it is that world itself and its opposite in a single unity. Only thus is it distinction as internal distinction, or distinction *per se*; in other words, only thus is it in the form of *Infinity*.

By means of infinity we see law attaining the form of inherent necessity, and so realizing its complete nature; and all moments of the sphere of appearance are thereby taken up into the inner realm. That the simple and ultimate nature of law is infinity means, according to the foregoing analysis, (*a*) that it is a self-identical element, which, however, is inherently distinction; or that it is selfsameness which repels itself from itself, breaks asunder into two factors. What was called simple force duplicates itself, and through its infinity is law. It means (*b*) that what is thus sundered, constituting as it does the parts which are thought of as in the law, puts itself forward as subsisting, as stable; and, if the parts are considered without the conception of internal distinction, then space and time, or distance and velocity, which appear as moments of gravity, are just as much indifferent and without necessary relation to one another as to gravity itself, or again as this bare gravity is indifferent to them, or as simple electricity is indifferent to positive and negative. But (*c*) by this conception of internal distinction, this unlike and indifferent factor, space and time, etc., becomes a distinction, which is no distinction, or merely a distinction of what is selfsame, and its essence is unity. They are reciprocally awakened into activity as positive and negative by each other, and their being lies rather in their putting themselves as not-being, and cancelling themselves in the common unity. Both the factors distinguished subsist; they are *per se*, and they are *per se* as opposites, that is are the opposites of themselves; they have their antithesis within them, and are merely *one* single unity.

This bare and simple infinity, or the absolute notion, may be called the ultimate nature of life, the soul of the world, the universal life-blood, which courses everywhere, and whose flow is neither disturbed nor checked by any obstructing distinction, but is itself every distinction that arises, as well as that into which all distinctions are dissolved; pulsating within itself, but ever motionless, shaken to its depths, but still at rest. It is self-identical, for the distinctions are tautological; they are distinctions that are none. This self-identical reality stands, therefore, in relation solely to itself. *To itself*; which means this is an other, to which the relation points; and relation to itself is, more strictly, breaking asunder; in other words, that very self-identity is internal distinction. These sundered factors have, hence, each a separate being of their own; each is an opposite—of an other; and thus with each the other is therein *ipso facto* expressly given; or it is not the opposite of an *other*, but only the pure opposite; and thus each is, therefore, in itself the opposite of itself. Or, again, each is not an opposite at all, but exists purely for itself, a pure self-identical reality, with no distinction in it. This being so, we do not need to *ask*, still less to treat *anxiety* over such a question as philosophy,—or even regard this as a question philosophy cannot answer,—"how distinction or otherness is to come out of this pure essence, how these are to be really got out of it." For the process of disruption has already taken place; distinction has been excluded from the self-identical entity, and put on one side so far as it is concerned; what was to have been the self-identical is thus already one of the sundered elements, instead of being the absolute essential reality. That the self-identical breaks asunder means, therefore, just as truly that it supersedes itself as *already* sundered, that it cancels itself *qua* otherness. The unity which people usually have in mind when they say distinction cannot come out of unity, is, in point of fact, itself merely one moment of the process of disruption; it is the abstraction of simplicity, which stands *in contrast with* distinction. But in that it is abstraction, is merely one of the two opposed elements, the statement thus already implies that the unity is the process of breaking asunder; for if the unity is a negative element, an opposite, then it is put forward precisely as that which contains opposition within it. The different aspects of diremption and of becoming self-identical are therefore likewise merely this process of self-cancelling. For since the self-identical element, which should first divide itself asunder or pass into its opposite, is an abstraction, i.e. is *already itself* a sundered element, its diremption is *eo ipso* a cancelling of what it is, and thus the cancelling of its being sundered. The process of becoming self-identical is likewise a process of diremption; what becomes identical with itself thereby opposes itself to disruption, that is, itself thereby puts itself on one side; in other words, it *becomes* really something sundered.

Infinitude, this absolute unrest of pure self-movement, such that whatever is determined in any way, e.g., as being, is really the opposite of this determinateness—has from the start been no doubt the very soul of all that has gone before; but it is in the inner world that it has first come out explicitly and definitely. The world of appearance, or the play of forces, already shows its operation; but it is in the first instance as Explanation that it comes openly forward. And since it is at length an object for consciousness, and consciousness is aware of it as what it is, consciousness is in this way *Self-consciousness*. Understanding's function of explaining furnishes in the first instance merely the description of what self-consciousness is. Understanding cancels the distinctions present in Law, distinctions which have already become pure distinctions but are still indifferent, and puts them inside a single unity, Force. This identification, however, is at the same time and immediately a process of diremption; for understanding removes the distinctions and sets up the oneness of force only by the fact that it creates a new distinction of force and law, which at the same time, however, is no distinction. And moreover in that this distinction is at the same time no distinction, it proceeds further and cancels this distinction again, since it lets force have just the same constitution as law. This process or necessity is, however, in this form, still a necessity and a process of understanding, or the process as such is not the *object* of understanding; instead, understanding has as its objects in that process positive and negative electricity, distance, velocity, force of attraction, and a thousand other things—objects which make up the content of the moments of the process. It is just for that reason that there is so much satisfaction in explanation, because consciousness being there, if we may use such an expression, in direct communion with itself, enjoys itself only. No doubt it there seems to be occupied with something else, but in point of fact it is busied all the while merely with itself.

In the opposite law, as the inversion of the first law, or in internal distinction, infinitude doubtless becomes itself object of understanding. But once more understanding fails to do justice to infinity as such, since understanding assigns again to two worlds, or to two substantial elements, that which is distinction *per se*,—the self-repulsion of the selfsame, and the self-attraction of unlike factors. To understanding the process, as it is found in experience, is here an event that happens, and the selfsame and the unlike are predicates, whose reality is an underlying substratum. What is for understanding an object in a covering veil of sense, now comes before us in its essential form as a pure notion. This apprehension of distinction as it truly is, the apprehension of infinitude as such, is something *for us* [observing the course of the process], or is implicit, immanent. The exposition of its notion belongs to science. Consciousness, however, in the way it immediately has this notion, again appears as a peculiar form or *new attitude* of consciousness, which does not recognize its own essential nature in what has gone before, but looks upon it as something quite different.

In that this notion of infinitude is its object, it is thus a consciousness of the distinction as one which at the same time is at once cancelled. Consciousness is for itself and on its own account, it is a distinguishing of what is undistinguished, it is Self-consciousness. I distinguish myself from myself; and therein I am immediately aware that this factor distinguished from me is not distinguished. I, the selfsame being, thrust myself away from myself; but this which is distinguished, which is set up as unlike me, is immediately on its being distinguished no distinction for me. Consciousness of an other, of an object in general, is indeed itself necessarily self-consciousness, reflectedness into self, consciousness of self in its otherness. The necessary advance from the previous attitudes of consciousness, which found their true content to be a thing, something other than themselves, brings to light this very fact that not merely is consciousness of a thing only possible for a self-consciousness, but that this self-consciousness alone is the truth of those attitudes. But it is only for us [who trace this process] that this truth is actually present; it is not yet so for the consciousness immersed in the experience. Self-consciousness has in the first instance become a specific reality on its own account (*für sich*), has come into being for itself; it is not yet in the form of unity with consciousness in general.

We see that in the inner being of the sphere of appearance, understanding gets to know in truth nothing else but appearance itself, not, however, appearance in the shape of a play of forces, but that play of forces in its absolutely universal moments and in the process of those moments; in fact, understanding merely experiences itself. Raised above perception, consciousness reveals itself united and bound up with the supersensible world through the mediating agency of the realm of appearance, through which it gazes into this background that lies behind appearance. The two extremes, the one that of the pure inner region, the other that of the inner being gazing into this pure inner region, are now merged together; and as they have disappeared *qua* extremes, the middle term, the mediating agency, *qua* something other than these extremes, has also vanished. This curtain [of appearance], therefore, hanging before the inner world is withdrawn, and we have here the inner being [the ego] gazing into the inner realm—the vision of the undistinguished selfsame reality, which repels itself from itself, affirms itself as a divided and distinguished inner reality, but as one for which at the same time the two factors have immediately no distinction; what we have here is Self-consciousness. It is manifest that behind the so-called curtain, which is to hide the inner world, there is nothing to be seen unless we ourselves go behind there, as much in order that we may thereby see, as that there may be something behind there which can be seen. But it is clear at the same time that we cannot without more ado go straightway behind there. For this knowledge of what is the truth of the idea of the realm of appearance and of its inner being, is itself only a result arrived at after a long and devious process, in the course of which the modes of consciousness, "meaning," "perception," and "understanding" disappear. And it will be equally evident that to get acquainted with what consciousness knows when it is knowing itself, requires us to fetch a still wider compass. What follows will set this forth at length.

B. SELF-CONSCIOUSNESS[1]

IV

THE TRUTH WHICH CONSCIOUS CERTAINTY OF SELF REALIZES

The analysis of experience up to this point has been occupied with the relation of consciousness to an object admittedly different in nature from the mind aware of it. This external opposition, however, breaks down under analysis, and we are left with the result that consciousness does and must find itself in unity with its object, a unity which implies identity of nature between consciousness and its object: consciousness becomes "certain of itself in its object." This is not merely a result, but the truest expression of the initial relation with which experience starts. It is, therefore, the ground of the possibility of any relation between the terms in question: "consciousness of self" is the basis of the consciousness of anything whatsoever. This is Hegel's re-interpretation of the Kantian analysis of experience.

But this result is, again, really the starting-point for a further analysis of experience, but of experience at a higher level of realization. Consciousness of self is to begin with a general attitude, a definite type of experience, which requires elucidation. It has its own conditions and forms of manifestation. Self-consciousness, being supreme, must realize itself in relation to nature, to other selves similar to the self, and to the Ultimate Being of the world. These are different kinds of content with which consciousness is to find its oneness, and they furnish different forms in which the same principle is manifested. The argument seeks to show that these forms are also different degrees of realization of self-consciousness. The outcome of the argument is that self-consciousness is truly realized only when it is universal self-consciousness, when consciousness is certain of itself throughout all reality, and explicitly finds there only itself. This result takes the form, as we shall see, of what is called *Reason*.

The immediately succeeding section takes up the first stage of the development of self-consciousness—the consciousness of self in relation to nature. This takes the shape of Desire, Instinct, Impulse, etc., and involves the category of Life. This relationship, while undoubtedly implying the sense of self in the object and consciousness of unity with it, is the least satisfying and the least complete of all the modes of self-consciousness. It points the way, therefore, to the fuller sense of self obtained when the self is aware of itself in relation to another self.

---

[1]Cp. *Propädeutik*, p. 84 ff.

IN the kinds of certainty hitherto considered, the truth for consciousness is something other than consciousness itself. The conception,
however, of this truth vanishes in the course of our experience of it.
What the object immediately was *in itself*—whether mere being in
sense-certainty, a concrete thing in perception, or force in the case of
understanding—it turns out, in truth, not to be this really; but instead,
this inherent nature (*Ansich*) proves to be a way in which it is for an
other. The abstract conception of the object gives way before the actual
concrete object, or the first immediate idea is cancelled in the course
of experience. Mere certainty vanished in favour of the truth. There
has now arisen, however, what was not established in the case of these
previous relationships, viz. a certainty which is on a par with its truth,
for the certainty is to itself its own object, and consciousness is to itself
the truth. Otherness, no doubt, is also found there; consciousness, that
is, makes a distinction; but what is distinguished is of such a kind that
consciousness, at the same time, holds there is no distinction made. If
we call the movement of knowledge conception, and knowledge, *qua*
simple unity or Ego, the object, we see that not only for us [tracing the
process], but likewise for knowledge itself, the object corresponds to the
conception; or, if we put it in the other form and call conception what
the object is in itself, while applying the term object to what the object
is *qua* object or *for an other*, it is clear that being "in-itself" and being
"for an other" are here the same. For the inherent being (*Ansich*) is
consciousness; yet it is still just as much that for which an other (viz.
what is "in-itself") is. And it is *for* consciousness that the inherent nature (*Ansich*) of the object, and its "being for an other" *are* one and the
same. Ego is the content of the relation, and itself the process of relating. It is Ego itself which is opposed to an other and, at the same time,
reaches out beyond this other, which other is all the same taken to be
only itself.

   With self-consciousness, then, we have now passed into the native
land of truth, into that kingdom where it is at home. We have to see
how the form or attitude of self-consciousness in the first instance appears. When we consider this new form and type of knowledge, the
knowledge of self, in its relation to that which preceded, namely, the
knowledge of an other, we find, indeed, that this latter has vanished,
but that its moments have, at the same time, been preserved; and the
loss consists in this, that those moments are here present as they are implicitly, as they are in themselves. The being which "meaning" dealt
with, particularity and the universality of perception opposed to it, as
also the empty, inner region of understanding—these are no longer
present as substantial elements (*Wesen*), but as moments of self-
consciousness, i.e. as abstractions or differences, which are, at the same

time, of no account for consciousness itself, or are not differences at all, and are purely vanishing entities (*Wesen*).

What seems to have been lost, then, is only the principal moment, viz. the simple fact of having independent subsistence for consciousness. But, in reality, self-consciousness is reflexion out of the bare being that belongs to the world of sense and perception, and is essentially the return out of otherness. As self-consciousness, it is movement. But when it distinguishes only its self as such from itself, distinction is straightway taken to be superseded in the sense of involving otherness. The distinction *is* not, and self-consciousness is only motionless tautology, Ego is Ego, I am I. When for self-consciousness the distinction does not also have the shape of *being*, it is *not* self-consciousness. For self-consciousness, then, otherness is a fact, it does exist as a distinct moment; but the unity of itself with this difference is also a fact for self-consciousness, and is a second distinct moment. With that first moment, self-consciousness occupies the position of consciousness, and the whole expanse of the world of sense is conserved as its object, but at the same time only as related to the second moment, the unity of self-consciousness with itself. And, consequently, the sensible world is regarded by self-consciousness as having a subsistence which is, however, only appearance, or forms a distinction from self-consciousness that *per se* has no being. This opposition of its appearance and its truth finds its real essence, however, only in the truth — in the unity of self-consciousness with itself. This unity must become essential to self-consciousness, i.e. self-consciousness is the state of *Desire* in general. Consciousness has, *qua* self-consciousness, henceforth a twofold object — the one immediate, the object of sense-certainty and of perception, which, however, is here found to be marked by the character of negation; the second, viz. itself, which is the true essence, and is found in the first instance only in the opposition of the first object to it. Self-consciousness presents itself here as the proces in which this opposition is removed, and oneness or identity with itself established.

For us or implicitly, the object, which is the negative element for self-consciousness, has on its side returned into itself, just as on the other side consciousness has done. Through this reflexion into self, the object has become *Life*. What self-consciousness distinguishes as having a being distinct from itself, has in it too, so far as it is affirmed to *be*, not merely the aspect of sense-certainty and perception; it is a being reflected into itself, and the object of immediate desire is something living. For the inherent reality (*Ansich*), the general result of the relation of the understanding to the inner nature of things, is the distinguishing of what cannot be distinguished, or is the unity of what is distinguished. This unity, however, is, as we saw, just as much its recoil from itself;

and this conception breaks asunder into the opposition of self-consciousness and life: the former is the unity *for which* the absolute unity of differences exists, the latter, however, *is* only this unity itself, so that the unity is not at the same time *for itself*. Thus, according to the independence possessed by consciousness, is the independence which its object in itself possesses. Self-consciousness, which is absolutely *for itself*, and characterizes its object directly as negative, or is primarily desire, will really, therefore, find through experience this object's independence.

The determination of the principle of life,[2] as obtained from the conception or general result with which we enter this new sphere, is sufficient to characterize it, without its nature being evolved further out of that notion. Its circuit is completed in the following moments. The essential element (*Wesen*) is infinitude as the supersession of all distinctions, the pure rotation on its own axis, itself at rest while being absolutely restless infinitude, the very self-dependence in which the differences brought out in the process are all dissolved, the simple reality of time, which in this self-identity has the solid form and shape of space. The differences, however, all the same hold as differences in this simple universal medium; for this universal flux exercises its negative activity merely in that it is the sublation of them; but it could not transcend them unless they had a subsistence of their own. Precisely this flux is itself, as self-identical independence, their subsistence or their substance, in which they accordingly are distinct members, parts which have being in their own right. Being no longer has the significance of mere abstract being, nor has their naked essence the meaning of abstract universality: their being now is just that simple fluent substance of the pure movement within itself. The difference, however, of these members *inter se* consists, in general, in no other characteristic than that of the moments of infinitude, or of the mere movement itself.

The independent members exist for themselves. To be thus for themselves, however, is really as much their reflexion directly into the unity, as this unity is the breaking asunder into independent forms. The unity is sundered because it is absolutely negative or infinite unity; and because it is subsistence, difference likewise has independence only in *it*. This independence of the form appears as a determinate entity, as what is for another, for the form is something disunited; and the cancelling of diremption takes effect to that extent through another. But this sublation lies just as much in the actual form itself. For just that flux is the substance of the independent forms. This substance, how-

---

[2]Cp. Hegel's *Logik*, T. II. Absch. 3. Kap. I. — "das Leben."

ever, is infinite, and hence the form itself in its very subsistence involves diremption, or sublation of its existence for itself.

If we distinguish more exactly the moments contained here, we see that we have as first moment the subsistence of the independent forms, or the suppression of what distinction inherently involves, viz. that the forms have no being *per se*, and no subsistence. The second moment, however, is the subjection of that subsistence to the infinitude of distinction. In the first moment there is the subsisting, persisting mode or form; by its being in its own right, or by its being in its determinate shape an infinite substance, it comes forward in opposition to the universal substance, disowns this fluent continuity with that substance, and insists that it is not dissolved in this universal element, but rather on the contrary preserves itself by and through its separation from this its inorganic nature, and by the fact that it consumes this inorganic nature. Life in the universal fluid medium, quietly, silently shaping and moulding and distributing the forms in all their manifold detail, becomes by that very activity the movement of those forms, or passes into life *qua Process*. The mere universal flux is here the inherent being; the outer being, the "other," is the distinction of the forms assumed. But this flux, this fluent condition, becomes itself the other in virtue of this very distinction; because now it exists "for" or in relation to that distinction, which is self-conditioned and self-contained (*an und für sich*), and consequently is the endless, infinite movement by which that stable medium is consumed—is life as living.

This inversion of character, however, is on that account again invertedness in itself as such. What is consumed is the essential reality: the Individuality, which preserves itself at the expense of the universal and gives itself the feeling of its unity with itself, precisely thereby cancels its contrast with the other, by means of which it exists for itself. The unity with self, which it gives itself, is just the fluent continuity of differences, or universal dissolution. But, conversely, the cancelling of individual subsistence at the same time produces the subsistence. For since the essence of the individual form—universal life—and the self-existent entity *per se* are simple substance, the essence, by putting the other within itself, cancels this its own simplicity or its essence, i.e. it sunders that simplicity; and this disruption of fluent undifferentiated continuity is just the setting up, the affirmation, of individuality. The simple substance of life, therefore, is the diremption of itself into shapes and forms, and at the same time the dissolution of these substantial differences; and the resolution of this diremption is just as much a process of diremption, of articulating. Thus both the sides of the entire movement which were before distinguished, viz., the *setting up of individual forms* lying apart and undisturbed in the universal medium of independent existence, and the *process* of life — collapse into one another. The latter is just as much a formation of independent individual shapes, as it is a way of cancelling a shape assumed; and the former, the setting up of individual forms, is as much a cancelling as an articulation of them. The fluent, continuous element is itself only the abstraction of the essential reality, or it is actual only as a definite shape or form; and that it articulates itself is once more a breaking up of the articulated form, or a dissolution of it. The *entire* circuit of this activity constitutes Life. It is neither what is expressed to begin with, the immediate continuity and concrete solidity of its essential nature; nor the stable, subsisting form, the discrete individual which exists on its own account; nor the bare process of this form; nor again is it the simple combination of all these moments. It is none of these; it is the *whole* which develops itself, resolves its own development, and in this movement simply preserves itself.

Since we started from the first immediate unity, and returned through the moments of form-determination, and of process, to the unity of both these moments, and thus again back to the first simple substance, we see that this *reflected* unity is other than the first. As opposed to that immediate unity, the unity expressed as a mode of being, this second is the universal unity, which holds all these moments sublated within itself. It is the simple genus, which in the movement of life itself does not exist in this simplicity for itself; but in this result points life towards what is other than itself, namely, towards Consciousness for which life exists as this unity or as genus.

This other life, however, for which the genus as such exists and which is genus for itself, namely, self-consciousness, exists in the first instance only in the form of this simple, essential reality, and has for object itself *qua* pure Ego. In the course of its experience, which we are now to consider, this abstract object will grow in richness, and will be unfolded in the way we have seen in the case of life.

The simple ego is this genus, or the bare universal, for which the differences are insubstantial, only by its being the negative essence of the moments which have assumed a definite and independent form. And self-consciousness is thus only assured of itself through sublating this other, which is presented to self-consciousness as an independent life; self-consciousness is *Desire*. Convinced of the nothingness of this other, it definitely affirms this nothingness to be for itself the truth of this other, negates the independent object, and thereby acquires the certainty of its own self, as *true* certainty, a certainty which it has become aware of in objective form.

In this state of satisfaction, however, it has experience of the independence of its object. Desire and the certainty of its self obtained in the gratification of desire, are conditioned by the object; for the certainty exists through cancelling this other; in order that this cancelling may be effected, there must be this other. Self-consciousness is thus unable by its negative relation to the object to abolish it; because of that relation it rather produces it again, as well as the desire. The object desired is, in fact, something other than self-consciousness, the essence of desire; and through this experience this truth has become realized. At the same time, however, self-consciousness is likewise absolutely for itself, exists on its own account; and it is so only by sublation of the object; and it must come to feel its satisfaction, for it is the truth. On account of the independence of the object, therefore, it can only attain satisfaction when this object itself effectually brings about negation within itself. The object must *per se* effect this negation of itself, for it is inherently (*an sich*) something negative, and must be for the other what it is. Since the object is in its very self negation, and in being so is at the same time independent, it is Consciousness. In the case of life, which is the object of desire, the negation *either* lies in an other, namely, in desire, *or* takes the form of determinateness standing in opposition to an other external individuum indifferent to it, *or* appears as its inorganic general nature. The above general independent nature, however, in the case of which negation takes the form of *absolute* negation, is the genus as such, or as self-consciousness. Self-consciousness attains its satisfaction only in another self-consciousness.

It is in these three moments that the notion of self-consciousness first gets completed: (*a*) pure undifferentiated ego is its first immediate object. (*b*) This immediacy is itself, however, thoroughgoing mediation; it has its being only by cancelling the independent object, in other words it is Desire. The satisfaction of desire is indeed the reflexion of self-consciousness into itself, is the certainty which has passed into objective truth. But (*c*) the truth of this certainty is really twofold reflexion, the reduplication of self-consciousness. Consciousness has an object which implicates its own otherness or affirms distinction as a void distinction, and therein is independent. The individual form distinguished, which is only a living form, certainly cancels its independence also in the process of life itself; but it ceases along with its distinctive difference to be what it is. The object of self-consciousness, however, is still independent in this negativity of itself; and thus it is for itself genus, universal flux or continuity in the very distinctiveness of its own separate existence; it is a living self-consciousness.

A self-consciousness has before it a self-consciousness. Only so and only then *is* it self-consciousness in actual fact; for here first of all it comes to have the unity of itself in its otherness. Ego which is the object of its notion, is in point of fact not "*object*." The object of desire, however, is only independent, for it is the universal, ineradicable substance, the fluent self-identical essential reality. When a self-consciousness is the object, the object is just as much ego as object.

With this we already have before us the notion of *Mind* or *Spirit*. What consciousness has further to become aware of, is the experience of what mind is—this absolute substance, which is the unity of the different self-related and self-existent self-consciousnesses in the perfect freedom and independence of their opposition as component elements of that substance: Ego that is "we," a plurality of Egos, and "we" that is a single Ego. Consciousness first finds in self-consciousness—the notion of mind—its turning-point, where it leaves the parti-coloured show of the sensuous immediate, passes from the dark void of the transcendent and remote super-sensuous, and steps into the spiritual daylight of the present.

A

INDEPENDENCE AND DEPENDENCE OF SELF-CONSCIOUSNESS

LORDSHIP AND BONDAGE

The selves conscious of self in another self are, of course, distinct and separate from each other. The difference is, in the first instance, a question of degree of self-assertion and self-maintenance: one is stronger, higher, more independent than another, and capable of asserting this at the expense of the other. Still, even this distinction of primary and secondary rests ultimately on their identity of constitution; and the course of the analysis here gradually brings out this essential identity as the true fact. The equality of the selves is the truth, or completer realization, of self in another self; the affinity is higher and more ultimate than the disparity. Still, the struggle and conflict of selves must be gone through in order to bring out this result. Hence the present section.

The background of Hegel's thought is the remarkable human phenomenon of the subordination of one self to another which we have in all forms of servitude—whether slavery, serfdom, or voluntary service. Servitude is not only a phase of human history, it is in principle a condition of the development and maintenance of the consciousness of self as a fact of experience.

SELF-CONSCIOUSNESS exists in itself and for itself, in that, and by the fact that it exists for another self-consciousness; that is to say, it *is* only by being acknowledged or "recognized." The conception of this its unity in its duplication, of infinitude realizing itself in self-consciousness, has many sides to it and encloses within it elements of varied significance. Thus its moments must on the one hand be strictly kept apart in detailed distinctiveness, and, on the other, in this distinction must, at the same time, also be taken as not distinguished, or must always be accepted and understood in their opposite sense. This double meaning of what is distinguished lies in the nature of self-consciousness:—of its being infinite, or directly the opposite of the determinateness in which it is fixed. The detailed exposition of the notion of this spiritual unity in its duplication will bring before us the process of Recognition.

Self-consciousness has before it another self-consciousness; it has come outside itself. This has a double significance. First it has lost its own self, since it finds itself as an *other* being; secondly, it has thereby sublated that other, for it does not regard the other as essentially real, but sees its own self in the other.

It must cancel this its other. To do so is the sublation of that first double meaning, and is therefore a second double meaning. First, it must set itself to sublate the other independent being, in order thereby to become certain of itself as true being, secondly, it thereupon proceeds to sublate its own self, for this other is itself.

This sublation in a double sense of its otherness in a double sense is at the same time a return in a double sense into its self. For, firstly, through sublation, it gets back itself, because it becomes one with itself again through the cancelling of *its* otherness; but secondly, it likewise gives otherness back again to the other self-consciousness, for it was aware of being in the other, it cancels this its own being in the other and thus lets the other again go free.

This process of self-consciousness in relation to another self-consciousness has in this manner been represented as the action of one alone. But this action on the part of the one has itself the double significance of being at once its own action and the action of that other as well. For the other is likewise independent, shut up within itself, and there is nothing in it which is not there through itself. The first does not have the object before it only in the passive form characteristic primarily of the object of desire, but as an object existing independently for itself, over which therefore it has no power to do anything for its own behoof, if that object does not *per se* do what the first does to it. The process then is absolutely the double process of both self-consciousnesses. Each sees the other do the same as itself; each itself does what it demands on the part of the other, and for that reason does what it does, only so far as the other does the same. Action from one side only would be useless, because what is to happen can only be brought about by means of both.

The action has then a *double entente* not only in the sense that it is an act done to itself as well as to the other, but also in the sense that the act *simpliciter* is the act of the one as well as of the other regardless of their distinction.

In this movement we see the process repeated which came before us as the play of forces; in the present case, however, it is found in consciousness. What in the former had effect only for us [contemplating experience], holds here for the terms themselves. The middle term is self-consciousness which breaks itself up into the extremes; and each extreme is this interchange of its own determinateness, and complete transition into the opposite. While *qua* consciousness, it no doubt comes outside itself, still, in being outside itself, it is at the same time restrained within itself, it exists for itself, and its self-externalization is for consciousness. *Consciousness* finds that it immediately is and is not another consciousness, as also that this other is for itself only when it cancels itself as existing for itself, and has self-existence only in the self-existence of the other. Each is the mediating term to the other, through which each mediates and unites itself with itself; and each is to itself and to the other an immediate self-existing reality, which, at the same time, exists thus for itself only through this mediation. They recognize themselves as mutually recognizing one another.

This pure conception of recognition, of duplication of self-consciousness within its unity, we must now consider in the way its process appears for self-consciousness. It will, in the first place, present the aspect of the disparity of the two, or the break-up of the middle term into the extremes, which, *qua* extremes, are opposed to one another, and of which one is merely recognized, while the other only recognizes.

Self-consciousness is primarily simple existence for self, self-identity by exclusion of every other from itself. It takes its essential nature and absolute object to be Ego; and in this immediacy, in this bare fact of its self-existence, it is individual. That which for it is other stands as unessential object, as object with the impress and character of negation. But the other is also a self-consciousness; an individual makes its appearance in antithesis to an individual. Appearing thus in their immediacy, they are for each other in the manner of ordinary objects. They are independent individual forms, modes of consciousness that have not risen above the bare level of life (for the existent object here has been determined as life). They are, moreover, forms of consciousness which have not yet accomplished for one another the process of absolute abstraction, of uprooting all immediate existence, and of being merely the bare, negative fact of self-identical consciousness; or, in other words, have not yet revealed themselves to each other as existing purely for themselves, i.e., as self-consciousness. Each is indeed certain of its own self, but not of the other, and hence its own certainty of itself is still without truth. For its truth would be merely that its own individual existence for itself would be shown to it to be an independent object, or, which is the same thing, that the object would be exhibited as this pure certainty of itself. By the notion of recognition, however, this is not possible, except in the form that as the other is for it, so it is for the other; each in its self through its own action and again through the action of the other achieves this pure abstraction of existence for self.

The presentation of itself, however, as pure abstraction of self-consciousness consists in showing itself as a pure negation of its objective form, or in showing that it is fettered to no determinate existence, that it is not bound at all by the particularity everywhere characteristic of existence as such, and is *not* tied up with life. The process of bringing all this out involves a twofold action—action on the part of the other and action on the part of itself. In so far as it is the other's action, each aims at the destruction and death of the other. But in this there is implicated also the second kind of action, self-activity; for the former implies that it risks its own life. The relation of both self-consciousnesses is in this way so constituted that they prove themselves and each other through a life-and-death struggle. They must enter into this struggle, for they must bring their certainty of themselves, the certainty of being for themselves, to the level of objective truth, and make this a fact both in the case of the other and in their own case as well. And it is solely by risking life that freedom is obtained; only thus is it tried and proved that the essential nature of self-consciousness is not bare existence, is not the merely immediate form in which it at first makes its appearance, is not its mere absorption in the expanse of life. Rather it is thereby guaranteed that there is nothing present but what might be taken as a vanishing moment—that self-consciousness is merely pure self-existence, being-for-self. The individual, who has not staked his life, may, no doubt, be recognized as a Person; but he has not attained the truth of this recognition as an independent self-consciousness. In the same way each must aim at the death of the other, as it risks its own life thereby; for that other is to it of no more worth than itself; the other's reality is presented to the former as an external other, as outside itself; it must cancel that externality. The other is a purely existent consciousness and entangled in manifold ways; it must view its otherness as pure existence for itself or as absolute negation.

This trial by death, however, cancels both the truth which was to result from it, and therewith the certainty of self altogether. For just as life is the natural "position" of consciousness, independence without absolute negativity, so death is the natural "negation" of consciousness, negation without independence, which thus remains without the requisite significance of actual recognition. Through death, doubtless, there has arisen the certainty that both did stake their life, and held it lightly both in their own case and in the case of the other; but that is not for those who underwent this struggle. They cancel their consciousness which had its place in this alien element of natural existence; in other words, they cancel themselves and are sublated as terms or extremes seeking to have existence on their own account. But along with this there vanishes from the play of change the essential moment, viz. that of breaking up into extremes with opposite characteristics; and the middle term collapses into a lifeless unity which is broken up into lifeless extremes, merely existent and not opposed. And the two do not mutually give and receive one another back from each other through consciousness; they let one another go quite indifferently, like things. Their act is abstract negation, not the negation characteristic of consciousness, which cancels in such a way that it preserves and maintains what is sublated, and thereby survives its being sublated.

In this experience self-consciousness becomes aware that *life* is as essential to it as pure self-consciousness. In immediate self-consciousness the simple ego is absolute object, which, however, is for us or in itself absolute mediation, and has as its essential moment substantial and solid independence. The dissolution of that simple unity is the result of the first experience; through this there is posited a pure self-consciousness, and a consciousness which is not purely for itself, but for another, i.e. as an existent consciousness, consciousness in the form and shape of thinghood. Both moments are essential, since, in the first instance, they are unlike and opposed, and their reflexion into unity has not yet come to light, they stand as two opposed forms or modes of consciousness. The one is independent, and its essential nature is to be for itself; the other is dependent, and its essence is life or existence for another. The former is the Master, or Lord, the latter the Bondsman.

The master is the consciousness that exists *for itself*; but no longer merely the general notion of existence for self. Rather, it is a consciousness existing on its own account which is mediated with itself through an other consciousness, i.e. through an other whose very nature implies that it is bound up with an independent being or with thinghood in general. The master brings himself into relation to both these moments, to a thing as such, the object of desire, and to the consciousness whose essential character is thinghood. And since the master, is (*a*) *qua* notion of self-consciousness, an immediate relation of self-existence, but (*b*) is now moreover at the same time mediation, or a being-for-self which is for itself only through an other—he [the master] stands in relation (*a*) immediately to both (*b*) mediately to each through the other. The master relates himself to the bondsman mediately through independent existence, for that is precisely what keeps the bondsman in thrall; it is his chain, from which he could not in the struggle get away, and for that reason he proved himself to be dependent, to have his independence in the shape of thinghood. The master, however, is the power controlling this state of existence, for he has shown in the struggle that he holds it to be merely something negative. Since he is the power dominating existence, while this existence again is the power controlling the other [the bondsman], the master holds, *par consequence*, this other in subordination. In the same way the master relates himself to the thing mediately through the bondsman. The bondsman being a self-consciousness in the broad sense, also takes up a negative attitude to things and cancels them; but the thing is, at the same time, independent for him, and, in consequence, he cannot, with all his negating, get so far as to annihilate it outright and be done with it; that is to say, he merely works on it. To the master, on the other hand, by means of this mediating process, belongs the immediate relation, in the sense of the pure negation of it, in other words he gets the enjoyment. What mere desire did not attain, he now succeeds in attaining, viz. to have done with the thing, and find satisfaction in enjoyment. Desire alone did not get the length of this, because of the independence of the thing. The master, however, who has interposed the bondsman between it and himself, thereby relates himself merely to the dependence of the thing, and enjoys it without qualification and without reserve. The aspect of its independence he leaves to the bondsman, who labours upon it.

In these two moments, the master gets his recognition through an other consciousness, for in them the latter affirms itself as unessential, both by working upon the thing, and, on the other hand, by the fact of being dependent on a determinate existence; in neither case can this other get the mastery over existence, and succeed in absolutely negating it. We have thus here this moment of recognition, viz. that the other consciousness cancels itself as self-existent, and, *ipso facto*, itself does what the first does to it. In the same way we have the other moment, that this action on the part of the second is the action proper of the first; for what is done by the bondsman is properly an action on the part of the master. The latter exists only for himself, that is his essential nature; he is the negative power without qualification, a power to which the thing is naught. And he is thus the absolutely essential act in this situation, while the bondsman is not so, he is an unessential activity. But for recognition proper there is needed the moment that what the master does to the other he should also do to himself, and what the bondsman does to himself, he should do to the other also. On that account a form of recognition has arisen that is one sided and unequal.

In all this, the unessential consciousness is, for the master, the object which embodies the truth of his certainty of himself. But it is evident that this object does not correspond to its notion; for, just where the master has effectively achieved lordship, he really finds that something has come about quite different from an independent consciousness. It is not an independent, but rather a dependent consciousness that he has achieved. He is thus not assured of self-existence as his truth; he finds that his truth is rather the unessential consciousness, and the fortuitous unessential action of that consciousness.

The truth of the independent consciousness is accordingly the consciousness of the bondsman. This doubtless appears in the first instance outside itself, and not as the truth of self-consciousness. But just as lordship showed its essential nature to be the reverse of what it wants to be, so, too, bondage will, when completed, pass into the opposite of what it immediately is: being a consciousness repressed within itself, it will enter into itself, and change round into real and true independence.

We have seen what bondage is only in relation to lordship. But it is a self-consciousness, and we have now to consider what it is, in this regard, in and for itself. In the first instance, the master is taken to be the essential reality for the state of bondage; hence, for it, the truth is the independent consciousness existing for itself, although this truth is not taken yet as inherent in bondage itself. Still, it does in fact contain within itself this truth of pure negativity and self-existence, because it has experienced this reality within it. For this consciousness was not in peril and fear for this element or that, nor for this or that moment of time, it was afraid for its entire being; it felt the fear of death, the sovereign master. It has been in that experience melted to its inmost soul, has trembled throughout its every fibre, and all that was fixed and steadfast has quaked within it. This complete perturbation of its entire substance, this absolute dissolution of all its stability into fluent continuity, is, however, the simple, ultimate nature of self-consciousness, absolute negativity, pure self-referent existence, which consequently is involved in this type of consciousness. This moment of pure self-existence is moreover a fact for it; for in the master it finds this as its object. Further, this bondsman's consciousness is not only this total dissolution in a general way; in serving and toiling the bondsman actually carries this out. By serving he cancels in every particular aspect his dependence on and attachment to natural existence, and by his work removes this existence away.

The feeling of absolute power, however, realized both in general and in the particular form of service, is only dissolution implicitly; and albeit the fear of the lord is the beginning of wisdom, consciousness is not therein aware of being self-existent. Through work and labour, however, this consciousness of the bondsman comes to itself. In the moment which corresponds to desire in the case of the master's consciousness, the aspect of the non-essential relation to the thing seemed to fall to the lot of the servant, since the thing there retained its independence. Desire has reserved to itself the pure negating of the object and thereby unalloyed feeling of self. This satisfaction, however, just for that reason is itself only a state of evanescence, for it lacks objectivity or subsistence. Labour, on the other hand, is desire restrained and checked, evanescence delayed and postponed; in other words, labour shapes and fashions the thing. The negative relation to the object passes into the *form* of the object, into something that is permanent and remains; because it is just for the labourer that the object has independence. This negative mediating agency, this activity giving shape and form, is at the same time the individual existence, the pure self-existence of that consciousness, which now in the work it does is externalized and passes into the condition of permanence. The consciousness that toils and serves accordingly attains by this means the direct apprehension of that independent being as its self.

But again, shaping or forming the object has not only the positive significance that the bondsman becomes thereby aware of himself as factually and objectively self-existent; this type of consciousness has also a negative import, in contrast with its first moment, the element of fear. For in shaping the thing it only becomes aware of its own proper negativity, existence on its own account, as an object, through the fact that it cancels the actual form confronting it. But this objective negative element is precisely alien, external reality, before which it trembled. Now, however, it destroys this extraneous alien negative, affirms and sets itself up as a negative in the element of permanence, and thereby becomes for itself a self-existent being. In the master, the bondsman feels self-existence to be something external, an objective fact; in fear self-existence is present within himself; in fashioning the thing, self-existence comes to be felt explicitly as his own proper being, and he attains the consciousness that he himself exists in its own right and on its own account (*an und für sich*). By the fact that the form is objectified, it does not become something other than the consciousness moulding the thing through work; for just that form is his pure self-existence, which therein becomes truly realized. Thus precisely in labour where there seemed to be merely some outsider's mind and ideas involved, the bondsman becomes aware, through this re-discovery of himself by himself, of having and being a "mind of his own."

For this reflexion of self into self the two moments, fear and service in general, as also that of formative activity, are necessary: and at the same time both must exist in a universal manner. Without the discipline of service and obedience, fear remains formal and does not

spread over the whole known reality of existence. Without the formative activity shaping the thing, fear remains inward and mute, and consciousness does not become objective for itself. Should consciousness
shape and form the thing without the initial state of absolute fear, then
it has a merely vain and futile "mind of its own"; for its form or negativity is not negativity *per se*, and hence its formative activity cannot furnish the consciousness of itself as essentially real. If it has endured not
absolute fear, but merely some slight anxiety, the negative reality has remained external to it, its substance has not been through and through
infected thereby. Since the entire content of its natural consciousness
has not tottered and shaken, it is still inherently a determinate mode of
being; having a "mind of its own" (*der eigene Sinn*) is simply stubbornness (*Eigensinn*), a type of freedom which does not get beyond the attitude of bondage. As little as the pure form can become its essential
nature, so little is that form, considered as extending over particulars, a
universal formative activity, an absolute notion; it is rather a piece of
cleverness which has mastery within a certain range, but not over the
universal power nor over the entire objective reality.

B

FREEDOM OF SELF-CONSCIOUSNESS

STOICISM: SCEPTICISM: THE UNHAPPY CONSCIOUSNESS

The previous section has established the self as ultimately a free self. But even
this is abstract at first, and hence the attempt to maintain it must pass through
different stages. These attempts have taken historical expression in European
civilization, but these are merely instances of an experience that is strictly
found in all mankind. Hegel, however, selects the forms assumed in European
history, and has these in mind throughout the succeeding analysis. The terms
Stoicism and Scepticism refer primarily to the forms which these assumed in
Greece and Rome. The last stage of independent and free self-hood he names
faute de mieux, the "unhappy consciousness." The background of historical
material for this type of mind is found in the religious life of the Middle Ages
and the mental attitude assumed under the dominion of the Roman Catholic
Church and the Feudal Hierarchy. The social and political dissolution of the
Roman Empire has its counterpart in the mental chaos and dissolution of
Scepticism; the craving of free mind for absolute stability and constancy amid
change and uncertainty found expression in an organized attempt on the part
of the Church to establish permanent connection between man's mental in-
security and an Immutable Reality. The two poles of the antithesis were far removed from each other, and the method or methods adopted to bring about
the union reflect the profound contrast of the opposing elements. It is the
inner process of free mind in this realm of abstract subjective piety which

Hegel analyses in the part termed the "unhappy consciousness"—"unhappy" because craving complete consciousness of self and never at this stage attaining it.

The end of this movement, and therefore the disappearance of all the onesidedness of abstract individual freedom of self, is found when, through the above struggle, there dawns on the self the consciousness of its complete and explicit unity with reality in every shape and form. This is the beginning of the absolute sovereignty of the Mind—Consciousness of Reason as supreme. The change to this new condition found historical expression in the Reformation and the Renaissance.

INDEPENDENT self-consciousness partly finds its essential reality in the bare abstraction of Ego. On the other hand, when this abstract ego develops further and forms distinctions of its own, this differentiation does not become an objective inherently real content for that self-consciousness. Hence this self-consciousness does not become an ego which truly differentiates itself in its abstract simplicity, or one which remains identical with itself in this absolute differentiation. The repressed and subordinate type of consciousness, on the other hand, becomes, in the formative activity of work, an object to itself, in the sense that the form, given to the thing when shaped and moulded, is his object; he sees in the master, at the same time, self-existence as a real mode of consciousness. But the subservient consciousness as such finds these two moments fall apart—the moment of itself as an independent object, and the moment of this object as a mode of consciousness, and so its own proper reality. Since, however, the form and the self-existence are for us, or objectively in themselves, one and the same, and since in the notion of independent consciousness the inherent reality is consciousness, the phase of inherent existence (*Ansichsein*) or thinghood, which received its shape and form through labour, is no other substance than consciousness. In this way, we have a new attitude or mode of consciousness brought about: a type of consciousness which takes on the form of infinitude, or one whose essence consists in unimpeded movement of consciousness. It is one which *thinks* or is free self-consciousness. For thinking does not mean being an abstract ego, but an ego which has at the same time the significance of inherently existing in itself; it means being object to itself or relating itself to objective reality in such a way that this connotes the self-existence of that consciousness for which it is an object. The object does not for thinking proceed by way of presentations or figures, but of notions, conceptions, i.e. of a differentiated reality or essence, which, being an immediate content of consciousness, is nothing distinct from it. What is presented, shaped and constructed, and existent as such, has the form of being something other than consciousness. A notion, however, is at the same time an existent, and this distinction, so far as it falls in consciousness itself, is its determinate content. But in that this content is, at the same time, a conceptually constituted, a comprehended (*begriffener*) content, consciousness remains immediately aware within itself of its unity with this determinate existent so distinguished; not as in the case of a presentation, where consciousness from the first has to take special note that this is its idea; on the contrary, the notion is for me *eo ipso* and at once *my* notion. In thinking I am free, because I am not in an other, but remain simply and solely in touch with myself; and the object which for me is my essential reality, is in undivided unity my self-existence; and my procedure in dealing with notions is a process within myself.

It is essential, however, in this determination of the above attitude of self-consciousness to keep hold of the fact that this attitude is thinking consciousness in general, that its object is immediate unity of the self's implicit, inherent existence, and of its existence explicitly for self. The selfsame consciousness which repels itself from itself, becomes aware of being an element existing in itself. But to itself it is this element to begin with only as universal reality in general, and not as this essential reality appears when developed in all the manifold details it contains, when the process of its being brings out all its fullness of content.

This freedom of self-consciousness, as is well known, has been called *Stoicism*, in so far as it has appeared as a phenomenon conscious of itself in the course of the history of man's spirit. Its principle is that consciousness is essentially that which thinks, is a thinking reality, and that anything is really essential for consciousness, or is true and good, only when consciousness in dealing with it adopts the attitude of a thinking being.

The manifold, self-differentiating expanse of life, with all its individualization and complication, is the object upon which desire and labour operate. This varied activity has now contracted itself into the simple distinction which is found in the pure process of thought. What has still essential reality is not a distinction in the sense of a determinate thing, or in the shape of a consciousness of a determinate kind of natural existence, in the shape of a feeling, or again in the form of desire and its specific purpose, whether that purpose be set up by the consciousness desiring or by an extraneous consciousness. What has still essential significance here is solely that distinction which is a thought-constituted distinction, or which, when made, is not distinguished from me. This consciousness in consequence takes a negative attitude towards the relation of lordship and bondage. Its action, in the case of the master, results in his not simply having his truth in and through the bondsman; and, in that of the bondsman, in not finding his truth in the will of his master and in service. The essence of this consciousness is to be free, on the throne as well as in fetters, throughout all the dependence that attaches to its individual existence, and to maintain that stolid lifeless unconcern which persistently withdraws from the movement of existence, from effective activity as well as from passive endurance, into the simple essentiality of thought. Stubbornness is that freedom which makes itself secure in a solid singleness, and keeps *within* the sphere of bondage. Stoicism, on the other hand, is the freedom which ever comes directly out of that sphere, and returns back into the pure universality of thought. It is a freedom which can come on the scene as a general form of the world's spirit only in a time of universal fear and bondage, a time, too, when mental cultivation is universal, and has elevated culture to the level of thought.

Now while this self-consciousness finds its essential reality to be neither something other than itself, nor the pure abstraction of ego, but ego which has within it otherness—otherness in the sense of a thought-constituted distinction—so that this ego in its otherness is turned back directly into itself; yet this essential nature is, at the same time, only an abstract reality. The freedom of self-consciousness is indifferent towards natural existence, and has, therefore, let this latter go and remain free. The reflexion is thus duplicated. Freedom of thought takes only pure thought as its truth, and this lacks the concrete filling of life. It is, therefore, merely the notion of freedom, not living freedom itself; for it is, to begin with, only thinking in general that is its essence, the form as such, which has turned away from the independence of things and gone back into itself. Since, however, individuality when acting should show itself to be alive, or when thinking should grasp the living world as a system of thought, there ought to lie in thought itself a content to supply the sphere of the ego, in the former case with what is good, and, in the latter, true, in order that there should throughout be no other ingredient in what consciousness has to deal with, except the notion which is the real essence. But here, by the way in which the notion as an abstraction cuts itself off from the multiplicity of things, the notion has *no content in itself*; the content is a datum, is given. Consciousness, no doubt, abolishes the content as an external, a foreign existent, by the fact that it thinks it, but the notion is a determinate notion, and this *determinateness* of the notion is the alien element the notion contains within it. Stoicism, therefore, got embarrassed, when, as the expression went, it was asked for the criterion of truth in general, i.e. properly speaking, for a *content* of thought itself. To the question what is good and true, it responded by giving again the abstract, contentless thought; the true and good are to consist in reasonableness. But this self-identity of thought is simply once more pure form, in which nothing is determinate. The general terms true and good, wisdom and virtue, with which Stoicism has to stop short, are, therefore, in a general way, doubtless elevating; but seeing that they cannot actually and in fact reach any expanse of content, they soon begin to get wearisome.

This thinking consciousness, in the way in which it is thus constituted, as abstract freedom, is therefore only incomplete negation of otherness. Withdrawn from existence solely into itself, it has not there fully vindicated itself as the absolute negation of this existence. The content is held indeed to be only thought, but is thereby also taken to be determinate thought, and at the same time determinateness as such.

Scepticism is the realisation of that of which Stoicism is merely the notion, and is the actual experience of what freedom of thought is; it is in itself and essentially the negative, and must so exhibit itself. With the reflexion of self-consciousness into the simple, pure thought of itself, independent existence or permanent determinateness has, in contrast to that reflexion, dropped as a matter of fact out of the infinitude of thought. In Scepticism, the entire unessentiality and unsubstantiality of this "other" becomes a reality for consciousness. Thought becomes thinking which wholly annihilates the being of the world with its manifold determinateness, and the negativity of free self-consciousness becomes aware of attaining, in these manifold forms which life assumes, real negativity.

It is clear from the foregoing that, just as Stoicism answers to the *notion* of independent consciousness, which appeared as a relation of lordship and bondage, Scepticism, on its side, corresponds to its *realization*, to the negative attitude towards otherness, to desire and labour. But if desire and work could not carry out for self-consciousness the process of negation, this polemical attitude towards the manifold substantiality of things will, on the other hand, be successful, because it turns against them as a free self-consciousness, and one complete within itself beforehand; or, expressed more definitely, because it has inherent in itself thought or the principle of infinitude, where the independent elements in their distinction from one another are held to be merely vanishing quantities. The differences, which, in the pure thinking of self are only the *abstraction* of differences, become here the whole of the differences; and every differentiated existent becomes a difference of self-consciousness.

With this we get determined the action of Scepticism in general, as also its mode and nature. It shows the dialectic movement, which is sense-certainty, perception, and understanding. It shows, too, the unessentiality of that which holds good in the relation of master and servant, and which for abstract thought itself passes as determinate.

That relation involves, at the same time, a determinate situation, in which there are found even moral laws, as commands of the sovereign lord. The determinations in abstract thought, however, are scientific notions, into which formal contentless thought expands itself, attaching the notion, as a matter of fact in merely an external fashion, to the existence independent of it, and holding as valid only determinate notions, albeit they are still pure abstractions.

Dialectic as a negative process, taken immediately as it stands, appears to consciousness, in the first instance, as something at the mercy of which it is, and which does not exist through consciousness itself. In Scepticism, on the other hand, this negative process is a moment of self-consciousness, which does not simply find its truth and its reality vanish, without self-consciousness knowing how, but rather which, in the certainty of its own freedom, itself makes this other, so claiming to be real, vanish. Self-consciousness here not only makes the objective as such to disappear before the negations of Scepticism but also its own function in relation to the object, where the object is held to be objective and made good—i.e. its function of perceiving as also its process of securing what is in danger of being lost, viz. sophistry and *its* self-constituted and self-established truth. By means of this self-conscious negation, self-consciousness procures for itself the certainty of its own freedom, brings about the experience of that freedom, and thereby raises it into the truth. What vanishes is what is determinate, the difference which, no matter what its nature or whence it comes, sets up to be fixed and unchangeable. The difference has nothing permanent in it, and must vanish before thought because to be differentiated just means not to have being in itself, but to have its essential nature solely in an other. Thinking, however, is the insight into this character of what is differentiated; it is the negative function in its simple, ultimate form.

Sceptical self-consciousness thus discovers, in the flux and alternation of all that would stand secure in its presence, its own freedom, as given by and received from its own self. It is aware of being this ἀταραξία of self-thinking thought, the unalterable and genuine certainty of its self. This certainty does not arise as a result out of something extraneous and foreign which stowed away inside itself its whole complex development; a result which would thus leave behind the process by which it came to be. Rather consciousness itself is thoroughgoing dialectical restlessness, this mêlée of presentations derived from sense and thought, whose differences collapse into oneness, and whose identity is similarly again resolved and dissolved—for this identity is itself determinateness as contrasted with non-identity. This consciousness, however, as a matter of fact, instead of being a selfsame consciousness, is here neither more nor less than an absolutely fortuitous embroglio, the giddy whirl of a perpetually self-creating disorder. This is what it takes itself to be; for itself maintains and produces this self-impelling confusion. Hence it even confesses the fact; it owns to being an entirely fortuitous *individual* consciousness—a consciousness which is empirical, which is directed upon what admittedly has no reality for it, which obeys what, in its regard, has no essential being, which realizes and does what it knows to have no truth. But while it passes in this manner for an individual, isolated. contingent, in fact animal life, and a lost self-consciousness, it also, on the contrary, again turns itself into universal selfsameness; for it is the negativity of all singleness and all difference. From this self-identity, or rather within its very self, it falls back once more into that contingency and confusion, for this very self-directed process of negation has to do solely with what is single and individual, and is occupied with what is fortuitous. This form of consciousness is, therefore, the aimless fickleness and instability of going to and fro, hither and thither, from one extreme of selfsame self-consciousness, to the other contingent, confused and confusing consciousness. It does not itself bring these two thoughts of itself together. It finds its freedom, at one time, in the form of elevation above all the whirling complexity and all the contingency of mere existence, and again, at another time, likewise confesses to falling back upon what is unessential, and to being taken up with that. It lets the unessential content in its thought vanish; but in that very act it is the consciousness of something unessential. It announces absolute disappearance but the announcement *is*, and this consciousness is the evanescence expressly announced. It announces the nullity of seeing, hearing, and so on, yet *itself* sees and hears. It proclaims the nothingness of essential ethical principles, and makes those very truths the sinews of its own conduct. Its deeds and its words belie each other continually; and itself, too, has the doubled contradictory consciousness of immutability and sameness, and of utter contingency and non-identity with itself. But it keeps asunder the poles of this contradiction within itself; and bears itself towards the contradiction as it does in its purely negative process in general. If sameness is shown to it, it points out unlikeness, non-identity; and when the latter, which it has expressly mentioned the moment before, is held up to it, it passes on to indicate sameness and identity. Its talk, in fact, is like a squabble among selfwilled children, one of whom says A when the other says B, and again B, when the other says A, and who, through being in contradiction with themselves, procure the joy of remaining in contradiction with one another.

In Scepticism consciousness gets, in truth, to know itself as a consciousness containing contradiction within itself. From the experience of this proceeds a new attitude which brings together the two thoughts which Scepticism holds apart. The want of intelligence which Scepticism manifests regarding itself is bound to vanish, because it is in fact *one* consciousness which possesses these two modes within it. This new attitude consequently is one which is *aware* of being the double consciousness of itself as self-liberating, unalterable, self-identical, and as utterly self-confounding, self-perverting; and this new attitude is the consciousness of this contradiction within itself.

In Stoicism, self-consciousness is the bare and simple freedom of itself. In Scepticism, it realizes itself, negates the other side of determinate existence, but, in so doing, really doubles itself, and is itself now a duality. In this way the duplication, which previously was divided between two individuals, the lord and the bondsman, is concentrated into one. Thus we have here that dualizing of self-consciousness within itself, which lies essentially in the notion of mind; but the unity of the two elements is not yet present. Hence the *Unhappy Consciousness*,[1] the Alienated Soul which is the consciousness of self as a divided nature, a doubled and merely contradictory being.

This unhappy consciousness, divided and at variance within itself, must, because this contradiction of its essential nature is felt to be a single consciousness, always have in the one consciousness the other also; and thus must be straightway driven out of each in turn, when it thinks it has therein attained to the victory and rest of unity. Its true return into itself, or reconciliation with itself, will, however, display the notion of mind endowed with a life and existence of its own, because it implicitly involves the fact that, while being an undivided consciousness, it is a double-consciousness. It is itself the gazing of one self-consciousness into another, and itself is both, and the unity of both is also its own essence; but objectively and consciously it is not yet this essence itself—is not yet the unity of both.

Since, in the first instance, it is the immediate, the implicit unity of both, while for it they are not one and the same, but opposed, it takes one, namely, the simple unalterable, as essential, the other, the manifold and changeable as the unessential. For it, both are realities foreign to each other. Itself, because consciousness of this contradiction, assumes the aspect of changeable consciousness and is to itself the unessential; but as consciousness of unchangeableness, of the ultimate essence, it must, at the same time, proceed to free itself from the

---

[1]The term "unglückliches Bewusstsein" is designed as a summary expression for the following movement, there being no recognized general term for this purpose, as in the case of "Stoicism." The term hardly seems fortunate: with the following analysis should be read Hegel's *Philosophy of History*, part 4, sec. 2, c. 1 and 2. (Eng. tr. pp. 380–415) and *History of Philosophy*, part 2, Introduction.

unessential, i.e. to liberate itself from itself. For though in its own view it is indeed only the changeable, and the unchangeable is foreign and extraneous to it, yet itself is simple, and therefore unchangeable consciousness, of which consequently it is conscious as its essence, but still in such wise that itself is again in its own regard not this essence. The position, which it assigns to both, cannot, therefore, be an indifference of one to the other, i.e. cannot be an indifference of itself towards the unchangeable. Rather it is immediately both itself; and the relation of both assumes for it the form of a relation of essence to the nonessential, so that this latter has to be cancelled; but since both are to it equally essential and are contradictory, it is only the conflicting contradictory process in which opposite does not come to rest in its own opposite, but produces itself therein afresh merely as an opposite.

Here, then, there is a struggle against an enemy, victory over whom really means being worsted, where to have attained one result is really to lose it in the opposite. Consciousness of life, of its existence and action, is merely pain and sorrow over this existence and activity; for therein consciousness finds only consciousness of its opposite as its essence—and of its own nothingness. Elevating itself beyond this, it passes to the unchangeable. But this elevation is itself this same consciousness. It is, therefore, immediately consciousness of the opposite, viz. of itself as single, individual, particular. The unchangeable, which comes to consciousness, is in that very fact at the same time affected by particularity, and is only present with this latter. Instead of particularity having been abolished in the consciousness of immutability, it only continues to appear there still.

In this process, however, consciousness experiences just this appearance of particularity in the unchangeable, and of the unchangeable in particularity. Consciousness becomes aware of particularity *in general* in the immutable essence, and at the same time it there finds its own particularity. For the truth of this process is precisely that the double consciousness is one and single. This unity becomes a fact to it, but in the first instance the unity is one in which the diversity of both factors is still the dominant feature. Owing to this, consciousness has before it the threefold way in which particularity is connected with unchangeableness. In one form it comes before itself as opposed to the unchangeable essence, and is thrown back to the beginning of that struggle, which is, from first to last, the principle constituting the entire situation. At another time it finds the unchangeable appearing in the form of particularity; so that the latter is an embodiment of unchangeableness, into which, in consequence, the entire form of existence passes. In the third case, it discovers *itself* to be this particular fact in the unchangeable. The first unchangeable is taken to be merely the alien, external Being,[2] which passes sentence on particular existence; since the second unchangeable is a form or mode of particularity like itself,[3] it, i.e. the consciousness, becomes in the third place spirit (*Geist*), has the joy of finding itself therein, and becomes aware within itself that its particularity has been reconciled with the universal.[4]

What is set forth here as a mode and relation of the unchangeable, came to light as the experience through which self-consciousness passes in its unhappy state of diremption. This experience is now doubtless not its own onesided process; for it is itself unchangeable consciousness; and this latter, consequently, is a particular consciousness as well; and the process is as much a process of that unchangeable consciousness, which makes its appearance there as certainly as the other. For that movement is carried on in these moments: an unchangeable now opposed to the particular in general, then, being itself particular, opposed to the other particular, and finally at one with it. But this consideration, so far as it is our affair,[5] is here out of place, for thus far we have only had to do with unchangeableness as unchangeableness of *consciousness*, which, for that reason, is not true immutability, but is still affected with an opposite; we have not had before us the unchangeable *per se* and by itself; we do not, therefore, know how this latter will conduct itself. What has here so far come to light is merely this, that to consciousness, which is our object here, the determinations above indicated appear in the unchangeable.

For this reason, then, the unchangeable consciousness also preserves, in its very form and bearing, the character and fundamental features of diremption and separate self-existence, as against the particular consciousness. For the latter it is thus altogether a contingency, a mere chance event, that the unchangeable receives the form of particularity; just as the particular consciousness merely happens to find itself opposed to the unchangeable, and therefore has this relation *per naturam*. Finally that it *finds itself* in the unchangeable appears to the particular consciousness to be brought about partly, no doubt, by itself, or to take place for the reason that itself is particular; but this union, both as regards its origin as well as in its being, appears partly also due to the unchangeable; and the opposition remains within this unity itself. In point of fact, through the unchangeable assuming a definite form, the "beyond," as a moment, has not only remained, but really is more securely established. For if the remote "beyond" seems indeed brought

---

[2]God as Judge.
[3]Christ.
[4]The religious communion.
[5]I.e. the philosophical observer.

closer to the individual by this particular form of realization, on the other hand, it is henceforward fixedly opposed to the individual, a sensuous, impervious unit, with all the hard resistance of what is actual. The hope of becoming one therewith must remain a hope, i.e. without fulfilment, without present fruition; for between the hope and fulfilment there stands precisely the absolute contingency, or immovable indifference, which is involved in the very assumption of determinate shape and form, the basis and foundation of the hope. By the nature of this existent unit, through the particular reality it has assumed and adopted, it comes about of necessity that it becomes a thing of the past, something that has been somewhere far away, and absolutely remote it remains.

If, at the beginning, the bare notion of the sundered consciousness involved the characteristic of seeking to cancel it, *qua* particular consciousness, and become the unchangeable consciousness, the direction its effort henceforth takes is rather that of cancelling its relation to the pure unchangeable, without shape or embodied form, and of adopting only the relation to the unchangeable which has form and shape.[6] For the oneness of the particular consciousness with the unchangeable is henceforth its object and the essential reality for it, just as in the mere notion of it the essential object was merely the formless abstract unchangeable: and the relation found in this absolute disruption, characteristic of its notion, is now what it has to turn away from. The external relation, however, primarily adopted to the formed and embodied unchangeable, as being an alien extraneous reality, must be transmuted and raised to that of complete and thoroughgoing fusion and identification.

The process through which the unessential consciousness strives to attain this oneness, is itself a triple process, in accordance with the threefold character of the relation which this consciousness takes up to its transcendent and remote reality embodied in specific form. In one it is a pure consciousness; at another time a particular individual who takes up towards actuality the attitude characteristic of desire and labour; and in the third place it is a consciousness of its self-existence, its existence for itself. We have now to see how these three modes of its being are found and are constituted in that general relation.

In the first place, then, regarded as pure consciousness, the unchangeable embodied in definite historical form seems, since it is an object for pure consciousness, to be established as it is in its self-subsistent reality. But this, its reality in and for itself, has not yet come to light, as we already remarked. Were it to be in consciousness as it is

---

[6]The historic Christ as worshipped, e.g. in the mediaeval church.

in itself and for itself, this would certainly have to come about not from the side of consciousness, but from the unchangeable. But, this being so, its presence here is brought about through consciousness only in a onesided way to begin with, and just for that reason is not found in a perfect and genuine form, but constantly weighted and encumbered with imperfection, with an opposite.

But although the "unhappy consciousness" does not possess this actual presence, it has, at the same time, transcended pure thought, so far as this is the abstract thought of Stoicism, which turns away from particulars altogether, and again the merely restless thought of Scepticism—so far, in fact, as this is merely particularity in the sense of aimless contradiction and the restless process of contradictory thought. It has gone beyond both of these; it brings and keeps together pure thought and particular existence, but has not yet risen to that level of thinking where the particularity of consciousness is harmoniously reconciled with pure thought itself. It rather stands midway, at the point where abstract thought comes in contact with the particularity of consciousness *qua* particularity. Itself *is* this act of contact; it is the union of pure thought and individuality; and this thinking individuality or pure thought also exists as object for it, and the unchangeable is essentially itself an individual existence. But that this its object, the unchangeable, which assumes essentially the form of particularity, is *its own self*, the self which is particularity of consciousness—this is *not* established *for it*.

In this first condition, consequently, in which we treat it as pure consciousness, it takes up towards its object an attitude which is not that of thought; but rather (since it is indeed in itself pure thinking particularity and its object is just this pure thought, but pure thought is not their relation to one another as such), it, so to say, merely gives itself up to thought, devotes itself to thinking (*geht an das Denken hin*), and is the state of Devotion (*Andacht*). Its thinking as such is no more than the discordant clang of ringing bells, or a cloud of warm incense, a kind of thinking in terms of music, that does not get the length of notions, which would be the sole, immanent, objective mode of thought. This boundless pure inward feeling comes to have indeed its object; but this object does not make its appearance in conceptual form, and therefore comes on the scene as something external and foreign. Hence we have here the inward movement of pure emotion (*Gemüth*) which feels itself, but feels itself in the bitterness of soul-diremption. It is the movement of an infinite Yearning, which is assured that its nature is a pure emotion of this kind, a pure thought which thinks itself as particularity—a yearning that is certain of being known and recognized by this object, for the very reason that this object thinks itself as particularity.

At the same time, however, this nature is the unattainable "beyond" which, in being seized, escapes or rather has already escaped. The "beyond" has already escaped for it is in part the unchangeable, thinking itself as particularity, and consciousness, therefore, attains itself therein immediately,—attains itself, but as something opposed to the unchangeable; instead of grasping the real nature consciousness merely *feels*, and has fallen back upon itself. Since, in thus attaining itself, consciousness cannot keep itself at a distance as this opposite, it has merely laid hold of what is unessential instead of having seized true reality. Thus, just as, on one side, when striving to find itself in the essentially real, it only lays hold of its own divided state of existence, so, too, on the other side, it cannot grasp that other [the essence] as particular or as concrete. That "other" cannot be found where it is sought; for it is meant to be just a "beyond," that which can *not* be found. When looked for as a particular it is not universal, a thought-constituted particularity, not notion, but particular in the sense of an object, or a concrete actual, an object of immediate sense-consciousness, of sense certainty; and just for that reason it is only one which has disappeared. Consciousness, therefore, can only come upon the *grave* of its life. But because this is itself an actuality, and since it is contrary to the nature of actuality to afford a lasting possession, the presence even of that tomb is merely the source of trouble, toil, and struggle, a fight which must be lost.[7] But since consciousness has found out by experience that the grave of its actual unchangeable Being has no concrete *actuality*, that the vanished particularity *qua* vanished is not true particularity, it will give up looking for the unchangeable particular existence as something actual, or will cease trying to hold on to what has thus vanished. Only so is it capable of finding particularity in a true form, a form that is universal.

In the first instance, however, the withdrawal of the emotional life into itself is to be taken in such a way that this life of feeling, in its own regard, *has* actuality *qua* particular existence. It is pure emotion which, for us or *per se*, has found *itself* and satiated itself, for although it is, no doubt, aware in feeling that the ultimate reality is cut off from it, yet in itself this feeling is *self-feeling*; it has felt the object of its own pure feeling, and this object is its own self. It thus comes forward here as self-feeling, or as something actual on its own account. In this return into self, we find appearing its second attitude, the condition of desire and labour, which ensures for consciousness the inner certainty of its own self (which, as we saw, it has obtained) by the process of cancelling and enjoying the alien external reality,—existence in the form of independent things. The unhappy consciousness, however, finds itself merely

---

[7]Cp. The Crusades.

desiring and toiling; it is not consciously and directly aware that so to find itself rests upon the inner certainty of its self, and that its feeling of real being is this self-feeling. Since it does not in its own view have that certainty, its inner life really remains still a shattered certainty of itself; that confirmation of its own existence which it would receive through work and enjoyment, is, therefore, just as tottering and insecure; in other words, it must consciously nullify this certification of its own being, so as to find therein confirmation indeed, but confirmation only of what it is *for itself*, viz. of its disunion.

The actual reality, on which desire and work are directed, is, from the point of view of this consciousness, no longer something in itself null and void, something merely to be destroyed and consumed; but rather something like that consciousness itself, a reality broken in sunder, which is only in one respect essentially null, but in another sense also a consecrated world. This reality is a form and embodiment of the unchangeable, for the latter has in itself preserved particularity; and because, *qua* unchangeable, it is a universal, its particularity as a whole has the significance of *all* actuality.

If consciousness were, for itself, an independent consciousness, and reality were taken to be in and for itself of no account, then consciousness would attain, in work and enjoyment, the feeling of its own independence, by the fact that its consciousness would be that which cancels reality. But since this reality is taken to be the form and shape of the unchangeable, consciousness is unable of itself to cancel that reality. On the contrary, seeing that consciousness manages to nullify reality and to obtain enjoyment, this must come about through the unchangeable itself when it disposes of its own form and shape and delivers this up for consciousness to enjoy.

Consciousness, on its part, appears here likewise as actual, though, at the same time, as internally shattered; and this diremption shows itself in the course of toil and enjoyment, to break up into a relation to reality, or existence for itself, and into an existence in itself. That relation to actuality is the process of alteration, or acting, the existence for itself, which belongs to the particular consciousness as such. But therein it is also in itself; this aspect belongs to the unchangeable "beyond." This aspect consists in faculties and powers: an external gift, which the unchangeable here hands over for the consciousness to make use of.

In its action, accordingly, consciousness, in the first instance, has its being in the relation of two extremes. On one side it takes its stand as the active present (*Diesseits*), and opposed to it stands passive reality: both in relation to each other, but also both withdrawn into the unchangeable, and firmly established in themselves. From both sides, therefore, there is detached merely a superficial element to constitute their opposition; they are only opposed at the surface, and the play of opposition, the one to the other, takes place there.

The extreme of passive reality is sublated by the active extreme. Actuality can, however, on its own side, be sublated only because its own changeless essence sublates it, repels itself from itself, and hands over to the mercy of the active extreme what is thus repelled. Active force appears as the power wherein actual reality is dissolved. For that reason, however, this consciousness, to which the inherent reality, or ultimate essence, is an "other," regards this power (which is the way it appears when active), as "the beyond," that which lies remote from its self. Instead, therefore, of returning out of its activity into itself, and instead of having confirmed itself as a fact for its self, consciousness reflects back this process of action into the other extreme, which is thereby represented as purely universal, as absolute might, from which the movement in every direction started, and which is the essential life of the self-disintegrating extremes, as they at first appeared, and of the process of change as well.

In that the unchangeable consciousness contemns its specific shape and form, and abandons it entirely, while, on the other hand, the individual consciousness "gives thanks," i.e. denies itself the satisfaction of being conscious of its independence, and refers the essential substance of its action to the "beyond" and not to itself: by these two moments, in which both parts give themselves up the one to the other, there certainly arises in consciousness a sense of *its own* unity with the unchangeable. But, at the same time, this unity is affected with division, is again broken within itself and out of this unity there once more comes the opposition of universal and particular. For consciousness, no doubt, in appearance renounces the satisfaction of its self-feeling, but it gets the actual satisfaction of that feeling, for it *has been* desire, work, and enjoyment; *qua* consciousness it has willed, has acted, has enjoyed. Its thanks similarly, in which it recognizes the other extreme as its true reality, and cancels itself, is itself its own act, which counterbalances the action of the other extreme, and meets with a like act the benefit handed over. If the former yields to consciousness merely its superficial content, yet consciousness still expresses thanks; and since it gives up its own action, i.e. its very essence, it, properly speaking, does more thereby than the other, which only renounces an outer surface. The entire process, therefore, is reflected into the extreme of particularity, not merely in actual desire, labour, and enjoyment, but even in the expression of thanks, where the reverse seems to take place. Consciousness feels itself therein as this particular individual, and does not let itself be deceived by the semblance of its renunciation; for the real truth of that procedure is that it has *not* given itself up. What has come about is merely the double reflection into both extremes; and the result is to repeat the cleavage into the opposed consciousness of the unchangeable and the consciousness of a contrasted opposite in the shape of willing, performing, enjoying, and of self-renunciation itself, or, in general, of self-existent particularity.

With this has come to light the third stage in the movement of this consciousness, a situation which follows from the second and one which in truth has, by its will and by its performance, proved itself independent. In the first situation we had only a "notion" of actual consciousness, the inward emotion, which is not yet real in action and enjoyment. The second is this actualization, as an external express action and enjoyment. With the return out of this stage, however, it is that which has got to know itself as a real and effective consciousness, or that whose truth consists in being in and for itself. But herein the enemy is discovered in its special and most peculiar form. In the battle of emotion this individual consciousness has the sense of being merely a tune, an abstract moment. In work and enjoyment, which are the realization of this unsubstantial existence, it can readily forget itself, and the consciousness of its own proper life found in this realization is overborne by grateful recognition, but this overthrow of its proper distinctiveness is in truth a return of consciousness into itself, and moreover into itself as the general reality.

This third attitude, wherein this genuine reality is one term, consists in so relating this reality to absolute universal Being, as to show it to be mere nothingness.[8] The course of this relation we have still to consider.

To begin with, as regards the contrasted relation of consciousness, in which its reality is taken to be immediately naught, its actual performance thus becomes a doing of nothing at all; its enjoyment becomes a feeling of its own unhappiness. In consequence, activity and enjoyment lose all universal content and significance; for in that case they would have a substantiality of their own: and both withdraw into the state of particularity, to which consciousness is directed in order to cancel them. Consciousness discovers itself as this concrete particular in the functions of animal life. These latter, instead of being performed unconsciously and naturally as something which, *per se*, is of no significance, and can acquire no importance and essential value for spirit,— these latter, since it is in them that the enemy is seen in his proper and peculiar shape, are rather an object of strenuous concern and serious occupation, and become precisely the most important consideration.[9] Since, however this enemy creates itself in its very defeat, conscious-

---

[8] The conception of the nothingness of the individual in the sight of God.
[9] Asceticism.

ness, by giving the enemy a fixedness of being and of meaning, instead of getting rid of him, really never gets away from him and finds itself constantly defiled. And since, at the same time, this object of its exertions, instead of being something essential, is the very meanest, instead of being a universal, is the merest particular—we have here before us merely a personality confined within its narrow self and its petty activity, a personality brooding over itself, as unfortunate as it is pitiably destitute.

But all the same both of these, both the feeling of its misfortune and the poverty of its own action, are points of connection to which to attach the consciousness of its unity with the unchangeable. For the attempted immediate destruction of its actual existence is affected through the thought of the unchangeable and takes place in this relation to the unchangeable. The mediate relation constitutes the essence of the negative process, in which this consciousness directs itself against its particularity of being, which, however, *qua* relation, is at the same time in itself positive, and will bring this its unity to light as an objective fact for this consciousness itself.

This mediate relation is consequently a connected inferential process (*Schluss*), in which particularity, establishing itself at first in opposition to the inherent essence, is bound together and united with this other term only through a third term. Through this middle term the one extreme, unchangeable consciousness, has a being for the unessential consciousness, in which, at the same time, is also involved that the latter likewise has a being for the former, solely through that middle term; and this middle term is thus one which presents both extremes to one another, and acts as the minister of each in turn in dealing with the other. This medium is itself a conscious being, for it is an action mediating consciousness as such; the content of this action is the destruction and annihilation, which consciousness has in view in dealing with its particularity.

In the middle term, then, this consciousness gets freed from action and enjoyment, in the sense of its own action and enjoyment. It puts away from itself, *qua* self-existent extreme, the substance of its will, and throws on to the mediating term, or the ministering agency,[10] its own proper freedom of decision, and herewith the guilt of its own act. This mediator, being in direct communication with the unchangeable Being, renders service by advising what is just and right. The act, since this follows upon obedience to a deliverance enunciated by another, ceases, as regards the performance or the willing of the act, to be the

---

[10]The Priesthood.

agent's own proper deed. There is still left, however, to the subordinate consciousness, its objective aspect, namely, the fruit of its labour, and enjoyment. These, therefore, it casts away as well, and just as it disclaimed its own will, so it contemns such reality as it received in work and in enjoyment. It renounces these, partly as being the accomplished truth of its self-conscious independence, when it seeks to do something quite foreign to itself, thinking and speaking what, for it, has no sense or meaning;[11] partly, too, as being external property—when it demits somewhat of the possession acquired through its toil. It also gives up the enjoyment it had—when with its fastings and its mortifications it once more absolutely denies itself that enjoyment.

Through these moments—the negative abandonment first of its own right and power of decision, then of its property and enjoyment, and finally the positive moment of carrying on what it does not understand— it deprives itself, completely and in truth, of the consciousness of inner and outer freedom, or reality in the sense of its own existence for itself. It has the certainty of having in truth stripped itself of its Ego, and of having turned its immediate self-consciousness into a "thing," into an objective external existence.

It could ensure its self-renunciation and self-abandonment solely by this real and vital sacrifice [of its self]. For only thereby is the deception got rid of, which lies in inner acknowledgment of gratitude through heart, sentiment, and tongue—an acknowledgment which indeed disclaims all power of independent self-existence, and ascribes this power to a gift from above, but in this very disclaimer retains for itself its own proper and peculiar life, outwardly in the possession it does not resign, inwardly in the consciousness of the decision which itself has resolved upon and in the consciousness of its own self-constituted content, which it has not exchanged for a content coming from without and filling it with meaningless ideas and phrases.

But in the sacrifice actually accomplished, while consciousness has cancelled the action as its own act, it has also implicitly demitted and put off its unhappy condition. Yet that this demission[12] *has* implicitly taken place, is effected by the other term of the logical process (*Schluss*) here involved, the term which is the inherent and ultimate reality. That sacrifice of the subordinate term, however, was at the same time not a onesided action; it involves the action of the other. For giving up one's own will is only in one aspect negative; in principle, or in itself, it is at the same time positive, positing and affirming the will as

---

[11]Cp. the use in the Church services of Latin instead of the vernacular: religious processions, etc.
[12]Absolution.

an *other*, and, specifically, affirming the will as *not* a particular, but universal. This consciousness takes this positive significance of the negatively affirmed particular will to be the will of the other extreme, the will, which, because it is simply an "other" for consciousness, assumes the form of advice, or counsel, not through itself, but through the third term, the mediator. Hence its will certainly becomes, for consciousness, universal will, inherent and essential will, but is not itself in its own view this inherent reality. The giving up of its own will as particular is not taken by it to be in principle the positive element of universal will. Similarly its surrender of possession and enjoyment has merely the same negative significance, and the universal which it thereby comes to find is, in its view, not its own doing proper. This unity of objectivity and independent self-existence which lies in the notion of action, and which therefore comes for consciousness to be the essential reality and object—as this is not taken by consciousness to be the principle of its action, neither does it become an object for consciousness directly and through itself. Rather, it makes the mediating minister express this still halting certainty, that its unhappy state is only *implicitly* the reverse, i.e. is only *implicitly* action bringing self-satisfaction in its act, or blessed enjoyment; that its pitiable action too is only *implicitly* the reverse, namely, absolute action; that in principle action is only really action when it is the action of some particular individual. But for its self, action and *its own* concrete action remain something miserable and insignificant, its enjoyment pain, and the sublation of these, positively considered, remains a mere "beyond." But in this object, where it finds its own action and existence, *qua* this particular consciousness, to be inherently existence and action as such, there has arisen the idea of Reason, of the certainty that consciousness is, in its particularity, inherently and essentially absolute, or is all reality.

C. [FREE CONCRETE MIND]¹

(AA)

REASON²

Reason is the first stage in the analysis of concrete mind—of universal self conscious of itself in its object and conscious of the object as universal. Reason is not a mere "function" of mind, but a stage of mind. It therefore possesses its own peculiar content and operates in a process peculiar to itself. Its aim is to become completely conscious of its own nature; and to acquire this it must develop itself through its various phases. The process of development is from immediate to mediate, from what it is implicitly to what it is explicitly. The first step therefore is reason as immediate—where universal self is simply and directly *aware of* itself in the universal object. The operation of concrete mind at this stage is found where reason "observes." The analysis of observation as this operates in the various domains covered by the empirical sciences is thus the subject-matter of the following section. The processes of these various sciences are assumed in Hegel's analysis. Observation must change in character with the objects observed; hence the difference between observation of inorganic and organic nature, observation of mind, and of the relation of mind and nature. The difficulties reason has to face in this operation, and the contradictions into which it falls in seeking to find laws, etc., to satisfy its aim, form the substance of the following analysis.

The nature of reason as here conceived is the source and origin of philosophical Idealism, whether the idealism be one-sided or absolute. Idealism is in fact the philosophical expression of the principle of reason, just as the various empirical sciences may be said to be the development, in the several ways which experience dictates, of the operation of rational observation. Hence the introductory pages of the following analysis are devoted to a statement of the character of true and false idealism.

The historical material behind the abstract argument elaborated here is provided by the awakened scientific spirit that appeared after the Reformation, and the methods and results of the empirical sciences at the time Hegel wrote. In particular the physiological conceptions of "irritability," "sensibility" and

---

¹Cp. Hegel's *Hist. of Philos.*, pt. 2, § 3, Introd. and C: pt. 3, Introd. *Philos. of Hist.*, pt. 4, § 3, c. 3 *ad fin.*
²Cp. *Naturphilos.*, W.W., vii. 1. § 246; *Logik*, W.W., v.

131

"reproduction," discussed on p. 152 ff., were first formulated by Haller, *Elementa Physiologiae* (1757–66). For a list of the chief scientific works which appeared shortly before or about the time the following analysis was written, and which doubtless provided part of the material for the analysis, see Merz, *History of European Thought*, Vol. I, pp. 82–83.

The polemical criticism which runs through this as through almost every section of the work is directed against the one-sided idealism of Hegel's predecessors and the imperfect conception of scientific method displayed by the current science of nature.

V

REASON'S CERTAINTY AND REASON'S TRUTH

WITH the thought which consciousness has laid hold of, that the individual consciousness is inherently absolute reality, consciousness turns back into itself. In the case of the unhappy consciousness, the inherent and essential reality is a "beyond" remote from itself. But the process of its own activity has in its case brought out the truth that individuality, when completely developed, individuality which is a concrete actual mode of consciousness, is made the negative of itself, i.e. the objective extreme;—in other words, has forced it to make explicit its self-existence, and turned this into an objective fact. In this process it has itself become aware, too, of its unity with the universal, a unity which, seeing that the individual when sublated is the universal, is no longer looked on *by us* as falling outside it, and which, since consciousness maintains itself in this its negative condition, is inherently in it as such its very essence. Its truth is what appears in the process of synthesis—where the extremes were seen to be absolutely held apart—as the middle term, proclaiming to the unchangeable consciousness that the isolated individual has renounced itself, and to the individual consciousness that the unchangeable consciousness is no longer for it an extreme, but is one with it and reconciled to it. This mediating term is the unity directly aware of both, and relating them to one another; and the consciousness of their unity, which it proclaims to consciousness and thereby to itself, is the certainty and assurance of being all truth.

From the fact that self-consciousness is Reason, its hitherto negative attitude towards otherness turns round into a positive attitude. So far it has been concerned merely with its independence and freedom; it has sought to save and keep itself for itself at the expense of the world or its own actuality, both of which appeared to it to involve the denial of its own essential nature. But *qua* reason, assured of itself, it is at peace so far as they are concerned, and is able to endure them; for it is certain its self is reality, certain that all concrete actuality is nothing else but it.

Its thought is itself *eo ipso* concrete reality; its attitude towards the latter is thus that of *Idealism*. To it, looking at itself in this way, it seems as if now, for the first time, the world had come into being. Formerly, it did not understand the world, it desired the world and worked upon it; then withdrew itself from it and retired into itself, abolished the world so far as itself was concerned, and abolished itself *qua* consciousness — both the consciousness of that world as essentially real, as well as the consciousness of its nothingness and unreality. Here, for the first time, after the grave of its truth is lost, after the annihilation of its concrete actuality is itself done away with, and the individuality of consciousness is seen to be in itself absolute reality, it discovers the world as its own new and real world, which in its permanence possesses an interest for it, just as previously the interest lay only in its transitoriness. The subsistence of the world is taken to mean the actual presence of its own truth; it is certain of finding only itself there.

Reason is the conscious certainty of being all reality. This is how Idealism expresses the principle of Reason.[3] Just as consciousness assuming the form of reason immediately and inherently contains that certainty within it, in the same way idealism also directly proclaims and expresses that certainty. I am I in the sense that the I which is object for me is sole and only object, is all reality and all that is present. The I which is object to me here is not what we have in self-consciousness in general, nor again what we have in free independent self-consciousness; in the former it is merely empty object in general, in the latter, it is merely an object that withdraws itself from other objects that still hold their own alongside it. In the present instance, the object-ego is object which is consciously known to exclude the existence of any other whatsoever. Self-consciousness, however, is not merely from its own point of view (*für sich*), but also in its very self (*an sich*) all reality, primarily by the fact that it becomes this reality, or rather demonstrates itself to be such. It demonstrates itself to be this by the way in which first in the course of the dialectic movement of "meaning" (*Meinen*),[4] perceiving, and understanding, otherness disappears as implicitly real (*an sich*); and then in the movement through the independence of consciousness in Lordship and Servitude, through the idea of freedom, sceptical detachment, and the struggle for absolute liberation on the part of the self-divided consciousness, otherness, in so far as it is only subjectively for self-consciousness, vanishes for the latter itself. There appeared two aspects, one after the other; the one where the essential reality or the truly real had for con-

---

[3]Cp. Fichte, *Grundlage d. Gesam. Wissenschaftslehre.*
[4]*v. sup.* p. 57 ff.

sciousness the character of (objective) existence, the other where it had the character of only being (subjectively) for consciousness. But both were reduced to one single truth, that what is or the real *per se* (*an sich*) only is so far as it is an object for consciousness, and that what is for consciousness is also objectively real. The consciousness, which is this truth, has forgotten the process by which this result has been reached; the pathway thereto lies behind it. This consciousness comes on the scene directly in the form of reason; in other words, this reason, appearing thus immediately, comes before us merely as the *certainty* of that truth. It merely gives the assurance of being all reality; it does not, however, itself *comprehend* this fact; for that forgotten pathway by which it arrives at this position is the process of comprehending what is involved in this mere assertion which it makes. And just on that account any one who has not taken this route finds the assertion unintelligible, when he hears it expressed in this abstract form—although as a matter of concrete experience he makes indeed the same assertion himself.

The kind of Idealism which does not trace the path to that result, but starts off with the bare assertion of this truth, is consequently a mere assurance, which does not understand its own nature, and cannot make itself intelligible to any one else. It announces an intuitive certainty, to which there stand in contrast other equally intuitive certainties that have been lost just along that very pathway. Hence the assurances of these other certainties are equally entitled to a place alongside the assurance of that certainty. Reason appeals to the self-consciousness of each individual consciousness: I am I, my object and my essential reality is ego; and no one will deny reason this truth. But since it rests on this appeal, it sanctions the truth of the other certainty, viz. there is for me an other; an other than "I" is to me object and true reality: or in that I am object and reality to myself, I am only so by my withdrawing myself from the other altogether and appearing alongside it as an actuality.

Only when reason comes forward as a reflexion from this opposite certainty does its assertion regarding itself appear in the form not merely of a certainty and an assurance but of a truth—and a truth not alongside others, but the only truth. Its appearing directly and immediately is the abstract form of its actual presence, the essential nature and inherent reality of which is an absolute notion, i.e. the process of its own development.

Consciousness will determine its relation to otherness or its object in various ways, according as it is at one or other stage in the development of the world-spirit into self-consciousness. How the world-spirit immediately finds and determines itself and its object at any given time, or how it appears to itself, depends on what it has already come to be, or on what it already implicitly and inherently is.

Reason is the certainty of being all reality. This its inherent nature, this reality, is still, however, through and through a universal, the pure abstraction of reality. It is the first positive character which self-consciousness *per se* is aware of being, and ego is, therefore, merely the pure, inner essence of existence, in other words, is the *Category* bare and simple. The category, which heretofore had the significance of being the inmost essence of existence—of existence indifferent to whether it is existence at all, or existence over against consciousness— is now the essential nature or simple unity of existence merely in the sense of a reality that thinks. To put it otherwise, the category means this, that existence and self-consciousness are the same being, the same not as a matter of comparison, but really and truly in and for themselves. It is only a onesided, unsound idealism which lets this unity again appear on one side as consciousness, with a reality *per se* over against it on the other.

But now this category, or simple unity of self-consciousness and being, has difference within it; for its very nature consists just in this— in being immediately one and identical with itself in otherness or in absolute difference. Difference therefore *is*, but completely transparent, a difference that is at the same time none. It appears in the form of a *plurality* of categories. Since idealism pronounces the simple unity of self-consciousness to be all reality, and makes it straightway the essentially real without first having comprehended its absolutely negative nature—only an absolutely negative reality contains within its very being negation, determinateness, or difference—still more incomprehensible is this second position, viz. that in the category there are differences, kinds or species of categories. This assurance in general, as also the assurance as to any determinate number of kinds of categories, is a new assurance, which, however, itself implies that we need no longer accept it as an assurance. For since difference starts in the pure ego, in pure understanding itself, it is thereby affirmed that here immediacy, making assurances, finding something given, must be abandoned and reflective comprehension begin. But to pick up the various categories again in any sort of way as a kind of happy find, hit upon, e.g. in the different judgments, and then to be content so to accept them, must really be regarded as an outrage on scientific thinking.[5] Where is understanding to be able to demonstrate necessity, if it is incapable of so doing in its own case, itself being pure necessity?

Now because, in this way, the pure essential being of things, as well

---

[5]This refers to Kant's "discovery" of his "table of categories."

as their aspect of difference, belongs to reason, we can, strictly speaking, no longer talk of things at all, i.e. of something which would only be present to consciousness by negatively opposing it. For the many categories are species of the pure category, which means that the pure category is still their genus or essential nature, and not opposed to them. But they are indeed that ambiguous being which contains otherness too, as opposed to the pure category in its plurality. They, in point of fact, contradict the pure category by this plurality, and the pure category must sublate them in itself, a process by which it constitutes itself the negative unity of the different elements. *Qua* negative unity, however, it puts away from itself and excludes both the diverse elements as such, and that previous immediate unity as such; it is then individual singleness—a new category, which is an exclusive form of consciousness, i.e. stands in relation to something else, an other. This individuality is its transition from its notion to an external reality, the pure "schema," which is at once a consciousness, and in consequence of its being a single individual and an excluding unit, points to the presence of an external other. But the "other" of this category is merely the "other" categories first mentioned, viz. pure essential reality and pure difference; and in this category, i.e. just in affirming the other, or in this other itself, consciousness is likewise itself too. Each of these various moments points and refers to an other; at the same time, however, they do not involve any absolute otherness. The pure category refers to the species, which pass over into the negative category, the category of exclusion, individuality; this latter, however, points back to them, it is itself pure consciousness, which is aware in each of them of being always this clear unity with itself—a unity, however, that in the same way is referred to an other, which in beng disappears, and in disappearing is once again brought into being.

We see pure consciousness here affirmed in a twofold form. In one case it is the restless activity which passes hither and thither through all its moments, seeing in them that otherness which is sublated in the process of grasping it; in the other case it is the imperturbable unity certain of its own truth. That restless activity constitutes the "other" for this unity, while this unity is the "other" for that activity; and within these reciprocally determining opposites consciousness and object alternate. Consciousness thus at one time finds itself seeking about hither and thither, and its object is what absolutely exists *per se*, and is the essentially real; at another time consciousness is aware of being the category bare and simple, and the object is the movement of the different elements. Consciousness, however, *qua* essential reality, is the whole of this process of passing out of itself *qua* simple category into individuality and the object, and of viewing this process in the object, cancelling it as distinct, appropriating it as its own, and declaring itself as this certainty of being all reality, of being both itself and its object.

Its first declaration is merely this abstract, empty phrase that everything is its own. For the certainty of being all reality is to begin with the pure category. Reason knowing itself in this sense in its object is what finds expression in abstract empty idealism;[6] it merely takes reason as reason appears at first, and by its pointing out that in all being there is this bare consciousness of a "mine," and by expressing things as sensations or ideas, it fancies it has shown that abstract "mine" of consciousness to be complete reality. It is bound, therefore, to be at the same time absolute Empiricism, because, for the filling of this empty "mine", i.e. for the element of distinction and all the further development and embodiment of it, its reason needs an impact (*Anstoss*) operating from without, in which lies the *fons et origo* of the multiplicity of sensations or ideas. This kind of idealism is thus just such a self-contradictory equivocation as scepticism, only, while the latter expresses itself negatively, the former does so in a positive way. But it fails just as completely as scepticism to link up its contradictory statements about pure consciousness being all reality, while all the time the alien impact, or sense-impressions and ideas, are equally reality. It oscillates hither and thither from one to the other and tumbles into the false, or the sensuous, infinite.[7] Since reason is all reality in the sense of the abstract "mine," and the "other" is an externality indifferent to it, there is here affirmed just that sort of knowledge of an "other" on the part of reason, which we met with before in the form of "intending" or "meaning" (*Meinen*),[8] "perceiving," and "understanding," which grasps what is "meant" and what is "perceived." Such a kind of knowledge is at the same time asserted by the very principle of this idealism itself not to be true knowledge; for only the unity of apperception is the real truth of knowledge. Pure reason as conceived by this idealism, if it is to get at this "other" which is essential to it, i.e. really is *per se*, but which it does not possess in itself—is thus thrown back on that knowledge which is not a knowledge of the real truth. It thus condemns itself knowingly and voluntarily to being an untrue kind of knowledge, and cannot get away from "meaning" and "perceiving," which for it have no truth at all. It falls into a direct contradiction; it asserts that the real has a twofold nature, consists of elements in sheer opposition, is the unity of apperception and a "thing" as well; whether a thing is called an alien impact, or an empirical entity, or sensibility, or the "thing in itself," it

---

[6]Fichte, Berkeley.
[7]Cp. *Wiss. d. Logik*, Pt. I, p. 253 ff.
[8]*v. sup.* p. 57 ff.

remains in principle precisely the same, viz. something external and foreign to that unity.

This idealism falls into such a contradiction because it asserts the abstract notion of reason to be the truth. Consequently reality comes directly before it just as much in a form which is not strictly the reality of reason at all, whereas reason all the while is intended to be all reality. Reason remains, in this case, a restless search, which in its very process of seeking declares that it is utterly impossible to have the satisfaction of finding. But actual concrete reason is not so inconsequent as this. Being at first merely the certainty that it is all reality, it is in this notion well aware that *qua* certainty, *qua* ego, it is not yet in truth all reality; and thus reason is driven on to raise its formal certainty into actual truth, and give concrete filling to the empty "mine."

A

OBSERVATION AS A PROCESS OF REASON

THIS consciousness, which takes being to mean what is its *own*, now seems, indeed, to adopt once again the attitude of "meaning"[1] and "perceiving"; but not in the sense that it is certain of what is a mere "other," but in the sense that it is certain of this "other" being itself. Formerly, consciousness merely happened to perceive various elements in the "thing," and had a certain experience in so doing. But here it itself settles the observations to be made and the experience to be had. "Meaning" and "perceiving," which formerly were superseded so far as *we* were concerned (*für uns*), are now superseded by consciousness in its own behalf (*für es*). Reason sets out to know the truth, to find in the form of a *notion* what, for "meaning" and "perceiving," is a "thing"; i.e. it seeks in thinghood to have merely the consciousness of its own self. Reason has, therefore, now a universal interest in the world, because it is certain of its presence in the world, or is certain that the actual present is rational. It seeks its "other," while knowing that it there possesses nothing else but itself: it seeks merely its own infinitude.

While, at first, merely surmising that it is in the world of reality, or knowing this only in a general way to be its own, it goes forward on this understanding and appropriates everywhere and at all points its own assured possession. It plants the symbol of its sovereignty on the heights and in the depths of reality. But this superficial "mine" is not its final and supreme interest. The joy of universal appropriation finds still in its property the alien other which abstract reason does not contain

---

[1] *v.* p. 57 ff.

within itself. Reason has the presentiment of being a deeper reality than pure ego is, and must demand that difference, the manifold diversity of being, should itself become its very own, that the ego should look at and see itself as concrete reality, and find itself present in objectively embodied form and in the shape of a "thing." But if reason probes and gropes through the inmost recesses of the life of things, and opens their every vein so that reason itself may gush out of them, then it will not achieve this desired result; it must, for its purpose, have first brought about in itself its own completion in order to be able after that to experience what its completion means.

Consciousness "observes," i.e. reason wants to find and to have itself in the form of existent object, to *be* in concrete sensuously-present form. The consciousness thus observing fancies (*meint*), and, indeed, says that it wants to discover not itself, but, on the contrary, the inner being of things *qua* things. That this consciousness "means" this and says so, lies in the fact that it is reason, but reason as such is for it not as yet object.

If it were to know reason to be equally and at once the essence of things and of itself, and knew that reason can only be actually present in consciousness in the form and shape peculiarly appropriate to reason, then it would descend into the depths of its own being, and seek reason there rather than in things. If it had found reason there, it would again turn from that and be directed upon concrete reality, in order to see therein its own sensuous expression, but would, at the same time, take that sensuous form to be essentially a notion.

Reason, as it immediately appears in the form of conscious certainty of being all reality, takes its reality in the sense of immediacy of being, and also takes the unity of ego with this objective existence in the sense of an *immediate* unity, a unity in which it (reason) has not yet separated and then again united the moments of being and ego, or, in other words, a unity which reason has not yet come to understand. It, therefore, when appearing as conscious observation, turns to things with the idea that it is really taking them as sensuous things opposed to the ego. But its actual procedure contradicts this idea, for it knows things, it transforms their sensuous character into conceptions, i.e. just into a kind of being which at the same time is ego; it transforms thought into an existent thought, or being into a thought-constituted being, and, in fact, asserts that things have truth merely as conceptions. In this process, it is only what the things are that consciousness in observation becomes aware of; we, however [who are tracing the nature of this experience], become aware of what conscious observation itself is. The outcome of its process, however, will be that this consciousness becomes aware of being for itself what it is in itself [i.e. becomes aware of being to itself what, in the meantime, it is to us].

We have to consider the operation of this observational phase of reason in all the various moments of its activity. It takes up this attitude towards Nature, Mind, and finally towards the relation of both in the form of sense-existence; and in all these it seeks to find itself as a definitely existing concrete actuality.

a (1)

OBSERVATION OF NATURE

WHEN the unreflective consciousness speaks of observation and experience as being the fountain of truth, the phrase may possibly sound as if the whole business were a matter of tasting, smelling, feeling, hearing, and seeing. It forgets, in its zeal for tasting, smelling, etc., to say that, in point of fact, it has really and rationally determined for itself already the object thus sensuously apprehended, and this determination of the object is at least as important for it as that apprehension. It will also as readily admit that its whole concern is not simply a matter of perceiving, and will not allow, e.g. the perception that this penknife lies beside this snuff-box to pass for an "observation." What is perceived should, at least, have the significance of a universal, and not of a sensuous particular "this."

The universal, here regarded, is, only in the first instance, what remains identical with itself; its movement is merely the uniform recurrence of the same operation. The consciousness, which thus far finds in the object merely universality or the abstract "mine," must take upon itself the movement peculiar to the object; and, since it is not yet at the stage of understanding that object, it must, at least, be the recollection of it, a recollection which expresses in a universal way what, in actual fact, is merely present in a particular form. This superficial way of educing from particularity, and the equally superficial form of universality into which the sense element is merely taken up, without the sense element having in itself become a universal—this description of things is not as yet a process effected in the object itself. The process really takes place solely in the function of *describing.* The object as it is described has consequently lost interest; when one object is being described another must be taken in hand and ever sought, so as not to put a stop to the process of description. If it is no longer easy to find new and whole things, then there is nothing for it but to turn back upon those already found, in order to divide them still further, break them up into component parts and look out for any new aspects of thinghood that still remain in them. There can never be an end to the material at the disposal of this restlessly active instinct. To find a new genus of distinctive significance, or even to discover a new planet, which although an individual entity yet possesses the nature of a universal, can only fall to the lot of those who are lucky enough. But the boundary line of what, like elephant, oak, gold, is markedly distinctive, the line of demarcation of what is genus and species, passes through many stages into the endless particularization of the chaos of plants and animals, kinds of rocks, or of metals, forms of earth, etc., etc., that only force and craft can bring to light. In this realm where universality means indeterminateness, where particularity now approximates to singleness, and again at this point and that even descends to it entirely, there is offered an inexhaustible supply of material for observation and description to deal with. Here, where a boundless field is opened up, at the boundary line of the universal it can have found not an immeasurable wealth, but instead, merely the limitations of nature and of its own operation. It can no longer know whether what seems to have being *per se* is not a chance accident. What bears the impress of a confused or immature feeble structure, barely evolving from the stage of elementary indeterminateness, cannot claim even to be described.

While this seeking and describing seem to be concerned merely with things, we see that in point of fact it does not continue in the form of sense-perception. Rather, what enables things to be *known* is more important for description than the range of sense properties still left over, qualities which, of course, the thing itself cannot do without, but which consciousness dispenses with. Through this distinction into what is essential and what is unessential, the notion rises out of the dispersion of sensibility, and knowledge thereby makes it clear that it has to do at least quite as essentially with its own self as with things. This twofold essentiality produces a certain hesitation as to whether what is essential and necessary for knowledge is also so in the case of the things. On the one hand, the qualifying "marks" have merely to serve the purpose of knowledge in distinguishing things *inter se*; on the other hand, however, it is not the unessential quality of things that has to be known, but that feature in virtue of which they themselves break away from the general continuity of being as a whole, separate themselves from others and stand by themselves. The distinguishing "marks" must not only have an essential relation to knowledge but also be the essential characteristics of the things, and the system of marks devised must conform to the system of nature itself, and merely express this system. This follows necessarily from the very principle and meaning of reason; and the instinct of reason—for it operates in this process of observation merely as an instinct—has also in its systems attained this unity, a unity where its objects are so constituted that they carry their own essential reality with them, involve an existence on their own account, and are not simply an incident of a given particular time, or a particular place. The distinguishing marks of animals, for example, are taken from their claws and teeth; for, in point of fact, not only does knowledge distinguish thus one animal from another, but each animal *itself* separates itself off thereby; it preserves itself independently by means of these weapons, and keeps itself detached from the universal nature. A plant, on the other hand, never gets the length of existing for itself; it touches merely the boundary line of individuality. This line is where plants show the semblance of diremption and separation by the possession of different sex-characters; this furnishes, therefore, the principle for distinguishing plants *inter se*. What, however, stands on a still lower level cannot of itself any longer distinguish itself from another; it gets lost when the contrast comes into play. Quiescent being and being in a relation come into conflict with one another; a "thing" in the latter case is something different from a "thing" in the former state; whereas the "individuum" consists in preserving itself in relation to another. What, however, is incapable of this and becomes in chemical fashion something other than it is empirically, confuses knowledge and gives rise to the same doubt as to whether knowledge is to hold to the one side or the other, since the thing has itself no self-consistency, and these two sides fall apart within it.

In those systems where the elements involve general selfsameness, this character connotes at once the selfsameness of knowledge and of things themselves as well. But this expansion of these self-identical characteristics, each of which describes undisturbed the entire circuit of its course and gets full scope to do as it likes, necessarily leads as readily to its very opposite, leads to the confusion of these characteristics. For the qualifying mark, the general characteristic is the unity of opposite factors, viz. of what is determinate, and of what is *per se* universal. It must, therefore, break asunder into this opposition. If, now, on one side the characteristic overmasters the universality in which its essence lies, on the other side, again, this universality equally keeps that characteristic under control, forces the latter on to its boundary line, and there mingles together its distinctions and its essential constituents. Observation which kept them apart in orderly fashion, and thought it had hold there of something stable and fixed, finds the principles overlapping and dominating one another, sees confusions formed and transitions made from one to another; here it finds united what it took at first to be absolutely separated, and there separated what it considered connected. Hence, when observation thus holds by the unbroken selfsameness of being, it has here, just in the most general determinations given—e.g. in the case of the essential marks of an animal or a plant—to see itself tormented with instances, which rob it of every determination, silence the universality it reached, and reduce it again to unreflective observation and description.

Observation, which confines itself in this way to what is simple, or restricts the sensuously dispersed elements by the universal, thus finds its principle confused by its object, because what is determined must by its very nature get lost in its opposite. Reason, therefore, must pass from that inert characteristic which had the semblance of stability, and go on to observe it as it really is in truth, viz. as relating itself to its opposite. What are called essential marks are passive characteristics, which, when expressed and apprehended as simple, do not bring out what constitutes their real nature—which is to be vanishing moments of its process of withdrawing and betaking itself into itself. Since the instinct of reason now arrives at the point of looking for the characteristic in the light of its true nature—that of essentially passing over into its opposite and not existing apart by itself and for its own sake—it seeks after the *Law* and the notion of law. It seeks for them, moreover, as existing reality; but this feature of concrete reality will in point of fact disappear before reason, and the aspects of the law will become for it mere moments or abstractions, so that the law comes to light in the nature of the notion, which has destroyed within itself the indifferent subsistence of sensuous reality.

To the consciousness observing, the truth of the law is given in "experience," in the way that sense existence is object for consciousness; the truth is not given in and for itself. If, however, the law does not have its truth in the notion, it is something contingent, not a necessity, in fact, not a law. But its being essentially in the form of a notion does not merely not contradict its being present for observation to deal with, but really gives it on that account necessary existence, and makes it an object for observation. The universal in the sense of a rational universality is also universal in the sense implied in the above notion: its being is *for* consciousness, it presents itself there as the real, the objective present; the notion sets itself forth in the form of thinghood and sensuous existence. But it does not, on that account, lose its nature and fall into the condition of immovable subsisting passivity, or mere adventitious (*gleichgültig*) succession. What is universally valid is also universally effective: what *ought to be*, as a matter of fact, *is* too; and what merely *should* be, and is *not*, has no real truth. The instinct of reason is entirely within its rights when it stands firm on this point, and refuses to be led astray by *entia intellectus* which merely *ought* to be and, *qua* ought, should be allowed to have truth even though they are to be met with nowhere in experience; and declines to be turned aside by the hypothetical suggestions and all the other impalpable unrealities designed in the interest of an everlasting "ought to be" which never *is*.[1] For reason is just this certainty of having reality; and what consciousness is not aware of as a real self (*Selbstwesen*), i.e. what does not appear, is nothing for consciousness at all.

The true nature of law, viz.: that it essentially is reality, no doubt again assumes for consciousness which remains at the level of observation, the form of an opposite over against the notion and the inherently universal; in other words, this consciousness does not take such an object as its law to be a reality of reason; it thinks it has got there something external and foreign. But it contradicts its own idea by actually and in fact not taking its universality to mean that all individual things of sense must have given evidence of the law to enable the truth of the law to be asserted. The assertion that stones, when raised from the ground and let go, fall, does not at all require us to make the experiment with all stones. It means most likely that this experiment must have been tried at least with a good many, and from that we can by analogy draw an inference about the rest with the greatest probability or with perfect right. Yet analogy not only gives no perfect right, but, on account of its nature, contradicts itself so often that the inference to be drawn from analogy itself rather is that analogy does not permit an inference to be drawn. Probability, which is what analogy would come to, loses, when face to face with truth, every distinction of less and greater; be the probability as great as it may it is nothing as against truth. The instinct of reason, however, takes, as a matter of fact, laws of that sort for truth. It is when reason does not find necessity in them that it resorts to making this distinction, and lowers the truth of the matter to the level of probability, in order to bring out the imperfect way in which truth is presented to the consciousness that as yet has no insight into the pure notion; for universality is before it merely in the form of simple immediate universality. But, at the same time, on account of this universality, the law has truth for consciousness. That a stone falls is true for consciousness, because it is aware of the stone being heavy, i.e. because in weight taken by itself as such, the stone has that essential relation to the earth expressed in the fact of falling. Consciousness thus finds in experience the objective being of the law, but has it there in the form of a notion as well; and only because of both factors together is the law true for consciousness. The law, therefore, is accepted as a law because it presents itself in the sphere of appearance and is, at the same time, in its very nature a notion.

The instinct of reason in this type of consciousness, because the law

---

[1]Directed against Kant and Fichte.

is at the same time inherently a notion, proceeds to give the law and its moments a purely conceptual form; and proceeds to do this of necessity, but without knowing that this is what it seeks to do. It puts the law to the test of experiment. As the law first appears, it is enveloped in particulars of sense, and the notion constituting its nature is involved with empirical elements. The instinct of reason sets to work to find out by experiment what follows in such and such circumstances. By so doing the law seems only to be plunged still further into sense; but sense existence really gets lost in the process. The inner purport of this investigation is to find pure conditions of the law; and this means nothing else (even if the consciousness stating the fact were to think it meant something different) than completely to bring out the law in conceptual shape and detach its moments entirely from determinate specific existence. For example, negative electricity, which is known at first, say, in the form of resin-electricity, while positive electricity comes before us as glass-electricity—these, by means of experiments, lose altogether such a significance, and become purely positive and negative electricity, neither of which is bound up any longer with things of a particular kind; and we can no longer say that there are bodies which are electrical positively, others electrical negatively. In the same way the relationship of acid and base and their reaction constitute a law in which these opposite factors appear as bodies. Yet these sundered things have no reality; the power which tears them apart cannot prevent them from entering forthwith into a process; for they are merely this relation. They cannot subsist and be indicated by themselves apart, like a tooth or a claw. That it is their very nature to pass over directly into a neutral product makes their existence lie in being cancelled and superseded, or makes it into a universal; and acid and base possess truth merely *qua* universal. Just, then, as glass and resin can be equally well positively as negatively electrified, in the same way acid and base are not attached as properties or qualities to this or that reality; each thing is only relatively acidulate and basic; what seems to be an absolute base or an absolute acid gets in the so-called Synsomates[2] the opposite significance in relation to an other.

The result of the experiments is in this way to cancel the moments or inner significations as properties of specific things, and free the predicates from their subjects. These predicates are found merely as uni-

---

[2]A term employed by a chemist, Winterl, at the beginning of the nineteenth century to denote combinations intermediate in character between physical mixtures and chemical combinations. In synsomates the bodies undergo in the product, e.g. a change of colour, specific density, and even weight; these changes do not take place in mere physical mixtures, and yet they do not constitute chemical combination. Examples of synsomates are the blending of water and alcohol, and amalgams of minerals.

versal, and in truth that is what they are. Because of this self-subsistence they therefore get the name of kinds of "matter," which is neither a body nor a property of a body; certainly no one would call acid, positive and negative electricity, heat,[3] etc., bodies.

Matter, on the contrary, is not a thing that exists, it is being in the sense of universal being, or being in the way the concept is being. Reason, still instinctive, correctly draws this distinction without being conscious that it (reason), by the very fact of its testing the law in every sense-particular, cancels the merely sensuous existence of the law; and, when it construes the moments of the law as forms of matter, their essential nature is taken to be something universal, and specifically expressed as a non-sensuous element of sense, an incorporeal and yet objective existence.

We have now to see what turn its result takes, and what new shape this activity of observation will, in consequence, assume. As the outcome and truth of this experimentation we find *pure law*, which is freed from sensuous elements; we see it as a concept, which, while present in sense, operates there independently and unrestrained, while enveloped in sense, is detached from it and is a concept bare and simple. This, which is in truth result and essence, now comes before this consciousness itself, but as an object; moreover, since the object is not exactly a result for it and is unrelated to the preceding process, the object is a specific kind of object, and the relation of consciousness to it takes the form of another kind of observation.

a (2)

OBSERVATION OF ORGANIC NATURE

Such an object which sustains the procedure in the simple activity of the notion is an organism.

Organic existence is this absolutely fluid condition wherein determinateness, which would only put it in relation to an other, is dissolved. Inorganic things involve determinateness in their very essence; and on that account a thing realizes the completeness of the moments of the notion only along with another thing, and hence gets lost when it enters the dialectic movement. In the case of an organic being, on the other hand, all determinate characteristics, by means of which it is palpable to another, are held under the control of the simple organic unity; none of them comes forward as essential and capable of detach-

---

[3]Heat, e.g. is a "mode of motion," a form of "energy."

ing itself from the rest and relating itself to an other being. What is organic, therefore, preserves itself in its very relation.

The aspects of law on which the instinct of reason directs its observation here are, as we see from the above, in the first instance organic nature and inorganic nature in their relation to one another. The latter means for organic nature just the free play—a freedom opposed to the simple notion of organic nature—of loosely connected characteristics in which individuated nature is at once dissolved, and out of the continuity of which the individuated unit of nature at the same time breaks away and exists separately. Air, water, earth, zones and climate are universal elements of this sort, which make up the indeterminate simple being of natural individualities, and in which these are at the same time reflected into themselves. Neither the individuality nor the natural element is absolutely self-contained. On the contrary: in the independent detachment, which observation finds these assuming towards one another, they stand at the same time in essential relation to one another, but in such a way that their independence and mutual indifference form the predominating feature, and only in part become abstractions. Here, then, law appears as the relation of an element to the formative process of the organic being, which at one moment has the element over against itself, at another exhibits it within its own self-determining organic structure. But laws like these: animals belonging to the air are of the nature of birds, those belonging to water have the constitution of fish, animals in northerly latitudes have thick coats of hair, and so on—such laws exhibit a degree of poverty which does not do justice to the manifold variety of organic nature. Besides the fact that the free activity of organic nature can readily divest its forms of determinate characters like these, and everywhere presents of necessity exceptions to such laws or rules, as we might call them; the characterization of those very animals to which they do apply is so very superficial that even the necessity of the "laws" can be nothing else but superfcial too, and does not carry us further than what is implied in speaking of the "great influence" of environment on the organism. And this does not tell us what properly is due to that influence and what is not. Such like relations of organic beings to the elements they live in cannot therefore be strictly called laws at all. For, on the one hand, such a relation, when we look at its content, does not exhaust, as we saw, the range of the organic beings considered, and on the other, the terms of the relation itself stand indifferently apart from one another and express no necessity. In the concept of an acid lies the notion of a base, just as the notion of positive electricity implies that of negative; but even though we do find as a fact a thick coat of hair associated with northerly latitudes, the structure of a fish with water, or that of birds with air, there is nothing in the notion of the north implying the notion of a thick covering of hair, the notion of the structure of fish does not lie in the notion of the sea, nor that of birds in that of the air. Because of this free detachment of the two notions from one another there *are* as a fact also land animals with the essential characters of a bird, of fish, and so on. The necessity, just because it cannot be conceived to be an inner necessity of the object, ceases also to have a foothold in sense, and can be no longer observed in actual reality, but has quitted the sphere of reality. Finding thus no place in the real object itself, it becomes what is called a "teleological relation," a relation which is *external* to what is related, and consequently the very reverse of a law of its constitution. It is an idea entirely detached from the necessity of nature, a thought which leaves this necessity of nature behind and floats above it all by itself.[4]

If the relation, above alluded to, of organic existence to the elemental conditions of nature does not express its true being, the notion of Purpose, on the other hand, does contain it. The observing attitude does not indeed take the τέλος to be the genuine essence of organic existence; this notion seems to it to fall outside the real nature of the organism, and is then merely that external teleological relation above mentioned. Yet looking at how the organic being was previously characterized, the organic is in point of fact just realized concrete purpose. For since *itself* maintains *itself* in relation to another, it is just that kind of natural existence in which nature reflects itself into the notion, and the moments of necessity separated out [by Understanding]—a cause and an effect, an active and a passive—are here brought together and combined into a single unity. In this way we have here not only something appearing as a *result* of necessity, but, because it has returned to itself, the last or the result is just as much the first which starts the process, and is to itself the purpose which it realizes. What is organic does not produce something, it merely conserves itself, or what *is* produced is as much there already as produced.

We must elucidate this principle more fully, both as it is in itself and as it is for the instinct of reason, in order to see how reason finds itself there, but does not know itself in what it finds. The concept of purpose, then, which rational observation has reached, is, while reason has apprehended it in consciousness, given to reason as something actually real as well; it is not merely an external relation of the actual, but its inner being. This actual, which is itself a purpose, is related purposively to an other, i.e. its relation is a contingent one with respect to what both

---

[4]Cp. with the above, the oscillation between the mechanical and teleological conception of "law" in theoretical biology.

are immediately; *prima facie* they are both self-subsistent and indifferent to one another. The real nature of their relation, however, is something different from what they thus appear to be, and its effect has another meaning than sense-perception directly finds. The necessity inherent in the process is concealed, and comes out at the end, but in such a way that this very end shows it to have been also the first. The end, however, shows this priority of itself by the fact that nothing comes out of the alteration the act produced, but what was there already. Or, again, if we start from what is first, this, in coming to the end or the result of its act, merely returns to itself, and, just by so doing, it demonstrates itself to be that which has itself as its end, that is to say, *qua* first it has already returned to itself, or is self-contained, is in and for itself. What, then, it arrives at by the process of its action is itself; and its arriving merely at itself means feeling itself, is its self-feeling. Thus we have here, no doubt, the distinction between what it is and what it seeks; but this is merely the semblance of a distinction, and consequently it is a notion in its very nature.

This is exactly, however, the way self-consciousness is constituted. It distinguishes itself in like manner from itself, without any distinction being thereby established. Hence it is that it finds in observation of organic nature nothing else than this kind of reality; it finds itself in the form of a thing, as a *life*, and yet, between what it is itself and what it has found, draws a distinction which is, however, no distinction. Just as the instinct of an animal is to seek and consume food, but thereby elicits nothing except itself; similarly too the instinct of reason in its search merely finds reason itself. An animal ends with self-feeling. The instinct of reason, on the other hand, is at the same time *self-consciousness*. But because it is merely instinct, it is put on one side as against consciousness, and in the latter finds its opposite. Its satisfaction is, therefore, broken in two by this opposite; it finds itself, viz. the purpose, and also finds this purpose in the shape of a thing. But the purpose is seen to lie, in the first instance, apart from the thing presenting itself as a purpose. In the second place, this purpose *qua* purpose is at the same time objective; it is taken to fall, therefore, not within the observing consciousness, but within another intelligence.

Looked at more closely, this character lies also just as much in the notion of the thing—that of being in itself purpose. It preserves itself; this means at one and the same time it is its nature to conceal the controlling necessity and to present that necessity in the form of a contingent relation. For its freedom, its being on its own account, means just that it behaves towards its necessary condition as something indifferent. It thus presents itself as if it were something whose notion falls apart from its existence. In this way reason is compelled to look on its own proper notion as falling outside it, to look at it as a thing, as that towards which it is indifferent, and which in consequence is reciprocally indifferent towards it [reason] and towards its own notion. *Qua* instinct it continues to remain within this state of being, this condition of indifference; and the thing expressing the notion remains for it something other than this notion, and the notion other than the thing. Thus for reason the thing organized is only *per se* a purpose in the sense that the necessity, which is presented as concealed within the action of the thing—for the active agency there takes up the attitude of being indifferent and independent—falls outside the organism itself.

Since, however, the organic *qua* purpose *per se* cannot behave in any other way than as organic, the fact of its being *per se* a purpose is also apparent and sensibly present, and as such it is observed. What is organic shows itself when observed to be something self-preserving, returning and returned into itself. But in this state of being, observation does not recognize the concept of purpose, or does not know that the notion of purpose is not in an intelligence anywhere else, but just exists here and in the form of a thing. Observation makes a distinction between the concept of purpose and self-existence and self-preservation, which is not a distinction at all. That it is no distinction is something of which it is not aware; what it is aware of is an activity which appears contingent and indifferent towards what is brought about by that activity, and towards the unity which is all the while the principle connecting both; that activity and this purpose are taken to fall asunder.

On this view the special function of the organic is the inner operating activity lying between its first and last stage, so far as this activity implies the character of singleness. So far, however, as the activity has the character of universality, and the active agent is equated with what is the outcome of its operation, this purposive activity as such would not belong to organic beings. That single activity, which is merely a means, comes, owing to its individual form, to be determined by an entirely individual or contingent necessity. What an organic being does for the preservation of itself as an individual, or of itself *qua* genus, is, therefore, quite lawless as regards this immediate content: for notion and universal fall outside it. Its activity would accordingly be empty functioning without any content in it; it would not even be the functioning of a machine, for this has a purpose and its activity in consequence a definite content. If it were deserted in this way by the universal, it would be an activity of a mere being *qua* being, i.e. would be an activity like that of an acid or a base, not forthwith reflected into itself—a function which could not be cut off from its immediate existence, nor give up this existence (which gets lost in the relation to its opposite), but could preserve itself. The kind of being whose functioning is here under consideration is, however, set down as a thing preserving itself in its relation to its opposite. The activity as such is nothing but the bare insubstantial form of its independent existence on its own account; and the purpose of the activity, its substances—a substance, which is not simply a determinate being, but the universal—does not fall outside the activity. It is an activity reverting into itself by its own nature, and is not turned back into itself by any alien, external agency.

This union of universality and activity, however, is not a matter for this attitude of observation, because that unity is essentially the inner movement of what is organic, and can only be apprehended conceptually. Observation, however, seeks the moments in the form of existence and duration; and because the organic whole consists essentially in not containing the moments in that form, and in not letting them be found within it in that way, this observing consciousness, by its way of looking at the matter, transforms the opposition into one which conforms and is adapted to its own point of view.

An organism comes before the observing consciousness in this manner as a relation of two fixed and existing moments—as a relation of elements in an opposition, whose two factors seem in one respect really given in observation, while in another respect, as regards their content, they express the opposition of the organic concept of purpose and actual reality. But because the notion, as such is there effaced, this takes place in an obscure and superficial way, where thought sinks to the level of mere ideal presentation. Thus we see the notion taken much in the sense of what is inner, reality in the sense of what is outer; and their relation gives rise to the law that "the outer is the expression of the inner."

Let us consider more closely this inner with its opposite and their relation to one another. In the first place we find that the two factors of the law no longer have such an import as we found in the case of previous laws, where the elements appeared as independent things, each being a particular body; nor, again, in the second place, do we find that the universal is to have its existence somewhere else outside what actually is. On the contrary, the organic being is, in undivided oneness and as a whole, the fundamental fact, it is the content of inner and outer, and is the same for both. The opposition is on that account of a purely formal character; its real sides have the same ultimate principle inherently constituting them what they are. At the same time, however, since inner and outer are also opposite *realities* and each is a distinct being for observation, they each seem to observation to have a peculiar content of their own. This peculiar content, since it consists of the same substance, or the same organic unity, can, however, in point of fact, be only a different form of that unity, of that substance; and this is indicated by observation when it says that the outer is merely the *expression* of the inner.

We have seen in the case of the concept of purpose the same characteristic features of the relation, viz. the indifferent independence of the diverse factors, and their unity in that independence, a unity in which they disappear.

We have now to see what shape and embodiment inner and outer assume in actually existing. The inner as such must have an outer being and an embodiment, just as much as the outer as such; for the inner is an object, or is affirmed as being, and as present for observation to deal with.

The organic substance *qua* inner is the *Soul* simply, the pure notion of purpose or the universal which in dividing into its discrete elements remains all the same a universal fluent continuity, and hence in its being appears as activity or the movement of vanishing reality; while, on the other hand, the outer, opposed to that existing inner, subsists in the passive being of the organic. The law, as the relation of that inner to this outer, consequently expresses it content, now by setting forth universal moments, or simple essential elements, and again by setting forth the realized essential nature or the form and shape actually assumed. Those first simple organic properties, to call them so, are Sensibility, Irritability, and Reproduction. These properties, at least the two first, seem indeed to refer not to any and every organism, but merely to the animal organism. Moreover, the vegetable level of organic life expresses in point of fact only the bare and simple notion of an organism, which does not develop and evolve its moments. Hence in regard to those moments, so far as observation has to take account of them, we must confine ourselves to the organism which presents them existing in developed form.

As to these moments, then, they are directly derived from the notion of self-purpose, of a being whose end is its own self. For Sensibility expresses in general the simple notion of organic reflexion into itself, or the universal continuity of this notion. Irritability, again, expresses organic elasticity, the capacity to exercise the function of reacting simultaneously with self-reflexion, and expresses, in contrast to the previous state of being passively and inertly within itself, the condition of being explicitly actualized—a realization, where that abstract existence for its own sake is an existence for something else. Reproduction, however, is the operation of this entire self-reflected organism, its activity as having its purpose in itself, its activity *qua* genus, wherein the individual repels itself from itself, where in procreating it repeats either the organic parts or the whole individual. Reproduction, taken in the sense of self-preservation in general, expresses the formal principle or conception of the organic, or the fact of Sensibility; but it is, properly speaking, the realized notion of organic existence, or the whole, which either *qua* individual returns into itself through the process of producing individual parts of itself, or *qua* genus does so through the production of distinct individuals.

The other significance of these organic elements, viz. as outer, is their embodiment in a given shape; here they assume the form of actual but at the same time universal parts, or appear as organic systems. Sensibility is embodied in the form, for instance, of a nervous system, irritability, of a muscular system, reproduction, of an intestinal system for the preservation of the individual and the species.

Laws peculiar to organic life, accordingly, concern a relation of the organic moments, taking account of their twofold significance—viz. of being in one respect a part of definite organic formation or embodiment, and in another respect a continuous universal element of a determinate kind, running through all those systems. Thus in giving expression to a law of that sort, a specific kind of sensibility, e.g. would find, *qua* moment of the whole organism, its expression in a determinately formed nervous system, or it would also be connected with a determinate reproduction of the organic parts of the individual or with the propagation of the whole, and so on. Both aspects of such a law can be observed. The external is in its very conception being for another; sensibility, e.g. finds its immediately realized form in the sensitive system; and, *qua* universal property, it is in its outer expressions an objective fact as well. The aspect which is called "inner" has its own "outer" aspect, which is distinct from what is in general called the outer.

Both the aspects of an organic law would thus certainly be open to observation, but not the laws of their relation. And observation is inadequate to perceive these laws, not because, *qua* observation, it is too short-sighted, i.e. not because, instead of proceeding empirically, we ought to start from the "Idea"—for such laws, if they were something real must, as a matter of fact, be actual, and must thus be observable; it is rather because the thought of laws of this sort proves to have no truth at all.

The relation assumed the role of a law in the case where the universal organic property had formed itself in an organic system into a thing and there found its own embodied image and copy, so that both were the same reality, present, in the one case, as universal moment, in the other, as thing. But besides, the inner aspect is also by itself a relation of several aspects; and hence to begin with there is presented the idea of a law as a relation of the universal organic activities or properties to one another. Whether such a law is possible has to be decided from the nature of such a property. Such a property, however, being universal and of a fluid nature, is, on the one hand, not something restricted like a thing, keeping itself within the distinction of a definite mode of existence, which is to constitute its shape and form: sensibility goes beyond the nervous system and pervades all the other systems of the organism. On the other hand, such a property is a universal moment, which is essentially undivided, and inseparable from reaction, or irritability, and reproduction. For, being reflection into self, it *eo ipso* already implies reaction. Merely to be reflected into itself is to be a passive, or lifeless being, and not sensibility; just as action—which is the same as reaction—when not reflected into self, is not irritability. Reflexion in action or reaction, and action or reaction in reflexion, is just that whose unity constitutes the organic being, a unity which is synonymous with organic reproduction. It follows from this that in every mode of the organism's actuality there must be present the same quantity of sensibility—when we consider, in the first instance, the relation of sensibility and irritability to one another—as of irritability, and that an organic phenomenon can be apprehended and determined or, if we like, explained, just as much in terms of the one as of the other. What one man takes for high sensibility, another may just as rightly consider high irritability. and an irritability of the *same* degree. If they are called factors, and this is not to be a meaningless phrase, it is thereby expressly stated that they are moments of the notion; in other words, the real object, the essential nature of which this notion constitutes, contains them both alike within it, and if the object is in one way characterized as very sensitive, it must be also spoken of in the other way as likewise very irritable.

If they are distinguished, as they must be, they are so in their true nature (*dem Begriffe nach*), and their opposition is *qualitative*. But when, besides this true distinction, they are also set down as different, *qua* existent and for thought, as they might be if made aspects of the law, then they appear quantitatively distinct. Their peculiar qualitative opposition thus passes into quantity; and hence arise laws of this sort, e.g. that sensibility and irritability stand in inverse quantitative relations, so that as the one increases the other diminishes; or better, taking directly the quantity itself as the content, that the magnitude of something increases as its smallness diminishes.

Should a specific content be given to this law, however, by saying, for example, that the size of a *hole* increases the more we decrease what it is filled with, then this inverse relation might be just as well changed into a direct relation and expressed in the form that the quantity of a hole increases in direct ratio to the amount of things we take away—a tautological proposition, whether expressed as a direct or an inverse relation; so expressed it comes merely to this that a quantity increases as this quantity increases. The hole and what fills it and is removed from it are qualitatively opposed, but the real content there and its specific quantity are in both one and the same, and similarly the increase of magnitude and decrease of smallness are the same, and their meaningless opposition runs into a tautology. In like manner the organic moments are equally inseparable in their real content, and in their quantity which is the quantity of that reality. The one decreases only with the other, and only increases with it, for one has literally a significance only so far as the other is present. Or rather, it is a matter of indifference whether an organic phenomenon is considered as irritability or as sensibility; this is so in general, and likewise when its magnitude is in question: just as it is indifferent whether we speak of the increase of a hole as an increase of the hole *qua* emptiness or as an increase of the filling removed from it. Or, again, a number, say three, is equally great, whether I take it positively or negatively; and if I increase the three to four, the positive as well as the negative becomes four: just as the south pole in the case of a magnet is precisely as strong as its north pole, or a positive electricity or an acid, is exactly as strong as its negative, or the base on which it operates.

An organic existence is such a quantum, like the number three or a magnet, etc. It is that which is increased or diminished, and if it is increased, then both its factors are increased, as much as both poles of the magnet or both kinds of electricity increase if the potential of a magnet or of one of the electric currents is raised.

That both are just as little different in intension and extension, that the one cannot decrease in extension and increase in intension, while the other conversely has to diminish its intension and increase in extension—this comes from the same notion of an unreal and empty opposition. The real intension is absolutely as great as the extension and vice versa.

What really happens in framing a law of this kind is obviously that at the outset irritability and sensibility are taken to constitute the specifically determinate organic opposition. This content, however, is lost sight of and the opposition goes off into a formal opposition of quantitative increase and diminution, or of different intension and extension—an opposition which has no longer anything to do with the nature of sensibility and irritability, and no longer expresses it. Hence this mere playing at law-making is not confined to organic moments, but can be carried on everywhere with everything and rests in general on want of acquaintance with the logical nature of these oppositions.

Lastly, if, instead of sensibility and irritability, reproduction is brought into relation with one or other of them, then there is wanting even the occasion for framing laws of this kind; for reproduction does not stand in any opposition to those moments, as they are opposed to one another; and since the making of such laws assumes this opposition, there is no possibility here of its even appearing to take place.

The law-making just considered implies the differences of the organism, taken in the sense of moments of its notion, and, strictly speaking, should be an *a priori* process. But it essentially involves this idea, that those differences have the significance of being present as something given, and the attitude of mere observation has in any case to confine itself merely to their actual *existence*. Organic reality necessarily has within it such an opposition as its notion expresses, and which can be determined as irritability and sensibility, as these again both appear distinct from reproduction. The aspect in which the moments of the notion of organism are here considered, their Externality, is the proper and peculiar immediate externality of the inner; not the outer which is the outer embodied form of the whole organism; the inner is to be considered in relation to this later on.

If, however, the opposition of the moments is apprehended as it is found in actual existence, then sensibility, irritability, reproduction sink to the level of common properties, which are universals just as indifferent towards one another as specific weight, colour, hardness, etc. In this sense, it may doubtless be observed that one organic being is more sensitive, or more irritable, or has a greater reproductive capacity than another: just as we may observe that the sensibility, etc., of one is in kind different from that of another, that one responds differently from another to a given simulus, e.g. a horse behaves differently towards oats from what it does towards hay, and a dog again differently towards both, and so on. These differences can as readily be observed as that one body is harder than another, and so on.

But these sense properties, hardness, colour, etc., as also the phenomena of responding to the stimulus of oats, of irritability under certain kinds of load, or of producing the number and kind of young—all such properties and phenomena, when related to one another and compared *inter se*, essentially defy the attempt to reduce them to law. For the characteristic of their being sensuous facts consists just in their existing in complete indifference to one another, and in manifesting the freedom of nature emancipated from the control of the notion, rather than the unity of a relation—in exhibiting nature's irrational way of playing up and down the scale of contingent quantity between the moments of the notion, rather than in setting forth these moments themselves.

It is the other aspect, in which the simple moments of the notion of organism are compared with the moments of the actual embodiment, that would first furnish the law proper for expressing the true outer as the copy of the inner.

Now because those simple moments are properties that permeate and pervade the whole, they do not find such a detached real expression in the organic thing as to form what we call an individual system with a definite structure (*Gestalt*). Or, again, if the abstract idea of organism is truly expressed in those three moments merely because they are nothing stable, but moments of the notion and its process, the organism, on the other hand, *qua* a definite embodiment, is not exhaustively expressed in those three determinate systems in the way anatomy analyses and describes them. So far as such systems are to be found in their actual reality and rendered legitimate by being so found, we must also bear in mind that anatomy not only puts before us three systems of that sort, but a good many others as well.

Further, apart from this, the sensitive system as a whole must mean something quite different from what is called a nervous system, the irritable system something different from the muscular system, the reproductive from the intestinal mechanism of reproduction. In the systems constituting an embodied form (*Gestalt*) the organism is apprehended from the abstract side of lifeless physical existence: so taken, its moments are elements of a corpse and fall to be dealt with by anatomy; they do not appertain to knowledge and to the living organism. *Qua* parts of that sort they have really ceased to *be*, for they cease to be processes. Since the being of an organism consists essentially in universality, or reflexion into self, the being of its totality, like its moments, cannot consist in an anatomical system. The actual expression of the whole, and the externalization of its moments, are really found only as a process and a movement, running throughout the various parts of the embodied organism; and in this process what is extracted as an individual system and fixated so, appears essentially as a fluid moment. So that the reality which anatomy finds cannot be taken for its real being, but only that reality as a process, a process in which alone even the anatomical parts have a significance.

We see, then, that the moments of the "inner" being of the organism taken separately by themselves are not capable of furnishing aspects of a law of being, since in a law of that sort they are predicated of an objective existence, are distinguished from one another, and thus each aspect would not be able to be equally named in place of the other. Further, we see that, when placed on one side, they do not find in the other aspect their realization in a fixed system; for this fixed system is as little something that could convey truly the general nature of organic existence, as it is the expression of those moments of the inner life of the organism. The essential nature of what is organic, since this is in-

herently something universal, lies altogether rather in having its moments equally universal in concrete reality, i.e. in having them as permeating processes, and not in giving a copy of the universal in an isolated thing.

In this manner the idea of a law in the case of organic existence slips
altogether from our grasp. The law wants to grasp and express the opposition as static aspects, and to attach as predicates of them the characteristic which is really their relation to one another. The inner, to
which falls the universality appearing in the process, and the outer, to
which belong the parts of the static structure of the organism, were
to constitute the corresponding sides of the law; but they lose, in being
kept asunder in this way, their organic significance. And at the bottom
of the idea of law lies just this, that its two aspects should have a subsistence each on its own account indifferent to the other, and the relation of the two sides should be shared between them, thus appearing as
a twofold characteristic corresponding to that relation. But really each
aspect of the organism consists inherently in being simple universality,
wherein all determinations are dissolved, and in being the process of
this resolution.

If we quite see the difference between this way of framing laws and
previous forms, it will clear up its nature completely. Turning back to
the process of perceiving and that of understanding (intelligence),
which reflects itself into itself, and by so doing determines its object, we
see that understanding does not there have before itself in its object the
relation of these abstract determinations, universal and individual, essential and external; on the contrary, it is itself the actual transition, the
relational process, and to itself this transition does not become objective. Here, on the other hand, the organic unity, i.e. just the relation of
those opposites, is itself the object; and this relation is a pure process of
transition. This process in its simplicity is directly universality; and in
that universality opens out into different factors, whose relation it is the
purpose of the law to express, the moments of the process take the form
of being *universal* objects of this mode of consciousness, and the law
runs, "the outer is an expression of the inner." Understanding has here
grasped the thought of the law itself, whereas formerly it merely looked
for laws in a general way, and their moments appeared before it in the
shape of a definite and specific content, and not in the form of thoughts
of laws.

As regards content, therefore, such laws ought not to have place in
this connexion which merely passively accept and put into the form of
universality purely existential distinctions; but such laws as directly
maintain in these distinctions the restless activity of the notion as well,
and consequently possess at the same time necessity in the relation of

the two sides. Yet, precisely because that object, organic unity, directly combines the endless superseding, or the absolute negation of, existence with inactive passive existence, and because the moments are essentially pure transition—there are thus not to be found any such merely existent aspects as are required for the law.

To get such aspects, intelligence must take its stand on the other moment of the organic relation, viz. on the fact that organic existence is reflected into itself. But this mode of being is so completely reflected into self that it has no specific character, no determinateness of its own as against something else, left over. The immediate sensuous being is directly one with the determinate quality as such, and hence inherently expresses a qualitative distinction, e.g. blue against red, acid against alkaloid, etc. But the *organic* being that has returned into itself is completely indifferent towards an other; its existence is simple universality, and refuses to offer observation any permanent sense distinctions, or, what is the same thing, shows its essential characteristic to be merely the changing flux of whatever determinate qualities there are. Hence, the way distinction *qua* actually existing expresses itself is just this, that it is an indifferent distinction, i.e. a distinction in the form of quantity. In this, however, the notion is extinguished and necessity disappears. If the content, however, and filling of this indifferent existence, the flux and interchange of sense determinations are gathered into the simplicity of an organic determination, then this expresses at the same time the fact that the content does not have that determinateness (the determinateness of the immediate property), and the qualitative feature falls solely within the aspect of quantity, as we saw above.

Although the objective element, apprehended in the form of a determinate character of organic existence, has thus the notion inherent in it, and thereby is distinguished from the object offered to understanding, which in apprehending the content of its laws proceeds in a purely perceptive manner, yet apprehension in the former case falls back entirely into the principle and manner of mere percipient understanding, for the reason that the object apprehended is used to constitute moments of a law. For by this means what is apprehended receives and keeps the character of a fixed determinate quality, the form of an immediate property or a passive phenomenon; it is, further, subsumed under the aspect of quantity, and the nature of the notion is suppressed.

The exchange of a merely perceived object for one reflected into itself, of a mere sense character for an organic, thus loses once more its value, and does so by the fact that understanding has not yet cancelled the process of framing laws.

If we compare what we find as regards this exchange in the case of a few examples, we see, it may be, something that perception takes for an animal with strong muscles characterized as an "animal organism of high irritability"; or, what perception takes to be a condition of great weakness, characterized as a "condition of high sensibility," or, if we prefer it, as an "abnormal affection," and, moreover, a raising of it to a "higher power"—expressions which translate sensuous facts into Teutonized Latin, instead of into terms of the notion. That an animal has strong muscles may also be expressed by understanding in the form that the animal "possesses a great muscular force"—great weakness meaning similarly "a slight force." Characterization in terms of irritability has this advantage over determination by reference to "force," that the latter expresses indeterminate, the former determinate reflexion into self; for the peculiar force characteristic of muscles is just irritability; and irritability is also a preferable determination to "strong muscles," in that, as in the case of force, reflexion into self is at once implied in it. In the same way "weakness," or "slight force," organic passivity, is expressed in a determinate manner by sensibility. But when this sensibility is so taken by itself and fixed, and the element of quality is in addition bound up with it, and *qua* greater or less sensibility is opposed to a greater or less irritability, each is reduced entirely to the level of sense, and degraded to the ordinary form of a sense property; their principle of relation is not the notion, but, on the contrary, it is the category of quantity into which the opposition is now cast, thus becoming a distinction not constituted by thought. While in this way the indeterminate nature of the expressions, "force," "strength," "weakness," would indeed be got rid of, there now arises the equally futile and indeterminate process of dealing with the oppositions of a higher and lower degree of sensibility and irritability, as they increase and decrease relatively to one another. The greater or less sensibility or irritability is no less a sensuous phenomenon, grasped and expressed without any reference to thought, than strength and weakness are sense determinations not constituted by thought. The notion has not taken the place of those non-conceptual expressions; instead, strength and weakness have been given a filling by a characteristic which, taken by itself alone, rests on the notion, and has the notion as its content, but loses entirely this origin and character.

Owing to the form of simplicity and immediacy, then, in which this content is made an element of a law, and through the element of quantity, which constitutes the principle of distinction for such determinations, the essential nature, which originally is a notion and is put forward as such, retains the character of sense perception, and remains as far removed from knowledge (*Erkennen*) as when characterized in terms of strength or weakness of force, or through immediate sense properties.

There is still left to consider what the outer side of the organic being is when taken by itself alone, and how in its case the opposition of *its* inner and outer is determined; just as at first we considered the inner of the whole in relation to its own proper outer.

The outer, looked at by itself, is the embodied form and shape (*Gestaltung*) in general, the system of life articulating itself in the element of existence, and at the same time essentially the existence of the organism as it is for an other—objective reality in its aspect of self-existence. This other appears in the first instance as its outer *inorganic nature*. If these two are looked at in relation to a law, the inorganic nature cannot, as we saw before, constitute the aspect of a law beside the organic being, because the latter exists absolutely for itself, and assumes a universal and free relation to inorganic nature.

To define more exactly, however, the relation of these two aspects in the case of the organic form, this form, in which the organism is embodied, is in one aspect turned against inorganic nature, while in another it is for itself and reflected into itself. The real organic being is the mediating agency, which brings together and unites the self-existence of life [its being *for* itself], with the outer in general, with what simply and inherently *is*.

The one extreme, self-existence, is, however, the inner in the sense of an infinite "one," which takes the moments of the embodied shape itself out of their subsistence and connexion with outer nature and withdraws these moments back into itself; it is that which, having no content, looks to the embodied form of the organism to provide its content, and appears there as the *process* of that form. In this extreme where it is mere negativity, or pure individual existence, the organism possesses its absolute freedom, whereby it is made quite secure and indifferent towards the fact of its being relative to another and towards the specific character belonging to the moments of the form of the organism. This free detachment is at the same time a freedom of the moments themselves; it is the possibility of their appearing and of being apprehended as existent. And just as they are therein detached and indifferent in regard to what is outer, so too are they towards one another; for the simplicity of this freedom is being or is their simple substance. This notion or pure freedom is one and the same life, no matter how varied and diverse the ways in which the shape assumed by the organism, its "being for another," may disport itself; it is a matter of indifference to this stream of life what sort of mills it drives.

In the first place, we must now note that this notion is not to be taken here, as it was formerly when we were considering the inner proper, in its character as the process or development of its moments; we must take it in its form as simple "inner," which constitutes the purely uni-

versal aspect as against the concrete living reality; it is the element in
which the existing members of the organic shape find their subsistence.
For it is this shape we are considering here, and in it the essential nature of life appears as the simple fact of subsistence. In the next place,
the existence for another, the specific character of the real embodied
form, is taken up into this simple universality, in which its nature lies,
a specificity that is likewise of a simple universal non-sensuous kind,
and can only be that which finds expression in *number*. Number is the
middle term of the organic form, which links indeterminate life with
actual concrete life, simple like the former, and determinate like the
latter. That which in the case of the former, the inner, would have the
sense of number, the outer would require to express after *its* manner as
multiform reality—kinds of life, colour, and so on, in general as the
whole host of differences which are developed as phenomena of life.

If the two aspects of the organic whole—the one being the inner,
while the other is the outer, in such a way that each again has in it an
inner and an outer—are compared with reference to the inner both
sides have, we find that the inner of the first is the notion, in the sense
of the restless activity of abstraction; the second has for its inner, however, inactive universality, which involves also the constant characteristic—number. Hence, if, because the notion develops its moments in
the former, this aspect made a delusive promise of laws owing to the
semblance of necessity in the relation, the latter directly disclaims
doing so, since number shows itself to be the determining feature of
one aspect of its laws. For number is just that entirely inactive, inert,
and indifferent characteristic in which every movement and relational
process is extinguished, and which has broken the bridge leading to the
living expression of impulses, manner of life, and whatever other sensuous existence there is.

This way of considering the embodied organic shape as such and the
inner *qua* inner merely of that embodied form, is, however, in point of
fact, no longer a consideration of organic existence. For both the aspects, which were to be related, are merely taken indifferent to one another, and thereby reflection into self, the essential nature of organism,
is done away with. What we have done here is rather to transfer that attempted comparison of inner and outer to the sphere of inorganic nature. The notion with its infinity is here merely the inner essence,
which lies hidden away within or falls outside in self-consciousness,
and no longer, as in the case of the organism, has its presence in an object. This relation of inner and outer has thus still to be considered in
its own proper sphere.

In the first place, that inner element of the form, being the simple
individual existence of an inorganic thing, is the *specific gravity*. As a

simply existing fact, this can be observed just as much as the characteristic of number, which is the only one of which it is capable; or properly speaking can be found by comparing observations; and it seems in this way to furnish one aspect of the law. The embodied form, colour, hardness, toughness, and an innumerable host of other properties, would together constitute the outer aspect, and would have to give expression to the characteristic of the inner, number, so that the one should find its counterpart in the other.

Now because negativity is here taken not in the sense of a movement of the process, but as an inoperative unity, or as simple self-existence, it appears really as that by which the thing resists the process, and maintains itself within itself, and in a condition of indifference towards it. By the fact, however, that this simple self-existence is an inactive indifference towards an other, specific gravity appears as one property alongside others; and therewith all necessary relation on its part to this plurality, or, in other words, all conformity to law, ceases.

The specific gravity in the sense of this simple inner aspect does not contain difference *in itself,* or the difference it has is merely non-essential; for its bare simplicity just cancels every distinction of an essential kind. This non-essential difference, quantity, was thus bound to find its other or counterpart in the other aspect, the plurality of properties, since it is only by doing so that it is difference at all. If this plurality itself is held together within the simple form of opposition, and is determined, say, as cohesion, so that this cohesion is self-existence in otherness, as specific gravity is pure self-existence, then cohesion here is in the first place this pure conceptually constituted characteristic as against the previous characteristic. The mode of framing the law would thus be what we discussed above, in dealing with the relation of sensibility to irritability. In the next place, cohesion, *qua* conception of self-existence in otherness, is merely the abstraction of the aspect opposed to specific gravity, and as such has no existential reality. For self-existence in otherness is the process wherein the inorganic would have to express its self-existence as a form of self-conservation, which on the other hand would prevent it emerging from the process as a constituent moment of a product. But this goes directly against its nature, which has no purpose or universality in it. Rather, its process is simply the determinate course of action by which its self-existence, in the sense of its specific gravity, cancels itself. This determinate action, which in that case would constitute the true principle implied in its cohesion, is itself however entirely indifferent to the other notion, that of the determinate quantity of its specific gravity. If the mode of action were left entirely out of account, and attention confined to the idea of quantity, we might be able to think of a feature like this: the greater specific weight, as it is a higher intensiveness of being (*Insichseyn*), would resist entering into the process more than a less specific weight. But on the contrary, freedom of self-existence (*Fürsichseyn*) shows itself only in facility to establish connexion with everything, and maintain itself throughout this manifold variety. That intensity without extension of relations is an abstraction with no substance in it, for extension constitutes the existence of intensity. The self-conservation of the inorganic element in its relation lies however, as already mentioned, outside its nature, since it does not contain the principle of movement within it or because its being is not absolute negativity and not a notion.

When this other aspect of the inorganic, on the other hand, is considered not as a process, but as an inactive being, it is ordinary cohesion. It is a simple sense property standing on one side over against the free and detached moment of otherness, which lies dispersed into a plurality of properties indifferent to and apart from one another, and which itself comes under this (cohesion) as does specific gravity. The multiplicity of properties together, then, constitutes the other side to cohesion. In its case, however, as in the case of the multiplicity, number is the only characteristic feature, which not merely does not bring out a relation and a transition from one to another of these properties, but consists essentially in having no necessary relation; its nature is rather to make manifest the absence of all conformity to law, for it expresses the determinate character as one that is non-essential. Thus we see that a series of bodies, whose difference is expressed as a numerical difference of their specific weights, by no means runs parallel to a series where the difference is constituted by the other properties, even if, for purposes of simplification, we select merely one or some of them. For, as a matter of fact, it could only be the *tout ensemble* of the properties which would have to constitute the other parallel aspect here. To bring this into orderly shape and to make it a connected single whole, observation finds at hand the quantitative determinations of these various properties; on the other hand, however, their differences come to light as qualitative. Now, in this collection, what would have to be characterized as positive or negative, and would be cancelled each by the other—in general, the internal arrangement and exposition of the equation, which would be very composite,—would belong to the notion. The notion however is excluded from operating just by the way in which the properties are found lying, and are to be picked up as mere existent entities. In this condition of mere being, none is negative in its relation to another: the one exists just as much as the other, nor does it in any other fashion indicate its position in the arrangement of the whole.

In the case of a series with concurrent differences—whether the relation is meant to be that of simultaneous increase on both sides or of increase in the one and decrease in the other—interest centres merely in the last simple expression of this combined whole, which would constitute the one aspect of the law with specific gravity for the opposite. But this one aspect, *qua* resultant fact, is nothing else than what has been already mentioned, viz. an individual property, say, like ordinary cohesion, alongside and indifferent to which the others, specific gravity among them, are found lying, and every other can be selected equally rightly, i.e. equally wrongly, to stand as representative of the entire other aspect; one as well as the other would merely "represent" or stand for [German *vorstellen*] the essential reality (*Wesen*), but would not actually be the fact (*Sache*) itself. Thus it seems that the attempt to find series of bodies which should in their two aspects run continuously and simply parallel, and express the essential nature of the bodies in a law holding of these aspects, must be looked at as an aim that is ignorant alike of what it is about and of the means for carrying it through.

Heretofore the relation between the inner and outer phases in the organic form set before observation was forthwith transferred to the sphere of the inorganic. The determinate condition to which this is due can now be stated more precisely; and there arises thence a further form and relation of this situation. What seems to present the possibility of such a comparison of inner and outer in the case of the inorganic, drops away altogether when we come to the organic. The inorganic inner is a simple inner, which comes before perception as a merely existent property. Its characteristic determination is therefore essentially quantity, and it appears as an existent property indifferent towards the outer, or the plurality of other sense properties. The self-existence of the living organism, however, does not so stand on one side opposed to its outer; it has the principle of otherness in itself. If we characterize self-existence as a simple self-preserving relation to self, its otherness is simple negativity; and organic unity is the unity of self-identical self-relation and pure negativity. This unity is *qua* unity the inwardness of the organic; the organic is thereby inherently universal, it is a *genus*. The freedom of the genus with reference to its realization is, however, something different from the freedom of specific gravity with reference to embodied form. That of the latter is freedom in the sphere of existence (*seyende Freiheit*), in the sense that it takes its stand on one side as a particular property. But because it is an existent freedom, it is also only a determinate character which belongs essentially to this embodied form, or by which this form *qua* essence is something determinate. The freedom, however, of the genus is a universal freedom, and indifferent to this embodied form, or towards its realization. The determinateness which attaches to self-existence *as such* of the inorganic, falls therefore in the case of the organic under its self-existence, while in the case of the inorganic it applies merely to the *existence* of the latter. Hence, although in the case of the latter that determinate characteristic appears at the same time only as a property, yet it possesses the value of being essential, because *qua* pure negative it stands over against concrete existence which is being for another; and this simple negative in its final and particular determinateness is a number. The organic, however, is a form of singleness, which is itself pure negativity, and hence abolishes within it the fixed determinateness of number, which is applicable to the indifference of mere being. So far as it has in it the moment of indifferent being and thereby of number, this numerical aspect can therefore only be regarded as an incident within it, but not as the essential nature of its living activity.

But now, though pure negativity, the principle of the process, does not fall outside the organic, and though the organic does not in its essence *possess* negativity as an adjectival characteristic, the singleness of the individual organism *being* instead inherently universal, yet this pure singleness is not therein developed and realized in its various moments as if these were themselves abstract or universal. On the contrary, this developed expression makes its appearance outside that universality, which thus falls back into mere inwardness; and between the concrete realization, the embodied form, i.e. the self-developing individual *singleness* of the organism, and the organic universal, the *genus*, appears the determinate or specific universal, the *species*. The existential form, to which the negativity of the universal, the negativity of the genus, attains, is merely the explicitly developed movement of a process, carried out among the parts of the given shape assumed by the organism. If the genus had the different parts within itself as an unbroken simple unity, so that its simple negativity as such were at the same time a movement, carried on through parts equally simple and directly universal in themselves, which were here actual as such moments, then the organic genus would be consciousness. But, as it is, the simple determinate character, *qua* determinateness of the species, is present in an unconscious manner in the genus; concrete realization *starts* from the genus; in other words, what finds express realization is not the genus as such, i.e. not really thought. This genus, *qua* actual organic fact, is merely represented by a deputy. Number, which is the representative here, seems to designate the transition from the genus into the individual embodiment, and to set before observation the two aspects of the necessary constitution, now in the form of a simple characteristic, and again in the form of an organic shape with all its manifold variety fully developed. This representative, however, really denotes the indifference and freedom of the universal and the individual as regards one another; the genus puts the individual at the mercy of mere quantitative difference, a non-essential element, but the individual *qua* living shows itself equally independent of this difference. True universality, in the way specified, is here merely *inner nature*; *qua* characteristic determining the species it is formal universality; and in contrast to the latter, that true universality takes its stand on the side of organic individual singleness, which is thereby a living individual entity, and owing to its inner nature is not concerned with its determinate character *qua* species. But this singleness is not at the same time a universal individual, i.e. one in which universality would have external realization as well; i.e. the universal individual falls outside the living organic whole. This universal individual, however, in the way it is immediately the individual of the natural embodiments of organic life, is not consciousness itself: its existence *qua* single organic living individual could not fall outside that universal if it were to be consciousness.

We have, then, here a connected system, where one extreme is the universal life *qua* universal or genus, the other being that same life *qua* a single whole, or universal individual: the mediating term, however, is a combination of both, the first seeming to fit itself into it as determinate universality or as species, the other as single whole proper or single individuality. And since this connected system belongs altogether to the aspect of the organic embodiment, it comprehends within it too what is distinguished as inorganic nature.

Since, now, the universal life *qua* the simple essence of the genus develops from its side the distinctions of the notion, and has to exhibit them in the form of a series of simple determining characteristics, this series is a system of distinctions set up indifferently, or is a numerical series. Whereas formerly the organic in the form of something individual and single was placed in opposition to this non-essential distinction [of quantity], a distinction which neither expresses nor contains its living nature: and while precisely the same has to be stated as regards the inorganic, taking into account its entire existence developed in the plurality of its properties: it is now the universal individual which is not merely to be looked on as free from every articulation of the genus, but also as the power controlling the genus. The genus disperses into species in terms of the universal characteristic of number, or again it may adopt as its principle of division particular characteristics of its existence like figure, colour, etc. While quietly prosecuting this aim, the genus meets with violence at the hands of the universal individual, the earth,[5] which in the role of universal negativity establishes the distinc-

---

[5] Cp. *Logik*, W. W., V. p. 153: "The earth as a concrete whole is at once a universal nature or genus as well as an individual." Cp. also *Naturphilosophie*, §§ 337, 338.

tions as they exist within itself,—the nature of which, owing to the substance they belong to, is different from the nature of those of the genus,—and makes good these distinctions as against the process of generic systematization. This action on the part of the genus comes to be quite a restricted business, which it can only carry on inside those mighty elements, and which is left with gaps and arrested and interrupted at all points through their unbridled violence.

It follows from all this that in the embodied, organic existence observation can only meet with reason in the sense of life in general, which, however, in its differentiating process involves really no rational sequence and organization, and is not an immanently grounded system of shapes and forms. If in the logical process of the moments involved in organic embodiment the mediating term, which contains the species and its realization in the form of a single individuality, had within it the two extremes of inner universality and universal individuality, then this middle term would have, in the movement of its reality, the expression and the nature of universality, and would be self-systematizing development. It is thus that consciousness takes as the middle term between universal spirit and its individuation or sense-consciousness, the system of shapes assumed by consciousness, as an orderly self-constituted whole of the life of spirit,—the system of forms of conscious life which is dealt with in this treatise, and which finds its objective existential expression as the history of the world. But organic nature has no history; it drops from its universal,—life,—immediately into the individuation of existence; and the moments of simple determinateness and individual living activity which are united in this realization, bring about the process of change merely as a contingent movement, wherein each plays its own part and the whole is preserved. But the energy thus exerted is restricted, so far as itself is concerned, merely to its own fixed centre, because the whole is not present in it; and the whole is not there because the whole is not as such here for itself.

Besides the fact, then, that reason in observing organic nature only comes to see itself as universal life in general, it comes to see the development and realization of this life merely by way of systems distinguished quite generally, in the determination of which the essential reality lies not in the organic as such, but in the universal individual [the earth]; and among these distinctions of earth [it comes to see that development and realization] in the form of sequences which the genus attempts to establish.

Since, then, in its realization, the universality found in organic life lets itself drop directly into the extreme of individuation, without any true self-referring process of mediation, the thing before the observing mind is merely a would-be "meaning"; and if reason can take an idle interest to observe what is thus "meant" here, it is confined to describing and recording nature's "meanings" and incidental suggestions. This irrational freedom of "fancying" doubtless will proffer on all sides beginnings of laws, traces of necessity, allusions to order and sequence, ingenious and specious relations of all kinds. But in relating the organic to the different facts of the inorganic, elements, zones, climates, so far as regards law and necessary connexion, observation never gets further than the idea of a "great influence." So, too, on the other side, where individuality has not the significance of the earth, but of the oneness immanent in organic life, and where this, in immediate unity with the universal, no doubt constitutes the genus, whose simple unity however, is just for that reason determined merely as a number and hence lets go the qualitative appearance;—here observation cannot get further than to make clever remarks, bringing out interesting points in connexion, a friendly condescension to the notion. But clever remarks do not amount to a knowledge of necessity; interesting points of connexion stop short at being simply of interest, while the interest is still nothing but fanciful "opinion" about the rational; and the friendliness of the individual in making allusion to a notion is a childlike friendliness, which is childish if, as it stands, it is to be or wants to be worth anything.

b

OBSERVATION OF SELF-CONSCIOUSNESS IN ITS PURE FORM AND IN ITS RELATION TO EXTERNAL REALITY—LOGICAL AND PSYCHOLOGICAL LAWS

Observation can be directed upon the self-conscious process of mind in two ways: it may consider the mind's thinking relation to reality, and it may consider the mind's active or biotic relation to reality. The result of observation here, as in the foregoing cases, finds expression in a number of laws, which it "frames." The "laws" in the first case are "laws of thought" or connected logical laws: in the latter case we have laws of psychic events, "psychological" laws.

The analysis in this section shows the inadequacy of observation as such to deal with its material in both cases. It fails in the first case because (1) "laws of thought" have no meaning apart from the reality with which thought is necessarily concerned; laws of thought are laws of "thinking," and thinking is both form and content: (2) observation gives each law an absolute being of its own, as if it were detached from the unity of self-consciousness, whereas this unity is the fundamental principle of each and all the laws, which only exist in and by the single process of that unity. Hence a type of logic confined to "observing" laws of thought is necessarily untrue. Observation again fails in the second case because it is impossible to separate mind from its total environment.

Observational or empirical psychology therefore is incapable of giving an adequate account of mind—the constitution of the environment enters into and in part determines the constitution of the psychic events, and the latter cannot be explained even as events without interpreting the former at the same time.

Observation of nature finds the notion realized in inorganic nature, laws, whose moments are things which at the same time are in the position of abstractions. But this notion is not a simplicity reflected into self. The life of organic nature, on the other hand, is only this self-reflected simplicity. The opposition within itself, in the sense of the opposition of universal and individual, does not make its appearance in the essential nature of this life itself with one factor apart from the other. Its essential nature is not the genus, self-sundered and self-moved in its undifferentiated element, and remaining at the same time for itself undifferentiated in its opposition. Observation finds this free notion, whose universality has just as absolutely within it developed individuality, only in the notion which itself exists as notion, i.e. in self-consciousness.

When observation now turns in upon itself and directs itself on the notion which is real *qua* free notion, it finds, to begin with, the *Laws of Thought*. This kind of individuality, which thought is in itself, is the abstract movement of the negative, a movement entirely introverted into simplicity; and the laws are outside reality.

To say "they have no reality" means in general nothing else than that they are without any truth. And in fact they do not claim to be entire truth, but still *formal* truth. But what is purely formal without reality is an *ens intellectus*, or empty abstraction without the internal diremption which would be nothing else but the content.

On the other hand, however, since they are laws of pure thought, while the latter is the inherently universal, and thus a kind of knowledge, which immediately contains being and therein all reality, these laws are absolute notions, and are in one and the same sense the essential principles of form as well as of things. Since self-directing, self-moving universality is the simple notion in a state of diremption, this notion has in this manner a content in itself, and one which is *all content*, except sensuous, not a being of sense. It is a content, which is neither in contradiction with the form nor at all separated from it; rather it is essentially the form itself; for the latter is nothing but the universal dividing itself into its pure moments.

In the way in which this form or content, however, comes before observation *qua* observation, it gets the character of a content that is found, given, i.e. one which merely *is*. It becomes a passively existing basis of relations, a multitude of detached necessities, which as a definitely fixed content are to have truth just as they stand with their specific character-istic, and thus, in point of fact, are withdrawn from the form.

This absolute truth of fixed characteristics, or of a plurality of differ-ent laws, contradicts, however, the unity of self-consciousness, contra-dicts the unity of thought and form in general. What is declared to be a fixed and inherently constant law can be merely a moment of the self-referring, self-reflecting unity, can come on the scene merely as a van-ishing element. When extricated, however, by the process of consider-ing them, from the movement imposing this continuous connexion, and when set out individually and separately, it is not content that they lack, for they have a specific content; they lack rather form, which is their essential nature. In point of fact it is not for the reason that they are to be merely formal and are not to have any content, that these laws are not the truth of thought; it is rather for the opposite reason. It is be-cause in their specificity, i.e. just as a content with the form removed, they want to pass for something absolute. In their true nature, as van-ishing moments in the unity of thought, they would have to be taken as knowledge or as thinking process, but not as laws of knowledge. Observing, however, neither is nor knows that knowledge itself; obser-vation converts its nature into the shape of an objective *being*, i.e. ap-prehends its negative character merely as laws of being.

It is sufficient for our purpose here to have indicated the invalidity of the so-called laws of thought from the consideration of the general na-ture of the case. It falls to speculative philosophy to go more intimately and fully into the matter, and there they show themselves to be what in truth they are, single vanishing moments, whose truth is simply the whole of the thinking process, knowledge itself.

This negative unity of thought exists for its own sake, or rather it is just being for itself and on its own account, the principle of individual-ity; and its reality consists in exercising a function, it is an active con-sciousness. Consequently the mental attitude of observation will by the nature of the case be led on towards this as being the reality of those laws of thought. Since this connexion is not a fact for observation, the latter supposes that thought with its laws remains standing separately on one side, and that, on the other side, it obtains another objective being in what is now the object observed, viz. that acting consciousness, which exists for itself in such a way as to cancel otherness and find its reality in this direct awareness of itself as the negative.

In the active practical reality of consciousness, observation thus finds opened up before it a new field. *Psychology* contains the collection of laws in virtue of which the mind takes up different attitudes towards the different forms of its reality given and presented to it in a condition of otherness. The mind adopts these various attitudes partly with a view to receiving these modes of its reality into itself, and conforming to the habits, customs, and ways of thinking it thus comes across, as being that wherein mind is reality and as such object to itself; partly with a view to knowing its own spontaneous activity in opposition to them, to follow the bent of its own inclinations, affections, and emotions, and carry off thence what is merely of particular and special moment for itself, and thus make what is objective conform to itself. In the former it behaves negatively towards itself as single and individual mind, in the latter negatively towards itself as the universal being.

In the former aspect independence [or self-dependence] gives what is met with merely the form of conscious individuality in general, and as regards the content remains within the general reality given; in the second aspect, however, it gives the reality at least a certain special modification, which does not contradict its essential content, or even a modification by which the individual *qua* particular reality and peculiar content sets itself against the general reality. This opposition becomes a form of wrongdoing when the individual cancels that reality in a merely particular manner, or when it does so in a manner that is general and thus for all, when it puts another world, another right, law, and custom in place of those already there.

Observational psychology, which in the first instance states what observation finds regarding the general forms brought to its notice in the active consciousness, discovers all sorts of faculties, inclinations, and passions; and since, while narrating what this collection contains, the remembrance of the unity of self-consciousness is not to be suppressed, observational psychology is bound to get the length at least of wonderment that such a lot and such a miscellany of things can happen to be somehow alongside one another in the mind as in a kind of bag, more especially when they are seen to be not lifeless inert things, but restless active processes.

In telling over these various faculties observation keeps to the universal aspect: the unity of these multifarious capacities is the opposite aspect to this universality, is the actual concrete individuality.

To take up again thus the different concrete individualities, and to describe how one man has more inclination for this, the other for that, how one has more intelligence than the other—all this is, however, something much more uninteresting than even to reckon up the species of insects, mosses, and so on. For these latter give observation the right to take them thus individually and disconnectedly (*begrifflos*), because they belong essentially to the sphere of fortuitous detailed particulars. To take conscious individuality on the other hand, as a particular phenomenal entity, and treat it in so wooden a fashion, is self-contradictory, because the essential nature of individuality lies in the universal element of mind. Since, however, the process of apprehending it causes it at the same time to pass into the form of universality, to apprehend it is to find its law, and seems in this way to have a rational purpose in view, and a necessary function to fulfil.

The moments constituting the content of the law are on the one hand individuality itself, on the other its universal inorganic nature, viz. the given circumstances, situation, habits, customs, religion, and so forth; from these the determinate individuality is to be understood and comprehended. They contain something specific, determinate, as well as universal, and are at the same time something lying at hand, which furnishes material for observation and on the other side expresses itself in the form of individuality.

The law of this relation of the two sides has now to contain and express the sort of effect and influence these determinate circumstances exert on individuality. This individuality, however, just consists both in being the universal, and hence in passively and directly assimilating and blending with the given universals, the customs, habits, etc., thus becoming conformed to them, as also in taking up an attitude of opposition towards them and thus transforming and transmuting them; and again in behaving towards them in its individual character with complete indifference, neither allowing them to exert an influence over it, nor setting itself actively against them. On that account *what* is to have an influence on individuality, and what *sort* of influence it is to have— which, properly speaking, mean the same thing—depend entirely on individuality itself: to say that by such and such an influence this individuality has become this specifically determinate individuality means nothing else than saying it has been this all along. Circumstances, situation, customs, and so on, which show themselves on one side as something given, and on the other as within this specific individuality, reveal merely indeterminate nature of individuality, which is not the point under consideration. If these circumstances, style of thought, customs, the whole state of the world, in short, had not been, then assuredly the individual would not have been what he is; for all the elements that find a place in this "state of the world" constitute this universal substance.

By the way, however, in which the state of the world has affected in particular any given individual—and it is such an individual that has to be comprehended—it must itself have assumed a particular shape on its own account, and have operated upon the individual in the specific character which it assumed. Only so could it have made the individual the specific particular individual he is. If the external element is so constituted in and for itself as it appears in individuality, the latter would be comprehended from the nature of the former. We should have a double gallery of pictures, one of which would be the reflexion of the other: the one the gallery of external circumstance completely encompassing, circumscribing, and determining the individual, the other the same gallery translated into the form in which those circumstances are in the conscious individual: the former the spherical surface, the latter the centre reflectively representing that surface within it.

But the spherical surface, the world for the individual, carries on the face of it this double meaning: it is in and for itself the actual world and situation, and it is the world of the individual. It is the world of the individual either in so far as this individual was merely fused and blended with it, had let that world, just as it is, pass into its own nature, and had taken up towards it merely the attitude of a formal consciousness; or, on the other hand, it is the world of the individual in the sense in which the given has been transformed and transmuted by that individual.

Since reality is capable of having this twofold meaning on account of this freedom of the individual, the world of the individual is only to be understood from the individual himself; and the influence of reality upon the individual, a reality which is represented as having a being all its own (*an und für sich*), receives through this individual absolutely the opposite significance—the individual either lets the stream of reality flowing in upon it have its way, or breaks off and diverts the current of its influence. In consequence of this, however, "psychological necessity" becomes an empty phrase, so empty that there is the absolute possibility that what is said to have this influence could equally well not have had it.

Herewith drops out of account that existence which was to be something all by itself, and was meant to constitute one aspect, and that the universal aspect, of a law. Individuality is what its world, in the sense of its own world, is. Individuality itself is the cycle of its own action, in which it has presented and established itself as reality, and is simply and solely a unity of what is given and what is constructed—a unity whose aspects do not fall apart, as in the idea of psychological law, into a world given *per se* and an individuality existing for itself. Or if those aspects are thus considered each by itself, there is no necessity to be found between them, and no law of their relation to one another.

c

OBSERVATION OF THE RELATION OF SELF-CONSCIOUSNESS TO
ITS IMMEDIATE ACTUALITY—PHYSIOGNOMY AND PHRENOLOGY[1]

In the previous section observation was directed upon the relation of mind to external reality—the natural environment of individuality. The relation of

---

[1]Cp. With Hegel's analysis Erdmann's *Psychologische Briefe*, Br. 9.

mind to its own physical embodiment furnishes a further object for observation to take up. How observation operates in dealing with this relation forms the subject of the analysis in the present section.

Up to and at the time at which Hegel wrote, the discussion of this relation took the form of what are now looked upon either as spurious sciences or at best as falling within the scope of physiology or psychophysics. Those pseudo-sciences were Physiognomy and Phrenology or Cranioscopy. Both had in one form or another engaged the attention of reflective minds from the earliest times. But about the latter half of the eighteenth century they gained unusual public prominence, in Germany, France and England, through the eloquence and conviction of their exponents; so much so that in Germany a law was passed forbidding the promulgation of phrenology as being dangerous to religion, and in England a law of George II re-enacted a statute of Elizabeth imposing the severest penalties on physiognomists. The chief exponents and propagandists of these studies of the human individual were Lavater (1741–1801), in physiognomy, and Gall (1758–1828), along with his pupil Spurzheim, in phrenology. The personal character and influence of the first, combined with his rhetorical eloquence, compelled the attention not only of the popular mind but of men of outstanding intelligence; while Gall lectured publicly and went from one University to another expounding the generalizations discovered or made.

It was impossible therefore for any philosopher who attempted to discuss comprehensively the methods and procedure of observational science to ignore the claims made by these pseudo-sciences or to refuse to examine the validity of the laws they proposed to formulate. This was all the more necessary because the object they dealt with—the relation of mind to its physical embodiment—was and is unquestionably an important fact of experience and presents a serious problem to philosophy, especially to idealism. Hence we have in the following section an elaborate analysis of the observational "sciences" of physiognomy and phrenology—an analysis the length of which can only be explained and justified by the historical circumstances above indicated.

PSYCHOLOGICAL observation discovers no law for the relation of self-consciousness to actuality or the world over against it; and owing to their mutual indifference it is forced to fall back on the peculiar determinate characteristic of real individuality, which has a being in and for itself or contains the opposition of subjective self-existence (*Fürsich-seyn*) and objective inherent existence (*Ansichseyn*) dissolved and extinguished within its own process of absolute mediation. Individuality is now the object for observation, or the object to which observation now passes.

The individual exists in himself and for himself. He is for himself, or is a free activity; he is, however, also in himself, or has himself an *original* determinate being of his own—a character which is in principle the same as what psychology sought to find outside him. Opposition thus breaks out in his own self; it has this twofold nature, it is a process or movement of consciousness, and it is the fixed being of a reality with a phenomenal character, a reality which in it is directly its own. This being, the "body" of the determinate individuality, is its original source, that in the making of which it has had nothing to do. But since the individual at the same time merely is what he has done, his body is also an "expression" of himself which he has brought about; a sign and indication as well, which has not remained a bare immediate fact, but through which the individual only makes known what is actually implied by his setting his original nature to work.

If we consider the moments we have here in relation to the view previously indicated, we find a general human shape and form, or at least the general character of a climate, of a portion of the world, of a people, just as formerly we found in the same way general customs and culture. In addition the particular circumstances and situation are within the universal reality; here this particular reality is a particular formation of the shape of the individual. On the other side, whereas formerly we were dealing with the free activity of the individual, and reality in the sense of his own reality was put in contrast and opposition to reality as given, here the shape assumed by the individual stands as an expression of his own actualization established by the individual himself, it bears the lineaments and forms of his spontaneously active being. But the reality, both universal as well as particular, which observation formerly found outside the individual, is here the actual reality of the individual, his connate body; and within this very body the expression due to his own action appears. From the psychological point of view objective reality in and for itself and determinate individuality had to be brought into relation to one another; here, however, it is the whole determinate individuality that is the object for observation, and each aspect of the opposition it entails is itself this whole. Thus, to the outer whole belongs not merely the original primordial being, the connate body, but the formation of the body as well, which is due to activity from the inner side; the body is a unity of unformed and formed existence, and is the reality of the individual permeated by his reference to self. This whole embraces the definite parts fixed originally and from the first, and also the lineaments which arise only as the result of action; this whole so formed *is*, and this being is an expression of what is inner, of the individual constituted as a consciousness and as a process.

This inner is, too, no longer formal, spontaneous activity without any content or determinateness of its own, an activity with its content and specific nature, as in the former case, lying in external circumstances; it is an original inherently determinate *Character*, whose form alone is the activity. What, then, we have to consider here is the relation subsisting between the two sides; the point to observe is how this relation is determined, and what is to be understood by the inner finding expression in the outer.

This outer, in the first place, does not act as an organ making the inner visible, or, in general terms, a being for another; for the inner, so far as it is in the organ, is the activity itself. The mouth that speaks, the hand that works, with the legs too, if we care to add them, are the operative organs effecting the actual realization, and they contain the action *qua* action, or the inner as such; the externality, however, which the inner obtains by their means is the deed, the act, in the sense of a reality separated and cut off from the individual. Language and labour are outer expressions in which the individual no longer retains possession of himself *per se*, but lets the inner get right outside him, and surrenders it to something else. For that reason we might just as truly say that these outer expressions express the inner too much as that they do so too little: too much — because the inner itself breaks out in them, and there remains no opposition between them and it; they not merely give an *expression* of the inner, they give the inner itself directly and immediately: too little — because in speech and action the inner turns itself into something else, into an other, and thereby puts itself at the mercy of the element of change, which transforms the spoken word and the accomplished act, and makes something else out of them than they are in and for themselves as actions of a particular determinate individual. Not only do the products of actions, owing to this externality, lose by the influence of others the character of being something constant *vis-à-vis* other individualities; but by their assuming towards the inner which they contain, the attitude of something external, separate, independent, and indifferent, they can, through the individual himself, be *qua* inner something other than they seem. Either the individual intentionally makes them in appearance something else than they are in truth; or he is too incompetent to give himself the outer aspect he really wanted, and to give them such fixity and permanence that the product of his action cannot become misrepresented by others. The action, then, in the form of a completed product has the double and opposite significance of being either the inner individuality and not its expression; or, *qua* external, a reality detached from the inner, a reality which is something quite different from the inner. On account of this ambiguity, we must look about for the inner as it still is within the individual himself, but in a visible or external form. In the organ, however, it exists merely as immediate activity as such, which attains its externalization in the act or deed, that either does or again does not represent the inner. The organ, in the light of this opposition, thus does not afford the expression which is sought.

If now the external shape and form were able to express the inner individuality only in so far as that shape is neither an organ nor action, hence only in so far as it is an inert passive whole, it would then play the rôle of a subsistent thing, which received undisturbed the inner as an alien element into its own passive being, and thereby became the sign and symbol of it—an external contingent expression, whose actual concrete aspect has no meaning of its own—a language whose sounds and tone-combinations are not the real fact itself, but are capriciously connected with it and a mere accident so far as it is concerned.

Such a capricious association of factors that are external for one another does not give a law. *Physiognomy*, however, would claim distinction from other spurious arts and unwholesome studies on the ground that in dealing with determinate individuality it considers the *necessary* opposition of an inner and an outer, of character as a conscious nature and character as a definitely embodied organic shape, and relates these moments to one another in the way they are related to one another by their very conception, and hence must constitute the content of a law. In astrology, on the other hand, in palmistry and similar "sciences," there appears merely external element related to external element, anything whatsoever to an element alien to it. A given constellation at birth, and, when the external element is brought closer to the body itself, certain given lines on the hand, are external factors making for long or short life, and the fate in general of the particular person. Being externalities they are indifferent towards one another, and have none of the necessity for one another which is supposed to lie in the relation of what is outer to what is inner.

The hand, to be sure, does not seem to be such a very external thing for fate; it seems rather to stand to it as something inner. For fate again is also merely the phenomenal manifestation of what the specifically determinate individuality inherently is as having originally an inner determinate constitution. Now to find out what this individuality is in itself, the palmist, as well as the physiognomist, takes a shorter cut than, e.g., Solon, who thought he could only know this from and after the course of the whole life: the latter looked at the phenomenal explicit reality, while the former considers the implicit nature (*das Ansich*). That the hand, however, must exhibit and reveal the inherent nature of individuality as regards its fate, is easily seen from the fact that after the organ of speech it is the hand most of all by which a man actualizes and manifests himself. It is the animated artificer of his fortune: we may say of the hand it *is* what a man does, for in it as the effective organ of his self-fulfilment he is there present as the animating soul; and since he is ultimately and originally his own fate, the hand will thus express this innate inherent nature.

From this peculiarity, that the organ of activity is at once a form of being and the operation going on within it, or again that the inner inherent being is itself explicitly present in it and has a being for others, we come upon a further aspect of it different from the preceding. For if the organs in general proved to be incapable of being taken as expressions of the inner for the reason that in them the action is present as a process, while the action as a deed or (finished) act is merely external, and inner and outer in this way fall apart and are or can be alien to one another, the organ must, in view of the peculiarity now considered, be again taken as also a middle term for both, since this very fact, that the operation takes place and is present in it, constitutes *eo ipso* an external attribute of it, and indeed one that is different from the deed or act; for the former holds by the individual and remains with him.

This mediating term uniting inner and outer is in the first place itself external too. But then this externality is at the same time taken up into the inner; it stands in the form of simple unbroken externality opposed to dispersed externality, which either is a single performance or condition contingent for the individuality as a whole, or else, in the form of a total externality, is fate or destiny, split up into a plurality of performances and conditions. The simple lines of the hand, then, the ring and compass of the voice, as also the individual peculiarity of the language used: or again this idiosyncrasy of language, as expressed where the hand gives it more durable existence than the voice can do, viz. in writing, especially in the particular style of "handwriting"—all this is an expression of the inner, so that, as against the multifarious externality of action and fate, this expression again stands in the position of simple externality, plays the part of an inner in relation to the externality of action and fate. Thus, then, if at first the specific nature and innate peculiarity of the individual along with what these become as the result of cultivation and development, are regarded as the inner reality, as the essence of action and of fate, this inner being finds its appearance in external fashion to begin with in his mouth, hand, voice, handwriting, and the other organs and their permanent characteristics. Thereafter and not till then does it give itself further outward expression in its realization in the world.

Now because this middle term assumes the nature of an outer expression, which is at the same time taken back into the inner, its existence is not confined to the immediate organ of action (the hand); this middle term is rather the movement and form of countenance and figure in general which perform no outward act. These lineaments and their move-

ments on this principle are the checked and restrained action that stops in
the individual and, as regards his relation to what he actually does, constitute his own personal inspection and observation of the action—outer
expression in the sense of reflexion upon the actual outer expression.

The individual, on the occasion of his external action, is therefore
not dumb and silent, because he is thereby at once reflected into himself, and he gives articulate expression to this self-reflexion. This theoretical action, the individual's conversing with himself on the matter, is
also perceptible to others, for his speaking is itself an outer expression.

In this inner, then, which in being expressed remains an inner, observation finds the individual reflected out of his actual reality; and we
have to see how the case stands with regard to the necessity which lies
in the unity here.

His being thus reflected is to begin with different from the act itself,
and therefore can *be*, and be taken for something other than the deed
is. We look at a man's face and see whether he is in earnest with what
he says or does. Conversely, however, what is here intended to be an
expression of the inner is at the same time an existent objective expression, and hence itself falls to the level of mere existence, which is
absolutely contingent for the self-conscious individual. It is therefore
no doubt an expression, but at the same time only in the sense of a sign,
so that to the content expressed the peculiar nature of that by which it
is expressed is completely indifferent. The inner in thus appearing is
doubtless an invisible made visible, but without being itself united to
this appearance. It can just as well make use of some other appearance
as another inner can adopt the same appearance. Lichtenberg,[2] therefore, is right in saying: "Suppose the physiognomist ever did have a
man in his grasp, it would merely require a courageous resolution on
the man's part to make himself again incomprehensible for centuries."

In the previous case[3] the immediately given circumstances formed a
sphere of existence from which individuality selected what it could or
what it wanted, either submitting to or transmuting this given existence, for which reason this did not contain the necessity and inner nature of individuality. Similarly here the immediate being in which individuality clothes its appearance is one which either expresses the fact
of its being reflected back out of reality and existing within itself, or
which is for it merely a sign indifferent to what is signified, and therefore signifying in reality nothing; it is as much its countenance as its
mask, which can be put off when it likes. Individuality permeates its
own shape, moves, speaks in the shape assumed; but this entire mode

---

[2]A critic of physiognomy in *Über Physiognomik*, 2Au f. Göttingen, 1778, p. 35.
[3]i.e. the relation of self-consciousness to external reality.

of existence equally well passes over into a state of being indifferent to the will and the act. Individuality effaces from it the significance it formerly had—of being that wherein individuality is reflected into itself, or has its true nature—and instead puts its real nature rather in the will and the deed.

Individuality abandons that condition of being reflected into self which finds expression in lines and lineaments, and places its real nature in the work done. Herein it contradicts the relationship which the instinct of reason, engaged in observing self-conscious individuality, establishes in regard to what its inner and outer should be. This point of view brings us to the special idea at the basis of the science of physiognomy—if we care to call it a "science." The opposition this form of observation comes upon is in form the opposition of practical and theoretical, both falling inside the practical aspect itself—the opposition of individuality, making itself real in action (in the most general sense of action), and individuality as being in this action at the same time reflected thence into self, and taking the action for its object. Observation apprehends and accepts this opposition in the same inverted form in which it is when it makes its appearance. To observation, the deed itself and the performance, whether it be that of speech or a more solid reality, stand for the non-essential outer, while the individuality's existence within itself passes for the essential inner. Of the two aspects which the practical mind involves, intention and act (the "meaning" regarding the action and the action itself), observation selects the former as the true inner; this (i.e. the intention or true inner) is supposed to have its more or less unessential externalization in the act, while its true outer expression is to be had in the form in which the individual is embodied. This latter expression is a sensuous immediate presence of the individual mind: the inwardness, which is intended to be the true internal aspect, is the particular point of the intention, and the singleness of self-existence: both together the mind subjectively "meant." Thus, what observation takes for its objects is an existence that is "meant"; and within this sphere it looks for laws.

The primary way of making conjectures (*meinen*) regarding the "presumptive" presence of mind is everyday (*natürlich*) physiognomy, hasty judgment formed at a glance about the inner nature and the character of its outer form and shape. The object of this guesswork thinking[4] is of such a kind that its very essence involves its being in truth something else than merely sensuous and immediate. Certainly what is really present is just this condition of being in sensuous form reflected out of sense into self; it is the visible as a sensuous presentment of the invisi-

---

[4]Cp. There is no art to find the mind's construction in the face. *Macbeth*, Act. I. 4.

ble, which constitutes the object of observation. But this very sensuous immediate presence is the mind's "reality" as that reality is approved by mere conjecture (*Meinung*); and observation from this point of view occupies itself with its "presumed" (*gemeint*) existence, with physiognomy, handwriting, sound of voice, etc.

Observation relates such and such a sensuous fact to just such a supposed or presumed (*gemeintes*) inner. It is not the murderer, the thief, that is to be known; it is the capacity to be a murderer, a thief. The definitely marked abstract attribute is thereby lost in the concrete indefinite characteristic nature of the particular individual, which now demands more skilful delineations than the former qualifications supply. Such skilful delineations no doubt say more than the qualification, "murderer," "thief," or "good-hearted," "unspoiled," and so on; but are a long way short of their aim, which is to express the being that is "meant," the single individuality; as far short as the delineations of the form and shape, which go further than a "flat brow," a "long nose," etc. For the individual shape and form, like the individual self-consciousness, is *qua* something "meant," inexpressible. The "science of knowing men,"[5] which is concerned about the supposed human being, like the "science" of physiognomy, which deals with his presumed reality and seeks to raise to the level of knowledge uncritical assertions of everyday (*natürlich*) physiognomy,[6] is therefore something with neither foundation nor finality; it cannot manage to say what it "means" because it merely "means," and its content is merely what is "presumed" or "meant."

The so-called "laws," this kind of science sets out to find, are relations holding between these two presumed or supposed aspects, and hence can amount to no more than an empty "fancying" (*meinen*). Again since this presumed knowledge, which takes upon itself to deal with the reality of mind, finds its object to be just the fact that mind is reflected from sense existence back into self, and that, for mind, a specific bodily expression is an indifferent accident, it is therefore bound to be aware at once that by the so-called "laws" discovered it really says nothing at all, but that, strictly speaking, this is mere chatter, or merely

---

[5]This refers to the claims put forward by Lavater, whose work was entitled *Physiognomische Fragmente zur Beförderung der Menschenkenntniss und Menschenliebe*. Leipzig, 1775–8.

[6]"Everyday Physiognomy" would be the familiar procedure of mankind, civilized and uncivilized, in divining or supposing what is in a man's mind from bodily expressions— e.g. the tone of his voice, the lineaments (natural and acquired) of his face, the play of his features, or even in general the conformation of his body. The procedure is instinctive; but it also leads to rough and ready judgments of experience which are used for guidance in everyday social life.

giving out a "fancy" or "opinion" (*Meinung*) of its own—(an assertion which has this amount of truth that to state one's "opinion," one's "fancy," and not to convey thereby the fact itself, but merely a "fancy of one's own," are one and the same thing). In content, however, such observations cannot differ in value from these: "It always rains at our annual fair," says the dealer; "And every time, too," says the housewife, "when I am drying my washing."

Lichtenberg, who characterizes physiognomic observation in this way, adds this remark: "If any one said, 'You act, certainly, like an honest man, but I can see from your face you are forcing yourself to do so, and are a rogue at heart,' without a doubt every brave fellow to the end of time when accosted in that fashion will retort with a box on the ear."

This retort is to the point, for the reason that it refutes the fundamental assumption of such a "science" of conjecture (*meinen*), viz. that the reality of a man is his face, etc.

The true being of a man is, on the contrary, his act; individuality is real in the deed, and a deed it is which cancels both the aspects of what is "meant" or "presumed" to be. In the one aspect where what is "presumed" or "imagined" takes the form of a passive bodily being, individuality puts itself forward in action as the negative essence which only *is* so far as it cancels *being*. Then furthermore the act does away with the inexpressibleness of what self-conscious individuality really "means"; in regard to such "meaning," individuality is endlessly determined and determinable. This false infinite, this endless determining, is abolished in the completed act. The act is something simply determinate, universal, to be grasped as an abstract, distinctive whole; it is murder, theft, a benefit, a deed of bravery, and so on, and what it *is* can be *said* of it. It *is* such and such, and its being is not merely a symbol, it is the fact itself. It *is* this, and the individual human being *is* what the *act is*. In the simple fact that the act *is*, the individual is for others what he really is and with a certain general nature, and ceases to be merely something that is "meant" or "presumed" to be this or that. No doubt he is not put there in the form of mind; but when it is a question of his being *qua* being, and the twofold being of bodily shape and act are pitted against one another, each claiming to be his true reality, the deed *alone* is to be affirmed as his genuine being—not his figure or shape, which would express what he "means" to convey by his acts, or what any one might "conjecture" he merely could do. In the same way, on the other hand, when his performance and his inner possibility, capacity, or intention are opposed, the former *alone* is to be regarded as his true reality, even if he deceives himself on the point and, after he has turned from his action into himself, means to be something else in his "inner mind" than what he is in the act. Individuality, which commits itself to the objective element, when it passes over into a deed no doubt puts itself to the risk of being altered and perverted. But what settles the character of the act is just this—whether the deed is a real thing that holds together, or whether it is merely a pretended or "supposed" performance, which is in itself null and void and passes away. Objectification does not alter the act itself; it merely shows what the deed *is*, i.e. whether it *is* or whether it is *nothing*.

The breaking up of this real being into intentions, and subtleties of that sort, by which the real man, i.e. his deed, is to be reduced again to, and explained in terms of, a "conjectured" being, as even the individual himself may produce out of himself particular intentions concerning his reality—all this must be left to idle "fancying" and "presuming" to furnish at its leisure. If this idle thinking *will* set its ineffective wisdom to work, and *will* deny the agent the character of reason, and use him so badly as to want to declare his figure and his lineaments to be his real being instead of his act, then it may expect to get the retort above spoken of, a retort which shows that figure is not the inherent being, but is on the contrary an object sufficiently on the surface to be roughly handled.

If we look now at the range of relations as a whole in which self-conscious individuality can be observed standing towards its outer aspect, there will be one left which has still to come before observation as an object. In psychology it is the external reality of things which in the life of mind is to have its counterpart conscious of itself and make the mind intelligible. In physiognomy, on the other hand, mind or spirit is to be known in its own proper outer (physical) aspect, a form of being which may be called the language or utterance of mind—the visible invisibility of its inner nature. There is still left the further character of the aspect of reality—that individuality expresses its nature in its immediate actuality, an actuality that is definitely fixed and purely existent.

This last relation [of mind to its reality] is distinguished from the physiognomic by the fact that this is the speaking presence of the individual, who in his practical active outer expression brings to light and manifests at the same time the expression wherein he reflects himself into himself and contemplates himself, an expression which is itself a movement, passive lineaments which are themselves essentially a mediated form of existence. In the character still to be considered, however, the outer element is finally an entirely inactive objectivity, which is not in itself a speaking sign, but presents itself on its own account, separate from the self-conscious process, and has the form of a bare thing.

In the first place in regard to the relation of the inner to this its outer, it is clear that that relation seems bound to be understood in the sense

of a causal connexion, since the relation of one immanent and inherent entity to another, *qua* a necessary relation, is causal connexion.

Now, for spiritual individuality to have an effect on the body it must
qua cause be itself corporeal. The corporeal element, however,
wherein it acts as a cause, is the organ, not the organ of action on external reality, but of the action of the self-conscious being within itself,
operating outward only on its own body. It is at the same time not easy
to see what these organs can be. If we merely think of organs in general, the general organ for work would at once occur to us, so, too, the
organ of sex, and so on. But organs of that sort are to be considered as
instruments or parts, which mind, *qua* one extreme, possesses as a
means for dealing with the other extreme, which is an outer object. In
the present case, however, an organ is to be understood to be one
wherein the self-conscious individual, as an extreme, maintains himself
on his own account and for himself against his *own* proper actuality
which is opposed to him, the individual not being at the same time
turned upon the outer world, but reflected in his own action, and
where, further, his aspect of existence is not an existence objective for
some other individual. In the case of physiognomy, too, the organ is no
doubt considered as an existence reflected into self and criticizing the
action. But in this case the existence is objective in character, and the
outcome of the physiognomical observation is that self-consciousness
treats precisely this its reality as something indifferent. This indifference disappears in the fact that this very state of being reflected into self
is itself active upon the other: thereby that existence occupies and
maintains a necessary relation to self-consciousness. But to operate effectually on that existence it must itself have a being, though not properly speaking an objective being, and it must be set forth as being this
organ.

In ordinary life, anger, e.g. as an internal action of that sort, is located
in the liver. Plato[7] even assigns the liver something still higher, something which to many is even the highest function of all, viz. prophesy-
ing, or the gift of uttering in an irrational manner things sacred and
eternal. But the process which the individual has in his liver, heart, and
so on, cannot be regarded as one wholly internal to the individual,
wholly reflected into his self; rather his process is there (viz. in the liver,
etc.) as something which has already become bodily and assumes a
physical animal existence, reacting on and towards external reality.

The nervous system, on the other hand, is the immediate stability of
the organism in its process of movement. The nerves themselves, no
doubt, are again organs of that consciousness which from the first is im-

---

[7]*Timæus*, 71, 72.

mersed in its outward impulses. Brain and spinal cord, however, may be looked at as the immediate presence of self-consciousness, a presence self-contained, not an object and also not transient. In so far as the moment of being, which this organ has, is a being for another, is an objective existence, it is a being that is dead, and is no longer the presence of self-consciousness. This self-contained existence, however, is by its very nature a fluent stream, wherein the circles that are made in it immediately break up and dissolve, and where no distinction is expressed as permanent or real. Meanwhile, as mind itself is not an abstractly simple entity, but a system of processes, wherein it distinguishes itself into moments, but in the very act of distinguishing remains free and detached; and as mind articulates its body as a whole into a variety of functions, and designates one particular part of the body for only one function:—so too one can represent to oneself the fluent state of its internal existence [its existence within itself] as something that is articulated into parts. Moreover, it seems bound to be thought of in this way, because the self-reflected being of mind in the brain itself is again merely a middle term between its pure essential nature and its bodily articulation, an intermediate link, which consequently must partake of the nature of both, and thus in respect of the latter must also again have in it actual articulation.

The psycho-organic being has at the same time the necessary aspect of a stable subsistent existence. The former must retire, *qua* extreme of self-existence, and have this latter as the other extreme over against it, an extreme which is then the object on which the former acts as a cause. If now brain and spinal cord are that bodily self-existence of mind, the skull and vertebral column form the other extreme separated off, viz. the solid fixed stable thing.

When, however, any one thinks of the proper place where mind exists, it is not the back that occurs to him, but merely the head. Since this is so, we can, in examining a form of knowledge like what we are at present dealing with, content ourselves with this reason—not a very bad one in the present case—in order to confine the existence of mind to the skull. Should it strike any one to take the vertebral column for the seat of mind, in so far as by it too knowledge and action doubtless are sometimes partly induced and partly educed, this would prove nothing in defence of the view that the spinal cord must be taken as well for the indwelling seat of mind, and the vertebral column for the existential counterpart, because this proves too much. For we may bear in mind that there are also other approved external ways for getting at the activity of mind in order to stimulate or inhibit its activity.

The vertebral column, then, if we like, drops rightly out of account; and it is as well made out as many another doctrine of the philosophy of nature that the skull alone does not indeed contain the "organs" of mind (but its existent embodiment). For this was previously excluded from the conception of this relation, and on that account the skull was taken for the aspect of existence; or, if we may not be allowed to recall the conception involved, then experience unquestionably teaches that, as we see with the eye *qua* organ, so it is not with the skull that we commit murder, steal, write poetry, etc.

We must on that account refrain from using the expression "organ" also when speaking of that significance of the skull which we have still to mention. For although it is a common thing to hear people say, that to reasonable men it is not words but facts that really matter, yet that does not give us permission to describe a thing in terms not appropriate to it. For this is at once stupidity and deceit, pretending merely not to have the right "word," and hiding from itself that in reality it has not got hold of the fact itself, the notion. If the latter were there, it would soon find the right word.

What has been here determined is, in the first instance, merely that just as the brain is the *caput vivum*, the skull is the *caput mortuum*.

It is in this *ens mortuum*, then, that the mental processes and specific functions of the brain would have to find their external reality manifested, a reality which is none the less in the individual himself. For the relation of those processes and functions to what, being an *ens mortuum*, does not contain mind indwelling within it, there is offered, in the first instance, the external and mechanical relation defined above, so that the organs proper—and these are in the brain—here press the skull out round, there make it broad, or force it flat, or in whatever way we care to state the effect thus exerted. Being itself a part of the organism, it must be supposed to have in it too, as is the case in every bone, an active, living, formative influence, so that, from this point of view, it really, from its side, presses the brain, and fixes its external boundary—which it is the better able to do being the harder. In that case, however, the relation of the activity of the one to the other would always maintain the same character; for whether the skull is the determining factor or the factor determined, this would effect no alteration in the general causal connexion, only that the skull would then be made the immediate organ of self-consciousness, because in it *qua* cause the aspect of existence-for-self would find expression. But, since self-existence in the sense of organic living activity belongs to both in the same manner, the causal connexion between them in point of fact drops altogether.

This development of the two, however, would be inwardly connected, and would be an organic pre-established harmony, which leaves the two interrelated aspects free as regards one another, each with its own proper form and shape, without this shape needing to correspond to that of the other; and still more so as regards the relation of the shape and the quality—just as the form of the grape and the taste of wine are mutually independent of one another.

Since, however, the character of self-existence appertains to the aspect of brain, while that of existence to the feature of skull, there is *also* a causal connexion to be set up between them inside the organic unity—a necessary relation between them as external for one another, i.e. a relation itself external, whereby their form and shape are determined the one through the other.

As regards the condition, however, in which the organ of self-consciousness would operate causally on the opposite aspect, all sorts of statements can be made. For the question concerns the constitution of a cause which is considered in regard to its indifferent existence, its shape and quantity, a cause whose inner nature and self-existence are to be precisely what leave quite unaffected the immediately existing aspect. The organic self-formation of the skull is, to begin with, indifferent to the mechanical influence exerted, and the relationship in which these two processes stand, since the former consists in relating itself to itself, is just this very indeterminateness and boundlessness. Furthermore, even though the brain accepted the distinctions of mind, and took them into itself as existential distinctions, and were a plurality of inner organs occupying each a different space, it would be left undecided whether a mental element would, according as it was originally stronger or weaker, either be bound to possess in the first case a more expanded brain-organ, or in the latter case a more contracted brain-organ, or just the other way about. But it is contradictory to nature for the brain to be such a plurality of internal organs; for nature gives the moments of the notion an existence of their own, and hence puts the fluent simplicity of organic life clear on one side, and its articulation and division with its distinctions on the other, so that, in the way they have to be taken here, they assume the form of particular anatomical facts.

The same holds good in regard to the question whether the improvement of the brain would enlarge or diminish the organ, whether it would make it coarser and thicker or finer. By the fact that it remains undetermined how the cause is constituted, it is left in the same way undecided how the effect exerted on the skull comes about, whether it is a widening or a narrowing and shrinking of it. Suppose this effect is named in perhaps more distinguished phrase a "solicitation," we cannot say whether this takes place by swelling like the action of a cantharides-plaster, or by shrivelling like the action of vinegar.

In defence of all views of that kind plausible reasons can be adduced; for the organic relation, which quite as much exerts its influence, finds one fit as well as another, and is indifferent to all this wit of mere understanding.

It is, however, not the interest of observation to seek to determine this relation. For it is in any case not the brain in the sense of a physical part which takes its stand on one side, but brain in the sense of the existential form of self-conscious individuality. This individuality, *qua* abiding character and self-moving conscious activity, exists for itself and within itself. Opposed to this existence within itself and on its own account stand its reality and its existence for another. Its own peculiar existence is the essential nature, and is subject, having a being in the brain; this being is subsumed under it, and gets its value merely through its indwelling significance. The other aspect of self-conscious individuality, however, that of its existence, is being *qua* independent and subject, or *qua* a thing, viz. a bone: the real existence of man is his skull-bone. This is the relationship and the sense which the two aspects of this relation have when the mind adopts the attitude of observation.

Observation has now to deal with the more determinate relation of these aspects. The skull-bone doubtless in general has the significance of being the immediate reality of mind. But the many-sidedness of mind gives its existence a corresponding variety of meanings. What we have to find out is the specific meaning of the particular regions into which this existence is divided; and we have to see how the reference to mind is denoted in them.

The skull-bone is not an organ of activity, nor even a process of utterance. We neither commit theft, murder, etc., with the skull-bone, nor does it in the least distort its face to suit the deed in such cases, so that the skull should express the meaning in the language of gesture. Nor does this existential form possess the value even of a symbol. Look and gesture, tone, even a pillar or a post stuck up on a desert island, proclaim at once that they stand for something else than what they merely are at first sight. They forthwith profess to be symbols, since they have in them a characteristic which points to something else by the fact that it does not belong peculiarly to them. Doubtless, even in the case of a skull, there is many an idea that may occur to us, like those of Hamlet over Yorick's skull; but the skull-bone by itself is such an indifferent object, such an innocent thing, that there is nothing else to be seen in it or to be thought about it directly as it is, except simply the fact of its being a skull. It no doubt reminds us of the brain and its specific nature, and skulls with other formations, but it does not recall a conscious process, since there is impressed on it neither a look or gesture, nor anything which would show traces of derivation from a conscious activity. For it is that sort of reality which, in the case of individuality, is intended to exhibit an aspect of another kind, one that would no longer be an existence reflecting itself into itself, but bare immediate existence.

While, further, the skull does not itself feel, there seems still a possibility of providing it with a more determinate significance in the fact that specific feelings might enable us, through their being in proximity to it, to find out what the skull may mean to convey; and when a conscious mode of mind has its feeling in a specific region of the skull, it may be thought perhaps that this spot of the skull may indicate by its shape what that mode is and what its peculiar nature. Just as, e.g., many people complain of feeling a painful tension somewhere in the head when thinking intensely, or even when thinking at all, so it might be that stealing, committing murder, writing poetry, and so on, could each be accompanied with its own proper feeling, which would over and above be bound to have its peculiar localization. This locality of the brain, which would in this manner be more disturbed and exercised, would also most likely develop further the contiguous locality of the bone of the skull; or again this latter locality would, from sympathy or conformity, not be inert, but would enlarge or diminish or in some other way assume a corresponding form.

What, however, makes such a hypothesis improbable is this: feeling in general is something indeterminate, and that feeling in the head as the centre might well be the general feeling that accompanies all suffering; so that mixed up with the thief's, murderer's, poet's tickling or pain in the head there would be other feelings too, and they would permit of being distinguished from one another, or from those we may call merely bodily feelings, as little as an illness can be determined from the symptom of headache, if we restrict its meaning merely to the bodily element.

In point of fact, from whatever side we look at the matter, all necessary reciprocal relation between them comes to nothing, as well as any intimation the one might give of the other in virtue of such a relation. If the relation is still to hold, what is left to form a sort of necessary relation is a pre-established harmony of the corresponding features of the two sides, a harmony which leaves the factors in question quite detached and rests on no inherent principle; for one of the aspects has to be a non-mental reality, a bare thing.

Thus then, on one side we have a number of passive regions of the skull, on the other a number of mental properties, the variety and character of which will depend on the condition of psychological investigation. The poorer the idea we have of mind, the easier the matter becomes in this respect; for, in part, the fewer become the mental properties, and, in part, the more detached, fixed, and ossified, and consequently more akin to features of the bone and more comparable with them. But, while much is doubtless made easier by this miserable representation of the mind, there still remains a very great deal to be found on both sides: there remains for observation to deal with the entire contingency of their relation. When every faculty of the soul, every passion and (for this, too, must be considered here) the various shades of characters, which the more refined psychology and "knowledge of mankind" are accustomed to talk about, are each and all assigned their place on the skull, and their contour on the skull-bone, the arbitrariness and artificiality of this procedure are just as glaring as if the children of Israel, who had been likened to "the sand by the seashore for multitude," had each assigned and taken to himself his own symbolic grain of sand!

The skull of a murderer has—not this organ or sign—but this "bump." But this murderer has in addition a lot of other properties, and other bumps too, and along with the bumps hollows as well. Bumps and hollows, there is room for selection! And again his murderous propensity can be referred to any bump or hollow, and this in turn to any mental quality; for the murderer is neither this abstraction of a murderer, nor does he have merely one protuberance and one depression. The observations offered on this point must therefore sound just about as sensible as those of the dealer about the rain at the annual fair, and of the housewife at her washing time.[8] Dealer and housewife might as well make the observation that it always rains when neighbour so-and-so passes by, or when they have roast pork. From the point of view of observation a given characteristic of mind is just as indifferent to a given formation of the skull as rain is indifferent to circumstances like these. For of the two objects thus under observation, the one is a barren isolated entity (*Fürsichsein*), an ossified property of mind, the other is an equally barren potentiality (*Ansichsein*). Such an ossified entity, as they both are, is completely indifferent to everything else. It is just as much a matter of indifference to a high bump whether a murderer is in close proximity, as to the murderer whether flatness is near him.

There is, of course, no getting over the *possibility* that still remains, that a bump at a certain place is connected with a certain property, passion, etc. We can think of the murderer with a high bump here at this place on the skull, the thief with one there. From this point of view phrenology is capable of much greater extension than it has yet had. For in the first instance it seems to be restricted merely to the connexion of a bump with a property in one and the same individual, in the sense that this individual possesses both. But phrenology *per naturam*—for there

---

[8] *v.* above, p. 183.

must be such a subject as well as a physiognomy *per naturam*—goes a long way beyond this restriction. It does not merely affirm that a cunning fellow has a bump like a fist lying behind the ear, but also puts forward the view that, not the unfaithful wife herself, but the other party to this conjugal transaction, has a bump on the brow.

In the same way, too, one may imagine the man living under the same roof with the murderer, or even his neighbour, or, going still further afield, imagine his fellow-citizens, etc., with high bumps on some part of the skull, just as well as one may picture to oneself the flying cow, that was first caressed by the crab riding on a donkey, and afterwards, etc., etc. But if possibility is taken not in the sense of a possibility of "imagining" but in the sense of *inner* possibility or possibility of *conceiving*, then the object is a reality of the kind which is a mere thing and is, and should be, deprived of a significance of this sort, and can thus only have it for imaginative or figurative thinking.

The observer may, in spite of the indifference of the two sides to one another, set to work to determine correlations, supported partly by the general rational principle that the outer is the expression of the inner, and partly by the analogy of the skulls of animals—which may doubtless have a simpler character than men, but of which at the same time it becomes just so much the more difficult to say what character they do have, in that it cannot be so easy for any man's imagination to think himself really into the nature of an animal. Should the observer do so, he will find, in giving out for certain the laws he maintains he has discovered, a first-rate means of assistance in a distinction which we too must necessarily take note of at this point.

The being of mind cannot be taken at any rate to be something completely rigid and immovable. Man is free. It will be admitted that the mind's original primordial being consists merely in *dispositions*, which mind has to a large extent under its control, or which require favourable circumstances to draw them out; i.e. an original "being" of mind must be equally well spoken of as what does not exist as a "being" at all. Were observations to conflict with what strikes any one as a warrantable law, should it happen to be fine weather at the annual fair or on the housewife's washing day—then dealer and housewife might say that it, properly speaking, should rain, and the conditions are really all that way. So too in the case of observing the skull, it might be said when those contradictory observations occur, that the given individual ought properly to be what according to the law his skull proclaims him to be, and that he has an original disposition which, however, has not been developed: this quality is not really present, but it *should* be there. The "law" and the "ought-to-be" rest on observation of actual showers of rain, and observation of the actual sense and meaning in the case of the given character of the skull; but if the *reality* is not present, the empty possibility is supposed to do just as well.

This mere possibility, i.e. the non-actuality of the law proposed, and hence the observations conflicting with the law, are bound to come out just for the reason that the freedom of the individual and the developing circumstances are indifferent towards what merely *is*, both in the sense of the original inner as well as the external ossiform structure, and also because the individual can be something else than he is in his original internal nature, and still more than what he is as a skull-bone.

We get, then, the possibility that a given bump or hollow on the skull may denote both something actual as well as a mere disposition, one indeed so little determined in any given direction as to denote something that is not actual at all. We see here, as always, the same result of a bad excuse, viz. that it is itself ready to be used *against* what it is intended to support. We see the thinking that merely "conjectures" brought by the very force of facts to say in unintelligent fashion the very opposite of what it holds to—to say that there is something indicated by such and such a bone, but also just as truly not indicated at all.

What hovers before this way of "conjecturing" when it makes this excuse is the true thought—a thought, however, which abolishes that way of "conjecturing,"—that being as such is not at all the truth of spirit. As the disposition is an original primordial being, having no share in the activity of mind, just such a being is the skull-bone on its side. What merely *is*, without participating in spiritual activity, is a thing for consciousness, and so little is it the essence of mind that it is rather the very opposite of it, and consciousness is only actual for itself by the negation and abolition of such a being.

From this point of view it must be regarded as a thorough denial of reason to give out a skull-bone as the actual existence of conscious life, and that is what it is given out to be when it is regarded as the outer expression of spirit; for the external expression is just the existent reality. It is no use to say we merely draw an inference from the outer as to the inner, which is something different, or to say that the outer is not the inner itself but merely its expression. For in the relation of the two to one another the character of the reality which thinks itself and is thought of by itself falls just on the side of the inner, while the outer has the character of existent reality.

When, therefore, a man is told, "You (your inner being) are so and so, because your skull-bone is so constituted," this means nothing else than that we regard a bone as the man's reality. To retort upon such a statement with a box on the ear—in the way mentioned above when dealing with physiognomy—removes primarily the "soft" parts of his head from their apparent dignity and position, and proves merely that *these* are no true inherent nature, are not the reality of mind; the retort here would, properly speaking, have to go the length of breaking the skull of the person who makes a statement like that, in order to demonstrate to him in a manner as palpable as his own wisdom that a bone is nothing of an inherent nature at all for a man, still less his true reality.

The untutored instinct of self-conscious reason will reject without examination phrenology—this other observing instinct of self-conscious reason, which having succeeded in making a guess at knowledge has grasped knowledge in the soulless form that the outer is an expression of the inner. But the worse the thought, the less sometimes does it strike us where its badness definitely lies, and the more difficult it is to explain it. For a thought is said to be the worse, the barer and emptier the abstraction, which thought takes to be the essential truth. But in the antithesis here in question the component parts are individuality conscious of itself, and the abstraction of a bare thing, to which externality has been reduced—the inner being of mind taken in the sense of a fixed soulless existence and in opposition to just such a being.

With the attainment of this, however, rational observation seems in fact to have also reached its culminating point, at which it must take leave of itself and turn right about; for it is only when anything is entirely bad that there is an inherent and immediate necessity in it to wheel round completely into its opposite. Just so it may be said of the Jews that it is precisely because they stand directly before the door of salvation, that they are and have been the most reprobate and abandoned:—what the nation should be in and for itself, this, the true inner nature of its self, it is not conscious of being, but puts away beyond itself. By this renunciation it creates for itself the *possibility* of a higher level of existence, if once it could get the object thus renounced back again to itself, than if it had never left its natural immediate state of existence—because spirit is all the greater the greater the opposition out of which it returns into itself; and such an opposition spirit brings about for itself, by doing away with its immediate unity, and laying aside its self-existence, a separate life of its own. But if such a consciousness does not mediate and reflect itself, the middle position or term where it has a determinate existence is the fatal unholy void, since what should give it substance and filling has been turned into a rigidly fixed extreme. It is thus that this last stage of reason's function of observation is its very worst, and for that reason its complete reversal becomes necessary.—

For the survey of the series of relations dealt with up to this point, which constitute the content and object of observation, shows that even in its first form, in observation of the relations of inorganic nature, sensuous being vanished from its ken. The moments of its relation (i.e. that of inorganic nature) present themselves as pure abstractions and as simple notions, which should be kept connected with the existence of things, but this gets lost, so that the abstract moment proves to be a pure movement and a universal. This free, self-complete process retains the significance of something objective; but now appears as a unit. In the process of the inorganic the unit is the inner with no existence. When the process does have existence *qua* unit, as one and single, it is an organism.

The unit *qua* self-existent or negative entity stands in antithesis to the universal, throws off its control, and remains independent by itself, so that the notion, being only realized in the condition of absolute dissociation, fails to find in organic existence its genuine expression, in the sense that it is not there, in the form of a universal; it remains an "outer," or, what is the same thing, an "inner" of organic nature.

The organic process is merely free implicitly (*an sich*); it is not so explicitly, "for itself" (*für sich*). The explicit phase of its freedom appears in the idea of purpose, has existence as another inner nature as a self-directing wisdom that lies outside that mere process. Reason's function of observation thus turns its attention to this wisdom, to mind, to the notion actually existing as universality, or to the purpose existing in the form of purpose; and what constitutes its own essential nature is now the object before it.

Reason here in the activity of observation is directed first to the pure abstract form of its essential nature. But since reason, in its apprehension of the object thus working and moving amidst its own distinctions takes this object as something that exists, observation becomes aware of laws of thought, relations of one constant factor to another constant factor. The content of these laws being, however, merely moments, they run together into the single one of self-consciousness.

This new object, taken in the same way as existent, is the contingent individual self-consciousness. The process of observation, therefore, keeps within the "conjectured" meaning of mind, and within the contingent relation of conscious to unconscious reality. Mind alone in itself is the necessity of this relation. Observation, therefore, attacks it at closer quarters, and compares its realization through will and action with its reality when it contemplates and is reflected into itself, a reality which is itself objective. This external aspect, although an utterance of the individual which he himself contains, is at the same time, *qua* symbol, something indifferent to the content which it is intended to denote, just as what finds for itself the symbol is indifferent to this symbol.

For this reason, observation finally passes from this variable form of utterance back to the permanent fixed being, and in principle declares that externality is the outer immediate reality of mind, not in the sense of an organ, and not like a language or a symbol, but in the sense of a lifeless thing. What the very first form of observation of inorganic nature did away with and superseded, viz. the idea that the notion should appear in the shape of a thing, this last form of observation reinstates so as to turn the reality of mind itself into a thing, or expressing it the other way about, so as to give lifeless being the significance of mind.

Observation has thus reached the point of explicitly expressing what our notion of observation was at the outset, viz. that rational certainty means objectivity of reason, that the certainty of reason seeks itself as an objective reality.

One does not, indeed, suppose that mind, which is represented by a skull, is defined as a thing. There is not meant to be any materialism, as it is called, in this idea; mind rather must be something very different from these bones of the skull. But that mind *is, means* nothing else than that it is a *thing*. When being as such, or thingness, is predicated of the mind, the true and genuine expression for this is, therefore, that mind is such an entity as a bone is. Hence it must be considered as supremely important that the true expression has been found for the bare statement regarding mind—that it *is*. When the statement is ever made about mind, that it *is*, has a being, is a *thing*, an individual reality, we do not *mean* it is something we can see, or knock about, or take in our hands, and so on, but that is what we *say*, and what the statement really amounts to is consequently conveyed in the expression that the existence of mind is a bone.

This result has now a twofold significance: one is its true meaning, in so far as the result is a completion of the outcome of the preceding movement of self-consciousness. The unhappy self-consciousness renounced its independence, and wrested its distinctive self-existence out into the shape of a thing. By doing so, it left the level of self-consciousness and reverted to the condition of mere consciousness, i.e. to that phase of conscious life for which the object is an existent, a thing. But what is "thing" in this case is self-consciousness; "thing" here is the unity of ego and being—the Category. When the object before consciousness is determined thus, consciousness possesses reason. Consciousness, as well as self-consciousness, is in itself properly reason in an implicit form; but only that consciousness can be said to *have* reason whose object has the character of being the category. From this, however, we must still distinguish the knowledge of what reason *is*.

The category, which is the immediate unity of being and self (*Seyn und Seinen*), must traverse both forms, and the conscious attitude of observation is just where the category is set forth in the form of being. In its result, consciousness expresses that, whose unconscious implicit certainty it is, in the shape of a proposition—the proposition which lies in the very notion of reason. This proposition is the infinite judgment that the self is a thing—a judgment that cancels and transcends itself.

Through this result, then, the category gets the added characteristic of being this self-cancelling opposition. The "pure" category, which is present to consciousness in the form of being or immediacy, is still an unmediated, a merely given object, and the attitude of consciousness is also direct, has no mediation in it. That infinite judgment is the moment which is the transition of immediacy into mediation or negativity. The given present object is therefore characterized as a negative object while consciousness in its relation towards it assumes the form of *self*-consciousness; or the category, which traversed the form of *being* in the process of observation, is now set up in the form of self-existence. Consciousness no longer seeks to find itself immediately, but to produce itself by its own activity. Consciousness itself is the purpose and end of its own action, as in the process of observation it had to do merely with things.

The other meaning of the result is the one already considered, that of unsystematic (*begrifflos*) observation. This has no other way of understanding and expressing itself than by declaring the reality of self-consciousness to consist in the skull-bone, just as it appears in the form of a thing of sense, still retaining its character as an object for consciousness. In stating this, however, it has no clear consciousness as to what the statement involves, and does not grasp the determinate character of the subject and predicate in the proposition and of their relation to one another, still less does it grasp the proposition in the sense of a self-resolving infinite judgment and a notion. Rather, in virtue of a deeper-lying self-consciousness of mind, which has the appearance here of being an innate decency and honesty of nature, it conceals from itself the ignominiousness of such an irrational crude thought as that of taking a bone for the reality of self-consciousness; and the very senselessness of introducing all sorts of relations of cause and effect, "symbol," "organ," etc., which are perfectly meaningless here, and of hiding away the glaring folly of the proposition behind distinctions derived from them—all this puts a gloss on that thought and whitewashes its naked absurdity.

Brain-fibres and the like, looked at as forms of the being of mind, are already an imagined, a merely hypothetical actuality of mind—not its presented reality, not its felt, seen, in short not its true reality. If they are present to us, if they are seen, they are lifeless objects, and then no longer pass for the being of mind. But its objectivity proper must take an immediate, a sensuous form, so that in this objectivity *qua* lifeless—

for the bone is lifeless so far as the lifeless is found in the living being itself—mind is established as actual.

The principle involved in this idea is that reason claims to be all thinghood, even thinghood of a purely objective kind. It is this, however, *in conceptu:* or, only this notion is the truth of reason; and the purer the notion itself is, the more silly an idea does it become, if its content does not take the shape of a notion (*Begriff*) but of a mere presentation or idea (*Vorstellung*)—if the self-superseding judgment is not taken with the consciousness of this its infinity, but is taken as a stable and permanent proposition, the subject and predicate of which hold good each on its own account, self fixed as self, thing as thing, while one has to be the other all the same.

Reason, essentially the notion, is immediately parted asunder into itself and its opposite, an opposition which just for that reason is immediately again superseded. But if it presents itself in this way as both itself and its opposite, and if it is held fast in the entirely isolated moment of this disintegration, reason is apprehended in an irrational form; and the purer the moments of this opposition are, the more glaring is the appearance of this content, which is either alone for consciousness, or alone expressed ingenuously by consciousness.

The "depth" which mind brings out from within, but carries no further than to make it a presentation (*Vorstellung*), and let it remain at this level—and the "ignorance" on the part of this consciousness as to what it really says, are the same kind of connexion of higher and lower which, in the case of the living being, nature naïvely expresses when it combines the organ of its highest fulfilment, the organ of generation, with the organ of urination. The infinite judgment *qua* infinite would be the fulfilment of life that comprehends itself, while the consciousness of the infinite judgment that remains at the level of presentation corresponds to urination.

B

THE REALIZATION OF RATIONAL SELF-CONSCIOUSNESS
THROUGH ITS OWN ACTIVITY

In this section we have the second form in which rational experience is realized. In "observation" mind is directly aware of itself as in conscious unity with its object: it makes no effort of its own to realize this unity: it finds the unity by looking on, so to say. But it may have the same experience by creating through its own effort an object constituted and determined solely by its self. Here it does not *find* the unity of itself and its object; it *makes* the object at one with itself by moulding the character and content of the object after its own nature.

As contrasted with observation, which may be called the operation of "theoretical" reason, this new way of having a rational experience may be called the operation of "practical" reason. In the first we have reason in the form of knowledge and science, in the second, reason in the sense of rational action and practice.

It is this second way of establishing the experience of reason which is analysed in the following sections. The immediately succeeding section describes the experience in its general features. We have here the sphere of conscious purpose and the foundation of moral and social life.

SELF-CONSCIOUSNESS found the "thing" in the form of itself, and itself in the form of a thing; that is to say, self-consciousness is explicitly aware of being in itself the objective reality. It is no longer the *immediate* certainty of being all reality; it is rather a kind of certainty for which the immediate in general assumes the form of something sublated, so that the objectivity of the immediate is regarded now merely as something superficial whose inner core and essence is self-conscious consciousness.

The object, therefore, to which self-consciousness is positively related, is a self-consciousness. The object has the form and character of thinghood, i.e. is independent: but self-consciousness has the conviction that this independent object is not alien to itself; it knows herewith that itself is inherently (*an sich*) recognized by the object. Self-consciousness is mind, which has the assurance of having, in the duplication of its self-consciousness and in the independence of both, its unity with its own self. This certainty has to be brought out now before the mind in all its truth; what self-consciousness holds as a fact, viz. that implicitly *in* itself and in its *inner* certainty it *is*, has to enter into its consciousness and become explicit *for* it.

What the general stages of this actualization will be can be indicated in a general way by reference to the road thus far traversed. Just as reason, when exercised in observation, repeated in the medium of the category the movement of "consciousness" as such, namely, sense-certainty,[1] perception,[2] and understanding,[3] the course of reason here, too, will again traverse the double movement of "self-consciousness," and from independence pass over into its freedom. To begin with, this active reason is aware of itself merely as "an individual," and must, being such, demand and bring forth its reality in an "other." Thereafter, however, its consciousness being lifted into universality, it becomes

---

[1] Viz. in descriptive observation of nature as such.
[2] Viz. in observation of living nature, the "organic."
[3] Viz. in observation of nature as the external reality of mind, laws of thought, psychology, physiognomy, phrenology.

universal reason, and is consciously aware of itself as reason, as something already recognized in and for itself, which within its pure
consciousness unites all self-consciousness. It is the simple ultimate
spiritual reality (*Wesen*), which, by coming at the same time to consciousness, is the real substance, into which preceding forms return
and in which they find their ground, so that they are, as contrasted with
reference to the latter, merely particular moments of the process of its
coming into being, moments which indeed break loose and appear as
forms on their own account, but have in fact only existence and actuality when borne and supported by it, and only retain their truth in so
far as they are and remain in it.

If we take this final result of the process as it is when really accomplished—this end, which is the notion that has already become manifest before us, viz. recognized self-consciousness, which has the certainty of itself in the other free self-consciousness, and finds its truth
precisely there; in other words, if we bring this still inward and un-
evolved mind to light as the substance that has developed into its concrete existence—we shall find that in this notion there is opened up the
realm of the Social Order, the Ethical World (*Sittlichkeit*). For this latter is nothing else than the absolute spiritual unity of the essential substance (*Wesen*) of individuals in their independent reality; it is an
inherently universal self-consciousness, which is aware of being so concrete and real in an other consciousness, that this latter has complete
independence, is looked on as a "thing," and the universal self-
consciousness is aware precisely therein of its unity with that "thing,"
and is only then self-consciousness, when thus in unity with this objective being (*Wesen*). This ethical substance when taken in its abstract
universality is only the conception of law, thought-constituted law; but
just as much it is immediately actual self-consciousness, it is Custom
(*Sitte*). The single individual conversely, is only a "this," a given existent unit, in so far as he is aware of the universal consciousness as his
own being in his own particular individuality, seeing that his action and
existence are the universal custom.

In point of fact the notion of the realization of self-conscious reason—of directly apprehending complete unity with another in his independence: of having for my object an other in the fashion of a
"thing" found detached and apart from me, and the negative of myself,
and of taking this as my own self-existence (*Fürmichseyn*)—finds its
complete reality in fulfilment in the life of a nation. Reason appears
here as the fluent universal substance, as unchangeable simple thinghood which yet breaks up into many entirely independent beings, just
as light bursts asunder into stars as innumerable luminous points, each
giving light on its own account, and whose absolute self-existence

(*Fürsichseyn*) is dissolved, not merely implicitly (*an sich*), but explicitly for themselves (*für sich*), within the simple independent substance. They are conscious within themselves of being these individual independent beings through the fact that they surrender and sacrifice their particular individuality, and that this universal substance is their soul and essence—as this universal again is the action of themselves as individuals, and is the work and product of their own activity.

The purely particular activity and business of the individual refer to needs which he has as a part of nature, i.e. as a mere existent particular. That even these, its commonest functions, do not come to nothing, but have reality, is brought about by the universal sustaining medium, the might of the entire nation.

It is not merely, however, this *form* of subsistence for his activity in general that the individual gets in the universal substance, but likewise also his *content*; what he does is what all are capable of doing, is the custom all follow. This content, in so far as it is completely particularized, is, in its concrete reality, confined within the limits of the activity of all. The labour of the individual for his own wants is just as much a satisfaction of those of others as of himself, and the satisfaction of his own he attains only by the labour of others.

As the individual in his own particular work *ipso facto* accomplishes unconsciously a universal work, so again he also performs the universal task as his *conscious* object. The whole becomes *in its entirety* his work, for which he sacrifices himself, and precisely by that means receives back his own self from it.

There is nothing here which may not be reciprocal, nothing in regard to which the independence of the individual may not, in dissipating its existence on its own account (*Fürsichseyn*), in negating itself, give itself its positive significance of existing for itself. This unity of existing for another, or making self a "thing," and of existence for self, this universal substance, utters its universal language in the *customs* and *laws* of a[4] nation. But this existent unchangeable nature (*Wesen*) is nothing else than the expression of the particular individuality which seems opposed to it: the laws give expression to that which each individual is and does; the individual knows them not merely to be what constitutes his universal objective nature as a "thing," but knows himself, too, in that form, or knows it to be particularized in his own individuality and in each of his fellow-citizens. In the universal mind, therefore, each has the certainty only of himself, the certainty of finding in the actual reality nothing but himself; he is as certain of the

---

[4]The first and succeeding editions read "seines" Volks: Lasson proposes "eines." This seems correct in the context.

others as of himself. I apprehend and see in all of them that they are in their own eyes (*für sich selbst*) only these independent beings just as I am. I see in their case the free unity with others in such wise that just as this unity exists through me, so it exists through the others too—I see them as myself, myself as them.

In a free nation, therefore, reason is in truth realized. It is a present living spirit, where the individual not only finds his destiny (*Bestimmung*), i.e. his universal and particular nature (*Wesen*), expressed and given to him in the fashion of a thing, but himself is this essential being, and has also attained his destiny. The wisest men of antiquity for that reason declared that wisdom and virtue consist in living in accordance with the customs of one's own nation.

From this happy state, however, of having attained its destiny, and of living in it, the self-consciousness, which in the first instance is only immediately and in principle spirit, has broken away; or perhaps it has not yet attained it: for both can be said with equal truth.

Reason must pass out of and leave this happy condition. For only implicitly or immediately is the life of a free nation the real objective ethical order (*Sittlichkeit*). In other words, the latter is an existent social order, and in consequence this universal mind is also an individualized mind. It is the totality of customs and laws of a particular people, a specifically determinate ethical substance, which casts off this limitation only when it reaches the higher moment, namely, when it becomes conscious regarding its own nature; only with this knowledge does it get its absolute truth, and not as it is immediately in its bare existence. In this latter form it is, on the one hand, a restricted ethical substance, on the other, absolute limitation consists just in this that mind is in the form of existence.

Hence, further, the individual, as he immediately finds his existence in the actual objective social order, in the life of his nation, has a solid imperturbable confidence; the universal mind has not for him resolved itself into its abstract moments, and thus, too, he does not think of himself as existing in singleness and independence. When however he has once arrived at this knowledge, as indeed he must, this immediate unity with mind, this undifferentiated existence in the substance of mind, his naïve confidence, is lost. Isolated by himself he is himself now the central essential reality—no longer universal mind. The element of this singleness of self-consciousness is no doubt in universal mind itself, but merely as a vanishing quantity, which, as it appears with an existence of its own, is straightway resolved within the universal, and only becomes consciously felt in the form of that confidence. When the individual gets fixity in the form of singleness (and every moment, being a moment of the essential reality, must manage to reveal itself as essential), the individual has thereby set himself over against the laws and customs. These latter are looked on as merely a thought without absolutely essential significance, an abstract theory without reality; while he *qua* this particular ego is in his own view the living truth.

Or, again [we can say, as above stated, that] self-consciousness has *not yet attained* this happy state of being ethical substance, the spirit of a people. For, after leaving the process of rational Observation, mind, at first, is not yet as such actually realized through itself; it is merely affirmed as *inner* nature and essence, or as abstraction. In other words, mind is first immediate. As immediately existing, however, it is individualized. It is *practical consciousness*, which steps into the world it finds lying ready-made with the intention of duplicating itself in the determinate form of an individual, of producing itself as this particular individual, and creating this its own existential counterpart, and thus becoming conscious of this unity of its own actual reality with the objective world. Self-consciousness possesses the *certainty* of this unity; it holds that the unity is implicitly (*an sich*) already present, or that this union and agreement between itself and "thinghood" (objective existence) is already an accomplished fact, and has only to become expressly so for it through its own agency; or that its making that unity is at the same time and as much its finding the unity. Since this unity means happiness, the individual is thus sent forth into the world by his own spirit to seek his happiness.

If, then, we for our part find the truth of this rational self-consciousness to be ethical substance, that self-consciousness on its part finds here the beginning of its ethical experience of the world. From the point of view that it has not yet attained to its ethical substance, this movement presses onwards to that end, and what is cancelled in the process are the particular moments which self-consciousness takes as valid in isolation. They have the form of an immediate will-process, or impulse of nature, which attains its satisfaction, this satisfaction itself being the content of a new impulse. Looking at self-consciousness, however, as having lost the happiness of being in the substance, these natural impulses are bound up with a consciousness that their purpose is the true destiny and essential nature of self-consciousness. Ethical substance has sunk to the level of a floating selfless adjective, whose living subjects are individuals, which have to fill up their universality through themselves, and to provide for their destiny out of the same source.

Taken in the former sense, then, those forms and modes are the process by which the ethical substance comes to be, and precede this substance: in the latter they succeed it, and disclose for self-consciousness what its destined nature is. In the former aspect the immediacy or raw brute impulses get lost in the process of finding out what their truth is, and their content passes over to a higher. In the latter aspect, however, the false idea of consciousness, which puts its characteristic nature in those impulses, passes to a higher idea. In the former case the goal which they attain is the immediate ethical substance; while, in the latter, the end is the consciousness of that substance, such a consciousness as knows the substance to be its own essential being; and to that extent this process would be the development of morality (*Moralität*), a higher state or attitude than the former (*Sittlichkeit*). But these modes at the same time constitute only one side of the development of morality, that, namely, which belongs to self-existence, or in which consciousness cancels *its* purposes; they do not constitute the side where morality arises out of the substance itself. Since these moments cannot yet have the signification of being made into purposes in opposition to the lost social order (*Sittlichkeit*), they hold here no doubt in their simple uncriticized content, and the end towards which they work is the ethical substance: but since with our time is more directly associated that form of these moments in which they appear after consciousness has lost its ethical custom-constituted (*sittliches*) life, and in the search for it repeats those forms, they may be represented more after this latter manner of expression.

Self-consciousness, which is as yet merely the notion of mind, takes this path with the specific characteristic of being to itself the essential reality *qua* individual mind, and its purpose, therefore, is to give itself actualization as individual, and to enjoy itself, *qua* individual, in so doing.

In existing for itself it is aware of itself as the essentially real. In this character it is the negativity of the other. There arises, therefore, within its consciousness an opposition between itself *qua* positive and something which no doubt exists, but *for it* not in the sense of existing substantially. Consciousness appears sundered into this objective reality found lying at its hand, and the purpose, which it carries out by the process of cancelling that objectivity, and which it makes the actual fact instead of the given object. Its primary purpose, however, is its immediate abstract existence for itself, in other words seeing itself as this particular individual in another, or seeing another self-consciousness as itself. The experience of what the truth of this purpose is, places self-consciousness on a higher plane, and henceforth it is to itself purpose, in so far as it is at once universal, and has the law immediately within it. In carrying out this law of its heart, however, it learns that here the individual cannot preserve himself, but rather the good can only be performed through the sacrifice of the individual: and so it passes into *Virtue*. The experience which virtue goes through can be no other than that of finding that its purpose is already implicitly (*an sich*) carried out, that happiness lies immediately in action itself, and action itself is the good. The principle or notion of this entire sphere of experience — viz. that "thinghood" is the independent self-existence of mind — becomes in the course of this experience an objective fact *for* self-consciousness. In that self-consciousness has found this principle, it is aware of itself as reality in the sense of directly self-expressing *Individuality*, which no longer finds any resistance in a reality opposed to it, and whose object and purpose are merely this function of self-expression.

a

PLEASURE AND NECESSITY

The succeeding three sections discuss the procedure of one-sided subjective individualism — the attempt to realize the individual and yet not transcend the particular individuality. The first thought of self-consciousness when it seeks to realize or objectify itself as a mere individual is to make the objective element return directly to itself and bring a sense of increase of its own individual being or private Pleasure. This is all its interest in the practical realization of its purposes. But the realization of purposes is an expression of the life of reason, and reason means *universality* and systematic connexion of the content realized. Hence to seek solely private satisfaction or pleasure by a process which is inherently universal is a contradiction in terms. This contradiction the individual discovers in the shape of a sharp and painful contrast between its private feeling of individuation on the one hand and a network of universal connexion on the other — the contrast between "pleasure" and "necessity." *Both* fall within the individual's experience as a *rational* agent, and hence this necessity is his own necessity as much as the pleasure is his own pleasure. In the opposition between these factors there is no question as to which must triumph, and which must surrender.

This is the type of experience analysed in the following section. It is an experience that constantly recurs in the life-history of most if not all human beings at one stage or another in their development. The analysis contained in this section is indirectly a searching criticism of Hedonism in all its forms.

SELF-CONSCIOUSNESS, which is aware of being the reality, has its object within itself, but an object which, at first, is merely its own (*für sich*), and is not yet in actual existence. Existence stands opposed to it as a reality other than its own; and the aim of self-consciousness consists in carrying out what it is "for itself" so as to see itself as another independent being. This first purpose is to become conscious, in that other self-consciousness, of itself as an individual, to turn this other into its own self. It has the assurance that this other already is essentially itself.

In so far as it has risen from out of the substance of ethical life and the quiescent state of thought, and attained its conscious independence, it has left behind the law of custom and of substantial existence, the kinds of knowledge acquired through observation, and the sphere of theory; these lie behind it as a gray shadow that is just vanishing. For this latter is rather a knowledge of something, the independent existence (*Fürsichseyn*) and actuality of which are other than those of self-consciousness. It is not the seemingly divine spirit of universality in knowledge and action, wherein (all individual) feeling and enjoyment are stilled, that has passed into and fills this new level of self-consciousness; but the spirit of the earth, a spirit which holds that being alone as true reality which is the reality of individual consciousness.

> It repudiates sense and science
> The highest gifts possessed by men—
> It has gone over to the devil,
> And must be o'erthrown.[1]

It plunges thus into life, and carries to its completion the pure individuality in which it appears. It does not so much make its own happiness as take it directly and enjoy it. The grey shades of science, laws and principles, which alone stand between it and its own reality, vanish like a lifeless mist that cannot contend against the living certainty of its reality. It takes to itself life much as a ripe fruit is plucked, which comes to meet the hand that takes it.[2]

Its action is only in one respect an act of Desire; it does not aim at abolishing the objective fact in its entirety, but only the form of its otherness or objectivity, which is an unreal appearance; for it holds this to be inherently and implicitly the same reality as its own self. The sphere in which desire and its object subsist independently and indifferent towards each other is that of living existence; the enjoyment of desire cancels this existence, so far as it belongs to the object of desire. But here this element, which gives to both separate and distinct actuality, is rather the category, a form of being which has essentially the character of a presented being. It (i.e. the element) is therefore the *consciousness* of independence—it may be natural consciousness, or the consciousness developed into a system of laws—which preserves the individuals each for himself. This separation does not *per se* hold for self-consciousness, which knows the other as its own proper self-hood. It attains therefore to the enjoyment of *Pleasure*, to the consciousness of its actualization in a consciousness which appears as independent, or to the intuition of the unity of both independent self-consciousnesses. It

---

[1] *Faust* (adapted).
[2] Cp. Spenser's *Faerie Queene*, Bk. 2: Canto 12, 54.

succeeds in its purpose, but only to learn there what the truth of that purpose is. It conceives itself as this individual self-existent (*Fürsichseinde*) being; but the actualization of this purpose is just the cancelling of the purpose. For it comes consciously to be, not object in the sense of a given particular individual, but rather as unity of its self and the other self-consciousness, consequently as cancelled and transcended individual, i.e. as universal.

The pleasure enjoyed has, indeed, the positive significance that the self has become aware of itself as objective self-consciousness: but the negative import is there as well—that of having cancelled itself. And since it took its realization in the former sense only, its experience comes consciously before it as contradiction, in which the acquired reality of its individual existence finds itself destroyed by the negative element, which stands without reality and without content over against the former, and yet is the force which consumes it. This negative element is nothing else than the notion of what this individuality inherently is. This individuality is, however, as yet the poorest form of self-realizing mind; for it is to itself still simply the abstraction of reason, or is the merely immediate unity of being-for-self and being-in-self (*Fürsich und Ansichseyns*), of explicit and implicit self. Its essential nature therefore is only the abstract category. Still it has no longer the form of immediate simple *being* as in the case of Observation, where it is abstract being, or, when affirmed as something alien, is thinghood in general. Here in the case before us there has entered into this thinghood self-existence (*Fürsichseyn*) and mediation. It comes on the scene here, therefore, in the form of a circular process, whose content is the developed pure relation of the simple essential elements. The actualization attained in the case of this individuality consists, therefore, in nothing else than its having turned out this cycle of abstractions from the restricted confines of simple self-consciousness, and put them into the sphere and condition of "being for consciousness" existence, where they appear spread out in detail as distinct objects.

The sort of object, then, that self-consciousness in its pleasurable enjoyment takes to be its true reality, is the detailed expansion of those bare essential elements—of pure unity, of pure difference, and of their relation. Further than this the object, which individuality experiences as its true nature, has no content. It is what is called *Necessity*. For Necessity, Fate, or the like, is just that about which we are unable to say what it is doing, what its definite laws and its positive content actually are, because it is the absolute pure notion itself, viewed as *being*, relation bare and simple, but imperturbable, irresistible, and immovable, whose work is merely the nothingness of individual existence. It is this firm unbending connexion, because that which is connected consists in pure essentialities or empty abstractions. Unity, Difference, and Relation are categories, each of which is nothing as it stands by itself, but only in its relation to its opposite, and they therefore cannot come apart from one another. They are by their own notion related to each other, for they are the pure notions themselves; and this absolute relation and abstract process constitute Necessity. The merely particular individuality, which has in the first instance only the pure notion of reason for its content, instead of having escaped from dead theory and plunged into actual life, has thus only precipitated itself into consciousness of its own lifelessness, and enjoys itself merely as naked and alien necessity, *lifeless* actuality.

The transition takes the place from the form of oneness to that of universality, from one absolute abstraction into the other; it proceeds from that purpose of pure explicit existence-for-self, which has cast off fellowship and communion with others, into the sheer opposite—i.e. into equally abstract implicit immanent existence—into mere being-in-itself. This appears consequently in such form that the individual is simply reduced to naught, and the utter atomicity of separate individual existence is pulverized on the equally hard but continuous actuality.

Since it is *qua* consciousness the unity of itself and its opposite, this transition is still a fact *for* it. Its purpose, and its realization as well as the contradiction of what constituted for it its essential nature, and what *inherently* that nature is—all this it is consciously aware of. It learns the double meaning which lies in what it did, when it sought to "take" and possess its life: it "took" life, but thereby rather laid hold on death.

This transition of its living being into lifeless necessity appears to it therefore a perversion which is mediated by no agency at all. The mediating factor would have to be that in which both sides would be one, where consciousness thus knew the one moment in the other, found its purpose and action in Fate, and its fate in its purpose and action, saw its own true nature in this Necessity. But, for consciousness the meaning of this unity here is just pleasure itself, or simple particular feeling; and the transition from the moment of this its purpose into the moment of its true nature is for it a mere leap into the opposite. For these moments are not contained and combined in feeling, but only in the bare pure self, which is a universal or thought. Consciousness, therefore, through the experience in which its truth ought to have come to light, has instead become to itself a dark riddle; the consequences of its deeds are to it not really its own deeds. What happens to it is found to be not the experience of what it inherently is; the transition is not a mere alteration in form of the same content and essential nature, presented now as content and true reality of consciousness, thereafter as object or intuitively perceived essence of itself. The abstract necessity thus gets the significance of the merely negative uncomprehended power of universality, on which individuality is broken in pieces.

The appearance of this mode of self-consciousness goes as far as this stage. The last moment of the existence of this mode is the thought of its loss and annihilation in necessity, or the thought of itself as a being (*Wesen*) entirely alien to itself. Self-consciousness in itself, however, has survived this loss; for this necessity or pure universality is its own proper nature (*Wesen*). This reflexion of consciousness into self, the knowledge that necessity is itself, is a new mode or attitude of consciousness.

b

THE LAW OF THE HEART, AND THE FRENZY OF SELF-CONCEIT

The following section is an analysis of the mood of moral Sentimentalism. It is a mood of all times and appears in many forms; but about Hegel's time it became prominent in the Romantic school and was frankly adopted as a practical attitude by certain of its representatives. Perhaps one of the most remarkable historic examples of sentimentalism was Rousseau, to whom so much in the romantic movement may be traced. In the literature of Hegel's time, and indeed in all literature, no more perfect type of sentimentalism can be found than Goethe's *Werther*. With such instances as these in our minds the succeeding analysis requires neither explanation nor comment.

NECESSITY is for this new mode of consciousness what in truth self-consciousness finds necessity in its own case to be. In its new attitude self-consciousness regards itself as the necessary element. It knows that it has the universal, the law, immediately within itself, a law which, because of this characteristic of being immediately within consciousness as it is for itself, is called the Law of the *Heart*. This mode or attitude of consciousness is for itself, *qua* individual, essential reality as the former mode similarly was; but in the present case it is richer by the characteristic that this self-existence is taken as necessary or universal.

The law, therefore, which is primarily the law proper of self-consciousness, or a "heart" which however has in it a law, is the purpose which the self proceeds to realize. It remains to be seen whether its realization corresponds to its notion, and whether it will therein come to find this its law to be the essential ultimate fact.

Opposed to this "heart" stands a reality. For in the "heart" the law is in the first place merely for itself; it is not yet actualized, and thus, too, is something other than what the notion is. This other is thereby characterized as a reality which is the antithesis of what is to be realized, and consequently is the contradiction of the law and the individual. This reality is thus on the one hand a law by which the particular individuality is crushed and oppressed, a violent ordinance of the world which contradicts the law of the heart, and, on the other hand, a humanity suffering under that ordinance—a humanity which does not follow the law of the heart, but is subjected to an alien necessity.

This reality, appearing in opposition to the present mode of consciousness is, as is evident, nothing but the foregoing diremption of individuality and its truth, a relation of gruesome necessity, under which the former is crushed. We, who trace the process, see the preceding movement, therefore, as in opposition to the new form, because the latter has essentially arisen from it, and the moment whence the new form comes is necessary for it. The new mode, however, looks on that moment as something simply met with, since it has no consciousness of its origin, and takes its real essence to consist rather in being independent, in being for itself, or negatively disposed toward this positive, implicit, immanent content.

The aim and object of this individuality is thus to cancel and transcend this necessity which contradicts the law of the heart, as also to do away with the suffering thereby arising. There is in consequence no longer here the frivolity of the former mode, which merely wanted private and particular pleasure; it is the earnestness of a high purpose, which seeks its pleasure in displaying the excellence of its own true nature, and in bringing about the welfare of mankind. What it realizes is itself the law, and its pleasure is at the same time universal, a pleasure which all hearts feel. To it both are inseparable; its pleasure is what conforms to the law and the realization of the law of all mankind affords it its particular pleasure. For within its own self individuality and necessity are immediately and directly one; the law is a law of the heart. Individuality is not yet removed from its place; and the unity of both has not been brought about by means of the development of individuality, has not yet been established by discipline. The realization of the immediate undisciplined nature passes for a display of excellence and for bringing about the well-being of mankind.

The law, again, which is opposed to the law of the heart is divided from the heart, and exists on its own account. Mankind, which is bound to it, does not live in the blissful unity of the law with the heart, but either lives in dismal separation and suffering, or at least in deprivation of the enjoyment of itself in obeying the law, and without the consciousness of its own excellence in overstepping it. Because that all-dominating divine and human ordinance is divided from the heart it is regarded by the latter as a delusion, which ought to lose what it still possesses, namely, power and actuality. It may, indeed, in its content agree by chance with the law of the heart, and then the latter can acquiesce in it. But, for the heart, it is not the bare conformity to law as such, which constitutes the essential fact (*Wesen*), but the consciousness of itself which the "heart" thereby obtains, the fact that it has therein found self-satisfaction. Where the content of universal necessity, however, does not agree with the heart, necessity is, as regards its content also, nothing in itself, and must give way before the law of the heart.

The individual, then, fulfils, carries out the law of his heart. This law becomes a universal ordinance, and pleasure becomes a reality which, as it stands, conforms to law. But in this realization, the law has, in point of fact, escaped the individual; and thus there arises immediately only that relation which ought to be cancelled. The law of the heart ceases through its very realization to be a law of the heart. For it thereby takes on the form of actually "being," and is now universal power, which holds this particular "heart" to be a matter of indifference; so that the individual, in establishing his own ordinance, no longer finds it to be his own. By realizing his law he consequently brings about, not *his* law, but—since the realization is inherently and implicitly his own, but explicitly alien and external—merely this: he gets involved and entangled in the actual ordinance, and, indeed, entangled in it, not merely as something alien to himself but as a hostile, overpowering dominion.

By his act he takes his place in, or rather as, the general element of existent actuality; and his act is, even in his own regard, intended to have the value of a universal ordinance. But thereby he has let himself get detached from his own self; *qua* universality he lives, grows on his own account, and purifies himself of individuality. The individual who will only recognize universality in the form of his own immediate self-subsistence (*Fürsichseyn*) does not, therefore, recognize himself in this liberated and independent universality, while all the same he belongs to it, because the latter is his doing. This doing thus has the reverse significance; it contradicts the universal ordinance. For the individual's act is intended to be that of his individual heart, and not independent universal reality; and at the same time he has, in fact, recognized and acknowledged this latter, for the act has the import of setting up his essential nature as free and independent reality, that is to say, of recognizing reality to be his own essential being.

The individual has, by the very principle of his action, determined the more special manner in which actual universality, to which he has leagued himself, gets turned against him. His act, *qua* actuality, belongs to the universal; its content, however, is his own individuality, which wants to preserve itself as this particular individuality in opposition to universality. It is not any specific law whose establishment is in question; on the contrary, the immediate unity of the individual heart with universality is the idea—raised to the dignity of a law and claiming to be valid—that every heart must recognize its own self in what is universal law. But only the heart of this individual has established its reality in his act, which, in his view, expresses his self-existence (*Fürsichseyn*) or his pleasure. The act is intended to stand immediately for what is universal; that is to say, it is in truth something particular, and has merely the form of universality: his particular content is, as such, to pass for universal. Hence others find in this content not the law of their heart fulfilled, but rather that of some one else; and precisely in accordance with the universal law, that each is to find *his own* heart in what is law, they turn against that reality which he set up, just as he on his side turned against theirs. The individual therefore finds, as at first merely the rigid law, so now the hearts of men themselves opposed to his excellent intentions, and to be detested and detestable.

Because this type of consciousness finds universality in the first place merely as immediate, and knows necessity as necessity of the heart, the nature of actualization and effective activity is to it unknown. This consciousness is unaware that effective realization involves objective existence, and is in its truth the inherently universal in which the particular life of consciousness, which commits itself to it in order to have being in the sense of this immediate individual life, is really submerged. Instead of obtaining this particular life of its own in that objective existence, it thus becomes estranged from itself. But that in which it does not know itself is no longer dead necessity, but necessity animated by universal individuality. It took this divine and human ordinance, which it found authoritative, to be a dead reality, wherein not only its own self—which claims the position of a particular individual, insists on being a particular "heart" with a life of its own and opposed to the universal—but those as well who were subject to this reality had no consciousness of themselves. Now, however, it finds that reality animated by the consciousness of all, and a law for all hearts. It learns through experience that the reality in question is an ordinance infused and endowed with life, and learns this, indeed, just by the fact that it actualizes the law of its own heart. For this means nothing else than that individuality becomes its own object in the form of universality, without however recognizing itself therein.

Thus, then, what the experience of this mode of self-consciousness reveals as the truth, contradicts what this mode takes itself to be. What, however, it takes itself to be has for it the form of absolute universality; and what is immediately one with consciousness of self is the law of the heart. At the same time the stable living ordinance is likewise its own true nature and work; it produces nothing else but that; the latter is in equally immediate union with self-consciousness. In this way self-consciousness here has the characteristic of belonging to a twofold antithetic essence; it is inherently contradictory and torn to distraction in its inmost being. The law of "this individual heart" is alone that wherein self-consciousness recognizes itself; but the universal and accepted ordinance has by actualizing that law become for self-consciousness likewise its own essential nature and its own reality. What thus contradicts itself within its consciousness has for it in both cases the character of essence, and of being its own reality.

In that it gives expression to this moment of its own conscious destruction, and thereby expresses the result of its experience, it shows itself to be this inner perversion of itself, to be consciousness gone crazy, its own essence being immediately not essence, its reality immediately unreality.

The madness here cannot be taken to mean that in general something unessential is regarded as essential, something unreal as real, so that what for one is essential or actual might not be so for another, and thus the consciousness of real and of unreal, or of essential and unessential, would fall apart. If something in point of fact is real and essential for consciousness in general, but for me is not so, then, in being conscious of its nothingness, I have, since I am consciousness in general, at the same time the consciousness of its reality; and since they both are fixed and rooted within me, this is a union which is madness in general. In this state, however, there is only an *object* deranged for consciousness—not consciousness as such within itself and for itself. But in the result of the process of experience, which has here come about, consciousness is in its law aware of its self as this individual reality; and at the same time, since precisely this same essential facts, this same reality, is estranged from it, it is *qua* self-consciousness, *qua* absolute realty—aware of its unreality. In other words, both aspects are held by it in their contradiction to be directly its essence, which is thus in its utmost being distracted.

The heart-throb for the welfare of mankind passes therefore into the rage of frantic self-conceit, into the fury of consciousness to preserve itself from destruction; and to do so by casting out of its life the perversion which it really is, and by straining to regard and to express that perversion as something else. The universal ordinance and law it, therefore, now speaks of as an utter distortion of the law of its heart and of its happiness, a perversion invented by fanatical priests, by riotous, revelling despots and their minions, who seek to indemnify themselves for their own degradation by degrading and oppressing in their turn—a distortion practised to the nameless misery of deluded mankind.

Consciousness in this its frenzy proclaims individuality to be deranging, mad, and perverted, but this is an alien and accidental individuality. It is the heart, however, or the particular consciousness immediately seeking to be universal, that is thus raving and perverted, and the outcome of its action is merely that this contradiction comes to its consciousness. For the truth in its view is the law of its heart, something merely *intended*, which has not stood the test of time as the permanent ordinance has done, but rather is overthrown, as time indeed discloses. This its law ought to have reality: herein the law *qua* reality, *qua* valid ordinance, is for it purpose and essential nature; but that reality, that very law as valid ordinance, is at once and at the same time for it nothingness and void.

Similarly its *own* reality, itself as individual consciousness, is in its view the essential truth. Its purpose, however, is to establish that particularity as existent. It thus in the first instance rather takes its self *qua not*-individual to be the truly real; or its self is purpose in the sense of law, and hence precisely a universality, which its self is held to be as object for its consciousness. This its notion comes by its own act to be its object. Its (individual) self is thus discovered to be unreal, and unreality it finds out to be *its* reality. It is thus not an accidental and alien individuality, but just this particular "heart," which is in every respect inherently perverted and perverting.

Since, however, the directly universal individuality is that which is perverted and perverting, this universal ordinance, being the law of all hearts, and so of the perverted consciousness, is no less itself in its very nature the perverted element, as indeed raging frenzy declared. On the one hand this ordinance proves itself to be a law for all hearts, by the resistance which the law of one heart meets with from other individuals. The accepted and established laws are defended against the law of a single individual because they are not empty necessity, unconscious and dead, but are spiritual substance and universality, in which those in whom this spiritual substance is realized live as individuals, and are conscious of their own selves. Hence, even when they complain of this ordinance, as if it went contrary to their own inmost law, and maintain in opposition to it the claims of the "heart," in point of fact they inwardly cling to it as being their essential nature; and if they are deprived of this ordinance, or put themselves outside the range of its influence, they lose everything. Since, then, it is precisely in this that the reality and power of public ordinance consist, the latter appears as the essence, self-identical and everywhere alive, and individuality appears as its form.

On the other hand, however, this ordinance is the sphere of perversion. For in that this ordinance is the law of all hearts, in that all individuals are immediately this universal, it is a reality which is only that of self-existing individuality, i.e. of the heart. When consciousness therefore sets up the law of its heart, it finds itself resisted by others because it conflicts with the equally individual laws of their heart; and the latter in opposing it are doing nothing else but setting up in their turn and making valid their own law. The universal here presented, therefore, is only a universal resistance and struggle of all against one another, in which each makes good his own individuality, but at the same time does not come off successfully, because each individuality meets with the same opposition, and each is reciprocally dissipated by the others. What appears as public ordinance is thus this state of war of each against all, in which every one for himself wrests what he can, executes even-handed justice upon the individual lives of others, and establishes his own individual existence, which in its turn vanishes at the hands of others. We have here the *Course of the World*, the mere semblance of a constant regular trend, which is only a pretence of universality, and whose content is rather the meaningless insubstantial sport of setting up individual beings as fixed and stable, and then dissipating them.

If we put both sides of the universal ordinance over against one another and consider them, we see that this later universality has for its content restless individuality, which regards opinion or mere individualism as law, the real as unreal, and the unreal as real. That universality is, however, at the same time the side of realization of the ordinance, for to it belongs the independent self-existence (*Fürsichseyn*) of individuality. The other side is the universal in the sense of stable passive essence; but, for that very reason, the universal is only something inner, which is not indeed absolutely non-existent, but still not an actual reality, and can itself only become actual by cancelling the individuality, that has presumed to claim actuality. This type of consciousness, which becomes aware of itself in the law; which finds itself in what is inherently true and good not as mere individual, but only as essentially real; and which knows individuality to be what is perverted and perverting, and hence feels bound to surrender and sacrifice individualism of consciousness—this type of consciousness is *Virtue*.

c

VIRTUE AND THE COURSE OF THE WORLD

The mood of moral sentimentalism is reduced to confusion and contradiction: but the subjective individualism in which it is rooted is not yet eradicated. Individualism now takes refuge in another attitude which claims to do greater justice to the inherent universality of rational self-realization, but yet clings to its particular individuality as an inalienable possession. It now tries to make the realization of universal purposes in the shape of the Good depend solely on its own activity, the objective sphere in which the good is to be carried out being regarded as at once external to its ends, opposing its activity, and yet requiring these ends to be carried out in order to have any moral significance. Individualism looks on the good as its private perquisite, and makes a personal merit and glory out of its action in carrying out the good. This external realm is the "Course of the World" which in itself is thought to contain no goodness, and which only gets a value if the good is realized in it. The world's course is thus to owe its goodness to the efforts of the individual. A struggle ensues, for the situation is contradictory; and the issue of the struggle goes to prove that the individual is not the *fons et origo boni*, that goodness does not await *his* efforts, and that in fact the course of the world is at heart good; the soul of the world is righteous.

The attitude analysed here is that of abstract moral idealism, the mood of moral strenuousness, the mood that constantly seeks the improvement and perfectibility of mankind. It is found in many forms, but particularly wherever there is any strong enmity between the "ideal" life and the "life of the world."

IN the first mode of active reason, self-consciousness felt it was pure individuality; and over against this stood empty universality. In the second the two factors in the antithesis had each both the moments within them, both law and individuality; but the one factor, the "heart," was their immediate unity, the other their opposition. Here, in the relation of virtue and the course of the world, both members are each severally unity and antithesis of the moments, are each a process, but in an opposite direction, of law and individuality *inter se*. For the virtuous consciousness law is the essential element, and individuality the one to be superseded and cancelled both in the case of its own conscious life, as well as in that of the course of the world. In the former case the private individuality claimed by any one has to be brought under the discipline and control of the universal, the inherently good and true.[1] It remains there, however, still a personal consciousness. True cultivation and discipline consist solely[2] in the surrender of the entire personality, as a way of making sure that in point of fact individual peculiarities are no longer asserted and insisted on. In this individual surrender, individuality, as it is found in the world's process, is at the same time annihilated; for individuality is also a simple moment common to both.

In the course of the world individuality adopts a position the reverse of what it is in the case of the virtuous consciousness, viz. that of

---

[1] Here the individual's *own* universal nature (his own good and true) has to control his private feelings and desires.

[2] Here, by contrast with ([1]), the only real discipline is to subdue the entire personality to the "course of the world" (i.e., the good and true in it.)

making itself the essential factor, and subordinating to itself the inherently good and true. Further, the course of the world, too, does not mean for virtue merely a universal thus overturned and perverted through individuality; absolute law and order form likewise a common moment: a moment, however, not present in the world's course in the sense of an existing actual fact for consciousness, but as the inmost essence of the process. That regulative order, therefore, has not, properly speaking, to be first produced by virtue, for production means, *qua* action, a consciousness of individuality, and individuality has, on the contrary, to be superseded. By thus cancelling individuality, however, the inherent nature of the world's process merely gets room, as it were, to enter real existence independently on its own account (*an und für sich selbst*).

The general content of the actual course of the world has already made itself known. Looked at more closely, it is again nothing else than the two proceeding movements of self-consciousness. From them have come virtue's shape and mould, for since they originate it, virtue has them before it; its aim, however, is to supersede its source and origin, and realize itself, or be "for itself," become objectively explicit. The way of the world is thus, from one point of view, particular individuality seeking its pleasure and enjoyment, finding itself overthrown in doing so, and as a result satisfying the demands of the universal. But this satisfaction, like the rest of the moments of this relationship, is a perverted state and process of the universal. The real fact is merely the particular pleasure and enjoyment, while the universal is opposed to it—a necessity which is only the empty shape of universality, a merely negative reaction, the form of an act without any content.

The other moment of the world's course is individuality, which wants to be a law independently and on its own account, and under the influence of this conceit upsets the established regular order. The universal law no doubt manages to hold its own against this sort of conceit, and no longer appears in the form of an empty opposite over against consciousness, does not play the rôle of a lifeless necessity, but is a necessity operating within the conscious life itself. But in the sense in which it is a reality existing in a *conscious* state of absolute contradiction, it is madness; while in the sense in which it is an objective reality it is simply utter perversion. The universal, then, in both aspects proves to be the might that moves them; but the way this might exists in fact is merely in the form of universal perversion.

It is from virtue that the universal is now to receive its true reality, by cancelling individuality, the principle of perversion. Virtue's purpose is by this means to transmute again the perverted world's process, and bring out its true inner nature. This true being is in the world-process merely in the form of its implicit inherent nature; it is not yet actual;

and hence virtue merely *believes* it. Virtue proceeds to raise this faith to sight, without, however, enjoying the fruit of its labour and sacrifice. For so far as it is individuality, it is the active carrying-on of the contest which it wages with the world's process. Its purpose and true nature, however, lie in conquering the reality of the world's process; and the existence of the good thereby effectuated carries with it the cessation of its action, i.e. of the consciousness of individuality.

How this struggle itself will come off, what virtue finds out in the course of it, whether, by the sacrifice which virtue takes upon itself to undergo, the world's process succumbs while virtue triumphs—all this must be decided from the nature of the living weapons the combatants carry. For the weapons are nothing else than the essential being of the combatants themselves, a being which only makes its appearance for them both reciprocally. What their weapons are is in this way already evident from what is inherently implied in this struggle.

The universal is an authentic element for the virtuous consciousness as a matter of belief; it is "implicitly" or "inherently" true; not yet an actual, but an abstract universality. It plays the rôle of purpose in the case of this consciousness itself, and of inner principle in that of the course of the world. It is also precisely in this character of inner principle that the universal manifests itself in the case of virtue, from the point of view of the world process; for virtue as yet only "wills" to carry out the good, and does not in the first instance claim reality for it. This characteristic can also be looked at in this way: the good, in that it comes on the scene in the struggle with the world process, thereby manifests itself in the form of what is for another, as something which is not self-contained (*an und für sich selbst*), for otherwise it would not want to win its own truth by vanquishing its opposites. By having its being only when it is for another, is meant the same as was shown in the opposite way of looking at it, viz. that it is to begin with an abstraction which only attains reality in a relation, and has no reality of itself as it stands.

The good or universal as it appears here, is, then, what is called *Gifts, Capacities, Powers*. It is a mode or form of spiritual life, where the spiritual life is presented as a universal, which requires the principle of individuality to give it life and movement, and in individuality finds its realization. This universal is *applied well* by the principle of individuality so far as this principle dwells in the consciousness of virtue, and *misused* by it as far as it is in the world's process—a passive instrument, which is regulated and directed by the hand of free individuality and is quite indifferent to the use it is put to, and can be misused for the production of a reality which means its ruin: a lifeless material deprived of any independence of its own—a material that can be formed in this way or that, or even to its own destruction.

Since this universal is at the beck and call equally of the virtuous consciousness as well as of the course of the world, it is not apparent whether with this equipment virtue will get the better of vice. The weapons are the same—these capacities and powers. Virtue has, it is true, carefully ensconced its belief in the original unity of its purpose and the essential nature of the world process, and the reserve thus placed in ambush is intended to fall on the rear of the enemy during the fight, and bring that purpose essentially (*an sich*) to fulfilment: so that thereby the knight of virtue finds as a matter of fact that his part in waging this warfare is, properly speaking, a mere sham-fight, which he cannot take seriously because he puts all his strength and confidence in the good being self-sufficient and real *per se*, i.e. in the good bringing about its own fulfilment—a sham-fight which he dare not even allow to become serious. For what he turns against the enemy, and finds turned against himself, and what, both in his own case and as regards his enemy as well, he runs the risk of getting wasted and damaged in the struggle, is not the good itself; he fights to keep and carry that out: what is exposed to the hazard of the contest is merely gifts and capacities that are indifferent to the issue. But these, in point of fact, are nothing else than just that universal from which individuality has been eliminated, and which is to be conserved and actualized by the struggle.

This universal, however, is at the same time directly realized and *ipso facto* made actual by the very notion of the contest; it is the inherent essential nature, the "universal," and its actualization means merely that it is at the same time for an other. The two aspects mentioned above, in each of which it became an abstraction, are no longer separated; it is in and through the struggle that the good is simultaneously established in both forms.

The virtuous consciousness, however, enters into conflict with the way of the world as if this were a factor opposed to the good. What the conflict brings to light is the universal, not merely as an abstract universal, but as one animated by individuality, and existing for an other, in other words the universal in the sense of the actually real good. Wherever virtue comes to grips with the world's process, it always hits upon places where goodness is found to exist; the good, as the inherent nature of the world's process, is inseparably interwoven with all the manifestations of it, with all the ways in which the world's process makes its appearance, and where it is real the good has its own existence too. Virtue thus finds the world's process invulnerable. All the moments which virtue was to jeopardize in itself when dealing with the world's process, all the moments which it was to sacrifice—these are just so many ways in which goodness exists, and consequently are invi-

olable relations. The conflict can, therefore, only be an oscillation between conserving and sacrificing; or rather there can be no place for
either sacrificing one's own or doing harm to what comes from elsewhere. Virtue is not merely like the combatant whose sole concern in
the fight is to keep his sword polished; but it has even started the fight
simply to preserve its weapons. And not merely is it unable to use its
own weapons, but it must also preserve intact those of its enemy, and
protect them against its own attack, seeing they are all noble parts of the
good, on behalf of which it entered the field of battle.

This enemy, on the other hand, has as its essential element not the
inherent universal, but individuality. Its force is thus the negative principle before which nothing stands, nothing is absolutely sacred, but
which can risk and endure the loss of everything and anything. In so
doing it feels victory to be assured, as much from its very nature as by
the contradiction in which its opponent gets entangled. What is to
virtue implicit and inherent is taken merely as an explicit objective fact
in the case of the world's process. The latter is detached from every moment which virtue finds fixed and to which it is fast secured. The world
process has such a moment under its power and has consequently in its
control the tethered knight of virtue bound thereto, by the fact that this
moment is held to be merely one which the world's process can as readily cancel as let be. This knight of valour cannot work himself loose
from it as he might from a cloak thrown round him, and get free by
leaving it behind; for it is to him the essential element which he cannot give up.

Finally, as to the ambush out of which the inherent good is cun-
ningly and craftily to fall on the rear of the world process, this hope is
vain and foolish from its very nature. The world process is the mind
sure of itself and ever on the alert, that can never be got at from behind,
but fronts breast-forward every quarter; for it consists in this that everything is an objective element *for* it, everything stands *before* it. But
when the inherent goodness is for its enemy, then it finds itself in the
struggle we have seen; so far, however, as it is *not* for its enemy, but subsists in itself, it is the passive instrument of gifts and capacities, material without reality. If represented as object, it would be a dormant consciousness, remaining in the background, no one knows where.

Virtue is thus overpowered by the world process, because the abstract unreal essence is in fact virtue's own purpose, and because its action as regards reality rests on distinctions that are solely a matter of
words. Virtue wanted to consist in the fact of bringing about the realization of goodness through sacrificing individuality; but the aspect of
reality is itself nothing else than the aspect of individuality. The good
was meant to be what is implicit and inherent, and opposed to what *is*;

but the implicit and inherent, taken in its real truth, is simply *being* it-self. The implicitly inherent element is primarily the abstraction of essence as against actual reality: but the abstraction is just what is not true, but a distinction merely for consciousness; this means, however, it is itself what is called actual, for the actual is what essentially is for an other—or it is being. But the consciousness of virtue rests on this dis-tinction of implicitness and explicit being, a distinction without any true validity.

The world process was supposed to be the perversion of the good, because it took individuality for its principle. But this latter is the prin-ciple of actual reality, for it is just that mode of consciousness by which what is implicit and inherent is for an other as well. The world process transmutes and perverts the unchangeable, but does so in fact by trans-forming it out of the nothingness of abstraction into the being of reality.

The course of the world is, then, victorious over what, in opposition to it, constitutes virtue; it is victorious over that which took an unreal abstraction to be the essential reality. But it is not victorious over some-thing real, but over the production of distinctions that are no distinc-tions, over this pompous talk about the best for mankind and the op-pression of humanity, about sacrifice for goodness' sake and the misuse of gifts. Imaginary idealities and purposes of that sort fall on the ear as idle phrases, which exalt the heart and leave the reason a blank, which edify but build up nothing that endures: declamations whose only def-inite announcement is that the individual who professes to act for such noble ends and indulges in such fine phrases holds himself for a fine creature: a swollen enlargement which gives itself and others a mighty size of a head, but big from inflation with emptiness.

Virtue in the olden time had its secure and determinate significance, for it found the fullness of its content and its solid basis in the substan-tial life of the nation, and had for its purpose and end a concrete good that existed and lay at its hand: it was also for that reason not directed against actual reality as a general perversity, and not turned against a world process. The virtue above considered, however, is removed from that substantial life, and is outside it, a virtue with no essential being, a virtue merely in idea and in words, and one that is deprived of all that content.

The vacuousness of this rhetorical eloquence in conflict with the world's process would be at once discovered if it were to be stated what all its eloquent phrases amount to. They are therefore assumed to be fa-miliar and well-understood. The request to say what, then, this "well-known" is would be either met by a new swell of phrases, or in reply there would be an appeal to the "heart" which "inwardly" tells what they mean—which is tantamount to an admission of inability to say what the meaning is.

The fatuousness of that style of eloquence seems, too, in a quasi-unconscious manner to have got the length of being an acknowledged certainty for the cultivated minds of our time, since all interest in the whole mass of those rhetorical spread-eagle phrases has disappeared—a loss of interest which is betrayed in the sheer wearisomeness they produce.

The result, then, arising from this opposition, consists in the fact that consciousness lets the idea of an inherent good, which yet has no actual reality, slip from it like a mere cloak. Consciousness has learned in the course of its struggle that the world's process is not so bad as it looked; for the reality of the world's process is that of the universal. With the discovery of this it is seen that there is no way of producing the good through the sacrifice of individuality, the means for doing so have gone; for individuality is precisely the explicit actualization of what is implicitly and inherently real (i.e. the universal); and the perversion ceases to be looked at as a perversion of goodness, for it is just the transmuting of the good, *qua* bare purpose, into actual reality. The movement of individuality is the reality of the universal.

In point of fact, however, what as world process stood opposed to the consciousness of the inherently and implicitly real, has likewise been vanquished and has disappeared with the attainment of the above result. The self-existence of individuality was there in opposition to the inner essential nature, the universal, and made its appearance as a reality cut off from the inherent implicit nature. Since, however, it has come out that reality is in undivided unity with the universal, the self-existence of the world's process proves not to be more than an aspect, just as the inherent nature (*Ansich*) of virtue is merely an aspect too (*Ansicht*). The individuality of the world's process may doubtless think it acts merely for itself or selfishly; it is better than it thinks; its action is at the same time one that is universal and with an inherent being of its own. If it acts selfishly, it does not know what it is doing; and if it insists that all men act selfishly, it merely asserts that all men are unaware as to what action is. If it acts for itself, this is just the explicit bringing into reality of what is at first implicit and inherent. The purpose of its self-existence, of its "being for itself," which it fancies opposed to the inherent nature—its futile ingenuity and cunning, as also its fine-spun explanations which so knowingly demonstrate the existence of selfishness everywhere—all these have as much vanished as the purpose of the inherent element and its rhetoric.

Thus, then, the effort, the struggle, the activity of individuality is inherently an end in itself; the use of powers, the play of their outward manifestations—that is what gives them life: otherwise they would be lifeless, potential, and merely implicit (*Ansich*). The inherent implicit nature is not an abstract universal without existence and never carried into effect; it is itself immediately this actual present and this living actuality of the process of individuality.

C

INDIVIDUALITY, WHICH TAKES ITSELF TO BE REAL IN AND FOR ITSELF

The following section gives a general description of individuality which seeks to realize itself, not in the one-sided ways analysed in the three preceding sections, but as a complete concrete whole. Here individuality does not regard itself abstractedly, and hence does not treat the sphere of its realization as in any way alien to itself. It is completely one with the objective world where it carries out its ends, and finds both itself adequate to its own realization, and the world sufficient and all-sufficient for the embodiment of its ends. In this sphere we have, as it were, the very antithesis of the preceding state of mind. There the good was opposed to the course of the "world," the latter being dependent for its goodness on individual effort. Here it is as if the "world" were made up of the activity of individuals and were wholly adequate to satisfy and embody all their ends. The real life of the individual is found simply in "self-expression." Naturally therefore individuals take themselves here to be "real just as they are," and have merely to express or develop their own content in order to objectify their ends. The objective world *is* their activity realized, is themselves "externalized."

This condition of individuality is the immediate preparation for the social order of the life of a free spiritual community, and is the anticipation of that community—a community where the individual is universalized through union with the whole, and the whole particularized in the individual.

SELF-CONSCIOUSNESS has now grasped its own principle, which at first was only *our* notion of it, viz. the notion that, when consciously certain of itself, it is all reality. Its purpose and nature henceforward consist in the interpenetration of the universal (its "gifts" and "capacities") and individuality. The individual moments of this process of complete concrete permeation preceding the unity into which they have now coalesced, were found in the purposes hitherto considered. These have now vanished—as being mere abstractions and chimeras, which belong to those first shallow modes of mind's self-consciousness, and which have their truth merely in the illusory "being" of the "heart," fancy and rhetoric, and not in reason. This reason is now sure of its own reality as it stands (*an und für sich*), and no longer views itself as an ideal purpose which it seeks to realize from the outset in opposition to immediately existent (sensible) reality, but, on the contrary, has the category as such as the object of its consciousness.

This means that the character of being for itself on its own account (*für sich*), or of negative self-consciousness, with which reason started, is cancelled. This self-consciousness at that stage fell in with a reality which was supposed to be its own negative, and by cancelling which it was to realize its purpose. Now that purpose and inherent nature (*Ansichseyn*) have proved to be the same as objective existence for another and the given reality, [objective] truth is no longer divided from [subjective] certainty—no matter whether the proposed purpose is taken as certainty of self and the realization of that purpose as the truth, or whether the purpose is taken for the truth and reality for certainty. The essential nature and purpose as it stands (*an und für sich*) constitute the certainty of immediate reality itself, the interpenetration of the inherent implicit nature (*ansich*), and the explicit distinctive nature (*fürsich*), of the universal and individuality. Action is *per se* its truth and reality, and the manifestation or expression of individuality is its purpose taken just as it stands.

With the attainment of such a conception, therefore, self-consciousness has returned into itself and passed from those opposite characteristics which the category presented, and which its relation to the category had, when it was "observing" and when it was "active." Its object is now the category pure and simple; in other words, it is itself the category become conscious of itself. Its account with its previous forms is now closed; they lie behind it in the forgotten past; they do not come forward against it as its world found ready to hand, but are developed solely within itself as transparent moments. Yet they still fall apart within its consciousness at this stage as a movement of distinct moments, which has not yet got combined into its own substantial unity. But throughout all these moments self-consciousness holds firmly to that simple unity of self with objective existence which is its constitutive generic nature.

Consciousness has in this way cast away all opposition and every condition limiting its activity. It starts anew from itself, and is occupied not with something external, but with itself. Since individuality is in itself actuality, the material of operation and the purpose of action lie in the action itself. Action consequently has the appearance of the movement of a circle, which moves itself within itself freely *in vacuo*, which, unimpeded, now enlarges and then contracts, and is quite content to play simply within itself and with itself. The element in which individuality manifests and displays its form and shape, is simply the day, in whose light consciousness wants to display itself. This element—the daylight—means nothing but the simple assuming of the form of individuality.

Action alters nothing, opposes nothing; it is the mere form of translation from a condition of being invisible to one of being visible, and the content, brought thus to daylight, and laid bare, is nothing else than what this action already is implicitly (*an sich*). It is *implicit*—that is its *form* as unity in *thought*: and it is *actual*—that is its form as unity in *existence*: while it is itself *content* merely in virtue of maintaining this character of simplicity in spite of its aspect of process and transition.

a

INTRODUCTORY NOTE

SELF-CONTAINED INDIVIDUALS ASSOCIATED AS A COMMUNITY
OF ANIMALS, AND THE DECEPTION THENCE ARISING: THE REAL FACT

The title of this section sounds unfamiliar; but the purpose of the analysis is plain, and the argument is essential as a stage in the unfolding of what rational self-contained individuality implies. It also, with the immediately succeeding sections, prepares the way for the constructive interpretation of organized society. Indeed, without individuals constituted as rational self-conscious units, each self-contained, a free self-conscious community could not exist. They form the component separate cells of the "organism" of a society, the elements out of which the compact structure of a society is made. In the first instance and as an abstract aspect of associated life, they can be regarded, and for certain purposes are in fact regarded, as merely distinct and detached units living together. Each functions as an individuality, endowed with certain powers and capacities for self-expression, pursuing his ends for his own interest, spontaneously putting forth his energies without being clearly aware of or concerned with any universal result which his essentially universal nature must bring about. In realizing his individuality he goes out of himself in one sense, in another sense he does not. By expressing himself he carries out some "end" in which he has an "interest"; he "does" something: he does a deed or a "work," which *qua* mere action is nothing more than a mode of purposed self-expression, and is not, as such, either good or bad (at this stage). What he does appears as external to himself, but is his own all the while, something which he has formed and in which he specifically is interested. Such a result at once objective, framed by himself and reflecting his interest, is "fact" as distinct from "thing" (which is an object of perception at the level of consciousness, not of self-consciousness). But by the nature of the case he can distinguish within this fact what is the real "intent" (*die Sache Selbst*)[1] he has in mind from the merely objective character of the fact (*Sache*); he can, if we may put it so, distinguish the "fact of the matter" from mere "matter of fact." But other indi-

---

[1]It is difficult to find a current English equivalent for this term (*die Sache Selbst*). "Fact itself" or "actual fact" does not seem to convey much meaning. It seems best to try to bring out the significance implied, even though at the sacrifice of literal translation.

viduals with whom he is associated and who are similarly constituted, carry on the same process of separate self-expression. Each is "honest" and "honourable" in so doing: each is concerned with his own "real intent" and his own "fact." By this association they necessarily are interrelated and intercommunicate. But communication on such a basis leads to misconception, transference of intent, and "deception" of each other as well as of themselves. Work, deeds, facts have a universal character as well as a particular nature: in the former aspect they cannot be one's own, in the latter aspect they cannot be another's: yet both aspects are inseparable. Intercommunication between these individuals thus inevitably leads to contradiction. It implies a common universal nature between the individuals: but such universality at this stage is implicit not explicit. The contradiction inherent at this level between the elements in the situation created by individuals merely coexisting together without a conscious common purpose controlling and guiding all, points the way and compels an advance to another stage in the evolution of rational individuality.

When self-conscious individuals are regarded as merely "together," as coexisting without consciously controlling common purposes, they resemble a community or herd of animals. Hence the title of the Section.

It is not an accidental but an essential aspect of the life of society; it is indeed the indispensable basis of community which is in one respect like a community of ants, the system of activity of its component individuals, though each may and does fulfil his purpose as his own private interest.

This aspect of social existence can be over-emphasized and may be regarded at times as the sole nature of society. The result can only lead to confusion. Such a conception of society may perhaps be said to be found where, as in certain economic conceptions of society, society is viewed as a herd of self-interested units each pursuing his own individual ends. It is also seen in certain historical forms of national polity which recur from time to time.

THE above substantial individuality, to begin with, is again single and determinate. Absolute reality, which it knows itself to be, is thus, in the way it becomes consciously aware of that reality, abstractly universal, without filling and content, merely the empty thought of this category. We have to see how this conception of substantial individuality is made explicit in its various moments, and how it comes to be conscious of its true nature.

The conception of this individuality, as it takes itself as such to be all reality, is in the first instance a mere *result*: its own movement and reality are not yet set forth; it is here in its immediacy as something purely and simply implicit. Negativity, however, which is the same as what appears as movement and process, is inherent in this implicit state as a determinate quality; and being, i.e. the simple implicit state, comes to be a determinate compass or range of being. Individuality confronts us, therefore, as an original determinate nature: *original*, in virtue of its being implicit: originally *determinate*, in virtue of the negative moment lying in that implicitness, which negative element is thereby a quality. This limitation cannot, however, limit the action of consciousness, for this consists at the present stage in thorough and complete relation of itself to itself: relation to what is other than itself, which its limitation would involve, is now overcome. The character inherent originally by nature is thus merely an undefined (simple) principle, a transparent universal element in which individuality finds itself free and at one with itself, as well as unfolds its diversity without restraint, and in realizing itself is simply in reciprocal relation with itself. We have here something similar to what we find in the case of indeterminate animal life: this breathes the breath of life, let us say, into water as its element, or air or earth, and within these again into still more determinate conditions: every aspect of its life is affected by the specific element, and yet animal life still keeps these aspects within its power and itself a unity in spite of the limitations of the element, and remains *qua* the given particular organization animal life throughout, the same general fact of animal life.

This determinate original nature of consciousness, in which it finds itself freely and wholly, appears as the immediate and only proper content of the purpose of the individual. That content is indeed a definite content, but is only content so far as we take the implicit nature in isolation. In truth, however, it is reality (*Realität*) permeated by individuality: actuality (*Wirklichkeit*) in the way consciousness *qua* individual contains this within itself, and is to begin with taken as existing, but not yet as acting. So far as action is concerned, however, that determinateness is, in one respect, not a limitation it wants to overcome; for, looked at as an existent quality, that determinateness is simply the colour of the element where it moves: in another respect, however, the negativity is determinateness merely in the case of what "exists." But acting is nothing else than negativity. Hence when individuality acts, its specific determinateness is dissipated into the general process of negation, into the sum and substance of all determinateness.

The simple "original nature" now breaks up, in action and the consciousness of action, into the distinction which action implies. To begin with, action is here an object, an object, too, still belonging to consciousness; it is present as a purpose, and thus opposed to a given reality. The other moment is the process of this statically presented purpose, the process of actualization of the purpose, bringing the purpose to bear on the entirely formal reality, and hence is the idea of the transition itself. In other words, this second moment is the "means." The third moment is, finally, the object, no longer as immediately and subjectively presented purpose, but as brought to light and established as something other than and external to the acting subject.

These various aspects must be viewed in the light of the general principle of this sphere of consciousness. The content throughout remains the same, without any difference, whether between individuality and existence in general, or between purpose as against individuality in the sense of an "original nature," or between purpose and the given reality: or between the means and that reality as absolute purpose: or finally between the reality moulded by the agent as against the purpose, the "original nature," of the means.

At the outset, then, the nature of individuality in its original determinate form, its immediate essence, is not yet affirmed as active; and in this shape is called special capacity, talent, character, and so on. This peculiar colouring of mind must be looked at as the only content of its purpose, and as the sole and only reality. If we thought of consciousness as going beyond that, as seeking to bring into reality another content, then we should think of it as a nothing working away towards nothing.

This original nature is, moreover, not merely the substance of its purpose, but implicitly the *reality* as well, which otherwise assumes the appearance of being a given material on which to act, of being found ready at hand for action to work up into some determinate form. That is to say, acting is simply transferring from a state not yet explicitly expressed to one fully expressed; the inherent being of that reality opposed to consciousness has sunk to the level of a mere empty appearance, a mere seeming. This mode of consciousness, by determining itself to act, thereby refuses to be led astray by the semblance of reality on the part of what is presented to it; and has likewise to abandon its dealings with idle thoughts and purposes, and keep its hold on the original content of its own nature. No doubt this content first exists as a fact for consciousness, when it has made that content actual; but the distinction between something which while *for* consciousness is only inside itself, and a reality outside consciousness existing in itself, has broken down. Consciousness must act solely that what it inherently and implicitly is, may be for it explicitly; or, acting is just the process of mind coming to be *qua* consciousness. What it is implicitly, therefore, it knows from its actual reality. Hence it is that an individual cannot know what he is till he has made himself real by action.

Consciousness, however, seems on this view to be unable to determine the purpose of its action before action has taken place; but before action occurs it must, in virtue of being consciousness, have the act in front of itself as entirely its own, i.e. as a purpose. The individual, therefore, who is going to act seems to find himself in a circle, where each moment already presupposes the others, and hence seems unable to find a beginning, because it only gets to know its own original nature, the nature which is to be its purpose, by first acting, while in order to act it must have that purpose beforehand. But just for that reason it has to start straight away and, whatever the circumstances are, without troubling further about beginning, means, or end, proceed to action at once. For its essential and implicit (*ansichseyende*) nature is beginning, means, and end all in one. As *beginning*, it is found in the circumstances of the action; and the *interest* which the individual finds in something is just the answer to the question, "whether he should act and what is to be done in a given case." For what seems to be a reality confronting him is implicitly his own original fundamental nature, which has merely the appearance of an objective being—an appearance which lies in the notion of action involving as this does self-diremption, but which expressly shows itself to be his own original nature by the interest the individual finds therein. Similarly the *how*, the means, is determined as it stands (*an und für sich*). Talent is likewise nothing but individuality with a definite original constitution, looked at as the subjective internal means, or transition of purpose into actuality. The actual means, however, and the real transition are the unity of talent with the nature of the fact as present in the interest felt. The former [talent] expresses that aspect of the means which concerns action, the latter [the fact found of interest] that which concerns content: both are individuality itself, as a fused whole of acting and existing. What we find, then, is *first* circumstances given ready to hand, which are implicitly the original nature of the individual; *next* the interest which affirms them as its own or as its purpose; and *finally* the connexion and sublation of these opposite elements in the means. This connexion itself still falls within consciousness, and the whole just considered is one side of an opposition. This appearance of opposition which still remains is removed by the transition, i.e. by the means. For the means is a unity of inner and outer, the antithesis of the determinate character it has *qua* inner means (viz. talent): it therefore abolishes this character, and makes itself—this unity of action and existence—equally an outer, viz.: the actually realized individuality, i.e. individuality which is established for individuality itself as the objectively existent. The entire act in this way does not go beyond itself, either as circumstances, or as purpose, or means, or as work performed.

In this notion of work, however, the distinction which lay within the original nature seems to enter. The work done is something determinate, like the original nature it expresses, because being cut loose by the process of acting and become an existing reality, the negation implied in this process remains in it as a quality. Consciousness, however, as against the work, is specifically that in which this quality is to be found as a general process of negation, as acting. It is thus the universal as opposed to the specific determinateness of the work performed; it can therefore compare one kind of work with another, and can thence apprehend individualities themselves as different; it can, e.g. regard an individual who is of wider compass in his work as possessing stronger energy of will or a richer nature, i.e. a nature whose original constitution (*Bestimmtheit*) is less limited; another again as a weaker and a poorer nature.

In contrast with this purely quantitative difference, which is not an essential difference, "good" and "bad" would express an absolute difference; but this is not in place here. Whether taken in one way or another, action is equally carried on; there is a process of displaying and expressing an individuality, and for that reason it is all good: it would, properly speaking, be impossible to say what "bad" is to be here. What would be called a bad work is the individual life of a certain specific nature, which is therein realized. It would only be degraded into a bad work by a reflective comparison, which, however, is quite empty and futile, since this goes beyond the essential meaning and nature of work (which is a self-expression of individuality), and then seeks to find and demand from it heaven knows what else.

The comparison could have to do only with the distinction above mentioned. But this, being a distinction of quantity, is *in itself* not an essential one; and here in particular is unessential because what are to be compared together are different works and individualities. But these do not affect one another; each is concerned simply with itself. The original nature is alone the essential fact, or what could be used as an ultimate standard of judgment regarding the work; and conversely. Both, however, correspond to each other: there is nothing *for* individuality which is not obtained *through* it: or there is no *reality* which is not *its* nature and *its* action, and no action nor inherent substance of individuality which is not real. And only these moments are to be compared.

There is, therefore, in general, no ground for feeling elevated or for lamenting or repenting: all that sort of thing arises from a reflection which imagines another content and another inner nature than is to be found in the original nature of the individual and the actual carrying of it out in reality. Whatever it is that the individual does, and whatever happens to him, that the individual has done, and is that himself. He can only have the consciousness of the mere transference of his self from the darkness of possibility to the daylight of the present, from a state abstract and implicit to the significance of actual being, and can have only the certainty that what seems to him in the second state is nothing else than what lay dormant in the former. The consciousness of this unity is no doubt likewise a comparison, but what is compared is just a mere appearance of opposition, a formal appearance which for reason, *qua* self-conscious and aware that individuality is inherently actuality, is nothing more than seeming. The individual, therefore, knowing that he can find in his objective actuality nothing but its unity with himself or can find only the certainty of himself in its very truth, and knowing that he thus always attains his purpose—can experience only a sense of joy in himself.

That, then, is the conception consciousness has of itself when it is sure of its being an absolute identification, a complete permeation, of individuality and existence. Let us see whether this notion is confirmed and supported by its experience, and whether its reality agrees with this notion.

The work produced is the reality which consciousness gives itself. It is there that the individual becomes consciously what he is implicitly, and in such wise that the consciousness which becomes aware of the individual in the work performed is not the particular consciousness but universal consciousness. He has placed himself by his work quite outside in the element of universality, in the characterless, qualityless region of existence. The consciousness which withdraws from its work is in point of fact universal—because it becomes, in this opposition between work and consciousness, absolute negativity, the process of action—and stands over against its work, which is determinate and particular. It thus goes beyond itself *qua* work, and is itself the indeterminate region which its work still leaves void and unfilled. If their unity was in the above notion still preserved, this took place just through the work being cancelled *qua* objectively existing product. But it has to *be*, and we have to see how individuality will retain its universality in the existence of the work, and will know how to get satisfaction.

To begin with we have to consider by itself the work which has come into being. It has received within it the entire nature of the individual. Its existence is therefore itself an action, in which all distinctions interpenetrate and are resolved. The work is thus thrown out into a subsisting form where the specific character of the original nature does in fact come out as against other determinate natures, encroaches on them, just as these in their turn encroach on it, and is lost as a vanishing moment in this general process. Although in the conception of individuality as here dealt with, the various moments (circumstances, purpose, means, and realization) are all alike, and the original specific nature stands for no more than a universal element, on the other hand, when this element takes on an objective existence, its determinate character as such comes to light in the work done, and obtains its truth in its dissolution. Looked at more closely, this dissolution is such that in this specific character the individual, *qua* this individual, has become consciously real; but the specific character is not merely the content of reality, but its form as well; or this reality as such is as a whole just this specific character, viz. being opposed to self-consciousness. On this view this reality is seen to be a reality which has disappeared out of the notion, and is merely found given as an alien reality. The work *is*, i.e. it is for other individuals, and for them it is an external, an alien reality, in whose place they have to put their own, in order to get by *their* action consciousness of *their* unity with reality. In other words, the interest which they take in that work owing to *their* original constitution is other than the peculiar interest of this work, which thereby is turned into something different. The work is, thus, in general something transitory, which is extinguished by the counter-action of other powers and interests, and displays the reality of individuality in a transitory form rather than as fulfilled and accomplished.

Consciousness, then, by doing work becomes aware of that contrast between being and acting, which in the earlier forms of consciousness was at the same time the beginning of action, and is here merely a result. This contrast, however, was in fact likewise the ultimate principle involved when consciousness proceeded to act as an implicitly real individuality; for action presupposed the determinate original nature as the ultimate implicit element, and the mere process of performing the act for the sake of this performance took that nature as its content. Mere action is, however, the self-identical form, with which, consequently, the specific determinateness of the original nature does not agree. It is a matter of indifference here, as elsewhere, which of the two is called notion and which reality. The original nature is the thought element, the implicit factor as against the action, in which it first gets its reality; or, again, the original nature is the existence both of individuality as such and of individuality in the form of work; while action is the original notion as pure and simple transition, as the process of becoming. This lack of correspondence between idea and reality, which lies in its essence, consciousness learns in its work; in work, therefore, consciousness becomes aware of itself as it in truth is, and its empty notion of itself disappears.

In this fundamental contradiction characteristic of work—which contains the truth of this individuality that takes itself to be inherently real—all the aspects of individuality thus appear again as contradictory. That is to say, in the work (done) the content of the entire individuality is put forth out of the process of doing (it), which is the negative unity holding fast all the moments of that content, into (objective) existence. So transferred and set forth, the work (done) lets the moments now go free; and in the element of factual subsistence they become indifferent to one another. The notion and its reality are thus separated into purpose and the original essential nature (*Wesenheit*). It is an accident that the purpose should have a true being, or that the implicit inherent nature should be made a purpose. Similarly, again, notion and reality fall apart as transition to actuality and as purpose; in other words, it is an accident that the means expressing the purpose should actually be chosen. While, finally, these inner moments taken together (whether they have some intrinsic unity or not)—i.e. the action of the individual—are again accidentally related to actuality in general: fortune decides equally in favour of a badly determined purpose and badly selected means, as well as against them.

If, now, consciousness hereby becomes aware in its work of the opposition between willing and performance, between purpose and means, and again between this inward nature, taken all together, and actual reality—an opposition which as a whole shows the fortuitous character of the action of consciousness—still the unity and the necessity of this action are just as much present too. This latter aspect transcends the former, and experience of the fortuitousness of the action is itself only a fortuitous experience. The necessity of the action consists in this, that purpose is directly related to actuality, and the unity of these is the very notion of action: the act takes place because action is *per se* and of itself the essence of actuality. In the work there is no doubt comes out the fortuitousness which characterizes accomplishment when contrasted with willing and the process of performing; and this experience, which seems as if it must be the truth, contradicts that notion of the act. Still, if we look at the content of this experience taken in its completeness, that content is seen to be the transitory work. What persists is not the transitoriness; rather this is itself actual and is bound up with the work, and vanishes with it; the negative falls away along with the positive whose negation it is.

The very notion of substantially and inherently real individuality contains within it this transience of transitoriness (*Verschwinden des Verschwindens*). For that wherein the work disappears, or what disappears in the work, is the objective reality; and this same reality was to give experience, as it was called, its supremacy over the notion which individuality has about itself. Objective reality, however, is a moment which itself has no longer independent truth in this mode of consciousness; it (i.e. the truth) consists solely in the unity of this consciousness with action, and the true work is only that unity of action and existence, of willing and performance. Because of the certainty fundamental to its actions, consciousness takes the actual reality opposed to that conscious certainty to be something which itself is only *for* consciousness. The opposition cannot any longer occur for consciousness in this form of its self-existence in contrast to reality, when consciousness is self-consciousness returned into itself and with all opposition gone. On the contrary, the opposition and the negativity manifested in the case of work then affect not only the content of the work *or* the content of consciousness as well, but the reality as such, and hence affect the opposition present merely in virtue of that reality and in it, and the disappearance of the work. In this way consciousness turns from its transitory work back upon itself, and asserts its own notion and its certainty to be what is permanent and abiding as opposed to the experience of the fortuitousness of action. In point of fact it comes to know its essential principle or notion, in which the reality is only a moment, something *for* consciousness, not something in and for itself; it finds that reality to be a passing moment, of significance therefore merely as being in general, whose universality is one and the same with action. This unity, this identity is the true work; it is the real intent, *the fact of the matter (die Sache selbst)*, which asserts iself at all costs and is felt to be the lasting element, independent of "fact" which is the accident of an individual action as such, the accident of circumstances, means, and actuality.

The main concern (*die Sache selbst*) stands opposed to these moments only so far as they claim to have a value in isolation, but is essentially their unity, because identifying, fusing, actuality with individuality. It is, too, an action, and, *qua* action, pure action in general, and thereby just as much action of *this* individual; and this action, because still appertaining to the individual in opposition to actuality, has the sense of a purpose. Similarly it is the transition from this specific character to the opposite: and finally it is a reality which is present objectively for consciousness. The main intent thus expresses the essential spiritual substance in which all these moments as independently valid are cancelled and transcended and so hold good only as universal; and in which the certainty consciousness has regarding itself is a "fact"—a real object before consciousness, an object born of self-consciousness as its *own*, without ceasing to be a free independent object in the proper sense. The "thing," found at the stage of sense-certainty and perception, now gets its significance through self-consciousness, and through it alone. On this rests the distinction between a thing (*Ding*) and a fact (*Sache*). A process is gone through here corresponding to what we find in the case of sense-experience and perception.

Self-consciousness, then, has attained its true conception of itself when this stage of the real intent is reached; it is the interpenetration of individuality and objectivity: an interpenetration which has become objective. In it self-consciousness has arrived at a consciousness of its own substance. At the same time, as we find self-consciousness here, it is a consciousness of its substance which has just arisen, and hence is immediate; and this is the specific way in which we find spirit at the present stage: it has not yet reached its truly real substance. The objectified intent takes in this immediate consciousness the form of bare and simple essence (*einfachen Wesens*), which being universal, contains all its various moments in itself and belongs to them, but, again, is also indifferent towards them taken as specific moments, and is independent by itself; and, as this free and objective simple abstract "fact," passes for the essentially real (*Wesen*). The various moments of the original determinateness, the moments of the "fact" of *this* particular individual, his purpose, means, action, and actual reality, are, on the one hand, particular moments for this consciousness, which it can abandon and give up for the objectified intent; on the other hand, however, they all have this object as their essential nature, but only in such a way that it, being their abstract universal, can find itself in each of these different moments and be their predicate. The objectified intent is not yet subject; but those moments stand for subject, because they belong to the aspect of individualness, while the object in mind is only at this stage bare universality. It is the genus which finds itself in all these moments as species of itself, and is equally independent of them.

Consciousness is called "honest," when it has on the one hand attained this idealization (*Idealismus*), which objectified intent expresses, and on the other possesses the truth in it *qua* this formal universality. Consciousness when so characterized is solely concerned with intended object, and hence occupies itself with its various moments or species. And when it does not reach this fact in one of these moments, does not find the real intent in one meaning, it just on that account lays hold of the fact in another; and consequently always really secures that satisfaction which should belong to this mode of consciousness by its very nature (*seinem Begriffe nach*). However things turn out, it achieves and secures the objectified intent, for the latter, being this universal *genus* of those moments, is the predicate of all.

Should it not bring a purpose into reality, it has at least *willed* the purpose, i.e. turns purpose *qua* purpose, mere doing which does nothing, into the real intent, and can therefore maintain and feel consoled that at least there has always been something attempted, something done. Since the universal contains within it even the negative or the transitoriness, this too, the self-annihilation of the work, is itself *its* doing. It has stimulated others towards this, and still finds satisfaction in the disappearance of its reality, just as bad boys enjoy a personal pleasure in getting their ears boxed because they are the cause of its being done. Or, again, suppose it has not so much as tried to carry out the real intent and done nothing at all, then it has not *cared*; the objectified intent is for it just the unity of its decision with reality; it asserts that the reality would be nothing else than its own wish in the matter (*sein*

Mögen). Finally, suppose something of interest has come its way entirely without its help, then for it this reality is the real intent just by the interest which it finds therein, although that reality has not been produced by its doing. If it is a piece of good luck, which has befallen the individual personally, he reckons it his own act and his own desert; if it is, on the other hand, a mere event in the world, which does not concern him further, he makes it likewise his own, and an interest, where he has done nothing, is held as a party interest which *he* has taken up and defended or maintained, for or against.

The "Honesty," or "Honourableness," of this mode of consciousness, as well as the satisfaction which it meets with at every point, really consists, as the above makes clear, in this, that it does not bring together its ideas regarding the objectified intent. Its own affair (*seine Sache*), no work at all, or mere action and bare purpose, or again a reality involving no action at all—all and every one of these are equally the real intent: it makes one meaning after another the subject of this predicate, and forgets one after the other. By its having merely willed or, again, in not having cared, the real intent has now the meaning of empty purpose, and of the merely ideal thought-unity of willing and performance. The consolation for the annihilation of the purpose which was at all events willed or at all events simply done, as well as the satisfaction of having given others something to do, makes simple doing, or entirely bad work, the essential reality; for that must be called a bad work which is no work at all. Finally, in the case of finding through good luck the reality at hand, this existence without any act becomes the real intent.

The true meaning of this "Honesty," however, lies in not being so honest as it seems. For it cannot be so unintelligent as to let these various moments fall apart in that way; it must have an immediate consciousness regarding their opposition, because they are absolutely related to one another. Bare action is essentially action of *this* individual, and this action is likewise essentially an actuality or a "fact." Conversely, actuality essentially is only as his own action, and as action in general as well; and just as his own action is action in general, so it is only reality in general. While, then, he thinks he has only to do with the objectified intent as abstract reality, there is also present this idea that he has to do with it as his own doing. But precisely so far as it is only a matter of being busy about doing something, he is not really in earnest in the matter, but rather is dealing with a "fact," and with fact as his own. Since, finally, he seems to will merely *his own* "fact" and his own action, it is again a matter of dealing with "fact" in general or actuality substantial and abiding (*an und für sich bleibende*).

Just as the real intent and its moments appear at this stage as *content,* they are likewise necessary also as *forms* in consciousness. They come forward as content merely to pass away again, each making room for the other. They have therefore to be present in the character of cancelled and sublated forms: so taken, however, they are aspects of *consciousness* itself. The real intent is present as the inherent nature or reflexion of consciousness into self; the ousting of the moments by each other there finds expression, however, in their being established in consciousness, not *per se*, but only for another consciousness. One of the moments of the content is exposed by it to the light, and presented as an object for others. Consciousness, however, is at the same time reflected therefrom back upon itself, and the opposite is thus equally present within it, is retained for itself as its own. There is, too, not one of them which could be *merely* and solely put outside, and another *merely* retained within; rather, consciousness operates alternately with them, for it has to make one as well as another essential for itself and for others. The *whole* is the moving process of permeating individuality with the universal. In that this consciousness finds this whole, however, to be merely the simple ultimate nature (*Wesen*) and thus the abstraction of the real intent, the moments of this whole appear as distinct outside that object and outside one another. As a single whole it is only exhaustively exhibited by the process of alternately exposing its elements to view and keeping them within itself. Since in this alternation consciousness has in its process of reflexion one moment for itself and keeps it as essential, while another is merely externally implied or is for *others*, there thus enters a play of individualities with one another, where they both deceive and find deceived themselves and one another reciprocally.

An individuality, then, sets to work to carry out something; by so doing it seems to have made something into an "actual fact." It acts; by so doing it comes out before others, and seems to be concerned to secure the reality of something. Others, therefore, take its action to be an interest in the "fact" as such, and take the end of the act to be the carrying out of the "fact" *per se*, regardless of whether this is done by the former individuality or by them. When on this account they point out that this "fact" has been already brought about by themselves, or, if not, offer and actually furnish their assistance, then they see that consciousness has rather left the position where they think it to be; it is its own action and effort, which arouses its interest in the "fact," and when they come to know that this was the real intent, the fact of the matter, they feel themselves deceived. In reality, however, their haste to render assistance was itself nothing else than their desire to see and manifest their own action and not the objectified intent, i.e. they wanted to deceive the other individual just in the way they complain of having been deceived. Since there has now been brought to light that its own action and effort, the play of its powers, is taken for the real intent, consciousness seems to be occupied in its own way on its own account and not on that of others, and only to be troubled about action *qua* its own action, and not about action *qua* an action of others, and hence seems to let the others in their turn keep to their own "fact." But they go wrong again; that consciousness has already left the point where they thought it was. It is not concerned with the matter in hand as "fact" in the sense of this its own *particular* fact, but as fact *qua* fact, *qua* something universal, which is for all. Hence it interferes in the action and work of others; and if consciousness can no longer take their work out of their hands, it is at least interested in the matter, and shows this by its concern to pass judgment. When it stamps the result with the mark of its approval and praise, this is meant to imply that in the work it does not merely praise the work itself, but at the same time its own generosity and moderation in not having destroyed the work as work nor spoiled it by finding fault. Since it shows an interest in the work, it enjoys its own self therein; and in the same way the work which it found fault with is welcomed for just this enjoyment of its own action which is thereby procured. Those, however, who regard themselves as, or profess to be, deceived by this interference from others wanted really themselves to deceive in the same way. They give out their efforts and doings as something only for themselves, in which they merely have themselves and their own nature in view. But since they do something, and thus express their nature, bring themselves to the light of day, they directly contradict by their deed the pretence of wanting to exclude the daylight, i.e. to exclude the publicity of universal consciousness, and participation by every one. Actualization is, on the contrary, an exposing of what is one's own in a universal element, where it comes to be and has to be "fact" for every one.

There is, then, as much deception of itself as of others, if it is pretended that the "bare fact" is one's sole concern. A consciousness that lays open a "fact" soon learns that others hurry to the spot and want to make themselves busy there, like flies to milk newly put out; and they in their turn find out in its case that it is not dealing with "fact" *qua* object, but with fact as "its own." On the other hand, if only action itself, the use of powers and capacities, or the expression of a given individuality, is to be the essential thing, they reciprocally learn that all are on the alert and consider themselves invited to deal with the matter, and that instead of a mere abstract action, or a single *peculiar* action, something has been elicited and exposed which was equally well *for others* or is a real intent. In both cases the same thing happens; and only appears to have a different significance by contrast with that which was accepted and assumed to hold on the matter. Consciousness finds both sides to be equally essential moments, and thereby learns what the nature of the "fact of the matter," the real intent, is, viz. that it is neither merely "fact," which is opposed to action in general and to individual action, nor action which is opposed to permanence and is the genus independent of these moments as its species. Rather it is an essential reality whose existence means the action of the single individual and of all individuals, and whose action is immediately for others, or is a "fact," and is only "fact" in the sense of an action of each and all—the essential reality which is the essence of all beings (*Wesen*), which is spiritual essence. Consciousness learns that no one of these moments is subject, but rather gets dissolved in the universal objectified intent. The moments of individuality, which were taken as subject one after another by this unreflective incoherent stage of consciousness, coalesce and concentrate into simple individuality, which *qua this*, is no less immediately universal. The real itent thereby ceases to stand in the relation of a predicate, loses the characteristic of lifeless abstract universality: it is substance permeated by individuality: it is subject, wherein is individuality just as much *qua* individual, or *qua* this, as *qua* all individuals: and it is the universal, which has an existence only as being this action of each and all, and gets an actual reality in that *this* consciousness knows it to be its own individual reality, and the reality of all. Pure objectified intent is what was characterized above as the "category"—being which is the ego, or ego which is being, but in the sense of thought, which is still distinguished from actual self-consciousness. Here, however, the moments of actual self-consciousness—both so far as we call them its content (purpose, action, and reality), and also in so far as we call them its form (being-for-self and being-for-another)—are made identical with the bare and simple category itself, and the category is thereby at the same time the entire content.

b

REASON AS LAWGIVER

The next step in the development of individuality is to bring out the universal conditions of its co-existence with other individualities. This it can do because it is complete in itself, and is essentially self-conscious reason. These conditions are many, because of the diversity of its own content and of the relations in which it stands; and are yet the conditions of individuality which is one and single. Hence their plurality never implies a separation; the conditions limit each other's operation and their precise operation must be determined.

These, then, are the two stages in determining the general conditions or laws

of co-existence of individuality: (1) the enunciation of different laws by and for
rational individuality, (2) the relation of these laws *inter se*, and to the single
principle from which they all proceed. Both stages owe their existence to the
activity of reason. Reason promulgates laws, and criticizes, tests the validity of,
the laws.

Hence the two following sections.

SPIRITUAL essential reality is, in its bare existence, pure consciousness,
and also *this* self-consciousness. The originally determinate nature of
the individual has lost its positive significance of being inherently the
element and purpose of his activity; it is merely a superseded moment,
while the individual is a self in the sense of a universal self. Conversely
the formal "real intent" gets its filling from active self-differentiating individuality; for the distinctions within individuality compose the content of that universal. The category is implicit (*an sich*) as the universal
of pure consciousness; it is also explicit (*für sich*), for the self of consciousness is likewise its moment. It is absolute being, for that universality is the bare self-identity of being.

Thus what is object for consciousness has (now) the significance of
being the true; it *is* and it *holds good*, in the sense of being and holding
good by itself as an independent entity (*an und für sich selbst*). It is the
"absolute fact," which no longer suffers from the opposition of certainty
and its truth, between universal and individual, between purpose and
its reality, but whose existence is the reality and action of self-
consciousness. This "fact" is therefore the *ethical substance*; and consciousness of it is *ethical* consciousness. Its object is likewise taken to
be the truth, for it combines self-consciousness and being in a single
unity. It stands for what is absolute, for self-consciousness cannot and
will not again go beyond this object because it is there at home with itself: it *cannot*, for the object is all power, and all being: it *will* not, because the object is its *self*, or the will of *this* self. It is the real object inherently as object, for it contains and involves the distinction which
consciousness implies. It divides itself into areas or spheres (*Massen*)
which are the determinate laws of the absolute reality [viz. the ethical
substance]. These spheres, however, do not obscure the notion, for the
moments (being, bare consciousness and self) are kept contained
within it—a unity which constitutes the inner nature of these spheres,
and no longer lets these moments in this distinction fall apart from one
another.

These laws or spheres (*Massen*) of the substance of ethical life are directly recognized and acknowledged. We cannot ask for their origin
and justification, nor is there something else to search for as their warrant; for something other than this independent self-subsistent reality

(*an und für sich seyendes Wesen*) could only be self-consciousness itself. But self-consciousness is nothing else than this reality, for itself is the self-existence of this reality, which is the truth just because it is as much the self of consciousness as its inherent nature (*sein Ansich*), or pure consciousness.

Since self-consciousness knows itself to be a moment of this substance, the moment of self-existence (of independence and self-determination), it expresses the existence of the law within itself in the form: "the healthy natural reason knows immediately what is right and good." As healthy reason knows the law immediately, so the law is valid for it also immediately, and it says directly: "this is right and good." The emphasis is on "*this*": there are determinate specific laws; there is the "fact itself" with a concrete filling and content.

What is thus given immediately must likewise be accepted and regarded as immediate. As in the case of the immediacy of sense-experience, so here we have also to consider the nature of the existence to which this immediate certainty in ethical experience gives expression—to analyse the constitution of the immediately existing areas (*Massen*) of ethical reality. Examples of some such laws will show what we want to know; and since we take them in the form of declarations of the healthy reason knowing them, *we* have not, in this connexion, to introduce the moment which has to be made good in their case when looked at as immediate ethical laws.

"Every one ought to speak the truth." In this duty, as expressed unconditionally, the condition will at once be granted, viz. *if* he knows the truth. The command will therefore now run: everyone should speak the truth, at all times according to his knowledge and conviction about it. The healthy reason, this very ethical consciousness which knows immediately what is right and good, will explain that this condition had all the while been so bound up with that universal maxim that it meant the command to be taken in that sense. It thereby admits, however, in point of fact, that in the very expression of the maxim it *eo ipso* really violated it. The healthy reason *said:* "each should speak the truth"; it *intended*, however: "he must speak the truth according to his knowledge and conviction." That is to say, it spoke otherwise than it intended, and to speak otherwise than one intends means not speaking the truth. The improved untruth, or inaptitude now takes the form: "each must speak the truth according to his knowledge and conviction about it on each occasion." Thereby, however, what was universally necessary and absolutely valid (and this the proposition wanted to express) has turned round into what is really a complete contingency. For speaking the truth is left to the chance whether I know it and can convince myself of it; and there is nothing more in the statement than that truth and falsehood are to be spoken, just as anyone happens to know, intend, and understand. This contingency in the content has universality merely in the propositional form of the expression; but as an ethical maxim the proposition promises a universal and necessary content, and thus contradicts itself by the content being contingent. Finally, if the maxim were to be improved by saying that the contingency of the knowledge and the conviction as to the truth should be dropped, and that the *truth*, too, "*ought*" to be known, then this would be a command which contradicts straightway what we started from. Healthy reason was at first assumed to have the immediate capacity of expressing the truth; now, however, we are saying that it "ought" to know the truth, i.e. that it does *not* immediately know how to express the truth. Looking at the content, this has dropped out in the demand that we "should" know the truth; for this demand refers to knowing in general—"we ought to *know*." What is demanded is, therefore, strictly speaking, something independent of every specific content. But here the whole point of the statement concerned a definite content, a distinction involved in the substance of the ethical life. Yet this immediate determination of that substance is a content of such a kind as turned out really to be a complete contingency; and when we try to get the required universality and necessity by making the law refer to the *knowledge* [instead of to the content], then the content really disappears altogether.

Another celebrated command runs: "Love thy neighbour as thyself." It is directed to an individual standing in relation to another individual, and asserts this law as a relation of a particular individual to a particular individual, i.e. a relation of sentiment or feeling (*Empfindung*). Active love—for an inactive love has no existence, and is therefore doubtless not intended here[1]—aims at removing evil from someone and bringing him good. To do this we have to distinguish what the evil is, what is the appropriate good to meet this evil, and what in general his well-being consists in; i.e. we have to love him intelligently. Unintelligent love will do him harm perhaps more than hatred. Intelligent, veritable (*wesentlich*) well-doing is, however, in its richest and most important form the intelligent universal action of the state— an action compared with which the action of a particular individual as such is something altogether so trifling that it is hardly worth talking about. The action of the state is in this connexion of such great weight and strength that if the action of the individual were to oppose it, and either sought to be straightway and deliberately (*für sich*) criminal, or out of love for another wanted to cheat the universal out of the right

---

[1] Cp. Kant, Groundwork of the Metaphysic of Morals: Sect. 1. Critique of Practical Reason: *Analytic* c. 3.

and claim which it has upon him, such action would be useless and
would inevitably be annihilated. Hence all that well-doing, which lies
in sentiment and feeling, can mean is an action wholly and solely particular, a help at need, which is as contingent as it is momentary.
Chance determines not merely its occasion, but also whether it is a
"work" at all, whether it is not at once dissipated again, and whether it
does not itself really turn to evil. Thus this sort of action for the good of
others, which is given out as necessary, is so constituted that it may just
as likely not exist as exist; is such that if the occasion by chance arises,
it may possibly be a "work," may possibly be good, but just as likely may
not. This law, therefore, has as little of a universal content as the first
above considered, and fails to express anything substantial, something
objectively real *per se* (*an und für sich*), which it should do if it is to be
an absolute ethical law. In other words, such laws never get further than
the "*ought to be*," they have no actual reality; they are not laws, but
merely commands.

It is, however, in point of fact, clear from the very nature of the case
that we must renounce all claim to an absolute universal content. For
every specific determination which the simple substance (and its very
nature consists in being simple) might obtain is inadequate to its
nature. The command itself in its simple absoluteness expresses immediate ethical existence; the distinction appearing in it is a specific
determinate element, and thus a content standing under the absolute
universality of this simple existence. Since, then, an absolute content
must thus be renounced, formal universality is the only kind that is possible and suitable, and this means merely that it is not to contradict itself. For universality devoid of content is formal; and an absolute content amounts to a distinction which is no distinction, i.e. means absence of content.[2]

In default of all content there is thus nothing left with which to make
a law but the bare form of universality, in fact, the mere tautology of
consciousness, a tautology which stands over against the content, and
consists in a knowledge, not of the content actually existing, the content proper, but of its ultimate essence only, a knowledge of its self-
identity.

The ethical inner essence is consequently not itself *ipso facto* a content, but only a standard for deciding whether a content is capable of
being a law or not, i.e. whether the content does not contradict itself.
Reason as law-giver is reduced to being reason as criterion; instead of
laying down laws reason now only tests *what is* laid down.

---

[2]The above criticism applies to Kant's "categorical imperative."

c

REASON AS TESTING LAWS

A DIFFERENCE within the bare and simple ethical substance is for it an accident, which, in the case of determinate commands, as we saw, appeared as contingency in the knowledge of the circumstances and contingency in action. The comparison of that simple existence with the determinateness which was inadequate to its nature took place in us; and the simple substance was then seen to be formal universality or pure consciousness, which holds itself free from and in opposition to the content, and is a knowledge of that content as something determinate. The universality in this way remains the same as what the objectified intent was. But in consciousness this universality is something different; it is no longer the genus, inert and void of thought, but is related to the particular and valid as its force and truth.

This consciousness at first seems the same process of testing which formerly *we* carried on, and its action seems unable to be anything else than has already taken place—a comparison of the universal with the determinate particular which would yield as formerly their mutual incongruity. But the relation of content to universal is different here, since this universal has got another significance. It is *formal* universality, of which the specific consent is *capable*; for in that universality the content is considered merely in relation to itself. When *we* were applying the test, the universal solid substance stood over against that specificity, which proved to be a contingent element of the consciousness into which the substance entered. *Here* one term of the comparison has vanished; the universal is no longer the existing substance with a value all its own, is no longer substantive right *per se*, but simple knowledge or form, which compares a content merely with itself, and looks at it to see if it is a tautology. Laws are no longer given, but examined and tested; and for that consciousness which applies the test the laws are already given. It picks up their content as simply there, without going into the consideration (as was done before) of the particularity and contingency attaching to its reality; instead of this it takes its stand by the command as command, and takes up an attitude towards this command just as direct and simple as [the fact of] its being a standard and criterion for criticizing it.

For that reason, however, this process of testing does not get very far. Just because the standard is a tautology and indifferent to the content, it accepts one content just as readily as the opposite. Suppose the question is:—ought it to be a law without qualification (*an und für sich*) that there should be property? Without qualification, and not because of utility for other ends:—the essential ethical truth consists just in the fact that the law should be merely a self-consistent whole (*sich selbst gleiche*), and through being identical with itself have its ground in its own essential nature, and not be something conditioned. Property *per se* does not contradict itself. It is a specifically determinate isolated element, or merely self-identical (*sich selbst gleich*). Absence of property, absence of ownership of things, or again, community of goods, contradicts itself just as little. That something belong to nobody at all, or to the first best man who puts himself in possession, or, again, to all together, and to each according to his need or in equal portions—that is a simple characteristic, a formal thought, like its opposite, property.

If indeed no one is master of a thing and it is looked at as a necessary object for human requirement, then it is necessary that it should become the possession of some particular individual; and the contradiction would rather lie in making a law out of the freedom of the thing. By the thing being without an owner is meant, however, not absolute freedom from ownership, but that it shall come into someone's possession according to the need of the individual, and, moreover, not in order to be kept but directly to be used. But to make provision for need in such an entirely haphazard manner is contradictory to the nature of the conscious being, with whom alone we have here to do. For such a being has to think of his need in a universal way, to look to his existence in its entirety, and procure himself a permanent lasting good. This being so, the idea that a thing is to become by chance the possession of the first self-conscious individual (*Leben*) who happens to need it, is inconsistent with itself.

In a communistic society, where provision would be made in a way which is universal and permanent, either each comes to have as much as he requires—in which case there is a contradiction between this inequality and the essential nature of consciousness, whose principle is the equality of individuals—or, acting on this last principle, there is an equal division of goods, and in this case the share each gets has no relation to his needs, and yet this is solely what "share," i.e. fair share, really means.

But if when taken in this way absence of property seems contradictory, this is only because it has not been left in the form of a simple determinate characteristic. The same result is found in the case of property if this is resolved into separate moments. The particular thing which is my property has by being so the value of something universal, established, and permanent. This, however, contradicts its nature, which consists in its being *used* and *passing away*. At the same time its value lies in being *mine*, which all others acknowledge and keep themselves away from. But just in my being acknowledged lies rather my equality, my identity, with every one—the opposite of exclusion.

Again, what I possess is a *thing*, i.e. an existence, which is there for others in general, quite universally and without any condition that it is for me alone. That I possess it contradicts the general nature of its thinghood. Property therefore contradicts itself on all hands just as much as absence of property; each has within it both these opposite and self-contradictory moments, universality and particularity.

But each of these determinate characteristics, presented simply as property or absence of property without further developing its implications, is as simple as the other, i.e. is not self-contradictory. The standard of law which reason has within itself therefore fits every case in the same way, and is in point of fact no standard at all. It would, too, turn out rather strange, if tautology, the principle of contradiction, which is allowed to be merely a formal criterion for knowledge of theoretical truth, i.e. something which is quite indifferent to truth and untruth alike, were to be more than this for knowledge of practical truth.

In both the above moments of what fills up the previous emptiness of spiritual reality (*geistigen Wesens*) the attempt to establish immediate determinate characteristics within the substance of the ethical life, and then to know whether these determinations are laws, has cancelled itself. The outcome, then, seems to be that neither determinate laws nor a knowledge of these can be obtained. But the substance in question is the consciousness of itself as absolute essentiality (*Wesenheit*), a consciousness therefore which can give up neither the difference falling within that substance, nor the knowledge of this difference. That giving laws and testing laws have turned out futile indicates that both, taken individually and in isolation, are merely unstable moments of the ethical consciousness; and the process in which they appear has the formal significance, that the substance of ethical life thereby expresses itself as consciousness.

So far as both these moments are more precise determinations of the consciousness of the real intent (*Sache selbst*) they can be looked on as forms of that honesty of nature (*Ehrlichkeit*) which now, as always with its formal moments, is much occupied with a content which "ought to be" good and right, and with testing definite fixed truth of this sort, and supposes itself to possess in healthy reason and intelligent insight the force and validity of ethical commands.

Without this honesty of nature, however, laws do not have validity as essential realities of consciousness, and the process of testing likewise does not hold good as an activity inside consciousness. Rather, these moments, when they appear directly as a reality each by itself, express in the one case an invalid establishment and mere *de facto* existence of actual laws, and in the other an equally invalid detachment from them. The law as determinate has an accidental content: this means here that it is a law made by a particular individual conscious of an arbitrary content. To legislate immediately in that way is thus tyrannical insolence and wickedness, which makes caprice into a law, and morality into obedience to such caprice—obedience to laws which are *merely* laws and not at the same time commands. So, too, the second process, testing the laws, so far as it is taken by itself, means moving the immovable, and the insolence of knowledge, which treats absolute laws in a spirit of intellectual detachment, and takes them for a caprice that is alien and external to it.

In both forms these moments are negative in relation to the ethical substance, to the real spiritual nature. In other words, the substance does not find in them its reality: but instead consciousness contains the substance still in the form of its own immediacy; and the substance is, as yet, only a process of willing and knowing on the part of *this* individual, or the "ought" of an unreal command and a knowledge of formal universality. But since these modes were cancelled, consciousness has passed back into the universal and those oppositions have vanished. The spiritual reality is actual substance precisely through these modes not holding good individually, but merely as cancelled and transcended; and the unity where they are merely moments is the self of consciousness which is henceforth established within the spiritual reality, and makes that spirit concrete, actual, and self-conscious.

Spiritual reality (*das geistige Wesen*) is thus, in the first place, for self-consciousness in the shape of a law implicitly existing. The universality present in the process of testing, which was of a formal kind and not inherently existent, is transcended. The law is, too, an eternal law, which does not have its ground in the will of a given individual, but has a being all its own (*an und für sich*), the pure and absolute will of all which takes the form of immediate existence. This will is, again, not a command which merely *ought to be*; it *is* and *has* validity; it is the universal ego of the category, ego which is immediately reality, and the world is only this reality. Since, however, this existing law is absolutely valid, the obedience given by self-consciousness is not service rendered to a master, whose orders are mere caprice and in which it does not recognize its own nature. On the contrary, the laws are thoughts of its own absolute consciousness, thoughts which are its own immediate possession. Moreover, it does not *believe* in them, for belief, while it no doubt sees the essential nature, still gazes at an alien essence—not its own. The ethical self-consciousness is directly at one with the essential reality, in virtue of the universality of its own self. Belief, on the other hand, begins with an individual consciousness; it is a process in which this consciousness is always approaching this unity, without ever being able to find itself at home with its essential nature. The above consciousness, on the other hand, has transcended itself as individual, this mediating process is completed, and only because of this, is it immediate self-consciousness of ethical substance.

The distinction, then, of self-consciousness from the essential nature (*Wesen*) is completely transparent. Because of this the distinctions found within that nature itself are not accidental characteristics. On the contrary, because of the unity of the essence with self-consciousness (from which alone discordance, incongruity, might have come), they are articulated groups (*Massen*) of the unity permeated by its own life, unsundered spirits transparent to themselves, stainless forms and shapes of heaven, that preserve amidst their differences the untarnished innocence and concord of their essential nature.

Self-consciousness, again, stands likewise in a simple and clear relation to those different laws. They *are* and nothing more—this is what constitutes the consciousness of its relation to them. Thus, Antigone takes them for the unwritten and unerring laws of the god—

> "Not now, indeed, nor yesterday, but for aye
> It lives, and no man knows what time it came."[1]

They are. If I ask for their origin, and confine them to the point whence they arose, that puts me beyond them, for it is I who am now the universal, while they are the conditioned and limited. If they are to get the sanction of my insight, I have already shaken their immovable nature, their inherent constancy, and regard them as something which is perhaps true, but possibly may also be not true, so far as I am concerned. True ethical sentiment consists just in holding fast and unshaken by what is right, and abstaining altogether from what would move or shake it or derive it. Suppose a deposit has been made over to me on trust, it is the property of another, and I recognize it because it is so, and remain immovable in this relation towards it. But if I keep the deposit for myself, then, according to the principle I use in testing laws—tautology—I undoubtedly do not commit a contradiction; for in that case I do not regard it any longer as the property of another. To keep anything which I do not look on as the property of some one else is perfectly consistent. Changing the point of view is not contradiction; for what we have to do with is not the point of view, but the object and content, which is not to contradict itself. Just as I can—as I do, when I give something away in a present—alter the view that something is mine into the view that it is the property of another, without being thereby guilty of a contradiction, so too I can proceed the other way about. It is not, then, because I find something not contradicting itself that it is

[1]Sophocles, *Antigone*, 1. 456–7.

right; but it is right because it is the right. That something is the property of another, this lies at the basis of what I do. I have not to "reason
why," nor to seek out or hit upon thoughts of all kinds, connexions, aspects; I have to think neither of giving laws nor of testing them. By all
such thought-processes on my part I should stultify that relation, since
in point of fact I could, if I liked, make the opposite suit my indeterminate tautological knowledge just as well, and make *that* the law. But
whether this or the opposite determination is the right, that is settled
just as it stands (*an und für sich*). I might, for my own part, have made
the law whichever I wanted, and neither of them just as well, and am,
by my beginning to test them, thereby already on an immoral track.
That the right is there for me just as it stands—this places me within
the substance of ethical reality: and in this way that substance is the
essence of self-consciousness. But self-consciousness, again, is *its* actualization and its existence, its self, and its will.

(BB)

SPIRIT[1]

In the preceding section there is analysed the attempt on the part of individuality to operate as its own legislator and judge of laws holding for individuals. Individuality may claim the privilege of enunciating laws universal in character but having their source and inspiration solely in the single individual. Such laws can at best only be regulative and cannot be constitutive of the substance of individuality; for the substance of individuality necessarily involves other individuals within it. In short individuality is itself only realized as a part of a concrete whole of individuals: its life is drawn from common life in and with others. To attempt to enunciate laws from itself as if it could create the conditions of its own inherent universality can only issue in one result: laws are furnished without the content which gives those laws any meaning, or else the laws and the content remain from first to last external to one another. But if laws are purely formal, they cease to *be* "laws," i.e. constitutive conditions of individuality. Hence the attempt above described is sure to break down by its own futility. What is wanted to give the laws meaning is the concrete substance of social life: and when this concrete substance is provided *ipso facto* the attempt of individuality to create laws disappears, for these laws are already found in operation in social life. Only such laws have reality. But this involves the further step that individuality is only realized, only finds its true universal content, in and with the order of a society. Here alone is individuality what it is in truth, at once a particular focus of self-consciousness, and a realization of universal mind. This condition where individuality is conscious of itself only in and with others, and conscious of the common life as its own, is the stage of spiritual existence. Spiritual existence and social life thus go together. The following section begins the analysis of this phase of experience, which extends from the simplest form of sociality—the Family—up to the highest experience of universal mind—Religion.

The immediately succeeding section may be taken as the keystone of the whole arch of experience traversed in the *Phenomenology*. Here it is pointed out that all the preceding phases of experience have not merely been prepar-

---

[1]The term "Spirit" seems better to render the word "*Geist*" used here, than the word "mind" would do. Up to this stage of experience the word "mind" is sufficient to convey the meaning. But spirit is mind at a much higher level of existence.

ing the way for what is to follow, but that the various aspects, hitherto treated as separate moments of experience, are in reality abstractions from the life of concrete spirit now to be discussed and analysed.

It is noteworthy that from this point onwards the argument is less negative in its result either directly or indirectly, and is more systematic and constructive. This is no doubt largely because hitherto individual mind as such has been under review, and this is an abstraction from social mind or spiritual existence.

VI

SPIRIT

REASON is spirit, when its certainty of being all reality has been raised to the level of truth, and reason is *consciously* aware of itself as its own world, and of the world as itself. The development of spirit was indicated in the immediately preceding movement of mind, where the object of consciousness, the category pure and simple, rose to be the notion of reason. When reason "observes," this pure unity of ego and existence, the unity of subjectivity and objectivity, of for-itself-ness and in-itself-ness—this unity is immanent, has the character of implicitness or of being; and consciousness of reason *finds itself*. But the true nature of "observation" is rather the transcendence of this instinct of *finding* its object lying directly at hand, and passing beyond this unconscious state of its existence. The directly perceived (*angeschaut*) category, the thing simply "found," enters consciousness as the self-existence of the ego— ego, which now knows itself in the objective reality, and knows itself there as the *self*. But this feature of the category, viz. of being for-itself as opposed to being—immanent—within—itself, is equally one-sided, and a moment that cancels itself. The category therefore gets for consciousness the character which it possesses in its universal truth—it is self-contained essential reality (*an und fürsichseyendes Wesen*). This character, still abstract, which constitutes the nature of absolute fact, of "fact itself," is the beginnings of "spiritual reality" (*das geistige Wesen*); and its mode of consciousness is here a formal knowledge of that reality, a knowledge which is occupied with the varied and manifold content thereof. This consciousness is still, in point of fact, a particular individual distinct from the general substance, and either prescribes arbitrary laws or thinks it possesses within its own knowledge as such the laws as they absolutely are (*an und für sich*), and takes itself to be the power that passes judgment on them. Or again, looked at from the side of the substance, this is seen to be the self-contained and self-sufficient spiritual reality, which is not yet a consciousness of its own self. The self-contained and self-sufficient reality, however, which is at once aware of being actual in the form of consciousness and presents itself to itself, is Spirit.

Its essential spiritual being (*Wesen*) has been above designated as the ethical substance; spirit, however, is concrete ethical actuality (*Wirklichkeit*). Spirit is the *self* of the actual consciousness, to which spirit stands opposed, or rather which appears over against itself, as an objective actual world that has lost, however, all sense of strangeness for the self, just as the self has lost all sense of having a dependent or independent existence by itself, cut off and separated from that world. Being substance and universal self-identical permanent essence (*Wesen*), spirit is the immovable irreducible basis and the starting point for the action of all and every one; it is their purpose and their goal, because the ideally implicit nature (*Ansich*) of all self-consciousnesses. This substance is likewise the universal product, wrought and created by the action of each and all, and constituting their unity and likeness and identity of meaning; for it is self-existence (*Fürsichseyn*), the self, action. *Qua* substance, spirit is unbending righteous selfsameness, self-identity; but *qua* for-itself, self-existent and self-determined (*Fürsichseyn*), its continuity is resolved into discrete elements, it is the self-sacrificing soul of goodness, the benevolent essential nature in which each fulfils his own special work, rends the continuum of the universal substance, and takes his own share of it. This resolution of the essence into individual forms is just the aspect of the separate action and the separate self of all the several individuals; it is the moving soul of the ethical substance, the resultant universal spiritual being. Just because this substance is a being resolved in the self, it is not a lifeless essence, but actual and alive.

Spirit is thus the self-supporting absolutely real ultimate being (*Wesen*). All the previous modes of consciousness are abstractions from it: they are constituted by the fact that spirit analyses itself, distinguishes its moments, and halts at each individual mode in turn. The isolating of such moments presupposes spirit itself and requires spirit for its subsistence, in other words, this isolation of modes only exists within spirit, which is existence. Taken in isolation they appear as if they existed as they stand. But their advance and return upon their real ground and essential being showed that they are merely moments or vanishing quantities; and this essential being is precisely this movement and resolution of these moments. Here, where spirit, the reflexion of these moments into itself, has become established, our reflexion may briefly recall them in this connexion: they were consciousness, self-consciousness, and reason. Spirit is thus *Consciousness* in general, which contains sense-certainty, perception and understanding, so far as in analysing its own self it holds fast by the moment of being a reality objective to itself, and by abstraction eliminates the fact that this reality is its own self objectified, its own self-existence. When again it holds fast by the other abstract moment produced by analysis, the fact that its object is its own self become objective to itself, is its self-existence, then it is *Self-consciousness*. But as immediate consciousness of its inherent and its explicit being, of its immanent self and its objective self, as the unity of consciousness and self-consciousness, it is that type of consciousness which has Reason: it is the consciousness which, as the word "have" indicates, has the object in a shape which is implicitly and inherently rational, or is categorized, but in such a way that the object is not yet taken by the consciousness in question to have the value of a category. Spirit here is that consciousness from the immediately preceding consideration of which we have arrived at the present stage. Finally, when this reason, which spirit *"has,"* is seen by spirit to be reason which actually *is*, to be reason which is actual in spirit, and is its world, then spirit has come to its truth; it *is* spirit, the essential nature of ethical life actually existent.

Spirit, so far as it is the immediate truth, is the ethical life of a nation:—the individual, which is a world. It has to advance to the consciousness of what it is immediately; it has to abandon and transcend the beautiful simplicity of ethical life, and get to a knowledge of itself by passing through a series of stages and forms. The distinction between these and those that have gone before consists in their being real spiritual individualities (*Geister*), actualities proper, and instead of being forms merely of consciousness, they are forms of a world.

The living ethical world is spirit in its truth. As it first comes to an abstract *knowledge* of its essential nature, ethical life (*Sittlichkeit*) is destroyed in the formal universality of right or legality (*Recht*). Spirit, being now sundered within itself, traces one of its worlds in the element of its objectivity as in a crass solid actuality; this is the realm of Culture and Civilization; while over against this in the element of thought is traced the world of Belief or Faith, the realm of the Inner Life and Truth (*Wesen*). Both worlds, however, when in the grip of the notion—when grasped by spirit which, after this loss of self through self-diremption, penetrates itself—are thrown into confusion and revolutionized through individual Insight (*Einsicht*), and the general diffusion of this attitude, known as the "Enlightenment" (*Aufklärung*). And the realm which had thus been divided and expanded into the "present" and the "remote beyond," into the "here" and the "yonder," turns back into self-consciousness. This self-consciousness, again, taking now the form of Morality (the *inner moral* life) apprehends itself as the essential truth, and the real essence as its actual self: no longer puts its world and its ground and basis away outside itself, but lets everything fade into itself, and in the form of Conscience (*Gewissen*) is spirit sure and certain (*gewiss*) of itself.

The ethical world, the world rent asunder into the "here" and the "yonder," and the moral point of view (*moralische Weltanschauung*), are, then, individual forms of spirit (*Geister*) whose process and whose return into the self of spirit, a self simple and self-existent (*fürsichseyend*), will be developed. As these attain their goal and final result, the actual self-consciousness of Absolute Spirit will make its appearance and be their outcome.

A

OBJECTIVE SPIRIT[1] — THE ETHICAL ORDER[2]

Spirit, in its ultimate simple truth, is consciousness, and breaks asunder its moments from one another. An act divides spirit into spiritual substance on the one side, and consciousness of the substance on the other; and divides the substance as well as consciousness. The substance appears in the shape of a universal inner nature and purpose standing in contrast to itself *qua* individualized reality. The middle or mediating term, infinite in character, is self-consciousness, which, being *implicitly* the unity of itself and that substance, becomes so, now, explicitly (*für sich*), unites the universal inner nature and its particular realization, raises the latter to the former and acts *ethically*: and, on the other hand, brings the former down to the latter and carries out the purpose, the substance presented merely in thought. In this way it brings to light the unity of its self and the substance, and produces this unity in the form of its "work," and thus as actual concrete fact (*Wirklichkeit*).

When consciousness breaks up into these elements, the simple substance has in part acquired the attitude of opposition to self-consciousness; in part it thereby manifests in itself the very nature of consciousness, which consists in distinguishing its own content within itself — manifests it as a world articulated into its spheres. The substance is thus an ethical being split up into distinct elemental forms, a human and a divine law. In the same way, the self-consciousness appearing over against the substance assigns itself, in virtue of its inner nature, to one of these powers, and, *qua* involving knowledge, gets broken up into ignorance of what it is doing on the one hand, and knowledge of this on the other, a knowledge which for that reason proves a deception. It learns, therefore, through its own act at once the contradictory nature of those powers into which the inner substance divided itself, and their mutual overthrow, as well as the contradiction between

---

[1]Der wahre Geist.
[2]Sittlichkeit.

its knowledge of the ethical character of its act and what is truly and essentially ethical, and so finds *its own* destruction. In point of fact, however, the ethical substance has by this process become actual concrete self-consciousness: in other words *this* particular self has become self-sufficient and self-dependent—(*Anund Fürsichseyenden*), but precisely thereby the ethical order has been overthrown and destroyed.

a

THE ETHICAL WORLD: LAW HUMAN AND DIVINE: MAN AND WOMAN

The first step in the analysis of spirit is to take spirit as a realized actual social order, immediately given as a historical fact, and present directly to the minds of the individuals composing it. This is social life as an established routine of human adjustments, where the natural characteristics and constitution of its moral individuals are absorbed and built into the single substance of the living social whole. It is spirit as an objectively embodied whole of essentially spiritual individuals, without any consciousness of opposition to one another or to the whole, and with an absolute unbroken sense of their own security and fulfilment within the substance of social mind. It is spirit at the level of naïve acquiescence in the law and order of conventional life.

But such a self-complete type of experience has various levels of realization. It cannot exist except through the union of opposing elements; and the central principle of all experience, self-consciousness, which assumes here such a concrete form, has abundant material on which to exercise its function of creating and uniting distinctions. The first level is determined by the fact that the substance of social life is constituted out of the quasi-natural phenomena of human genus and species, of race and nationality, on the one hand, and the purely natural element of specialized individual sex on the other. These two aspects go together; the sex-relations of individuals maintain race and nationality, the nation lives in and through its sexually distinct individuals. The social order as an order is realized and maintained in the medium of these elements. The fact that this order is an order of universal mind gives it a permanence, an inviolability, an absoluteness, which are inseparable from it, so inseparable that the order is looked on as having its roots in the Absolute Mind, and as deriving its authority from it. The social order on this aspect consists of a divinely established and divinely sanctioned *régime*; the gods are the guardians of the city, of the hearth and the home. On the other hand the expression of this order varies, and is enunciated from time to time in the history of a community. The order in this sense is made by man; the law of the social order thus becomes a human law, determined by human conditions and human ends; it is a round of conventions and customs. These two forms of order are inseparable in the life of a community, and they subsist together and side by side at this level of social consciousness. They may lead to conflict in the life of the individual in the community, and have to be reconciled by force or otherwise; and they become associated and connected with the fundamental differences of individuality above referred to.

The analysis of this level of social life constituted as above furnishes the argument of the following section. With Hegel's treatment of the relationships holding between Husband and Wife, Parents and Children, Brothers and Sisters should be read Aristotle's discussion of social fellowship in Eth. Nicom. Bks. VIII, IX.

THE simple substance of spirit, being consciousness, divides itself into parts. In other words, just as consciousness of abstract sensuous existence passes over into perception, so does immediate certainty of real ethical existence; and just as for sense-perception bare "being" becomes a "thing" with many properties, so for ethical perception a given act becomes a reality involving many ethical relations. For the former, again, the unnecessary plurality of properties concentrates itself into the form of an essential opposition between individual and universal; and still more for the latter, which is consciousness purified and substantial, the plurality of ethical moments is reduced to and assumes a twofold form, that of a law of individuality and a law of universality. Each of these areas or "masses" of the substance remains, however, spirit in its entirety. If in sense-perception "things" have no other substantial reality than the two determinations of individual and universal, these determinations express, in the present instance, merely the superficial opposition of both sides to one another.

Individuality, in the case of the subject (*Wesen*) we are here considering, has the significance of self-consciousness in general, not of any particular consciousness we care to take. The ethical substance is, thus, in this determination actual concrete substance, Absolute Spirit realized in the plurality of distinct consciousnesses definitely existing. It [this spirit] is the community (*Gemeinwesen*) which, as we entered the stage of the practical embodiment of reason in general, came before us as the absolute and ultimate reality, and which here comes objectively before itself in its true nature as a conscious ethical reality (*Wesen*), and as the essential reality for that mode of consciousness we are now dealing with. It is spirit which is *for itself*, since it maintains itself by being reflected in the minds of the component individuals; and which is *in itself* or substance, since it preserves them within itself. *Qua* actual substance, that spirit is a Nation (*Volk*); *qua* concrete consciousness, it is the Citizens of the nation. This consciousness has its essential being in simple spirit, and is certain of itself in the actual realization of this spirit, in the entire nation; it has its truth there directly, not therefore in something unreal, but in a spirit which exists and makes itself felt.

This spirit can be named Human Law, because it has its being essentially in the form of self-conscious actuality. In the form of universality, that spirit is the law known to everybody, familiar and recognized, and is the everyday Customary Convention (*Sitte*); in the form of particularity it is the concrete certainty of itself in any and every individual; and the certainty of itself as a single individuality is that spirit in the form of Government. Its true and complete nature is seen in its authoritative validity openly and unmistakably manifested, an existence which takes the form of unconstrained independent objective fact, and is immediately apprehended with conscious certainty in this form.

Over against this power and publicity of the ethical secular human order there appears, however, another power, the Divine Law. For the ethical power of the state, being the movement of self-conscious action, finds its opposition in the simple immediate essential being of the ethical order; *qua* actual concrete universality, it is a force exerted against the independence of the individual; and, *qua* actuality in general, it finds inherent in that essential being something other than the power of the state.

We mentioned before that each of the opposite ways in which the ethical substance exists contains that substance in its entirety, and contains all moments of its contents. If, then, the community is that substance in the form of self-consciously realized action, the other side has the form of immediate or directly existent substance. The latter is thus, on the one hand, the inner principle (*Begriff*) or universal possibility of the ethical order in general, but, on the other hand, contains within it also the moment of self-consciousness. This moment which expresses the ethical order in this element of immediacy or mere being, which, in other words, is an immediate consciousness of self (both as regards its essence and its particular thisness) in an "other"—and hence, is a *natural* ethical community—this is the *Family*. The family, as the inner indwelling principle of sociality operating in an unconscious way, stands opposed to its own actuality when explicitly conscious; as the basis of the actuality of a nation, it stands in contrast to the nation itself; as the *immediate* ethical existence, it stands over against the ethical order which shapes and preserves itself by work for universal ends; the Penates of the family stand in contrast to the universal spirit.

Although the ethical existence of the family has the character of immediacy, it is within itself an *ethical* entity, but not so far as it is the natural relation of its component members, or so far as their connexion is one immediately holding between individual concrete beings. For the *ethical* element is intrinsically universal and this relation established by nature is essentially just as much a spiritual fact, and is only ethical by being spiritual. Let us see wherein its peculiar ethical character consists.

In the first place, because the ethical element is the intrinsically universal element, the *ethical* relation between the members of the family is not that of sentiment or the relationship of love. The ethical element in this case seems bound to be placed in the relation of the individual member of the family to the *entire* family as the real substance, so that the purpose of his action and the content of his actuality are taken from this substance, are derived solely from the family life. But the conscious purpose which dominates the action of this whole, so far as that purpose concerns that whole, is itself the individual member. The procuring and maintaining of power and wealth turn, in part, merely on needs and wants, and are a matter that has to do with desire; in part, they become in their higher object something which is merely of mediate significance. This object does not fall within the family itself, but concerns what is truly universal, the community; it acts rather in a negative way on the family, and consists in setting the individual outside the family, in subduing his merely natural existence and his mere particularity and so drawing him on towards virtue, towards living in and for the universal. The positive purpose peculiar to the family is the individual as such. Now in order that this relationship may be ethical, neither the individual who does an act nor he to whom the act refers must show any trace of contingency such as obtains in rendering some particular help or service. The content of the ethical act must be substantial in character, or must be entire and universal; hence it can only stand in relation to the entire individual, to the individual *qua* universal. And this, again, must not be taken as if it were merely in idea that an act of service furthered his entire happiness, whereas the service, taken as an immediate or concrete act, only does something particular in regard to him. Nor must we think that the ethical act, like a process of education, really takes him as its object, and, dealing with him as a whole, in a series of efforts, produces him as a kind of work; for there, apart from the purpose, which operates in a negative way on the family, the real act has merely a limited content. Finally, just as little should we take it that the service rendered is a help in time of need, by which in truth the entire individual is saved; for such help is itself an entirely casual act, the occasion of which is an ordinary actuality which can as well be as not be. The act, then, which embraces the entire existence of the blood relation does not concern the citizen, for he does not belong to the family, nor does it deal with one who is going to be a citizen and so will cease to have the significance of a mere particular individual: it has as its object and content this specific individual belonging to the family, takes him as a universal being, divested of his sensuous, or particular reality. The act no longer concerns the living but the dead, one who has passed through the long sequence of his broken and diversified existence and gathered up his being into its one completed embodiment, who has lifted himself out of the unrest of a life of chance and change into the peace of simple universality. Because it is only as citizen that he is real and substantial, the individual, when not a citizen, and belonging to the family, is merely unreal insubstantial shadow.

This condition of universality, which the individual *as such* reaches, is mere being, death; it is the immediate issue of the process of nature, and is not the action of a conscious mind. The duty of the member of a family is on that account to attach this aspect too, in order that this last phase of being also (this universal being), may not belong to nature alone, and remain something irrational, but may be something actually *done*, and the right of consciousness be asserted in it. Or rather the significance of the act is that, because in truth the peace and universality of a self-conscious being does not belong to nature, the apparent claim which nature has made to act in this way may be given up and the truth reinstated.

What nature did in the individual's case concerns the aspect in which his process of becoming universal is manifested as the movement of an existent. It takes effect no doubt within the ethical community, and has this in view as its purpose: death is the fulfilment and highest task which the individual as such undertakes on its behalf. But so far as he is essentially a particular individual, it is an accident that his death was connected directly with his labour for the universal whole, and was the outcome of his toil; partly because, if it was so, it is the *natural* course of the negativity of the individual *qua* existent, in which consciousness does not return into itself and become self-conscious; or, again, because, since the process of the existent consists in becoming cancelled and transcended and attaining the stage of independent self-existence, death is the aspect of diremption, where the self-existence, which is obtained, is something other than that being which entered on the process.

Because the ethical order is spirit in its immediate truth, those aspects into which its conscious life breaks up fall also into this form of immediacy; and the individual's particularity passes over into this abstract negativity, which, being in itself without consolation or reconcilement, must receive them essentially through a concrete and external act.

Blood-relationship therefore supplements the abstract natural process by adding to it the process of consciousness, by interrupting the work of nature, and rescuing the blood-relation from destruction; or better, because destruction, the passing into mere being, is necessary, it takes upon itself the act of destruction.

Through this it comes about that the universal being, the sphere of death, is also something which has returned into itself, something self-existent; the powerless bare particular unity is raised to universal individuality. The dead individual, by his having detached and liberated his being from his action or his negative unity, is an empty particular, merely existing passively for some other, at the mercy of every lower irrational organic agency, and the [chemical, physical] forces of abstract material elements, both of which are now stronger than himself, the former on account of the life which they have, the latter on account of their negative nature.[1] The family keeps away from the dead this dishonouring of him by the desires of unconscious organic agencies and by abstract elements, puts its own action in place of theirs, and weds the relative to the bosom of the earth, the elemental individuality that passes not away. Thereby the family makes the dead a member of a community[2] which prevails over and holds under control the powers of the particular material elements and the lower living creatures, which sought to have their way with the dead and destroy him.

This last duty thus accomplishes the complete divine law, or constitutes the positive ethical act towards the given individual. Every other relation towards him which does not remain at the level of love, but is ethical, belongs to human law, and has the negative significance of lifting the individual above the confinement within the natural community to which he belongs as a concrete individual. But, now, though human right has for its content and power the actual ethical substance consciously aware of itself, the entire nation, while divine right and law derive theirs from the particular individual who is beyond the actual, yet he is still not without power. His power lies in the abstract pure universal, the elemental individual, which seizes upon the individuality that cuts itself loose from the element and constitutes the self-conscious reality of the nation, and draws it back into the pure abstraction which is its essential nature: draws it back just as that essence is its ultimate ground and source. How this power is made explicit in the nation itself will come out more fully as we proceed.

Now in the one law as in the other there are differences and stages. For since these laws involve the element of consciousness in both cases, distinction is developed within themselves: and this is just what constitutes the peculiar process of their life. The consideration of these differences brings out the way they operate, and the kind of self-consciousness at work in both the universal essential principles (*Wesen*) of the ethical world, as also their connexion and transition into one another.

The community, the upper law whose validity is open to the light of

---

[1] The description here refers to the process of bodily corruption.
[2] i.e. the earth?

day, has its concrete vitality in government; for in government it is an individual whole. Government is concrete actual spirit reflected into itself, the self pure and simple of the entire ethical substance. This simple force allows, indeed, the community to unfold and expand into its component members, and to give each part subsistence and self-existence of its own (*Fürsichseyn*). Spirit finds in this way its realization or its objective existence, and the family is the medium in which this realization takes effect. But spirit is at the same time the force of the whole, combining these parts again within the unity which negates them, giving them the feeling of their want of independence, and keeping them aware that their life only lies in the whole. The community may thus, on the one hand, organize itself into the systems of property and of personal independence, of personal right and right in things; and, on the other hand, articulate the various ways of working for what in the first instance are particular ends—those of gain and enjoyment—into their own special guilds and associations, and may thus make them independent. The spirit of universal assemblage and association is the single and simple principle, and the negative essential factor at work in the segregation and isolation of these systems. In order not to let them get rooted and settled in this isolation and thus break up the whole into fragments and let the common spirit evaporate, government has from time to time to shake them to the very centre by War. By this means it confounds the order that has been established and arranged, and violates their right to independence, while the individuals (who, being absorbed therein, get adrift from the whole, striving after inviolable self-existence (*Fürsichseyn*) and personal security), are made, by the task thus imposed on them by government, to feel the power of their lord and master, death. By thus breaking up the form of fixed stability, spirit guards the ethical order from sinking into merely natural existence, preserves the self of which it is conscious, and raises that self to the level of freedom and its own powers. The negative essential being shows itself to be the might proper of the community and the force it has for self-maintenance. The community therefore finds the true principle and corroboration of its power in the inner nature of divine law, and in the kingdom of the nether world.

The divine law which holds sway in the family has also on its side distinctions within itself, the relations among which make up the living process of its realization. Amongst the three relationships, however, of husband and wife, parents and children, brothers and sisters, the relationship of husband and wife is to begin with the primary and immediate form in which one consciousness recognizes itself in another, and in which each knows that reciprocal recognition. Being natural self-knowledge, knowledge of self on the basis of nature and not on that of ethical life, it merely represents and typifies in a figure the life of spirit, and is not spirit itself actually realized. Figurative representation, however, has its reality in an other than it is. This relationship, therefore, finds itself realized not in itself as such, but in the child—an other, in whose coming into being that relationship consists, and with which it passes away. And this change from one generation onwards to another is permanent in and as the life of a nation.

The reverent devotion (*Pietät*) of husband and wife towards one another is thus mixed up with a natural relation and with feeling, and their relationship is not inherently self-complete; similarly, too, the second relationship, the reverent devotion of parents and children to one another. The devotion of parents towards their children is affected with emotion just by their being consciously realized in what is external to themselves (viz. the children), and by their seeing them become something on their own account without this returning to the parents; independent existence on the part of the children remains a foreign reality, a reality all their own. The devotion of children, again, towards their parents is conversely affected by their coming into being from, or having their essential nature in, what is external to themselves (viz. the parents) and passes away; and by their attaining independent existence and a self-consciousness of their own solely through separation from the source whence they came—a separation in which the spring gets exhausted.

Both these relationships are constituted by and hold within the transience and the dissimilarity of the two sides, which are assigned to them.

An unmixed intransitive form of relationship, however, holds between brother and sister. They are the same blood, which, however, in them has entered into a condition of stable equilibrium. They therefore stand in no such natural relation as husband and wife, they do not desire one another; nor have they given to one another, nor received from one another, this independence of individual being; they are free individualities with respect to each other. The feminine element, therefore, in the form of the sister, premonizes and foreshadows most completely the nature of ethical life (*sittliches Wesen*). She does not become conscious of it, and does not actualize it, because the law of the family is her inherent implicit inward nature, which does not lie open to the daylight of consciousness, but remains inner feeling and the divine element exempt from actuality. The feminine life is attached to these household divinities (*Penates*), and sees in them both her universal substance, and her particular individuality, yet so views them that this relation of her individuality to them is at the same time not the natural one of pleasure.

As a daughter, the woman must now see her parents pass away with natural emotion and yet with ethical resignation, for it is only at the cost of this condition that she can come to that individual existence of which she is capable. She thus cannot see her independent existence positively attained in her relation to her parents. The relationships of mother and wife, however, are individualized partly in the form of something natural, which brings pleasure; partly in the form of something negative, which finds simply its own evanescence in those relationships; partly again the individualization is just on that account something contingent which can be replaced by an other particular individuality. In a household of the ethical kind, a woman's relationships are not based on a reference to this particular husband, this particular child, but to *a* husband, to children *in general*, —not to feeling, but to the universal. The distinction between her ethical life (*Sittlichkeit*) (while it determines her particular existence and brings her pleasure) and that of her husband consists just in this, that it has always a directly universal significance for her, and is quite alien to the impulsive condition of mere particular desire. On the other hand, in the husband these two aspects get separated; and since he possesses, as a citizen, the self-conscious power belonging to the universal life, the life of the social whole, he acquires thereby the rights of desire, and keeps himself at the same time in detachment from it. So far, then, as particularity is implicated in this relationship in the case of the wife, her ethical life is not purely ethical; so far, however, as it is ethical, the particularity is a matter of indifference, and the wife is without the moment of knowing herself as *this* particular self in and through an other.

The brother, however, is in the eyes of the sister a being whose nature is unperturbed by desire and is ethically like her own; her recognition in him is pure and unmixed with any sexual relation. The indifference characteristic of particular existence and the ethical contingency thence arising are, therefore, not present in this relationship; instead, the moment of individual selfhood, recognizing and being recognized, can here assert its right, because it is bound up with the balance and equilibrium resulting from their being of the same blood, and from their being related in a way that involves no mutual desire. The loss of a brother is thus irreparable to the sister, and her duty towards him is the highest.[3]

This relationship at the same time is the limit, at which the circumscribed life of the family is broken up, and passes beyond itself. The brother is the member of the family in whom its spirit becomes individualized, and enabled thereby to turn towards another sphere, towards what is other than and external to itself, and pass over into con-

---

[3]Cp. *Antigone*, 1. 910.

sciousness of universality. The brother leaves this immediate, rudimentary, and, therefore, strictly speaking, negative ethical life of the family, in order to acquire and produce the concrete ethical order which is conscious of itself.

He passes from the divine law, within whose realm he lived, over to the human law. The sister, however, becomes, or the wife remains, director of the home and the preserver of the divine law. In this way both the sexes overcome their merely natural being, and become ethically significant, as diverse forms dividing between them the different aspects which the ethical substance assumes. Both these universal factors of the ethical world have their specific individuality in naturally distinct self-consciousnesses, for the reason that the spirit at work in the ethical order is the immediate unity of the substance [of ethical life] with self-consciousness—an immediacy which thus appears as the existence of a natural difference, at once as regards its aspect of reality and of difference. It is that aspect which, in the notion of spiritual reality, came to light as "original determinate nature," when we were dealing with the stage of "Individuality which is real to itself." This moment loses the indeterminateness which it still has there, and the contingent diversity of "constitution" and "capacities." It is now the specific opposition of the two sexes, whose natural character acquires at the same time the significance of their respective ethical determinations.

The distinction of the sexes and of their ethical content remains all the same within the unity of the ethical substance, and its process is just the constant development of that substance. The husband is sent forth by the spirit of the family into the life of the community, and finds there his self-conscious reality. Just as the family thereby finds in the community its universal substance and subsistence, conversely the community finds in the family the formal element of its own realization, and in the divine law its power and confirmation. Neither of the two is alone self-complete. Human law as a living and active principle proceeds from the divine, the law holding on earth from that of the nether world, the conscious from the unconscious, mediation from immediacy; and returns too whence it came. The power of the nether world, on the other hand, finds its realization upon earth; it comes through consciousness to have existence and efficacy.

The universal elements of the ethical life are thus the (ethical) substance *qua* universal, and that substance *qua* particular consciousness. Their universal actuality is the nation and the family; while they get their natural self, and their operative individuality, in man and woman. Here in this content of the ethical world we see attained those purposes which the previous insubstantial modes of conscious life set before them. What Reason apprehended only as an object has become Self-consciousness, and what self-consciousness merely contained within it is here explicit true reality. What Observation knew—an object given externally and picked up, and one in the constitution of which the subject knowing had no share—is here a given ethical condition, a custom found lying ready at hand, but a reality which is at the same time the deed and product of the subject finding it. The individual who seeks the "pleasure" of enjoying his particular individuality finds it in the family life, and the "necessity"[4] in which that pleasure passes away is his own self-consciousness as a citizen of his nation. Or, again, it is knowing the "law of his own heart"[5] as the law of all hearts, knowing the consciousness of self to be the recognized and universal ordinance of society: it is "virtue,"[6] which enjoys the fruits of its own sacrifice, which brings about what it sets out to do, viz. to bring the essential nature into the light of the actual present,—and its enjoyment is this universal life. Finally, consciousness of "fact as such" (*der Sache selbst*)[7] gets satisfaction in the real substance, which contains and maintains in positive form the abstract aspects of that empty category. That substance finds a genuine content in the powers of the ethical order, a content that takes the place of those insubstantial commands which the "healthy human reason"[8] wanted to give and to know: and in consequence thus gets a concrete inherently determinate standard for "testing," not the laws, but what is done.

The whole is a stable equilibrium of all the parts, and each part a spirit in its native element, a spirit which does not seek its satisfaction beyond itself, but has the satisfaction within itself for the reason that itself is in this balanced equipoise with the whole. This condition of stable equilibrium can, doubtless, only be living by inequality arising within it, and being brought back again to equipoise by Righteousness and Justice. Justice, however, is neither an alien principle (*Wesen*) holding somewhere remote from the present, nor the realization (unworthy of the name of justice) of mutual malice, treachery, ingratitude, etc., which, in the unintelligent way of chance and accident, would fulfil the law by a kind of irrational connexion without any controlling idea, action by commission and omission, without any consciousness of what was involved. On the contrary, being justice in human law, it brings back to the whole, to the universal life of society, what has broken away separately from the harmony and equilibrium of the whole:—the independent classes and individuals. In this way justice is

[4]Cp. p. 205 ff.
[5]Cp. p. 209 ff.
[6]Cp. p. 216 ff.
[7]Cp. p. 226 ff.
[8]Cp. p. 240 ff.

the government of the nation, and is its all-pervading essential life in a consciously present individual form, and is the personal self-conscious will of all.

That justice, however, which restores to equilibrium the universal when getting the mastery over the particular individual, is similarly the simple single spirit of the individual who has suffered wrong; it is not broken up into the two elements, one who has suffered wrong and a far-away remote reality (*Wesen*). The individual himself is the power of the "nether" world, and that reality is *his* "fury," wreaking vengeance upon him.[9] For his individuality, his blood still lives in the house, his substance has a lasting actuality. The wrong, which can be brought upon the individual in the realm of the ethical world, consists merely in this, that a bare something by chance happens to him. The power which perpetrates on the conscious individual this wrong of making him into a mere thing is "nature"; it is the universality not of the community, but the abstract universality of mere existence. And the particular individual, in wiping out the wrong suffered, turns not against the community—for he has not suffered at its hands—but against the latter. As we saw,[10] the consciousness of those who share the blood of the individual removes this wrong in such a way that what has happened becomes rather a work of their own doing, and hence bare existence, the last state, gets also to be something willed, and thus an object of gratification.

The ethical realm remains in this way permanently a world without blot or stain, a world untainted by any internal dissension. So, too, its process is an untroubled transition from one of its powers to the other, in such a way that each preserves and produces the other. We see it no doubt divided into two ultimate elements and their realization: but their opposition is rather the confirming and substantiation of one through the other; and where they directly come in contact with each other as actual factors, their mediating common element is the immediate permeation of the one with the other. The one extreme, universal spirit conscious of itself, becomes, through the individuality of man, linked together with its other extreme, its force and its element, with *unconscious* spirit. On the other hand, divine law is individualized, the unconscious spirit of the particular individual finds its existence, in woman, through the mediation of whom the unconscious spirit comes out of its unrealizedness into actuality, and rises out of the state of un-knowing and unknown, into the conscious realm of universal spirit. The union of man with woman constitutes the operative mediating agency for the whole, and constitutes the element which, while sepa-

---

[9]The reference here is to Orestes.
[10]P. 259 *sup.*

rated into the extremes of divine and human law, is, at the same time, their immediate union. This union, again, turns both those first mediate connexions (*Schlusse*) into one and the same synthesis, and unites into one process the twofold movement in opposite directions—one from reality to unreality, the downward movement of human law, organized into independent members, to the danger and trial of death,— the other, from unreality to reality, the upward movement of the law of the nether world to the daylight of conscious existence. Of these movements the former falls to man, the latter to woman.

b

ETHICAL ACTION. KNOWLEDGE, HUMAN AND DIVINE. GUILT AND DESTINY

A fundamental condition of social order is that it is maintained by action on the part of the individual members of a society; action is a fundamental principle of distinction between individuals, is the way they make their contribution to social life, and is also the way by which the continuance of social life is ceaselessly broken and reconstituted. In a comprehensive sense therefore action is the principle by which distinction in unity is carried out in social life. The consideration of its significance is thus an essential problem of social mind. Action must be considered at once with reference to individuality and also with reference to those conceptions of social order as containing both "divine" and "human" law. In the following section, this analysis is undertaken.

The specific historical background of Hegel's thought in this section, and to some extent in the preceding section, is supplied by the social life of the Greek city state. The Greek city state has been taken as the type, so to say, of spiritual existence realized as a self-complete ethical order. But the social life of Greece is here in large measure read and interpreted in the light of the dramatization of Greek ethical conceptions by the great Greek tragedians, especially Sophocles. This accounts for the repeated reference to the purely dramatic conception of the "destiny" or the "pathic" element in the life of the individual whose spiritual existence is completely bound up with the established social order. It is in Greece that we find most fully realized the all-sufficiency of the state for the individual, which Hegel has here in view, a sufficiency which was at once the strength and beauty, as well as the pathos and weakness, of Greek social life.

With this and the preceding section should be read Hegel's *Philosophy of History*, Part II, "The Greek World."

In the form presented by the opposition of elements in the realm just dealt with, self-consciousness has not yet come to its rights as a single individuality. Individuality there has, on one side, the sense of merely universal will, on the other, of consanguinity of the family. *This* particular individual has merely the significance of shadowy unreality. There is as yet no performance of an act. The act, however, is the realized self. It breaks in upon the untroubled stable organization and movement of the ethical world. What there appears as ordinance and harmony between both its constituent elements, each of which confirms and complements the other, becomes through the performing of an act a transition of opposites into one another, by which each proves to be the annihilation rather than the confirmation of its self and its opposite. It becomes the process of negation or destruction, the eternal necessity of awful destiny, which engulfs in the abyss of its bare identity divine and human law alike, as well as both the self-conscious factors in which these powers subsist; and, to our view, passes over into the absolute self-existence of mere single self-consciousness.

The basis from which this movement proceeds, and on which it takes effect, is the kingdom of the ethical order. But the activity at work in this process is self-consciousness. Being ethical consciousness, it is the pure and simple direction of activity towards the essential principle of the ethical life—it is *Duty*. There is no caprice, and likewise no struggle, no indecision in it, since it has given up legislating and testing laws: the essential ethical principle is, for it, something immediate, unwavering, without contradiction. There is therefore neither the painful spectacle of finding itself in a collision between passion and duty, nor the comic spectacle of a collision between duty and duty—a collision, which so far as content goes is the same as that between passion and duty; for passion can also be presented as a duty, because duty, when consciousness withdraws into itself and leaves its immediate essential substance (*Wesenheit*), comes to be the formal universal, into which one content fits equally well with another, as we found before. The collision of duties is, however, comical, because it brings out the contradiction inherent in the idea of an absolute standing opposed to another absolute, expresses something absolute and then directly the annihilation of this so-called absolute or duty. The ethical consciousness, however, knows what it has to do; and is decided, whether it is to belong to divine or human law. This directness which characterizes its decision is something immanent and inherent (*Ansichseyn*), and hence has at the same time the significance of a natural condition of being, as we saw. Nature, not the accident of circumstances or choice, assigns one sex to one law, the other to the other law; or conversely both the ethical powers themselves establish their individual existence and actualization in the two sexes.

Thus, then, because on the one side the ethical order consists essentially in this immediate directness of decision, and therefore only the one law is *for consciousness* the essential reality; while, on the other side, the powers of the ethical order are actual in the self of conscious life — in this way these forces acquire the significance of excluding one another and of being opposed to one another. They are explicit in self-consciousness just as they were merely implicit in the realm of the ethical order. The ethical consciousness, because it is decisively on the side of one of them, is essentially *Character*. There is not for it equal essentiality in both. The opposition therefore appears as an unfortunate collision of duty merely with reality, on which right has no hold. The ethical consciousness is *qua* self-consciousness in this opposition, and being so, it at once proceeds either to subdue by force this reality opposed to the law which it accepts, or to get round this reality by craft. Since it sees right only on its own side, and wrong on the other, so, of these two, that which belongs to divine law detects, on the other side, mere arbitrary fortuitous human violence, while what appertains to human law finds in the other the obstinacy and disobedience of subjective self-sufficiency. For the commands of government have a universal sense and meaning open to the light of day; the will of the other law, however, is the inner concealed meaning of the realm of darkness (*unterirdisch*), a meaning which appears expressed as the will of a particular being, and in contradicting the first is malicious offence.

There arises in this way in consciousness the opposition between what is known and what is not known, just as, in the case of substance, there was an opposition between the conscious and the unconscious; and the absolute right of ethical self-consciousness comes into conflict with the divine right of the essential reality. Self-consciousness, *qua* consciousness, takes the objective actuality, as such, to have essential being. Looking at its substance, however, it is the unity of itself and this opposite, and the ethical self-consciousness is consciousness of that substance: the object, *qua* opposed to self-consciousness, has, therefore, entirely lost the characteristic of having essential being by itself. Just as the spheres [of conscious life] where the object is merely a "thing" are long past and gone, so, too, are these spheres, where consciousness sets up and establishes something from out itself, and turns a particular moment into the essential reality (*Wesen*). Against such one-sidedness actual concrete reality has a power of its own; it takes the side of truth against consciousness and shows consciousness itself what the truth is. The ethical consciousness, however, has drunk from the cup of the absolute substance, forgotten all the one-sidedness of isolating self-existence, all its purposes and peculiar notions, and has, therefore, at the same time drowned in this Stygian stream all essentiality of nature and all the independence claimed by the objective reality. Its absolute right, therefore, when it acts in accordance with ethical law, is to find in this actualization nothing else than the fulfilment and performance of this law itself: and that the deed should manifest nothing but ethical action.

The ethical, being absolute essence and absolute power at once, cannot endure any perversion of its content. If it were merely absolute essence without power, it might undergo perversion at the hands of individuality. But this latter, being ethical consciousness, has renounced all perverting when it gave up its one-sided subjectivity (*Fürsichseyn*). Conversely, again, mere power might be perverted by the essential reality, if power were still a subjectivity of that kind. On account of this unity, individuality is a pure form of the substance which is the content, and action consists in transition from thought over into reality, merely as the process of an unreal opposition, whose moments have no special and particular content distinct from one another, and no essential nature of their own. The absolute right of ethical consciousness is, therefore, that the deed, the mode and form of its realization, should be nothing else than it *knows*.

But the essential ethical reality has split asunder into two laws, and consciousness, taking up an undivided single attitude towards law, is assigned only to one. Just as this simple consciousness takes its stand on the absolute right that the essential reality has appeared to it *qua* ethical as that reality inherently is, so, too, this essence insists on the right belonging to its reality, i.e. the right of having a double form.[1] This right of the essential reality does not, however, at the same time stand over against and opposed to self-consciousness, as if it were to be found anywhere else; rather it is the essential nature of self-consciousness. Only there has it its existence and its power; and its opposition is the act of self-consciousness itself. For the latter, just in that it is a self to itself, and proceeds to act, lifts itself out of the state of simple immediacy, and itself sets up the division into two. By the act it gives up the specific character of the ethical life, that of being pure and simple certainty of immediate truth, and sets up the division of itself into self as active and reality over against it, and for it, therefore, negative. By the act it thus becomes *Guilt*. For the deed is its doing, and doing is its inmost nature. And the guilt acquires also the meaning of Crime; for as simple ethical consciousness it has turned to and conformed itself to the one law, but turned away from the other and thus violates the latter by its deed.

Guilt is not an external indifferent entity (*Wesen*) with the double meaning, that the deed, as actually manifested to the light of day, may be an action of the guilty self, or may not be so, as if with the doing of it there could be connected something external and accidental that did

---

[1] Viz. divine and human law.

not belong to it, from which point of view, therefore, the action would be innocent. Rather the act is itself this diremption, this affirming itself for itself, and establishing over against this an alien external reality. That such a reality exists is due to the deed itself, and is the outcome of it. Hence, innocence is an attribute merely of the want of action (*Nicht-thun*), a state like the mere being of a stone, and one which is not even true of a child.   ✳ guilt = one-sidedness ??

Looking at the content, however, the ethical act contains the element of wrongdoing, because it does not cancel and transcend the natural allotment of the two laws to the two sexes; but rather, being an undivided attitude towards the law, keeps within the sphere of natural immediacy, and, *qua* acting, turns this one-sidedness into guilt, by merely laying hold of one side of the essential reality and taking up a negative relation towards the other, i.e. violating it. Where, in the general ethical life, guilt and crime, deeds and actions, come in, will be more definitely brought out later. Meantime, so much is at once clear, that it is not *this* particular individual who acts and becomes guilty. For he, *qua* this particular self, is merely a shadowy unreality; he *is* merely *qua* universal self, and individuality is purely the formal aspect of doing anything at all, while its content is the laws and customs, which, for the individual, are, specifically, the laws and customs of his class or station. He is the substance *qua* genus, which by its determinateness becomes, no doubt, a species, but the specific form remains at the same time the generic universal. Self-consciousness within the life of a nation descends from the universal only down as far as specific particularity, but not as far as the single individuality, which sets up an exclusive self, establishes in its action a reality negative to itself. On the contrary, the action of that self-consciousness rests on secure confidence in the whole, into which there enters nothing alien or foreign, neither fear nor hostility.

Ethical self-consciousness now comes to find in its deed the full explicit meaning of concrete real action as much when it followed divine law as when it followed human. The law manifest to it is, in the essential reality, bound up with its opposite; the essential reality is the unity of both; but the deed has merely carried out one as against the other. But being bound up with this other in the inner reality, the fulfilment of the one calls forth the other, in the shape of something which, having been violated and now become hostile, demands revenge—an attitude which the deed has made it take up. In the case of action, only one phase of the decision is in general in evidence. The decision, however, is inherently something negative, which plants an "other" in opposition to it, something foreign to the decision, which is clear knowledge. Actual reality, therefore, keeps concealed within itself this other aspect alien to clear knowledge, and does not show itself to consciousness as it fully and truly is (*an und für sich*). In the story of Œdipus the son does not see his own father in the person of the man who has insulted him and whom he strikes to death, nor his mother in the queen whom he makes his wife. In this way a hidden power shunning the light of day, waylays the ethical self-consciousness, a power which bursts forth only after the deed is done, and seizes the doer in the act. For the completed deed is the removal of the opposition between the knowing self and the reality over against it. The ethical consciousness cannot disclaim the crime and its guilt. The deed consists in setting in motion what was unmoved, and in bringing out what in the first instance lay shut up as a mere possibility, and thereby linking on the unconscious to the conscious, the non-existent to the existent. In this truth, therefore, the deed comes to the light;—it is something in which a conscious element is bound up with what is unconscious, what is peculiarly one's own with what is alien and external:—it is an essential realty divided in sunder, whose other aspect consciousness experiences and also finds to be its own aspect, but as a power violated by its doing, and roused to hostility against it.

It may well be that the right, which kept itself in reserve, is not in its peculiar form present to the consciousness of the doer, but is merely implicit, present in the subjective inward guilt of the decision and the action. But the ethical consciousness is more complete, its guilt purer, if it knows beforehand the law and the power which it opposes, if it takes them to be sheer violence and wrong, to be a contingency in the ethical life, and wittingly, like Antigone, commits the crime. The deed when accomplished transforms its point of view; the very performance of it *eo ipso* expresses that what is ethical has to be actual; for the realization of the purpose is the very purpose of acting. Acting expresses precisely the unity of reality and the substance; it expresses the fact that actuality is not an accident for the essential element, but that, in union with that element, it is given to no right which is not true right. On account of this actuality and on account of its deed ethical consciousness must acknowledge its opposite as its own actuality; it must acknowledge its guilt.

> Because of our sufferings we acknowledge we have erred.[2]

To acknowledge this is expressly to indicate that the severance between ethical purpose and actuality has been done away; it means the return to the ethical frame of mind, which knows that nothing counts but right. Thereby, however, the agent surrenders his character and the re-

---

[2]An adaptation from *Antigone*, 926.

ality of his self, and has utterly collapsed. His being lies in belonging to his ethical law, as his substance; in acknowledging the opposite law, however, he has ceased to find his substance in this law; and instead of reality this has become an unreality, a mere *sentiment*, a frame of mind. The substance no doubt appears as the "pathic" element[3] in the individuality, and the individuality appears as the factor which animates the substance, and hence stands above it. But the substance is a "pathic" element which is at the same time his character; the ethical individuality is directly and inherently one with this its universal, exists in it alone, and is incapable of surviving the destruction which this ethical power suffers at the hands of its opposite.

This individuality, however, has all the same the certainty that that individuality, whose "pathic" element is this opposite power [the opposed law], suffers no more harm than it has inflicted. The opposition of the ethical powers to one another, and the process of the individualities setting up these powers in life and action, have reached their true end only in so far as both sides undergo the same destruction. For neither of the powers has any advantage over the other that it should be a more essential moment of the substance common to both. The fact of their being equally and to the same degree essential, and subsisting independently beside each other, means their having no separate self; in the act they have a self-nature, but a different self,—which contradicts the unity of the self and cancels their claim to independent right, and thus brings about their necessary destruction. Character too, in part, looking at its "pathic" element, the substance, belongs to one alone; in part, when we look at the aspect of knowledge, the one character like the other is divided into a conscious element and an unconscious: and since each itself calls forth this opposition, and the want of knowledge is by the act also its doing, each falls into the guilt which consumes it. The victory of one power and its character, and the defeat of the other side, would thus be merely the part and the incomplete work, which steadily advances till the equilibrium between the two is attained. It is in the equal subjection of both sides that absolute right is first accomplished, and the ethical substance, as the negative force devouring both sides, in other words omnipotent and righteous Destiny, makes its appearance.

If both powers are taken according to their specific content and its individualization, we have the scene presented of a contest between them as individuated. On its formal side, this is the struggle of the ethical order and of self-consciousness with unconscious nature and a con-

---

[3]The element that so permeates his being as to constitute his controlling necessity and destiny.

tingency due to this nature. The latter has a right as against the former, because this is only objective spirit, merely in immediate unity with its substance. On the side of content, the struggle is the rupture of divine and human law. The youth goes forth from the unconscious life of the family and becomes the individuality of the community [i.e. Ruler]. But that he still shares the natural life from which he has torn himself away is seen in the fact that he emerges there from only to find his claim affected by the contingency that there are *two* brothers[4] who with equal right take possession of the community;[5] the inequality due to the one having been born earlier and the other later, an inequality which is a natural difference, has no importance for them when they enter the ethical life of society. But government, as the single soul, the self of the national spirit, does not admit of a duality of individuality; and in contrast to the ethical necessity of this unity, nature appears as by accident providing more than one. These two [brothers], therefore, become disunited; and their equal right in regard to the power of the state is destructive to both, for they are equally wrong. Humanly considered, he has committed the crime who, not being in actual possession, attacks the community, at the head of which the other stood. While again he has right on his side who knew how to seize the other merely *qua* particular individual, detached from the community, and who banished him, while thus powerless, out of the community; he has merely laid hands on the individual as such, not the community, not the essential nature of human right. The community, attacked and defended from a point of view which is merely particular, maintains itself; and both brothers find their destruction reciprocally through one another. For individuality, which involves peril to the whole in the maintenance of its own self-existence (*Fürsichseyn*), has thrust its own self out of the community, and is disintegrated in its own nature. The community, however, will do honour to the one who is found on its side; the government, the reestablished singleness of the self of the community, will punish by depriving of the last honour him who already proclaimed its devastation on the walls of the city. He who came to affront the highest spiritual form of conscious life, the spirit of the community, must be stripped of the honour of his entire and complete nature, the honour due to the spirit of the departed.[6]

But if the universal thus lightly knocks off the highest point of its pyramid, and doubtless triumphs victoriously over the family, the rebellious principle of individuation, it has thereby merely put itself into

---

[4]Eteocles and Polynices: *v. Œdipus at Colonus.*
[5]viz. the throne of their Father Œdipus.
[6]*v. Antigone.*

divine law: ? unconscious law of weakness + darkness,
nether realm, not on earth +
The Phenomenology of Mind *light of day?* 275

conflict with divine law, the self-conscious with the unconscious spirit. For the latter, this unconscious spirit, is the other essential power, and therefore the power undestroyed, and only insulted by the former. It finds, however, only a bloodless shade to lend it help towards actually carrying itself out in the face of that masterful and openly enunciated law. Being the law of weakness and of darkness, it therefore gives way, to begin with, before law which has force and publicity; for the strength of the former is effective in the nether realm, not on earth and in the light of day. But the actual and concrete, which has taken away from what is inward its honour and its power, has thereby consumed its own real nature. The spirit which is manifest to the light of day has the roots of its power in the lower world: the certainty felt by a nation, a certainty which is sure of itself and which makes itself assured, finds the truth of its oath binding all its members into one, solely in the mute unconscious substance of all, in the waters of forgetfulness. In consequence, the fulfilment of the public spirit turns round into its opposite, and learns that its supreme right is supreme wrong, its victory rather its own defeat. The slain, whose right is injured, knows, therefore, how to find means of vengeance which are equally as real and strong as the power at whose hands it has suffered. These powers are other communities,[7] whose altars the dogs or birds defiled with the corpse of the dead, which is not raised into unconscious universality by being restored, as is its due, to the ultimate individuum, the elemental earth, but instead has remained above ground in the sphere of reality, and has now received, as the force of divine law, a self-conscious actual universality. They rise up in hostility, and destroy the community which has dishonoured and destroyed its own power, the sacred claims, the "piety" of the family.

Represented in this way, the movement of human and divine law finds the expression of its necessity in individuals, in whom the universal appears as a "pathic" element, and the activity of the movement as action of individuals, which gives the appearance of contingency to the necessity of the process. But individuality and action constitute the principle of individuation in general, a principle which in its pure universality was called inner divine law. As a moment of the visible community it does not merely exhibit that unconscious activity of the nether world, its operation is not simply external in its existence; it has an equally manifest visible existence and process, actual in the actual nation. Taken in this form, what was represented as a simple process of the "pathic" element as embodied in individuals, assumes another

---

[7]Refers to the attack of Argos against Thebes: *v. Antigone.*

look, and crime and the resulting ruin of the community assume the proper form of their existence.

Human law, then, in its universal mode of existence is the community, in its efficient operation in general is the manhood of the community, in its actual efficient operation is the government. It has its being, its process, and its subsistence by consuming and absorbing into itself the separatist action of the household gods (*Penates*), the individualization into insular independent families which are under the management of womankind, and by keeping them dissolved in the fluent continuum of its own nature. The family at the same time, however, is in general its element, the individual consciousness its universal operative basis. Since the community gets itself subsistence only by breaking in upon family happiness, and dissolving [individual] self-consciousness into the universal, it creates its enemy for itself within its own gates, creates it in what it suppresses, and what is at the same time essential to it—womankind in general. Womankind—the everlasting irony in the life of the community—changes by intrigue the universal purpose of government into a private end, transforms its universal activity into a work of this or that specific individual, and perverts the universal property of the state into a possession and ornament for the family. Woman in this way turns to ridicule the grave wisdom of maturity, which, being dead to all particular aims, to private pleasure, personal satisfaction, and actual activity as well, thinks of, and is concerned for, merely what is universal; she makes this wisdom the laughing-stock of raw and wanton youth, an object of derision and scorn, unworthy of their enthusiasm. She asserts that it is everywhere the force of youth that really counts; she upholds this as of primary significance; extols a son as one who is the lord and master of the mother who has borne him; a brother as one in whom the sister finds man on a level with herself; a youth as one through whom the daughter, freed from her dependence (on the family unity), acquires the satisfaction and the dignity of wifehood.

The community, however, can preserve itself only by suppressing this spirit of individualism; and because the latter is an essential element, the community likewise creates it as well, and creates it, too, by taking up the attitude of seeking to suppress it as a hostile principle. Nevertheless, since, by cutting itself off from the universal purpose, this hostile element is merely evil, and in itself of no account, it would be quite ineffective if the community itself did not recognize the force of youth, (manhood, which, while immature, still remains in the condition of particularity), as the force of the whole. For the community, the whole, is a nation, it is itself individuality, and really only is something for itself by other individualities being for *it*, by its excluding these from itself and knowing itself independent of them. The negative side of the community, suppressing the isolation of individuals within its own bounds, but originating activity directed beyond those bounds, finds the weapons of its warfare in individuals. War is the spirit and form in which the essential moment of ethical substance, the absolute freedom of ethical self-consciousness from all and every kind of existence, is manifestly confirmed and realized. While, on the one hand, war makes the particular spheres of property and personal independence, as well as the personality of the individual himself, feel the force of negation and destruction, on the other hand this engine of negation and destruction stands out as that which preserves the whole in security. The individual who provides pleasure to woman, the brave youth, the suppressed principle of ruin and destruction, comes now into prominence, and is the factor of primary significance and worth. It is now physical strength and what seems like the chance of fortune, that decide as to the existence of ethical life and spiritual necessity. Because the existence of the ethical life thus rests on physical strength and the chances of fortune, it is *eo ipso* settled that its overthrow has come. While only household gods, in the former case, gave way before and were absorbed in the national spirit, here the living individual embodiments of the national spirit fall by their own individuality and disappear in one universal community, whose bare universality is soulless and dead, and whose living activity is found in the particular individual *qua* particular. The ethical form and embodiment of the life of spirit has passed away, and another mode appears in its place.

This disappearance of the ethical substance, and its transition into another mode are thus determined by the ethical consciousness being directed upon the law essentially in an immediate way. It lies in this character of immediacy that nature at all enters into the acts which constitute the ethical life. Its realization simply reveals the contradiction and the germ of destruction, which lie hid within that very peace and beauty belonging to the gracious harmony and peaceful equilibrium of the ethical spirit. For the essence and meaning of this immediacy contains a contradiction: it is at once the unconscious peace of nature and the self-conscious unresting peace of spirit. On account of this "naturalness," this ethical nation is, in general, an individuality determined by nature, and therefore limited, and thus finds its dissolution in, and gives place to, another individuality. This determinateness being given a positive existence, is a limitation, but at the same time is the negative element in general and the self of individuality. In so far, however, as this determinateness passes away, the life of spirit and this substance, conscious of itself in all its component individuals, are lost. The substance comes forth and stands apart as a formal universality of all the component individuals, and no longer dwells within them as a living spirit; instead, the uniform solidarity of their individuality has burst into a plurality of separate points.

c

THE CONDITION OF RIGHT OR LEGAL STATUS

A further step in the realization of the principle of coherent sociality is reached when the individual is invested with the universality of the social order by definite enactments of the controlling agency of the social whole. His contingency as an individual is removed by his being expressly treated as a focal unity of the whole order, whose very existence is staked on maintaining him as a unit with a universal significance, and which stands or falls by maintaining him in this condition. The universal order is in this case no longer merely implicit, merely a matter of routine and custom; it is openly and objectively expressed in and through each individual component of society. The form this takes is the differentiation of the social substance into a totality of "persons," each and all invested with express universal, or legally acknowledged, significance. This is the sphere of legal personality, or of individuality constituted by a system of Rights. It is a supreme achievement of social existence, and the highest attainment of coherent social experience. Hence the present section.

This is a condition or stage in every developed community. But the specific historical material for this section is derived from the law-constituted social order of the Roman Empire, especially the Empire under the Antonines. Here, whether by coincidence or otherwise, the culmination of imperial rule and the "golden age" of law synchronized. The triumph of Roman imperial government and the perfecting of the system of Roman jurisprudence were accomplished during the same period of time, about A.D. 131–235. There is every reason to suppose that the two necessarily arose and fell together, and that the decline and disappearance of the Roman law-constituted state should thus prepare the way for a further achievement of the social spirit of humanity. Hence the historical justification for the transition to the next stage of social life, that of self-discordant spiritual existence.

With this section should be read Hegel's *Philosophy of History*, Part III, especially the introduction to this part, and Sect. III, c. 1., "Rome under the Emperors."

THE general comprehensive unity, into which the living immediate unity of individuality and the ethical substance falls back, is the soulless (*geistlos*) community, which has ceased to be the unselfconscious[1] substance of individuals, and in which they now, each in his separate individual existence, count as selves and substances with a being of their own. The universal being thus split up into the atomic units of a

---

[1]Reading "selbstbewusstlose" (1st ed.).

sheer plurality of individuals, this inoperative, lifeless spirit is a principle of equality in which all count for as much as each, i.e. have the significance of *Persons*. What in the realm of the ethical life was called the
hidden divine law has in fact come out of concealment to the light of
actuality. In the former the individual was, and was counted, actual
merely as a blood relation, merely as sharing in the general life of the
family. *Qua* particular individual, he was the selfless departed spirit;
now, however, he has come out of his unreality. Because the ethical
substance is only objective, "true," spirit, the individual on that account
turns back to the immediate certainty of his own self; he is that substance *qua* positive universal, but his actuality consists in being a negative universal self.

We saw the powers and forms of the ethical world sink in the bare
necessity of mere Destiny. This power of the ethical world is the substance turning itself back into its ultimate and simple nature. But that
absolute being turning back into itself, that very necessity of characterless Destiny, is nothing else than the Ego of self-consciousness.

This, therefore, is taken henceforth as the absolutely real, as the ultimate self-contained reality. To be so acknowledged is its substantiality; but this is abstract universality, because its content is this rigid self,
not the self dissolved in the substance.

Personality, then, has here risen out of the life and activity of the ethical substance. It is the condition in which the independence of consciousness has *actual concrete validity*. The unrealized abstract thought
of such independence, which arises through renouncing actuality, was
at an earlier stage before our notice in the form of "Stoical self-
consciousness." Just as the latter was the outcome of "Lordship and
Bondage,"[2] the mode in which self-consciousness exists immediately—
so personality is the outgrowth of the immediate life of spirit which is
the universal controlling will of all, as well as their dutiful obedience
and submissive service. What in Stoicism was implicit merely in an abstract way, is now an explicit concrete world. Stoicism is nothing else
than the mood of consciousness which reduces to its abstract form the
principle of legal status, the principle of the sphere of right—an independence devoid of the qualities of spirit (*geistlos*). By its flight from actuality it attained merely the idea of independence: it is absolutely subjective, exists solely for itself, in that it does not link its being to anything
that exists, but is prepared to give up every kind of existence, and places
its essential meaning in the unity of mere thinking. In the same manner, the "right" of a "person" is not linked on to a richer or more pow-
erful existence of the individual *qua* individual, nor again connected

---

[2]*v.* p. 104 ff.

with a universal living spirit, but, rather, is attached to the mere unit of its abstract reality, or to that unit *qua* self-consciousness in general.

Now just as the abstract independence of Stoicism set forth the stages of its actualization, so, too, this last form of independence [Personality] will recapitulate the process of the former mode. The former [Stoicism] passes over into the state of sceptical confusion, into a broken gibber of negation, which without adopting any permanent form strays from one contingent mode of being and thinking to another, dissipates them indeed in absolute independence, but just as readily creates them again once more. In fact, it is simply the contradiction of consciousness claiming to be at once independent and yet devoid of independence. In like manner, the personal independence characteristic of the sphere of right is really a similar universal confusion and reciprocal dissolution of this kind. For what passes for the absolute essential reality is self-consciousness in the sense of the bare empty unit of the person. As against this empty universality, the substance has the form of what supplies the filling and the content; and this content is now left completely detached and disconnected; for the spirit, which kept it in subjection and held it together in its unity, is no longer present. The empty unit of the person is, therefore, as regards its reality, an accidental existence, a contingent insubstantial process and activity that comes to no durable subsistence. Just as was the case in Scepticism, the formalism of "right" is, thus, by its very conception, without special content; it finds at its hand the fact of "possession," a fact subsisting in multiplicity, and imprints thereon the abstract universality, by which it is called "property"—the same sort of abstraction as Scepticism made use of. But while the reality so determined is in Scepticism called a mere appearance, "mere semblance," and has merely a negative value, in the case of right it has a positive significance. The negative value in the former case consists in the real having the meaning of self *qua* thought, *qua* inherent universal; the positive significance in the latter case, however, consists in its being mine in the sense of the category, as something whose validity is admitted, recognized, and actual. Both are the same abstract universal. The actual content, the proper value of what is "mine"—whether it be an external possession, or again inner riches or poverty of mind and character—is not contained in this empty form and does not concern it. The content belongs, therefore, to a peculiar specific power, which is something different from the formal universal, is chance and caprice. Consciousness of right, therefore, even in the very process of making its claim good, experiences the loss of its own reality, discovers its complete lack of inherent substantiality; and to describe an individual as a "person" is to use an expression of contempt.

The free and unchecked power possessed by the content takes determinate shape in this way. The absolute plurality of dispersed atomic personalities is, by the nature of this characteristic feature, gathered at the same time into a single centre, alien to them and just as devoid of the life of spirit (*geistlos*). That central point is, in one respect, like the atomic rigidity of their personality, a merely single reality; but in contrast to their empty singleness, it has the significance of the entire content, and hence is taken to be the essential element; while again, in contrast to their pretended absolute, but inherently insubstantial, reality it is the universal power, and absolute actuality. This "lord and master of the world" takes himself in this way to be the absolute person, comprising at the same time all existence within himself, for whom there exists no higher type of spirit. He is a person: but the solitary single person who has taken his stand confronting all. These all constitute and establish the triumphant universality of the one person; for the single being, as such, is truly what it is only *qua* universal plurality of single units: cut off from this plurality, the solitary and single self is, in fact, a powerless and unreal self. At the same time, it is the consciousness of the content which is antithetically opposed to that universal personality. This content, however, when liberated from its negative power, means chaos of spiritual powers, which, when let loose, become elemental independent agencies, break out into wild extravagances and excesses, and fall on one another in mad destruction. Their helpless self-consciousness is the powerless inoperative enclosure and the arena of their chaotic tumult. But this master and lord of the world, aware of his being the sum and substance of all actual powers, is the titanic self-consciousness, which takes itself to be the living God. Since, however, he exists merely *qua* formal self, which is unable to tame and subdue those powers, his procedure and his self-enjoyment are equally titanic excess.[3]

The lord of the world becomes really conscious of what he is—viz. the universal might of actuality—by that power of destruction which he exercises against the contrasted selfhood of his subjects. For his power is not the spiritual union and concord in which the various persons might get to know their *own* self-consciousness. Rather they exist as persons separately for themselves, and all continuity with others is excluded from the absolute punctual atomicity of their nature. They are, therefore, in a merely negative relation, a relation of exclusion both to one another and to him, who *is* their principle of connexion or continuity. *Qua* this continuity, he is the essential being and content of their

---

[3]Cp. with the above Hobbes' *Leviathan*. The historical reference here is to the "apotheosis" of the Roman Emperors.

formal nature—a content, however, foreign to them, and a being hostile in character, which abolishes just what they take to be their very essence, viz. bare self-existence without any content, mere empty independent existence each on its own account. And, again, *qua* the continuity of their personality, he destroys this very personality itself. Juridical personality thus finds itself, rather, without any substance of its own, since content alien to it is imposed on it and holds good within it—and does so there, because such content is the reality of that type of personality. On the other hand the passion for destroying and turning over everything on this unreal field gains for itself the consciousness of its complete supremacy. But this self is sheer devastation, and hence is merely beside itself, and is indeed the very abandonment and rejection of its own self-consciousness.

Such, then, is the constitution of that aspect in which self-consciousness *qua* absolute being is *actual*. The consciousness, however, that is driven back into itself out of this actuality, *thinks* this its insubstantiality, makes it an object of *thought*. Formerly we saw the stoical independence of pure thought pass through Scepticism and find its true issue in the "unhappy consciousness"—the truth about what constitutes its inherent and explicit nature, its final meaning. If this knowledge appeared at that stage merely as the one-sided view of a consciousness *qua* consciousness, here the actual truth of that view has made its appearance. The truth consists in the fact that this universal accepted objectivity of self-consciousness is reality estranged from it. This objectivity is the universal actuality of the self; but this actuality is directly the perversion of the self as well—it is the loss of its essential being. The reality of the self that was not found in the ethical world, has been gained by its reverting into the "person." What in the case of the former was all harmony and union, comes now on the scene, no doubt in developed form, but self-estranged.

B

SPIRIT IN SELF-ESTRANGEMENT—
THE DISCIPLINE OF CULTURE

The life of spirit as found in the social self-consciousness has two fundamental factors, the universal spirit or social whole as such, and the individual member as such. The interrelation of these constitutes the spiritual existence of society. Each by itself is abstract, but the realization of complete spiritual life through and in each is absolutely essential for spiritual fulfilment. In the preceding analysis of spirit, one form of this process has been considered, the realization of the objective social order in and through individuals. In the succeeding section, with its various subsections, the other process of securing the same general result is analysed: we have the movement by which, starting from the individual spirit, the realization of complete spiritual existence is established. The former starts from the compact solidarity of the social substance, and results in the establishment of separate and individually complete legal personalities. The latter process starts from the rigidly exclusive unity of the individual self and issues in the establishment of a social order of absolutely universal and therefore absolutely free wills. Both processes are *per se* abstract, necessary though they are: hence, as we shall find, a further stage in the evolution of spirit has still to appear.

The process of spirit in this second stage assumes from the start a conscious contrast between the individual spirit and a universal spiritual whole, a contrast, which, while profound, the individual seeks to remove, because the universality of spiritual existence which he seeks to attain is implicitly involved in his very being as a spiritual entity. His spiritual life seems, to begin with, rent in twain, so complete is the sense of the opposition of these factors constituting his life. His true life, his objective embodiment, seems outside him altogether and yet is felt to be his own self. He seems "estranged" from his complete self, and the estrangement seems his own doing, because the substance from which he is cut off is felt to be his own. The contrast is the deepest that spirit can possibly experience, just because spirit is and knows itself to be self-contained and self-complete, "the only reality." The contrast can only be removed by effort and struggle, for the individual spirit has to create or recreate for itself and by its own activity a universal objective spiritual realm, which it implies and in which alone it can be free and feel itself at home. The struggle spirit goes through is thus the greatest in the whole range of its experience, for the opposition to be overcome is the profoundest that exists. Since its aim is to achieve the highest for itself, nothing sacred can be allowed to stand in its way. It will make any sacrifice, and, if necessary, produce the direst spiritual disaster, a spiritual "reign of terror," to accomplish its result.

The movement of spirit here analysed covers every form of the individual's "struggle for a substantial spiritual life." It embraces the "intellectual," "economic," "religious," and the "ethical" in the narrower sense of these terms; it embraces all that we mean by "culture" and "civilization." Hence the various parts of the argument:—spiritual "discipline," "enlightenment," the pursuit of "wealth," "belief" and "superstition," "absolute freedom."

The process of spiritual life passed under critical review here is familiar to a greater or less extent in every age and every society. But the actual historical material present to the mind of the writer is derived from (1) the period of European history embracing the entrance of Christianity and Christian philosophy into European civilization after the fall of the Roman Empire, and the intellectual, "humanistic," awakening of the Renaissance which led on to the ecclesiastical revolution known as the Reformation: (2) the rationalistic movement of the eighteenth century, the so-called "Enlightenment" which proceded and culminated in the French Revolution, the supreme outburst of spiritual emancipation known in European history. These two periods, far removed as they are in time, have much in common. They embody principles of spiritual development fundamentally alike, and are therefore freely drawn upon in the analysis, regardless of historicity.

Much of Hegel's analysis of the first stage of this spiritual movement has also directly in view the character of Rameau in Diderot's *Le neveu de Rameau*. This remarkable work was written in 1760, but was first brought to the notice of the literary public by Goethe, who translated and published the work in 1805. It thus came into Hegel's hands while he was writing the *Phenomenology:* and this perhaps accounts for the repeated references to it in the argument. The term "self-estranged spirit" with which he heads this section occurs in Goethe's translation. Rameau is an extreme type of such a spirit.

With this section should be read Hegel's *Philosophy of History*, Pt. III, §3, c. 2; Pt. IV, §2, c. 1, §3, c. 1, 3: the *History of Philosophy*, Pt. 3, Introduction, and c. 2, "The French Philosophy and the German Enlightenment."

The ethical substance preserved and kept opposition enclosed within its simple conscious life; and this consciousness was in immediate unity with its own essential nature. That nature has therefore the simple characteristic of something merely existing for the consciousness which is directed immediately upon it, and whose "custom" (*Sitte*) it is. Consciousness does not take itself to be particular excluding self, nor does the substance mean for it an existence shut out from it, with which it would have to establish its identity only through estranging itself and thus at the same time have to produce that substance. But that spirit, whose self is absolutely insular, absolutely discrete, finds its content over against itself in the form of a reality that is just as impenetrable as itself, and the world here gets the characteristic of being something external, negative to self-consciousness. Yet this world is a spiritual reality, it is essentially the fusion of individuality with being. This its existence is the work of self-consciousness, but likewise an actuality immediately present and alien to it, which has a peculiar being of its own, and in which it does not know itself. This reality is the external element and the free content[1] of the sphere of legal right. But this external reality, which the lord of the world of legal right takes control of, is not merely this elementary external entity casually lying before the self; it is his work, but not in a positive sense, rather negatively so. It acquires its existence by self-consciousness of its own accord relinquishing itself and giving up its essentiality, the condition which, in that waste and ruin which prevail in the sphere of right, the external force of the elements let loose seems to bring upon self-consciousness. These elements by themselves are sheer ruin and destruction, and cause their own overthrow. This overthrow, however, this their negative nature, is just the *self*; it is their subject, their action, and their process.

---

[1]*v.* p. 278 ff.

Such process and activity again, through which the substance becomes actual, are the estrangement of personality, for the immediate self, i.e. the self without estrangement and holding good as it stands, is without substantial content, and the sport of these raging elements. Its substance is thus just its relinquishment, and the relinquishment is the substance, i.e. the spiritual powers forming themselves into a coherent world and thereby securing their subsistence.

The substance in this way is spirit, self-conscious unity of the self and the essential nature; but both also take each other to mean and to imply alienation. Spirit is consciousness of an objective reality which exists independently on its own account. Over against this consciousness stands, however, that unity of the self with the essential nature, consciousness pure and simple over against actual consciousness. On the one side actual self-consciousness by its self-relinquishment passes over into the real world, and the latter back again into the former. On the other side, however, this very actuality, both person and objectivity, is cancelled and superseded; they are purely universal. This their alienation is pure consciousness, or the essential nature. The "present" has directly its opposite in its "beyond," which is its thinking and its being thought; just as this again has its opposite in what is here in the "present," which is the actuality of the "beyond" but alienated from it.

Spirit in this case, therefore, constructs not merely one world, but a twofold world, divided and self-opposed. The world of the ethical spirit is its own proper present; and hence every power it possesses is found in this unity of the present, and, so far as each separates itself from the other, each is still in equilibrium with the whole. Nothing has the significance of a negative of self-consciousness; even the spirit of the departed is in the life-blood of his relative, is present in the self of the family, and the universal power of government is the will, the self of the nation. Here, however, what is present means merely objective actuality, which has its consciousness in the beyond; each single moment, as an essential entity, receives this, and thereby actuality, from an other, and so far as it is actual, its essential being is something other than its own actuality. Nothing has a spirit self-established and indwelling within it; rather, each is outside itself in what is alien to it. The equilibrium of the whole is not the unity which abides by itself, nor its inwardly secured tranquillity, but rests on the estrangement of its opposite. The whole is, therefore, like each single moment, a self-estranged reality. It breaks up into two spheres: in one kingdom self-consciousness is actually both the self and its object, and in another we have the kingdom of pure consciousness, which, being beyond the former, has no actual present, but exists for Faith, is matter of Belief. Now just as the ethical world passes from the separation of divine and human law, with its various forms, and its consciousness gets away from the division into knowledge and the absence of knowledge, and returns into the principle which is its destiny, into the self which is the power to destroy and negate this opposition, so, too, both these kingdoms of self-alienated spirit will return into the self. But if the former, the first self holding good directly, was the single person, this second, which returns into itself from its self-relinquishment, will be the universal self, the consciousness grasping the conception; and these spiritual worlds, all of whose moments insist on having a fixed reality and an unspiritual subsistence, will be dissolved in the light of pure Insight. This insight, being the self grasping itself, completes the stage of culture. It takes up nothing but the self, and everything as the self, i.e. it comprehends everything, extinguishes all objectiveness, and converts everything implicit into something explicit, everything which has a being *in itself* into what is *for* itself. When turned against belief, against faith, as the alien realm of inner being lying in the distant beyond, it is Enlightenment (*Aufklärung*). This enlightenment completes spirit's self-estrangement in this realm too, whither spirit in self-alienation turns to seek its safety as to a region where it becomes conscious of the peace of self-equipoise. Enlightenment upsets the household arrangements, which spirit carries out in the house of faith, by bringing in the goods and furnishings belonging to the world of the Here and Now, a world which that spirit cannot refuse to accept as its own property, for its conscious life likewise belongs to that world. In this negative task pure insight realizes itself at the same time, and brings to light its own proper object, the "unknowable absolute Being" and utility.[2] Since in this way actuality has lost all substantiality, and there is nothing more implicit in it, the kingdom of faith, as also that of the real world, is overthrown; and this revolution brings about absolute freedom, the stage at which the spirit formerly estranged has gone back completely into itself, leaves behind this sphere of culture, and passes over into another region, the land of the inner or subjective moral consciousness (*moralischen Bewusstsein*).

I

THE WORLD OF SPIRIT IN SELF-ESTRANGEMENT

THE sphere of spirit at this stage breaks up into two regions. The one is the actual world, that of self-estrangement, the other is that which spirit constructs for itself in the ether of pure consciousness, raising itself

---

[2]Cp. Eighteenth century Deism and utilitarianism.

above the first. This second world, being constructed in opposition and contrast to that estrangement, is just on that account not free from it; on the contrary, it is only the other form of that very estrangement, which consists precisely in having a conscious existence in two sorts of worlds, and embraces both. Hence it is not self-consciousness of Absolute Being in and for itself, not Religion, which is here dealt with: it is Belief, Faith, in so far as faith is a flight from the actual world, and thus is not a self-complete experience (*an und für sich*). Such flight from the realm of the present is, therefore, directly in its very nature a dual state of mind. Pure consciousness is the sphere into which spirit rises: but it is not only the element of faith, but of the notion as well. Consequently both appear on the scene together at the same time, and the former comes before us only in antithesis to the latter.

a

CULTURE AND ITS REALM OF ACTUAL REALITY[1]

THE spirit of this world is spiritual essence permeated by a self-consciousness which knows itself to be directly present as a self-existent particular, and knows that essence as an objective actuality over against itself. But the existence of this world, as also the actuality of self-consciousness, depends on the process that self-consciousness divests itself of its personality, by so doing creates its world, and treats it as something alien and external, of which it must now take possession. But the renunciation of its self-existence is itself the production of the actuality, and in doing so, therefore, self-consciousness *ipso facto* makes itself master of this world.

To put the matter otherwise, self-consciousness is only something definite, it only has real existence, so far as it alienates itself from itself. By doing so, it puts itself in the position of something universal, and this its universality is its validity, establishes it, and is its actuality. This equality of the self with all selves is, therefore, not the equality that was found in the case of right; self-consciousness does not here, as there, get immediate validity and acknowledgment merely because it is; on the contrary, its claim to be valid rests on its having made itself, by that mediating process of self-alienation, conform to what is universal. The spiritless formal universality which characterizes the sphere of right takes up every natural form of character as well as of existence, and sanctions and establishes them. The universality which holds good

---

[1]It will be observed that "culture" embraces all means of self-development, "ideas" as well as material factors such as "wealth."

here, however, is one that has undergone development, and for that
reason it is concrete and actual.

The means, then, whereby an individual gets objective validity and
concrete actuality here is the formative process of Culture. The estrangement on the part of spirit from its natural existence is here the individual's true and original nature, his very substance. The relinquishment of this natural state is, therefore, both his purpose and his mode
of existence; it is at the same time the mediating process, the transition
of the thought-constituted substance to concrete actuality, as well as,
conversely, the transition of determinate individuality to its essential
constitution. This individuality moulds itself by culture to what it inherently is, and only by so doing is it then something *per se* and possessed of concrete existence. The extent[2] of its culture is the measure
of its reality and its power. Although the self, *qua* this particular self,
knows itself here to be real, yet its concrete realization consists solely in
cancelling and transcending the natural self. The original determinateness of its nature is, therefore, reduced to a matter of quantity, to a
greater or less energy of will, a non-essential principle of distinction.
But purpose and content of the self belong to the universal substance
alone, and can only be something universal. The specific particularity
of a given nature, which becomes purpose and content, is something
powerless and unreal: it is a "kind of being" which exerts itself foolishly
and in vain to attain embodiment: it is the contradiction of giving reality to the bare particular, while reality is, *ipso facto*, something universal. If, therefore, individuality is falsely held to consist in particularity
of nature and character, then the real world contains no individualities
and characters; individuals are all alike for one another; the pretence
(*vermeint*) of individuality in that case is precisely the mere presumptive (*gemeint*) existence which has no permanent place in this world
where only renunciation of self and, therefore, only universality get actual reality. What is presumed or conjectured to be (*Das Gemeinte*)
passes, therefore, simply for what it is, for a *kind* of being. "Kind" is not
quite the same as *Espèce*,[3] "the most horrible of all nicknames, for it
signifies mediocrity, and denotes the highest degree of contempt."[4] "A
kind" and "to be good of its kind" are German expressions, which add
an air of honesty to this meaning, as if it were not so badly meant and
intended after all; or which, indeed, do not yet involve a clear consciousness of what "kind" and what culture and reality are.

That which, in reference to the single individual, appears as his cul-

---

[2]Bacon's phrase, "Knowledge is power."
[3]"Espèce se dit de personnes auxquelles on ne trouve ni qualité ni mérite."—Littré.
[4]Diderot's *Rameau's Neffe*.

ture, is the essential moment of spiritual substance as such, viz.: the direct transition of its ideal, thought-constituted, universality into actual reality; or otherwise put, culture is the single soul of this substance, in virtue of which the essentially inherent (*Ansich*) becomes something explicitly acknowledged, and assumes definite objective existence. The process in which an individuality cultivates itself is, therefore, *ipso facto*, the development of individuality *qua* universal objective being; that is to say, it is the development of the actual world. This world, although it has come into being by means of individuality, is in the eyes of self-consciousness something that is directly and primarily estranged, and, for self-consciousness, takes on the form of a fixed, undisturbed reality. But at the same time self-consciousness is sure this is its own substance, and proceeds to take it under control. This power over its substance it acquires by culture, which, looked at from this aspect, appears as self-consciousness making itself conform to reality, and doing so to the extent permitted by the energy of its original character and talents. What seems here to be the individual's power and force, bringing the substance under it, and thereby doing away with that substance is the same thing as the actualization of the substance. For the power of the individual consists in conforming itself to that substance, i.e. in emptying itself of its own self, and thus establishing itself as the objectively existing substance. Its culture and its own reality are, therefore, the process of making the substance itself actual and concrete.

The self is conscious of being actual only as transcended, as cancelled.[5] The self does not here involve the unity of consciousness of self and object; rather this object is negative as regards the self. By means of the self *qua* inner soul of the process, the substance is so moulded and worked up in its various moments, that one opposite puts life into the other, each opposite, by its alienation from the other, gives the other stability, and similarly gets stability from the other. At the same time, each moment has its own definite nature, in the sense of having an insuperable worth and significance; and has a fixed reality as against the other. The process of thought fixes this distinction in the most general manner possible, by means of the absolute opposition of "good" and "bad," which are poles asunder, and can in no way become one and the same. But the very soul of what is thus fixed consists in its immediate transition to its opposite; existence consists really in transmuting each determinate element into its opposite; and it is only this estrangement that constitutes the essential nature and the preservation of the whole. We must now consider this process by which the moments are thus made actual and give each other life; the alienation will be

---

[5] Cp. Hume's view of "personal identity," *Treatise*, pt. IV, c. 6.

cf Blackburn on projectionism?

found to alienate itself, and the whole thereby will take all its contents back into the ultimate principle it implies (*seinen Begriff*).

At the outset we must deal with the simple substance itself in its immediate unconscious organization of its moments; they exist there, but are lifeless, their soul is wanting. We have here something like what we find in nature. Nature, we find, is resolved and spread out into separate and general elements—air, water, fire, earth. Of these air is the unchanging factor, purely universal and transparent; water, the reality that is for ever being resolved and given up; fire, their animating unity which is ever dissolving opposition into unity, as well as breaking up their simple unity into opposite constituents: earth is the tightly compact knot of this articulated whole, the subject in which these realities *are*, where their processes take effect, that which they start from and to which they return. In the same way the inner essential nature, the simple life of spirit that pervades self-conscious reality, is resolved, spread out into similar general areas or masses, spiritual masses in this case, and appears as a whole organized world. In the case of the first mass it is the inherently universal spiritual being, self-identical; in the second it is self-existent being, it has become inherently self-discordant, sacrificing itself, abandoning itself; the third which takes the form of self-consciousness is subject, and possesses in its very nature the fiery force of dissolution. In the first case it is conscious of itself, as immanent and implicit, as existing *per se*; in the second it finds independence, self-existence (*Fürsichseyn*) developed and carried out by means of the sacrifice of what is universal. But spirit itself is the self-containedness and self-completeness of the whole, which splits up into substance *qua* constantly enduring and substance *qua* self-sacrificing, and which at the same time resumes substance again into its own unity; a whole which is at once a flame of fire bursting out and consuming the substance, as well as the abiding form of the substance consumed. We can see that the areas of spiritual reality here referred to correspond to the Community and the Family in the ethical world, without, however, possessing the native indwelling spirit which the latter have. On the other hand, while destiny is alien to this spirit, here self-consciousness is and knows itself to be the real power underlying them.

We have now to consider these separate members of the whole, in the first instance as regards the way they are presented *qua* thoughts, *qua* essential inherent entities falling within pure consciousness, and also secondly as regards the way they appear as objective realities in concrete conscious life.

In the *first* form, the simplicity of content found in pure consciousness, the first member, being the self-identical, immediate and unchanging nature of every consciousness is the Good:—the independent spiritual power inherent in the essence, alongside which the activity of the mere self-existent consciousness is only by-play. Its other is the passive spiritual being, the universal so far as it parts with its own claims, and lets individuals get in it the consciousness of their particular existence; it is a state of nothingness, a being that is null and void, the Bad. This absolute break-up of the real into these *disjecta membra* is itself a permanent condition; while the first member is the foundation, starting-point, and result of individuals, which are there purely universal, the second member, on the other hand, is a being partly sacrificing itself for another, and, on that very account, is partly their incessant return to self *qua* individual, and their constant development of a separate being of their own.

But, *secondly*, these bare ideas of Good and Bad are similarly and immediately alienated from one another; they are actual, and in actual consciousness appear as moments that are objective. In this sense the first state of being is the Power of the State, the second its Resources or Wealth. The state-power is the simple spiritual substance, as well as the achievement of all, the absolutely accomplished fact, wherein individuals find their essential nature expressed, and where their particular existence is simply and solely a consciousness of their own universality. It is likewise the achievement and simple result from which the sense of its having been their doing has vanished: it stands as the absolute basis of all their action, where all their action securely subsists. This simple ethereal substance of their life, owing to its thus determining their unalterable self-identity, has the nature of objective being, and hence only stands in relation to and exists for "another." It is thus, *ipso facto*, inherently the opposite of itself—Wealth or Resources. Although wealth is something passive, is nothingness, it is likewise a universal spiritual entity, the continuously created result of the labour and action of all, just as it is again dissipated into the enjoyment of all. In enjoyment each individuality no doubt becomes aware of self-existence, aware of itself as single; but this enjoyment is itself the result of universal action, just as, reciprocally, wealth calls forth universal labour, and produces enjoyment for all. The actual has through and through the spiritual significance of being directly universal. Each individual doubtless thinks he is acting in his own interests when getting this enjoyment; for this is the aspect in which he gets the sense of being something on his own account, and for that reason he does not take it to be something spiritual. Yet looked at even in external fashion, it becomes manifest that in his own enjoyment each gives enjoyment to all, in his own labour each works for all as well as for himself, and all for him. His self-existence is, therefore, inherently universal, and self-interest is merely a supposition that cannot get the length of making concrete and actual what it means or supposes, viz. to do something that is not to further the good of all.

Thus, then, in these two spiritual powers self-consciousness finds its own substance, content, and purpose; it has there a direct intuitive consciousness of its twofold nature; in one it sees what it is inherently in itself, in the other what it is explicitly for itself. At the same time *qua* spirit, it is the negative unity, uniting the subsistence of these powers with the separation of individuality from the universal, or that of reality from the self. Dominion and wealth are, therefore, before the individual as objects he is aware of, i.e. as objects from which he knows himself to be detached and between which he thinks he can choose, or even decline to choose either. In the form of this detached bare consciousness he stands over against the essential reality as one which is merely there for him. He then has the reality *qua* essential reality within himself. In this bare consciousness the moments of the substance are taken to be not state-power and wealth, but thoughts, the thoughts of Good and Bad. But further, self-consciousness is a relation of his pure consciousness to his actual consciousness, of what is thought to the objective being; it is essentially Judgment. What is Good and what is Bad has already been brought out in the case of the two aspects of actual reality by determining what the aspects immediately are; the Good is state-power, the Bad, wealth. But this first judgment, this first distinction of content, cannot be looked at as a "spiritual" judgment; for in that first judgment the one side has been characterized as only the inherently existing or positive, and the other side as only the explicit self-existent and negative. But *qua* spiritual realities, each permeates both moments, pervades both aspects; and thus their nature is not exhausted in those specific characteristics [positive and negative]. And the self-consciousness that has to do with them is self-complete, is in itself and for itself. It must, therefore, relate itself to each in that twofold form in which they appear; and by so doing, this nature of theirs, which consists in being self-estranged determinations, will come to light.

Now self-consciousness takes that object to be good, and to exist *per se*, in which it finds itself; and that to be bad when it finds the opposite of itself there. Goodness means identity of objective reality with it, badness their disparity. At the same time what is for it good and bad, is *per se* good and bad; because it is just that in which these two aspects—of being *per se*, and of being for it—are the same: it is the real indwelling soul of the objective facts, and the judgment is the evidence of its power within them, a power which makes them into what they are in themselves. What they are when spirit is actively related to them, their identity or non-identity with spirit—that is their real nature and the test of their true meaning, and not how they are identical or diverse taken immediately in themselves apart from spirit, i.e. not their inherent being and self-existence *in abstracto*. The active relation of spirit to these moments—which are first put forward as objects to it and there-after pass by its action into what is essential and inherent—becomes at the same time their reflexion into themselves, in virtue of which they obtain actual spiritual existence, and their spiritual meaning comes to light. But as their first immediate characteristic is distinct from the re-lation of spirit to them, the third determinate moment—their own proper spirit—is also distinguished from the second moment. Their second inherent nature (*Das zweite Ansich derselben*)—their essential-ity which comes to light through the relation of spirit to them—in the first instance, must surely turn out different from the immediate inher-ent nature; for indeed this mediating process of spiritual activity puts in motion the immediate characteristic, and turns it into something else.

As a result of this process, then, the self-contained conscious mind doubtless finds in the Power of the State its bare and simple reality, and its subsistence; but it does not find its individuality as such; it finds its inherent and essential being, but not what it is for itself. Rather, it finds there action *qua* individual action rejected and denied, and subdued into obedience. The individual thus recoils before this power and turns back into himself; it is for him the reality that suppresses him, and is the bad. For instead of being identical with him, that with which he is at one, it is something utterly in discordance with individuality. In con-trast with this, Wealth is the good; wealth tends to the general enjoy-ment, it is there simply to be disposed of, and it ensures for every one the consciousness of his particular self. Riches means in its very nature universal beneficence: if it refuses any benefit in a given case, and does not gratify every need, this is merely an accident which does not detract from its universal and necessary nature of imparting to every individual his share and being a thousand-handed benefactor.

These two judgments provide the ideas of Goodness and Badness with a content which is the reverse of what they had for us. Self-consciousness had up till now, however, been related to its objects only incompletely, viz. only according to the criterion of the self-existent. But consciousness is also real in its inherent nature, and has likewise to take this aspect for its point of view and criterion, and by so doing round off completely the judgment of self-conscious spirit. According to this aspect state-power expresses its essential nature: the power of the state is in part the quiet insistence of law, in part government and pre-scription, which appoints and regulates the particular processes of uni-versal action. The one is the simple substance itself, the other its action which animates and sustains itself and all individuals. The individual thus finds therein his ground and nature expressed, organized, and exercised. As against this, the individual, by the enjoyment of wealth, does not get to know his own universal nature: he only gets a transitory consciousness and enjoyment of himself *qua* particular and self-existing, and discovers his discordance, his want of agreement with his own essential nature. The conceptions Good and Bad thus receive here a content the opposite of what they had before.

These two ways of judging find each of them an identity and a disagreement. In the first case consciousness finds the power of the state out of agreement with it, and the enjoyment that came from wealth in accord with it; while in the second case the reverse holds good. There is a twofold attainment of identity and a twofold form of disagreement: there is an opposite relation established towards both the essential realities. We must pass judgment on these different ways of judging as such; to this end we have to apply the criterion already brought forward. The conscious relation which finds identity or agreement, is, according to this standard, the Good; that which finds want of agreement, the Bad. These two types of relation must henceforth be regarded as diverse forms of conscious existence. Conscious life, through taking up a different kind of relation, thereby becomes itself characterized as different, comes to be itself good or bad. It is not thus distinct in virtue of the fact that it took as its constitutive principle either existence for itself, or mere being in itself; for both are equally essential moments of its life: that dual way of judging, above discussed, presented those principles as separated, and contained, therefore, merely abstract ways of judging. Concrete actual conscious life has within it both principles, and the distinction between its forms falls solely within its own nature, viz. inside the relation of itself to the real.

This relation takes opposite forms; in the one there is an active attitude towards state-power and wealth as to something with which it is in accord, in the other it is related to these realities as to something with which it is at variance. A conscious life which finds itself at one with them has the attribute of Nobility. In the case of the public authority of the state, it regards what is in accord with itself, and sees that it has there its own nature pure and simple and the sphere for the exercise of its own powers, and stands in the position of actually rendering obedient service in its interests, as well as that of inner reverence towards it. In the same way in the sphere of wealth, it sees that wealth secures for it the consciousness of self-existence, of realizing the other essential aspect of its nature: hence it looks upon wealth likewise as something essential in relation to itself, acknowledges him from whence the enjoyment comes as a benefactor, and considers itself under a debt of obligation.

The conscious life involved in the other relation, again, that of disagreement, has the attribute of Baseness. It holds to its discordance
with both those essential elements. It looks upon the authoritative
power of the state as a chain, as something suppressing its separate existence for its own sake, and hence hates the ruler, obeys only with secret malice, and stands ever ready to burst out in rebellion. It sees, too,
in wealth, by which it attains to the enjoyment of its own independent
existence, merely something discordant, i.e. its disagreement with its
permanent nature; since through wealth it only gets a sense of its particular isolated existence and a consciousness of passing enjoyment,
since it loves wealth but despises it, and, with the disappearance of enjoyment, of what is inherently evanescent, regards its relation to the
man of wealth as having ceased too.

These relations now express, in the first instance, a judgment, the determinate characterization of what both those facts [state-power and
wealth] are as objects for consciousness; not as yet what they are in their
complete objective nature (*an und für sich*). The reflexion which is presented in this judgment is partly at first for *us* [who are philosophizing]
an affirmation of the one characteristic along with the other, and hence
is a simultaneous cancelling of both; it is not yet the reflexion of them
for consciousness itself. Partly, again, they are at first immediate essential entities; they have not become this, nor is there in them consciousness of self: that *for* which they are is not yet their animating principle:
they are predicates which are not yet themselves subject. On account of
this separation, the entirety of the spiritual process of judgment also
breaks asunder and falls into two modes of consciousness, each of which
has a one-sided character. Now, just as at the outset the indifference of
the two aspects in the process of self-estrangement—one of which was
the inherent essential being of pure consciousness, viz. the determinate
ideas of good and bad, the other their actual existence in the form of
state-power and wealth—passed to the stage of being related the one to
the other, passed to the level of judgment; in the same way this external
relation must be raised to the level of their inner unity, must become a
relation of thought to actual reality, and also the spirit animating both
the forms of judgment will make its appearance. This takes place when
judgment passes into inference, becomes the mediating process in
which the middle term necessitating and connecting both sides of the
judgment is brought into relief.

The noble type of consciousness, then, finds itself in the judgment
related to state-power, in the sense that this power is indeed not a self
as yet but at first is universal substance, in which, however, this form of
mind feels its own essential nature to exist, is conscious of its own purpose and absolute content. By taking up a positive relation to this sub-

stance, it assumes a negative attitude towards its own special purposes, its particular content and individual existence, and lets them disappear. This type of mind is the heroism of Service; the virtue which sacrifices individual being to the universal, and thereby brings this into existence; the type of personality which of itself renounces possession and enjoyment, acts for the sake of the prevailing power, and in this way becomes a concrete reality.

Through this process the universal becomes united and bound up with existence in general, just as the individual consciousness makes itself by this renunciation essentially universal. That from which this consciousness estranges itself by submitting to serve is its consciousness immersed in mere existence: but the being alienated from itself is the inherent nature. By thus shaping its life in accord with what is universal, it acquires a Reverence for itself, and gets reverence from others. The power of the state, however, which to start with was merely universal in thought, the inherent nature, becomes through this very process universal in fact, becomes actual power. It is actually so only in getting that actual obedience which it obtains through self-consciousness judging it to be the essential reality, and through the self being freely sacrificed to it. The result of this action, binding the essential reality and self indissolubly together, is to produce a twofold actuality— a self that is truly actualized, and a state-power whose authority is accepted as true.

Owing to this alienation [implied in the idea of sacrifice] state-power, however, is not yet a self-consciousness that knows itself as state-power. It is merely the law of the state, its inherent principle, that is accepted; the state-power has as yet no particular will. For as yet the self-consciousness rendering service has not surrendered its pure selfhood, and made it an animating influence in the exercise of state-power; the serving attitude merely gives the state its bare being, sacrifices merely its existence to the state, not its essential nature. This type of self-consciousness has a value as one that is in conformity with the essential nature, and is acknowledged and accepted because of its inherent reality. The others find their essential nature operative in it, but not their independent existence—find their thinking, their pure consciousness fulfilled, but not their specific individuality. It has a value, therefore, in their thoughts, and is honoured accordingly. Such a type is the haughty vassal; he is active in the interests of the state-power, so far as the latter is not a personal will [a monarch] but merely an essential will. His self-importance lies only in the honour thus acquired, only in the general mind which directs its thoughts to what is essential, not in an individuality thinking gratefully of services rendered; for he has not helped this individuality [the monarch] to get independence.

The language he would use, were he to occupy a direct relation to the personal will of the state-power, which thus far has not arisen, would take the form of "counsel" imparted in the interests of what is best for all.

State-power has, therefore, still at this stage no will to oppose the advice, and does not decide between the different opinions as to what is universally the best. It is not yet governmental control, and on that account is in truth not yet real state-power. Individual self-existence, the possession of an individual will that is not yet *qua* will surrendered, is the inner secretly reserved spiritual principle of the various classes and stations, a spirit which keeps for its own behoof what suits itself best, in spite of its words about the universal best, and tends to make this clap-trap about what is universally the best a substitute for action bringing it about. The sacrifice of existence, which takes place in the case of service, is indeed complete when it goes so far as death. But the endurance of the danger of death which the individual survives, leaves him still a specific kind of existence, and hence a particular self-reference; and this makes the counsel imparted in the interests of the universally best ambiguous and open to suspicion; it really means, in point of fact, retaining the claim to a private opinion of his own, and a separate individual will as against the power of the state. Its relation to the latter is, therefore, still one of discordance; and it possesses the characteristic found in the case of the base type of consciousness—it is ever at the point of breaking out into rebellion.

This contradiction, which has to be overcome, in this form of discordance and opposition between the independence of the individual conscious life and the universality belonging to state-authority, contains at the same time another aspect. That renunciation of existence, when it is complete, as it is in death, is one that does not revert to the consciousness that makes the sacrifice; it simply is: this consciousness does not survive the renunciation and exist in its own self-completeness (*an und für sich*), it merely passes away into the unreconciled opposite. That alone is true sacrifice of individuality, therefore, in which it gives itself up as completely as in the case of death, but all the while preserves itself in the renunciation. It comes thereby to be actually what it is implicitly—the identical unity of self with its opposed self. In this way, by the inner withdrawn and secret spiritual principle, the self as such, coming forward and abrogating itself, the state-power becomes *ipso facto* raised into a proper self of its own; without this estrangement of self the deeds of honour, the actions of the noble type of consciousness, and the counsels which its insight reveals, would continue to maintain the ambiguous character which, as we saw, kept that secret reserve of private intention and self-will, in spite of its overt pretensions.

This estrangement, however, takes place in Language, in words alone, and language assumes here its peculiar role. Both in the sphere of the general social order (*Sittlichkeit*), where language embodies laws and commands, and in the sphere of actual life, where it appears as conveying advice, the content of what it expresses is the essential reality, and language is the form of that essential content. Here, however, it takes the form in which *qua* language it exists to be its content, and possesses authority, *qua* spoken word; it is the power of utterance *qua* utterance which, just in speaking, performs what has to be performed. For it is the existence of the pure self *qua* self; in speech the self-existent singleness of self-consciousness comes as such into existence, so that its particular individuality is something for others. Ego *qua* this particular pure ego is non-existent otherwise; in every other mode of expression it is absorbed in some concrete actuality, and appears in a shape from which it can withdraw; it turns reflectively back into itself, away from its act, as well as from its physiognomic expression, and leaves such an incomplete existence (in which there is always at once too much as well as too little), lying soulless behind. Speech, however, contains this ego in its purity; it alone expresses I, I itself. Its existence in this case is, *qua* existence, a form of objectivity which has in it its true nature. Ego is this particular ego, but at the same time universal; its appearing is *ipso facto* and at once the alienation and disappearance of this particular ego, and in consequence its remaining all the while universal. The I, that expresses itself, is apprehended as an ego; it is a kind of infection in virtue of which it establishes at once a unity with those who are aware of it, a spark that kindles a universal consciousness of self. That it is apprehended as a fact by others means *eo ipso* that its existence is itself dying away: this its otherness is taken back into itself; and its existence lies just in this, that, *qua* self-conscious Now, as it exists, it has no subsistence and that it subsists just through its disappearance. This disappearance is, therefore, itself *ipso facto* its continuance; it is its own cognition of itself, and its knowing itself as something that has passed into another self that has been apprehended and is universal.

Spirit acquires this form of reality here, because the extremes, too, whose unity spirit is, have directly the character of being realities each on its own account. Their unity is disintegrated into rigid aspects, each of which is an actual object for the other, and each is excluded from the other. The unity, therefore, appears in the rôle of a mediating term, which is excluded and distinguished from the separated reality of the two sides; it has, therefore, itself the actual character of something objective, apart, and distinguished from its aspects, and objective for them, i.e. the unity is an existent objective fact. The spiritual substance comes as such into existence only when it has been able to take as its

aspects those self-consciousnesses, which know this pure self to be a reality possessing immediate validity, and therein immediately know, too,
that they are such realities merely through the mediating process of
alienation. Through that pure self the moments of substance get the
transparency of a self-knowing category, and become clarified so far as
to be moments of spirit; through the mediating process spirit comes to
exist in spiritual form. Spirit in this way is the mediating term, presup-
posing those extremes and produced through their existence; but it is
also the spiritual whole breaking out between them, which sunders its
self into them, and, solely in virtue of that contact, creates each into the
whole in terms of its principle. The fact that both extremes are from the
start and in their very nature transcended and disintegrated produces
their unity; and this is the process which fuses both together, interchanges their characteristic features, and binds them together, and
does so in each extreme. This mediating process consequently actualizes the principle of each of the two extremes, or makes what each is
inherently in itself its controlling and moving spirit.

Both extremes, the state-authority and the noble type of consciousness, are disintegrated by this latter. In state-power, the two sides are the
abstract universal which is obeyed, and the individual will existing on
its own account, which, however, does not yet belong to the universal
itself. In nobility, the two sides are the obedience in giving up existence, or the inherent maintenance of self-respect and honour, and, on
the other hand, a self which exists purely for its own sake and whose
self-existence is not yet done away with, the self-will that remains always in reserve. These two moments into which the extremes are refined, and which, therefore, find expression in language, are the abstract universal, which is called the "universal best," and the pure self
which by rendering service abrogated the life of absorption in the manifold variety of existence. Both in principle are the same; for pure self
is just the abstract universal, and hence their unity acts as their mediating term. But the self is, at first, actual only in consciousness, the one
extreme, while the inherent nature (*Ansich*) is actualized in the other
extreme, state-authority. That state-power not merely in the form of honour but in reality should be transferred to it, is lacking in the case of
consciousness; while in the case of state-authority there is lacking the
obedience rendered to it not merely as a so-called universal best, but as
will, in other words, as state-power which is the self regulating and deciding. The unity of the principle in which state-power still remains,
and into which consciousness has been refined, becomes real in this
mediating process, and this exists *qua* mediating term in the simple
form of speech. All the same, the aspects of this unity are not yet present in the form of two selves as selves; for state-power has first to be in-

spired with active self-hood. This language is, therefore, not yet spiritual existence in the sense in which spirit completely knows and expresses itself.

The noble consciousness, being the extreme which is the self, assumes the rôle of producing the language by which the separate factors related are formed into active spiritual wholes. The heroism of dumb service passes into the heroism of flattery. This reflexion of service in express language constitutes the spiritual self-disintegrating mediating term, and reflects back into itself not only its own special extreme, but reflects the extreme of universal power back into this self too, and makes that power, which is at first implicit, into an independent self-existence, and gives it the individualistic form of self-consciousness. Through this process the indwelling spirit of this state-power comes into existence—that of an unlimited monarch. It is unlimited; the language of flattery raises this power into its transparent, purified universality; this moment being the product of language, of purified spiritualized existence, is a purified form of self-identity. It is a monarch; for flattering language likewise puts individualistic self-consciousness on its pinnacle; what the noble consciousness abandons as regards this aspect of pure spiritual unity is the pure essential nature of its thought, its ego itself. More definitely expressed:—flattery raises the individual singleness, which otherwise is only imagined, into its purist form as an actual existence, by giving the monarch his proper name. For it is in the name alone that the distinction of the individual from every one else is not imagined but is actually made by all. By having a name the individual passes for a pure individual not merely in his own consciousness of himself, but in the consciousness of all. By its name, then, the monarch becomes absolutely detached from every one, exclusive and solitary, and in virtue of it is unique as an atom that cannot communicate any part of its essential nature, and has no equal. This name is thus its reflexion into itself, or is the actual reality which universal power has inherently within itself: through the name the power is the monarch.[6] Conversely he, this particular individual, thereby knows himself, this individual self, to be the universal power, knows that the nobles not only are ready and prepared for the service of the state-authority, but are grouped as an ornamental setting round the throne, and that they are for ever telling him who sits thereon what he is.

The language of their proffered praise is in this way the spirit that unites together the two extremes in the case of state-power itself. This language turns the abstract power back into itself, and gives to it the moment peculiar to the other extreme, an isolated self of its own,

---

[6]Cp. "L'état c'est moi."

willing and deciding on its own account, and consequently gives it self-conscious existence. Or again, by that means this actual individual self-consciousness comes to be aware of itself for certain as the supreme authority. This power is the central focal self into which, through relinquishing their own inner certainty of self, the many separate centres of selfhood are fused together into one.

Since, however, this proper spirit of state-power subsists by getting its realization and its nourishment from the homage of action and thought rendered by the nobility, it is a form of independence in internal self-estrangement. The noble, the extreme form of self-existence, receives the other extreme of actual universality in return for the universality of thought which he relinquished. The power of the state has passed over to and fallen upon the noble. It falls to the noble primarily to make the state-authority truly effective: in his existence as a self on his own account, that authority ceases to be the inert being it appeared to be *qua* extreme of abstract and merely implicit reality.

Looked at *per se*, state-power reflected back into itself, or becoming spiritual, means nothing else than that it has come to be a moment of self-conscious life, i.e. *is* only by being sublated. Consequently it is now the real in the sense of something whose spiritual meaning lies in being sacrificed and squandered; it exists in the sense of wealth. It continues, no doubt, to subsist at the same time as a form of reality over against wealth, into which in principle it is forever passing; but it is a reality, whose inherent principle is this very process of passing over—owing to the service and the reverence rendered to it, and by which it arises—into its opposite, into the condition of relinquishing its power. Thus from its point of view (*Fürsich*) the special and peculiar self, which constitutes its will, becomes, by the self-abasement of the nobility, a universal that renounces itself, becomes completely an isolated particular, a mere accident, which is the prey of every stronger will. What remains to it of the universally acknowledged and incommunicable independence is the empty name.

While, then, the noble consciousness adopted the attitude of something that stood in concord with the universal power,[7] its true nature lies rather in retaining its own independence of being when rendering its service, but, when really and properly abnegating its personality, its true being lies in actually cancelling and rending in pieces the universal substance. Its spirit is the attitude of thoroughgoing discordance: on one side it retains its own will in the honour it receives; on the other hand it gives up its will, but in part it therein alienates from itself its inner nature, and arrives at the extreme of discordance with itself, in

---

[7] *v.* p. 294.

part it subdues the universal substance to itself, and puts this entirely at variance with itself. It is obvious that, as a result, its own specific nature, which made it distinct from the so-called base type of mind, disappears, and with that this latter type of mind too. The base type has gained its end, that of subordinating universal power to self-centred isolation of self.

Endowed in this way by the universal power, self-consciousness exists in the form of universal beneficence: or, from another point of view, universal power is wealth that again is itself an object for consciousness. For wealth is here taken to be the universal put indeed in subjection, but which is not yet absolutely returned into the self through this first transcendence. Self has not as yet its self as such for object, but the universal essential reality in a state of sublation. Since this object has first come into being, the relation of consciousness towards it is immediate, and consciousness has thus not yet set forth its discordance with this object: we have here nobility acquiring its own self-centred existence in the universal that has become non-essential, and hence acknowledging the object and feeling grateful to its benefactor.

Wealth has within it from the first the aspect of self-existence (*Fürsichsein*). It is not the self-less universal of state-power, or the unconstrained simplicity of the natural life of spirit; it is state-power as holding its own by effort of will in opposition to a will that wants to get the mastery over it and get enjoyment out of it. But since wealth has merely the form of being essential, this one-sided self-existent life—which has no being in itself, which is rather the sublation of inherent being—is the return of the individual into himself to find no essential reality in his enjoyment. It thus itself needs to be given animation; and its reflective process of bringing this about consists in its becoming something real in itself as well as for itself, instead of being merely for itself; wealth, which is the sublated essential reality, has to become the essentially real. In this way it preserves its own spiritual principle in itself.

It will be sufficient here to describe the *content* of this process since we have already explained at length its form. Nobility, then, stands here in relation not to the object in the general sense of something essential; what is alien to it is self-existence itself. It finds itself face to face with its own self as such in a state of estrangement, as an objective solid actuality which it has to take from the hands of another self-centred being, another equally fixed and solid entity. Its object is self-existence, i.e. its own being: but by being an object this is at the same time *ipso facto* an alien reality, which is a self-centred being on its own account, has a will of its own; i.e. it sees its self under the power of an alien will on which it depends for the concession of its self.

From every particular aspect self-consciousness can abstract, and for that reason, even when under an obligation to one of these aspects, retains the recognition and inherent validity of self-consciousness as an independent reality. Here, however, it finds that, as regards its own ego, its own proper and peculiar actuality, it is outside itself and belongs to an other, finds its personality as such dependent on the chance personality of another, on the accident of a moment, of an arbitrary caprice, or some other utterly irrelevant circumstance.

In the sphere of legal right, what lies in the power of the objective being appears as an incidental content from which it is possible to make abstraction; and the governing force does not affect the self as such; rather this self is recognized. But here the self sees its self-certainty as such to be the most unreal thing of all, finds its pure personality to be absolutely without the character of personality. The spirit of its gratitude is, therefore, one in which it feels profoundly this condition of humiliation, and feels also the deepest revolt as well. Since the pure ego sees itself outside self, and torn in sunder, everything that has continuity and universality, everything that bears the name of law, good, and right, is thereby torn to pieces at the same time, and goes to rack and ruin: all identity and concord break up, for what holds sway is the purest discord and disunion, what was absolutely essential is absolutely unessential, what has a being on its own account has its being outside itself: the pure ego itself is absolutely disintegrated.

Thus although this consciousness receives back from the sphere of wealth the objective form of being a separate self-existence, and transcends that objective character, yet it is not only, like the preceding reflexion, not completed in principle, but is consciously unsatisfied: the reflexion, wherein the self receives itself as an objective fact, is sheer direct contradiction that has taken root in the pure ego as such. *Qua* self, however, it at the same time *ipso facto* rises above this contradiction; it is absolutely elastic, and again cancels this sublation of itself, repudiates this repudiation of itself, wherein its self-existence is made to be something alien to it, revolts against this acceptance of itself and in the very reception of itself is self-existent.

Since, then, the attitude of this type of consciousness is bound up with this condition of utter disintegration, the distinction constituting its spiritual nature — that of being nobility and opposed to baseness — falls away and both aspects are the same.

The spirit of well-doing that characterizes the action of wealth may, further, be distinguished from that of the conscious life accepting the benefit it confers, and deserves special consideration.

The spirit animating wealth had an unreal insubstantial independence; wealth was something given freely to all. By communicating what it has, however, it passes into something essential and inherent; since it fulfilled its destiny, that of sacrificing itself, it cancels the aspect of singleness, that of merely seeking enjoyment for one's own self, and, being thus sublated *qua* single, spirit here is universality or essentially real.

What it imparts, what it gives to others, is self-existence. It does not hand itself over, however, as a natural self-less object, as the frankly and freely offered condition of unconscious life, but as self-conscious, as a reality keeping hold of itself: it is not like the power of an inorganic element which is felt by the consciousness receiving its force to be inherently transitory; it is the power over self, a power aware that it is independent and voluntary, and knowing at the same time that what it dispenses becomes the self of someone else.

Wealth thus shares repudiation with its clientele; but in place of revolt appears arrogance. For in one aspect it knows, as well as the self it benefits, that its self-existence is a matter of accident; but itself is this accident in whose power personality is placed. In this mood of arrogance—which thinks it has secured through a dole an alien ego-nature, and thereby brought its inmost being into submission—it overlooks the secret rebellion of the other self: it overlooks the fact of all bonds being completely cast aside, overlooks this pure disintegration, in which, the self-identity of what exists for its own sake having become sheer internal discordance, all oneness and concord, all subsistence is rent asunder, and in which in consequence the repute of and respect for the benefactor are the first to be shattered. It stands directly in front of this abyss, cleaving it to the innermost, this bottomless pit, where every solid base and stay have vanished: and in the depths it sees nothing but a common thing, a plaything for its whims, a chance result of its own caprice. Its spirit consists in quite unreal imagining, in being superficiality forsaken of all true spiritual import.

Just as self-consciousness had its own manner of speech in dealing with state-power, in other words, just as spirit took the form of expressly and actually mediating between these two extremes, self-consciousness has also a mode of speech in dealing with wealth; but still more when in revolt does it adopt a language of its own. The form of utterance which supplies wealth with the sense of its own essential significance, and thereby makes itself master of it, is likewise the language of flattery, but of ignoble flattery; for what it gives out to be the essential reality, it knows to be a reality without an inherent nature of its own, to be something at the mercy of others. The language of flattery, however, as already remarked, is that of a spirit still one-sided. To be sure its constituent elements are, on the one hand, a self moulded by service into a shape where it is reduced to bare existence, and, on the other, the inherent reality of the power dominating the self. Yet the bare principle, the pure conception, in which the simple self and the inherent reality (*Ansich*), that pure ego and this pure reality or thought, are one and the same thing—this conceptual unity of the two aspects between which the reciprocity takes effect, is not consciously felt when this language is used. The object is consciously still the inherent reality in opposition to the self; in other words, the object is not for consciousness at the same time its own proper self as such.

The language expressing the condition of disintegration, wherein spiritual life is rent asunder, is, however, the perfect form of utterance for this entire realm of spiritual culture and development, of the formative process of moulding self-consciousness (*Bildung*), and is the spirit in which it most truly exists. This self-consciousness, which finds befitting the rebellion that repudiates its own repudiation, is *eo ipso* absolute self-identity in absolute disintegration, the pure activity of mediating pure self-consciousness with itself. It is the oneness expressed in the identical judgment, where one and the same personality is subject as well as predicate. But this identical judgment is at the same time the infinite judgment; for this personality is absolutely split in two, and subject and predicate are entities utterly indifferent one to the other, which have nothing to do with each other, with no necessary unity, so much so that each has the power of an independent personality of its own. What exists as a self on its own account has for its object its own self-existence, which is object in the sense of an absolute other, and yet at the same time directly in the form of itself—itself in the sense of an other, not as if this had an other content, for the content is the same self in the form of an absolute opposite, with an existence completely all its own and indifferent.

We have, then, here the spirit of this real world of formative culture, conscious of its own nature as it truly is, and conscious of its ultimate and essential principle (*Begriff*).

This type of spiritual life is the absolute and universal inversion of reality and thought, their entire estrangement the one from the other; it is pure culture. What is found out in this sphere is that neither the concrete realities, state-power and wealth, nor their determinate conceptions, good and bad, nor the consciousness of good and bad (the consciousness that is noble and the consciousness that is base) possess real truth; it is found that all these moments are inverted and transmuted the one into the other, and each is the opposite of itself.

The universal power, which is the substance, when it gains a spiritual nature peculiarly its own through the principle of individuality, accepts the possession of a self of its own merely as a name by which it is described, and, even in being actual power, is really so powerless as to have to sacrifice itself. But this self-less reality given over to others, this self that is turned into a thing, is in fact the return of the reality into itself; it is a self-existence that is there for its own sake, it is the existence of spirit.   *when substance / universality returns to itself.*

The principles belonging to these realities, the thoughts of good and bad, are similarly transmuted and reversed in this process; what is characterized as good is bad, and vice versa. The consciousness of each of these moments by itself, the conscious types judged as noble and base—these are rather in their real truth similarly the reverse of what these specific forms intend to be; nobility is base and repudiated, just as what is repudiated as base turns round into the nobleness that characterizes the most highly developed form of free self-consciousness.

Looked at formally, everything is likewise in its external aspects the reverse of what it is internally for itself; and again it is not really and in truth what it is for itself, but something else than it wants to be; its existence on its own account is, strictly speaking, the loss of self, and alienation of self is really self-preservation.

The state of things brought about here, then, is that all moments execute justice on one another all round, each is just as much in a condition of inherent self-alienation as it moulds itself into its opposite, and in this way reverses the nature of that opposite.

Spirit truly objective, however, is just this unity of absolutely separate moments, and in fact comes into existence as the common ground, the mediating agency, just through the independent reality of these self-less extremes. Its existence consists in universal talk and depreciatory judgment rending and tearing everything, before which all those moments are broken up that are meant to signify something real and to stand for actual members of the whole, and which at the same time plays with itself this game of self-dissolution. This judging and talking is, therefore, the real truth, which cannot be got over, while it overpowers everything—it is that which in this real world is alone truly of importance. Each part of this world comes to find there its spirit expressed, or gets to be spoken of with *esprit* and finds said of it what it is.

The honest[8] soul takes each moment as a permanent and essential fact, and is the uncultivated thoughtless condition that does not think and does not know that it is likewise doing the very inverse. The distraught and disintegrated soul is, however, aware of inversion; it is, in fact, a consciousness of absolute inversion: the conceptual principle predominates there, brings together into a single unity the thoughts that lie far apart in the case of the honest soul, and the language conveying its meaning is, therefore, full of *esprit* and wit (*geistreich*).

---

[8]v. p. 235 ff.

The content uttered by spirit and uttered about itself is, then, the inversion and perversion of all conceptions and realities, a universal deception of itself and of others. The shamelessness manifested in stating this deceit is just on that account the greatest truth. This style of speech is the madness of the musician "who piled and mixed up together some thirty airs, Italian, French, tragic, comic, of all sorts and kinds; now, with a deep bass, he descended to the depths of hell, then, contracting his throat to a high, piping falsetto, he rent the vault of the skies, raving and soothed, haughtily imperious and mockingly jeering by turns."[9] The placid soul[10] that in simple honesty of heart takes the melody of the good and true to consist in harmony of sound and uniformity of tones, i.e. in a single note, regards this style of expression as a "fantastic mixture of wisdom and folly, a *melée* of as much skill as low cunning, composed of ideas as likely to be right as wrong, with as complete a perversion of sentiment, with as much consummate shamefulness in it, as absolute frankness, candour, and truth. It will not be able to refrain from breaking out into all these tones, and running up and down the whole gamut of feeling, from the depths of contempt and repudiation to the highest pitch of admiration and stirring emotion. A vein of the ridiculous will be diffused through the latter, which takes away from their nature"; the former will find in their very candour a strain of atoning reconcilement, will find in their shuddering depths the all-powerful strain which gives to itself spirit.

If we consider, by way of contrast to the mode of utterance indulged in by this self-transparent distracted type of mind, the language adopted by that simple, placid consciousness of the good and the true, we find that it can only speak in monosyllables when face to face with the frank and self-conscious eloquence of the mind developed under the influence of culture; for it can say nothing to the latter that the latter does not know and say. If it gets beyond speaking in monosyllables, then it says the same thing that the cultivated mind expresses, but in doing so commits, in addition, the folly of imagining that it is saying something new, something different. Its very syllables, "disgraceful," "base," are this folly already, for the other says them of itself. This latter type of spirit perverts in its mode of utterance everything that sounds monotonous, because this selfsameness is merely an abstraction, but in its actual reality is intrinsically and inherently perversion. On the other hand, again, the unsophisticated mind takes under its protection the good and the noble (i.e. what retains its identity of meaning in being objectively expressed), and defends it in the only way here possible—

---

[9]Diderot, *Rameau's Neffe*.
[10]The "philosopher" in Diderot's Dialogue.

that is to say, the good does not lose its value because it may be linked with what is bad or mingled with it, for to be thus associated with badness is its condition and necessity, and the wisdom of nature lies in this fact. Yet this unsophisticated mind, while it intended to contradict, has merely, in doing so, gathered into a trifling form the meaning of what spirit said, and put it in a manner which, by turning the opposite of noble and good into the necessary condition of noble and good, thoughtlessly supposes itself to convey something else than that the so-called noble and good is by its very nature the reverse of itself, or that what is bad is, conversely, something excellent.

If the naïve consciousness makes up for this barren, soulless idea by the concrete reality of what is excellent, by adducing an example of what is excellent, whether in the form of a fictitious case or a true story, and thus shows it to be not an empty name, but an actual fact, then it has against it the universal reality of the perverted action of the entire real world, where that example constitutes merely something quite isolated and particular, merely an *espèce*, a *sort* of thing. And to represent the existence of the good and the noble as an isolated particular anecdote, whether fictitious or true, is the bitterest thing that can be said about it.

Finally, should the naïve mind require this entire sphere of perversion to be dissolved and broken up, it cannot ask the individual to withdraw out of it, for even Diogenes in his tub [with his pretence of withdrawal] is under the sway of that perversion; and to ask this of the particular individual is to ask him to do precisely what is taken to be bad, viz. to care for himself as individual. But if the demand to withdraw is directed at the universal individual, it cannot mean that reason must again give up the culture and development of spiritual conscious life which it has reached, that reason should let the extensive riches of its moments sink back into the *naïveté* of natural emotion, and revert and approximate to the wild condition of the animal consciousness, which is also called the natural state of innocence. On the contrary, the demand for this dissolution can only be addressed to the spirit of culture itself, and can only mean that it must *qua* spirit return out of its confusion into itself, and win for itself a still higher level of conscious life.

In point of fact, however, spirit has already accomplished this result. To be conscious of its own distraught and torn condition and to express itself accordingly,—this is to pour scornful laughter on existence, on the confusion pervading the whole and on itself as well: it is at the same time this whole confusion dying away and yet apprehending itself to be doing so. This self-apprehending vanity of all reality and of every definite principle reflects the real world into itself in a twofold form: in the

particular self of consciousness *qua* particular, and in the pure universality of consciousness, in thought. According to the first aspect, mind
thus come to itself has directed its gaze into the world of actual reality,
and still has that reality as its own purpose and its immediate content:
from the other side, its gaze is in part turned solely on itself and against
that world of reality, in part turned away from it towards heaven, and its
object is the region beyond the world.

In respect of that return into self the vanity of all things is its own peculiar vanity, it is itself vain. It is self existing for its own sake, a self that
knows not only how to sum up and chatter about everything, but cleverly
to state the contradiction that lies in the heart of the solid elements of reality, and in the fixed determinations which judgment sets up; and this
contradiction is their real truth. Looked at formally it knows everything
to be estranged from itself; self-existence is cut off from essential being
(*Ansich*), what is intended and the purpose are separated from real truth,
and from both again existence for another, what is ostensibly put forward
is cut off from the proper meaning, the real fact, the true intention.

It thus knows exactly how to put each moment in antithesis to every
other, knows in short how to express correctly the perversion that dominates all of them: it knows better than each what each is, no matter
how it is constituted. Since it apprehends what is substantial from the
side of that disunion and contradiction of elements combined within
its nature, but not from the side of this union itself, it understands very
well how to pass judgment on this substantial reality, but has lost the
capacity of truly grasping it. Its ultimate unity

This vanity needs at the same time the vanity of all things, in order
to get from them consciousness of itself; it therefore itself creates this
vanity, and is the soul that supports it. State-power and wealth are the
supreme purposes of its strenuous exertion, it is aware that through renunciation and sacrifice it is moulded into universal shape, that it attains universality, and in possessing universality finds general recognition and acceptance: state-power and wealth are the real and actually
acknowledged forms of power. But its gaining acceptance thus is itself
vain, and just by the fact that it gets the mastery over them it knows
them to be not real by themselves, knows rather itself to be the power
within them, and them to be vain and empty. That in possessing them
it thus itself is able to stand apart from and outside them—this is what
it expresses in witty phrases; and to express this is, therefore, its supreme
interest, and the true meaning of the whole process. In such utterance
this self—in the form of a pure self not associated with or bound by determinations derived either from reality or thought—comes consciously to be a spiritual entity having a truly universal significance and
value. It is the condition in which the nature of all relationships is rent

asunder, and it is the conscious rending of them all. But only by self-consciousness being roused to revolt does it know its own peculiar torn and shattered condition; and in its knowing this it has *ipso facto* risen above that condition. In that state of self-conscious vanity all substantial content comes to have a negative significance, which can no longer be taken in a positive sense. The positive object is merely the pure ego itself; and the consciousness that is rent in sunder is inherently and essentially this pure self-identity of self-consciousness returned to itself.

b

BELIEF AND PURE INSIGHT[1]

THE spiritual condition of self-estrangement exists in the sphere of culture as a fact. But since this whole has become estranged from itself, there lies beyond this sphere the nonactual realm of pure consciousness, of thought. Its content consists of what has been reduced purely to thought, its absolute element is thinking. Since, however, thinking is in the first instance the *element* of this world, consciousness *has* merely these thoughts, but it does not as yet *think* them or does not know that they are thoughts: to consciousness they appear in the form of presentations, they are objects in the form of ideas. For it comes out of the sphere of actuality into that of pure consciousness, but is itself still to all intents and purposes in the sphere of actuality with the determinateness that implies. The conscious state of contrition and abasement is still essentially and inherently the self-identity of pure consciousness, not as a fact that *itself* is aware of but only as presented to *us* who are considering its condition. It has thus not as yet completed within itself the process of spiritual exaltation, it is simply there; and it still has within itself the opposite principle by which it is conditioned, without as yet having become master of that principle through the mediating process. Hence the essential content of its thought is not taken to be an essential object merely in the form of abstract immanence (*Ansich*), but in the form of a common object, an object that has merely been elevated into another element, without having lost the character of an object that is not constituted by thought.

It is essentially distinct from the immanent nature which constitutes the essential being of the stoic type of consciousness. The significant factor for Stoicism was merely the form of thought as such, which has

---

[1]The contrast between these two elements is found both in the pre-Reformation period and in the eighteenth-century period; in the latter the contrast assumes perhaps its acutest form.

any content foreign to it that is drawn from actuality. In the case of the consciousness just described, however, it is not the form of thought which counts. Similarly it is essentially distinct from the inherent principle of the virtuous type of conscious life; here the essential fact stands, no doubt, in a relation to reality; it is the essence of reality itself: but it is no more than an unrealized essence of it. In the above type of consciousness the essence, although no doubt beyond reality, stands all the same for an actual real essence. In the same way, the inherently right and good which reason as lawgiver establishes, and the universal operating—when consciousness tests and examines laws—neither of these has the character of actual reality.

Hence while pure thought fell within the sphere of spiritual culture as an aspect of the estrangement characteristic of this sphere, as the standard, in fact, for judging abstract good and abstract bad, it has become enriched, by having gone through the process of the whole, with the element of reality and thereby with content. This reality of its essential being, however, is at the same time merely a reality of pure consciousness, not of concrete actual consciousness: it is no doubt lifted into the element of thought, but this concrete consciousness does not yet take it for a thought; it is beyond the reality peculiar to this consciousness, for it means flight from the latter.

In the form in which Religion here appears—for it is religion obviously that we are speaking about—as the belief which belongs to the realm of culture, religion does not yet appear as it is truly and completely (an und für sich). It has already come before us in other phases, viz. as the unhappy consciousness, as a form of conscious process with no substantial content in it. So, too, in the case of the ethical substance, it appeared as a belief in the nether-world. But a consciousness of the departed spirit is, strictly speaking, not belief, not the inner essence subsisting in the element of pure consciousness away beyond the actual: there the belief has itself an immediate existence in the present; its element is the family.

But at the stage we are now considering, religion is in part the outcome of the substance, and is the pure consciousness of that substance; in part this pure consciousness is alienated from its concrete actual consciousness, the essence from its existence. It is thus doubtless no longer the insubstantial process of consciousness; but it has still the characteristic of opposition to actuality qua this actuality in general, and of opposition to the actuality of self-consciousness in particular. It is essentially, therefore, merely a belief.

This pure consciousness of Absolute Being is a consciousness in estrangement. Let us see more closely what is the characteristic of that whose other it is; we can only consider it in connexion with this other.

In the first instance this pure consciousness seems to have over against it merely the world of actuality. But since its nature is to flee from this actuality, and thereby is characterized by opposition, it has this actuality inherent within its own being; pure consciousness is, therefore, essentially in its very being self-alienated, and belief constitutes merely one side of it. The other side has already arisen too. For pure consciousness is reflexion out of the world of culture in such a way that the substantial content of this sphere, as also the separate areas into which it falls, are shown to be what they inherently are—essential modes of spiritual life, absolutely restless processes or determinate moments which are at once cancelled in their opposite. Their essential nature, bare consciousness, is thus the bare simplicity of absolute distinction, distinction which as it stands is no distinction. Consequently it is pure self-existence not of this single self, but essentially universal self, whose being consists in a restless process invading and pervading the stable existence of actual fact. In it is thus found the certainty that knows itself at once as the truth: there we have pure thought in the sense of absolute notion with all its power of negativity, which annihilates every objective existence that would claim to stand over against consciousness, and turns it into a form of conscious existence.

This pure consciousness is at the same time simple and undifferentiated as well, just because its distinction is no distinction. Being this form of bare and simple reflexion into self, however, it is the element of belief, in which spirit has the character of positive universality, of what is inherent and essential in contrast with that self-existence of self-consciousness.

Forced back upon itself away from this unsubstantial world whose being is mere dissolution, spirit when we consider its true meaning is, in undivided unity, at once the absolute movement, the ceaseless process of negating its appearance, as well as the essential substance thereof satisfied within itself, and the positive stability of that process. But, bearing as they inherently do the characteristic of alienation, these two moments fall apart in the shape of a twofold consciousness. The former is pure Insight, the spiritual process concentrated and focussed in self-consciousness, a process which has over against it the consciousness of something positive, the form of objectivity or presentation, and which directs itself against this presented object. The proper and peculiar object of this insight is, however, merely pure ego.[2] The bare consciousness of the positive element, of unbroken self-identity, finds its object, on the other hand, in the inner reality as such.

Pure insight has, therefore, in the first instance, no content within it,

---

[2]Kant: "Pure ego is the absolute unity of apperception."

because it exists for itself by negating everything in it; to belief, on the other hand, belongs the content, but without insight. While the former does not get away from self-consciousness, the latter to be sure has its content as well in the element of pure self-consciousness, but only in thought, not in conceptions—in pure consciousness, not in pure self-consciousness. Belief is, as a fact, in this way pure consciousness of the essential reality, i.e. of the bare and simple inner nature, and is thus *thought*—the primary factor in the nature of belief, which is generally overlooked.[3] The immediateness which characterizes the presence of the essential reality within it is due to the fact that its object is essence, inner nature, i.e. pure thought.[4] This immediateness, however, so far as thinking enters consciousness, or pure consciousness enters into self-consciousness, acquires the significance of an objective being that lies beyond consciousness of self. It is because of the significance which immediacy and simplicity of pure thought thus acquire in consciousness that the essential reality, the object of belief, drops into being an imaginatively presented idea (*Vorstellung*), instead of being the content of thought, and comes to be looked at as a supersensible world, which is essentially an "other" than self-consciousness.

In the case of pure insight, on the other hand, the passage of pure thought into consciousness has the opposite character: objectivity has the significance of a content that is merely negative, that cancels itself and returns into the self; that is to say, only the self is properly object to self, or, to put it otherwise, the object only has truth so far as it has the form of self.

As belief and pure insight fall in common within pure consciousness, they also in common involve the mind's return out of the concrete sphere of spiritual culture. There are three aspects, therefore, from which they show what they are. In one aspect each is outside every relation, and has a being all its own; in another each takes up an attitude towards the concrete actual world standing in antithesis to pure consciousness; while in the third form each is related to the other inside pure consciousness.

In the case of belief the aspect of complete being, of being in-and-for-itself, is its absolute object, whose content and character we have already come to know. For it lies in the very notion of belief that this object is nothing else than the real world lifted into the universality of pure consciousness. The articulation of this world, therefore, constitutes the organization belonging to pure universality also, except that the parts in the latter case do not alienate one another when spiritual-

---

[3]"Belief is a kind of knowledge."—*Encycl.*: §554.
[4]Kant: "I am the essential reality when conscious of myself in pure thought."

ized, but are complete realities all by themselves, are spirits[5] returned into themselves and self-contained.

The process of their transition from one into the other is, therefore, only for us [who are analysing the process] an alienation of the characteristic nature in which their distinction lies, and only for us, the observers, does it constitute a necessary series; for belief, however, their distinction is a static diversity, and their movement simply a historical fact.

To deal shortly with the external character of their form: as in the world of culture state-power or the good was primary, so here the first and foremost moment is Absolute Being, spirit absolutely self-contained, so far as it is simple eternal substance.[6] But in the process of realizing its constitutive notion, which consists in being spirit, that substance passes over into a form where it exists for an other; its self-identity becomes actual Absolute Being, actualized in self-sacrifice; it becomes a self, but a self that is transitory and passes away.[7] Hence the third stage is the return of self thus alienated, the substance thus abased, into its first primal simplicity. Only when this is done is spirit presented and manifested as spirit.[8]

These distinct ultimate Realities, when brought back by thought into themselves out of the flux of the actual world, are changeless, eternal spirits, whose being lies in thinking the unity which they constitute. While thus torn away from self-consciousness, these Realities all the same lay hold on it; for if the Ultimate Reality were to be fixed and unmoved in the form of the first bare and simple substance, it would remain alien to self-consciousness. But the laying aside, the "emptying," of this substance, and afterwards its spirit, involves the element of concrete actuality, and thereby participates in the believing self-consciousness, or the believing attitude of consciousness belongs to the real world.

According to this second condition, the believing type of consciousness partly finds its actuality in the real world of culture, and constitutes its spirit and its existence, which have been described; partly, however, belief takes up an attitude of opposition to this its own actuality, looks on this as something vain, and is the process of cancelling and transcending it. This process does not consist in the believing consciousness making witty remarks about the perverted condition of that reality; for it is the naïve simple consciousness, which reckons *esprit* and wit as

---

[5]The "persons" of the "Trinity."
[6]God transcendent, God as Substance, God the Father.
[7]The God-man, Christ.
[8]God as Absolute Spirit, God the Holy Ghost.

emptiness and vanity, because this still has the real world for its purpose. On the contrary, in opposition to its placid realm of thought
stands concrete actuality as a soulless form of existence, which on that
account has to be overcome in external fashion. This obedience
through service and praise, by cancelling sense-knowledge and action,
produces the consciousness of unity with the self-complete and self-
existing Being, though not in the sense of an actual perceived unity.
This service is merely the incessant process of producing the sense of
unity, a process that never completely reaches its goal in the actual present. The religious communion no doubt does so, for it is universal self-
consciousness. But for the individual self-consciousness the realm of
pure thought necessarily remains something away beyond its actuality;
or, again, since this remote region by the emptying, the "kenosis," of
the eternal Being, has entered the sphere of actuality, its actuality is
sensuous, uncomprehended. But one sensuous actuality is ever indifferent and external to another, and what lies beyond has thus only received the further character of remoteness in space and time. The
essential notion, however—the concrete actuality of spirit directly present to itself—remains for belief an inner principle, which is all and
effects all, but never itself comes to the light.

In the case of pure insight, however, the concept, the essential notion (*Begriff*), is alone the real; and this third aspect of belief—that of
being an object for pure insight—is the specific relation in which belief here appears. Pure insight itself has like belief to be considered
partly by itself (*an und für sich*), partly in relation to the real world—so
far as the real world is still present in positive shape, viz. in the form of
a vain consciousness—and lastly in that relation to belief just
mentioned.

We have already seen what pure insight by itself is. Belief is unperturbed pure consciousness of spirit as the essentially real; pure insight
is the self-consciousness of spirit as the essentially real; it knows the essentially real, therefore, not *qua* essence but *qua* Absolute Self. Its aim
thus is to cancel every kind of independence which falls without self-
consciousness, whether that be the independence of the actually objective or of the inherently real, and to mould it into conceptual form.
It not merely is the certainty of self-conscious reason assured of being
all truth; it knows that it is so.

In the form, however, in which the notion of pure insight meets us
first, it is not yet realized. As a phase of consciousness it appears in consequence as something contingent, as something isolated and particular, and its inmost constitutive nature appears as some purpose that it
has to carry out and realize. It has to begin with the *intention* of
making pure insight universal, i.e. of making everything that is actual

into a notion, and one and the same notion for every self-consciousness.[9] The intention is pure, for its content is pure insight; and this insight is similarly pure, for its content is solely the absolute notion, which finds no opposition in an object, and is not restricted in itself. In the unrestricted notion there are found at once both the aspects—that everything objective is to signify only the self-existent, self-consciousness, and that this is to signify something universal, that pure insight is to be the property of all self-consciousnesses. This second feature of the intention is so far a result of culture, in that in culture both the distinctions of objective spirit, the parts and express determinations of its world, have come to naught, as well as the distinctions which appeared as originally determinate natures. Genius, talent, special capacities one and all, belong to the world of actuality, in so far as this world contains still the aspect of being a herd of self-conscious individuals, where, in confusion and mutual violence, individuals cheat and struggle with one another over the contents of the real world.

The above distinctions doubtless have no place in it as genuine *espèces*. Individuality neither is contented with unreal "fact," nor has special content and purposes of its own. It counts merely as something universally acknowledged and accepted, viz. *qua* cultivated and developed; and the fact of distinction is reduced to a matter of less or more energy, a distinction of quantity, i.e. a non-essential distinction. This last difference, however, has come to nothing, by the fact that the distinction in the state where consciousness was completely torn asunder, turned round into an absolutely qualitative distinction. What is there the other for the ego is merely the ego itself. In this infinite judgment all the one-sidedness and peculiarity of the original self-existing self is extinguished; the self knows itself *qua* pure self to be its own object; and this absolute identity of both sides is the element of pure insight.

Pure insight, therefore, is the simple ultimate being undifferentiated within itself, and at the same time the universal achievement and result and a universal possession of all. In this simple spiritual substance self-consciousness gives itself and maintains for itself in every object the sense of this its own individual being or of action, just as conversely the individuality of self-consciousness is there identical with itself and universal.

This pure insight is, then, the spirit that calls to every consciousness: be *for* yourselves what you are all essentially *in* yourselves—rational.

---

[9] "Kant's philosophy is the enlightenment adapted so as to become a philosophical method."—Hegel, W.W. 15, p. 502.

II

ENLIGHTENMENT[1]

THE peculiar object against which pure insight directs the active force of the notion is belief, this being a form of pure consciousness like itself and yet opposed to it in that element. But at the same time pure insight has a relation to the actual world, for, like belief, it is a return from the actual world into pure consciousness. We have first of all to see how its activity is constituted as operating against the impure motives and the perverted forms of insight found in the actual world.[2]

We have touched already on the placid type of consciousness, which stands in contrast to this turmoil of alternate self-dissolution and self-recreation; it constitutes the aspect of pure insight and intention. This unperturbed consciousness, however, as we saw, has no special insight regarding the sphere of culture. The latter has itself rather the most painful feeling, and the truest insight about itself—the feeling that everything made secure crumbles to pieces, that every limb of its existence is wracked and rent, and every bone broken: moreover, it consciously expresses this feeling in words, pronounces judgment and gives sparkling utterance concerning all aspects of its condition. Pure insight, therefore, can have here no activity and content of its own, and thus can only take up the attitude of formally and truly apprehending this witty insight peculiar to the world and the language it adopts. Since this language is a scattered and broken utterance and the pronouncement a fickle mood of the moment, which is again quickly forgotten, and is only known to be a whole by a third consciousness, this latter can be distinguished as pure insight only if it gathers those several scattered traces into a universal picture, and then makes them the insight of all.

By this simple means pure insight will resolve the confusion of this world. For we have found that the areas and determinate conceptions and individualities are not the essential nature of this actuality, but that it finds its substance and support alone in the spirit which exists *qua* judging and discussing, and that the interest of having a content for this ratiocination and parleying to deal with alone preserves the whole and the areas of its articulation. In this language which insight adopts, its self-consciousness is still this isolated individual, a self existing for itself; but the emptiness of its content is at the same time emptiness of the self knowing that content to be vain and empty. Now, when the consciousness placidly apprehending all these sparkling utterances of vanity

---

[1]Enlightenment (*Aufklärung*) is the universalization of the principle of "pure insight," and hence is logically the outcome of the preceding analysis.
[2]Cf. pp. 305 ff.

makes a collection of the most striking and penetrating phrases, the soul that still preserves the whole, the vanity of witty criticism, goes to ruin with the other form of vanity, the previous vanity of existence. The collection shows most people a better wit, or at least shows every one a more varied wit than their own, and shows that "knowing-better" and "judging" generally are something universal and are now universally familiar. Thereby the sole and only surviving interest is done away with; and individual light is resolved into universal insight.

Still, however, knowledge of essential reality stands secure above vain and empty knowledge; and pure insight only appears in genuinely active form in so far as it enters into conflict with belief.

a

THE STRUGGLE OF ENLIGHTENMENT WITH SUPERSTITION[1]

THE various negative forms which consciousness adopts, the attitude of scepticism, and that of theoretical and practical idealism, are inferior attitudes compared with that of pure insight and the expansion of pure insight—enlightenment; for pure insight is born of the substance of spirit, it knows the pure self of consciousness to be absolute, and enters into conflict with the pure consciousness of the Absolute Being of all reality.

Since belief and insight are the same pure consciousness, but in form are opposed—the reality in the case of belief being a thought, not a notion, and hence something absolutely opposed to self-consciousness, while the reality in the case of pure insight is the self—they are such that *inter se* the one is the absolute negative of the other.

As appearing the one against the other, all content falls to belief; for in its unperturbed element of thought every moment obtains definite subsistence. Pure insight, however, is in the first instance without any content; it is rather the sheer disappearance of content; but by its negative attitude towards what it excludes it will make itself real and give itself a content.

It knows belief to be opposed to insight, opposed to reason and truth. Just as, for it, belief is in general a tissue of superstitious prejudices and errors; so it further sees the consciousness embracing this content organized into a realm of error, in which false insight is the general sphere of consciousness, immediate, naïvely unperturbed, and inherently unreflective. Yet all the while this false insight does have within

---

[1] "We live in an age of enlightenment" (Kant). Cp. Hegel W. W. 15 introduction to "French Philosophy."

it the moment of self-reflexion, the moment of self-consciousness, separated from its simple *naïveté*, and keeps this reflexion in the background as an insight remaining by itself, and as an evil intention by which that former conscious state is befooled. That mental sphere is the victim of the deception of a Priesthood, which carries out its envious vain conceit of being alone in possession of insight, and carries out its other selfish ends as well. At the same time this priesthood conspires with Despotism, which takes up the attitude of being the synthetic crude (*begrifflos*) unity of the real and this ideal kingdom—a singularly amorphous and inconsistent type of being—and stands above the bad insight of the multitude, and the bad intention of the priests, and even combines both of these within itself. As the result of the stupidity and confusion produced amongst the people by the agency of priestly deception, despotism despises both and draws for itself the advantage of undisturbed control and the fulfilment of its lusts, its humours, and its whims. Yet at the same time it is itself in this same state of murky insight, is equally superstition and error.

Enlightenment does not attack these three forms of the enemy without distinction. For since its essential nature is pure insight, which is *per se* universal, its true relation to the other extreme is that in which it is concerned with the common and identical element in both. The aspect of individual existence isolating itself from the universal naïve consciousness is the antithesis of it, and cannot be directly affected by it. The will of the deceiving priesthood and the oppressive despot is, therefore, not primarily the object on which it directs its activity; its object is the insight that is without will and without individualized isolated self-existence, the notion (*Begriff*) of rational self-consciousness, which has its existence in the total conscious area, but is not yet there in the fullness of its true meaning (*Begriff*). Since, however, pure insight rescues this genuinely honest form of insight, with its naïve simplicity of nature, from prejudices and errors, it wrests from the hands of bad intention the effective realization of its powers of deception, for whose realm the incoherent and undeveloped (*begrifflos*) consciousness of the general area provides the basis and raw material, while the self-existence of each power finds its substance in the simple consciousness.

The relation of pure insight to the naïve consciousness of absolute Being has now a double aspect. On one side pure insight is inherently one and the same with it. On the other side, however, this naïve consciousness lets absolute Being as well as its parts dispose themselves at will in the simple element of its thought, and subsist there, and lets them hold only as its inherent nature and hence hold good in objective form. In accepting this inherent nature it disowns, however, its own independent existence. In so far as, according to the first aspect, this belief is for pure insight inherently and essentially pure self-consciousness, and has merely to become so expressly for itself, pure insight finds in this constitutive notion of belief the element in which, in place of false insight, it realizes itself.

Since, from this point of view, both are essentially the same, and the relation of pure insight takes effect through and in the same element, the communication between them is direct and immediate, and their give and take an unbroken interfusion. Whatever pins and bolts may be otherwise driven into consciousness, it is in itself this simplicity of nature in which everything is resolved, forgotten, and unconstrained, and which, therefore, is absolutely receptive to the activity of the notion. The communication of pure insight is on that account comparable to a silent extension or the expansion, say, of a scent in the unresisting atmosphere. It is a penetrating infection, which did not previously make itself noticeable as something distinct from and opposed to the indifferent medium into which it insinuates its way, and hence cannot be averted. Only when the infection has become widespread is that consciousness alive to it, which unconcernedly yielded to its influence. For what this consciousness received into itself was doubtless something simple, homogeneous, and uniform throughout it, but was at the same time the simplicity of self-reflected negativity, which later on also develops by its nature into something opposed, and thereby reminds consciousness of its previous state. This simple uniformity is the notion, which is simple knowledge that knows both itself and its opposite, this opposite being, however, cancelled as opposite within the self-knowledge of the notion. In the condition, therefore, in which consciousness becomes aware of pure insight, this insight is already widespread. The struggle with it betrays the fact that the infection has done its work. The struggle is too late; and every means taken merely makes the disease worse; for the disease has seized the very marrow of spiritual life, viz. consciousness in its ultimate principle (*Begriff*), or its pure inmost nature itself. There is therefore no power left in conscious life to surmount the disease. Because it affects the very inmost being, it manifestations, so long as they remain isolated, are repressed and subside and its superficial symptoms are smothered. This is immensely to its advantage; for it does not now squander its power in useless fashion, nor does it show itself unworthy of its true nature—which is the case when it breaks out into symptoms and isolated eruptions antithetic to the content of belief and to the connexion of its external reality. Rather, being now an invisible and unperceived spirit, it insinuates its way through and through the noble parts, and soon has got complete hold over all the vitals and members of the unconscious idol; and then "some fine morning it gives its comrade a shove with the elbow, when, bash! crash!—and the idol is lying on the floor."[2] On some "fine morning," whose noon is not red with blood, if the infection has penetrated to every organ of spiritual life. It is then the memory alone that still preserves the dead form of the spirit's previous state, as a vanished history, vanished men know not how. And the new serpent of wisdom, raised on high before bending worshippers, has in this manner painlessly sloughed merely a shrivelled skin.

But this silent steady working of the loom of spirit in the inner region of its substance,[3] spirit's own action being hidden from itself, is merely one side of the realizing of pure insight. Its expansion does not only consist in like combining with like; and its realization is not merely an unresisted expansion. The action of the principle of negation is just as essentially a developed process of self-distinction, which, being a conscious action, must set forth its moments in a definitely manifested expression, and must make its appearance in the form of a great noise, and a violent struggle with an opposite as such.

We have, therefore, to see how pure insight and pure intention manifests its negative attitude towards that other which it finds standing opposed to it.

Pure insight and intention, operating negatively, can only be—since its very principle is all essentiality and there is nothing outside it—the negative of itself. As insight, therefore, it passes into the negative of pure insight, it becomes untruth and unreason; and as intention it passes into the negative of pure intention, becomes a lie and sordid impurity of purpose.

It involves itself in this contradiction by the fact that it engages in a strife and thinks to do battle with some alien external other. It merely imagines this, for its nature as absolute negativity lies in having that otherness within its own self. The absolute notion is the category; it is the principle that knowledge and the object of knowledge are the same. In consequence, what pure insight expresses as its other, what it pronounces to be an error or a lie, can be nothing else than its own self; it can only condemn what itself is. What is not rational has no truth, or what is not comprehended through a notion, conceptually determined, *is* not. When reason thus speaks of some other than itself is, it in fact speaks merely of itself; it does not therein go beyond itself.

This struggle with the opposite, therefore, combines in its meaning the significance of being insight's own actualization. This consists just in the process of unfolding its moments and taking them back into it-

---

[2]*Rameau's Neffe.*
[3]In the life of "feeling" and "emotion."

self. One part of this process is the making of the distinction in which the insight of reason opposes itself as object to itself; so long as it remains in this condition, it is at variance with itself. *Qua* pure insight it is without any content; the process of its realization consists in itself becoming content to itself; for no other can be made its content, because it is the category become self-conscious. But since this insight in the first instance thinks of the content as in its opposite, and knows the content merely as a content, and does not as yet think of it as its own self, pure insight misconceives itself in it. The complete attainment of insight, therefore, has the sense of a process of coming to know that content as its own, which was to begin with opposite to itself. Its result, however, will be thereby neither the reestablishment of the errors it fights with, nor merely its original notion, but an insight which knows the absolute negation of itself to be its own proper reality, to be its self, or an insight which is its self-understanding notion.

This feature of the struggle of enlightenment with errors—that of fighting itself in them, and of condemning that in them which it asserts—this is something for us who observe the process, or is what enlightenment and its struggle are in themselves implicitly. The first aspect of this struggle, however—the contamination and defilement of enlightenment through its pure self-identity accepting the attitude and function of destructive negation—this is how belief looks upon it; belief finds it simply lying unreason and malicious intent, just as enlightenment in the same way regards belief as error and prejudice.

As regards its content, it is in the first instance empty insight, whose content appears an external other to it. It meets this content, consequently, in the shape of something not yet its own, as something that exists quite independent of it, and is found in belief.

Enlightenment, then, conceives its object in the first instance and generally in such a way as to take it as pure insight, and failing to recognize itself there, interprets it as error. In insight as such consciousness apprehends an object in such a manner that it becomes the inner being of conscious life, or becomes an object which consciousness permeates, in which consciousness maintains itself, keeps within itself, and is present to itself, and, by its thus being the process of that object, brings the object into being. It is precisely this which enlightenment rightly declares belief to be, when enlightenment says that the Absolute Reality professed by belief is a being that comes from belief's own consciousness, is its own thought, something produced from and by consciousness.[4] Enlightenment, consequently, explains and declares it to

---

[4] Cp. the view of God held by Fichte: also Feuerbach:—*Wesen der Religion*.

be error, to be a made-up invention about the very same thing as enlightenment itself is.

Enlightenment that seeks to teach belief this new wisdom does not, in doing so, tell it anything new. For the object of belief itself is just this too, viz. a pure essential reality of its own peculiar consciousness; so that this consciousness does not put itself down for lost and negated in that object, but rather puts trust in it; and this just means that it finds itself there as this particular consciousness, finds itself therein to be self-consciousness. If I put my trust in anyone, his certitude of himself is for me the certitude of myself; I know my self-existence in him, I know that he acknowledges it, and that it is for him both his purpose and his real nature. Belief, however, is trust, because the believing consciousness has a direct relation to its object, and thus sees at once that it is one with the object, and in the object.

Further, since what is object for me is something in which I know myself, I am at the same time in that object really in the form of another self-consciousness, i.e. one which has become in that object alienated from its own particular individuation, from its natural and contingent existence, but which partly continues therein to be self-consciousness, and partly is there an essential consciousness just like pure insight.

In the notion of insight there lies not merely this, that consciousness knows itself in the object it looks at, and finds itself directly there, without first quitting the thought element and then returning into itself; the notion implies as well that consciousness is aware of itself as being also the mediating process, aware of itself as active, as the agency of production. Through this it gets the thought of this unity of self as self and object.

Belief also is this very consciousness. Obedience and action make a necessary moment, through which the certainty of existence in Absolute Being comes about. This action of belief does not indeed make it appear as if Absolute Being is itself produced thereby. But the Absolute Being for belief is essentially not the abstract being that lies beyond the believing consciousness; it is the spirit of the religious communion, it is the unity of that abstract being and self-consciousness. The action of the communion is an essential moment in bringing about that it is this spirit of the communion. That spirit is what it is by the productive activity of consciousness, or rather it does not exist without being produced by consciousness. For essential as this process of production is, it is as truly not the only basis of Absolute Being; it is merely a moment. The Absolute Being is at the same time self-complete and self-contained (*an und für sich selbst*).

On the other side the notion of pure insight is seen to be something else than its own object; for just this negative character constitutes the object. Thus from the other side it also expresses the ultimate Being of belief as something foreign to self-consciousness, something that is not a bone of its bone, but is surreptitiously foisted on it like a changeling child. But here enlightenment is entirely foolish; belief experiences it as a way of speaking which does not know what it is saying, and does not understand the facts of the case when it talks about priestly deception, and deluding the people. It speaks about this as if by means of some hocus-pocus of conjuring priestcraft there were foisted on consciousness as true Reality something that is absolutely foreign, and absolutely alien to it; and yet says all the while that this is an essential reality for consciousness, that consciousness believes in it, trusts in it, and seeks to make it favourably disposed towards itself, i.e. that consciousness therein sees its pure ultimate Being just as much as its own single and universal individuality, and creates by its own action this unity of itself with its essential reality. In other words, it directly declares that to be the very inmost nature of consciousness which it declares to be something alien to consciousness.

How, then, can it possibly speak about deception and delusion? By the fact that it directly expresses about belief the very opposite of what it asserts of belief, it *ipso facto* really reveals itself to belief as the conscious lie. How are deception and delusion to take place, where consciousness in its very truth has directly and immediately the certitude of itself, where it possesses itself in its object, since it just as much finds as produces itself there? The distinction no longer exists, even in words.

When the general question has been raised, whether it is permissible to delude a people, the answer, as a fact, was bound to be that the question is pointless, because it is impossible to deceive a people in this matter. Brass in place of gold, counterfeit instead of genuine coin may doubtless have swindled individuals many a time; lots of people have stuck to it that a battle lost was a battle won; and lies of all sorts about things of sense and particular events have been plausible for a time; but in the knowledge of that inmost reality where consciousness finds the direct certainty of its own self, the idea of delusion is entirely baseless.

Let us see further how belief undergoes enlightenment in the case of the different moments of its own conscious experience, to which the view just noted referred in the first instance only in a general way. These moments are pure thought, or, *qua* object, absolute Being *per se* (*an und für sich*); then its relation, as a form of knowledge, to absolute Being, the ultimate basis of its belief; and finally its relation to absolute Being in its acts, i.e. its "worship" and service.[5] Just as pure insight has

---

[5]Enlightenment attacks the *object* and the *basis* of belief, and the mode of *worship*.

failed to recognize itself in belief as a whole and denied its own nature, we shall find it taking up in these moments, too, an attitude similarly perverted and distorted.

Pure insight assumes towards the absolute Being of the believing mind a negative attitude. This Being is pure thought, and pure thought established within itself as object or as the true Being; in the believing consciousness this immanent and essential reality of thought acquires at the same time for the self-existent consciousness the form of objectivity, but merely the empty form; it exists in the character of something "presented" to consciousness. To pure insight, however, since it is pure consciousness in its aspect of self existing for itself, this other appears as something negative of self-consciousness. This might still be taken either as the pure essential reality of thought, or also as the being found in sense-experience, the object of sense-certainty. But since it is at the same time for the self, and this self, *qua* self which has an object, is an actual consciousness, for insight the peculiar object as such is an ordinary existing thing of sense. This its object appears before it in the picture-presentation found in belief. It condemns this idea and in doing so condemns its own proper object. It really commits a wrong, however, against belief in so apprehending the object of belief as if it were its own object. Accordingly it states regarding belief that its absolute Being is a piece of stone, a block of wood, having eyes and seeing not, or again a bit of bread-dough, which is obtained from grain grown on the field and transformed by men and is returned to earth again; or in whatever other ways belief may be said to anthropomorphize absolute Being, making it objective and representable.

Enlightenment, proclaiming itself as the pure and true, here turns what is held to be eternal life and holy spirit into a concrete passing thing of sense, and contaminates it with what belongs to sense-certainty—with an aspect inherently worthless and one which is not to be found at all in the worshiping attitude of belief, so that enlightenment simply calumniates it by introducing such an aspect. What belief reveres is for belief assuredly neither stone nor wood, nor bread-dough, nor any other sort of thing of time and sense. If enlightenment thinks it worth while to say its object all the same is this *as well*, or even that it is this in its inherent nature and in truth, then belief also knows that something which it is "as well," but for it this something lies outside its worship; on the other hand, however, belief does not look on such things as stones, etc., as having an inherent and essential being at all, the essential nature as grasped by pure thought is alone for it something inherently real.

The second moment is the relation of belief as a form of knowing consciousness to this ultimate Being. As pure thinking consciousness belief has this Being immediately before it. But pure consciousness is just as much a mediate relation of conscious certainty to truth, a relation constituting the ground of belief. For enlightenment this ground comes similarly to be regarded as a chance knowledge of chance occurrences. The ground of knowledge, however, is the conscious universal, and in its ultimate meaning is absolute spirit, which in abstract pure consciousness, or thought as such, is merely absolute Being, but *qua* self-consciousness is the knowledge of itself. Pure insight treats this conscious universal, self-knowing spirit pure and simple, likewise as an element negative of self-consciousness. Doubtless this insight is itself pure mediate thought, i.e. thought mediating itself with itself, it is pure knowledge; but since it is pure insight, or pure knowledge, which does not yet know itself, i.e. for which as yet there is no awareness that it is this pure process of mediation, this process seems to insight, like everything else constituting it, to be something external, an other. When realizing its inherent principle, then, it develops this moment essential to it; but that moment seems to it to belong to belief, and to be, in its character of an external other, a fortuitous knowledge of stories of "real" events in this ordinary sense of "real." It thus here charges religious belief with basing its certainty on some particular historical evidences, which, considered as historical evidences, would assuredly not even warrant that degree of certainty about the matter which we get regarding any event mentioned in the newspapers. It further makes the imputation that the certainty in the case of religious belief rests on the accidental fact of the preservation of all this evidence: on the preservation of this evidence partly by means of paper, and partly through the skill and honesty in transferring what is written from one paper to another, and lastly rests upon the accurate interpretation of the sense of dead words and letters. As a matter of fact, however, it never occurs to belief to make its certainty depend on such evidences and such fortuitous circumstances. Belief in its conscious assurance occupies a naïve unsophisticated attitude towards its absolute object, knows it with a purity, which never mixes up letters, paper, or copyists with its consciousness of the Absolute Being, and does not make use of things of that sort to affect its union with the Absolute. On the contrary, this consciousness is the self-mediating, self-relating ground of its knowledge; it is spirit itself which bears witness of itself both in the inner heart of the individual consciousness, as well as through the presence everywhere and in all men of belief in it. If belief wants to appeal to historical evidences in order to get also that kind of foundation, or at least confirmation, for its content which enlightenment speaks of, and is really serious in thinking and acting as if that were an important matter, then it has *eo ipso* allowed itself to be corrupted and led astray by the insinuations of enlightenment; the efforts it makes to secure a basis or support in this way are merely indications that show how it has been affected and infected by enlightenment.

There still remains the third aspect, the active relation of consciousness to Absolute Being, its forms of service.[6] This action consists in cancelling the particularity of the individual, or the natural form of its self-existence, whence arises its certainty of being pure self-consciousness, of being, as the result of its action, i.e. as a self-existing conscious individual, one with ultimate Reality.

Since in this action purposiveness and end are distinguished, and pure insight likewise takes up a negative attitude towards this action, and denies itself just as it did in the other moments, it must as regards purposiveness present the appearance of being stupid and unintelligent, since insight united with intention, accordance of end with means, appears to it as an other, as really the opposite of what insight is. As regards the end, however, it has to make badness, enjoyment, and possession, its purpose, and prove itself in consequence to be the impurest kind of intention, since pure intention, *qua* external, an *other*, is similarly impure intention.

Accordingly we find that, so far as concerns purposiveness, enlightenment thinks it foolish if the believing individual seeks to obtain the higher consciousness of freedom from entanglement with natural enjoyment and pleasure, by positively denying itself natural enjoyment and pleasure, and proving through its acts that there is no lie in its open contempt for them, but rather that the contempt is quite genuine.

In the same way enlightenment finds it foolish for consciousness to absolve itself of its characteristic of being absolutely individual, excluding all others, and possessing property of its own, by itself demitting its own property, for thereby it shows in reality that this isolation is not really serious. It shows rather that itself is something that can rise above the natural necessity of isolating itself and of denying, in this absolute isolation of its own individual existence, that the others are one and the same with itself.

Pure insight finds both purposeless as well as wrong. It is purposeless to renounce a pleasure and give away a possession, in order to show oneself independent of pleasure and possession; hence, in the converse case, insight will be obliged to proclaim the man a fool, who, in order to eat, employs the expedient of actually eating. Insight again thinks it wrong to deny oneself a meal, and give away butter and eggs not for money, nor money for butter and eggs, but just to give them away and get no return at all; it declares a meal, or the possession of things of that

---

[6]The cult.

sort, to be an end in itself, and hence in fact declares itself to be a very *impure* intention which ascribes essential value to enjoyment and possessions of this kind. As pure intention it further maintains the necessity of rising above natural existence, above covetousness as to the means for such existence; it only finds it foolish and wrong that this supremacy should be demonstrated by action. In other words this pure intention is in reality a deception, which pretends to and demands an inner elevation, but declares that it is superfluous, foolish, and even wrong to be in earnest in the matter, to put this uplifting into concrete expression, into actual shape and form, and demonstrate its truth.

Pure insight thus denies itself both as pure insight—for it denies directly purposive action, and as pure intention—for it denies the intention of proving its independence of the ends of individual existence.

Thus, then, enlightenment makes belief learn what it means. It takes on this appearance of being bad, because just by the fact of relation to an external other it gives itself a negative reality, it presents itself as the opposite of itself. Pure insight and intention have to adopt this relational attitude, however, for that is their actualization.

This realization appeared, in the first instance, as a negative reality. Perhaps its positive reality is better constituted. Let us see how this stands.

If all prejudice and superstition have been banished, the question arises what next? What is the truth enlightenment has diffused in their stead? It has already given expression to this positive content in its process of exterminating error, for that alienation of itself is equally its positive reality.

In dealing with what for belief is Absolute Spirit, it interprets whatever sort of determination it discovers there as being wood, stone, etc., as particular concrete things of sense. Since in this way it conceives in general every characteristic, i.e. every content and filling, to be a finite fact, to be a human entity and a mental presentation, absolute Being on its view turns out to be a mere vacuum, to which can be attributed no characteristics, no predicates at all. In fact to marry such a vacuity with universal predicates would be essentially reprehensible; and it is just through such a union that the monstrosities of superstition have been produced. Reason, pure insight, is doubtless not empty itself, since the negative of itself is present consciously to it, and is its content; it is, on the contrary, rich in substance, but only in particularity and restrictions. The enlightened function of reason, of pure insight, consists in allowing nothing of that sort to appertain to Absolute Being, nor attributing anything of that kind to it: this function well knows how to put itself and the wealth of finitude in their place, and deal with the Absolute in a worthy manner.

In contrast with this colourless empty Being there stands, as a second aspect of the positive truth of enlightenment, the singleness in general of conscious life and of all that it is:—a singleness excluded from an absolute Being, and standing by itself as something entirely self-contained. Consciousness, which in its very earliest expression is sense-certainty and mere "opining," here comes back, after the whole course of its experience, to this same point, and is once again a *knowledge* of what is purely negative of itself, a knowledge of sense things, i.e. of existent entities which stand in indifference over against its own self-existence. But here it is not an *immediate* natural consciousness; it has *become* such for itself. While at first the prey to every sort of entanglement, into which it is plunged by its gradually unfolding, and now led back to its first form by pure insight, it has arrived at this first state as the result and outcome of the process. This sense-certainty, resting as it does on an insight into the nothingness of all other forms of consciousness, and hence the nothingness of whatever is beyond sense-experience—this sense-certainty is no longer a mere "opining," it is rather absolute truth. This nothingness of everything that transcends sense is doubtless merely a negative proof of this truth. But no other is admissible or possible, for the positive truth of sense-experience in itself is just the unmediated self-existence of the notion itself *qua* object and an object in the form of otherness—the positive truth is that it is absolutely certain to every consciousness that it is and that there are other real things outside it, and that in its natural existence it, as well as these things too, are in and for themselves or absolute.

Lastly, the third moment of the truth of enlightenment is the relation of the particular beings to Absolute Being, is the relation of the first two moments to one another. Insight, *qua* pure insight of what is identical or unrestricted, also transcends the unlike or diverse, i.e. transcends finite reality, or transcends itself *qua* mere otherness. The "beyond" of this otherness it takes to be the void, to which it therefore relates the facts of sense. In determining this relation both the terms do not enter the relation as its content; for the one is the void, and thus a content is only to be had through the other, through sense reality. The form the relation assumes, however, to the determination of which the aspect of immanent and ultimate being (*Ansich*) contributes, can be shaped just as we please; for the form is something inherently and essentially negative, and therefore something self-opposed, being as well as nothing, inherent and ultimate (*Ansich*) as well as the opposite; or, what is the same thing, the relation of actuality to an inherent essential being *qua* something beyond, is as much a negating as a positing of that actuality. Finite actualities can, therefore, properly speaking, be taken just in the way people have need of them. Sense facts are thus related now posi-

tively to the Absolute *qua* something ultimate (*Ansich*), and sense reality is itself ultimate *per se*; the Absolute makes them, fosters and cher-
ishes them. Then, again, they are related to it as an opposite, that is to
their own non-being; in this case they are not something ultimate, they
have being only for an other. Whereas in the preceding mode of consciousness the conceptions involved in the opposition took shape as
good and bad, in the case of pure insight they pass into the more abstract forms of what is *per se* (*Ansich*) and what is for an other.

Both ways of dealing with the positive as well as the negative relation
of finitude to what is *per se* (*Ansich*) are, however, equally necessary
as a matter of fact, and everything is thus as much something *per se*
(*an sich*) as it is something for an other: in other words everything is
"useful."

Everything is now at the mercy of other things, lets itself now be used
by others, and exists for them; and then again it, so to say, gets up on its
hind legs, fights shy of the other, exists for itself on its own account.,
and on its side uses the other too.

From this, as a result, man, being the thing *conscious* of this relation,
derives his true nature and place. As he is immediately, man is good,
qua natural consciousness *per se*, absolute *qua* individual, and all else
exists for him: and further,—since the moments have the significance
of universality for him *qua* self-conscious animal,—everything exists to
pleasure and delight him, and, as he first comes from the hand of God,
he walks the earth as in a garden planted for him. He is bound also to
have plucked the fruit of the tree of knowledge of good and evil; he
claims to have a use for it which distinguishes him from every other
being, for, as it happens, his inherently good nature is also so constituted that the superfluity of delight does it harm, or rather his singleness contains as a factor in its constitution a principle that goes beyond
it; his singleness can overreach itself and destroy itself. To prevent
this, he finds reason a useful means for duly restraining this self-
transcendence, or rather for preserving himself when he does go beyond
the determinate: for such is the force of consciousness. The enjoyment
of this conscious and essentially universal being must, in manifold variety and duration, be itself universal and not something determinate.
The principle of measure or proportion has, therefore, the determinate
function of preventing pleasure in its variety and duration from being
quite broken off: i.e. the function of "measure" is immoderation.

As everything is useful for man, man is likewise useful too, and his
characteristic function consists in making himself a member of the
human herd, of use for the common good, and serviceable to all. The
extent to which he looks after his own interests is the measure with
which he must also serve the purpose of others, and so far as he serves

their turn, he is taking care of himself: the one hand washes the other. But wherever he finds himself there he is in his right place: he makes use of others and is himself made use of.

Different things are serviceable to one another in different ways. All things, however, have this reciprocity of utility by their very nature, by being related to the Absolute in the twofold manner, the one positive, whereby they have a being all their own, the other negative, and thereby exist for others. The relation to Absolute Being, or Religion, is therefore of all forms of profitableness the most supremely profitable;[7] for it is profiting pure and simple; it is that by which all things stand — by which they have a being all their own — and that by which all things fall — have an existence for something else.

Belief, of course, finds this positive outcome of enlightenment as much an abomination as its negative attitude towards belief. This enlightened insight into absolute Being, that sees nothing in it but just absolute Being, the *être suprême*, the great Void — this intention to find that everything in its immediate existence is inherently real (*an sich*) or good, and finally to find the relation of the individual conscious entity to the Absolute Being, Religion, exhaustively summed up in the conception of profitableness — all this is for belief utterly and simply revolting. This special and peculiar wisdom of enlightenment necessarily seems at the same time to the believing mind to be sheer insipidity and the confession of insipidity; because it consists in knowing nothing of absolute Being, or, what amounts to the same thing, in knowing this entirely accurate platitude regarding it — that it is merely absolute Being, and, again, in knowing nothing but finitude, taking this, moreover, to be the truth, and thinking this knowledge about finitude as the truth to be the highest knowledge attainable.

Belief has a divine right as against enlightenment, the right of absolute self-identity or of pure thought; and it finds itself utterly wronged by enlightenment; for enlightenment distorts all its moments, and makes them something quite different from what they are in it. Enlightenment, on the other hand, has merely a human right as against belief, and can only put in a human claim for its own truth; for the wrong it commits is the right of disunion, of discordance, and consists in perverting and altering, a right that belongs to the nature of self-consciousness in opposition to the simple ultimate essence or thought. But since the right of enlightenment is the right of self-consciousness, it will not merely retain its own right, too, in such a way that two equally valid rights of spirit would be left standing in opposition to one another without either satisfying the claims of the other; it will main-

---

[7]Cp. 1 Timothy iv. 8: "Godliness is profitable unto all things."

tain the absolute right, because self-consciousness is the negative function of the notion (*Begriff*), a function which does not merely operate in independence, but also gets control over its opposite. And because belief is a mode of consciousness, it will not be able to baulk enlightenment of that right.

For enlightenment does not operate against the believing mind with special principles of its own, but with those which belief itself implies and contains. Enlightenment merely brings together and presents to belief its own thoughts, the thoughts that lie scattered and apart within belief, all unknown to it. Enlightenment merely reminds belief, when one of its own forms is present, of others it also has, but which it is always forgetting when the one is there. Enlightenment shows itself to belief to be pure insight, by the fact that it, in a given determinate moment, sees the whole, brings forward the opposite element standing in direct relation to that moment and, converting the one in the other, brings out the negative principle which is the essence of both thoughts—the notion. It appears, therefore, to belief to be distortion and lies, because it shows up the other side in the moments of belief. Enlightenment seems, in consequence, directly to make something else out of them than they are in their own singleness; but this other is equally essential, and in reality is to be found in the believing mind itself, only the latter does not think about it, but keeps it somewhere else. Hence neither is it foreign to belief nor can it be denied of belief.

Enlightenment itself, however, which reminds belief of the opposite of its various separate moments, is just as little enlightened regarding its own nature. It takes up a purely negative attitude to belief, so far as it excludes its own content from its own pure activity and takes that content to be negative of itself. Consequently, neither in this negative, in the content of belief, does it recognize itself, nor, for this reason, does it bring together the two thoughts, the one which it contributes and the one against which it brings the first. Since it does not recognize that what it condemns in the case of belief is directly its very own thought, it has its own being in the opposition of both moments, only one of which—viz. in every case the one opposed to belief—it acknowledges, but cuts off the other from the first, just as belief does. Enlightenment, consequently, does not produce the unity of both as their unity, i.e. the notion; but the notion *arises* before it and comes to light of its own accord, in other words, enlightenment finds the notion merely as something there at hand. For in itself the process of realizing pure insight is just this, that insight, whose essential nature is the notion, first comes to be for itself in the shape of an absolute other, and repudiates itself (for the opposite of the notion is an absolute opposite), and then out of this otherness comes to itself or comes to its notion.

Enlightenment, however, is merely this process, it is the activity of the notion in still unconscious form, an activity which no doubt arrives at itself *qua* object, but takes this object for an external other, and does not even know the nature of the notion, i.e. does not know that it is the undifferentiated, the self-identical, which absolutely divides itself.

As against belief, then, insight is the power of the notion in so far as this is the active process of relating the moments lying apart from one another in belief; a way of relating them in which the contradiction in them comes to light. Herein lies the absolute right of the power which insight exercises over belief; but the actuality on which it brings this power to bear lies just in the fact that the believing consciousness is itself the notion and thus itself recognizes and accepts the opposite which insight presents before it. Insight, therefore, has and retains right against belief, because it makes valid in belief what is necessary to belief itself, and what belief contains within it.

At first enlightenment emphasizes the moment that the notion is an act of consciousness; it maintains in the face of belief that the absolute Being belief accepts is a Being of the believer's consciousness *qua* a self, or that this absolute Being is produced by consciousness. To the believing mind its absolute Being, while it is in itself objective for the believer, is also and at the same time not like a foreign thing standing therein, having come there no one knows how or whence. The trust of belief consists just in finding itself as a particular personal consciousness in absolute Being, and its obedience and service consist in producing, through its activity, that Being as *its own* Absolute. Enlightenment, strictly speaking, only reminds belief of this, if belief affirms without qualification the ultimate nature (*Ansich*) of absolute Being to be something beyond the action of consciousness.

But while enlightenment no doubt puts alongside the one-sidedness of belief the opposite moment, viz.:—the action of belief in contrast to being—and being is all belief thinks about here—and yet does not itself in doing so bring those opposite thoughts together, enlightenment isolates the pure moment of action, and declares that what belief takes to be *per se* ultimate (*Ansich*) is merely a product of consciousness. Isolated action, action opposed to this ultimate Being (*Ansich*), is, however, a contingent action, and, *qua* presentative activity, is a creating of fictions—presented figurative ideas that have no being in themselves. And this is how enlightenment regards the content of belief.

Conversely, however, pure insight equally says the very opposite. When insight lays stress on the moment of otherness which the notion involves, it declares the essential Reality for belief to be one which does not in any way concern consciousness, is away beyond consciousness, foreign to it, and unknown. To belief, too, that Reality has the same character. On one side belief trusts in it, and gets, in doing so, the assurance of its own self, on the other side it is unsearchable in all its ways and unattainable in its being.

Further, enlightenment maintains against the believing mind a right which the latter concedes, when enlightenment treats the object of the believer's veneration as stone and wood, or, in short, some finite anthropomorphic feature. For, since this consciousness is divided within itself in having a "beyond" remote from actuality and an immediate present embodiment of that remote beyond, there is also found in it, as a matter of fact, the view that sense-things have a value and significance in and for themselves (*an und für sich*). But belief does not bring together these two ideas of what is "in and for itself," viz. that at one time what is "in and for itself" is for belief pure essential Reality and at another time is an ordinary thing of sense. Even its own pure consciousness is affected by this last view; for the distinctions of its supersensuous world, because this is without the notion, are a series of independent shapes and forms, and their activity is a happening, i.e. they exist merely in figurative presentation, and have the characteristic of sense-existence.

Enlightenment on its side isolates actuality in the same way, treating it as a reality abandoned by spirit; isolates specific determinateness and makes it a fixed finite element, as if it were not a moment in the spiritual process of the real itself, a something which is not nothing, nor possessed of a being all its own, but evanescent and transitory.

It is clear that the same is the case with regard to the ground of knowledge. The believing mind itself recognizes an accidental knowledge; for in belief the mind adopts an attitude towards contingencies, and absolute Being itself comes before belief in the form of a pictorial presentation of an ordinary actual fact. Consequently belief is *also* a certainty which does not carry the truth within it, and it confesses itself to be an unsubstantial consciousness of this kind, holding of *this* world and separated from the spirit that is self-assuring and assured of itself. This moment, however, belief forgets in its immediate spiritual knowledge of absolute Reality.

Enlightenment, however, which reminds belief of all this, thinks again merely of the contingency of the knowledge and forgets the other—thinks only of the mediating process which takes effect through an alien third term, and does not think of that process wherein the immediate is for itself its own third term through which it mediates itself with the other, viz. with itself.

Finally, on the view enlightenment takes of the action of belief, the rejection of enjoyment and possessions is looked upon as wrong and purposeless.

As to the wrong thus done, enlightenment preserves its harmony with the believing mind in this:—that belief itself acknowledges the actual reality of possessing property, keeping hold of it, and enjoying it. In insisting on its property, it behaves with all the more stubborn independence and exclusiveness, and in its enjoyment with all the more frank self-abandonment, since its religious act of giving up pleasure and property takes effect beyond the region of this actuality, and purchases for it freedom to do as it likes so far as that other sphere is concerned. This service, the service of sacrificing natural activities and enjoyments, in point of fact has no truth, owing to this opposition. The retention and the sacrifice subsist together side by side. The sacrifice is merely a "sign" which performs real sacrifice only as regards a small part, and hence in point of fact is only a figurative idea of sacrifice.

As for purposiveness, enlightenment finds it pointless and stupid to throw away *a* possession in order to feel and to prove oneself to be free from all possession, to renounce *an* enjoyment in order to think and demonstrate that one is rid of all enjoyment. The believing mind itself takes the absolute act for a universal one. Not only does the action of its absolute Reality as its object appear something universal, but the individual consciousness, too, has to prove itself detached entirely and altogether from its sensuous nature. But throwing away a single possession, giving up and disclaiming a single enjoyment, is not acting universally in this way. And since in the action the purpose, which is a universal, and the performance, which is a singular process, were bound to stand before consciousness, as essentially incompatible, that action shows itself to be of a kind in which consciousness has no share, and consequently this way of acting is seen to be too naïve to be an action at all. It is too naïve to fast in order to prove oneself quite indifferent to the pleasures of the table; too naïve to rid the body of some other pleasure, as Origen did, in order to show that pleasure is finished and done with. The act itself proves an external and a single operation. But desire is deeply rooted within the inner life, and is a universal element; its pleasure neither disappears with the instrument for getting pleasure nor by abstention from particular pleasures.

But enlightenment on its side here isolates the unrealized inwardness as against the concrete actuality; just as in the case of the devotion and direct intuition of belief, enlightenment held fast to the externality of things of sense as against the inward attitude of belief. Enlightenment finds the main point in the intention, in the thought, and thereby finds no need for actually bringing about the liberation from natural ends. On the contrary, this inner sphere is itself the formal element that has its concrete fulfilment in natural impulses, which are justified simply by the fact that they fall within, that they belong to universal being, to nature.

Enlightenment, then, holds irresistible sway over belief by the fact that the latter finds in its own consciousness the very moments to which enlightenment gives significance and validity. Looking more closely at the action exerted by this force, its operation on belief seems to rend asunder the beautiful unity of trustfulness and immediate confidence, to pollute its spiritual life with lower thoughts drawn from the sphere of sense, to destroy the feeling of calm security in its attitude of submission by introducing the vanity of understanding, of self-will, and self-fulfilment. But in point of fact, enlightenment really brings to pass the abolition of that state of unthinking, or rather unreflective (*begrifflos*) cleavage, which finds a place in the nature of belief. The believing mood weighs and measures by a twofold standard, it has two sorts of eyes and ears, uses two voices to express its meaning, it duplicates all ideas, without comparing and relating the sense and meaning in the two forms used. Or we may say belief lives its life amidst two sorts of perceptions, the one the perceptions of thought which is asleep, purely uncritical and uncomprehending, the other those of waking consciousness living solely and simply in the world of sense; and in each of them it manages to conduct a household of its own.

Enlightenment illuminates that world of heaven with ideas drawn from the world of sense, pointing out there this element of finitude which belief cannot deny or repudiate, because it is self-consciousness, and in being so is the unity to which both kinds of ideas belong, and in which they do not fall apart from one another; for they belong to the same indivisible simple self into which belief has passed, and which constitutes its life.

Belief has by this means lost the content which furnished its filling, and collapses into an inarticulate state where the spirit works and weaves within itself.[8] Belief is banished from its own kingdom; this kingdom is sacked and plundered, since the waking consciousness has forcibly taken to itself every distinction and expansion of it and claimed every one of its parts for earth, and returned them to the earth that owns them. Yet belief is not on that account satisfied, for this illumination has everywhere brought to light only what is individual, with the result that only insubstantial realities and finitude forsaken of spirit make any appeal to spirit.

Since belief is without content and cannot continue in this barren condition, or since, in getting beyond finitude, which is the sole content, it finds merely the empty void, it is a sheer longing: its truth is an

---

[8] i.e. the life of feeling.

empty beyond, for which there is no longer any appropriate content to be found, for everything is appropriated and applied in other ways.

Belief in this manner has in fact become the same as enlightenment—the conscious attitude of relating a finite that inherently exists to an unknown and unknowable Absolute without predicates; the difference is merely that the one is enlightenment satisfied, while belief is enlightenment unsatisfied.[9] It will yet be seen whether enlightenment can continue in its state of satisfaction; that longing of the troubled, beshadowed spirit, mourning over the loss of its spiritual world, lies in the background. Enlightenment has on it this stain of unsatisfied longing:—in its empty Absolute Being we find this in the form of the pure abstract object; in passing beyond its individual nature to an unfulfilled beyond, the stain appears as an act and a process; in the selflessness of what is "useful" it is seen in the form of a sensuous concrete object. Enlightenment will remove this stain: by considering more closely the positive result which constitutes the truth for it, we shall find that the stain is implicitly removed already.

b

THE TRUTH OF ENLIGHTENMENT[1]

THE spirit that sullenly works and weaves without further distinctions within itself has thus passed into itself away beyond consciousness, which, on the other hand, has arrived at clearness as to itself. The first moment of this clearness of mind is determined, in regard to its necessity and condition, by the fact that pure insight, or insight that is implicitly and *per se* notion, actualizes itself; it does so when it gives otherness or determinateness a place in its own nature. In this manner it is negative pure insight, i.e. the negation of the notion; this negation is equally pure; and herewith has arisen the pure and simple "thing," the Absolute Being, that has no further determination of any sort. If we define this more precisely, insight in the sense of absolute notion is a distinguishing of distinctions that are not so any longer, of abstractions or pure notions that no longer support themselves but find a fixed hold and a distinction only by means of the whole life of the process. This distinguishing of what is not distinguished consists just in the fact that the absolute notion makes itself its object, and as against that process

---

[9]i.e. the contrast between belief and enlightenment becomes a contrast inside enlightenment itself.

[1]The outcome is at once positive and negative—materialism and agnosticism: on the secular side, it is pure utilitarianism.

asserts itself to be the essence. The essence hereby is without the aspect wherein abstractions or distinctions are kept apart, and hence becomes pure thought in the sense of a pure thing.

This, then, is just the dull, silent, unconscious working and weaving of the spirit at the loom of its own being, to which belief, as we saw, sank back when it lost all distinction in its content. And this is at the same time that movement of pure self-consciousness, in regard to which the essence is intended to be the absolutely external beyond. For, because this pure self-consciousness is a movement working in pure notions, in distinctions that are no distinctions, pure self-consciousness collapses in fact into that unconscious working and weaving of spirit, i.e. into pure feeling, or pure thinghood.

The self-alienated notion—for the notion still stands here at the level of such alienation—does not, however, recognize this identical nature constituting both sides,—the movement of self-consciousness and its absolute Reality,—does not recognize the identity of their nature, which, in point of fact, is their very substance and subsistence. Since the notion is not aware of this unity, absolute Reality has significance for it merely in the form of an objective beyond, while the consciousness making these distinctions, and in this way keeping the ultimate reality outside itself, is treated as a finite consciousness.

Regarding that Absolute Being, enlightenment itself falls out with itself in the same way as it did formerly with belief, and is divided between the views of two parties. One party proves itself to be victorious by the fact that it breaks up into two parties; for in that fact it shows it possesses within it the principle it combats, and consequently shows it has abolished the one-sidedness with which it formerly made its appearance. The interest which was divided between it and the other, now falls entirely within it, and forgets the other, because that interest finds lying in it alone the opposition on which its attention is directed. At the same time, however, the opposition has been lifted into the higher victorious element, where it manifests itself in a clarified form. So that the schism that arises in one party, and seems a misfortune, demonstrates rather its good fortune.

The pure essence itself has in it no distinction; consequently distinction is reached by two such pure essences being put forward for consciousness to be aware of, or by a twofold consciousness of the pure reality. The pure absolute essence is only in pure thought, or rather it is pure thought itself, and thus absolutely beyond the finite, beyond self-consciousness, and is merely the ultimate essence in a negative sense. But in this way it is just being, the negative of self-consciousness. Being negative of self-consciousness, it is also related to self-consciousness. It is *external being*, which, placed in relation to self-consciousness within which distinctions and determinations fall, acquires within it the distinctions, of being tasted, seen, and so on; and the relationship is that of sense-experience and perception.

Taking the point of departure from this sense-existence, into which that negative beyond necessarily passes, but abstracting from those various ways in which consciousness is related to sense-existence, there is left pure *matter* as that in which consciousness weaves and moves inarticulately within itself. In dealing with this, the essential point to note is that pure matter is merely what remains over when we abstract from seeing, feeling, tasting, etc., i.e. it is not what is seen, tasted, felt, and so on; it is not matter that is seen, felt, or tasted, but colour, a stone, a salt, and so on. Matter is really pure abstraction; and, being so, we have here the pure essential nature of thought, or pure thought itself, as the Absolute without predicates, undetermined, having no distinctions within it.[2]

The one kind of enlightenment calls absolute Being that predicateless Absolute, which exists in thought beyond the actual consciousness from which this enlightenment started; the other calls it matter. If they were distinguished as Nature and Spirit or God, the unconscious inner working and weaving would have nothing of the wealth of developed life required in order to be nature, while Spirit or God would have no self-distinguishing consciousness. Both, as we saw, are entirely the same notion; the distinction lies not in the objective fact, but purely in the diversity of starting-point adopted by the two developments of thought, and in the fact that each stops at its own special point in the thought-process. If they rose above that, their thoughts would coincide, and they would find what to the one is, as it professes, a horror, and to the other a folly, is one and the same thing. For to the one, absolute Being is in its pure thought, or is immediately *for* pure consciousness—is outside finite consciousness, is the negative beyond of finite mind. If it would reflect that in part that simple immediacy of thought is nothing else than pure being, that in part, again, what is negative for consciousness is at the same time related to consciousness—that in the negative judgment the copula "is" connects as well as separates the two factors—it would come to see that this beyond, having the character of an external existence, stands in a relation to consciousness, and that in so doing it means the same as what is called pure matter. The missing moment of *presence* would then be secured.

The other enlightenment starts from sense-existence; it then abstracts from the sensuous relation of tasting, seeing, etc., and turns sense-existence into purely inherent being (*Ansich*), absolute matter,

---

[2]Cp. Schopenhauer: "The absolute without predicates is just matter."

something neither felt nor tasted. This being has in this way become the inner reality of pure consciousness, the ultimately simple without predicates; it is the pure notion, *qua* notion whose being is implicit, or it is pure thought within itself. This insight in its conscious activity does not go through the reverse process of passing from being, which is purely being, to an opposite in thought, which is the same as mere being, or does not go from the pure positive to the opposite pure negative; although after all the positive is really pure simply and solely through negation, while the negative *qua* pure is self-identical and one within itself, and precisely on that account positive.

Or again, these two have not come to the notion found in Descartes' metaphysics that being and thought are inherently the same; they have not arrived at the thought that being, pure being, is not a concrete actual reality, but pure abstraction, and conversely that pure thought, self-identity or inner essence, is partly the negative of self-consciousness, and consequently is being, and partly, *qua* immediate simple entity, is likewise nothing else than being. Thought is thinghood, or thinghood is thought.

The real essence is here divided asunder in such a way that, to begin with, it appertains to two specifically distinct modes of thinking. In part, the real must hold distinction in itself; in part, just by so doing, both ways of considering it merge into one; for then the abstract moments, of pure being and the negative, by which their distinction is expressed, are united in the object with which these modes of treatment deal.

The universal common to both is the abstraction of pure self-thinking, of pure quivering within the self. This simple motion of rotating on its own axis is bound to resolve itself into separate moments, because it is itself only motion by distinguishing its own moments. This distinguishing of the moments leaves the unmoved [unity] behind as the empty shell of pure being, that is no longer actual thought, has no more life within it; for *qua* distinction this process is all the content. The process, which thus puts itself outside that unity thereby constitutes, however, the shifting change—a change that does not return into itself—of the moments of being-in-itself, of being-for-another, and of being-for-self: it is actual reality in the way this is object for the concrete consciousness of pure insight—viz. Utility.

Bad as utility may look to belief or sentimentality, or even to the abstraction that calls itself speculation, and deals with the inherent nature in fixed isolation; yet it is that in which pure insight finds its realization and is itself the object for itself, an object which insight now no longer repudiates, and which, too, it does not consider as the void or the pure beyond. For pure insight, as we saw, is the living notion itself, the selfsame pure personality, distinguishing itself within itself in such a way that each of the distinguished elements is itself pure notion, i.e. is *eo ipso* not distinct; it is simple undifferentiated pure self-consciousness, which is for itself as well as in itself within an immediate unity. Its inherent being (*Ansichsein*) is therefore not fixed and permanent, but at once ceases, in its distinction, to be something distinctive. A being of that kind, however, which is immediately without support and cannot stand of itself, has no being in itself, no inherent existence, it is essentially for something else, which is the power that consumes and absorbs it. But this second moment, opposed to that first one, disappears just as immediately as the first; or, rather, *qua* being merely for some other, it is the very process of disappearing, and there is thus affirmed being that has turned back into itself, being for itself. This simple being-for-self, however, *qua* self-identity, is rather an objective being, or is thereby for an other.

This nature of pure insight in thus unfolding and making explicit its moments, in other words insight *qua* object, finds expression in the useful, the profitable. What is useful is a thing, something that subsists in itself; this being in itself is at the same time only a pure moment: it is in consequence absolutely for something else, but is equally for an other merely as it is in itself: these opposite moments have returned into the indivisible unity of being-for-self. While, however, the useful doubtless expresses the notion of pure insight, it is all the same not insight as such, but insight as conscious presentation, or as object for insight. It is merely the restless shifting change of those moments, of which one is indeed Being-returned-into-itself, but merely as being-for-itself, i.e. as abstract moment, appearing on one side over against the others. The useful itself does not consist in the negative fact of having these moments in their opposition at the same time undivided in one and the same respect, of having them as a form of thought *per se* in the way they are *qua* pure insight. The moment of being-for-self is doubtless a phase of usefulness, but not in the sense that it swamps the other moments, being-*per-se* and being-for-another; if so, it would be the whole self. In the useful, pure insight thus possesses as its object its own peculiar notion in the pure moments constituting its nature; it is the consciousness of this metaphysical principle, but not yet its conceptual comprehension, it has not yet itself reached the unity of being and notion. Because the useful still appears before insight in the form of an object, insight has a world, not indeed any longer a world all by itself and self-contained, but still a world all the same, which it distinguishes from itself. Only, since the opposites have appeared at the supreme point of the notion, the next step will be for them to collide and collapse together and for enlightenment to experience the fruits of its deeds.

When we looked at the object reached in relation to this entire sphere of spiritual life, we found the actual world of culture summed up in the vanity of self-consciousness—in independent self-existence, whose content is drawn from the confusion characteristic of culture, and which is still the individual notion, not yet the self-conscious (*für sich*) universal notion. Returned into itself, however, that (individual) notion is pure insight—pure consciousness *qua* pure self or negativity, just as belief, too, is pure consciousness, *qua* pure thought or positivity. Belief finds in that self the moment that makes it complete;—but, perishing through being thus completed, it is in pure insight that we now see both moments as absolute Being, which is purely thought-constituted or is a negative entity, and as matter, which is the positive entity.

This completion still lacks that actual reality of self-consciousness, which belongs to the vain and empty type of consciousness—the world out of which thought raised itself up to itself. What is thus wanting is reached in the fact of utility so far as pure insight secures positive objectivity there; pure insight is thereby a concrete actual consciousness satisfied within itself. This objectivity now constitutes its world, and is become the final and true outcome of the entire previous world, ideal as well as real. The first world of spirit is the expanded realm of spirit's self-dispersing existence and of certainty of self in separate individual shapes and forms: just as nature disperses its life in an endless multiplicity of forms and shapes, without the generic principle of all the forms being present therein. The second world contains the generic principle, and is the realm of the ultimate inherent nature (*Ansichseyns*) or the essential truth, over against that individual certainty. The third world, however, that of the useful, is the truth which is certainty of self as well. The realm of the truth of belief lacks the principle of concrete actuality, or of certainty of self in the sense of this individual self. But, again, concrete actuality, or certainty of self *qua* this individual, lacks the ultimate inherent nature (*Ansich*). In the object of pure insight both worlds are united. The useful is the object so far as self-consciousness sees through it, and individual certainty of self finds its enjoyment (its self-existence) in it; self-consciousness sees into it in this manner, and this insight contains the true essence of the object (which consists in being something seen through, in other words, in being for an other). This insight is thus itself true knowledge; and self-consciousness directly finds in this attitude universal certainty of itself as well, has its pure consciousness in this attitude, in which truth as well as immediateness and actuality are united. Both worlds are reconciled and heaven is transplanted to the earth below.

III

ABSOLUTE FREEDOM AND TERROR[1]

CONSCIOUSNESS has found its notion in the principle of utility. But that notion is partly an object still, partly, for that very reason, still a purpose, of which consciousness does not yet find itself to be immediately possessed. Utility is still a predicate of the object, not a subject, not its immediate and sole actuality. It is the same thing that appeared before when we found that self-existence (being-for-self) had not yet shown itself to be the substance of the remaining moments, a process by which the useful would be directly nothing else than the self of consciousness and this latter thereby in its possession.

This revocation of the form of objectivity which characterizes the useful has, however, already taken effect implicitly, and as the outcome of this immanent internal revolution there comes to light the actual revolution of concrete actuality, the new mode of conscious life—absolute freedom.

This is so because in point of fact there is here no more than an empty semblance of objectivity separating self-consciousness from actual possession. For, in part, all the validity and permanence of the various specific members of the organization of the world of actuality and belief have as a whole returned into this simple determination, as into their ground and their indwelling spirit: in part, however, this organized world has nothing peculiarly its own left for itself, it is instead pure metaphysic, pure notion or knowledge of self-consciousness. That is to say, from the whole and complete being of the useful *qua* object consciousness recognizes that its inherent nature, its being-in-itself, is essentially a being for another; mere being-in-itself, since it is self-less, is ultimately and in truth a passive entity, or something that is for another self. The object, however, is present to consciousness in this abstract form of purely inherent being, of pure being-in-itself; for consciousness is the activity of pure insight, the separate moments of which take the pure form of notions.

Self-existence, being-for-self, however, into which being for another returns, in other words the self, is not a self of what is called object, a self all its own and different from the ego: for consciousness *qua* pure insight is not an individual self, over against which the object, in the sense of having a self all its own, could stand, but the pure notion, the gazing of the self into self, the literal and absolute seeing itself doubled. The certainty of itself is the universal subject, and its notion knowing itself is the essential being of all reality. If the useful was merely the

---

[1]Refers primarily to the *régime* under the French revolutionaries.

shifting change of the moments, without returning into its own proper unity, and was still hence an object for knowledge to deal with, then *it* ceases to be this now. For knowing is itself the process and movement of those abstract moments; it is the universal self, the self of itself as well as of the object, and, being universal, is the unity of this process, a unity that returns into itself.

This brings on the scene spirit in the form of absolute freedom. It is the mode of self-consciousness which clearly comprehends that in its certainty of self lies the essence of all the component spiritual spheres of the concrete sensible as well as of the supersensible world, or, conversely, that essential being and concrete actuality consist in the knowledge consciousness has of itself.

It is conscious of its pure personality and with that of all spiritual reality; and all reality is solely spirituality; the world is for it absolutely its own will, and this will is universal will. And further, this will is not the empty thought of will, which is constituted by giving a silent assent, or an assent through a representative, a mere symbol of willing; it is concretely embodied universal will, the will of all individuals as such. For will is in itself the consciousness of personality, of every single one; and it has to be as this true concrete actual will, as self-conscious essential being of each and every personality, so that each single and undivided does everything, and what appears as done by the whole is at once and consciously the deed of every single individual.

This undivided substance of absolute freedom puts itself on the throne of the world, without any power being able to offer effectual resistance. For since in very truth consciousness is alone the element which furnishes spiritual beings or powers with their substance, their entire system, which is organized and maintained through division into separate spheres and distinct wholes, has collapsed into a single whole, when once the individual consciousness conceives the object as having no other nature than that of self-consciousness itself, or conceives it to be absolutely the notion. What made the notion an existential object was the distinguishing it into separate and separately subsisting spheres; when, however, the object becomes a notion there is nothing fixedly subsisting left in it; negativity has pervaded all its moments. It exists in such a way that each individual consciousness rises out of the sphere assigned to it, finds no longer its inmost nature and function in this isolated area, but grasps itself as the notion of will, grasps all the various spheres as the essential expression of this will, and is in consequence only able to realize itself in a work which is a work of the whole. In this absolute freedom all social ranks or classes, which are the component spiritual factors into which the whole is differentiated, are effaced and annulled; the individual consciousness that belonged to any such group and exercised its will and found its fulfilment there, has removed the barriers confining it; its purpose is the universal purpose, its language universal law, its work universal achievement.

The object and the element distinguished have here lost the meaning of utility, which was a predicate of all real being; consciousness does not commence its process with the object as a sort of alien element after dealing with which it then and only then returns into itself; the object is for it consciousness itself. The opposition thus consists solely in the distinction of individual and universal consciousness. But the individual itself is directly on its own view that which had merely the semblance of opposition; it is universal consciousness and will. The remote beyond that lies remote from this its actual reality, hovers over the corpse of the vanished independence of what is real or believed to be, and hovers there merely as an exhalation of stale gas, of the empty *être suprême*.

By doing away with the various distinct spiritual spheres, and the restricted and confined life of individuals, as well as both its worlds, there thus remains merely the process of the universal self-consciousness within itself—a process which consists in a reciprocal interaction between its universal form and personal consciousness. The universal will goes into itself, is subjectivized, and becomes individual will, to which the universal law and universal work stand opposed. But this individual consciousness is equally and immediately conscious of itself as universal will; it is fully aware that its object is a law given by that will, a work performed by that will; in exercising and carrying out its activity, in creating objectivity, it is thus doing nothing individual, but executing laws and functions of the state.

This process is consequently the interaction of consciousness with itself, in which it lets nothing break away and assume the shape of a detached object standing over against it. It follows from this, that it cannot arrive at a positive accomplishment of anything, either in the way of universal works of language or of those of actual reality, either in the shape of laws and universal regulations of conscious freedom, or of deeds and works of active freedom.

The accomplished result at which this freedom, that gives itself consciousness, might manage to arrive, would consist in the fact that such freedom *qua* universal substance made itself into an object and an abiding existence. This objective otherness would there be the differentiation which enabled it to divide itself into stable spiritual spheres and into the members of distinct powers. These spheres would partly be the thought-constituted factors of a power that is differentiated into legislative, judicial and executive; but partly they would be the substantial elements we found in the real world of spiritual culture; and, since the content of universal action would be more closely taken note of, they would be the particular spheres of labour, which are further distinguished as more specific "estates" or social ranks. Universal freedom, which would have differentiated itself in this manner into its various parts, and by the very fact of doing so would have made itself an existing substance, would thereby be free from particular individualities, and could apportion the plurality of individuals to its several organic parts.

The activity and being of personality would, however, find itself by this process confined to a branch of the whole, to one kind of action and existence; when placed in the element of existence, personality would bear the meaning of a determinate personality; it would cease to be in reality universal self-consciousness. Neither by the idea of submission to self-imposed laws, which would assign to it only a part of the whole work, nor by its being represented when legislation and universal action take place, does self-consciousness here let itself be cheated out of the actual reality—the fact that *itself* lays down the law and itself accomplishes a universal and not a particular task. For in the case where the self is merely represented and ideally presented (*vorgestellt*), there it is not actual: where it is by proxy, it *is* not.[2]

Just as the individual self-consciousness does not find itself in this universal work of absolute freedom *qua* existing substance, as little does it find itself in the deeds proper, and specific individual acts of will, performed by this substance. For the universal to pass into a deed, it must gather itself into the single unity of individuality, and put an individual consciousness in the forefront; for universal will is an actual concrete will only in a self that is single and one. Thereby, however, all other individuals are excluded from the entirety of this deed, and have only a restricted share in it, so that the deed would not be a deed of real universal self-consciousness.

Universal freedom can thus produce neither a positive achievement nor a deed; there is left for it only negative action; it is merely the rage and fury of destruction.

But the highest reality of all and the reality most of all opposed to absolute freedom, or rather the sole object it is yet to become aware of, is the freedom and singleness of actual self-consciousness itself. For that universality which does not let itself attain the reality of organic articulation, and whose purpose is to maintain itself in unbroken continuity, distinguishes itself within itself all the while, because it is process or consciousness in general. Moreover, on account of its own peculiar abstraction, it divides itself into extremes equally abstract, into the cold

---

[2] The essential principle of anarchy.

unbending bare universality, and the hard discrete absolute rigidity and stubborn atomic singleness of actual self-consciousness. Now that it is done with destroying the organization of the actual world, and subsists in isolated singleness, this is its sole object, an object that has no other content left, no other possession, existence and external extension, but is merely this knowledge of itself as absolutely pure and free individual self. The point at which this object can be laid hold of is solely its abstract existence in general.

The relation, then, of these two, since they exist for themselves indivisibly and absolutely and thus cannot arrange for a common part to act as a means for connecting them, is pure negation entirely devoid of mediation, the negation, moreover, of the individual as a factor existing within the universal. The sole and only work and deed accomplished by universal freedom is therefore *death* — a death that achieves nothing, embraces nothing within its grasp; for what is negated is the unachieved, unfulfilled punctual entity of the absolutely free self. It is thus the most cold-blooded and meaningless death of all, with no more significance than cleaving a head of cabbage or swallowing a draught of water.

In this single expressionless syllable consists the wisdom of the government, the intelligence of the universal will; this is how it fulfils itself. The government is itself nothing but the self-established focus, the individual embodiment of the universal will. Government, a power to will and perform proceeding from a single focus, wills and performs at the same time a determinate order and action. In doing so it, on the one hand, excludes other individuals from a share in its deed, and, on the other, thereby constitutes itself a form of government which is a specifically determinate will and *eo ipso* opposed to the universal will. By no manner of means, therefore, can it exhibit itself as anything but a *faction*. The victorious faction only is called the government; and just in that it is a faction lies the direct necessity of its overthrow; and its being government makes it, conversely, into a faction and hence guilty. When the universal will fastens on this concrete action of the government and treats this as the crime which the government has committed against the universal will, then the government on its side has nothing tangible and external left whereby to establish and show the guilt of the will opposing itself to it; for what thus stands opposed to it as concrete actual universal will is merely unreal pure will, mere intention. Being suspected, therefore, takes the place, or has the significance and effect, of being guilty; and the external reaction against this reality that lies in bare inward intention, consists in the arid barren destruction of this particular existent self, in whose case there is nothing else to take away but its mere existence.

In this its characteristically peculiar performance, absolute freedom becomes objective to itself, and self-consciousness finds out what this freedom is. In itself it is just this abstract self-consciousness, which destroys all distinction and all subsistence of distinction within itself. It is object to itself in this shape; the terror of death is the direct apprehension (*Anschauung*) of this its negative nature. This its reality, however, absolute free self-consciousness finds quite different from what its own notion of itself was, viz. that the universal will is merely the positive substance of personality, and that this latter knows itself in it only positively, knows itself preserved there. Rather for this self-consciousness, which *qua* pure insight completely separates its positive and negative nature—separates the unpredicated Absolute *qua* pure thought and *qua* pure matter—the absolute transition of the one into the other is found here present in its reality. The universal will, *qua* absolutely positive concrete self-consciousness—because it is this self-conscious actuality raised to the level of pure thought or abstract matter—turns round into the negative entity, and shows itself at the same time to be what cancels and does away with self-thinking or self-consciousness.

Absolute freedom *qua* pure self-identity of universal will thus carries with it negation; but in doing so contains distinction in general, and develops this again as concrete actual difference. For pure negativity finds in the self-identical universal will the element of subsistence, or the substance in which its moments get their realization; it has the matter which it can convert into the specific nature of its own being; and in so far as this substance has manifested itself to be the negative element for the individual consciousness, the organization of the spiritual spheres or "masses" of the substance, to which the plurality of conscious individuals is assigned, thus takes shape and form once more. These individuals, who felt the fear of death, their absolute lord and master, submit to negation and distinction once more, arrange themselves under the "spheres," and return to a restricted and apportioned task, but thereby to their substantial reality.

Out of this tumult spirit would be, hurled back upon its starting-point, the ethical world and the real world of spiritual culture, which would thus have been merely refreshed and rejuvenated by the fear of the lord, that has again entered men's hearts. Spirit would have anew to traverse and continually repeat this cycle of necessity, if only complete interpenetration of self-consciousness and the substance were the final result: an interpenetration in which self-consciousness, which has experienced the force of its universal nature operating negatively upon it, would try to know and find itself not as this particular self-consciousness but only as universal, and hence, too, would be able to endure the objective reality of universal spirit, a reality, excluding self-consciousness *qua* particular.

But this is not the form the final result assumed. For in absolute freedom there was no reciprocal interaction either between an external world and consciousness, which is absorbed in manifold existence or sets itself determinate purposes and ideas, or between consciousness and an external objective world, be it a world of reality or of thought. What that freedom contained was the world absolutely in the form of consciousness, as a universal will, and, along with that, self-consciousness gathered out of all the dispersion and manifoldness of existence or all the manifold ends and judgments of mind, and concentrated into the bare and simple self. The form of culture, which it attains in interaction with that essential nature, is, therefore, the grandest and the last, is that of seeing its pure and simple reality immediately disappear and pass away into empty nothingness.[3] In the sphere of culture itself it does not get the length of viewing its negation or alienation in this form of pure abstraction; its negation is negation with a filling and a content—either honour and wealth, which it gains in the place of the self that it has alienated from itself; or the language of *esprit* and insight, which the distraught consciousness acquires; or, again, the negation is the heaven of belief or the principle of utility belonging to the stage of enlightenment. All these determinate elements disappear with the disaster and ruin that overtake the self in the state of absolute freedom;[4] its negation is meaningless death, sheer horror of the negative which has nothing positive in it, nothing that gives a filling.

At the same time, however, this negation in its actual manifestation is not something alien and external. It is neither that universal background of necessity in which the moral world is swamped, nor the particular accident of private possession, the whims and humours of the owner, on which the distraught consciousness finds itself dependent; it is universal will, which in this its last abstraction has nothing positive, and hence can give nothing in return for the sacrifice. But just on that account this will is in unmediated oneness with self-consciousness, it is the pure positive because it is the pure negative; and that meaningless death, the unfilled, vacuous negativity of self, in its inner constitutive principle, turns round into absolute positivity. For consciousness, the immediate unity of itself with universal will, its demand to know itself as this particular determinate centre in the universal will, is changed and converted into the absolutely opposite experience. What it loses there, is abstract being, the immediate existence of that insubstantial

---

[3]Kant's "thing in itself"?
[4]In the sense of abstract autonomy.

centre; and this vanished immediacy is the universal will as such which it now knows itself to be, so far as it is superseded and cancelled immediacy, so far as it is pure knowledge or pure will. By this means it knows that will to be itself, and knows itself to be essential reality; but not as the immediate essence, not will as revolutionary government or anarchy struggling to establish an anarchical constitution, nor itself as a centre of this faction or the opposite; the universal will is its pure knowing and willing, and *it* is universal will *qua* this pure knowledge and volition. It does not lose itself there, for pure knowledge and volition *is* it far more than that atomic point of consciousness. It is thus the interaction of pure knowledge with itself; pure knowledge *qua* essential reality is universal will, while this essence is simply and solely pure knowledge. Self-consciousness is thus pure knowledge of essential reality in the sense of pure knowledge. Furthermore, *qua* single self it is merely the form of the subject or concrete real action, a form which by it is known as form. In the same way objective reality, "being," is for it absolutely self-less form; for that objective reality would be what is not known: this knowledge, however, knows knowledge to be the essential fact.

Absolute freedom has thus squared and balanced the self-opposition of universal and single will. The self-alienated type of mind, driven to the acme of its opposition, where pure volition and the purely volitional agent are still kept distinct, reduces that opposition to a transparent form, and therein finds itself.

Just as the realm of the real and actual world passes over into that of belief and insight, absolute freedom leaves its self-destructive sphere of reality, and passes over into another land of self-conscious spirit, where in this unreality freedom is taken to be and is accepted as the truth. In the thought of this truth spirit refreshes and revives itself (so far as spirit is thought and remains so), and knows this being which self-consciousness involves [viz. thought] to be the complete and entire essence of everything. The new form and mode of experience that now arises is that of the Moral Life of Spirit.

C

SPIRIT IN THE CONDITION OF BEING CERTAIN OF ITSELF: MORALITY

The following section deals with the final and highest stage in the life of finite spiritual experience as realized in the concrete form of a historical society. Here the substance of the social order is the real content of the self-conscious individual: that substance has become subjectified; we have therefore a self-contained spiritual subject. The discordance involved in the sphere of culture and enlightenment is overcome by the self knowing and realizing itself as a completely universal self-determining free will, its world within itself, and its self its own world. Each reflects the whole (the totality of social life) in itself so perfectly that what it does is transparently the doing of the whole as much as its own doing. Such a sphere of spiritual existence is Morality, the all-sufficient spiritual order of the finite spirit as an individual. The meaning assigned to "morality" here is that expressed by Kant when he says that morality is "the relation of actions to the autonomy of the will, i.e. to possible universal legislation through maxims of the will." In other words, all the universality constituting the interrelations of finite spirits in a society is epitomized in the soul of the acting individual, who can thus quite legitimately look upon itself as the self-regulating source of all universal conditions of action.

It is inevitable that such a concrete mode of experience should have various aspects and should pass through various stages in the process of fully realizing its nature. The individual may lay exclusive stress on the self-completeness which he possesses through being the source and origin of his own laws. His self-legislative function, just because it carries with it the sense of universality, may appear so supremely important that all the actual detail of his life comes to be treated as external, indifferent, and contingent. This detail no doubt is essential to give body and substance to his spiritual individuality, but the universality of his will so far transcends each and every detail of content as to seem by itself the sole and all-sufficient reality of his being. The content of his life only enters into consideration as an element to be regulated and made to conform to the universal: the relation so constituted between content and universal is found in the consciousness of Duty. Since the content is thus subordinate, though absolutely essential to give even meaning to the idea and the "fulfilment" of duty, and since the universal is the supremely important fact, not merely is duty to be fulfilled for duty's sake, but the duty in question is pure duty. The "good will" is the purely universal will, and is the only will in the world from this point of view.

In the first section (a) Hegel analyses this phase of the moral life.

The historical material the writer has in mind is a moral attitude which came into prominence at the time of the Romantic movement towards the end of the eighteenth and the beginning of the nineteenth centuries. It found its philosophical expression in the moral theories of Kant and Fichte; and Lessing may be taken as a typical representative in literature of the same attitude.

THE ethical order of the community found its destiny consummated and its truth realized in the spirit that merely passed away within it— the individual self. This legal person, however, has its substance and its fulfilment outside the ethical order. The process of the world of culture and belief does away with this abstraction of a mere person; and by the completion of the process of estrangement, by reaching the extremity of abstraction, the self of spirit finds the substance become first the universal will, and finally its own possession. Here, then, knowledge seems at last to have become entirely adequate to the truth at which it aims; for its truth is this knowledge itself. All opposition between the two sides has vanished, and that, too, not *for us* (who are tracing the process), not merely *implicitly*, but actually for self-consciousness itself. That is to say, self-consciousness has itself got the mastery over the opposition which consciousness involves. This latter rests on the opposition between certainty of self and the object. Now, however, the object for it *is* the certainty of self, knowledge: just as the certainty of itself as such has no longer ends of its own, is no longer conditioned and determinate, but is pure knowledge.

Self-consciousness thus now takes its knowledge to be the substance itself. This substance is, for it, at once immediate and absolutely mediated in one indivisible unity. It is *immediate* — just like the "ethical" consciousness, it knows and itself does its duty, and is bound to its duty as to its own nature: but it is not *character*, as that ethical consciousness was, which in virtue of its immediacy is a determinate type of spirit, belongs merely to one of the essential features of ethical life, and has the characteristic of not being conscious explicit knowledge. It is, again, absolute *mediation*, like the consciousness developing itself through culture and like belief; for it is essentially the movement of the self to transcend the abstract form of immediate existence, and become consciously universal — and yet to do so neither by simply estranging and rending itself as well as reality, nor by fleeing from it. Rather, it is for itself directly and immediately present in its very substance; for this substance is its knowledge, it is the pure certainty of self become transparently visible. And just this very immediacy, which constitutes its own actual reality, is the entire actuality; for the immediate is being, and *qua* pure immediacy, immediacy purified by thoroughgoing negativity, this immediacy is pure being, is being in general, is all being.

Absolute essential Being is, therefore, not exhausted by the characteristic of being the simple essence of thought; it is all actuality, and this actuality exists merely as knowledge. What consciousness did not know would have no sense and can be no power in its life. Into its self-conscious knowing will, all objectivity, the whole world, has withdrawn. It is absolutely free in that it knows its freedom; and just this very knowledge of its freedom is its substance, its purpose, its sole and only content.

a

THE MORAL VIEW OF THE WORLD

SELF-CONSCIOUSNESS knows and accepts duty as the Absolute. It is bound by that alone, and this substance is its own pure conscious life;

duty cannot, for it, take on the form of something alien and external. When thus shut up and confined within itself, however, moral self-consciousness is not yet affirmed and looked at as *consciousness*.[1] The object is immediate knowledge, and being thus permeated purely by the self, is not *object*. But, self-consciousness being essentially mediation and negativity, there is implied in its very conception relation to some otherness; and thus it is *consciousness*. This other, because duty constitutes the sole essential purpose and object of self-consciousness, is a reality completely devoid of significance for self-consciousness. But again because this consciousness is so entirely confined within itself, it takes up towards this otherness a perfectly free and detached attitude; and the existence of this other is, therefore, an existence completely set free from self-consciousness, and in like manner relating itself merely to itself. The freer self-consciousness becomes, the freer also is the negative object of its consciousness. The object is thus a complete world within itself, with an individuality of its own, an independent whole of laws peculiar to itself, as well as an independent procedure and an unfettered active realization of those laws. It is a *nature* in general, a nature whose laws and also whose action belong to itself as a being which is not disturbed about the moral self-consciousness, just as the latter is not troubled about it.

Starting with a specific character of this sort, there is formed and established a moral outlook on the world which consists in a process of relating the implicit aspect of morality (*moralisches Ansichseyn*) and the explicit aspect (*moralisches Fürsichseyn*). This relation presupposes both thorough reciprocal indifference and specific independence as between nature and moral purposes and activity; and also, on the other side, a conscious sense of duty as the sole essential fact, and of nature as entirely devoid of independence and essential significance of its own. The moral view of the world, the moral attitude, consists in the development of the moments which are found present in this relation of such entirely antithetic and conflicting presuppositions.

To begin with, then, the moral consciousness in general is presupposed. It takes duty to be the essential reality: itself is actual and active, and in its actuality and action fulfils duty. But this moral consciousness, at the same time, finds before it the assumed freedom of nature: it learns by experience that nature is not concerned about giving consciousness a sense of the unity of its reality with that of nature, and hence discovers that nature may let it become happy, but perhaps also may not. The non-moral consciousness on the other hand finds, by chance perhaps, its realization where the moral consciousness sees

---

[1] i.e. there is not the opposition of an object to subject which consciousness requires.

merely an occasion for acting, but does not see itself obtaining through its action the happiness of performance and of the enjoyment of achievement. It therefore finds reason for bewailing a situation where there is no correspondence between itself and existence, and lamenting the injustice which confines it to having its object merely in the form of pure duty, but refuses to let it see this object and itself actually realized.

The moral consciousness cannot renounce happiness and drop this element out of its absolute purpose. The purpose, which is expressed as pure duty, essentially implies retention of individual self-consciousness and maintenance of its claims. Individual conviction and knowledge thereof constituted a fundamental element in morality. This moment in the objectified purpose, in duty fulfilled, is the individual consciousness seeing itself as actually realized. In other words, this moment is that of enjoyment, which thus lies in the very principle of morality, not indeed of morality immediately in the sense of a frame of mind, but in the principle of the *actualization* of morality. Owing to this, however, enjoyment is also involved in morality, as a mood, for morality seeks, not to remain a frame of mind as opposed to action, but to act or realize itself. Thus the purpose, expressed as a whole along with the consciousness of its elements or moments, is that duty fulfilled shall be both a purely moral act and a realized individuality, and that nature, the aspect of individuality in contrast with abstract purpose, shall be one with this purpose.

While experience must necessarily bring to light the disharmony between the two aspects, seeing that nature is detached and free, nevertheless duty is alone the essential fact and nature by contrast is devoid of selfhood. That purpose in its entirety, which the harmony of the two constitutes, contains within it actuality itself. It is, at the same time, the thought of actuality. The harmony of morality and nature, or—seeing that nature is taken account of merely so far as consciousness finds out nature's unity with it—the harmony of morality and happiness, is thought of as necessarily existing; it is *postulated*. For to postulate or demand means that something is *thought as being* which is not yet actual—a necessity affecting, not the conception *qua* conception, but existence. But necessity is at the same time essentially relation through the conception. The postulated existence thus is not something that concerns the imagination of some chance individual consciousness, but is implied in the very notion of morality itself, whose true content is the unity of pure with individual consciousness. It falls to the individual consciousness to see that this unity is, for it, an actuality:— which means happiness as regards the content of the purpose, and existence in general as regards its form. The existence thus demanded—

the unity of both—is therefore not a wish, nor, looked at *qua* purpose, is it of such a kind as to be still uncertain of attainment; the purpose is rather a demand of *reason*, or an immediate certainty and presupposition of reason.

The first experience above referred to and this postulate are not the only experience and postulate; a whole round of postulates comes to light. For nature is not merely this completely free external mode in which, as a bare pure object, consciousness has to realize its purpose. Consciousness is *per se* essentially something *for* which this other detached reality exists, i.e. it is *itself* something contingent and natural. This nature, which is properly its own, is *sensibility*, which, taking the form of volition, in the shape of Impulses and Inclinations, has by itself a determinate essential being of its own, i.e. has specific single purposes, and thus is opposed to pure will with its pure purpose. In contrast with this opposition, however, pure consciousness rather takes the relation of sensibility to it, the absolute unity of sensibility with it, to be the essential fact. Both of these, pure thought and sensibility, are essentially and inherently *one* consciousness, and pure thought is just that for which and in which this pure unity exists; but for it *qua* consciousness the opposition between itself and its impulses holds. In this conflict between reason and sensibility, the essential thing for reason is that the conflict should be resolved, and that the unity of both should come out as a result: not the original unity which consisted in both the opposites being in one individual, but a unity which arises out of the *known* opposition of the two. So attained, such a unity is then actual morality; for in it is contained the opposition through which the self is a consciousness, or first becomes concrete and in actual fact self, and at the same time universal. In other words, we find there expressed that process of mediation which, as we see, is essential to morality.

Since, of the two factors in opposition, sensibility is otherness out and out, is the negative, while, on the other hand, pure thought of duty is the ultimate essence which cannot possibly be surrendered in any respect, it seems as if the unity produced can be brought about only by doing away with sensibility. But since sensibility is itself a moment of this process of producing the unity, is the moment of actuality, we have, in the first instance, to be content to express the unity in this form— sensibility should be in conformity with morality.

This unity is likewise a *postulated* existence; it is not there as a fact; for what is there is consciousness, or the *opposition* of sensibility and pure consciousness. All the same, the unity is not a something *per se* like the first postulate, in which free external nature constitutes an aspect and the harmony of nature with moral consciousness in consequence falls outside the latter. Rather, nature is here that which lies within consciousness; and we have here to deal with morality (*Moralität*) as such, with a harmony which is the active self's very own. Consciousness has, therefore, of itself to bring about this harmonious unity, and "to be always making progress in morality." The completion of this result, however, has to be pushed away into the remote infinite, because if it actually entered the life of consciousness as an actual fact, the moral consciousness would be done away with. For morality is only moral consciousness *qua* negative force; sensibility has merely a negative significance for the consciousness of pure duty, it is something merely "*not* in conformity with" duty. By attaining that harmony, however, morality *qua* consciousness, i.e. its actuality, passes away, just as in the moral consciousness or actuality its harmony vanishes. The completion is, therefore, not to be reached as an actual fact; it is to be thought of merely as an absolute task or problem, i.e. one which remains a problem pure and simple. Nevertheless, its content has to be thought as something which unquestionably has to be, and must not remain a problem: whether we imagine the moral consciousness quite cancelled in the attainment of this goal, or not. Which of these exactly is the case, can no longer be clearly distinguished in the dim distance of infinitude, to which the attainment of the end has to be postponed, just because we cannot decide the point. We shall be, strictly speaking, bound to say that a definite idea on the matter ought to be of no interest and ought not to be sought for, because this leads to contradictions—the contradiction involved in an undertaking that at once ought to remain an undertaking and yet ought to be carried out, and the contradiction involved in the morality which is to be no longer consciousness, i.e. no longer actual. By adopting the view, however, that morality when completed would contain a contradiction, the sacredness of moral truth would be seriously affected, and the unconditional duty would appear something unreal.

The first postulate was the harmony of morality and objective nature—the final purpose of the world: the other was the harmony of morality and will in its sensuous form, in the form of impulse, etc.— the final purpose of self-consciousness as such. The former is the harmony in the form of implicit immanent existence; the latter, the harmony in the form of explicit self-existence. That, however, which connects these two extreme final purposes which are thought, and operates as their mediating ground, is the process of concrete action itself. They are harmonies whose moments have not yet become definitely objective in their abstract distinctiveness from each other: this takes place in concrete actuality, in which the aspects appear in consciousness proper, each as the other of the other. The postulates arising by this means contain harmonies which are now both immanent and self-existent, whereas formerly they were postulated merely separately, the one being the immanent harmony, the other self-existent.

The moral consciousness, *qua* simple knowledge and willing of pure duty, is brought, by the process of acting, into relation with an object opposed to that abstract simplicity, into relation with the manifold actuality which various cases present, and thereby assumes a moral attitude varied and manifold in character. Hence arise, on the side of content, the plurality of laws generally, and, on the side of form, the contradictory powers of intelligent knowing consciousness and of a being devoid of consciousness.

To begin with, as regards the plurality of duties, it is merely the aspect of pure or bare duty in them which the moral consciousness in general recognizes as having validity: the many duties *qua* many are determinate and, therefore, are not, as such, anything sacred for the moral consciousness. At the same time, however, being necessary, in virtue of the notion of action which implicates a manifold actuality, and hence manifold types of moral attitude, those many duties must be looked on as having a substantial existence and value. Furthermore, since they can only exist in a moral *consciousness*, they exist at the same time in another consciousness than that for which only pure duty *qua* pure duty is sacred and substantial.

It is thus postulated that there is *another* consciousness which renders them sacred, or which knows them as duties and wills them so. The first maintains pure duty indifferent towards all specific content, and duty consists merely in being thus indifferent towards it. The other, however, contains the equally essential relation to the process of action, and the *necessity*, therefore, of determinate content: since duties for this other mean determinate duties, the content is thus, for it, just as essential as the form in virtue of which the content is a duty at all. This consciousness is, consequently, such that in it the universal and the particular are, through and through, one; its essential principle is thus the same as that of the harmony of morality and happiness. For this opposition between morality and happiness expresses in like manner the separation of the self-identical moral consciousness from that actuality which, *qua* manifold existence, opposes and conflicts with the simple nature of duty. While, however, the first postulate expresses merely the objective existential harmony between morality and nature, because nature is therein the negative of self-consciousness, is the moment of existence, this inherent harmony, on the other hand, is now affirmed essentially as a type of consciousness. For existence now appears as the content of duty, as that in the determinate duty which gives it specific determinateness. The immanent harmony is thus the unity of elements which, *qua* simple ultimate elements, are essentially thought-created, and hence cannot exist except in a consciousness. This latter becomes now a master and ruler of the world, who brings about the harmony of morality and happiness, and at the same time sanctifies duties in their multiplicity. To sanctify these duties means this much, that the consciousness of pure duty cannot straightway and directly accept the determinate or specific duty as sacred; but because a specific duty, owing to the nature of concrete action which is something specific and definite, is likewise necessary, its necessity falls outside that consciousness and holds inside another consciousness, which thus mediates or connects determinate and pure duty, and is the reason why that specific duty also has validity.

In the concrete act, however, consciousness proceeds to work as this particular self, as completely individual: it directs its activity on actual reality as such, and takes this as its purpose, for it wants to perform something definite. "Duty in general" thus falls outside it and within another being, which is a consciousness and the sacred lawgiver of pure duty. The consciousness which acts, just because it acts, accepts the other consciousness, that of pure duty, and admits its validity immediately; this pure duty is thus a content of another consciousness, and is only indirectly or in a mediate way sacred for the active consciousness, viz. in virtue of this other consciousness.

Because it is established in this manner that the validity, the bindingness, of duty as something wholly and absolutely sacred, falls outside the actual consciousness, this latter thereby stands altogether on one side as the incomplete moral consciousness. Just as, in regard to its *knowledge*, it is aware of itself as that whose knowledge and conviction are incomplete and contingent; in the same way, as regards its *willing*, it feels itself to be that whose purposes are affected with sensibility. On account of its "unworthiness," therefore, it cannot look on happiness as something necessary, but as a something contingent, and can only expect happiness as the result of "grace."

But though its actuality is incomplete, duty is still, so far as its pure will and knowledge are concerned, held to be the essential truth. In principle, therefore, so far as the notion is opposed to actual reality, in other words, in *thought*, it *is* perfect. The absolute Being [God] is, however, just this object of thought, and is something postulated beyond the actual. It is therefore the thought in which the morally imperfect knowledge and will are held to be perfect; and the Absolute, since it takes this imperfection to have full weight, distributes happiness according to "worthiness," i.e. according to the "merit" ascribed to the imperfect consciousness.

This completes the meaning of the moral attitude. For in the conception of moral self-consciousness the two aspects, pure duty and actual reality, are affirmed of a single unity, and thereby the one, like the other, is put forward, not as something self-complete, but as a moment, or as cancelled and transcended. This becomes consciously explicit in the last phase of the moral attitude or point of view. Consciousness, we there saw, places pure duty in another form of being than its own consciousness, i.e. it regards pure duty partly as something ideally presented, partly as what does not by itself hold good—indeed, the non-moral is rather what is held to be perfect. In the same way it affirms itself to be that whose actuality, not being in conformity with duty, is transcended, and, *qua* transcended, or in the idea of the Absolute [God's view], no longer contradicts morality.

For the moral consciousness itself, however, its moral attitude does not mean that consciousness therein develops its own proper notion and makes this its object. It has no consciousness of this opposition either as regards the form or the content thereof; the elements composing this opposition it does not relate and compare with one another, but goes forward on its own course of development, without being the connecting principle of those moments. For it is only aware of the essence pure and simple, i.e. the object so far as this is duty, so far as this is an abstract object of its pure consciousness—in other words, it is only aware of this object as pure knowledge or as itself. Its procedure is thus merely that of *thinking*, not *conceiving*, is by way of thoughts not notions. Consequently it does not yet find the object of its actual consciousness transparently clear to itself; it is not the absolute notion, which alone grasps otherness as such, its absolute opposite, as its very self. Its own reality, as well as all objective reality, no doubt is held to be something unessential; but its freedom is that of pure thought, in opposition to which, therefore, nature has likewise arisen as something equally free. Because both are found in like manner within it—both the freedom which belongs to [external] being and the inclusion of this existence within consciousness—its object comes to be an existing object, which is at the same time merely a thought-product. In the last phase of its attitude or point of view, the content is essentially so affirmed that its being has the character of something presented, and this union of being and thinking is expressed as what in fact it is, viz.— Imagining (*Vorstellen*).

When we look at the moral view of the world and see that this objective condition is nothing else than the very principle or *notion* of moral self-consciousness which it makes objective to itself, there arises through this consciousness concerning the form of its origin another mode of exhibiting this view of the world.

The first stage, which forms the starting-point, is the actual moral self-consciousness, or is the fact that there is such a self-consciousness at all. For the *notion* establishes moral self-consciousness in the form that, for it, all reality in general has essential being only so far as such reality is in conformity with duty; and that notion establishes this essential element as knowledge, i.e. in immediate unity with the actual self. This unity is thus itself actual, is a moral actual consciousness. The latter, now, *qua* consciousness, pictures its content to itself as an object, viz. as the final purpose of the world, as the harmony of morality with all reality. Since, however, it pictures this unity as object and is not yet the complete notion, which has mastery over the object as such, this unity is taken to be something negative of self-consciousness, i.e. the unity falls outside it, as something beyond its actual reality, but at the same time of such a nature as to be also existent, though merely thought of.

This self-consciousness, which, *qua* self-consciousness, is something other than the object, thus finds itself left with the *want* of harmony between the consciousness of duty and actual reality, and indeed its own reality. The proposition consequently now runs thus: "there is no morally complete actual self-consciousness"; and, since what is moral only is at all so far as it is complete,—for duty is the pure unadulterated ultimate element (*Ansich*), and morality consists merely in conformity to this pure principle—the second proposition runs: "there is no actual existence which is moral."

Since, however, in the third place, it is a self, it is inherently the unity of duty and actual reality. This unity thus becomes its object, as completed morality—but as something beyond its actual reality, and yet a "beyond" which still ought to be real.

In this final goal or aim of the synthetic unity of the two first propositions, the self-conscious actuality, as well as duty, is only affirmed as a transcended or superseded moment. For neither of them is alone, neither is isolated; on the contrary, these factors, whose essential characteristic lies in being free from one another, are thus each in that unity no longer free from the other; each is transcended. Hence, as regards content, they become, as such, object, each of them holds good for the other; and, as regards form, they become object in suchwise that this reciprocal interchange is, at the same time, merely pictured—a mere idea. Or, again, the actually non-moral, because it is, at the same time, pure thought and elevated above its own actual reality, is in idea *still* moral, and is taken to be entirely valid. In this way the first proposition, that there *is* a moral self-consciousness, is reinstated, but bound up with the second that there is *none*; that is to say, there is one, but merely in idea. In other words, there is indeed none, but it is all the same allowed by some other consciousness to pass for one.

b

DISSEMBLANCE[1]

The first stage fails as it stands to do complete justice to the full meaning of morality. Both elements in the spiritually complete individual are essential, and each has to be recognized. The universal must be objectified in nature ("external nature" and "sensibility"), and nature must be subjectivized in spirit. Another condition or stage of the moral consciousness, therefore, is found where the equality of value of the elements of the moral consciousness is admitted, without these elements being completely fused into a single and total attitude. The universal is realized in many ways and forms, and each is accepted in turn as the true moral reality. The mind passes from one to the other; when one is accepted the other is set aside. The moral consciousness tries, so to say, to hide from itself the endless diversity of its appearances, simply because it clings tenaciously to the idea that the inherent self-completeness of itself is a unity *per se* which can only admit diversity on sufferance. Formerly it eliminated all diversity by eliminating the source of diversity—nature. Here it is forced to admit diversity, and yet cannot give up the claim to be an abstract single unity independent of difference. Thus its condition here is a mixture of self-realization and self-sophistication—a condition which Hegel characterizes as "Dissemblance," and which borders upon and may pass into "Hypocrisy." Hegel regards this attitude as the inevitable outcome of the preceding.

IN the moral attitude of experience we see, on one side, consciousness itself produce its object in a conscious way. We find that neither does it pick up the object as something external, nor does the object come before it in an unconscious manner. Rather, consciousness throughout proceeds on an explicit ground, and from this establishes the objective reality. It thus knows this objective reality to be itself, for it is aware of itself as the active agent producing this object. It seems, in consequence, to attain here its peace and satisfaction, for this can only be found where it does not need to go any more beyond its object, because this object no longer goes beyond it. On the other side, however, it really puts the object away outside itself, as something beyond itself. But this latter self-contained entity is at the same time put there as something that is not free from self-consciousness, but really there on behalf of and by means of it.

The moral attitude is, therefore, in fact nothing else than the developed expression of this fundamental contradiction in its various as-

---

[1]*Verstellung*: It is not possible to bring out exactly by an English word the verbal play involved in Hegel's interpretation of the state of mind here discussed. Hegel has, in the course of his analysis, used the meaning implied in the general term *"stellen"* to explain by contrast the specific nuance of the purely moral attitude conveyed by the term *verstellen*.

pects. It is—to use a Kantian phrase which is here most appropriate—
a "perfect nest" of thoughtless contradictions.[2] Consciousness, in developing this situation, proceeds by fixing definitely one moment, passing
thence immediately over to another and doing away with the first. But,
as soon as it has now set up this second moment, it also "shifts" (*verstellt*)
this again, and really makes the opposite the essential element. At the
same time, it is conscious of its contradiction and of its shuffling, for it
passes from one moment, immediately in its relation to this very moment, right over to the opposite. Because a moment has for it no reality
at all, it *affirms* that very moment as real: or, what comes to the same
thing, in order to assert one moment as *per se* existent, it asserts the opposite as the *per se* existent. It thereby confesses that, as a matter of fact,
it is in earnest about neither of them. The various moments of this ver-
tiginous fraudulent process we must look at more closely.

Let us, to begin with, agree to accept the assumption that there is an
actual moral consciousness, because the assumption is made directly
and not with reference to something preceding; and let us turn to the
harmony of morality and nature—the first postulate. It is to be immanent, not explicitly for actual conscious life, not really present; the present is rather simply the contradiction between the two. In the present,
morality is taken to be something at hand, and actual reality to be so
situated or "placed" that it is not in harmony with morality. The concrete moral consciousness, however, is an active one; that is precisely
what constitutes the actuality of its morality. In the very process of acting, however, that "place" or semblance is immediately "displaced," is
dissembled; for action is nothing else than the actualization of the
inner moral purpose, nothing but the production of an actuality constituted and determined by the purpose; in other words, the production
of the harmony of moral purpose and reality itself. At the same time the
performance of the action is a *conscious* fact, it is the "presence" of this
unity of reality and purpose; and because in the completed act consciousness realizes itself as a given individual consciousness, or sees existence returned into itself—and in this consists the nature of enjoyment—there is, *eo ipso*, contained in the realization of moral purpose
also that form of its realization which is called enjoyment and
happiness.

Action thus, as a fact, fulfils directly what it was asserted could not
take place at all, fulfils what was to be merely a postulate, was to lie
merely "beyond." Consciousness, therefore, expresses through its deed
that it is not in earnest in making the postulate, since the meaning of
acting is really that it makes a present fact of what was not to be in the

---

[2]An expression used by Kant of the "cosmological proof."

present. And, since the harmony is postulated for the sake of the action—for what is to become actual through action must *be* implicit, otherwise the actuality would not be *possible*—the connexion of action with the postulate is so constituted that, for the sake of the action, i.e. *for the sake of the actual harmony of purpose and reality*, this harmony is put forward as *not* actual, as far away, as "beyond."

In that action takes place, the want of adaptation between purpose and reality is thus not taken seriously at all. Action itself, on the other hand, does seem to be taken seriously. But, as a matter of fact, the actual deed done is only the action of an individual consciousness, and so is itself merely something individual, and the result contingent. The end of reason, however, being the all-comprehensive universal end, is nothing short of the entire world—a final purpose which goes far beyond the content of this individual act, and therefore is to be placed altogether beyond anything actually done. Because the universal best ought to be carried out, nothing good is done. In point of fact, however, the nothingness of actual action and the reality of the entire purpose alone, which are here upheld—these are on all hands again "shifted" or dissembled. The moral act is not something contingent and restricted; its essential nature lies in pure duty. This pure duty constitutes the sole entire purpose; and the act, whatever may be the limitation of the content, being the actualization of that purpose, is the accomplishment of the entire absolute purpose. Or, if again we take the reality in the sense of nature, which has laws of its own and stands over against pure duty, and take it in such a way that duty cannot realize its law within nature, then, since duty as such is the essential element, we are, when acting, not in fact concerned about the accomplishment of pure duty which is the whole purpose; for the accomplishment would then rather have as its end not pure duty, but the opposite, viz. reality. But there is again a "shifting" from the position that it is not reality with which we have to do. For by the very notion of moral action, pure duty is essentially an active consciousness. Action thus *ought* certainly to take place, absolute duty ought to be expressed in the whole of nature, and "moral law" to become "natural law."

If, then, we allow this highest good to stand for the essentially real, consciousness is altogether not in earnest with morality. For, in this highest good, nature has not a different law from what morality has. Moral action itself, in consequence, drops, for action takes place only under the assumption of a negative element which is to be cancelled by means of the act. But if nature conforms to the moral law, then assuredly this moral law would be violated by acting, by cancelling what already exists.

On that mode of interpretation, then, there has been admitted as the essential situation one which renders moral action superfluous and in which moral action does not take place at all. Hence the postulate of the harmony between morality and reality—a harmony posited by the very notion of moral action, which means bringing the two into agreement—finds on this view, too, an expression which takes the form:—"because moral action is the absolute purpose, the absolute purpose is—that moral action do not take place at all."

If we put these moments together, through which consciousness has moved in presenting its ideas of its moral life, we see that it cancels each one again in its opposite. It starts from the position that, *for it*, morality and reality do not make a harmony; but it is not in earnest with that, for in the moral act it is *conscious* of the presence of this harmony. But neither is it in earnest with this action, since the action is something individual; for it has such a high purpose, the highest good. This, however, is once more merely a dissemblance of the actual fact, for thereby all action and all morality would fall to the ground. In other words, it is not strictly in earnest with moral action; on the contrary, it really feels that, what is most to be wished for, the absolutely desirable, is that the highest good were carried out and moral action superfluous.

From this result consciousness must go on still further in its contradictory process, and must of necessity again dissemble the abolition of moral action. Morality is the inherently essential (*Ansich*); in order that it may have place, the final end of the world cannot be carried out; rather, the moral consciousness must exist for itself, and must find lying before it a nature opposing it. But it must *per se* be completed. This leads to the second postulate of the harmony of itself and sensibility, the "nature" immediately within it. Moral self-consciousness sets up its purpose as pure purpose, as independent of inclinations and impulses, so that this bare purpose has abolished within itself the ends of sensibility. But this cancelling of the element of sense is no sooner set up than it is again dissembled. The moral consciousness acts, it brings its purpose into reality; and self-conscious sensibility, which should be done away with, is precisely the mediating element between pure consciousness and reality—is the instrument used by the former for the realization of itself, or is the organ, and what is called impulse, inclination. It is thus not really in earnest in cancelling inclinations and impulses, for these are just self-consciousness making itself actual. Moreover, they ought not to be suppressed, but merely to be in conformity with reason. They *are*, too, in conformity with it; for moral action is nothing else than self-realizing consciousness—consciousness taking on the form of an impulse, i.e. it is immediately the realized actually present harmony of impulse and morality. But, in point of fact, impulse is not only this empty conscious form, which might possibly have within itself a spring of action other than the impulse in question, and be driven on by that. For sensibility is a kind of nature, which contains within itself its own laws and springs of action: consequently, morality cannot seriously mean to be the inciting motive (*Triebfeder*) for impulses (*Triebe*), the angle of inclination for inclinations. For, since these latter have their own fixed character and peculiar content, the consciousness, to which *they* were to conform, would rather be in conformity with *them*—a conformity which moral self-consciousness declines to adopt. The harmony between the two is thus merely implicit and postulated.

In moral action the realized or present harmony of morality and sensibility was set up just now, and is now again "displaced." The harmony is in a misty distance beyond consciousness, where nothing can any more be accurately distinguished or grasped; for, to grasp this unity, which we have just tried to do, has proved impossible.

In this merely immanent or implicit harmony, however, consciousness gives up itself altogether. This immanent state is its moral completion, where the struggle of morality and sensibility has ceased, and the latter is in conformity to the former in a way which cannot be made out. On that account this completion is again merely a dissemblance of the actual case; for in point of fact morality would be really giving up itself in that completion, because it is only consciousness of the absolute purpose *qua* pure purpose, i.e. in opposition to all other purposes. Morality is both the activity of this pure purpose, and at the same time the consciousness of rising above sensibility, of being mixed up with sensibility and of opposing and struggling with it. That this moral completion is not taken seriously is directly expressed by consciousness itself in the fact that it shifts this completion away into infinity, i.e. asserts that the completion is never completed.

Thus it is really only the middle state of being incomplete that is admitted to have any value: a state nevertheless which at least is supposed to be one of progress towards completion. Yet it cannot be so; for advancing in morality would really mean approaching its disappearance. For the goal would be the nothingness above mentioned, the abolition of morality and consciousness itself: but to come ever nearer and nearer to nothing means to decrease. Besides, "advancing" would, in general, in the same way as "decreasing," assume distinctions of quantity in morality: but these are quite inadmissible in such a sphere. In morality as the consciousness which takes the ethical end to be pure duty, we cannot think at all of difference, least of all of the superficial difference of quantity: there is only one virtue, only one pure duty, only one morality.

Since, then, it is not moral completion that is taken seriously, but rather the middle state, i.e. as just explained, the condition of no morality, we thus come by another way back to the content of the first postulate. For we cannot perceive how happiness is to be demanded for this moral consciousness on the ground of its worthiness to be happy. It is well aware of its not being complete, and cannot, therefore, in point of fact, demand happiness as a desert, as something of which it is worthy. It can ask happiness to be given merely as an act of free grace, i.e. it can only ask for happiness as such and as a substantive element by itself; it cannot expect it except as the result of chance and caprice, not because there is any absolute reason of the above sort. The condition of non-morality herein expresses just what it is—that it is concerned, not about morality, but about happiness alone, without reference to morality.

By this second aspect of the moral point of view, the assertion of the first aspect, wherein disharmony between morality and happiness is presupposed, is also cancelled. One may pretend to have found by experience that in the actual present the man who is moral often fares badly, while the man who is not, often comes off happily. Yet the middle state of incomplete morality, the condition which has proved to be the essential one, shows clearly that this perception that morality fares badly, this supposed experience of it, is merely a dissemblance of the real facts of the case. For, since morality is not completed, i.e. since morality in point of fact is *not*, what can there be in the "experience" that morality fares badly?

Since, at the same time, it has turned out that the point at issue concerns happiness alone, it is manifest that, in making the criticism, "the man without morality comes off well," there was no intention to convey thereby that there is something wrong in such a case. The designation of an individual as one devoid of morality necessarily falls to the ground, when morality in general is incomplete; such a characterization rests, indeed, on pure caprice. Hence the sense and content of that judgment of experience is simply this, that happiness as such should not have fallen to some who have got it, i.e. the judgment is an expression of envy, which covers itself up in the cloak of morality. The reason, however, why we think good luck, as we call it, should fall to the lot of others is good friendship, which ungrudgingly grants and wishes them, and wishes itself too, this favour, this accident of good fortune.

Morality, then, in the moral consciousness, is not completed. This is what is now established. But its essence consists in being only what *is* complete, and so pure morality: incomplete morality is, therefore, impure, in other words, is Immorality. Morality itself thus exists in another being than the actual concrete consciousness. This other is a *holy moral legislator*.

Morality which is not completed in consciousness, the morality which is the reason for making those postulates, means, in the first instance, that morality, when it is set up as actual in consciousness, stands in relation to something else, to an existence, and thus itself acquires otherness or distinction, whence arises a manifold plurality of moral commands. The moral self-consciousness at the same time, however, looks on these many duties as unessential; for it is concerned with merely the one pure duty, and this plurality of duties, so far as they are determinate duties, has no true reality for self-consciousness. They can thus have their real truth only in another consciousness, and are (what they are not for the actual moral self-consciousness) sacred through a holy law-giver.

But this, too, is again merely a dissembling of the actual fact. For moral self-consciousness is to itself the absolute, and duty is simply and solely what *it* knows to be duty. It, however, knows only pure duty as duty: what is not sacred in its view is not *per se* sacred at all, and what is not *per se* sacred cannot be rendered so by the being that is sacred. Moral consciousness, further, is not really serious in allowing something to be made sacred by another consciousness than its own. For, only that is without qualification sacred in its eyes which is made sacred through its own action, and is sacred within it. It is thus just as little in earnest in treating this other being as a holy being; for this would mean that, within that holy being something was to attain an essential significance, which, for the moral consciousness, i.e. in itself, has none.

If the sacred being was postulated, in order that duty might have binding validity within the moral consciousness, not *qua* pure duty, but as a plurality of specific duties, then this must again be dissembled and this other being must be solely sacred in so far as only pure duty has binding validity within it. Pure duty has also, in point of fact, binding validity only in another being, not in the moral consciousness. Although, within the latter, pure morality seems alone to hold good, still this must be put in another form, for it is, at the same time, a natural consciousness. Morality is, in it, affected and conditioned by sensibility, and thus is not something substantial, but a contingent result of free will; in it, however, *qua* pure will, morality is a contingency of knowledge. Taken by itself, therefore, morality is in another being, is self-complete only in another reality than the actual moral consciousness.

This other being, then, is here absolutely complete morality, because in it morality does not stand in relation to nature and sensibility. Yet the reality of pure duty is its actualization in nature and sensibility. The moral consciousness accounts for its incompleteness by the fact that morality, in its case, has a positive relation to nature and sensibility, since it holds that an essential moment of morality is that morality should have simply and solely a negative relation towards nature and sensibility. The pure moral being, on the other hand, because far above the struggle with nature and sense, does not stand in a negative relation to them. Thus, in point of fact, the positive relation to them alone remains in *its* case, i.e. there remains just what a moment ago passed for the incomplete, for what was *not* moral. Pure morality, however, entirely cut off from actual reality so as likewise to be even without positive relation to reality, would be an unconscious unreal abstraction, where the very notion of morality, which consists in thinking of pure duty and in willing and doing, would be absolutely done away with. This other being, so purely and entirely moral, is again, therefore, a mere dissemblance of the actual fact, and has to be given up.

In this purely moral being, however, the moments of the contradiction, in which this synthetic imaginative process is carried on, come closer together. So, likewise, do the opposites taken up alternately, now this and *also* that, and *also* the other, opposites which are allowed to follow one after the other, the one being constantly supplanted by the other, without these ideas being brought together. So close do they come, that consciousness here has to give up its moral view of the world and retreat within itself.

It knows its morality as incomplete because it is affected by an opposing sensibility and nature, which partly perturb morality as such, and partly give rise to a plurality of duties, by which, in concrete cases of real action, consciousness finds itself embarrassed. For each case is the concrete focus of many moral relations, just as an object of perception in general is a thing with many qualities. And since the determinate duty is its purpose, it has a *content*; its content is a part of the purpose, and so morality is not pure morality. This latter, then, has its real existence in some other being. But such reality means nothing else than that morality is here self-complete, in itself and for itself—*for itself*, i.e. is morality of a consciousness: *in itself*, i.e. has existence and actuality.

In that first incomplete consciousness, morality is not realized and carried out. It is there something immanent and implicit, in the sense of a mere thought-entity; for it is associated with nature and sensibility, with the actuality of [external] existence and conscious life, which constitutes its content; and nature and sensibility are morally nothing. In the second, morality is present as completed, and not in the form of an unrealized thought-element. But this completion consists just in the fact that morality has reality in a consciousness, as well as free reality, objective existence in general, is not something empty, but filled out, full of content. That is to say, the completion of morality is placed in this, that what a moment ago was characterized as morally nothing is found present in morality and inherent in it. It is at one time to have validity simply and solely as the unrealized thought-element, a product of pure abstraction; but, on the other hand, is just as certainly to have in this form no validity at all: its true nature is to consist in being opposed to reality, detached altogether therefrom, and empty, and then again to consist in being actual reality.

The syncretism, or fusion, of these contradictions, which is expressed *in extenso* in the moral attitude of experience, collapses internally, since the distinction on which it rests—viz. the conception of something which must be thought and posited as necessary, and is yet at the same time not essential—passes into one which does not any longer exist even in words. What, at the end, is affirmed to be something with different aspects, both to be nothing and also real, is one and the very same—existence and reality. And what is to be absolute only as something beyond actual existence and actual consciousness, and at the same time to be only in consciousness and so, *qua* beyond, nothing at all—this absolute is pure duty and the knowledge that pure duty is the essentially real. The consciousness, which makes this distinction that is no distinction, which announces actuality to be at once what is nothing and what is real, pronounces pure morality to be both the ultimate truth and also to be devoid of all true reality—such a consciousness expresses together in one and the same breath ideas which it formerly separated, and itself proclaims that it is not in earnest with this characterization and separation of the moments of self and inherent reality. It shows, on the contrary, that, what it announces as absolute existence apart from consciousness, it really keeps enclosed within the self of self-consciousness; and that, what it gives out as the absolute object of thought or absolutely inherent and implicit, it just for that reason takes to be something which has no truth at all.

It becomes clear to consciousness that placing these moments apart from each other is "*dis*-placing" them, is a dissemblance, and it would be *hypocrisy* were it really to keep to this. But, being pure moral self-consciousness, it flees from this discordance between its way of imagining and what constitutes its essential nature, flees from this untruth, which gives out as true what it holds to be untrue, and, turning away with abhorrence, it hastens back into itself. The consciousness, which scorns such a moral idea of the world, is pure *Conscience* (*Gewissen*): it is, in its inmost being, simply spirit consciously assured or "certain" (*gewiss*) of itself, spirit which acts directly in the light of this assurance, which acts conscientiously (*gewissenhaft*), without the intervention of those ideas, and finds its true nature in this direct immediacy.

While, however, this sphere of dissemblance is nothing else than the development of moral self-consciousness in its various moments and is consequently its reality, so too this self-consciousness, by returning into itself, will become, in its inmost nature, nothing else. This returning into itself, indeed, simply means that it has come to be conscious that its truth is a pretended truth, a mere pretence. As returning into itself it would have to be always giving out this pretended truth as its real truth, for it would have to express and display itself as an objective idea; but it would know all the same that this is merely a dissemblance. It would consequently be, in point of fact, hypocrisy, and its abhorrence of such dissemblance would be itself the first expression of hypocrisy.

CONSCIENCE: THE "BEAUTIFUL SOUL": EVIL AND THE FORGIVENESS OF IT

The one-sidedness of each of the preceding stages is removed when the moral consciousness assumes the attitude of Conscience. Here the individual is at once self-legislating and yet sure of the unity and self-completeness of its own will in the midst of all diversity of moral content. The immediacy involved in the idea of a "self-legislating" will appears in the perceptual directness of the action of conscience: it "sees" what is right and does the right without hesitation. But it is not an abstract "faculty" of willing independent of the varied content of the individual's moral experience. The universality of the individual permeates and pervades all the content of his being and makes him a concrete moral individuality, at home with himself in the smallest detail as well as in the larger issues of his self-complete spiritual existence. Conscience, as Butler says, is a "system" or "constitution," analogous in the case of the individual to the objectified system of the state and its institutions. The self-deception of the second one-sided phase of moral experience seems also to have no place in Conscience, for Conscience is the transparent and self-revealing unity in all the content of moral individuality. Only on this condition can it be absolutely confident and certain of itself in all its functions, and this certainty of itself is the inalienable characteristic of conscience. It thinks it cannot be deceived about itself, can neither delude itself nor others, but freely realizes all that it professes to be and professes to be all that it realizes. It is thus the supreme achievement of finite spiritual existence; but it has no meaning apart from the existence of finite spirit in the form of society.

Its very conditions, however, give rise to delusion and deception of another kind. For, so complete is its world and its life, that it may attempt to cut itself off from the concrete substance of actual society which alone makes possible the existence of conscience. It then tries to cultivate goodness in solitary isolation from the actual social whole. This is the attitude of the "beautiful soul," a type of spiritual life cultivated by the "Moravians," and familiar during the Romantic movement. Novalis is the best-known example; the classical interpretation of the mood was given in Goethe's *Meister's Lehrjahre*, Bk. 6. It has the self-confidence and individual inspiration of Conscience, but frankly rejects the concrete objectivity which secures for Conscience liberation from mere subjectivity. The very rejection of objectivity is the only achievement of the "beautiful soul," and is held to be the greatest triumph of its self-conscious freedom. It flees from concrete moral action, and luxuriates in a state of self-hypnotized inactivity. Still it takes up this attitude in the interests of "pure goodness," and hence in withdrawing from the lowly deeds of the daily moral life it indulges all the more in the self-cloistered cult of the beauty of holiness. It is moral individualism turned into mystic self-absorption. Hegel's analysis brings out that this type of spirit is in principle as it was in fact the direct ally of moral evil. For (1) its refusal to act means indifference to all action, good and bad alike, and the rejection of the demands of duty is precisely immorality: (2) its self-closed isolation destroys the very principle of true morality, universality of will, recognition and acknowledgment by others of the claims of the individual will.

But this extremity of finite spiritual experience is the opportunity of Absolute Spirit. The attitude of this mystical moral individuality is indirectly an indication of the finitude of the moral point of view and therefore of its failure to supply the absolute self-completeness which spirit requires. The very consciousness by finite spirit of its inherent incompleteness is implicitly a consciousness of the Absolute Spirit. The consciousness of Absolute Spirit is the attitude of experience known as Religion.

The antinomy in the moral view of the world—viz. that there is a moral consciousness and that there is none, or that the validity, the bindingness of duty has its ground beyond consciousness, and conversely *only* takes effect *in* consciousness—these contradictory elements had been combined in the idea, in which the non-moral consciousness is to pass for moral, its contingent knowledge and will to be accepted as fully sufficing, and happiness to be its lot as a matter of grace. Moral self-consciousness took this self-contradictory idea not upon itself, but transferred it to another being. But this putting outside itself of what it must think as necessary is as much a contradiction in form as the other was in content. But that which appears as contradictory, and that in the division and resolution of which lies the round of activity peculiar to the moral attitude, are inherently the same: for pure duty *qua* pure knowledge is nothing else than the self of consciousness, and the self of consciousness is existence and actuality; and, in the same way, what is to be beyond actual consciousness is nothing else than pure thought, is, in fact, the self. Because this is so, self-consciousness, for us or *per se*, passes back into itself, and becomes aware that that being is its self, in which the actual is at once pure knowledge and pure duty. It takes itself to be absolutely valid in its contingency, to be that which knows its immediate individual being as pure knowledge and action, as the true objective reality and harmony.

This self of Conscience, the mode of spirit immediately certain of itself as absolute truth and objective being, is the third type of spiritual self. It is the outcome of the third sphere of the spiritual world,[1] and may be shortly compared with the two former types of self.

The totality or actuality which is revealed as the truth of the ethical world, the world of the social order, is the self of a Person [the legal self]: its existence lies in being recognized and acknowledged. As the person is the self devoid of substance, this its existence is abstract reality too. The person has a definite standing, and that directly and immediately: its self is the point in the sphere of its existence which is immediately at rest. That point is not torn away from its universality; the two [the particular focus and its universality] are therefore not in a relational process with regard to one another: the universal is in it without distinction, and is neither the content of the self, nor is the self filled by itself.

The second self is the truth and outcome of the world of culture, is spirit that has recovered itself after and through disruption, is absolute freedom. In this self, the former immediate unity of individual existence and universality breaks up into its component elements. The universal, which remains at the same time a purely spiritual entity, the state of recognition or universal will and universal knowledge — the universal is object and content of the self, and its universal actuality. But the universal has not there the form of existence detached from the self: in this mode of self it therefore gets no filling, no positive content, no world.

Moral self-consciousness, indeed, lets its universal aspect get detached, so that this aspect becomes a nature of its own; and at the same time it retains this universality within itself in a superseded form. But it is merely a game of dissembling; it constantly interchanges these two characteristics. In the form of Conscience, with its certainty of itself, it first finds the content to fill the former emptiness of duty as well as the emptiness of right and the empty universal will. And because this certainty of self is at the same time immediacy, it finds in conscience definite existence.

Having reached this level of its truth, moral self-consciousness then leaves, or rather supersedes, this state of internal division and self-separation, whence arose "dissemblance" — the separation of its inherent being from the self, of pure duty, *qua* pure purpose, from reality *qua* a nature and a sensibility opposed to pure purpose. It is, when thus returned into itself, concrete moral spirit, which does not make for itself a bare abstract standard out of the consciousness of pure duty, a

---

[1] Viz. Morality, the first being the *Ethical Order* of Society, the second the sphere of *Culture*.

standard to be set up against actual conscious life; on the contrary, pure duty, as also the sensuous nature opposed to pure duty, are superseded moments. This mode of spirit, in its immediate unity, is a moral being making itself actual, and an act is immediately a concrete embodiment of morality.

Given a case of action; it is an objective reality for the knowing mind. The latter, *qua* conscience, knows it in a direct concrete manner; and at the same time it *is* merely as conscience knows it to be. When knowledge is something other than its object, it is contingent in character. Spirit, however, which is sure of its self, is no longer an accidental knowledge of that kind, is not a way of producing inside its own being ideas from which reality is divorced. On the contrary; since the separation between what is essential and self has been given up, a case of moral action falls, just as it is essentially, directly within immediate conscious certainty, the sensible [feeling] form of knowledge, and it is essentially only as it is in this form of knowledge.

Action, then, *qua* realization, is in this way the pure form of will — the bare conversion of reality in the sense of a given case, into a reality that is enacted, the conversion of the bare state of objective knowledge into one of knowledge about reality as something produced and brought about by consciousness. Just as sensuous certainty is directly taken up, or rather converted, into the essential life and substance of spirit, this other transformation is also simple and unmediated, a transition made through the pure conception without changing the content, the content being conditioned by some interest on the part of the consciousness knowing it.

Further, conscience does not break up the circumstances of the case into a variety of duties. It does not operate as the positive general medium, in which the manifold duties, each for itself, would acquire immovable substantial existence. If it did so, *either* no action could take place at all, because each concrete case involves opposition in general, and, in the specific case of morality, opposition of duties — and hence there would always be one side injured, one duty violated, by the very nature of concrete action: *or* else, if action does take place, the violation of one of the conflicting duties would be the actual result brought about. Conscience is rather the negative single unity, it is the absolute self, which does away with this variety of substantial moral constituents. It is simple action in accordance with duty, action which does not fulfil this or that duty, but knows and does what is concretely right. It is, therefore, in general, and for the first time in moral experience, moral action as action, and into this the previous stage of mere consciousness of morality without action has passed.

The concrete shape which the act takes may be analysed by a conscious process of distinction into a variety of properties, i.e. in this case into a variety of moral relationships; and these may either be each expressly held to be absolute (as each must be if it is to be duty) or, again, subjected to comparison and criticism. In the simple moral action arising from conscience, duties are so piled and commingled that the isolated independence of all these separate entities is immediately destroyed, and the process of critically considering and worrying about what our duty is finds no place at all in the unshaken certainty of conscience.

Just as little, again, do we find in conscience that fluctuating uncertainty of mind, which puts now so-called "pure" morality away from itself, assigning it to some other holy being, and takes itself to be unholy, and then again, on the other hand, puts this moral purity within itself, and places in that other the connexion of the sensuous with the moral element.

It renounces all these semblances and dissemblances (*Stellungen und Verstellungen*) characteristic of the moral point of view, when it gives up thinking that there is a contradiction between duty and actual reality. According to this latter state of mind, I act morally when I am conscious of performing merely pure duty and nothing else but that: i.e. in fact, when I do *not* act. When, however, I really act, I am conscious of an "other," of a reality which is there before me, and one which I want to bring about; I have a definite end and fulfil a definite duty. There is something else therein than the pure duty, which alone was supposed to be kept in view.

Conscience, on the other hand, is the sense that, when the moral consciousness declares pure duty to be the essence of its action, this pure purpose is a dissemblance of the actual fact. For the real fact is that pure duty consists in the empty abstraction of pure thought, and finds its reality and content solely in some definite actual existence, an actuality which is actuality of consciousness itself—not of consciousness in the sense of a thought-entity, but as an individual. Conscience for its own part, finds its truth to lie in the direct certainty of itself. This immediate concrete certainty of itself is the real essence. Looking at this certainty from the point of view of the opposition which consciousness involves, the agent's own immediate individuality constitutes the content of moral action; and the form of moral action is just this very self as a pure process, viz. as the process of knowing, in other words, is private individual conviction.

Looking more closely at the unity and the significance of the moments of this stage, we find that moral consciousness conceived itself merely in the form of the inherent principle, or as ultimate essence; *qua* conscience, however, it lays hold of its explicit individual self-existence (*Fürsichseyn*), or its self. The contradiction involved in the moral point of view is resolved, i.e. the distinction, which lay at the basis of its peculiar attitude, proves to be no distinction, and melts into the process of pure negativity. This process of negativity is, however, just the self: a single simple self which is at once pure knowledge and knowledge of itself as this individual conscious life. This self constitutes, therefore, the content of what formerly was the empty essence; for it is something actual and concrete, which no longer has the significance of being a nature alien to the ultimate essence, a nature independent and with laws of its own. As the negative element, it introduces distinction into the pure essence, a definite content, and one, too, which has a value in its own right as it stands.

Further, this self is, *qua* pure self-identical knowledge, the universal without qualification, so that just this knowledge, being its very own knowledge, being conviction, constitutes *duty*. Duty is no longer the universal appearing over against and opposed to the self; duty is known to have in this condition of separation no validity. It is now the law which exists for the sake of the self, and not the law for the sake of which the self exists. The law and duty, however, have for that reason not only the significance of existing on their own account, but also of being inherent and essential; for this knowledge is, in virtue of its identity with itself, just what is inherently essential. This inherent being gets also separated in consciousness from that direct and immediate unity with self-existence: so contrasted and opposed, it is objective being, it is being for something else.

Duty itself now, *qua* duty deserted by the self, is known to be merely a moment; it has ceased to mean absolute being, it has become degraded to something which is not a self, does not exist on its own account, and is thus what exists for something else. But this existing-for-something-else remains an essential moment just for the reason that self, *qua* consciousness, constitutes and establishes the opposition between existence-for-self and existence-for-another; and now duty essentially means something immediately actual, and is no longer a mere abstract pure consciousness.

This existence for something else is, then, the inherently essential substance distinguished from the self. Conscience has not given up pure duty, the abstract implicit essence: pure duty is the essential moment of relating itself, *qua* universality, to others. Conscience is the common element of distinct self-consciousnesses; and this is the substance in which the act secures subsistence and reality, the moment of being recognized by others. The moral self-consciousness does not possess this moment of recognition, of pure consciousness which has definite existence; and on that account really does not "act" at all, does not effectually actualize anything. Its inherent nature is for it either the abstract unreal essence, or else existence in the form of a reality which has no spiritual character. The actual reality of conscience, however, is one which is a self, i.e. an existence conscious of itself, the spiritual element of being recognized. Doing something is, therefore, merely the translation of its individual content into that objective element where it is universal and is recognized, and this very fact, that the content is recognized, makes the deed an actuality. The action is recognized and thereby real, because the actual reality is immediately bound up with conviction or knowledge; or, in other words, knowledge of one's purpose is immediately and at once the element of existence, is universal recognition. For the essence of the act, duty, consists in the conviction conscience has about it. This conviction is just the inherent principle itself; it is inherently universal self-consciousness—in other words, is recognition and hence reality. The result achieved under conviction of duty is therefore directly one which has substantial solid existence. Thus, we hear nothing more there about good intention not coming to anything definite, or about the good man faring badly. What is known as duty is carried out completely and becomes an actual fact, just because what is dutiful is the universal for all self-consciousnesses, that which is recognized, acknowledged, and thus objectively *is*. Taken separately and alone, however, without the content of self, this duty is existence-for-another, the transparent element, which has merely the significance of an unsubstantial essential factor in general.

If we look back on the sphere where spiritual reality first made its appearance, we find that the principle involved was that the utterance of individuality is the absolutely real, the ultimately substantial. But the shape which, in the first instance, gave expression to this principle, was the "honest consciousness"[2] which was occupied and concerned with abstract "fact itself." This "fact itself" was there a predicate. In conscience, however, it is for the first time a Subject, which has affirmed within it all aspects of consciousness, and for which all these moments, substantiality in general, external existence, and essence of thought, are contained in this certainty of itself. The "fact itself" has substantiality in general in the ethical order (*Sittlichkeit*), external existence in culture, self-knowing essence of thought in morality; and in conscience it is the Subject, which knows these moments within itself. While the "honest consciousness" is for ever grasping merely the bare and empty "fact itself," conscience, on the other hand, secures the "fact itself" in its fullness, a fullness which conscience of itself supplies. Conscience has this power through its knowing the moments of consciousness as

---

[2] *v.* p. 235 ff.

moments, and controlling them because it is their negative essential principle.

When conscience is considered in relation to the single features of the opposition which appears in action, and when we consider its consciousness regarding the nature of those features, its attitude towards the reality of the situation where action has to take place is, in the first instance, that of knowledge. So far as the aspect of universality is present in such knowledge, it is the business of conscientious action *qua* knowledge, to compass the reality before it in an unrestricted exhaustive manner, and thus to know exactly the circumstances of the case, and give them due consideration. This knowledge, however, since it is aware of universality as a moment, is in consequence a kind of knowledge of these circumstances which is conscious all the while of not embracing them, is conscious of not being conscientious in its procedure. The genuinely universal and pure relation of knowledge would be one towards something not opposed, a relation to itself. But action through the opposition essentially implied in action is related to what negates consciousness, to a reality existing *per se*. This reality—being, as contrasted with the simple nature of pure consciousness, the absolute other, multiplicity *per se*—is a sheer plurality of circumstances which breaks up indefinitely and spreads in all directions—backwards into their conditions, sidewards in their associations, forwards in their consequences.

The conscientious mind is aware of this nature of "the fact" and of its relation thereto, and knows it is not acquainted to the full and complete extent required with the situation in which its action takes place, and knows that its pretence of conscientiously weighing and considering *all* the circumstances is futile. This acquaintance with and consideration of all the circumstances, however, are not entirely absent: but they are merely present as a moment, as something which is only for others: and the conscientious mind holds its *incomplete* knowledge to be sufficient and complete, *because* it is its *own* knowledge.

In a similar way the process is constituted in connexion with the universality of the essential principle, that is, with the characterization of the content as determined through pure consciousness. Conscience, when it goes on to act, takes up a relation to the various sides of the case. The case breaks up into separate elements, and the relation of pure consciousness towards it does the same: whereby the multiplicity characteristic of the case becomes a multiplicity of duties. Conscience knows that it has to select and decide amongst them; for none of them specifically, in its content, is an absolute duty; only pure duty is so. But this abstract entity has, in its realization, come to denote self-conscious ego. Spirit certain of itself is at rest within itself in the form of conscience, and its real universality, its duty, lies in its pure conviction concerning duty. This pure conviction as such is as empty as pure duty, pure in the sense that nothing within it, no definite content, is duty. Action, however, has to take place, the individual must determine to do something or other; and spirit which is certain of itself, in which the inherent principle has attained the significance of self-conscious ego, knows it has this determination, this specific content, in the immediate certainty of its own self. This certainty, being a determination and a content, is "natural" consciousness, i.e. the various impulses and inclinations.

Conscience admits no content as absolute for it, because it is absolute negativity of all that is definite. It determines from itself alone. The circle of the self, however, within which determinateness as such falls, is so-called "sensibility": in order to get a content out of the immediate certainty of self, there is no other element to be found except sensibility.

Everything that in previous modes of experience was presented as good or bad, law and right, is something other than immediate certainty of self; it is a universal, which is now a relative entity, an existence-for-another. Or, looked at otherwise, it is an object which, while connecting and relating consciousness with itself, comes between consciousness and its own proper truth, and instead of that object being the immediacy of consciousness, it rather cuts consciousness off from itself.

For conscience, however, certainty of self is the pure, direct, and immediate truth: and this truth is thus its immediate certainty of self presented as content; i.e. its truth is altogether the caprice of the individual, and the accidental content of his unconscious natural existence [his sensibility].

This content at the same time passes for essential moral reality, for duty. For pure duty, as was found when testing and examining laws,[3] is utterly indifferent to every content, and gets along with any. Here it has at the same time the essential form of self-existence, of existing on its own account: and this form of individual conviction is nothing else than the sense of the emptiness of pure duty, and the consciousness that this is merely a moment, that its substantiality is a predicate which finds its subject in the individual, whose caprice gives pure duty content, can connect every content with this form, and attach its feeling of conscientiousness to any content.

An individual increases his property in a certain way. It is a duty that each should see to the maintenance of himself and family, and no less

---

[3] v. p. 244 ff.

ensure the possibility of his being serviceable to his neighbours and of doing good to those standing in need. The individual is aware that this is a duty, for this content is directly contained in the certainty he has of himself. He perceives, further, that he fulfils this particular duty in this particular case. Other people possibly consider the specific way he adopts as fraud: they hold by other sides of the concrete case presented, while he holds firmly to this particular side of it by the fact of his being conscious that the increase of property is a pure and absolute duty.

In the same way there is fulfilled by the individual, as a duty, what other people call violence and wrongdoing—the duty of asserting one's independence against others: and, again, the duty of preserving one's life, and the possibility of being useful to one's neighbours. Others call this cowardice, but what they call courage really violates both these duties. But cowardice must not be so stupid and clumsy as not to know that the maintenance of life and the possibility of being useful to others are duties—so inept as not to be convinced of the dutifulness of its action, and not to know that dutifulness consists in knowledge. Otherwise it would commit the stupidity of being immoral. Since morality lies in the consciousness of having fulfilled one's duty, this will not be lacking when the action is what is called cowardice any more than when it is what is called courage. As the abstraction called "duty" is capable of every content, it is quite equal to that of cowardice. The agent knows what he does to be duty, and since he knows this, and *conviction* as to duty is just *dutifulness*, he is thus recognized and acknowledged by others. The act thereby becomes accepted as valid and has actual existence.

It is of no avail to object to this freedom—which puts any and every kind of content into this universal inert receptacle of pure duty and pure knowledge—by asserting that another content ought to have been put there. For whatever the content be, each content has upon it the stain of determinateness from which pure knowledge is free, which pure knowledge can despise just as readily as it can take up every determinateness in turn. Every content, through its being determinate, stands on the same footing with every other, even though it seems to have precisely the character that the particularity in the content is cancelled. It may well seem—since in concrete cases duty breaks regularly into opposition, and, by doing so, sunders the opposites individuality and universality—that the duty, whose content is the universal as such, contains on that account, *ipso facto*, the nature of pure duty, and that thus form and content are here entirely in accord. On this view, it might seem that, e.g. acting for the universal good, for what is the best for all, is to be preferred to acting for what is the best for the individual. But this universal duty is precisely what is present as self-contained actual substance, in the form of [established] law and right, and holds good independently of the individual's knowledge and conviction as well as of his immediate interest. It is thus precisely that against the form of which morality as a whole is directed. As regards its content, however, this too is determinate in character, in so far as the "universally best" is opposed to the "individual best." Consequently, its law is one from which conscience knows itself to be absolutely free, and it gives itself the absolute privilege to add and pare, to neglect as well as fulfil it.

Then, again, the above distinction of duty towards the individual and duty towards the universal is not something fixed and final, when we look at the nature of the opposition in question. On the contrary, what the individual does for himself is to the advantage of the universal as well. The more he looks after his own good, not only is there the greater *possibility* of his usefulness to others: his very reality consists merely in his living and existing in connexion with others. His individual enjoyment means ultimately and essentially putting what is his own at the disposal of others, and helping them to secure *their* enjoyment. In fulfilling duty to individuals, and hence duty to self, duty to the general thus also gets fulfilled. Weighing, considering, comparing duties, should this appear here, would take the line of calculating the advantage which the general would get from any given action. But there can be no such process; partly because morality would thereby be handed over to the inevitable contingency characteristic of mere "insight"; partly because it is precisely the nature of conscience to have done with all this calculating and weighing of duties, and to decide directly from itself without any such reasons.

In this way, then, conscience acts and maintains itself in the unity of its essential being and its objective existence for itself, in the unity of pure thought and individuality: it is spirit certain of itself, which inherently possesses its own truth, within itself, in its knowledge, a knowledge in the sense of knowledge of its duty. It maintains its being therein by the fact that the positive element in the act, the content as well as form of duty and the knowledge of duty, belong to the self, to the certainty of itself. What, however, seeks to come before the self with an inherent being of its own is held to be not truly real, merely a transcended element, only a moment. Consequently, it is not universal knowledge in general that has a value, but what is known of the circumstances. It puts into duty, which is the universal immanent essence, the content which it derives from its natural individuality; for the content is one that is present in its own being. This content, in virtue of the universal medium wherein it exists, becomes the duty which it carries out, and empty pure duty is, through this very fact, affirmed to be something transcended, a moment. This content is its emptiness, transcended and cancelled, i.e. is the fulfilling of pure duty.

But at the same time conscience is detached from every possible content. It absolves itself from every specific duty, which would try to pass for a law. In the strength of its certainty of itself, it has the majesty of absolute self-sufficiency, of absolute αὐτάρκεια, to bind or to loose. This self-determination is at once, therefore, absolute conformity to duty. Duty is the knowledge itself; this pure and simple selfhood, however, is the immanent principle and essence; for this inherent principle is pure self-identity, and self-identity lies in this consciousness.

This pure knowledge is immediately objective, is existence-for-another; for, *qua* pure self-identity, it is immediacy, it is objective being. This being, however, is at the same time pure universality, the selfhood of all: in other words, action is acknowledged, and hence actual. This being forms the element by which conscience directly stands on a footing of equality with every self-consciousness; and this relation means not an abstract impersonal law, but the self of conscience.

In that this right which conscience does is at the same time, however, a fact for others, a disparity seems to affect conscience. The duty which it fulfils is a determinate content; that content is, no doubt, the self of consciousness, and so its knowledge of itself, its identity with its self. But when fulfilled, when planted in the general element of existence, this identity is no longer knowledge, no longer this process of distinction which directly and at the same time does away with its distinctions. Rather, in the sphere of existence, the distinction is set up as subsistent, and the act is a determinate specific one, not identical with the element of everybody's self-consciousness, and hence *not* necessarily acknowledged and recognized. Both aspects, conscience *qua* acting, and the general consciousness acknowledging this act to be duty, stand equally loose from the specific character belonging to this deed. On account of this freedom and detachment, the relation of the two within the common medium of their connexion is rather a relationship of complete disparity—as a result of which, the consciousness, which is aware of the act, finds itself in complete *uncertainty* regarding the spirit which does the act and is "certain of itself." This spirit acts and places in existence a determinate characteristic; others hold to this existence, as its truth, and are therein certain of this spirit; it has therein expressed *what* it takes to be its duty. But it is detached and free from any specific duty; it has, therefore, left the point where other people think it actually to be; and this very medium of existence and duty as inherently existing are held by it to be merely transitory moments. What it thus places before them, it also "displaces" again, or rather has, *eo ipso*, immediately "displaced." For its reality is, for it, not the duty and determinate content thus put forward, but rather is the reality which it has in its absolute certainty of itself.

The other self-consciousnesses do not know, then, whether this particular conscience is morally good or is wicked; or, rather, not merely can they not know this conscience, but they must take it to be also wicked. For just as it stands loose to the determinate content of duty, and detached from duty as inherently existing, so do they likewise. What it places before them, they themselves know how to "displace" or dissemble: it is something expressing merely the self of another individual, not their own: they do not merely know themselves to be detached and free from it, but have to resolve and analyse it within their own consciousness, reduce it to nothingness by judgments and explanations in order to preserve their own self.

But the act of conscience is not merely this determination of existence, a determinate content forsaken by the pure self. What is to be binding and to be recognized as duty, only is so through knowledge and conviction as to its being duty, by knowledge of self in the deed done. When the deed ceases to have this self in it, it ceases to be what is alone its essential nature. Its existence, if deserted by this consciousness of self, would be an ordinary reality, and the act would appear to us a way of fulfilling one's pleasure and desire. What ought to exist has here essentiality only by its being known to be individuality giving itself expression. And its being thus known is what is acknowledged and recognized by others, and is that which as such ought to have existence.

The self enters existence as self. The spirit which is certain of itself exists as such for others; its immediate act is not what is valid and real; what is acknowledged by others is, not the determinate element, not the inherent being, but solely and simply the self knowing itself as such. The element which gives permanence and stability is universal self-consciousness. What enters this element cannot be the effect of the act: the latter does not last there, and acquires no permanence: only self-consciousness is what is recognized and gains concrete reality.

Here again,[4] then, we see Language to be the form in which spirit finds existence. Language is self-consciousness existing *for others*; it is self-consciousness which as such is there immediately present, and which in its individuality is universal. Language is self separating itself from itself, which as the pure ego identical with ego becomes an object to itself, which at once maintains itself in this objective form as *this* actual self, and at the same time fuses directly with others and is *their* self-consciousness. The self perceives itself at the same time that it is per-

---

[4]v. p. 297 ff.

ceived by others: and this perceiving is just existence which has become a self.

The content, which language has here obtained, is no longer the self we found in the world of culture, perverted, perverting, and distraught. It is spirit which, having returned to itself, is certain of itself, certain in itself of its truth, or of its own act of recognition, and which is recognized as this knowledge. The language of the ethical spirit of society is law, and simple command and complaint, which is but a tear shed over necessity. Moral consciousness, on the other hand, remains dumb, shut up within its inner life; for self has no existence as yet in its case: rather existence and self there stand as yet only in external relation to each other. Language, however, comes forward merely as the mediating element only between self-consciousnesses independent and recognized; and the existent self means immediately universal recognition, means manifold recognition and in this very manifoldness simple recognition. What the language of conscience contains is the self knowing itself as essential reality. This alone is what that language expresses, and this expression is the true realization of "doing," of action, and is the validation of the act. Consciousness expresses its conviction: in this conviction alone is the action duty: it holds good as duty, too, solely by the conviction being *expressed*. For universal self-consciousness stands detached from the specific act which merely exists: the act *qua* existence means nothing to it: what it holds of importance is the *conviction* that the act is a duty; and this appears concretely in language.

To realize the act means here not translating its content from the form of purpose, or self-existence, into the form of abstract reality: it means translating it from the form of immediate certainty of self, which takes its knowledge, its self-existence, to be the essential fact, into the form of the assurance that consciousness is convinced of its duty, and, being conscience, knows of itself what duty is. This assurance thus guarantees that consciousness is convinced of its conviction being the essential fact.

Whether the assurance, that it acts from conviction of duty, is true, whether it really is *duty* which is done — these questions or doubts have no meaning as directed against conscience. In the case of the question, whether the assurance is true, it would be assumed that the inner attention is different from the one put forward, i.e. that the willing of the individual self can be separated from duty, from the will of the universal and pure consciousness: the latter will would in that case be a matter of words, while the former would be strictly the real moving principle of the act. But such a distinction between the universal consciousness and the individual self is precisely what has been cancelled, and the superseding of it constitutes conscience. Immediate knowledge on the part of self which is certain of itself is law and duty. Its intention, by being *its own* intention, is what is right. All that is required is that it should know this, and state its conviction that its knowledge and will are the right. The expression of this assurance *ipso facto* cancels the form of its particularity. It recognizes thereby the necessary universality of the self. In that it calls itself *conscience*, it calls itself pure self-knowledge and pure abstract will, i.e. it calls itself a universal knowledge and will which acknowledges and recognizes others, is like them—for they are just this pure self-knowledge and will—and which is on that account also recognized by *them*. In the willing of the self which is certain of itself, in this knowledge of the self as the essential reality, lies the essence of the right.

When any one says, therefore, he is acting from conscience, he is saying what is true, for his conscience is the self which knows and wills. But it is essential he should *say* so, for this self has to be at the same time universal self. It is not universal in the content of the act: for this content is *per se* indifferent on account of its being specific and determinate. The universality lies in the form of the act. It is this form which is to be affirmed as real: the form is the self, which as such is actual in language, pronounces itself to be the truth, and just by so doing acknowledges all other selves, and is recognized by them.

Conscience, then, in its majestic sublimity above any specific law and every content of duty, puts whatever content it pleases into its knowledge and willing. It is moral genius and originality, which knows the inner voice of its immediate knowledge to be a voice divine; and since in such knowledge it directly knows existence as well, it is divine creative power, which contains living force in its very conception. It is in itself, too, divine worship, "service of God," for its action is the contemplation of this its own proper divinity.

This solitary worship, this "service of God" in solitude of soul, is at the same time essentially "service of God" on the part of a religious community; and pure inward self-knowledge and perception of self pass to being a moment of consciousness.[5] Contemplation of itself is its objective existence, and this objective element is the utterance of its knowledge and will as a universal. Through such expression the self becomes established and accepted, and the act becomes an effective deed, a deed carrying out a definite result. What gives reality and subsistence to its deed is universal self-consciousness. When, however, conscience finds expression, this puts the certainty of itself in the form of pure self and thereby as universal self. Others let the act hold as valid, owing to the explicit terms in which the self is thus expressed and

---

[5] i.e. into a state which implies distinction and opposition of subject and object.

acknowledged to be the essential reality. The spirit and the substance of their community are, thus, the mutual assurance of their conscientiousness, of their good intentions, the rejoicing over this reciprocal purity of purpose, the quickening and refreshment received from the glorious privilege of knowing and of expressing, of fostering and cherishing, a state so altogether admirable.

So far as this sphere of conscience still distinguishes its abstract consciousness from its self-consciousness, its life is merely hid in God. God is indeed immediately present to its mind and heart, to its self. But what is revealed, its actual consciousness and the mediating process of this consciousness, is, to it, something other than that hidden inner life and the immediacy of God's presence. But, with the completion of conscience, the distinction between its abstract consciousness and its self-consciousness is done away. It knows that the abstract consciousness is just this self, this individual self-existence which is certain of itself: that the very difference between the terms is abolished in the *immediateness* of the relation of the self to the ultimate Being, which, when placed outside the self, is the abstract essence, and a Being concealed from it. For a relation is mediate when the terms related are not one and the same, but each is a different term for the other, and is one only with the other in some third term: an *immediate* relation, however, means, in fact, nothing else than the unity of the terms. Having risen above the meaningless position of holding these distinctions, which are not distinctions at all, to be still such, consciousness knows the immediateness of the presence of ultimate Being within it to be the unity of that Being and its self: it thus knows itself to be the living inherent reality, and knows its knowledge to be Religion, which, *qua* knowledge viewed as an object or knowledge with an objective existence, is the utterance of the religious communion regarding its own spirit.

We see then, here, self-consciousness withdrawn into the inmost retreats of its being, with all externality, as such, gone and vanished from it—returned into the intuition of ego as altogether identical with ego, an intuition where this ego is all that is essential, and all that exists. It is swamped in this conception of itself; for it has been driven to the extreme limit of its extreme positions, and in such a way that the moments distinguished, moments through which it is real or still consciousness, are not merely *for us* these bare extremes; rather what it is for itself, and what, to it, is inherent, and what is, for it, existence—all these moments have evaporated into abstractions. They have no longer stability, no substantial existence for this consciousness itself. Everything, that was hitherto for consciousness essential, has reverted into these abstractions. When clarified to this degree of transparency, consciousness exists in its poorest form, and the poverty, constituting its sole and only possession, is itself a process of disappearance. This absolute *certainty* into which the substance has been resolved is absolute *untruth*, which collapses within itself; it is absolute self-consciousness, in which consciousness [with its relation of self and object] is submerged and goes under.

Looking at this submergence and disappearance from within, the inherent and essential substance is, for consciousness, knowledge in the sense of *its* knowledge. Being consciousness, it is split up into the opposition between itself and the object, which is, for it, the essentially real. But this very object is what is perfectly transparent, is its self; and its consciousness is merely knowledge of itself. All life and all spiritual truth have returned into this self, and have lost their difference from the ego. The moments of consciousness are therefore these extreme abstractions, of which none holds its ground, but each loses itself in the other and produces it. We have here the process of the "unhappy soul,"[6] in restless change with self; in the present case, however, this is a conscious experience going on inside itself, fully conscious of being the notion of reason, while the "unhappy soul" above spoken of was only reason implicitly. The absolute certainty of self thus finds itself, *qua* consciousness, converted directly into a dying sound, a mere objectification of its subjectivity or self-existence. But this world so created is the utterance of its own voice, which in like manner it has directly heard, and only the echo of which returns to it. This return does not therefore mean that the self is there in its true reality (*an und für sich*): for the real is, for it, not an inherent being, is no *per se*, but its very self. Just as little has consciousness itself existence, for the objective aspect does not succeed in becoming something negative of the actual self, in the same way as this self does not reach complete actuality. It lacks force to externalize itself, the power to make itself a thing, and endure existence. It lives in dread of staining the radiance of its inner being by action and existence. And to preserve the purity of its heart, it flees from contact with actuality, and steadfastly perseveres in a state of self-willed impotence to renounce a self which is pared away to the last point of abstraction, and to give itself substantial existence, or, in other words, to transform its thought into being, and commit itself to absolute distinction [that between thought and being]. The hollow object, which it produces, now fills it, therefore, with the feeling of emptiness. Its activity consists in yearning, which merely loses itself in becoming an unsubstantial shadowy object, and, rising above this loss and falling back on itself, finds itself merely as lost. In this transparent purity of its moments it becomes a sorrow-laden "beautiful soul," as it is called; its

---

[6]*v.* p. 119 ff.

light dims and dies within it, and it vanishes as a shapeless vapour dissolving into thin air.[7]

This silent fusion of the pithless unsubstantial elements of evaporated life has, however, still to be taken in the other sense of the reality of conscience, and in the way its process actually appears. Conscience has to be considered as *acting*. The objective moment in this phase of consciousness took above the determinate form of universal consciousness. The knowing of self is, *qua this* particular self, different from the other self. Language in which all reciprocally recognize and acknowledge each other as acting conscientiously—this general equality breaks up into the inequality of each individual existing for himself; each consciousness is just as much reflected out of its universality absolutely into itself as it is universal. By this means there necessarily comes about the opposition of individuality to other individuals and to the universal. And this relation and its process we have to consider.

Or, again, this universality and duty have the absolutely opposite significance; they signify determinate individuality, exempting itself from what is universal, individuality which looks on pure duty as universality that has appeared merely on the surface and is turned outwards: "duty is merely a matter of words," and passes for that whose being is for something else. Conscience, which in the first instance takes up merely a negative attitude towards duty, *qua* a given determinate duty, knows itself detached from it. But since conscience fills empty duty with a determinate content drawn from its own self, it is positively aware of the fact that it, *qua* this particular self, makes its own content. Its pure self, as it is empty knowledge, is without content and without definiteness. The content which it supplies to that knowledge is drawn from its own self, *qua* this determinate self, is drawn from itself as a natural individuality. In affirming the conscientiousness of its action, it is doubtless aware of its pure self, but in the purpose of its action—a purpose which brings in a concrete content—it is conscious of itself as this particular individual, and is conscious of the opposition between what it is for itself and what it is for others, of the opposition of universality or duty and its state of being reflected into self away from the universal.

While in this way the opposition, into which conscience passes when it acts, finds expression in its inner life, the opposition is at the same time disparity on its outer side, in the sphere of existence—the lack of correspondence of its particular individuality with reference to another individual. Its special peculiarity consists in the fact that the two elements constituting its consciousness—viz. the self and the inherent nature (*Ansich*)—are unequal in value and significance within

---

[7] Cf. Hegel's remarks on Jacobi's conception of the "beautiful soul": W.W., X., 1, p. 303.

it; an inequality in which they are so determined that certainty of self is the essential fact as against the inherent nature, or the universal, which is taken to be merely a moment. Over against this internal determination there thus stands the element of existence, the universal consciousness; for this latter it is rather universality, duty, that is the essential fact, while individuality, which exists for itself and is opposed to the universal, has merely the value of a superseded moment. The first consciousness is held to be *Evil* by the consciousness which thus stands by the fact of duty, because of the lack of correspondence of its internal subjective life with the universal; and since at the same time the first consciousness declares its act to be congruency with itself, to be duty and conscientiousness, it is held by that universal consciousness to be *Hypocrisy*.

The course taken by this opposition is, in the first instance, the formal establishment of correspondence between what the evil consciousness is in its own nature and what it expressly says. It has to be made manifest that it is evil, and its objective existence thus made congruent with its real nature; the hypocrisy must be unmasked. This return of the discordance, present in hypocrisy, into the state of correspondence is not at once brought to pass by the mere fact that, as people usually say, hypocrisy just proves its reverence for duty and virtue through assuming the appearance of them, and using this as a mask to hide itself from its own consciousness no less than from another—as if, in this acknowledgment and recognition in itself of its opposite, *eo ipso* congruency and agreement were implied and contained. Yet even then it is just as truly done with this recognition in words and is reflected into self; and in the very fact of its using the inherent and essential reality merely as something which has a significance for another consciousness, there is really implied its own contempt for that inherent principle, and the demonstration of the worthlessness of that reality for all. For what lets itself be used as an external instrument shows itself to be a thing, which has within it no proper weight and worth of its own.

Moreover, this correspondence is not brought about either by the evil consciousness persisting onesidedly in its own state, or by the judgment of the universal consciousness. If the former denies itself as against the consciousness of duty, and maintains that what the latter pronounces to be baseness, to be absolute discordance with universality, is an action according to inner law and conscience, then, in this onesided assurance of identity and concord, there still remains its discordance with the other, since this other universal consciousness certainly does not believe the assurance and does not acknowledge it. In other words, since onesided insistence on one extreme destroys itself, evil would indeed thereby confess to being evil, but in so doing would at once cancel itself and cease to be hypocrisy, and so would not *qua* hypocrisy be unmasked. It confesses itself, in fact, to be evil by asserting that, while opposing what is recognized as universal, it acts according to its own inner law and conscience. For were this law and conscience not the law of its individuality and caprice, it would not be something inward, something private, but what is universally accepted and acknowledged. When, therefore, any one says he acts towards others from a law and conscience of his own, he is saying, in point of fact, that he is abusing and wronging them. But actual conscience is not this insistence on a knowledge and a will which are opposed to what is universal; the universal is the element of its existence, and its very language pronounces its action to be *recognized* duty.

Just as little, when the universal consciousness persists in its own judgment, does this unmask and dissipate hypocrisy. When that universal consciousness stigmatizes hypocrisy as bad, base, and so on, it appeals, in passing such a judgment, to its *own* law, just as the evil consciousness appeals to *its* law. For the former law makes its appearance in opposition to the latter, and thereby as a particular law. It has, therefore, no antecedent claim over the other law; rather it legitimizes this other law. Hence the universal consciousness, by its zeal in abusing hypocrisy, does precisely the opposite of what it means to do: for it shows that its so-called "true duty," which ought to be universally acknowledged, is something *not* acknowledged and recognized, and consequently it grants the other an equal right of independently existing on its own account.

This judgment [of universal consciousness], however, has, at the same time, another side to it, from which it leads the way to the dissolution of the opposition in question. Consciousness of the universal does not proceed, *qua real* and *qua acting*, to deal with the evil consciousness; for this latter, rather, is the real. In opposing the latter, it is a consciousness which is not entangled in the opposition of individual and universal involved in action. It stays within the universality of thought, takes up the attitude of an apprehending intelligence, and its first act is merely that of judgment. Through this judgment it now places itself, as was just observed, alongside the first consciousness, and the latter, through this likeness between them, comes to see itself in this other consciousness. For the consciousness of duty maintains the passive attitude of apprehension. Thereby it is in contradiction with itself as the absolute will of duty, as the self that determines absolutely from itself. It may well preserve itself in its purity, for it does not act; it is hypocrisy, which wants to see the fact of judging taken for the actual deed, and instead of proving its uprightness and honesty by acts does so by expressing fine sentiments. It is thus constituted entirely in the same

way as that against which the reproach is made of putting its phrases in
place of duty. In both alike the aspect of reality is distinct from the express statements—in the one owing to the selfish purpose of the action,
in the other through failure to act at all, although the necessity of acting is involved in the very speaking of duty, for duty without deeds is altogether meaningless.

The act of judging, however, has also to be looked at as a positive act
of thought and has a positive content: this aspect makes the contradiction present in the apprehending consciousness, and its identity with
the first consciousness, still more complete. The active consciousness
declares its specific deed to be its duty, and the consciousness that
passes judgment cannot deny this; for duty as such is form void of all
content and capable of any. In other words, concrete action, inherently
implying diversity in its manysidedness, involves the universal aspect,
which is that which is taken as duty, just as much as the particular,
which constitutes the share and interest the individual has in the act.
Now the judging consciousness does not stop at the former aspect of
duty and rest content with the knowledge which the active agent has of
this, viz. that this is his duty, the condition and the status of his reality.
It holds on to the other aspect, diverts the act into the inner realm, and
explains the act from selfish motives and from its inner intention, an intention different from the act itself. As every act is capable of treatment
in respect of its dutifulness, so, too, each can be considered from this
other point of view of particularity; for as an act it is the reality of an
individual.

This process of judging, then, takes the act out of the sphere of its
objective existence, and turns it back into the inner subjective sphere,
into the form of private or individual particularity. If the act carries
glory with it, then the inner sphere is judged as love of fame. If it is altogether conformity with the position of the individual, without going
beyond this position, and is so constituted that the individuality in question does not have the position attached to it as an external feature, but
through itself supplies concrete filling to this universality, and by that
very process shows itself to be capable of a higher station—then the
inner nature of the act is judged as ambition; and so on. Since, in the
act in general, the individual who acts comes to see himself in objective form, or gets the feeling of his own being in his objective existence
and thus attains enjoyment, the judgment on the act finds the inner nature of it to be an impulse towards personal happiness, even though this
happiness were to consist merely in inner moral vanity, the enjoyment
of a sense of personal excellence, and in the foretaste and hope of a
happiness to come.

No act can escape being judged in such a way; for "duty for duty's sake," this pure purpose, is something unreal. What reality it has lies in the deed of some individuality, and the action thereby has in it the aspect of particularity. No hero is a hero to his valet, not, however, because the hero is not a hero, but because the valet is—the valet, with whom the hero has to do, not as a hero, but as a man who eats, drinks, and dresses, who, in short, appears as a private individual with certain personal wants and ideas of his own. In the same way, there is no act in which that process of judgment cannot oppose the personal aspect of the individuality to the universal aspect of the act, and play the part of the "moral" valet towards the agent.[8]

The consciousness, that so passes judgment, is in consequence *itself* base and mean, because it divides the act up, and produces and holds to the act's self-discordance. It is, furthermore, hypocrisy, because it gives out this way of judging, not as another fashion of being wicked, but as the correct consciousness of the act; sets itself up, in its unreality, in this vanity of knowing well and better, far above the deeds it decries; and wants to find its mere words without deeds taken for an admirable kind of reality.

On this account, then, putting itself on a level with the agent on whom it passes judgment, it is recognized by the latter as the same as himself. This latter does not merely find himself apprehended as something alien to, and discordant with, that other: but rather finds the other in its peculiar constitutive character identical with himself. Seeing this identity and giving this expression, he openly confesses himself to the other, and expects in like manner that the other, having in point of fact put itself on the same level, will respond in the same language, will therein give voice to this identity, and that thus the state of mutual recognition will be brought about. His confession is not an attitude of abasement or humiliation before the other, is not throwing himself away. For to give the matter expression in this way has not the one-sided character which would fix and establish his disparity with the other: on the contrary, it is solely because of seeing the identity of the other with him that he gives himself utterance. In making his confession he announces, from his side, their common identity, and does so for the reason that language is the existence of spirit as an immediate self. He thus expects that the other will make its own contribution to this manner of existence.

But the admission on the part of the one who is wicked, "I am so," is not followed by a reply making a similar confession. This was not what that way of judging meant at all: far from it! It repels this community of nature, and is the "hardheartedness," which keeps to itself and rejects

---

[8]Cp. with above *Philosophy of History*, Intro. (Eng. trans., p. 32 ff.)

all continuity with the other. By so doing the scene is changed. The one who made the confession sees himself thrust off, and takes the *other* to be in the wrong when he refuses to let his own inner nature go forth in the objective shape of an express utterance, when he contrasts the beauty of his own soul with the wicked individual, and opposes to the confession of the penitent the stiffnecked attitude of the self-consistent equable character, and the rigid silence of one who keeps himself to himself and refuses to throw himself away for some one else. Here we find asserted the highest pitch of revolt to which a spirit certain of itself can reach. For it beholds itself, *qua* this simple self-knowledge, in another conscious being, and in such a way that even the external form of this other is not an unessential "thing," as in the case of an object of wealth, but thought; knowledge itself is what is held opposed to it. It is this absolutely fluid continuity of pure knowledge which refuses to establish communication with an other, which had, *ipso facto*, by making its confession, renounced separate isolated self-existence, had affirmed its particularity to be cancelled, and thereby established itself as continuous with the other, i.e. established itself as universal. The other however, in its own case reserves for itself its uncommunicative, isolated independence: in the case of the individual confessing, it reserves for him the very same independence, though the latter has already cast that away. It thereby proves itself to be a form of consciousness which is forsaken by and denies the very nature of spirit; for it does not understand that spirit, in the absolute certainty of itself, is master and lord over every deed, and over all reality, and can reject and cast them off and make them as if they had never been. At the same time, it does not see the contradiction it is committing in not allowing a rejection, which has been made in express language, to pass for genuine rejection, while itself has the certainty of its own spiritual life, not in a concrete real act, but in its inner nature, and finds the objective existence of this inner being in the language of its own judgment. It is thus its own self which checks that other's return from the act to the spiritual objectivity of language, and to spiritual identity, and by its harshness produces the discordance which still remains.

Now, so far as the spirit which is certain of itself, in the form of a "beautiful soul," does not possess the strength to relinquish the self-absorbed uncommunicative knowledge of itself, it cannot attain to any identity with the consciousness that is repulsed, and so cannot succeed in seeing the unity of its self in another life, cannot reach objective existence. The identity comes about, therefore, merely in a negative way, as a state of being devoid of spiritual character. The "beautiful soul," then, has no concrete reality; it subsists in the contradiction between its pure self and the necessity felt by this self to externalize itself and turn into something actual; it exists in the immediacy of this rooted and fixed opposition, an immediacy which alone is the middle term reconciling an opposition which has been intensified to its pure abstraction, and is pure being or empty nothingness. Thus the "beautiful soul," being conscious of this contradiction in its unreconciled immediacy, is unhinged, disordered, and runs to madness, wastes itself in yearning, and pines away in consumption.[9] Thereby it gives up, as a fact, its stubborn insistence on its own isolated self-existence, but only to bring forth the soulless, spiritless unity of abstract being.

The true, that is to say the self-conscious and actual adjustment of the two sides is necessitated by, and already contained in the foregoing. Breaking the hard heart and raising it to the level of universality is the same process which was expressed in the case of the consciousness that openly made its confession. The wounds of the spirit heal and leave no scars behind. The deed is not the imperishable element; spirit takes it back into itself; and the aspect of individuality present in it, whether in the form of an intention or of an existential negativity and limitation, is that which immediately passes away. The self which realizes, i.e. the form of the spirit's act, is merely a moment of the whole; and the same is true of the knowledge functioning through judgment, and establishing and maintaining the distinction between the individual and universal aspects of action. The evil consciousness, above spoken of, affirms this externalization of itself or asserts itself as a moment, being drawn into the way of express confession by seeing itself in another. This other, however, must have its onesided, unaccepted and unacknowledged judgment broken down, just as the former has to abandon its onesided unacknowledged existence in a state of particularity and isolation. And as the former displays the power of spirit over its reality, so this other must manifest the power of spirit over its constitutive, determinate notion.

The latter, however, renounces the thought that divides and separates, and the harshness of the self-existence which holds to such thought, for the reason that, in point of fact, it sees itself in the first. That which, in this way, abandons its reality and makes itself into a *superseded* particular "this" (*Diesen*), displays itself thereby as, in fact, universal. It turns away from its external reality back into itself as inner essence; and there the universal consciousness thus knows and finds itself.

The forgiveness it extends to the first is the renunciation of self, of its *unreal* essence, since it identifies with this essence that other which was

---

[9]This was the actual fate of Novalis, the "St. John of Romanticism" (d. 1801, æt 29). Cp. Hegel's remarks on Novalis W.W., X., 1, p. 201; XVI., p. 500.

real action, and recognizes what was called bad—a determination assigned to action by thought—to be good; or rather it lets go and gives up this distinction of determinate thought with its self-existent determining judgment, just as the other forgoes determining the act in isolation and for its own private behoof. The word of reconciliation is the objectively existent spirit, which immediately apprehends the pure knowledge of itself *qua* universal essence in its opposite, in the pure knowledge of itself *qua* absolutely self-confined single individual—a reciprocal recognition which is Absolute Spirit.

Absolute Spirit enters existence merely at the culminating point at which its pure knowledge about itself is the opposition and interchange with itself. Knowing that its pure knowledge is the abstract essential reality, Absolute Spirit is this knowing duty in absolute opposition to the knowledge which knows itself, *qua* absolute singleness of self, to be the essentially real. The former is the pure continuity of the universal, which knows the individuality, that knows itself the real, to be inherently naught, to be evil. The latter, again, is absolute discreteness, which knows itself absolute in its pure oneness, and knows the universal is the unreal which exists only for others. Both aspects are refined and clarified to this degree of purity, where there is no self-less existence left, no negative of consciousness in either of them, where, instead, the one element of "duty" is the self-identical character of its self-knowledge, and the other element of "evil" equally has its purpose in its own inner being and its reality in its own mode of utterance. The content of this utterance is the substance that gives this spirit subsistence; the utterance is the assurance of the certainty of spirit within its own self.

These spirits, both certain of themselves, have each no other purpose than its own pure self, and no other reality and existence than just this pure self. But they are still different, and the difference is absolute, because holding within this element of the pure notion. The difference is absolute, too, not merely for *us* [tracing the experience], but for the notions themselves which stand in this opposition. For while these notions are indeed determinate and specific relatively to one another, they are at the same time in themselves universal, so that they fill out the whole range of the self; and this self has no other content than this its own determinate constitution, which neither transcends the self nor is more restricted than it. For the one factor, the absolutely universal, is pure self-knowledge as well as the other, the absolute discreteness of single individuality, and both are merely this pure self-knowledge. Both determinate factors, then, are cognizing pure notions which know *qua* notions, whose very determinateness is immediately knowing, or, in other words, whose relationship and opposition is the Ego. Because of

this they are *for one another* these absolute opposites; it is what is completely inner that has in this way come into opposition to itself and entered objective existence; they constitute pure knowledge, which,
owing to this opposition, takes the form of consciousness. But as yet it
is not *self-consciousness*. It obtains this actualization in the course of the
process through which this opposition passes. For this opposition is
really itself the indiscrete continuity and identity of ego=ego; and each
by itself inherently cancels itself just through the contradiction in its
pure universality, which, while implying continuity and identity, at the
same time still resists its identity with the other, and separates itself
from it. Through this relinquishment of separate selfhood, the knowledge, which in its existence is in a state of diremption, returns into the
unity of the self; it is the concrete actual Ego, universal knowledge of
self in its absolute opposite, in the knowledge which is internal to and
within the self, and which, because of the very purity of its separate subjective existence, is itself completely universal. The reconciling affirmation, the "yes," with which both egos desist from their existence in
opposition, is the existence of the ego expanded into a duality, an ego
which remains therein one and identical with itself, and possesses the
certainty of itself in its complete relinquishment and its opposite: it is
God appearing in the midst of those who know themselves in the form
of pure knowledge.

(CC)

VII

RELIGION

The appearance of Absolute Spirit as a principle constituting on its own account a distinctive stage of experience is at once a demand of the preceding development and a condition of making experience self-complete. Finite or socialized spiritual existence is at its best incapable of establishing the truth that "Spirit is the only reality"; for the more finite spirit approximates to the state of claiming to be self-contained the more is it dependent on universal self-consciousness. A trans-finite or Absolute Spiritual Being as such is thus necessary to realize and sustain the fullness of meaning which finite spirit possesses. Moreover, if "the truth is the whole," and only so is truth self-complete and self-explaining, and if reality is essentially spiritual—then experience only finds its complete meaning realized in the principle of Absolute Spirit. Hence the final stage of the *Phenomenology* of experience is the appearance therein of Absolute Spirit. Moreover, Absolute Spirit, in its own distinctive existence, could only appear at the end of the process of experience, for the whole of that process is required to reveal and to constitute the substance of which the Absolute consists. But the peculiarity of the stage now reached is that here the Absolute operates in its undivided totality to form a definite type of experience; or, in the language of the text, we have the Absolute here "conscious of its self." No doubt, in all the previous stages, "consciousness," "self-consciousness," "reason," "spirit," the Absolute has been implied as a limiting principle, at once substantiating and determining the boundaries of each stage: hence each stage had an Absolute of its own, the character of which was derived in each case from the peculiarity of the stage in question. Now, however, we have the Absolute by itself, in its single self-completeness, as the sole formative factor of a certain type of experience.

The Absolute, then, in its own self-complete reality appears as the constitutive principle of experience. The experience here is the self-consciousness of Absolute Spirit; it appears to itself in all its objects. Since all the modes of finitude hitherto considered (consciousness, self-consciousness, etc.) are embraced in its single totality, it may use each and all of these various modes as the media through and in which to appear. When it appears in and through these modes of finitude we have the attitude of *Religion*. Since these modes, as we saw, differ, the religious attitude differs; and accordingly we have various types or forms of religion.

Each of these forms, in and through which the Absolute appears, is circumscribed in its nature and process; each is *per se* inadequate to the revelation of complete absolute self-consciousness: hence the variety of religions is necessitated by and is indirectly due to the failure of any one type and the inadequacy of every single type to reveal the Absolute completely. A form of appearance or self-manifestation of the Absolute is therefore demanded which will reveal Absolute Spirit adequately to itself as it essentially is in itself. Here it will know itself, so to say, face to face, and with perfect completeness. This form is *Absolute Knowledge*. Hence Religion and Absolute Knowledge are the final stages in the argument of the *Phenomenology*. The former is dealt with in the immediately succeeding section (VII) and its various subsections; the latter forms the subject of the concluding section (VIII) of the work.

RELIGION IN GENERAL

IN the forms of experience hitherto dealt with—which are distinguished broadly as Consciousness, Self-consciousness, Reason, and Spirit—Religion also, the consciousness of Absolute Being in general, has no doubt made its appearance. But that was from the point of view of consciousness, when it has the Absolute Being for its object. Absolute Being, however, in its own distinctive nature, the Self-consciousness of Spirit, has not appeared in those forms.

Even at the plane of Consciousness, viz. when this takes the shape of "Understanding," there is a consciousness of the supersensuous, of the inner being of objective existence. But the supersensible, the eternal, or whatever we care to call it, is devoid of selfhood. It is merely, to begin with, something universal, which is a long way still from being spirit knowing itself as spirit.

Then there was Self-consciousness, which came to its final shape in the "unhappy consciousness"; that was merely the pain and sorrow of spirit wrestling to get itself out into objectivity once more, but not succeeding. The unity of individual self-consciousness with its unchangeable Being, which is what this stage arrives at, remains, in consequence, a "beyond," something afar off.

The immediate existence of Reason (which we found arising out of that state of sorrow), and the special shapes which reason assumes, have no form of religion, because self-consciousness in the case of reason knows itself or looks for itself in the direct and immediate present.

On the other hand, in the world of the Ethical Order, we met with a type of religion, the religion of the nether world. This is belief in the fearful and unknown darkness of Fate, and in the Eumenides of the spirit of the departed: the former being pure negation taking the form of universality, the latter the same negation but in the form of individuality. Absolute Being is, then, in the latter shape no doubt the self and is present, as there is no other way for the self to *be* except present. But the individual self is this individual ghostly shade, which keeps the universal element, Fate, separated from itself. It is indeed a shade, a ghost, a cancelled and superseded particular, and so a universal self. But that negative meaning has not yet turned round into this latter positive significance, and hence the self, so cancelled and transcended, still directly means at the same time this particular being, this insubstantial reality. Fate, however, without self remains the darkness of night devoid of consciousness, which never comes to draw distinctions within itself, and never attains the clearness of self-knowledge.

This belief in a necessity that produces nothingness, this belief in the nether world, becomes belief in Heaven, because the self which has departed must be united with its universal nature, must unfold what it contains in terms of this universality, and thus become clear to itself. This kingdom of belief, however, we saw unfold its content merely in the element of reflective thought (*Denken*), without bringing out the true notion (*Begriff*); and we saw it, on that account, perish in its final fate, viz. in the religion of enlightenment. Here in this type of religion, the supersensible beyond, which we found in "understanding," is reinstated, but in such a way that self-consciousness rests and feels satisfied in the mundane present, not in the "beyond," and knows the supersensible beyond, void and empty, unknowable, and devoid of all terrors, neither as a self nor as power and might.

In the religion of Morality it is at last reinstated that Absolute Reality is a positive content; but that content is bound up with the negativity characteristic of the enlightenment. The content is an objective being, which is at the same time taken back into the self, and remains there enclosed, and is a content with internal distinctions, while its parts are just as immediately negated as they are posited. The final destiny, however, which absorbs this contradictory process, is the self conscious of itself as the controlling necessity (*Schicksal*) of what is essential and actual.

Spirit knowing its self is in religion primarily and immediately its own pure self-consciousness. Those modes of it above considered—"objective spirit," "spirit estranged from itself" and "spirit certain of its self"—together constitute what it is in its condition of consciousness, the state in which, being objectively opposed to its own world, it does not therein apprehend and consciously possess itself. But in Conscience it brings itself as well as its objective world as a whole into subjection, as also its idea[1] and its various specific conceptions;[2] and is

---

[1] *Vorstellung.*
[2] *Begriff.*

now self-consciousness at home with itself. Here spirit, represented as an object, has the significance for itself of being Universal Spirit, which contains within itself all that is ultimate and essential and all that is concrete and actual; yet is not in the form of freely subsisting actuality, or of the apparent independence of external nature. It has a shape, no doubt, the form of objective being, in that it is object of its own consciousness; but because this consciousness is affirmed in religion with the essential character of being self-consciousness, the form or shape assumed is one perfectly transparent to itself; and the reality spirit contains is enclosed in it, or transcended in it, just in the same way as when we speak of "all reality"; it is "all reality," but universal reality only in the sense of an object of thought.

Since, then, in religion, the peculiar characteristic of what is properly consciousness of spirit does not have the form of detached independent otherness, the existence of spirit is distinct from its self-consciousness, and its actual reality proper falls outside religion. There is no doubt one spirit in both, but its consciousness does not embrace both together; and religion appears as a part of existence, of acting, and of striving, whose other part is the life lived within spirit's own actual world. As we now know that spirit in its own world and spirit conscious of itself as spirit, i.e. spirit in the sphere of religion, are the same, the completion of religion consists in the two forms becoming identical with one another: not merely in its reality being grasped and embraced by religion, but conversely—it, as spirit conscious of itself, becomes actual to itself, and real object of its own consciousness.

So far as spirit in religion *presents* itself to itself, it is indeed consciousness, and the reality enclosed within it is the shape and garment in which it clothes its idea of itself. The reality, however, does not in this presentation get proper justice done to it, that is to say, it does not get to be an independent and free objective existence and not merely a garment. And conversely, because that reality lacks within itself its completion, it is a determinate shape or form, which does not attain to what it ought to reveal, viz. spirit conscious of itself. That spirit's shape might express spirit itself, the shape would have to be nothing else than spirit, and spirit would have to appear to itself, or to be actual, as it is in its own essential being. Only thereby, too, would be attained—what may seem to demand the opposite—that the object of its consciousness has, at the same time, the form of free and independent reality. But only spirit which is object to itself in the shape of Absolute Spirit, is as much aware of being a free and independent reality as it remains therein conscious of itself.

Since in the first instance self-consciousness and consciousness simply, religion, and spirit as it is externally in its world, or the objective existence of spirit, are distinct, the latter consists in the totality of spirit, so far as its moments are separated from each other and each is set forth by itself. These moments, however, are consciousness, self-consciousness, reason, and spirit—spirit, that is, *qua* immediate spirit, which is not yet consciousness of spirit. Their totality, taken all together, constitutes the mundane existence of spirit as a whole; spirit as such contains the previous separate embodiments in the form of universal determinations of its own being, in those moments just named. Religion presupposes that these have completely run their course, and is their simple totality, their absolute Self and soul.

The course which these traverse is, moreover, in relation to religion, not to be pictured as a temporal sequence. It is only spirit in its entirety that is in time, and the shapes assumed, which are specific embodiments of the whole of spirit as such, present themselves in a sequence one after the other. For it is only the whole which properly has reality, and hence the form of pure freedom relatively to anything else, the form which takes expression as time. But the moments of the whole, consciousness, self-consciousness, reason, and spirit, have, because they are moments, no existence separate from one another.

Just as spirit was distinct from *its* moments, we have further, in the third place, to distinguish from these moments their specific individuated character. Each of those moments, in itself, we saw broke up again in a process of development all its own, and took various shapes and forms: as e.g. in the case of consciousness, sensuous certainty and perception were distinct phases. These latter aspects fall apart in time from one another, and belong to a specific particular whole. For spirit descends from its universality to assume an individual form through specific determination. This determination, or mediate element, is consciousness, self-consciousness, and so on. But *individuality* is constituted just by the forms assumed by these moments. Hence these exhibit and reveal spirit in its individuality or concrete reality, and are distinguished in time from one another, though in such a way that the succeeding retains within it the preceding.

While, therefore, religion is the completion of the life of spirit, its final and complete expression, into which, as being their ground, its individual moments, consciousness, self-consciousness, reason, and spirit, return and have returned, they, at the same time, together constitute the objectively existing realization of spirit in its totality; as such spirit is real only as the moving process of these aspects which it possesses, a process of distinguishing them and returning back into itself. In the process of these universal moments is contained the development of religion generally. Since, however, each of these attributes was set forth and presented, not only in the way it in general determines itself, but as it is in and for itself, i.e. as, within its own being, running its course as a distinct whole—there has thus arisen not merely the development of religion *generally*; those independently complete processes pursued by the individual phases or moments of spirit contain at the same time the determinate forms of religion itself. Spirit in its entirety, spirit in religion, is once more the process from its immediacy to the attainment of a knowledge of what it implicitly or immediately is; and is the process of attaining the state where the shape and form, in which it appears as an object for its own consciousness, will be perfectly adequate to its essential nature, and where it will behold itself as it is.

In this development of religion, then, spirit itself assumes definite shapes, which constitute the distinctions involved in this process: and at the same time a determinate or specific form of religion has likewise an actual spirit of a specific character. Thus, if consciousness, self-consciousness, reason, and spirit belong to self-knowing spirit in general, in a similar way the specific shapes, which self-knowing spirit assumes, appropriate and adopt the distinctive forms which were specially developed in the case of each of the stages—consciousness, self-consciousness, reason, and spirit. The determinate shape, assumed in a given case by religion, appropriates, from among the forms belonging to each of its moments, the one adapted to it, and makes this its actual spirit. Any one determinate attitude of religion pervades and permeates all aspects of its actual existence, and stamps them with this common feature.

In this way the arrangement now assumed by the forms and shapes which have thus far appeared, is different from the way they appeared in their own order. On this point we may note shortly at the outset what is necessary. In the series we considered, each moment, exhaustively elaborating its entire content, evolved and formed itself into a single whole within its own peculiar principle. And knowledge was the inner depth, or the spirit, wherein the moments, having no subsistence of their own, possessed their substance. This substance, however, has now at length made its appearance; it is the deep life of spirit certain of itself; it does not allow the principle belonging to each individual form to get isolated, and become a whole within itself: rather it collects all these moments into its own content, keeps them together, and advances within this total wealth of its concrete actual spirit; while all its particular moments take into themselves and receive together in common the like determinate character of the whole. This spirit certain of itself and the process it goes through—this is their true reality, the independent self-subsistence, which belongs to each individually.

Thus while the previous linear series in its advance marked the retrogressive steps in it by knots, but thence went forward again in one linear stretch, it is now, as it were, broken at these knots, these universal moments, and falls asunder into many lines, which, being bound together into a single bundle, combine at the same time symmetrically, so that the similar distinctions, in which each separately took shape within its own sphere, meet together.

For the rest, it is self-evident from the whole argument, how this co-ordination of universal directions, just mentioned, is to be understood; so that it becomes superfluous to remark that these distinctions are to be taken to mean essentially and only moments of the process of development, not parts. In the case of actual concrete spirit they are attributes of its substance; in religion, on the other hand, they are only predicates of the subject. In the same way, indeed, all forms in general are, in themselves or for us, contained in spirit and contained in every spirit. But the main point of importance, in dealing with its reality, is solely what determinate character it has in its consciousness, in which specific character it has expressed its self, or in what shape it knows its essential nature.

The distinction made between actual spirit and that same spirit which knows itself as spirit, or between itself *qua* consciousness and *qua* self-consciousness, is transcended and done away with in the case where spirit knows itself in its real truth. Its consciousness and its self-consciousness have come to terms. But, as religion is here to begin with and immediately, this distinction has not yet reverted to spirit. It is merely the conception, the principle, of religion that is established at first. In this the essential element is self-consciousness, which is conscious of being all truth, and which contains all reality within that truth. This self-consciousness, being consciousness [and so aware of an object], has itself for its object. Spirit, which knows itself in the first instance immediately, is thus to itself spirit in the form of immediacy; and the specific character of the shape in which it appears to itself is that of pure simple being. This being, this bare existence, has indeed a filling drawn neither from sensation or manifold matter, nor from any other one-sided moments, purposes, and determinations; its filling is solely spirit, and is known by itself to be all truth and reality. Such filling is in this first form not in adequate agreement with its own shape, spirit *qua* ultimate essence is not in accord with its consciousness. It is actual only as Absolute Spirit, when it is also for itself in its truth as it is in its certainty of itself, or, when the extremes, into which spirit *qua* consciousness falls, exist for one another in spiritual shape. The embodiment adopted by spirit *qua* object of its own consciousness, remains filled by the certainty of spirit, and this self-certainty constitutes its substance. Through this content, the degrading of the object to bare objectivity, to the form of something that negates self-consciousness, disappears. The immediate unity of spirit with itself is the fundamental basis, or pure consciousness, inside which consciousness breaks up into its constituent elements [viz. an object with subject over against it]. In this way, shut up within its pure self-consciousness, spirit does not exist in religion as the creator of a nature in general; rather what it produces in the course of this process are its shapes *qua* spirits, which together constitute all that it can reveal when it is completely manifested. And this process itself is the development of its perfect and complete actuality through the individual aspects thereof, i.e. through its imperfect modes of realization.

The first realization of spirit is just the principle and notion of religion itself—religion as immediate and thus Natural Religion. Here spirit knows itself as its object in a "natural" or immediate shape. The second realization, is, however, necessarily that of knowing itself in the shape of transcended and superseded natural existence, i.e. in the form of self. This therefore is Religion in the form of Art. For the shape it adopts is raised to the form of self through the productive activity of consciousness, by which this consciousness beholds in its object its own action, i.e. sees the self. The third realization, finally, cancels the one-sidedness of the first two: the self is as much an immediate self as the immediacy is a self. If spirit in the first is in the form of consciousness, and in the second in that of self-consciousness, it is in the third in the form of the unity of both; it has then the shape of what is completely self-contained (*An-und-Fürsichseyns*); and in being thus presented as it is in and for itself, this is Revealed Religion. Although spirit, however, here reaches its true shape, the very shape assumed and the conscious presentation are an aspect or phase still unsurmounted; and from this spirit has to pass over into the life of the Notion, in order therein completely to resolve the form of objectivity, in the notion which embraces within itself this its *own* opposite.

It is then that spirit has grasped its own principle, the notion of itself, as so far only we [who analyse spirit] have grasped it; and its shape, the element of its existence, in being the notion, is then spirit itself.

A

NATURAL RELIGION[1]

The arrangement of the analysis of Religion and the divisions into the various subsections are, as indicated in the preceding note (p. 396), determined by the general development of experience. That development is from the immediate

---

[1] Primarily Oriental religion.

through mediation to the fusion of immediacy and mediation. The stages of the development of experience are Consciousness, Self-consciousness, Reason, the latter leading to its highest level—finite Spiritual existence. The development of Religion follows these various ways in which objects are given in experience, and the three chief divisions of Religion are determined accordingly: Natural Religion is religion at the level of Consciousness; Art, Religion at the level of Self-consciousness; Revealed Religion is Religion at the level of Reason and Spirit. Each of these is again subdivided, and the subdivision follows more or less closely the various subdivisions of these three ultimate levels of experience—Consciousness, etc. Thus, in Natural Religion, we have Religion at the level of Sense-certainty—"Light": Religion at the level of Perception—"Life": and Religion at the level of Understanding—the reciprocal relation constituted by the "play of forces" appears as the relation of the "Artificer" to his own product.

The general principle is not worked out in detail, with the same obviousness, in the case of the other two primary types of Religion—Art and Revealed Religion. But the same general method of development is pursued in these cases.

The historical material before the mind of the writer is, as might be expected, the various religions which have historically appeared amongst mankind. These religions are treated, however, as illustrations of principles dominating the religious consciousness m general, rather than as merely historical phenomena.

With the succeeding argument should be read Hegel's *Philosophy of Religion*, Part II, Sections I and II, and Part III.

SPIRIT knowing spirit is consciousness of itself; and is to itself in the form of objectivity. It *is*; and is at the same time self-existence (*Fürsichsein*). It is for itself; it is the aspect of self-consciousness, and is so in contrast to the aspect of its consciousness, the aspect by which it relates itself to itself as object. In its consciousness there is the opposition and in consequence the determinateness of the form in which it appears to itself and knows itself. It is with this determinateness of shape that we have alone to do in considering religion; for its essential unembodied principle, its pure notion, has already come to light. The distinction of consciousness and self-consciousness, however, falls at the same time within this notion. The form or shape of religion does not contain the existence of spirit in the sense of its being nature detached and free from thought, nor in the sense of its being thought detached from existence. The shape assumed by religion *is* existence contained and preserved in thought as well as a something thought which is consciously existent.

It is by the determinate character of this form, in which spirit knows itself, that one religion is distinguished from another. But we have at the same time to note that the systematic exposition of this knowledge about itself, in terms of this individual specific character, does not as a fact exhaust the whole nature of an actual religion. The series of different religions, which will come before us, just as much sets forth again merely the different aspects of a single religion, and indeed of every single religion, and the imagery, the conscious ideas, which seem to mark off one concrete religion from another, make their appearance in each. All the same the diversity must also be looked at as a diversity of religion. For while spirit lives in the distinction of its consciousness and its self-consciousness, the process it goes through finds its goal in the transcendence of this fundamental distinction and in giving the form of self-consciousness to the given shape which is object of consciousness. This distinction, however, is not *eo ipso* transcended by the fact that the shapes, which that consciousness contains, have *also* the moments of self in them, and that God is *presented* as self-consciousness. The consciously presented self is not the actual concrete self. In order that this, like every other more specific determination of the shape, may in truth belong to this shape, it has partly to be put into this shape by the action of self-consciousness, and partly the lower determination must show itself to be cancelled and transcended and comprehended by the higher. For what is consciously presented (*vorgestellt*) only ceases to be something "*presented*" and alien to spirit's knowledge, by the self having produced it, and so viewing the determination of the object as its own determination, and hence seeing itself in that object. By this operation, the lower determination [that of being something "presented"] has at once vanished; for doing anything is a negative process which is carried through at the expense of something else. So far as that lower determination still continues to appear, it has withdrawn into the condition of unessentiality: just as, on the other hand, where the lower still predominates, while the higher is also present, the one coexists in a self-less way alongside of the other. While, therefore, the various ideas falling within a single religion no doubt exhibit the whole course taken by the forms of religion, the character of each is determined by the particular unity of consciousness and self-consciousness; that is to say, by the fact that the self-consciousness has taken into itself the determination belonging to the object of consciousness, has, by its own action, made that determination altogether its own, and knows it to be the essential one as compared with the others.

The truth of belief in a given determination of the religious spirit shows itself in this, that the actual spirit is constituted after the same manner as the shape in which spirit beholds itself in religion; thus e.g. the incarnation of God, which is found in Eastern religion, has no truth, because the concrete actual spirit of this religion is without the reconciliation this principle implies.

It is not in place here to return from the totality of specific determinations back to the individual determination, and show in what shape the plenitude of all the others is contained within it and within its particular form of religion. The higher form, when put back under a lower, is deprived of its significance for self-conscious spirit, belongs to spirit merely in a superficial way, and is for it at the level of presentation. The higher form has to be considered in its own peculiar significance, and dealt with where it is the principle of a particular religion, and is certified and approved by its actual spirit.

a

GOD AS LIGHT[2]

SPIRIT, as the absolute Being, which is self-consciousness—or the self-conscious absolute Being, which is all truth and knows all reality as itself—is, to begin with, merely its notion and principle in contrast to the reality which it gives itself in the process of its conscious activity. And this notion is, as contrasted with the clear daylight of that explicit development, the darkness and night of its inner life; in contrast to the existence of its various moments as independent forms or shapes, this notion is the creative secret of its birth. This secret has its revelation within itself; for existence has its necessary place in this notion, because this notion is spirit knowing itself, and thus possesses in its own nature the moment of being consciousness and of presenting itself objectively. We have here the pure ego, which in its externalization, in itself *qua* universal object, has the certainty of self; in other words, this object is, for the ego, the interfusion of all thought and all reality.

When the first and immediate cleavage is made within self-knowing Absolute Spirit, its shape assumes that character which belongs to immediate consciousness or to sense-certainty. It beholds itself in the form of *being*; but not being in the sense of what is without spirit, containing only the contingent qualities of sensation—the kind of being that belongs to sense-certainty. Its being is filled with the content of spirit. It also includes within it the form which we found in the case of immediate self-consciousness, the form of lord and master,[3] in regard to the self-consciousness of spirit which retreats from its object.

This being, having as its content the notion of spirit, is, then, the shape of spirit in relation simply to itself—the form of having no special shape at all. In virtue of this characteristic, this shape is the pure

---

[2]Parsee religion.
[3]Term applied in e.g. Judaism and Mohammedanism.

all-containing, all-suffusing Light of the Sunrise, which preserves itself in its formless indeterminate substantiality. Its counterpart, its otherness, is the equally simple negative—Darkness. The process of its own externalization, its creations in the unresisting element of its counterpart, are bursts of Light. At the same time in their ultimate simplicity they are its way of becoming something for itself, and its return from its objective existence, streams of fire consuming its embodiment. The distinction, which it gives itself, no doubt thrives abundantly on the substance of existence, and shapes itself as the diverse forms of nature. But the essential simplicity of its thought rambles and roves about inconstant and inconsistent, enlarges its bounds to measureless extent, and its beauty heightened to splendour is lost in its sublimity.[4]

The content, which this state of pure being evolves, its perceptive activity, is, therefore, an unreal by-play on this substance which merely rises, without setting into itself to become subject and secure firmly its distinctions through the self. Its determinations are merely attributes, which do not succeed in attaining independence; they remain merely names of the One, called by many names. This One is clothed with the manifold powers of existence and with the shapes of reality, as with a soulless, selfless ornament; they are merely messengers of its mighty power,[5] claiming no will of their own, visions of its glory, voices in its praise.

This revel of heaving life[6] must, however, assume the character of distinctive self-existence, and give enduring subsistence to its fleeting shapes. Immediate being, in which it places itself over against its own consciousness, is itself the negative destructive agency which dissolves its distinctions. It is thus in truth the Self; and spirit therefore passes on to know itself in the form of self. Pure Light scatters its simplicity as an infinity of separate forms, and presents itself as an offering to self-existence, that the individual may take sustainment to itself from its substance.

b

PLANTS AND ANIMALS AS OBJECTS OF RELIGION[7]

SELF-CONSCIOUS spirit, passing away from abstract, formless essence and going into itself—or, in other words, having raised its immediacy to the level of Self—makes its simple unity assume the character of a

[4]Cp. *Philos. of Relig.*, W.W., XI, 403, 404, 411.
[5]Angels.
[6]Cp. *Ency.*, §389.
[7]Primarily religions of India.

manifold of self-existing entities, and is the religion of spiritual sense-perception. Here spirit breaks up into an innumerable plurality of weaker and stronger, richer and poorer spirits. This Pantheism, which, to begin with, consists in the quiescent subsistence of these spiritual atoms, passes into a process of active internal hostility. The innocence, which characterizes the flower and plant religions, and which is merely the selfless idea of Self, gives way to the seriousness of struggling warring life, to the guilt of animal religions; the quiescence and impotence of contemplative individuality pass into the destructive activity of separate self-existence.

It is of no avail to have removed the lifelessness of abstraction from the things of perception, and to have raised them to the level of realities of spiritual perception: the animation of this spiritual kingdom has death in the heart of it, owing to the determinateness and the negativity, which overcome and trench upon the innocent indifference [of the various species of plants] to one another. Owing to this determinateness and negativity, the dispersion of spirit into the multiplicity of the passive plant-forms becomes a hostile process, in which the hatred stirred up by their independent self-existence rages and consumes.

The actual self-consciousness at work in this dispersed and disintegrated spirit, takes the form of a multitude of individualized mutually-antipathetic folk-spirits, who fight and hate each other to the death, and consciously accept certain specific forms of animals as their essential being and nature:[8] for they are nothing else than spirits of animals, or animal lives separate and cut off from one another, and with no universality consciously present in them.

The characteristic of purely negative independent self-existence, however, consumes itself in this active hatred towards one another; and through this process, involved in its very principle, spirit enters into another shape. Independent self-existence cancelled and abolished is the form of the object, a form which is produced by the self, or rather is the self produced, the self-consuming self, i.e. the self that becomes a "thing." The agent at work, therefore, retains the upper hand over these animal spirits merely tearing each other to pieces; and his action is not merely negative, but composed and positive. The consciousness of spirit is, thus, now the process which is above and beyond the immediate inherent [universal] nature, as well as transcends the abstract self-existence in isolation. Since the implicit inherent nature is reduced, through opposition, to the level of a specific character, it is no longer the proper form of Absolute Spirit, but a reality which its consciousness finds lying over against itself as an ordinary existing fact and cancels; at

---

[8]Sacred animals in Indian religion.

the same time this consciousness is not merely this negative cancelling self-existent being, but produces its own objective idea of itself,—self-existence put forth in the form of an object. This process of production is, all the same, not yet perfect production; it is a conditioned activity, the forming of a given material.

c

THE ARTIFICER[9]

SPIRIT, then, here takes the form of the artificer, and its action, when producing itself as object, but without having as yet grasped the thought of itself, is an instinctive kind of working, like bees building their cells.

The first form, because immediate, has the abstract character of "understanding," and the work accomplished is not yet in itself endued with spirit. The crystals of Pyramids and Obelisks, simple combinations of straight lines with even surfaces and equal relations of parts in which the incommensurability of roundness is set aside—these are the works produced by this artificer, the worker of the strict form. Owing to the purely abstract intelligible nature of the form, the work is not in itself its own true significance; it is not the spiritual self. Thus, either the works produced only receive spirit into them as an alien, departed spirit, one that has forsaken its living suffusion and permeation with reality, and, being itself dead, enters into these lifeless crystals; or they take up an external relation to spirit as something which is itself there externally and not as spirit—they are related to it as to the Orient Light, which throws its significance on them.

The separation of elements from which spirit as artificer starts—the separation of the implicit essential nature, which becomes the material it works upon, and independent self-existence, which is the aspect of the self-consciousness at work—this division has become objective to spirit in its work. Its further endeavour has to be directed to cancelling and doing away with this separation of soul and body; it must strive to clothe and give embodied shape to soul *per se*, and endow the body with soul. The two aspects, in that they are brought closer to one another, bear towards each other, in this condition, the character of ideally presented spirit and of enveloping shell. Spirit's oneness with itself contains this opposition of individuality and universality. As the work comes closer to itself in the coming together of its aspects, there comes about thereby at the same time the other fact, that the work comes

---

[9]Egyptian religions.

closer to the self-consciousness performing it, and that the latter attains in the work knowledge of itself as it truly is. In this way, however, the work merely constitutes to begin with the abstract side of the activity of spirit, which does not yet know the content of this activity within itself but in its work, which is a "thing." The artificer as such, spirit in its entirety, has not yet appeared; the artificer is still the inner, hidden reality, which *qua* entire is present only as broken up into active self-consciousness and the object it has produced.

The surrounding habitation, then, external reality, which has so far been raised merely to the abstract form of the understanding, is worked up by the artificer into a more animated form. The artificer employs plant life for this purpose, which is no longer sacred as in the previous case of inactive impotent pantheism; rather, the artificer, who grasps *himself* as the self-existent reality, takes that plant life as something to be used and degrades it to an external aspect, to the level of an ornament. But it is not turned to use without some alteration: for the worker producing the self-conscious form destroys at the same time the transitoriness, inherently characteristic of the immediate existence of this life, and brings its organic forms nearer to the more exact and more universal forms of thought. The organic form, which, left to itself, grows and thrives in particularity, being on its side subjugated by the form of thought, elevates in turn these straight-lined and level shapes into more animated roundness—a blending which becomes the root of free architecture.[10]

This dwelling, (the aspect of the universal element or inorganic nature of spirit), also includes within it now a form of individuality, which brings nearer to actuality the spirit that was formerly separated from existence and external or internal thereto, and thus makes the work to accord more with active self-consciousness. The worker lays hold, first of all, on the form of self-existence in general, on the forms of animal life. That he is no longer directly aware of himself in animal life, he shows by the fact that in reference to this he constitutes himself the productive force, and knows himself in it as being his own work, whereby the animal shape at the same time is one which is superseded and becomes the hieroglyphic symbol of another meaning, the hieroglyph of a thought. Hence also this shape is no longer solely and entirely used by the worker, but becomes blended with the shape embodying thought, with the human form.[11] Still, the work lacks the form and existence where self exists as self: it also fails to express in its very nature that it includes within itself an inner meaning; it lacks language, the element

---

[10]The Egyptian columns and architecture.
[11]The representations of the gods with forms half animal, half human.

in which the sense and meaning contained are actually present. The work done, therefore, even when quite purified of the animal aspect, and bearing the form and shape of self-consciousness alone, is still the silent soundless shape, which needs the rays of the rising sun in order to have a sound which, when produced by light, is even then merely noise and not speech, shows merely an outer self, not the inner self.[12]

Contrasted with this outer self of the form and shape, stands the other form, which indicates that it has in it an inner being. Nature, turning back into its essential being, degrades its multiplicity of life, ever individualizing itself and confounding itself in its own process, to the level of an unessential encasing shell, which is the covering for the inner being. And as yet this inner being is still simple darkness, the unmoved, the black formless stone.[13]

Both representations contain inwardness and existence—the two moments of spirit: and both kinds of manifestation contain both moments at once in a relation of opposition, the self both as inward and as outward. Both have to be united. The soul of the statue in human form does not yet come out of the inner being, is not yet speech, objective existence of self which is inherently internal,—and the inner being of multiform existence is still without voice or sound, still draws no distinctions within itself, and is still separated from its outer being, to which all distinctions belong. The artificer, therefore, combines both by blending the forms of nature and self-consciousness; and these ambiguous beings, a riddle to themselves—the conscious struggling with what has no consciousness, the simple inner with the multiform outer, the darkness of thought mated with the clearness of expression—these break out into the language of a wisdom that is darkly deep and difficult to understand.[14]

With the production of this work, the instinctive method of working ceases, which, in contrast to self-consciousness, produced a work devoid of consciousness. For here the activity of the artificer, which constitutes self-consciousness, comes face to face with an inner being equally self-conscious and giving itself expression. He has therein raised himself by his work up to the point where his conscious life breaks asunder, where spirit greets spirit. In this unity of self-conscious spirit with itself, so far as it is aware of being embodiment and object of its own consciousness, its blending and mingling with the unconscious state of immediate shapes of nature become purified. These monsters in form and shape, word and deed, are resolved and dissolved into a

---

[12]The statues of Memnon which gave forth a moaning harp-like noise at sunrise.
[13]The Black Stone of Mecca: a fetish still worshipped by the faithful.
[14]Sphinxes.

shape which is spiritual—an outer which has entered into itself, an inner which expresses itself out of itself and in itself,—they pass into thought, which brings forth itself, preserves the shape and form suited to thought, and is transparent existence. Spirit is *Artist*.

B

RELIGION IN THE FORM OF ART[1]

SPIRIT has raised the shape in which it is object for its own conscious-ness into the form of consciousness itself; and spirit produces such a shape for itself. The artificer has given up the synthesizing activity, that blending of the heterogeneous forms of thought and nature. When the shape has gained the form of self-conscious activity, the artificer has be-come a spiritual workman.

If we next ask, what the actual spirit is, which finds in the religion of art the consciousness of its Absolute, it turns out that this is the ethical or objective spirit. This spirit is not merely the universal substance of all individuals; but when this substance is said to have, as an objective fact for actual consciousness, the form of consciousness, this amounts to saying that the substance, which is individualized, is known by the individuals within it as their proper essence and their own achieve-ment. It is for them neither the Light of the World, in whose unity the self-existence of self-consciousness is contained only negatively, only transitorily, and beholds the lord and master of its reality; nor is it the restless waste and destruction of hostile nations; nor their subjection to "castes," which together constitute the semblance of organization of a completed whole, where, however, the universal freedom of the indi-viduals concerned is wanting. Rather this spirit is a free nation, in which custom and order constitute the common substance of all, whose reality and existence each and every one knows to be his own will and his own deed.

The religion of the ethical spirit, however, raises it above its actual realization, and is the return from its objectivity into pure knowledge of itself. Since an ethically constituted nation lives in direct unity with its own substance, and does not contain the principle of pure individ-ualism of self-consciousness, the religion characteristic of its sphere first appears in complete form in its parting from its stable security. For the reality of the ethical substance rests partly on its quiet unchange-ableness as contrasted with the absolute process of self-consciousness; and consequently on the fact that this self-consciousness has not yet left

---

[1]Greek religion.

its serene life of customary convention and its confident security therein, and gone into itself. Partly, again, that reality rests on its organization into a plurality of rights and duties, as also on its organized distribution into the spheres of the various classes, each with its particular way of acting which co-operates to form the whole; and hence rests on the fact that the individual is contented with the limitation of his existence, and has not yet grasped the unrestricted thought of his free self. But that serene immediate confidence in the substance of this ethical life turns back into trust in self and certainty of self; and the plurality of rights and duties, as well as the restricted particular action this involves, is the same dialectic process in the sphere of the ethical life as the plurality of "things" and their various "qualities"—a process which only comes to rest and stability in the simplicity of spirit certain of self.

The complete fulfilment of the ethical life in free self-consciousness, and the destined consummation (*Schicksal*) of the ethical world, are therefore that individuality which has entered into itself; the condition is one of absolute levity on the part of the ethical spirit; it has dissipated and resolved into itself all the firmly established distinctions constituting its own stability, and the separate spheres of its own articulated organization, and, being perfectly sure of itself, has attained to boundless cheerfulness of heart and the freest enjoyment of itself. This simple certainty of spirit within itself has a double meaning; it is quiet stability and solid truth, as well as absolute unrest, and the disappearance of the ethical order. It turns round, however, into the latter; for the truth of the ethical spirit lies primarily just in this substantial objectivity and trust, in which the self does not know itself as free individual, and which, therefore, in this inner subjectivity, in the self becoming free, falls into ruins. Since then its trust is broken, and the substance of the nation cracked, spirit, which was the connecting medium of unstable extremes, has now come forward as an extreme—that of self-consciousness grasping itself as essential and ultimate. This is spirit certain within itself, which mourns over the loss of its world, and now out of the purity of self produces its own essential being, raised above actual reality.

At such an epoch art in absolute form[2] comes on the scene. At the earlier stage it is instinctive in its operation; its operation is steeped in existence, works its way out of existence and works right into the existent; it does not find its substance in the free life of an ethical order, and hence, too, as regards the self operating does not exercise free spiritual activity.

Later on, spirit goes beyond art in order to gain its higher manifesta-

---

[2] The religion of pure beauty.

tion, viz. that of being not merely the substance born and produced out of the self, but of being, in its manifestation as object, this very self; it seeks at that higher level not merely to bring forth itself out of its own notion, but to have its very notion as its shape, so that the notion and the work of art produced may know each other reciprocally as one and the same.[3]

Since, then, the ethical substance has withdrawn from its objective existence into its pure self-consciousness, this is the aspect of the notion, or the activity with which spirit brings itself forth as object. It is pure form, because the individual in ethical obedience and service has so worked off every unconscious existence and every fixed determination, as the substance has itself become this fluid and undifferentiated essence. This form is the night in which the substance was betrayed, and made itself subject. It is out of this night of pure certainty of self that the ethical spirit rises again in a shape freed from nature and its own immediate existence.

The existence of the pure notion into which spirit has fled from its bodily shape, is an individual, which spirit selects as the vessel for its sorrow. Spirit acts in this individual as his universal and his power, from which he suffers violence, as his element of "Pathos," by having given himself over to which his self-consciousness loses freedom. But that positive power belonging to the universal is overcome by the pure self of the individual, the negative power. This pure activity, conscious of its inalienable force, wrestles with the unembodied essential being. Becoming its master, this negative activity has turned the element of pathos into its own material, and given itself its content; and this unity comes out as a work, universal spirit individualized and consciously presented.

a

THE ABSTRACT WORK OF ART

THE first work of art is, because immediate, abstract and particular. As regards itself, it has to move away from this immediate and objective phase towards self-consciousness, while, on the other side, the latter for itself endeavours in the "cult" to do away with the distinction, which it at first gives itself in contrast to its own spirit, and by so doing to produce a work of art inherently endowed with life.

The first way in which the artistic spirit keeps as far as possible removed from each other its shape and its active consciousness, is

---

[3]This paragraph may be regarded as a parenthetical note.

immediate in character—the shape assumed is there as a "thing" in general. It breaks up into the distinction of individualness which has the shape of the self, and universality, which presents the inorganic nature in reference to the shape adopted, and is its environment and habitation. This shape assumed obtains its pure form, the form belonging to spirit, by the whole being raised into the sphere of the pure notion. It is not the crystal, belonging as we saw to the level of understanding, a form which housed and covered a lifeless element, or is shone upon externally by a soul. Nor, again, is it that commingling of the forms of nature and thought, which first arose in connexion with plants, thought's activity here being still an imitation. Rather the notion strips off the remnant of root, branches, and leaves, still clinging to the forms, purifies the forms, and makes them into figures in which the crystal's straight lines and surfaces are raised into incommensurable relations, so that the animation of the organic is taken up into the abstract form of understanding, and, at the same time, its essential nature—incommensurability—is preserved for understanding.

The indwelling god, however, is the black stone extracted from the animal encasement,[1] and suffused with the light of consciousness. The human form strips off the animal character with which it was mixed up. The animal form is for the god merely an accidental vestment; the animal appears alongside its true form,[2] and has no longer a value on its own account, but has sunk into being a significant sign of something else, has become a mere symbol. By that very fact, the form assumed by the god in itself casts off even the restrictions of the natural conditions of animal existence, and hints at the internal arrangements of organic life melted down into the surface of the form, and pertaining only to this surface.

The essential being of the god, however, is the unity of the universal existence of nature and of self-conscious spirit which in its actuality appears confronting the former. At the same time, being in the first instance an individual shape, its existence is one of the elements of nature, just as its self-conscious actuality is a particular national spirit.[3] But the former is, in this unity, that element reflected back into spirit, nature made transparent by thought and united with self-conscious life. The form of the gods retains, therefore, within it its nature element as something transcended, as a shadowy, obscure memory. The utter chaos and confused struggle amongst the elements existing free and detached from each other, the non-ethical disordered realm of the Titans,

---

[1] *v. sup.*, p. 410.
[2] e.g. the eagle as the "bird of Zeus."
[3] e.g. Athene.

is vanquished and banished to the outskirts of self-transparent reality, to the cloudy boundaries of the world which finds itself in the sphere of spirit and is there at peace. These ancient gods, first-born children of the union of Light with Darkness, Heaven, Earth, Ocean, Sun, earth's blind typhonic Fire, and so on, are supplanted by shapes, which do but darkly recall those earlier titans, and which are no longer things of nature, but clear ethical spirits of self-conscious nations.

This simple shape has thus destroyed within itself the dispeace of endless individuation, the individuation both in the life of nature, which operates with necessity only *qua* universal essence, but is contingent in its actual existence and process; and also in the life of a nation, which is scattered and broken into particular spheres of action and into individual centres of self-consciousness, and has an existence manifold in action and meaning. All this individuation the simplicity of this form has abolished, and brought together into an individuality at peace with itself. Hence the condition of unrest stands contrasted with this form; confronting quiescent individuality, the essential reality, stands self-consciousness, which, being its source and origin, has nothing left over for itself except to be pure activity. What belongs to the substance, the artist imparted entirely to his work; to himself, however, as a specific individuality he gave in his work no reality. He could only confer completeness on it by relinquishing his particular nature, divesting himself of his own being, and rising to the abstraction of pure action.

In this first and immediate act of production, the separation of the work and his self-conscious activity is not yet healed again. The work is, therefore, not by itself really an animated thing; it is a whole only when its process of coming to be is taken along with it. The obvious and common element in the case of a work of art, that it is produced in consciousness and is made by the hand of man, is the moment of the notion existing *qua* notion, and standing in contrast to the work produced. And if this notion, *qua* the artist or spectator, is unselfish enough to declare the work of art to be *per se* absolutely animated, and to forget himself *qua* agent or onlooker, then, as against this, the notion of spirit has to be insisted on; spirit cannot dispense with the moment of being conscious of itself. This moment, however, stands in contrast to the work, because spirit, in this its primary disruption, gives the two sides their abstract and specifically contrasted characteristics of "doing" something and of being a "thing"; and their return to the unity they started from has not yet come about.

The artist finds out, then, in his work, that he did not produce a reality like himself. No doubt there comes back to him from his work a consciousness in the sense that an admiring multitude honours it as the spirit, which is their own true nature. But this way of animating his work, since it renders him his self-consciousness merely in the way of admiration, is rather a confession to the artist that the animated work is not on the same level as himself. Since his self comes back to him in the form of gladness in general, he does not find therein the pain of his self-discipline and the pain of production, nor the exertion and strain of his own toil. People may, moreover, judge the work, or bring it offerings and gifts, or endue it with their consciousness in whatever way they like—if they with their knowledge set themselves *over* it, he knows how much more his act is than what they understand and say; if they put themselves *beneath* it, and recognize in it their own dominating essential reality, he knows himself as the master of this.

The work of art hence requires another element for its existence; God requires another way of going forth than this, in which, out of the depths of his creative night, he drops into the opposite, into externality, to the character of a "thing" with no self-consciousness. This higher element is that of Language—a way of existing which is directly self-conscious existence. When individual self-consciousness exists in that way, it is at the same time directly a form of universal contagion; complete isolation of independent self-existent selves is at once fluent continuity and universally communicated unity of the many selves; it is the soul existing as soul. The god, then, which takes language as its medium of embodiment, is the work of art inherently animated, endowed with a soul, a work which directly in its existence contains the pure activity which was apart from and in contrast to the god when existing as a "thing." In other words, self-consciousness, when its essential being becomes objective, remains in direct unison with itself. It is, when thus at home with itself in its essential nature, pure thought or devotion, whose inwardness gets at the same time express existence in the Hymn. The hymn keeps within it the individuality of self-consciousness, and this individual character is at the same time perceived to be there universal. Devotion, kindled in every one, is a spiritual stream which in all the manifold self-conscious units is conscious of itself as one and the same function in all alike and a simple state of being. Spirit, being this universal self-consciousness of every one, holds in a single unity its pure inwardness as well as its objective existence for others and the independent self-existence of the individual units.

This kind of language is distinct from another way God speaks, which is not that of universal self-consciousness. The Oracle, both in the case of the god of the religions of art as well as of the preceding religions, is the necessary and the first form of divine utterance. For God's very principle implies that God is at once the essence of nature and of spirit, and hence has not merely natural but spiritual existence as well.

In so far as this moment is merely implied as yet in God's principle and is not realized in religion, the language used is, for the religious self-consciousness, the speech of an alien and external self-consciousness. The self-consciousness which remains alien and foreign to its religious communion, is not yet there in the way its essential principle requires it should be. The self is simple self-existence, and thereby is altogether universal self-existence; that self, however, which is cut off from the self-consciousness of the communion, is primarily a mere individual self.

The content of this its own peculiar and individual form of speech results from the general determinate character which the Absolute Spirit is affirmed to have in its religion as such. Thus the universal spirit of the Sunrise, which has not yet particularized its existence, utters about the Absolute equally simple and universal statements, whose substantial content is sublime in the simplicity of its truth, but at the same time appears, because of this universality, trivial to the self-consciousness developing further.

The further developed self, which advances to being distinctively *for* itself, rises above the pure "pathos" of [unconscious] substance, gets the mastery over the objectivity of the Light of the rising Sun, and knows that simplicity of truth to be the inherent reality (*das Ansichseyende*) which does not possess the form of contingent existence through an utterance of an alien self, but is the sure and unwritten law of the gods, a law that "lives for ever, and no man knows what time it came."

As the universal truth, revealed by the "Light" of the world, has here returned into what is within or what is beneath, and has thus got rid of the form of contingent appearance; so too, on the other hand, in the religion of art, because God's shape has taken on consciousness and hence individuality in general, the peculiar utterance of God, who is the spirit of an ethically constituted nation, is the Oracle, which knows its special circumstances and situation, and announces what is serviceable to its interests. Reflective thought, however, claims for itself the universal truths enunciated, because these are known as the essential inherent reality of the nation's life; and the utterance of them is thus for such reflexion no longer a strange and alien speech, but is its very own. Just as that wise man of old[4] searched in his own thought for what was worthy and good, but left it to his "Daimon" to find out and decide the petty contingent content of what he wanted to know—whether it was good for him to keep company with this or that person, or good for one of his friends to go on a journey, and such like unimportant things; in the same way the universal consciousness draws the knowledge

---

[4] Socrates.

about the contingent from birds, or trees, or fermenting earth, the steam from which deprives the self-conscious mind of its sanity of judgment. For what is accidental is not the object of sober reflexion, and is extraneous; and hence the ethical consciousness lets itself, as if by a throw of the dice, settle the matter in a manner that is similarly unreflective and extraneous. If the individual, by his understanding, determines on a certain course, and selects, after consideration, what is useful for him, it is the specific nature of his particular character which is the ground of this self-determination. This basis is just what is contingent; and that knowledge which his understanding supplies as to what is useful for the individual, is hence just such a knowledge as that of "oracles" or of the "lot"; only that he who questions the oracle or lot, thereby shows the ethical sentiment of indifference to what is accidental, while the former, on the contrary, treats the inherently contingent as an essential concern of his thought and knowledge. Higher than both, however, is to make careful reflexion the oracle for contingent action, but yet to recognize that this very act reflected on is something contingent, because it refers to what is opportune and has a relation to what is particular.

The true self-conscious existence, which spirit receives in the form of speech, which is not the utterance of an alien and so accidental, i.e. not universal, self-consciousness, is the work of art which we met with before. It stands in contrast to the statue, which has the character of a "thing." As the statue is existence in a state of rest, the other is existence in a state of transience. In the case of the former, objectivity is set free and is without the immediate presence of a self of its own; in the latter, on the other hand, objectivity is too much confined within the self, attains insufficiently to definite embodiment, and is, like time, no longer there just as soon as it is there.

The religious Cult constitutes the process of the two sides—a process in which the divine embodiment in motion within the pure feeling-element of self-consciousness, and its embodiment at rest in the element of thinghood, reciprocally abandon the different character each possesses, and the unity, which is the underlying principle of their being, becomes an existing fact. Here in the Cult, the self gives itself a consciousness of the Divine Being descending from its remoteness into it, and this Divine Being, which was formerly the unreal and merely objective, thereby receives the proper actuality of self-consciousness.

This principle of the Cult is essentially contained and present already in the flow of the melody of the Hymn. These hymns of devotion are the way the self obtains immediate pure satisfaction through and within itself. It is the soul purified, which, in the purity it thus attains, is immediately and only absolute Being, and is one with absolute

Being. The soul, because of its abstract character, is not consciousness distinguishing its object from itself, and is thus merely the night of the object's existence and the place prepared for its shape. The abstract Cult, therefore, raises the self into being this pure divine element. The soul fulfils the attainment of this purity in a conscious way. Still the soul is not yet the self, which has descended to the depths of its being, and knows itself as evil. It is something that merely *is*, a soul, which cleanses its exterior with the washing of water, and robes it in white, while its innermost traverses the imaginatively presented path of labour, punishment, and reward, the way of spiritual discipline in general, of relinquishing its particularity—the road by which it reaches the mansions and the fellowship of the blest.

This ceremonial cult is, in its first form, merely in secret, i.e. is a fulfilment accomplished merely in idea, and unreal in fact. It has to become a real act, for an unreal act is a contradiction in terms. Consciousness proper thereby raises itself to the level of its pure self-consciousness. The essential Being has in it the significance of a free object; through the actual cult this object turns back into the self; and in so far as, in pure consciousness, it has the significance of absolute Being dwelling in its purity beyond actual reality, this Being descends, through this mediating process of the cult, from its universality into individual form, and thus combines and unites with actual reality.

The way the two sides make their appearance in the act is of such a character that the self-conscious aspect, so far as it is actual consciousness, finds the absolute Being manifesting itself as actual nature. On the one hand, nature belongs to self-consciousness as its possession and property, and stands for what has no existence *per se*. On the other hand, nature is its proper immediate reality and particularity, which is equally regarded as not essential, and is superseded. At the same time, that external nature has the opposite significance for its pure consciousness—viz. the significance of being the inherently real, for which the self sacrifices its own [relative] unreality, just as, conversely, the self sacrifices the unessential aspect of nature to itself. The act is thereby a spiritual movement, because it is this double-sided process of cancelling the abstraction of absolute Being (which is the way devotion determines the object), and making it something concrete and actual, and, on the other hand, of cancelling the actual (which is the way the agent determines the object and the self acting), and raising it into universality.

The practice of the religious Cult begins, therefore, with the pure and simple "offering up" or "surrender" of a possession, which the owner, apparently without any profit whatsoever to himself, pours away or lets rise up in smoke. By so doing he renounces before the absolute

Being of his pure consciousness all possession and right of property and enjoyment thereof; renounces personality and the reversion of his action to his self; and instead, reflects the act into the universal, into the absolute Being rather than into himself. Conversely, however, the objective ultimate Being too is annihilated in that very process. The animal offered up is the symbol of a god; the fruits consumed are the actual living Ceres and Bacchus. In the former die the powers of the upper law the [Olympians] which has blood and actual life, in the latter the powers of the lower law [the Furies] which possesses in bloodless form secret and crafty power.

The sacrifice of the divine substance, so far as it is active, belongs to the side of self-consciousness. That this concrete act may be possible, the absolute Being must have from the start *implicitly* sacrificed *itself*. This it has done in the fact that it has given itself definite existence, and made itself an individual animal and fruit of the earth. The self actively sacrificing demonstrates in actual existence, and sets before its own consciousness, this already implicitly completed self-renunciation on the part of absolute Being; and replaces that immediate reality, which absolute Being has, by the higher, viz. that of the self making the sacrifice. For the unity which has arisen, and which is the outcome of transcending the singleness and separation of the two sides, is not merely negative destructive fate, but has a positive significance. It is merely for the abstract Being of the nether world that the sacrifice offered to it is wholly surrendered and devoted; and, in consequence, it is only for that Being that the reflexion of personal possession and individual self-existence back into the Universal is marked distinct from the self as such. At the same time, however, this is only a trifling part; and the other act of sacrifice is merely the destruction of what cannot be used, and is really the preparation of the offered substance for a meal, the feast that cheats the act out of its negative significance. The person making the offering at that first sacrifice reserves the greatest share for his own enjoyment; and reserves from the latter sacrifice what is useful for the same purpose. This enjoyment is the negative power which cancels the absolute Being as well as the singleness; and this enjoyment is, at the same time, the positive actual reality in which the objective existence of absolute Being is transmuted into self-conscious existence, and the self has consciousness of its unity with its Absolute.

This cult, for the rest, is indeed an actual act, although its meaning lies for the most part only in devotion. What pertains to devotion is not objectively produced, just as the result when confined to the feeling of enjoyment[5] is robbed of its external existence. The Cult, therefore,

---

[5] i.e. at the feast.

goes further, and replaces this defect, in the first instance by giving its devotion an objective subsistence, since the cult is the common task— or the individual task for each and all to do—which produces for the honour and glory of God a House for Him to dwell in and adornment for His presence. By so doing, partly the external objectivity of statuary is cancelled; for by thus dedicating his gifts and his labours the worker makes God well disposed towards him and looks on his self as detached and appertaining to God. Partly, too, this action is not the individual labour of the artist; this particularity is dissolved in the universality. But it is not only the honour of God which is brought about, and the blessing of His countenance and favour is not only shed in idea and imagination on the worker; the work also has a meaning the reverse of the first which was that of self-renunciation and of honour done to what is alien and external. The Halls and Dwellings of God are for the use of man, the treasures preserved there are in time of need his own; the honour which God enjoys in his decorative adornment, is the honour and glory of the artistic and magnanimous nation. At the festival season, the people adorn their own dwellings, their own garments, as well as God's establishments with furnishings of elegance and grace. In this manner they receive a return for their gifts from a responsive and grateful God; and receive the proofs of His favour—wherein the nation became bound to the God because of the work done for Him—not as a hope and a deferred realization, but rather, in testifying to His honour and in presenting gifts, the nation finds directly and at once the enjoyment of its own wealth and adornment.

b

THE LIVING WORK OF ART

THAT nation which approaches its god in the cult of the religion of art is an ethically constituted nation, knowing its State and the acts of the State to be the will and the achievement of its own self. This universal spirit, confronting the self-conscious nation, is consequently not the "Light-God," which, being selfless, does not contain the certainty of the individual selves, but is only their universal ultimate Being and the dominating imperious power, wherein they disappear. The religious cult of this simple unembodied ultimate Being gives back, therefore, to its votaries in the main merely this: that they are the nation of their god. It secures for them merely their stable subsistence, and their simple substance as a whole; it does not secure for them their actual self; this is indeed rejected. For they revere their god as the empty profound, not as spirit. The cult, however, of the religion of art, on the other hand, is

without that abstract simplicity of the absolute Being, and therefore
without its "profundity." But that Being, which is directly at one with
the self, is inherently spirit and comprehending truth, although not yet
truth known explicitly, in other words not knowing the "depths" of its
nature. Because this Absolute, then, implies self, consciousness finds itself at home with it when it appears; and, in the cult, this consciousness
receives not merely the general title to its own subsistence, but also its
self-conscious existence within it: just as, conversely, the Absolute has
no being in a despised and outcast nation whose mere substance is acknowledged, whose reality is selfless, but in the nation whose self is acknowledged as living in its substance.

From the ceremonial cult, then, self-consciousness that is at peace
and satisfied in its ultimate Being turns away, as also does the god that
has entered into self-consciousness as into its place of habitation. This
place is, by itself, the night of mere "substance," or its pure individuality; but no longer the strained and striving individuality of the artist,
which has not yet reconciled itself with its essential Being that is striving to become objective; it is the night [substance] satisfied, having its
"pathos" within it and in want of nothing, because it comes back from
intuition, from objectivity which is overcome and superseded.

This "pathos" is, by itself, the Being of the Rising Sun,[1] a Being, however, which has now "set" and disappeared within itself, and has its own
"setting," self-consciousness, within it, and so contains existence and
reality.

It has here traversed the process of its actualization. Descending
from its pure essentiality and becoming an objective force of nature
and the expressions of this force, it is an existence relative to an other,
an objective existence for the self by which it is consumed. The silent
inner being of selfless nature attains in its fruits the stage where nature,
duly self-prepared and digested, offers itself as material for the life
which has a self. In its being useful for food and drink it reaches its
highest perfection. For therein it is the possibility of a higher existence,
and comes in touch with spiritual existence. In its metamorphosis the
spirit of the earth has developed and become partly a silently energiz-
ing substance, partly spiritual ferment; in the first case it is the feminine
principle, the nursing mother, in the other the masculine principle, the
self-driving force of self-conscious existence.

In this enjoyment, then, that orient "Light" of the world is discovered for what it really is: Enjoyment is the Mystery of its being. For mys-
ticism is not concealment of a secret, or ignorance; it consists in the self
knowing itself to be one with absolute Being, and in this latter, there-

---

[1]The "Light" of the world.

fore, becoming revealed. Only the self is revealed to itself; or what is manifest is so merely in the immediate certainty of itself. But it is just in such certainty that simple absolute Being has been placed by the cult. As a thing that can be used, it has not only existence which is seen, felt, smelt, tasted; it is also object of desire, and, by actually being enjoyed, it becomes one with the self, and thereby disclosed completely to this self, and made manifest.

When we say of anything, "it is manifest to reason, to the heart," it is in point of fact still secret, for it still lacks the actual certainty of immediate existence, both the certainty regarding what is objective, and the certainty of enjoyment, a certainty which in religion, however, is not only immediate and unreflecting, but at the same time purely cognitive certainty of self.

What has thus been, through the cult, revealed to self-conscious spirit within itself, is simple absolute Being; and this has been revealed partly as the process of passing out of its dark night of concealment up to the level of consciousness, to be there its silently nurturing substance; partly, however, as the process of losing itself again in nether darkness, in the self, and of waiting above merely with the silent yearning of motherhood. The more conspicuous moving impulse, however, is the variously named "Light" of the Rising Sun and its tumult of heaving life, which, having likewise desisted from its abstract state of being, has first embodied itself in objective existence in the fruits of the earth,[2] and then, surrendering itself to self-consciousness,[3] attained there to its proper realization; and now it curvets and careers about in the guise of a crowd of excited, fervid women, the unrestrained revel of nature in self-conscious form.[4]

Still, however, it is only Absolute Spirit in the sense of this simple abstract Being, not as spirit *per se*, that is discovered to consciousness: i.e. it is merely immediate spirit, the spirit of nature. Its self-conscious life is therefore merely the mystery of the Bread and the Wine, of Ceres and Bacchus, not of the other, the strictly higher, gods [of Olympus], whose individuality includes, as an essential moment, self-consciousness as such. Spirit has not yet *qua* self-conscious spirit offered itself up to it, and the mystery of bread and wine is not yet the mystery of flesh and blood.

This unstable divine revel must come to rest as an object, and the enthusiasm, which did not reach consciousness, must produce a work which confronts it as the statue stands over against the enthusiasm of

---

[2] As found in the mysteries of Demeter.
[3] As found in the mysteries of Bacchus and Dionysus.
[4] The Maenads; *cp.* Euripides, *Bacchae*.

the artist in the previous case,—a work indeed that is equally complete and finished, yet not as an inherently lifeless but as a living self. Such a cult is the Festival which man makes in his own honour, though not yet imparting to a cult of that kind the significance of the Absolute Being; for it is the ultimate Being that is first revealed to him, not yet Spirit—not such a Being as *essentially* takes on human form. But this cult provides the basis for this revelation, and lays out its moments individually and separately. Thus we here get the abstract moment of the living embodiment of ultimate Being, just as formerly we had the unity of both in the state of unconstrained emotional fervency. In the place of the statue man thus puts himself as the figure elaborated and moulded for perfectly free movement, just as the statue is the perfectly free state of quiescence. If every individual knows how to play the part at least of a torchbearer, one of them comes prominently forward who is the very embodiment of the movement, the smooth elaboration, the fluent energy and force of all the members. He is a lively and living work of art, which matches strength with its beauty; and to him is given, as a reward for his force and energy, the adornment, with which the statue was honoured [in the former type of religion], and the honour of being, amongst his own nation, instead of a god in stone, the highest bodily representation of what the essential Being of the nation is.

In both the representations, which have just come before us, there is present the unity of self-consciousness and spiritual Being; but they still lack their due balance and equilibrium. In the case of the bacchic[5] revelling enthusiasm the self is beside itself; in bodily beauty of form it is spiritual Being that is outside itself. The dim obscurity of consciousness in the one case and its wild stammering utterance, must be taken up into the transparent existence of the latter; and the clear but spiritless form of the latter, into the emotional inwardness of the former. The perfect element in which the inwardness is as external as the externality is inward, is once again Language. But it is neither the language of the oracle, entirely contingent in its content and altogether individual in character; nor is it the emotional hymn sung in praise of a merely individual god; nor is it the meaningless stammer of delirious bacchantic revelry. It has attained to its clear and universal content and meaning. Its content is *clear*, for the artificer has passed out of the previous state of entirely substantial enthusiasm, and worked himself into a definite shape, which is his own proper existence, permeated through all its movements by self-conscious soul, and is that of his contemporaries. Its content is *universal*, for in this festival, which is to the honour of man, there vanishes the onesidedness peculiar to figures represented in

---

[5]As distinct from the worship of Apollo.

statues, which merely contain a national spirit, a determinate character of the godhead. The finely built warrior is indeed the honour and glory of his particular nation; but he is a physical or corporeal individuality in which are sunk out of sight the expanse and the seriousness of meaning, and the inner character of the spirit which underlies the particular mode of life, the peculiar petitions, the needs and the customs of his nation. In relinquishing all this for complete corporeal embodiment, spirit has laid aside the particular impressions, the special tones and chords of that nature which it, as the actual spirit of the nation, includes. Its nation, therefore, is no longer conscious in this spirit of its special particular character, but rather of having laid this aside, and of the universality of its human existence.

c

THE SPIRITUAL WORK OF ART

THE national spirits, which become conscious of their being in the shape of some particular animal, coalesce into one single spirit.[1] Thus it is that the separate artistically beautiful national spirits combine to form a Pantheon, the element and habitation of which is Language. Pure intuition of self in the sense of universal human nature takes, when the national spirit is actualized, this form: the national spirit combines with the others (which with it constitute, through nature and natural conditions, one people), in a common undertaking, and for this task builds up a collective nation, and, with that, a collective heaven. This universality, to which spirit attains in its existence, is, nevertheless, merely this first universality, which, to begin with, starts from the individuality of ethical life, has not yet overcome its immediacy, has not yet built up a single state out of these separate national elements. The ethical life of an actual national spirit rests partly on the immediate confiding trust of the individuals in the whole of their nation, partly in the direct share which all, in spite of differences of class, take in the decisions and acts of its government. In the union, not in the first instance to secure a permanent order but merely for a common act, that freedom of participation on the part of each and all is for the nonce set aside. This first community of life is, therefore, an assemblage of individualities rather than the dominion and control of abstract thought, which would rob the individuals of their self-conscious share in the will and act of the whole.

The assembly of national spirits constitutes a circle of forms and

---

[1] *v. sup.*, A., *b.*

shapes, which now embraces the whole of nature, as well as the whole ethical world. They too are under the supreme command rather than the supreme dominion of the One. By themselves, they are the universal substances embodying what the self-conscious essential reality inherently is and does. This, however, constitutes the moving force, and, in the first instance, at least the centre, with which those universal entities are concerned, and which, to begin with, seems to unite in a merely accidental way all that they variously accomplish. But it is the return of the divine Being to self-consciousness which already contains the reason that self-consciousness forms the centre for those divine forces, and conceals their essential unity in the first instance under the guise of a friendly external relation between both worlds.

The same universality, which belongs to this content, attaches necessarily also to that form of consciousness in which the content appears. It is no longer the concrete acts of the cult; it is an action which is not indeed raised as yet to the level of the notion, but only to that of ideas, the synthetic connexion of self-conscious and external existence. The element in which these presented ideas exist, language, is the earliest language, the *Epic* as such, which contains the universal content, at any rate universal in the sense of completeness of the world presented, though not in the sense of universality of thought. The Minstrel is the individual and actual spirit from whom, as a subject of this world, it is produced, and by whom it is borne. His "pathos" is not the deafening power of nature, but Mnemosyne, Recollection, a gradually evolved inwardness, the memory of an essential mode of being once directly present. He is the organ and instrument whose content is passing away; it is not his own self which is of any account, but his muse, his universal song. What, however, is present in fact, has the form of an inferential process, where the one extreme of universality, the world of gods, is connected with individuality, the minstrel, through the middle term of particularity. The middle term is the nation in its heroes, who are individual men like the minstrel, but only ideally presented, and thereby at the same time universal like the free extreme of universality, the gods.

In this Epic, then, what is inherently established in the cult, the relation of the divine to the human, is set forth and displayed as a whole to consciousness. The content is an "act"[2] of the essential Being conscious of itself. Acting disturbs the peace of the substance, and awakens the essential Being; and by so doing its simple unity is divided into parts, and opened up into the manifold world of natural powers and ethical forces. The act is the violation of the peaceful earth; it is the trench which, vivified by the blood of the living, calls forth the spirits

---

[2] A "drama."

of the departed, who are thirsting for life, and who receive it in the action of self-consciousness.[3] There are two sides to the business the universal activity is concerned to accomplish: the side of the self—in virtue of which it is brought about by a collection of actual nations with the prominent individualities at the head of them; and the side of the universal—in virtue of which it is brought about by their substantial forces. The relation of the two, however, took, as we saw just now, the character of being the synthetic connexion of universal and individual, i.e. of being a process of ideal presentation. On this specific character depends the judgment regarding this world.

The relation of the two is, by this means, a commingling of both, which illogically divides the unity of the action, and in a needless fashion throws the act from one side over to the other. The universal powers have the form of individual beings, and thus have in them the principle from which action comes; when they effect anything, therefore, this seems to proceed as entirely from them and to be as free as in the case of men. Hence both gods and men have done one and the same thing. The seriousness with which those divine powers go to work is ridiculously unnecessary, since they are in point of fact the moving force of the individualities engaged in the acts; while the strain and toil of the latter again is an equally useless effort, since the former direct and manage everything. Overzealous mortal creatures, who are as nothing, are at the same time the mighty self that brings into subjection the universal beings, offends the gods, and procures for them actual reality and an interest in acting. Just as, conversely, these powerless gods, these impotent universal beings, who procure their sustenance from the gifts of men and through men first get something to do, are the natural inner principle and the substance of all events, as also the ethical material, and the "pathos" of action. If their cosmic natures first get reality and a sphere of effectual operation through the free self of individuality, it is also the case that they are the universal, which withdraws from and avoids this connexion, remains unrestricted and unconstrained in its own character, and, by the unconquerable elasticity of its unity, extinguishes the atomic singleness of the individual acting and his various features, preserves itself in its purity, and dissolves all that is individual in the current of its own continuity.

Just as the gods fall into this contradictory relation with the antithetic nature having the form of self, in the same way their universality comes into conflict with their own specific character and the relation in which it stands to others. They are the eternal and resplendent individuals, who exist in their own calm, and are removed from the changes of time

---

[3]The Epic exorcises the dead past; *v. Odyssey*, XI.

and the influence of alien forces. But they are at the same time determinate elements, particular gods, and thus stand in relation to others. But that relation to others, which, in virtue of the opposition it involves, is one of strife, is a comic self-forgetfulness of their eternal nature. The determinateness they possess is rooted in the divine subsistence, and in its specific limitation has the independence of the whole individuality; owing to this whole, their characters at once lose the sharpness of their distinctive peculiarity, and in their ambiguity blend together.

One purpose of their activity and their activity itself, being directed against an "other" and so against an invincible divine force, are a contingent and futile piece of bravado, which passes away at once, and transforms the pretence of seriousness in the act into a harmless, self-confident piece of sport with no result and no issue. If, however, in the nature of their divinity, the negative element, the specific determinateness of that nature, appears merely as the inconsistency of their activity, and as the contradiction between the purpose and result, and if that independent self-confidence outweighs and overbalances the element of determinateness, then, by that very fact, the pure force of negativity confronts and opposes their nature, and moreover with a power to which it must finally submit, and over which it can in no way prevail. They are the universal, and the positive, as against the individual self of mortals, which cannot hold out against their power and might. But the universal self, for that reason, hovers over them [the gods in Homer] and over this whole world of imagination to which the entire content belongs; and is for them the unintelligible void of Necessity,—a mere happening to which they stand related selfless and sorrowing, for these determinate natures do not find themselves in this purely formal necessity.

This necessity, however, is the unity of the notion, a unity dominating and controlling the contradictory independent subsistence of the individual moments, a unity in which the inconsistency and fortuitousness of their action is coherently regulated, and the sportive character of their acts receives its serious value in those acts themselves. The content of the world of imagination carries on its process in the middle element [term] detached by itself, gathering round the individuality of some hero, who, however, feels the strength and splendour of his life broken, and mourns the early death he sees ahead of him. For individuality, firmly established and real in itself, is isolated and excluded to the utmost extreme, and severed into its moments, which have not yet found each other and united. The one individual element, the abstract unreal moment, is necessity which shares in the life of the mediating term just as little as does the other, the concrete real individual element, the minstrel, who keeps himself outside it, and disappears in what he imaginatively presents. Both extremes must get nearer the content; the one, necessity, has to get filled with it, the other, the language of the minstrel, must have a share in it. And the content formerly left to itself must acquire in itself the certainty and the fixed character of the negative.

This higher language, that of *Tragedy*, gathers and keeps more closely together the dispersed and scattered moments of the inner essential world and the world of action. The substance of the divine falls apart, in accordance with the nature of the notion, into its shapes and forms, and their movement is likewise in conformity with that notion. In regard to form, the language here ceases to be narrative, in virtue of the fact that it enters into the content, just as the content ceases to be merely one that is ideally imagined. The hero is himself the spokesman, and the representation given brings before the audience—who are also spectators—*self-conscious* human beings, who know their own rights and purposes, the power and the will belonging to their specific nature, and who know how to state them. They are artists who do not express with unconscious naïveté and naturalness the merely external aspect of what they begin and what they decide upon, as is the case in the language accompanying ordinary action in actual life; they make the very inner being external, they prove the righteousness of their action, and the "pathos" controlling them is soberly asserted and definitely expressed in its universal individuality, free from all accident of circumstance and the particular peculiarities of personalities. Lastly, it is in actual human beings that these characters get existence, human beings who impersonate the heroes, and represent them in actual speech, not in the form of a narrative, but speaking in their own person. Just as it is essential for a statue to be made by human hands, so is the actor essential to his mask—not as an external condition, from which, artistically considered, we have to abstract; or so far as abstraction must certainly be made, we thereby state just that art does not yet contain in it the true and proper self.

The general ground, on which the movement of these shapes produced from the notion takes place, is the consciousness expressed in the imaginative language of the Epic, where the detail of the content is loosely spread out with no unifying self. It is the commonalty in general, whose wisdom finds utterance in the Chorus of the Elders; in the powerlessness of this chorus the generality finds its representative, because the common people itself compose merely the positive and passive material for the individuality of the government confronting it. Lacking the power to negate and oppose, it is unable to hold together and keep within bounds the riches and varied fullness of divine life; it allows each individual moment to go off its own way, and in its hymns of honour and reverence praises each individual moment as an independent god, now this god and now again another. Where, however, it detects the seriousness of the notion, and perceives how the notion marches onward shattering these forms as it goes along; and where it comes to see how badly its praised and honoured gods come off when they venture on the ground where the notion holds sway;—there it is not itself the negative power interfering by action, but keeps itself within the abstract selfless thought of such power, confines itself to the consciousness of alien and external destiny, and produces the empty wish to tranquillize, and feeble ineffective talk intended to appease. In its terror before the higher powers, which are the immediate arms of the substance; in its terror before their struggle with one another, and before the simple self of that necessity, which crushes them as well as the living beings bound up with them; in its compassion for these living beings, whom it knows at once to be the same with itself—it is conscious of nothing but ineffective horror of this whole process, conscious of equally helpless pity, and, as the end of all, the mere empty peace of resignation to necessity, whose work is apprehended neither as the necessary act of the character, nor as the action of the absolute Being within itself.

Spirit does not appear in its dissociated multiplicity on the plane of this onlooking consciousness [the chorus], the indifferent ground, as it were, on which the presentation takes place; it comes on the scene in the simple diremption of the notion. Its substance manifests itself, therefore, merely torn asunder into its two extreme powers. These elementary universal beings are, at the same time, self-conscious individualities—heroes who put their conscious life into one of these powers, find therein determinateness of character, and constitute the effective activity and reality of these powers. This universal individualization descends again, as will be remembered, to the immediate reality of existence proper, and is presented before a crowd of spectators, who find in the chorus their image and counterpart, or rather their own thought giving itself expression.

The content and movement of the spirit, which is object to itself here, have been already considered as the nature and realization of the substance of ethical life. In its form of religion spirit attains to consciousness about itself, or reveals itself to its consciousness in its purer form and its simpler mode of embodiment. If, then, the ethical substance by its very principle broke up, as regards its content, into two powers—which were defined as divine and human law, law of the nether world and law of the upper world, the one the family, the other state sovereignty, the first bearing the impress and character of woman, the other that of man—in the same way, the previously multiform circle of gods, with its wavering and unsteady characteristics, confines itself to these powers, which owing to this feature are brought closer to individuality proper. For the previous dispersion of the whole into manifold abstract forces, which appear hypostatized, is the dissolution of the subject which comprehends them merely as moments in its self; and individuality is therefore only the superficial form of these entities. Conversely, a further distinction of characters than that just named is to be reckoned as contingent and inherently external personality.

At the same time, the essential nature [in the case of ethical substance] gets divided in its form, i.e. with respect to knowledge. Spirit when acting, appears, *qua* consciousness, over against the object on which its activity is directed, and which, in consequence, is determined as the negative of the knowing agent. The agent finds himself thereby in the opposition of knowing and not knowing. He takes his purpose from his own character, and knows it to be essential ethical fact; but owing to the determinateness of his character, he knows merely the one power of substance; the other remains for him concealed and out of sight. The present reality, therefore, is one thing in itself, and another for consciousness. The higher and lower right come to signify in this connexion the power that knows and reveals itself to consciousness, and the power concealing itself and lurking in the background. The one is the aspect of light, the god of the Oracle, who as regards its natural aspect [Light] has sprung from the all-illuminating Sun, knows all and reveals all, Phœbus and Zeus, who is his Father. But the commands of this truth-speaking god, and his proclamations of what *is*, are really deceptive and fallacious. For this knowledge is, in its very principle, directly *not* knowledge, because consciousness in acting is inherently this opposition. He,[4] who had the power to unlock the riddle of the sphinx, and he too who trusted with childlike confidence,[5] are, therefore, both sent to destruction through what the god reveals to them. The priestess, through whose mouth the beautiful god speaks,[6] is in nothing different from the equivocal sisters of fate,[7] who drive their victim to crime by their promises, and who, by the double-tongued, equivocal character of what they gave out as a certainty, deceive the King when he relies upon the manifest and obvious meaning of what they say. There is a type of consciousness that is purer than the latter[8] which believes in witches, and more sober, more thorough, and more solid than the former which puts its trust in the priestess and the beautiful god. This type of con-

---

[4]Oedipus.
[5]Orestes.
[6]In the Delphic Oracle.
[7]The witches in "Macbeth."
[8]Macbeth.

sciousness,[9] therefore, lets his revenge tarry for the revelation which the spirit of his father makes regarding the crime that did him to death, and institutes other proofs in addition—for the reason that the spirit giving the revelation might possibly be the devil.

This mistrust has good grounds, because the knowing consciousness takes its stand on the opposition between certainty of itself on the one hand, and the objective essential reality on the other. Ethical rightness, which insists that actuality is nothing *per se* in opposition to absolute law, finds out that its knowledge is onesided, its law merely a law of its own character, and that it has laid hold of merely one of the powers of the substance. The act itself is this inversion of what is known into its opposite, into objective existence, turns round what is right from the point of view of character and knowledge into the right of the very opposite with which the former is bound up in the essential nature of the substance—turns it into the "Furies" who embody the right of the other power and character awakened into hostility. The lower right sits *with* Zeus enthroned, and enjoys equal respect and homage with the god revealed and knowing.

To these three supernatural Beings the world of the gods of the chorus is limited and restricted by the acting individuality. The one is the substance, the power presiding over the hearth and home and the spirit worshipped by the family, as well as the universal power pervading state and government. Since this distinction belongs to the substance as such, it is, when dramatically presented, not individualized in two distinct shapes [of the substance], but has in actual reality the two persons of its characters. On the other hand, the distinction between knowing and not knowing falls within each of the actual self-consciousnesses; and only in abstraction, in the element of universality, does it get divided into two individual shapes. For the self of the hero only exists as a whole consciousness, and hence includes essentially the whole of the distinction belonging to the form; but its substance is determinate, and only one side of the content distinguished belongs to him. Hence the two sides of consciousness, which have in concrete reality no separate individuality peculiarly their own, receive, when ideally represented, each its own particular form: the one that of the god revealed, the other that of the Furies keeping themselves concealed. In part both enjoy equal honour, while again, the form assumed by the substance, Zeus, is the necessity of the relation of the two to one another. The substance is the relation [1] that knowledge is for itself, but finds its truth in what is simple; [2] that the distinction, through and in which actual consciousness exists, has its basis in that inner being which destroys it;

---

[9]Hamlet.

[3] that the clear conscious assurance of certainty has its confirmation in forgetfulness.

Consciousness disclosed this opposition by action, through doing something. Acting in accordance with the knowledge revealed, it finds out the deceptiveness of that knowledge, and being committed, as regards its inner nature, to one of the attributes of substance, it did violence to the other and thereby gave the latter right as against itself. When following that god who knows and reveals himself, it really seized hold of what is not revealed, and pays the penalty for having trusted the knowledge, whose equivocal character (since this is its very nature) it also had to discover, and an admonition thereanent to be given. The frenzy of the priestess, the inhuman shape of the witches, the voices of trees and birds, dreams, and so on, are not ways in which truth appears; they are admonitory signs of deception, of want of judgment, of the individual and accidental character of knowledge. Or, what comes to the same thing, the opposite power, which consciousness has violated, is present as express law and authentic right, whether law of the family or law of the state; while consciousness, on the other hand, pursued its own proper knowledge, and hid from itself what was revealed. The truth, however, of the opposing powers of content and consciousness is the final result, that both are equally right, and, hence, in their opposition (which comes about through action) are equally wrong. The process of action proves their unity in the mutual overthrow of both powers and both self-conscious characters. The reconciliation of the opposition with itself is the Lethe of the nether world in the form of Death—or the Lethe of the upper world in the form of absolution, not from guilt (for consciousness cannot deny its guilt, because the act was done), but from the crime, and in the form of the peace of soul which atones for the crime. Both are forgetfulness, the disappearance of the reality and action of the powers of the substance, of their component individualities, and of the powers of the abstract thought of good and evil. For none of them by itself is the real essence: this consists in the undisturbed calm of the whole within itself, the immovable unity of Fate, the quiescent existence (and hence want of activity and vitality) of the family and government, and the equal honour and consequent indifferent unreality of Apollo and the Furies, and the return of their spiritual life and activity into Zeus solely and simply.

This destiny completes the depopulation of Heaven—of that unthinking blending of individuality and ultimate Being—a blending whereby the action of this absolute Being appears as something incoherent, contingent, unworthy of itself; for individuality, when attaching in a merely superficial way to absolute Being, is unessential. The expulsion of such unreal insubstantial ideas, which was demanded by the philosophers of antiquity, thus already has its beginning in tragedy in general, through the fact that the division of the substance is controlled by the notion, and hence individuality is the essential individuality, and the specific determinations are absolute characters. The self-consciousness represented in tragedy knows and acknowledges on that account only one highest power, Zeus. This Zeus is known and acknowledged only as the power of the state or of the hearth and home, and, in the opposition belonging to knowledge, merely as the Father of the knowledge of the particular,—a knowledge assuming a figure in the drama:—and again as the Zeus of the oath and of the Furies, the Zeus of what is universal, of the inner being dwelling in concealment. The further moments taken from the notion (*Begriff*) and dispersed in the form of ideal presentation (*Vorstellung*), moments which the chorus permits to hold good one after the other, are, on the other hand, not the "pathos" of the hero; they sink to the level of passions in the hero—to the level of accidental, insubstantial moments, which the impersonal chorus no doubt praises, but which are not capable of constituting the character of heroes, nor of being expressed and revered by them as their real nature.

But, further, the persons of the divine Being itself, as well as the characters of its substance, coalesce into the simplicity of what is devoid of consciousness. This necessity has, in contrast to self-consciousness, the characteristic of being the negative power of all the shapes that appear, a power in which they do not recognize themselves, but perish therein. The self appears as merely allotted amongst the different characters, and not as the mediating factor of the process. But self-consciousness, the simple certainty of self, is in point of fact the negative power, the unity of Zeus, the unity of the substantial essence and abstract necessity; it is the spiritual unity into which everything returns. Because actual self-consciousness is still distinguished from the substance and fate, it is partly the chorus, or rather the crowd looking on, whom this movement of the divine life fills with fear as being something alien and strange, or in whom this movement, as something closely touching themselves, produces merely the emotion of passive pity. Partly again, so far as consciousness co-operates and belongs to the various characters, this alliance is of an external kind, is a hypocrisy—because the true union, that of self, fate, and substance, is not yet present. The hero, who appears before the onlookers, breaks up into his mask and the actor, into the person of the play and the actual self.

The self-consciousness of the heroes must step forth from its mask and be represented as knowing itself to be the fate both of the gods of the chorus and of the absolute powers themselves, and as being no longer separated from the chorus, the universal consciousness.

Comedy has, then, first of all, the aspect that actual self-consciousness represents itself as the fate of the gods. These elemental Beings are, *qua* universal moments, no definite self, and are not actual. They are, indeed, endowed with the form of individuality, but this is in their case merely put on, and does not really and truly belong to them. The actual self has no such abstract moment as its substance and content. The subject, therefore, is raised above such a moment, as it would be above a particular quality, and when clothed with this mask gives utterance to the irony of such a property trying to be something on its own account. The pretentious claims of the universal abstract nature are shown up and discovered in the actual self; it is seen to be caught and held in a concrete reality, and lets the mask drop, just when it wants to be something genuine. The self, appearing here in its significance as something actual, plays with the mask which it once puts on, in order to be its own person; but it breaks away from this seeming and pretence just as quickly again, and comes out in its own nakedness and commonness, which it shows not to be distinct from the proper self, the actor, nor again from the onlooker.

This general dissolution, which the formally embodied essential nature as a whole undergoes when it assumes individuality, becomes in its content more serious, and hence more petulant and bitter, in so far as the content possesses its more serious and necessary meaning. The divine substance combines the meaning of natural and ethical essentiality.

As regards the natural element, actual self-consciousness shows in the very fact of applying elements of nature for its adornment, for its abode and so on, and again in feasting on its own offering, that *itself* is the Fate to which the secret is betrayed, no matter what may be the truth as regards the independent substantiality of nature. In the mystery of the bread and wine it makes its very own this self-subsistence of nature together with the significance of the inner reality; and in Comedy it is conscious of the irony lurking in this meaning.

So far, again, as this meaning contains the essence of ethical reality, it is partly the nation in its two aspects of the state, or Demos proper, and individual family life; partly, however, it is self-conscious pure knowledge, or rational thought of the universal. Demos, the general mass, which knows itself as master and governor, and is also aware of being the insight and intelligence which demand respect, exerts compulsion and is befooled through the particularity of its actual life, and exhibits the ludicrous contrast between its own opinion of itself and its immediate existence, between its necessity and contingency, its universality and its vulgarity. If the principle of its individual existence, cut off from the universal, breaks out in the proper figure of an actual man and openly usurps and administers the commonwealth, to which it is a secret harm and detriment, then there is more immediately disclosed the contrast between the universal in the sense of a theory, and that with which practice is concerned; there stand exposed the entire emancipation of the ends and aims of the mere individual from the universal order, and the scorn the mere individual shows for such order.[10]

Rational thinking removes contingency of form and shape from the divine Being; and, in opposition to the uncritical wisdom of the chorus—a wisdom, giving utterance to all sorts of ethical maxims and stamping with validity and authority a multitude of laws and specific conceptions of duty and of right—rational thought lifts these into the simple Ideas of the Beautiful and the Good. The process of this abstraction is the consciousness of the dialectic involved in these maxims and laws themselves, and hence the consciousness of the disappearance of that absolute validity with which they previously appeared. Since the contingent character and superficial individuality which imagination lent to the divine Beings, vanish, they are left, as regards their natural aspect, with merely the nakedness of their immediate existence; they are Clouds,[11] a passing vapour, like those imaginative ideas. Having passed in accordance with their essential character, as determined by thought, into the simple thoughts of the Beautiful and the Good, these latter submit to being filled with every kind of content. The force of dialectic knowledge[12] puts determinate laws and maxims of action at the mercy of the pleasure and levity of youth, led astray therewith, and gives weapons of deception into the hands of solicitous and apprehensive old age, restricted in its interests to the individual details of life. The pure thoughts of the Beautiful and the Good thus display a comic spectacle:—through their being set free from the opinion, which contains both their determinateness in the sense of content and also their absolute determinateness, the firm hold of consciousness upon them, they become empty, and, on that very account, the sport of the private opinion and caprice of any chance individuality.

Here, then, the Fate, formerly without consciousness, consisting in empty rest and forgetfulness, and separated from self-consciousness, is united with self-consciousness. The individual[13] self is the negative force through which and in which the gods, as also their moments, (nature as existent fact and the thoughts of their determinate characters), pass away and disappear. At the same time, the individual self is not the mere vacuity of disappearance, but preserves itself in this very nothing-

---

[10]Cp. Cleon in Aristophanes, *Knights*.
[11]Cp. Aristophanes, *Clouds*.
[12]Cp. the arguments in the *Clouds*.
[13]In comedy.

ness, holds to itself and is the sole and only reality. The religion of art is fulfilled and consummated in it, and is come full circle. Through the fact that it is the individual consciousness in its certainty of self which manifests itself as this absolute power, this latter has lost the form of something ideally presented (*vorgestellt*), separated from and alien to consciousness in general—as were the statue and also the living embodiment of beauty or the content of the Epic and the powers and persons of Tragedy. Nor again is the unity the unconscious unity of the cult and the mysteries; rather the self proper of the actor coincides with the part he impersonates, just as the onlooker is perfectly at home in what is represented before him, and sees himself playing in the drama before him. What this self-consciousness beholds, is that whatever assumes the form of essentiality as against self-consciousness, is instead dissolved within it—within its thought, its existence and action,—and is quite at its mercy. It is the return of everything universal into certainty of self, a certainty which, in consequence, is this complete loss of fear of everything strange and alien, and complete loss of substantial reality on the part of what is alien and external. Such certainty is a state of spiritual good health and of self-abandonment thereto, on the part of consciousness, in a way that, outside this kind of comedy, is not to be found anywhere.[14]

C

REVEALED RELIGION[1]

THROUGH the Religion of Art spirit has passed from the form of substance into that of Subject; for art brings out its shape and form, and imbues it with the nature of action, or establishes in it the self-consciousness which merely disappears in the awesome substance and in the attitude of simple trust does not itself comprehend itself. This incarnation in human form of the Divine Being begins with the statue, which has in it only the outward shape of the self, while the inner life thereof, its activity, falls outside it. In the case of the cult, however, both aspects have become one; in the outcome of the religion of art this unity, in being completely attained, has at the same time also passed over to the extreme of self; in the spirit, which is perfectly certain of itself in the individual existence of consciousness, all essential content is swallowed up and submerged. The proposition, which gives this light-hearted folly expression, runs thus: "The Self is Absolute Being." The

---

[14]Cp. Hegel's *Aesthetik*, W W., X., 3, 560.

[1]Christianity.

Being which was substance, and in which the self was the accidental element, has dropped to the level of a predicate; and in this self-consciousness, over against which nothing appears in the form of objective Being, spirit has lost its aspect of consciousness.[2]

This proposition, "The Self is Absolute Being," belongs, as is evident on the face of it, to the non-religious, the concrete actual spirit; and we have to recall what form of spirit it is which gives expression to it. This form will contain at once the movement of that proposition and its conversion, which lowers the self to a predicate and raises substance into subject. This we must understand to take place in such a way that the converse statement does not *per se*, or for us, make substance into subject, or, what is the same thing, does not reinstate substance again so that the consciousness of spirit is carried back to its commencement in natural religion; but rather in such a way that this conversion is brought about *for* and *through* self-consciousness itself. Since this latter *consciously* gives itself up, it is preserved and maintained in thus relinquishing itself, and remains the subject of the substance; but as being likewise *self*-relinquished, it has at the same time the consciousness of this substance. In other words, since, by thus offering itself up, it produces substance as subject, this subject remains its own very self. If, then, taking the two propositions, in the first the subject merely disappears in substantiality, and in the second the substance is merely a predicate, and both sides are thus present in each with contrary inequality of value—the result hereby effected is that the union and transfusion of both natures [subject and substance] become apparent. In this union both, with equal value and worth, are at once essential and also merely moments. Hence it is that spirit is equally consciousness of itself as its *objective* substance, as well as simple self-contained self-consciousness.

The religion of art belongs to the spirit animating the ethical sphere, the spirit which we formerly saw sink and disappear in the condition of right,[3] i.e. in the proposition: "The self as such, the abstract person, is absolute Being." In ethical life the self is absorbed in the spirit of its nation, it is universality filled to the full. Simple abstract individuality, however, rises out of this content, and its lightheartedness clarifies and rarifies it till it becomes a "person" and attains the abstract universality of right. Here the substantial reality of the ethical spirit is lost, the abstract insubstantial spirits of national individuals are gathered together into a pantheon; not into a pantheon represented in idea (*Vorstellung*), whose impotent form lets each alone to do as it likes, but into the

[2]Which implies such opposition.
[3]The Roman State.

pantheon of abstract universality, of pure thought, which disembodies them, and bestows on the spiritless self, on the individual person, complete existence on its own account.

But this self, through its being empty, has let the content go; this consciousness is Being merely within itself. Its own existence, the legal recognition of the person, is an unfulfilled empty abstraction. It thus really possesses merely the thought of itself; in other words, as it there exists and knows itself as object, it is something unreal. Consequently, it is merely stoic independence, the independence of thought; and this finds, by passing through the process of scepticism, its ultimate truth in that form we called the "unhappy self-consciousness"—the soul of despair.

This knows how the case stands with the actual claims to validity which the abstract [legal] person puts forward, as also with the validity of this person in pure thought [in Stoicism]. It knows that a vindication of such validity means really being altogether lost; it is just this loss become conscious of itself, and is the surrender and relinquishment of its knowledge about itself. We see that this "unhappy consciousness" constituted the counterpart and the complement of the perfectly happy consciousness, that of comedy. All divine reality goes back into this latter type of consciousness; it means, in other words, the complete relinquishment and emptying of substance. The former, on the contrary, is conversely the tragic fate that befalls certainty of self which aims at being absolute, at being self-sufficient. It is consciousness of the loss of everything of significance in this certainty of itself, and of the loss even of this knowledge or certainty of self—the loss of substance as well as of self; it is the bitter pain which finds expression in the cruel words, "God is dead."[4]

In the condition of right or law, then, the ethical world has vanished, and its type of religion has passed away in the mood of Comedy. The "unhappy consciousness," the soul of despair, is just the knowledge of all this loss. It has lost both the worth and dignity it attached to its immediate personality [as a legal person] as well as that attaching to its personality when reflected in the medium of thought [in the case of Stoicism]. Trust in the eternal laws of the Gods is likewise silenced, just as the oracles are dumb, who pretended to know what to do in particular cases. The statues set up are now corpses in stone whence the animating soul has flown, while the hymns of praise are words from which all belief has gone. The tables of the gods are bereft of spiritual food and drink, and from his games and festivals man no more receives the joyful sense of his unity with the divine Being. The works of the

---

[4]From a hymn of Luther.

muse lack the force and energy of the spirit which derived the certainty and assurance of itself just from the crushing ruin of gods and men. They are themselves now just what they are for us—beautiful fruit broken off the tree; a kindly fate has passed on those works to us, as a maiden might offer such fruit off a tree. Their actual life as they exist is no longer there, not the tree that bore them, not the earth, and the elements, which constituted their substance, nor the climate that determined their constitutive character, nor the change of seasons which controlled the process of their growth. So too it is not their living world that Fate preserves and gives us with those works of ancient art, not the spring and summer of that ethical life in which they bloomed and ripened, but the veiled remembrance alone of all this reality. Our action, therefore, when we enjoy them is not that of worship, through which our conscious life might attain its complete truth and be satisfied to the full: our action is external; it consists in wiping off some drop of rain or speck of dust from these fruits, and in place of the inner elements composing the reality of the ethical life, a reality that environed, created and inspired these works, we erect in prolix detail the scaffolding of the dead elements of their outward existence,—language, historical circumstances, etc. All this we do, not in order to enter into their very life, but only to represent them ideally or pictorially (*vorstellen*) within ourselves. But just as the maiden who hands us the plucked fruits is more than the nature which presented them in the first instance—the nature which provided all their detailed conditions and elements, tree, air, light, and so on—since in a higher way she gathers all this together into the light of her self-conscious eye, and her gesture in offering the gifts; so too the spirit of the fate, which presents us with those works of art, is more than the ethical life realized in that nation. For it is the *inwardizing* in *us*, in the form of conscious memory (*Er-Innerung*), of the spirit which in them was manifested in a still *external* way;—it is the spirit of the tragic fate which collects all those individual gods and attributes of the substance into the one Pantheon, into the spirit which is itself conscious of itself as spirit.

All the conditions for its production are present, and this totality of its conditions constitutes the development of it, its notion, or the inherent production of it. The cycle of the creations of art embraces in its scope all forms in which the absolute substance relinquishes itself. The absolute substance is in the form of individuality as a thing; as an object existing for sense experience; as pure language, or the process of that form whose existence does not get away from the self, and is a purely evanescent object; as immediate unity with universal self-consciousness when inspired with enthusiasm; as mediated unity when performing the acts of the cult; as corporeal embodiment of the self in a form of beauty; and finally as existence lifted into ideal representation (*Vorstellung*) and the expansion of this existence into a world which at length gathers its content together into universality, a universal which is at the same time pure certainty and assurance of itself. These forms, and, on the other side, the world of personality and legal right, the wild and desert waste of content with its constituent elements set free and detached, as also the thought-constituted personality of Stoicism, and the unresting disquiet of Scepticism—these compose the periphery of the circle of shapes and forms, which attend, an expectant and eager throng, round the birthplace of spirit as it becomes self-consciousness. Their centre is the yearning agony of the unhappy despairing self-consciousness, a pain which permeates all of them and is the common birthpang at its production,—the simplicity of the pure notion, which contains those forms as its moments.

Spirit, here, has in it two sides, which are above represented as the two converse propositions: one is this, that substance empties itself of itself, and becomes self-consciousness; the other is the converse, that self-consciousness empties itself of itself and makes itself into the form of "thing," or makes itself universal self. Both sides have in this way met each other, and, in consequence, their true union has arisen. The re-linquishment or "kenosis" on the part of the substance, its becoming self-consciousness, expresses the transition into the opposite, the un-conscious transition of necessity, in other words, that it is *implicitly* self-consciousness. Conversely, the emptying of self-consciousness ex-presses this, that implicitly it is Universal Being, or—because the self is pure self-existence, which is at home with itself in its opposite—that the substance is self-consciousness explicitly *for the self*, and, just on that account, is spirit. Of this spirit, which has left the form of sub-stance behind, and enters existence in the shape of self-consciousness, we may say, therefore—if we wish to use terms drawn from the process of natural generation—that it has a real mother but a potential or an implicit father. For actual reality, or self-consciousness, and implicit being in the sense of substance are its two moments; and by the reci-procity of their kenosis, each relinquishing or "emptying" itself of itself and becoming the other, spirit thus comes into existence as their unity.

In so far as self-consciousness in a one-sided way grasps only its *own* relinquishment, although its object is thus for it at once both existence and self and it knows all existence to be spiritual in nature, yet true spirit has not become thereby objective for it. For, so far, being in gen-eral or substance, would not essentially *from its side* be also emptied of itself, and become self-consciousness. In that case, then, all existence is spiritual reality merely from the standpoint of consciousness, not in-herently in itself. Spirit in this way has merely a fictitious or imaginary

existence.[5] This imagination is fantastic extravagance of mind, which
introduces into nature as well as history, the world and the mythical
ideas of early religions, another inner esoteric meaning different from
what they, on the face of them, bear directly to consciousness, and, in
particular, in the case of religions, another meaning than the self-
consciousness, whose religions they were, actually knew to be there.
But this meaning is one that is borrowed, a garment, which does not
cover the nakedness of the outer appearance, and secures no belief and
respect; it is no more than murky darkness and a peculiar crazy con-
tortion of consciousness.

If then this meaning of the objective is not to be bare fancy and
imagination, it must be inherent and essential (an sich), i.e. must in the
first place arise in consciousness as springing from the very notion, and
must come forth in its necessity. It is thus that self-knowing spirit has
arisen; it has arisen through the knowledge of immediate consciousness, i.e. of consciousness of the existing object, by means of its necessary process. This notion, which, being immediate, had also, for its consciousness, the shape of immediacy, has, in the second place, taken on
the form of self-consciousness essentially and inherently, i.e. by just the
same necessity of the notion by which being or immediacy, the abstract
object of self-consciousness, renounces itself and becomes, for consciousness, Ego. The immediate entity (Ansich), or [objectively] existent necessity, is, however, different from the [subjective] thinking entity, or the knowledge of necessity—a distinction which, at the same
time, does not lie outside the notion, for the simple unity of the notion
is itself immediate being. The notion is at once what empties or relinquishes itself, or the explicit unfolding of directly apprehended
(angeschaut) necessity, and is also at home with itself in that necessity,
knows it and comprehends it. The immediate inherent nature of spirit,
which takes on the form of self-consciousness, means nothing else than
that the concrete actual world-spirit has reached this knowledge of itself.
It is then too that this knowledge first enters its consciousness, and enters it as truth. How that came about has already been explained.

That Absolute Spirit has taken on the shape of self-consciousness inherently, and therefore also consciously to itself—this appears now as
the belief of the world, the belief that spirit exists in fact as a definite
self-consciousness, i.e. as an actual human being; that spirit is an object
for immediate experience; that the believing mind sees, feels, and hears
this divinity.[6] Taken thus it is not imagination, not a fancy; it is actual
in the believer. Consciousness in that case does not set out from its own

---

[5]As in neo-Platonism.
[6]e.g. in Christianity.

inner life, does not start from thought, and in itself combine th thought of God with existence; rather it sets out from immediate pre ent existence, and recognizes God in it.

The moment of immediate existence is present in the content of the notion, and present in such a way that the religious spirit, on the return of all ultimate reality into consciousness, has become simple positive self, just as the actual spirit as such, in the case of the "unhappy consciousness," was just this simple self-conscious negativity. The self of the existent spirit has in that way the form of complete immediacy. It is neither set up as something thought, or imaginatively represented, nor as something produced, as is the case with the immediate self in natural religion, or again in religion as art. Rather, this concrete God is beheld sensuously and immediately as a self, as a real individual human being; only so is it a self-consciousness.

This incarnation of the Divine Being, its having essentially and directly the shape of self-consciousness, is the simple content of Absolute Religion. Here the Divine Being is known as Spirit; this religion is the Divine Being's consciousness concerning itself that it is Spirit. For spirit is knowledge of self in a state of alienation of self: spirit is the Being which is the process of retaining identity with itself in its otherness. This, however, is Substance, so far as in its accidents substance at the same time is turned back into itself; and is so, not as being indifferent towards something unessential and, consequently, as finding itself in some alien element, but as being there within itself, i.e. so far as it is subject or self.

In this form of religion the Divine Being is, on that account, revealed. Its being revealed obviously consists in this, that what it is, is known. It is, however, known just in its being known as spirit, as a Being which is essentially self-consciousness.

There is something in its object concealed from consciousness if the object is for consciousness an "other," or something alien, and if consciousness does not know the object as its self. This concealment, this secrecy, ceases when the Absolute Being *qua* spirit is object of consciousness. For here in its relation to consciousness the object is in the form of self; i.e. consciousness immediately knows itself there, or is manifest, revealed, to itself in the object. Itself is manifest to itself only in its own certainty of self; the object it has is the self; self, however, is nothing alien and extraneous, but inseparable unity with itself, the *immediately universal*. It is the pure notion, pure thought, or self-existence, (being-for-self), which is immediately *being*, and, therewith, being-for-another, and, *qua* this being-for-another, is immediately turned back into itself and is at home with itself (*bei sich*). It is thus the truly and solely revealed. The Good, the Righteous, the Holy, Creator of Heaven and Earth, etc.—all these are predicates of a subject, universal moments, which have their support on this central point, and only *are* when consciousness goes back into thought.

As long as it is *they* that are known, their ground and essential being, the Subject itself, is not yet revealed; and in the same way the specific determinations of the universal are not this universal itself. The Subject itself, and consequently this pure universal too, is, however, revealed as self; for this self is just this inner being reflected into itself, the inner being which is immediately given and is the proper certainty of that self, for which it is given. To be in its notion that which reveals and is revealed—this is, then, the true shape of spirit; and moreover, this shape, its notion, is alone its very essence and its substance. Spirit is known as self-consciousness, and to this self-consciousness it is directly revealed, for it is this self-consciousness itself. The divine nature is the same as the human, and it is this unity which is intuitively apprehended (*angeschaut*).

Here, then, we find as a fact consciousness, or the general form in which Being is aware of Being—the shape which Being adopts—to be identical with its self-consciousness. This shape is itself a self-consciousness; it is thus at the same time an existent object; and this existence possesses equally directly the significance of pure thought, of Absolute Being.

The absolute Being existing as a concrete actual self-consciousness, seems to have descended from its eternal pure simplicity; but in fact it has, in so doing, attained for the first time its highest nature, its supreme reach of being. For only when the notion of Being has reached its simple purity of nature, is it *both* the absolute abstraction, which is pure thought and hence the pure singleness of self, *and* immediacy or objective being, on account of its simplicity.

What is called sense-consciousness is just this pure abstraction; it is this kind of thought for which being is the immediate. The lowest is thus at the same time the highest: the revealed which has come forth entirely to the surface is just therein the deepest reality. That the Supreme Being is seen, heard, etc., as an existent self-consciousness,— this is, in very truth, the culmination and consummation of its notion. And through this consummation, the Divine Being is given and exists immediately in its character as Divine Being.

This immediate existence is at the same time not solely and simply immediate consciousness; it is *religious* consciousness. This immediacy means not only an existent self-consciousness, but also the purely thought-constituted or Absolute Being; and these meanings are inseparable. What we [the philosophers] are conscious of in our conception,—that objective being is ultimate essence,—is the same as what the religious consciousness is aware of. This unity of being and essence, of thought which is immediately existence, is immediate knowledge on the part of this religious consciousness just as it is the inner thought or the mediated reflective knowledge of this consciousness. For this unity of being and thought is self-consciousness and actually exists; in other words, the thought-constituted unity has at the same time this concrete shape and form of what it is. God, then, is here revealed, as He is; He actually exists as He is in Himself; He is real as Spirit. God is attainable in pure speculative knowledge alone, and only *is* in that knowledge, and is merely that knowledge itself, for He is spirit; and this speculative knowledge is the knowledge furnished by revealed religion. That knowledge knows God to be thought, or pure Essence; and knows this thought as actual being and as a real existence, and existence as the negativity of itself, hence as Self, an individual "this" and a universal self. It is just this that revealed religion knows.

The hopes and expectations of preceding ages pressed forward to, and were solely directed towards this revelation, the vision of what Absolute Being is, and the discovery of themselves therein. This joy, the joy of seeing itself in Absolute Being, becomes realized in self-consciousness, and seizes the whole world. For the Absolute is Spirit, it is the simple movement of those pure abstract moments, which expresses just this—that Ultimate Reality is then, and not till then, known as Spirit when it is seen and beheld as immediate self-consciousness.

This conception of spirit knowing itself to be spirit, is still the immediate notion; it is not yet developed. The ultimate Being is spirit; in other words, it has appeared, it is revealed. This first revelation is itself immediate; but the immediacy is likewise thought, or pure mediation, and must therefore exhibit and set forth this moment in the sphere of immediacy as such.

Looking at this more precisely, spirit, when self-consciousness is immediate, is "this" individual self-consciousness set up in contrast to the universal self-consciousness. It is a one, an excluding unit, which appears to that consciousness, for which it exists, in the as yet impervious form of a sensuous other, an unresolved entity in the sphere of sense. This other does not yet know spirit to be its own; in other words, spirit, in its form as an individual self, does not yet exist as equally universal self, as *all* self. Or again, the shape it assumes has not as yet the form of the notion, i.e. of the universal self, of the self which in its immediate actual reality is at once transcended, is thought, universality, without losing its reality in this universality.

The preliminary and similarly immediate form of this universality is, however, not at once the form of thought itself, of the notion as notion; it is the universality of actual reality, it is the "allness," the collective totality, of the selves, and is the elevation of existence into the sphere of figurative thought (*Vorstellung*); just as in general, to take a concrete example, the "this" of sense, when transcended, is first of all the "thing" of "perception," and is not yet the "universal" of "understanding."

This individual human being, then, which Absolute Being is revealed to be, goes through in its own case as an individual the process found in sense existence. He is the *immediately* present God; in consequence, His being passes over into His *having been*. Consciousness, for which God is thus sensuously present, ceases to see Him, to hear Him: it *has* seen Him, it *has* heard Him. And it is because it only *has* seen and heard Him, that it first becomes itself spiritual consciousness;[7] or, in other words, He has now arisen in Spirit, as He formerly rose before consciousness as an object existing in the sphere of sense. For, a consciousness which sees and hears Him by sense, is one which is itself merely an immediate consciousness, which has not cancelled and transcended the disparateness of objectivity, has not withdrawn it into pure thought, but knows this objectively presented individual, and not itself, as spirit. In the disappearance of the immediate existence of what is known to be Absolute Being, immediacy acquires its negative moment. Spirit remains the immediate self of actual reality, but in the form of the universal self-consciousness of a religious communion,[8] a self-consciousness which rests in its own proper substance, just as in it this substance is universal subject: it is not the individual subject by himself, but the individual along with the consciousness of the communion, and what he is for this communion is the complete whole of the individual spirit.

The conditions "past" and "distance" are, however, merely the imperfect form in which the immediateness gets mediated or made universal; this is merely dipped superficially in the element of thought, is kept there as a sensuous mode of immediacy, and not made one with the nature of thought itself. It is lifted out of sense merely into the region of pictorial presentation; for this is the synthetic [external] connexion of sensuous immediacy and its universality or thought.

Pictorial presentation constitutes the characteristic form in which spirit is conscious of itself in this its religious communion. This form is not yet the self-consciousness of spirit which has reached its notion as notion; the mediating process is still incomplete. In this connexion of being and thought, then, there is a defect; spiritual life is still cumbered with an unreconciled diremption into a "here" and a "beyond." The

---

[7]Cp. "He that hath seen me hath seen the Father" (John xiv.). "If I go not away the Comforter will not come unto you" (*ibid.* xvi.).

[8]"Lo, I am with you always, even unto the end of the world" (Matt. xxviii.; also xviii. 20).

content is the true content; but all its moments, when placed in the element of mere imaginative presentation, have the character, not of being conceptually comprehended, but of appearing as completely independent aspects, externally related to one another.

In order that the true content may also obtain its true form for consciousness, the latter must necessarily pass to a higher plane of mental development, where the absolute Substance is not intuitively apprehended but conceptually comprehended and where consciousness is *for itself* brought to the level of its self-consciousness;—as this has already taken place objectively or for us [who have analysed the process of experience].

We have to consider this content as it exists in its consciousness. Absolute Spirit is content; that is how it exists in the shape of its truth. But its truth consists not merely in being the substance or the inherent reality of the religious communion; nor again in coming out of this inwardness into the objectivity of imaginative thought; but in becoming concrete actual self, reflecting itself into self, and being *Subject*. This, then, is the process which spirit realizes in its communion; this is its *life*. What this self-revealing spirit is in and for itself, is therefore not brought out by the rich content of its life being, so to say, untwined and reduced to its original and primitive strands, to the ideas, for instance, presented before the minds of the first imperfect religious communion, or even to what the actual human being [incarnating the Divine Spirit] has spoken.[9] This reversion to the primitive is based on the instinct to get at the notion, the ultimate principle; but it confuses the origin, in the sense of the immediate existence of the first historical appearance, with the simplicity of the notion. By thus impoverishing the life of spirit, by clearing away the idea of the communion and its action with regard to its idea, there arises, therefore, not the notion, but bare externality and particularity, merely the historical manner in which spirit once upon a time appeared, the soulless recollection of a presumably (*gemeinten*) individual historical figure and its past.[10]

Spirit is content of its consciousness to begin with in the form of pure substance; in other words, it is content of its pure consciousness. This element of thought is the process of descending into existence, or individuality. The middle term between these two is their synthetic connexion, the consciousness of passing into otherness, the process of imaginative presentation as such. The third stage is the return from this presentation and from that otherness; in other words, it is the element of self-consciousness itself.

---

[9]viz. Christ.
[10]The life and work of the historical Jesus.

These three moments constitute the life of spirit. Its resolution in imaginative thought consists in its taking on a determinate mode of being; this determinateness, however, is nothing but one of its moments. Its detailed process thus consists in spreading its nature out in each of its moments as in an element in which it lives: and in so far as each of these spheres completes itself in itself, this reflexion into itself is at the same time the transition into another sphere of its being. Imaginative presentation constitutes the middle term between pure thought and self-consciousness as such, and is merely *one* of the determinate forms. At the same time however, as has been shown, the character belonging to such presentation—that of being "synthetic connexion"—is spread over all these elements and is their common characteristic.

The content itself, which we have to consider, has partly been met with already, as the idea of the "unhappy" and the "believing" consciousness. In the case of the "unhappy" consciousness, however, the content has the characteristic of being produced from consciousness and for which it yearns, a content wherein the spirit can never be satiated nor find rest because the content is not yet its own content inherently and essentially, or in the sense of being its substance. In the case of the "believing" consciousness, again, this content was regarded as the impersonal Being of the World, as the essentially objective content of imaginative thought—a pictorial thinking that seeks to escape the actual world altogether, and consequently has not the certainty of self-consciousness, a certainty which is cut off from it, partly as being conceit of knowledge, partly as being pure insight. The consciousness of the religious communion, on the other hand, possesses the content as its substance, just as the content is the certainty the communion has of its own spirit.

Spirit, represented at first as substance in the element of pure thought, is, thus, primarily the eternal essential Being, simple, self-identical, which does not, however, have this abstract meaning of essential Being, but the meaning of Absolute Spirit. Yet spirit consists, not in being a meaning, not in being the inner, but in being the actual, the real. "Simple eternal essential Being" would, therefore, be spirit merely in empty phrase, if we remained at the level of pictorial thought, and went no further than the expression of "simple eternal essential Being." "Simple essential Being," however, because it is abstraction, is in point of fact the inherently negative, is indeed the negativity of reflective thought, or negativity as found in Being *per se*; i.e. it is absolute distinction from itself, is pure process of becoming its other. *Qua* essential Being, it is merely implicit, or for us: but since this purity of form is just abstraction or negativity, it is *for itself*, it is the self, the notion. It is thus objective; and since pictorial thinking apprehends and expresses as an event what has just been expressed as the *necessity* of the notion, it will be said that the eternal Being begets for itself an other. But in this otherness it has likewise, *ipso facto*, returned into itself again; for the distinction is distinction in itself, i.e. the distinction is directly distinguished merely from itself, and is thus the unity returned into itself.

There are thus three moments to be distinguished: Essential Being; explicit Self-existence, which is the express otherness of essential Being, and for which that Being is object; and Self-existence or Self-knowledge *in* that other. The essential Being beholds only itself in its Self-existence, in its objective otherness. In thus emptying itself, in this kenosis, it is merely within itself: the independent Self-existence which excludes itself from essential Being is the knowledge of itself on the part of essential Being. It is the "Word," the Logos, which when spoken empties the speaker of himself, outwardizes him, and leaves him behind emptied, but is as immediately perceived, and only this act of self-perceiving himself is the actual existence of the "Word." Hence, then, the distinctions which are set up are just as immediately resolved as they are made, and are just as directly made as they are resolved, and the truth and the reality consist precisely in this self-closed circular process.

This movement within itself expresses the absolute Being *qua* Spirit. Absolute Being, when not grasped as Spirit, is merely the abstract void, just as spirit which is not grasped as this process is merely an empty word. Since its moments are grasped *purely as* moments, they are notions in restless activity, which *are* merely in being inherently their own opposite, and in finding their rest in the whole. But the pictorial thought of the religious communion is not this notional thinking; it has the content without its necessity; and instead of the form of the notion it brings into the realm of pure consciousness the natural relations of Father and Son. Since it thus, even when thinking, proceeds by way of figurative ideas, absolute Being is indeed revealed to it, but the moments of this Being, owing to this [externally] synthetic pictorial thinking, partly fall of themselves apart from one another, so that they are not related to each other through their own very notion, while, partly again, this figurative thinking retreats from the pure object it deals with, and takes up a merely external relation towards it. The object is externally revealed to it from an alien source, and in this thought of Spirit it does not recognize its own self, does not recognize the nature of pure self-consciousness. In so far as the form of figurative thinking and that way of thinking by means of relationships derived from nature have to be transcended, and especially the method of taking the moments of the process, which Spirit is, as isolated immovable substances or subjects, instead of transient moments—this transcendence is to be looked at as a compulsion on the part of the notion, in the way we formerly pointed out when dealing with another aspect.[11] But since it is only an instinct, it mistakes its own real character, rejects the content along with the form, and, what comes to the same thing, degrades the content into a historical imaginative idea and an heirloom handed down by tradition. In this way there is retained and preserved only what is purely external in belief, and the retention of it as something dead and devoid of knowledge; while the inner element in belief has passed away, because this would be the notion knowing itself as notion.

The Absolute Spirit, as pictured in the element of pure essential Being, is not indeed the abstract pure essential Being; rather, just by the fact that this is merely a moment in the life of Spirit, abstract essential Being has sunk to the level of a mere element (in which Spirit lives). The representation of Spirit in this element, however, has inherently the same defect, as regards form, which essential Being as such has. Essential Being is abstraction, and, therefore, the negative of its simplicity, is an *other*: in the same way, Spirit in the element of essential Being is the form of simple unity, which, on that account, is just as essentially a process of becoming something else. Or, what is the same thing, the relation of the eternal Being to its self-existence, (its objective existence for Itself), is that of pure thought, an immediately simple relation. In this simple beholding of itself in the Other, otherness therefore is not as such set up independently; it is distinction in the way of distinction, in pure thought, is immediately no distinction—a recognition of Love, where lover and beloved are by their very nature not opposed to each other at all. Spirit, which is expressed in the element of pure thought, is essentially just this: not to be merely *in* that element, but to be *concrete*, *actual*; for otherness itself, i.e. cancelling and superseding its own pure thought-constituted notion, lies in the very notion of Spirit.

The element of pure thought, because it is an abstract element, is itself rather the other of its own simplicity, and hence passes over into the proper element of imagination—the element where the moments of the pure notion at once acquire a substantial existence in opposition to each other and are subjects as well, which do not exist in indifference towards each other, merely for a third, but, being reflected into themselves, break away from one another and stand confronting each other.

Merely eternal, or *abstract* Spirit, then, becomes an other to itself: it enters existence, and, in the first instance, enters *immediate* existence. It creates a World. This "Creation" is the word which pictorial thought

---

[11]*v.* p. 448.

uses to convey the notion itself in its absolute movement; or to express
the fact that the simple which has been expressed as absolute, or pure
thought, just because it is abstract, is really the negative, and hence opposed to itself, *the other* of itself; or because, to state the same in yet another way, what is put forward as essential Being is simple immediacy,
bare existence, but *qua* immediacy or existence, is without Self, and,
lacking thus inwardness, is passive, or exists *for* another. This existence
for another is at the same time a world. Spirit, in the character of existing for another, is the undisturbed separate subsistence of those moments formerly enclosed within pure thought, is, therefore, the dissolution of their simple universality, and their dispersion into their own
particularity.

The world, however, is not merely Spirit thus thrown out and dispersed into the plenitude of existence and the external order imposed
on it; for since Spirit is essentially the simple Self, this self is likewise
present therein. The world is objectively existent spirit, which is *individual* self, that has consciousness and distinguishes itself as other, as
world, from itself. In the way this individual self is thus immediately established at first it is not yet conscious of being Spirit; it thus does not
exist as Spirit; it may be called "innocent," but not strictly "good." In
order that in fact it may be self and Spirit, it has first to become objectively an other to itself, in the same way that the Eternal Being manifests itself as the process of being self-identical in its otherness. Since
this spirit is determined as yet only as immediately existing, or dispersed
into the diverse multiplicity of its conscious life, its becoming "other"
means that knowledge concentrates itself upon itself. Immediate existence turns into thought, or merely sense-consciousness turns round
into consciousness of thought; and, moreover, because that thought has
come from immediacy or is conditioned thought, it is not pure knowledge, but thought which contains otherness, and is, thus, the self-
opposed thought of good and evil. Man is pictorially represented by the
religious mind in this way: it happened once as an event, with no necessity about it, that he lost the form of harmonious unity with himself
by plucking the fruits of the tree of the knowledge of good and evil, and
was driven from the state of innocence, from Paradise, from the garden
with all its creatures, and from nature offering its bounties without
man's toil.

Since this self-concentration on the part of the existent consciousness has straightway the character of becoming discordant with itself,
Evil appears as the first actual expression of the self-concentrated consciousness. And because the thoughts of good and evil are utterly opposed, and this opposition is not yet broken down, this consciousness is
essentially and merely evil. At the same time, however, owing to just

this very opposition, there is present also the good consciousness opposing the one that is evil, and again their relation to each other. In so far as immediate existence turns round into thought, and self-concentration is partly itself thought, while partly again the transition to otherness on the part of the inner self (*Wesen*), is thereby more precisely determined,—the fact of becoming evil can be removed further backwards away out of the actually existing world and transferred to the very earliest realm of thought. It may thus be said that it was the very first-born Son of Light [Lucifer] who, by becoming self-concentrated, fell, but that in his place another was at once created. Such a form of expression as "fallen," belonging merely to figurative thought, and not to the notion, just like the term "Son," either (we may say) transmutes and lowers the moments of the notion to the level of imaginative thought, or transfers pictures into the realm of thought.

In the same way, it is matter of indifference to coordinate a multiplicity of other shapes and forms[12] with the simple thought of otherness in the Being of the Eternal, and transfer to them that condition of self-concentration. This co-ordination must, all the same, win approval, for the reason that, through it, this moment of otherness does express diversity, as it should do: not indeed as plurality in general, but as determinate diversity, so that one part is the Son, that which is simple and knows itself to be essential Being, while the other part is the abandonment, the emptying, of self-existence, and merely lives to praise that Being. To this part may then also be assigned the resumption once again of the self-existence relinquished, and that "self-centredness" characteristic of evil. In so far as this condition of otherness falls into two parts, Spirit might, as regards its moments, be more exactly expressed numerically as a Quaternity, a four in one, or (because the multiplicity breaks up itself again into two parts, viz. one part which has remained good, the other which has become evil), might even be expressed as a Quinity.

Counting the moments, however, can be regarded as altogether useless, since, for one thing, what is distinguished is itself just as truly one and single—viz. the thought of distinction which is only *one* thought—as the thought is this element distinguished, the second over against the first. For another thing it is useless to count, because the thought which grasps the many in one has to be dissolved out of its universality and must be distinguished into more than three or four distinct components. This universality appears, in contrast to the absolute determinateness of the abstract unit—the principle of number—as indeterminateness in relation to number as such; so that in this connexion we

---

[12]The angelic hosts.

can speak only of numbers in general, i.e. not of a specific number of distinctions. Hence, in general, it is here quite superfluous to think of number and counting, just as, in other connexions, the bare difference of magnitude and multitude says nothing at all and falls outside conceptual thought.

Good and Evil were the specific distinctions of thought which we found. Since their opposition is not yet broken down, and they are represented as essential realities of thought, each of them independent by itself, man is the self with no essential reality of his own and the mere ground which couples them together, and on which they exist and war with one another. But these universal powers of good and evil belong all the same to the self, or the self is their actuality. From this point of view it thus comes about that, as evil is nothing else than the self-concentration of the natural existence of spirit, conversely, good enters into actual reality and appears as an (objectively) existing self-consciousness. That which, when Spirit is interpreted in terms of pure thought, is in general merely hinted at as the Divine Being's transition into otherness, here, for figurative thinking, comes nearer its realization: the realization is taken to consist in the Divine Being "humbling" Itself, and renouncing its abstract nature and unreality. The other aspect, that of evil, is taken by imagination as an event extraneous and alien to the Divine Being: to grasp evil in the Divine Being itself as the wrath of God—that is the supreme effort, the severest strain, of which figurative thought, wrestling with its own limitations, is capable, an effort which, since it is devoid of the notion, remains a fruitless struggle.

The alienation of the Divine Nature is thus set up in its double-sided form: the self of Spirit, and its simple thought, are the two moments whose absolute unity is Spirit itself. Its alienation with itself consists in the two falling apart from each other, and in the one having an unequal value as against the other. This disparateness is, therefore, twofold in character, and two connexions arise, which have in common the moments just given. In the one, the Divine Being stands for what is essential, while natural existence and the self are unessential and are to be cancelled. In the other, on the contrary, it is self-existence which passes for what is essential and the simply Divine for unessential. Their mediating, though still empty, ground is existence in general, the bare community of their two moments.

The dissolution of this opposition does not take effect through the struggle between the two elements, which are pictured as separate and independent Beings. Just in virtue of their independence each must inherently, through its own notion, dissolve itself in itself. The struggle only takes place where both cease to be this mixture of thought and independent existence, and confront each other merely as thoughts. For there, being determinate notions, they essentially exist merely in the relation of opposition; *qua* independent, on the other hand, they have their essential nature outside their opposition; their movement is thus free, self-determined, and peculiar to themselves. If, then, we consider the movement of both as it is in themselves—i.e. as it is essentially—their movement starts only in that one of the two which has the character of being inherently essential as contrasted with the other. This is pictured as a spontaneous action; but the necessity for its self-abandonment lies in the notion that what is inherently essential, and gets this specific character merely through opposition, has just on that account no real independent subsistence. Therefore that element which has for its essence, not independent self-existence, but simple being, is what empties and abandons itself, gives itself unto death, and so reconciles Absolute Being with its own self. For in this process it manifests itself as spirit: the abstract Being is estranged from itself, it has natural existence and the reality of an actual self. This its otherness, or its being sensuously present, is taken back again by the second process of becoming "other," and is affirmed as superseded, as universal. Thereby the Divine Being has come to itself in the sphere of the sensuous present; the immediate existence of actual reality has ceased to be something alien or external to the Divine, by being sublated, universal: this death (of immediacy) is therefore its rising anew as spirit. When the self-conscious Being cancels and transcends its immediate present, it is as universal self-consciousness. This notion of the transcended individual self which is Absolute Being, immediately expresses therefore the establishment of a communion which, while hitherto having its abode in the sphere of pictorial thought, now returns into itself as the Self: and Spirit thus passes from the second element constituting it,—figurative thought—and goes over to the third-self—consciousness as such.

If we further consider the kind of procedure that pictorial thinking adopts as it goes along, we find in the first place the expression that the Divine Being "takes on" human nature. Here it is *eo ipso* asserted that implicitly and inherently the two are not separate: just as in the statement, that the Divine Being from the beginning empties Itself of Itself, that its objective existence becomes concentrated in Itself and becomes evil, it is not asserted but implied that *per se* this evil existence is *not* something alien to the Divine nature. Absolute Being would be merely an empty name if in very truth there were any other being external to it, if there were a "fall" from it. The aspect of self-concentration really constitutes the essential moment of the self of Spirit.

That this self-centredness, whence primarily comes its reality, belongs to the Divine Being—while this is for *us* a notion, and so as far as it *is* a notion,—appears to pictorial thinking as an inconceivable happening. The inherent and essential nature assumes for figurative thought the form of an indifferent objective fact. The thought, however, that those apparently mutually repugnant moments, absolute Being and self-existent Self, are not inseparable, comes also before this figurative way of thinking (since it does possess the real content), but that thought appears *afterwards*, in the form that the Divine Being empties Itself of Itself and is made flesh. This figurative idea, which in this manner is still immediate and hence not spiritual, i.e. it knows the human form assumed by the Divine as merely a particular form, not yet as a universal form—becomes spiritual for this consciousness in the process whereby God, who has assumed shape and form, surrenders again His immediate existence, and returns to His essential Being. The essential Being is then Spirit only when it is reflected into itself.

The reconciliation of the Divine Being with its other as a whole, and, specifically, with the *thought* of this other—evil—is thus presented here in a figurative way. If this reconciliation is expressed *conceptually*, by saying it consists in the fact that evil is inherently the same as what goodness is, or again that the Divine Being is the same as nature in its entire extent, just as nature separated from God is simply nothingness,—then this must be looked at as an unspiritual mode of expression which is bound to give rise to misunderstandings. When evil is the *same* as goodness, then evil is just *not* evil nor goodness good; on the contrary, both are really done away with—evil in general, self-centred self-existence, and goodness, self-less simplicity. Since in this way they are both expressed in terms of their notion, the unity of the two is at once apparent; for self-centred self-existence is simple knowledge; and what is self-less simplicity is similarly pure self-existence centred within itself. Hence, if it must be said that good and evil in this their conception, i.e. so far as they are *not* good and evil, are the same, just as certainly it must be said that they are not the same, but absolutely different; for simple self-existence, or again pure knowledge, are equally pure negativity or *per se* absolute distinction. It is only these two propositions that make the whole complete; and when the first is asserted and asseverated, it must be met and opposed by insisting on the other with immovable obstinacy. Since both are equally right, they are both equally wrong, and their wrong consists in taking such abstract forms as "the same" and "not the same," "identity" and "non-identity," to be something true, fixed, real, and in resting on them. Neither the one nor the other has truth; their truth is just their movement, the process in which simple sameness is abstraction and thus absolute distinction, while this again, being distinction *per se*, is distinguished from itself and so is self-identity. Precisely this is what we have in sameness of the Divine Being and Nature in general and human nature in particular: the former is Nature so far as it is not essential Being; Nature is Divine in its essential Being. But it is in Spirit that we find both abstract aspects affirmed as they truly are, viz. as cancelled and preserved at once: and this way of affirming them cannot be expressed by the judgment, by the soulless word "is," the copula of the judgment. In the same way Nature is nothing outside its essential Being [God]; but this nothing itself *is* all the same; it is absolute abstraction, therefore pure thought or self-centredness, and with its moment of opposition to spiritual unity it is the principle of Evil. The difficulty people find in these conceptions is due solely to sticking to the term "is," and forgetting the character of thought, where the moments as much *are* as they *are not*,—are only the process which is Spirit. It is this spiritual unity,— unity where the distinctions are merely in the form of moments, or as transcended—which became known to pictorial thinking in that atoning reconciliation spoken of above. And since this unity is the universality of self-consciousness, self-consciousness has ceased to be figurative or pictorial in its thinking; the process has turned back into it.

Spirit thus takes up its position in the third element, in universal self-consciousness: Spirit is its own community. The movement of this community being that of self-consciousness, which distinguishes itself from its figurative idea, consists in explicitly bringing out what has implicitly become established. The dead Divine Man, or Human God, is implicitly universal self-consciousness; he has to become explicitly so for this self-consciousness. Or, since this self-consciousness constitutes one side of the opposition involved in figurative thought, viz. the side of evil, which takes natural existence and individual self-existence to be the essential reality—this aspect, which is pictured as independent, and not yet as a moment, has, on account of its independence, to raise itself in and for itself to the level of spirit; it has to reveal the process of Spirit in its self.

This particular self-consciousness is Spirit in natural form, natural spirit: self has to withdraw from this natural existence and enter into itself, become self-centred; that would mean, it has to become evil. But this aspect is already *per se* evil: entering into itself consists, therefore, in persuading itself that natural existence is what is evil. By picture-thinking the world is supposed actually to become evil and be evil as an actual fact, and the atoning reconcilement of the Absolute Being is viewed as an actual existent phenomenon. By self-consciousness as such, however, this pictured truth, as regards its form, is considered to be merely a moment that is already superseded and transcended; for the self is the negative, and hence knowledge—a knowledge which is a pure act of consciousness within itself. This moment of the negative must in like manner find expression in the content. Since, that is to say,

the essential Being is inherently and from the start reconciled with itself and is a spiritual unity, in which what are parts for figurative
thought are sublated, are moments, what we find is that each part of figurative thought receives here the opposite significance to that which it
had before. By this means each meaning finds its completion in the
other, and the content is then and thereby a spiritual content. Since the
specific determinateness of each is just as much its opposite, unity in
otherness—spiritual reality—is achieved: just as formerly we saw the
opposite meanings combined objectively (*für uns*), or in themselves,
and even the abstract forms of "the same" and "not-the-same," "identity" and "non-identity" cancelled one another and were transcended.

If, then, from the point of view of figurative thought, the becoming
self-centred on the part of the natural self-consciousness was actually
existing evil, that process of becoming fixed in itself is in the sphere of
self-consciousness, the *knowledge of evil* as something that *per se* belongs to existence. This knowledge is certainly a process of becoming
evil, but merely of the *thought* of evil, and is therefore recognized as
the first moment of reconciliation. For, being a return into self out of
the immediacy of nature, which is specifically characterized as evil, it
is a forsaking of that immediacy, and a dying to sin. It is not natural existence as such that consciousness forsakes, but natural existence that is
at the same time known to be evil. The immediate process of becoming self-centred, is just as much a mediate process: it presupposes itself,
i.e. is its own ground and reason: the reason for self-concentrating is because nature has *per se* already done so. Because of evil man must be
self-centred (*in sich gehen*); but evil is itself the state of self-concentration. This first movement is just on that account itself merely immediate, is its simple notion, because it is the same as what its ground or reason is. The movement, or the process of passing into otherness, has
therefore still to come on the scene in its own more peculiar form.

Beside this immediacy, then, the mediation of figurative thought is
necessary. The knowledge of nature as the untrue existence of spirit,
and this universality of self which has arisen within the life of the self—
these constitute implicitly the reconciliation of spirit with itself. This
implicit state is apprehended by the self-consciousness, that does not
comprehend (*begreifen*), in the form of an objective existence, and as
something presented to it figuratively. Conceptual comprehension
(*Begreifen*), therefore, does not mean for it a grasping (*Ergreifen*) of this
conception (*Begriff*) which knows natural existence when cancelled
and transcended to be universal and thus reconciled with itself; but
rather a grasping of the imaginative idea (*Vorstellung*) that the Divine
Being is reconciled with its existence through an event,—the event of
God's emptying Himself of His Divine Being through His factual

Incarnation and His Death. The grasping of this idea now expresses more specifically what was formerly called in figurative thinking spiritual resurrection, or the process by which God's individual self-consciousness[13] becomes the universal, becomes the religious communion. The death of the Divine Man, qua death, is abstract negativity, the immediate result of the process which terminates only in the universality belonging to nature. In spiritual self-consciousness death loses this natural significance; it passes into its true conception, the conception just mentioned. Death then ceases to signify what it means directly—the non-existence of this individual—and becomes transfigured into the universality of the spirit, which lives in its own communion, dies there daily, and daily rises again.

That which belongs to the sphere of pictorial thought—viz., that Absolute Spirit presents the nature of spirit in its existence, qua individual or rather qua particular,—is thus here transferred to self-consciousness itself, to the knowledge which maintains itself in its otherness. This self-consciousness does not therefore really die, as the particular person[14] is pictorially imagined to have really died; its particularity expires in its universality, i.e. in its knowledge, which is essential Being reconciling itself with itself. That immediately preceding element of figurative thinking is thus here affirmed as transcended, has, in other words, returned into the self, into its notion. What was in the former merely an (objective) existent has come to assume the form of Subject. By that very fact the first element too, pure thought and the spirit eternal therein, are no longer away beyond the mind thinking pictorially nor beyond the self; rather the return of the whole into itself consists just in containing all moments within itself. When the death of the mediator is grasped by the self, this means the sublation of his factuality, of his particular independent existence: this particular self-existence has become universal self-consciousness.

On the other side, the universal, just because of this, is self-consciousness, and the pure or non-actual Spirit of bare thought has become actual. The death of the mediator is death not merely of his natural aspect, of his particular self-existence: what dies is not merely the outer encasement, which, being stripped of essential Being, is eo ipso dead, but also the abstraction of the Divine Being. For the mediator, as long as his death has not yet accomplished the reconciliation, is something one-sided, which takes as essential Being the simple abstract element of thought, not concrete reality. This one-sided extreme of self has not yet equal worth and value with essential Being; the self first gets

---

[13] The Christ.
[14] Christ.

this as Spirit. The death of this pictorial idea implies at the same time the death of the abstraction of Divine Being, which is not yet affirmed as a self. That death is the bitterness of feeling of the "unhappy consciousness," when it feels that God Himself is dead. This harsh utterance is the expression of inmost self-knowledge which has simply self for its content; it is the return of consciousness into the depth of darkness where Ego is nothing but bare identity with Ego, a darkness distinguishing and knowing nothing more outside it. This feeling thus means, in point of fact, the loss of the Substance and of its objective existence over against consciousness. But at the same time it is the pure subjectivity of Substance, the pure certainty of itself, which it lacked when it was object or immediacy, or pure essential Being. This knowledge is thus spiritualization, whereby Substance becomes Subject, by which its abstraction and lifelessness have expired, and Substance therefore has become real, simple, and universal self-consciousness.

In this way, then, Spirit is Spirit knowing its own self. It knows itself; that, which is for it object, exists, or, in other words, its figurative idea is the true absolute content. As we saw, the content expresses just Spirit itself. It is at the same time not merely content of self-consciousness, and not merely object *for* self-consciousness; it is also actual Spirit. It is this by the fact of its passing through the three elements of its nature: this movement through its whole self constitutes its actual reality. What moves itself, that is Spirit; it is the subject of the movement, and it is likewise the moving process itself, or the substance through which the subject passes. We saw how the notion of spirit arose when we entered the sphere of religion: it was the process of spirit certain of its self, which forgives evil, and in so doing puts aside its own simplicity and rigid unchangeableness: it was, to state it otherwise, the process, in which what is absolutely in opposition recognizes itself as the same as its opposite, and this knowledge breaks out into the "yea, yea," with which one extreme meets the other. The religious consciousness, to which the Absolute Being is revealed, beholds this notion, and does away with the distinction of its self from what it beholds; and as it is Subject, so it is also Substance; and is thus itself Spirit just because and in so far as it is this process.

This religious communion, however, is not yet fulfilled in this its self-consciousness. Its content, in general, is put before it in the form of a pictorial idea; so that this disruption still attaches even to the actual spiritual character of the communion—to its return out of its figurative thinking; just as the element of pure thought itself was also hampered with that opposition.[15] This spiritual communion is not also con-

---

[15] I.e. between spiritual consciousness and objective idea.

sciously aware what it is; it is spiritual self-consciousness, which is not object to itself as this self-consciousness, or does not develop into clear consciousness of itself. Rather, so far as it is consciousness, it has before it those picture-thoughts which were considered.

We see self-consciousness at its last turning point become inward to itself and attain to knowledge of its inner being, of its self-centredness. We see it relinquish its natural existence, and reach pure negativity. But the positive significance—viz. that this negativity, or pure inwardness of knowledge is just as much the self-identical essential Being: put otherwise, that Substance has here attained to being absolute self-consciousness—this is, for the devotional consciousness, an external other. It grasps this aspect—that the knowledge which becomes purely inward is inherently absolute simplicity, or Substance—as the pictorial idea of something which is not thus by its very conception, but as the act of satisfaction obtained from an (alien) other. In other words, it is not really aware as a fact that this depth of pure self is the power by which the abstract essential Being is drawn down from its abstractness and raised to the level of self by the force of this pure devotion. The action of the self hence retains towards it this negative significance, because the relinquishment of itself on the part of substance is for the self something *per se*; the self does not at once grasp and comprehend it, or does not find it in its *own* action as such.

Since this unity of Essential Being and Self has been inherently brought about, consciousness has this idea also of its reconciliation, but in the form of an imaginative idea. It obtains satisfaction by attaching, in an external way, to its pure negativity the positive significance of the unity of itself with essential Being. Its satisfaction thus itself remains hampered with the opposition of a beyond. Its own peculiar reconciliation therefore enters its consciousness as something remote, something far away in the future, just as the reconciliation, which the other self achieved, appears as away in the distance of the past. Just as the individual divine man[16] has an implied (essential, *an sich*) father and only an actual mother, in like manner the universal divine man, the spiritual communion, has as its father its own proper action and knowledge, while its mother is eternal Love, which it merely *feels*, but does not behold in its consciousness as an actual immediate object. Its reconciliation, therefore, is in its heart, but still with its conscious life sundered in twain and its actual reality shattered. What falls within its consciousness as the immanent essential element, the aspect of pure mediation, is the reconciliation that lies beyond: while what appears as actually present, as the aspect of immediacy and of existence, is the

---

[16]The historical Christ.

world which has yet to await transfiguration. The world is no doubt implicitly reconciled with the essential Being; and that Being no doubt knows that it no longer regards the object as alienated from itself, but as one with itself in its Love. But for self-consciousness this immediate presence has not yet the form and shape of spiritual reality. Thus the spirit of the communion is, in its immediate consciousness, separated from its religious consciousness, which declares indeed that these two modes of consciousness inherently are *not* separated; but this is an implicitness which is not realized, or has not yet become an equally absolute explicit self-existence.

ABSOLUTE KNOWLEDGE*

VIII

ABSOLUTE KNOWLEDGE[1]

THE Spirit manifested in revealed religion has not as yet surmounted its attitude of consciousness as such; or, what is the same thing, its actual self-consciousness is not at this stage the object it is aware of. Spirit as a whole and the moments distinguished in it fall within the sphere of figurative thinking, and within the form of objectivity. The *content* of this figurative thought is Absolute Spirit. All that remains to be done now is to cancel and transcend this bare form; or better, because the form appertains to consciousness as such, its true meaning must have already come out in the shapes or modes consciousness has assumed.

The surmounting of the object of consciousness in this way is not to be taken one-sidedly as meaning that the object showed itself returning into the self. It has a more definite meaning: it means that the object as such presented itself to the self as a vanishing factor; and, furthermore, that the emptying of self-consciousness itself establishes thinghood, and that this externalization of self-consciousness has not merely negative, but positive significance, a significance not merely *for us* or *per se*, but for self-consciousness itself. The negative of the object, its cancelling its own existence, gets, for self-consciousness, a positive significance; or, self-consciousness knows this nothingness of the object because on the one hand self-consciousness itself externalizes itself; for in doing so it establishes itself as object, or, by reason of the indivisible unity characterizing its self-existence, sets up the object as its self. On

---

*On the nature of absolute knowledge, or philosophy in Hegel's sense, cp. above, pp. 20 ff., 45, 80 ff., 96 f., 105 ff., 125 f.; on the distinction between the special sciences, everyday knowledge and philosophy, see the *Preface* and *Introduction* to the *Phenomenology*. Reference may also be made to W. Wallace, *The Logic of Hegel, Prolegomena*, c. vi., and the same author's edition of Hegel's *Philosophy of Mind.*

[1] *v. sup.* p. 397. "Absolute Knowledge" is at once the consummation of experience and, when developed, constructive philosophy: *v. infra*, p. 472 ff.

the other hand, there is also this other moment in the process, that self-consciousness has just as really cancelled and superseded this self-relinquishment and objectification, and has resumed them into itself, and is thus at home with itself in its otherness as such. This is the movement of consciousness, and in this process consciousness is the totality of its moments.

Consciousness, at the same time, must have taken up a relation to the object in all its aspects and phases, and have grasped its meaning from the point of view of each of them. This totality of its determinate characteristics makes the object *per se* or inherently a spiritual reality; and it becomes so in truth for consciousness, when the latter apprehends every individual one of them as self, i.e. when it takes up towards them the spiritual relationship just spoken of.

The object is, then, partly immediate existence, a *thing* in general — corresponding to immediate consciousness; partly an alteration of itself, its relatedness, (or existence-for-another and existence-for-self), *determinateness* — corresponding to perception; partly essential being or in the form of a *universal* — corresponding to understanding. The object as a whole is the mediated result [the syllogism] or the passing of universality into individuality through specification, as also the reverse process from individual to universal through cancelled individuality or specific determination.

These three specific aspects, then, determine the ways in which consciousness must know the object as itself. This knowledge of which we are speaking is, however, not knowledge in the sense of pure conceptual comprehension of the object; here this knowledge is to be taken only in its development, has to be taken in its various moments and set forth in the manner appropriate to consciousness as such; and the moments of the notion proper, of pure knowledge, assume the form of shapes or modes of consciousness. For that reason the object does not yet, when present in consciousness as such, appear as the inner essence of Spirit in the way this has just been expressed. The attitude consciousness adopts in regard to the object is not that of considering it either in this totality as such or in the pure conceptual form; it is partly that of a mode or shape of consciousness in general, partly a multitude of such modes which *we* [who analyze the process] gather together, and in which the totality of the moments of the object and of the process of consciousness can be shown merely resolved into their moments.

To understand this method of grasping the object, where apprehension is a shape or mode of consciousness, we have here only to recall the previous shapes of consciousness which came before us earlier in the argument.

As regards the object, then, so far as it is immediate, an indifferent objective entity, we saw Reason, at the stage of "Observation," seeking and finding itself in this indifferent thing—i.e. we saw it conscious that its activity is there of an external sort, and at the same time conscious of the object merely as an immediate object. We saw, too, its specific character take expression at its highest stage in the infinite judgment: "the being of the ego is a thing." And, further, the ego is an immediate thing of sense. When ego is called a soul, it is indeed represented also as a thing, but a thing in the sense of something invisible, impalpable, etc., i.e. in fact *not* as an immediate entity, and not as that which is generally understood by a thing. That judgment, then, "ego is a thing," taken at first glance, has no spiritual content, or rather, is just the absence of spirituality. In its conception, however, it is in fact the most luminous and illuminating judgment; and this, its inner significance, which is not yet made evident, is what the two other moments to be considered express.

The thing is ego. In point of fact, thing is transcended in this infinite judgment. The thing is nothing in itself; it only has significance in relation, only through the ego and its reference to the ego. This moment came before consciousness in pure insight and enlightenment. Things are simply and solely useful, and only to be considered from the point of view of their utility. The trained and cultivated self-consciousness, which has traversed the region of spirit in self-alienation, has, by giving up itself, produced the thing as its self; it retains itself, therefore, still in the thing, and knows the thing to have no independence, in other words knows that the thing has essentially and solely a relative existence. Or again—to give complete expression to the relationship, i.e. to what here alone constitutes the nature of the object—the thing stands for something that is self-existent; sense-certainty (sense-experience) is announced as absolute truth; but this self-existence is itself declared to be a moment which merely disappears, and passes into its opposite, into a being at the mercy of an "other."

But knowledge of the thing is not yet finished at this point. The thing must become known as self not merely in regard to the immediateness of its being and as regards its determinateness, but also in the sense of essence or inner reality. This is found in the case of Moral Self-consciousness. This mode of experience knows its knowledge as the absolute essential element, knows no other objective being than pure will or pure knowledge. It is nothing but merely this will and this knowledge. Any other possesses merely non-essential being, i.e. being that has no inherent nature *per se*, but only its empty husk. In so far as the moral consciousness, in its view of the world, lets existence drop out of the self, it just as truly takes this existence back again into its self. In the form of conscience, finally, it is no longer this incessant alternation between the "placing" and the "displacing" [dissembling] of existence and self; it knows that its existence as such is this pure certainty of its own self; the objective element, into which *qua* acting it puts forth itself, is nothing else than pure knowledge of itself by itself.

These are the moments which compose the reconciliation of spirit with its own consciousness proper. By themselves they are single and isolated; and it is their spiritual unity alone which furnishes the power for this reconciliation. The last of these moments is, however, necessarily this unity itself, and, as we see, binds them all in fact into itself. Spirit certain of itself in its objective existence takes as the element of its existence nothing else than this knowledge of self. The declaration that what it does it does in accordance with the conviction of duty—this statement is the warrant for its own action, and makes good its conduct.

Action is the first inherent division of the simple unity of the notion, and the return out of this division. This first movement turns round into the second, since the element of recognition puts itself forward as simple knowledge of duty in contrast to the distinction and diremption that lie in action as such and, in this way, form a rigid reality confronting action. In pardon, however, we saw how this rigid fixity gives way and renounces its claims. Reality has here, *qua immediate existence*, no other significance for self-consciousness than that of being pure knowledge; similarly, *qua determinate existence*, or *qua* relation, what is self-opposed is a knowledge partly of this purely individual self, partly of knowledge *qua* universal. Herein it is established, at the same time, that the third moment, universality, or the essence, means for each of the two opposite factors merely knowledge. Finally they also cancel the empty opposition that still remains, and are the knowledge of ego as identical with ego:—this individual self which is immediately pure knowledge or universal.

This reconciliation of consciousness with self-consciousness thus proves to be brought about in a double-sided way; in the one case, in the religious mind, in the other case, in consciousness itself as such. They are distinguished *inter se* by the fact that the one is this reconciliation in the form of implicit immanence, the other in the form of explicit self-existence. As we have considered them, they at the beginning fall apart. In the order in which the modes or shapes of consciousness came before us, consciousness has reached the individual moments of that order, and also their unification, long before ever religion gave its object the shape of actual self-consciousness. The unification of both aspects is not yet brought to light; it is this that winds up this series of embodiments of spirit, for in it spirit gets to the point where it knows itself not only as it is inherently in itself, or in terms of its absolute content, nor only as it is (objectively) for itself in terms of its bare form devoid of content, or in terms of self-consciousness, but as it is in its self-completeness, as it is in itself and for itself.

This unification has, however, already taken place by implication, and has done so in religion in the return of the figurative idea (*Vorstellung*) into self-consciousness, but not according to the proper form, for the religious aspect is the aspect of the essentially independent (*Ansich*) and stands in contrast to the process of self-consciousness. The unification therefore belongs to this other aspect, which by contrast is the aspect of reflexion into self, is that side therefore which contains its self and its opposite, and contains them not only implicitly, (*an sich*) or in a general way, but explicitly (*für sich*) or expressly developed and distinguished. The content, as well as the other aspect of self-conscious spirit, so far as it is the *other* aspect, have been brought to light and are here in their completeness: the unification still a-wanting is the simple unity of the notion. This notion is also already given with the aspect of self-consciousness; but as it previously came before us above, it, like all the other moments, has the form of being a particular mode or shape of consciousness. It is that part of the embodiment of self-assured spirit which keeps within its essential principle and was called the "beautiful soul." That is to say, the "beautiful soul" is its own knowledge of itself in its pure transparent unity—self-consciousness, which knows this pure knowledge of pure inwardness to be spirit, is not merely intuition of the divine, but the self-intuition of God Himself.

Since this notion keeps itself fixedly opposed to its realization, it is the one-sided shape which we saw before disappear into thin air, but also positively relinquish itself and advance further. Through this act of realization, this objectless self-consciousness ceases to hold fast by itself, the determinateness of the notion in contrast with its fulfilment is cancelled and done away with. Its self-consciousness attains the form of universality; and what remains is its true notion, the notion that has attained its realization—the notion in its truth, i.e. in unity with its externalization. It is knowledge of pure knowledge, not in the sense of an abstract essence such as duty is, but in the sense of an essential being which *is this* knowledge, this individual pure self-consciousness which is therefore at the same time a genuine *object*; for this notion is the self-existing self.

This notion gave itself its fulfilment partly in the acts performed by the spirit that is sure of itself, partly in religion. In the latter it won the absolute content *qua* content, or in the form of a figurative idea or of otherness for consciousness. On the other hand, in the first the form is just the self, for that mode contains the active spirit sure of itself; the self accomplishes the life of Absolute Spirit. This shape (mode), as we see, is that simple notion, which however gives up its eternal essential

Being, takes upon itself objective existence, or acts. The power of diremption or of coming forth out of its inwardness lies in the purity of
the notion, for this purity is absolute abstraction of negativity. In the
same way the notion finds its element of reality, or the objective being
it contains, in pure knowledge itself; for this knowledge is simple immediacy, which is being and existence as well as essence, the former
negative thought, the latter positive thought. This existence, finally, is
just as much that state of reflexion into self which comes out of pure
knowledge—both *qua* existence and *qua* duty—and this is the state of
evil. This process of "going into self" constitutes the opposition lying in
the notion, and is thus the appearance on the scene of pure knowledge
of the essence, a knowledge which does not act and is not real. But to
make its appearance in this opposition is to participate in it; pure
knowledge of essence has inherently relinquished its simplicity, for it is
the diremption of negativity which constitutes the notion. So far as this
process of diremption is the process of becoming self-centred, it is the
principle of evil: so far as it is the inherently essential, it is the principle which remains good.

Now what in the first instance takes place implicitly is at once for
consciousness, and is duplicated as well—is both for consciousness
and is its self-existence or its own proper action. The same thing that
is already inherently established, thus repeats itself now as knowledge
thereof on the part of consciousness and as conscious action. Each
lays aside for the other the independence of character with which
each appears confronting the other. This waiving of independence is
the same renunciation of the one-sidedness of the notion as constituted implicitly the beginning; but it is now its own act of renunciation, just as the notion renounced is its own notion. That implicit
nature of the beginning is in truth as much mediated, because it is
negativity; it now establishes itself as it is in its truth; and the negative
element exists as a determinate quality which each has for the other,
and is essentially self-cancelling, self-transcending. The one of the
two parts of the opposition is the disparity between existence within
itself, in its individuality, and universality; the other, disparity between its abstract universality and the self. The former dies to its self-
existence, and relinquishes itself, makes confession; the latter renounces the rigidity of its abstract universality, and thereby dies to its
lifeless self and its inert universality; so that the former is completed
through the moment of universality, which is the essence, and the latter through universality, which is self. By this process of action spirit
has come to light in the form of pure universality of knowledge,
which is self-consciousness as self-consciousness, which is simple
unity of knowledge. It is through action that spirit is spirit so as defi-

nitely to exist; it raises its existence into the sphere of thought and hence into absolute opposition, and returns out of it through and within this very opposition.

Thus, then, what was in religion content, or a way of imagining (*Vorstellen*) an other, is here the action proper of the self. The notion is the connecting principle securing that the content is the action proper of the self. For this notion is, as we see, the knowledge that the action of the self within itself is all that is essential and all existence, the knowledge of this Subject as Substance and of the Substance as this knowledge of its action. What we have done here, in addition, is simply to gather together the particular moments, each of which in principle exhibits the life of spirit in its entirety, and again to secure the notion in the form of the notion, whose content was disclosed in these moments, and which had already presented itself in the form of a mode or shape of consciousness.

This last embodiment of spirit—spirit which at once gives its complete and true content the form of self, and thereby realizes its notion, and in doing so remains within its own notion—this is *Absolute Knowledge*. It is spirit knowing itself in the shape of spirit, it is knowledge which comprehends through notions. Truth is here not merely *in itself* absolutely identical with certainty; it has also the shape, the character of certainty of self; or in its existence—i.e. for spirit knowing it—it is in the *form* of knowledge of itself. Truth is the content, which in religion is not as yet at one with its certainty. This identification, however, is secured when the content has received the shape of self. By this means, what constitutes the very essence, viz. the notion, comes to have the nature of existence, i.e. assumes the form of what is objective to consciousness. Spirit, appearing before consciousness in this element of existence, or, what is here the same thing, produced by it in this element, is systematic Science.

The nature, moments, and process of this knowledge have then shown themselves to be such that this knowledge is pure self-existence of self-consciousness.

It is ego, which is *this* ego and no other, and at the same time, immediately is mediated, or sublated, universal ego. It has a content, which it distinguishes from itself; for it is pure negativity, or self-diremption; it is consciousness. This content in its distinction is itself the ego, for it is the process of superseding itself, or the same pure negativity which constitutes ego. Ego is in it, *qua* distinguished, reflected into itself; only then is the content comprehended (*begriffen*) when ego in its otherness is still at home with itself. More precisely stated, this content is nothing else than the very process just spoken of; for the content is the spirit which traverses the whole range of its own being, and does this for itself *qua* spirit, by the fact that it possesses the shape of the notion in its objectivity.

As to the actual existence of this notion, science does not appear in time and in reality till spirit has arrived at this stage of being conscious regarding itself. *Qua* spirit which knows what it is, it does not exist before, and is not to be found at all till after the completion of the task of mastering and constraining its imperfect embodiment—the task of procuring for its consciousness the shape of its inmost essence, and in this manner bringing its self-consciousness level with its consciousness. Spirit in and for itself is, when distinguished into its separate moments, self-existent knowledge, comprehension (*Begreifen*) *in general*, which *as such* has not yet reached the substance, or is not in itself absolute knowledge.

Now in actual reality the knowing substance exists, is there earlier than its form, earlier than the shape of the notion. For the substance is the undeveloped inherent nature, the ground and notion in its inert simplicity, the state of inwardness or the self of spirit which is not yet there. What is there, what does exist, is in the shape of still unexpressed simplicity, the undeveloped immediate, or the object of imagining (*Vorstellen*) consciousness in general. Because knowledge (*Erkennen*) is a spiritual state of consciousness, which admits as real what essentially is only so far as this is a being for the self and a being *of* the self or a notion—knowledge has on this account merely a barren object to begin with, in contrast to which the substance and the consciousness of this substance are richer in content. The revelation which substance has in such a consciousness is, in fact, concealment; for the substance is here still self-less existence and nothing but certainty of self is revealed. To begin with, therefore, it is only the abstract moments that belong to self-consciousness concerning the substance. But since these moments are pure activities and must move forward by their very nature, self-consciousness enriches itself till it has torn from consciousness the entire substance, and absorbed into itself the entire structure of the substance with all its constituent elements. Since this negative attitude towards objectivity is positive as well, establishes and fixes the content, it goes on till it has produced these elements out of itself and thereby reinstated them once more as objects of consciousness. In the notion, knowing itself as notion, the moments thus make their appearance prior to the whole in its complete fulfilment; the movement of these moments is the process by which the whole comes into being. In consciousness, on the other hand, the whole—but not as comprehended conceptually—is prior to the moments.

Time is just the notion definitely existent, and presented to consciousness in the form of empty intuition. Hence spirit necessarily appears in time, and it appears in time so long as it does not grasp its pure notion, i.e. so long as it does not annul time. Time is the pure self in external form, apprehended in intuition, and not grasped and understood by the self, it is the notion apprehended only through intuition. When this notion grasps itself, it supersedes its time character, (conceptually) comprehends intuition, and is intuition comprehended and comprehending. Time therefore appears as spirit's destiny and necessity, where spirit is not yet complete within itself; it is the necessity compelling spirit to enrich the share self-consciousness has in consciousness, to put into motion the immediacy of the inherent nature (which is the form in which the substance is present in consciousness); or, conversely, to realize and make manifest what is inherent, regarded as inward and immanent, to make manifest that which is at first within—i.e. to vindicate it for spirit's certainty of self.

For this reason it must be said that nothing is known which does not fall within experience, or (as it is also expressed) which is not *felt* to be true, which is not given as an inwardly revealed eternal verity, as a sacred object of belief, or whatever other expressions we care to employ. For experience just consists in this, that the content—and the content is spirit—in its inherent nature is substance and so object of consciousness. But this substance, which is spirit, is the development of itself explicitly to what it is inherently and implicitly; and only as this process of reflecting itself into itself is it essentially and in truth spirit. It is inherently the movement which is the process of knowledge—the transforming of that inherent nature into explicitness, of Substance into Subject, of the object of consciousness into the object of self-consciousness, i.e. into an object that is at the same time transcended—in other words, into the notion. This transforming process is a cycle that returns into itself, a cycle that presupposes its beginning, and reaches its beginning only at the end. So far as spirit, then, is of necessity this self-distinction, it appears as a single whole, intuitively apprehended, over against its simple self-consciousness. And since that whole is what is distinguished, it is distinguished into the intuitively apprehended pure notion, Time, and the Content, the inherent, implicit, nature. Substance, *qua* subject, involves the necessity, at first an *inner* necessity, to set forth in itself what it inherently is, to show itself to be spirit. The completed expression in objective form is—and is only when completed—at the same time the reflexion of substance, the development of it into the self. Consequently, until and unless spirit inherently completes itself, completes itself as a world-spirit, it cannot reach its completion as self-conscious spirit. The content of religion, therefore, expresses earlier in time than (philosophical) science what spirit is; but this science alone is the perfect form in which spirit truly knows itself.

The process of carrying forward this form of knowledge of itself is the task which spirit accomplishes as actual History. The religious communion, in so far as it is at the outset the substance of Absolute Spirit, is the crude form of consciousness, which has an existence all the harsher and more barbaric the deeper is its inner spirit; and its inarticulate self has all the harder task in dealing with its essence, the content of its consciousness alien to itself. Not till it has surrendered the hope of cancelling that foreignness by an external, i.e. alien, method does it turn to itself, to its own peculiar world, in the actual present. It turns thither because to supersede that alien method means returning into self-consciousness. It thus discovers this world in the living present to be its own property; and so has taken the first step to descend from the ideal intelligible world, or rather to quicken the abstract element of the intelligible world with concrete self-hood. Through "observation," on the one hand, it finds existence in the shape of thought, and comprehends existence; and, conversely, it finds in its thought existence.[2] When, in the first instance, it has thus itself expressed in an abstract way the immediate unity of thought and existence, of abstract Essential Reality and Self; and when it has expressed the primal principle of "Light" in a purer form, viz. as unity of extension and existence—for "existence" is an ultimate simple term more adequate to thought than "Light"—and in this way has revived again in thought the Substance of the Orient;[3] thereupon spirit at once recoils in horror from this abstract unity, from this self-less substantiality, and maintains as against it the principle of Individuality.[4] But after Spirit has externalized this principle in the process of its culture, has thereby made it an objective existence and established it throughout the whole of existence, has arrived at the idea of "Utility"[5] and in the sphere of absolute freedom has grasped existence as its Individual Will,[6]—after these stages, spirit then brings to light the thought that lies in its inmost depths, and expresses essential Reality in the form Ego=Ego.[7]

This "Ego identical with Ego" is, however, the self-reflecting process; for since this identity *qua* absolute negativity is absolute distinction, the self-identity of the Ego stands in contrast to this absolute distinction, which—being pure distinction and at the same time objective to the self that knows itself—has to be expressed as Time. In this way, just as formerly Essential Reality was expressed as unity of thought and *extension*, it would here be interpreted as unity of thought and

----

[2]Descartes.
[3]Spinoza.
[4]Leibnitz.
[5]The principle of the "*Aufklärung.*"
[6]Kant.
[7]Fichte.

time. But distinction left to itself, unresting, unhalting time, really collapses upon itself; it is the objective quiescence of extension; while this latter is pure identity with self—is Ego.

Again, Ego is not merely self, it is identity of self with itself. This identity, however, is complete and immediate unity with self; in other words this Subject is just as much Substance. Substance by itself alone would be void and empty Intuition (*Anschauen*), or the intuition of a content which *qua* specific would have merely a contingent character and would be devoid of necessity. Substance would only stand for the Absolute in so far as Substance was thought of or "intuited" as absolute unity; and all content would, as regards its diversity, have to fall outside the Substance and be due to reflexion, a process which does not belong to Substance, because Substance would not be Subject, would not be conceived as Spirit, as reflecting about self and reflecting itself into self. If, nevertheless, a content were to be spoken of, then on the one hand it would only exist in order to be thrown into the empty abyss of the Absolute, while on the other it would be picked up in external fashion from sense perception. Knowledge would appear to have come by things, by what is distinct from knowledge itself, and to have got at the distinctions between the endless variety of things, without any one understanding how or where all this came from.[8]

Spirit, however, has shown itself to us to be neither the mere withdrawal of self-consciousness into its pure inwardness, nor the mere absorption of self-consciousness into Substance and the nothingness of its (self-) distinction. Spirit is the movement of the self which empties (externalizes) itself of self and sinks itself within its own substance, and *qua* subject, both has gone out of that substance into itself, making its substance an object and a content, and also supersedes this distinction of objectivity and content. That first reflexion out of immediacy is the subject's process of distinction of itself from its substance, the notion in a process of self-diremption, the going-into-itself and the coming into being of the pure ego. Since this distinction is the pure action of Ego=Ego, the notion is the necessity for and the rising of existence, which has the substance for its essential nature and subsists on its own account. But this subsisting of existence for itself is the notion established in determinate form, and is thereby the notion's own inherent movement—that of descending into the simple substance, which is only subject by being this negativity and going through this process.

Ego has not to take its stand on the form of self-consciousness in opposition to the form of substantiality and objectivity, as if it were afraid of relinquishing or externalizing itself. The power of spirit lies rather in

---

[8]Schelling.

remaining one with itself when giving up itself, and, because it is self-contained and self-subsistent, in establishing as mere moments its explicit self-existence as well as its implicit inherent nature. Nor again is Ego a *tertium quid* which casts distinctions back into the abyss of the Absolute, and declares them all to mean the same there. On the contrary, true knowledge lies rather in the seeming inactivity which merely watches how what is distinguished is self-moved by its very nature and returns again into its own unity.

With absolute knowledge, then, Spirit has wound up the process of its embodiment, so far as the assumption of those various shapes or modes is affected with the insurmountable distinction which consciousness implies [i.e. the distinction of consciousness from its object or content]. Spirit has attained the pure element of its existence, the notion. The content is, in view of the freedom of its own existence, the self that empties (externalizes) itself; in other words, that content is the *immediate* unity of self-knowledge. The pure process of thus externalizing itself constitutes—when we consider this process in its content—the *necessity* of this content. The diversity of content is, *qua* determinate, due to relation, and is not inherent; and its restless activity consists in cancelling and superseding itself, or is negativity. Thus the necessity or diversity, like its free existence, is the self too; and in this self-form, in which existence is immediately thought, the content is a notion. Seeing, then, that Spirit has attained the notion, it unfolds its existence and develops its processes in this ether of its life and is (*Philosophical*) *Science.*[9] The moments of its process are set forth therein no longer as determinate modes or shapes of consciousness, but—since the distinction, which consciousness implies, has reverted to and has become a distinction within the self—as determinate notions, and as the organic self-explaining and self-constituted process of these notions. While in the *Phenomenology of Mind* each moment is the distinction of knowledge and truth, and is the process in which that distinction is cancelled and transcended, Absolute Knowledge does not contain this distinction and supersession of distinction. Rather, since each moment has the form of the notion, it unites the objective form of truth and the knowing self in an immediate unity. Each individual moment does not appear as the process of passing back and forward from consciousness or figurative (imaginative) thought to self-consciousess and conversely: on the contrary, the pure shape, liberated from the condition of being an appearance in mere consciousness,—the pure notion with its further development,—depends solely on its pure characteristic nature. Conversely, again, there corresponds to

---

[9] I.e. Absolute or completely coherent Knowledge.

every abstract moment of Absolute Knowledge a mode in which mind as a whole makes its appearance. As the mind that actually exists is not richer than it,[10] so, too, mind in its actual content is not poorer. To know the pure notions of knowledge in the form in which they are modes or shapes of consciousness—this constitutes the aspect of their reality, according to which their essential element, the notion, appearing there in its simple mediating activity as thinking, breaks up and separates the moments of this mediation and exhibits them to itself in accordance with their immanent opposition.

Absolute Knowledge contains within itself this necessity of relinquishing itself from the form of the pure notion, and necessarily involves the transition of the notion into consciousness. For Spirit that knows itself is, just for the reason that it grasps its own notion, immediate identity with itself; and this, in the distinction that it implies, is the certainty of what is immediate or is sense-consciousness—the beginning from which we started. This process of releasing itself from the form of its self is the highest freedom and security of its knowledge of itself.

All the same, this relinquishment (externalization) of self is still incomplete. This process expresses the relation of the certainty of its self to the object, an object which, just by being in a relation, has not yet attained its full freedom. Knowledge is aware not only of itself, but also of the negative of itself, or its limit. Knowing its limit means knowing how to sacrifice itself. This sacrifice is the self-abandonment, in which Spirit sets forth, in the form of free fortuitous happening, its process of becoming Spirit, intuitively apprehending outside it its pure self as Time, and likewise its existence as Space.[11] This last form into which Spirit passes, *Nature*, is its living immediate process of development. Nature—Spirit divested of self (externalized)—is, in its actual existence, nothing but this eternal process of abandoning its (Nature's) own independent subsistence, and the movement which reinstates Subject.

The other aspect, however, in which Spirit comes into being, *History*, is the process of becoming in terms of knowledge, a conscious self-mediating process—Spirit externalized and emptied into Time. But this form of abandonment is, similarly, the emptying of itself by itself; the negative is negative of itself. This way of becoming presents a slow procession and succession of spiritual shapes (*Geistern*), a gallery of pictures, each of which is endowed with the entire wealth of Spirit, and moves so slowly just for the reason that the self has to permeate and assimilate all this wealth of its substance. Since its accomplishment consists in Spirit knowing what it is, in fully comprehending its substance, this knowledge

---

[10]Absolute Knowledge.
[11]Cp. *Ency.* §244; also *Naturphilos.*, Introd.

means its concentrating itself on itself (*Insichgehen*), a state in which Spirit leaves its external existence behind and gives its embodiment over to Recollection (*Erinnerung*). In thus concentrating itself on itself, Spirit is engulfed in the night of its own self-consciousness; its vanished existence is, however, conserved therein; and this superseded existence—the previous state, but born anew from the womb of knowledge—is the new stage of existence, a new world, and a new embodiment or mode of Spirit. Here it has to begin all over again at its immediacy,[12] as freshly as before, and thence rise once more to the measure of its stature, as if, for it, all that preceded were lost, and as if it had learned nothing from the experience of the spirits that preceded. But re-collection (*Erinnerung*) has conserved that experience, and is the inner being, and, in fact, the higher form of the substance. While, then, this phase of Spirit begins all over again its formative development, apparently starting solely from itself, yet at the same time it commences at a higher level. The realm of spirits developed in this way, and assuming definite shape in existence, constitutes a succession, where one detaches and sets loose the other, and each takes over from its predecessor the empire of the spiritual world. The goal of the process is the revelation of the depth of spiritual life, and this is the Absolute Notion. This revelation consequently means superseding its "depth," is its "extension" or *spatial* embodiment, the negation of this inwardly self-centred (*insichseiend*) ego—a negativity which is its self-relinquishment, its externalization, or its substance: and this revelation is also its *temporal* embodiment, in that this externalization in its very nature relinquishes (externalizes) itself, and so exists at once in its spatial "extension" as well as in its "depth" or the self. The goal, which is Absolute Knowledge or Spirit knowing itself as Spirit, finds its pathway in the recollection of spiritual forms (*Geister*) as they are in themselves and as they accomplish the organization of their spiritual kingdom. Their conservation, looked at from the side of their free existence appearing in the form of contingency, is *History*; looked at from the side of their intellectually comprehended organization, it is the *Science* of the ways in which knowledge appears.[13] Both together, or History (intellectually) comprehended (*begriffen*), form at once the recollection and the Golgotha of Absolute Spirit, the reality, the truth, the certainty of its throne, without which it were lifeless, solitary, and alone. Only

> The chalice of this realm of spirits
> Foams forth to God His own Infinitude.[14]

---

[12]Cp. Aristotle, *Metaph.*, 1071*b*, "Movement can neither come into being, nor cease to be; nor can time come into being, or cease to be."

[13]"*Phenomenology*."

[14]Adaptation of Schiller's *Die Freundschaft* ad fin.; cp. also Schiller's *Philos. Briefe*, "*Gott.*"

Index